PASSING WEALTH ON DEATH

Wealth can be transferred on death in a number of different ways, most commonly by will. Yet a person can also use a variety of other means to benefit someone on death. Examples include *donationes mortis causa*, joint tenancies, trusts, life insurance contracts, and nominations in pension and retirement plans. In the US, these modes of transfer are grouped under the category of 'will-substitutes' and are generally treated as testamentary dispositions.

Much has been written about the effect of the use of will-substitutes in the US, but little is generally known about developments in other jurisdictions. For the first time, this collection of contributions looks at will-substitutes from a comparative perspective. It examines mechanisms that pass wealth on death across a number of common law, civil law and mixed legal jurisdictions, and explores the rationale behind their use. It analyses them from different viewpoints, including those of owners of businesses, investors, as well as creditors, family members and dependants. The aims of the volume are to show the complexity and dynamics of wealth transfers on death across jurisdictions, to identify patterns between jurisdictions, and to report the attitudes towards the different modes of transfer in light of their utility and the potential frictions they give rise to with policies and principles underpinning current laws.

Volume 22 Studies of the Oxford Institute of European and Comparative Law

Studies of the Oxford Institute of European and Comparative Law

Recent titles in this Series

Volume 12: Article 82 EC: Reflections on its Recent Evolution
Edited by Ariel Ezrachi

Volume 13: Prohibition of Abuse of Law: A New General Principle of EU Law?
Edited by Rita de la Feria and Stefan Vogenauer

Volume 14: Constitutional Pluralism in the European Union and Beyond
Edited by Matej Avbelj and Jan Komárek

Volume 15: The Protection of Fundamental Rights in the EU after Lisbon
Edited by Sybe de Vries, Ulf Bernitz and Stephen Weatherill

Volume 16: The Involvement of EU Law in Private Law Relationships
Edited by Dorota Leczykiewicz and Stephen Weatherill

Volume 17: Current Problems in the Protection of Human Rights: Perspectives from Germany and the UK
Edited by Katja S Ziegler and Peter M Huber

Volume 18: Legal Challenges in the Global Financial Crisis: Bail-outs, the Euro and Regulation
Edited by Wolf-Georg Ringe and Peter M Huber

Volume 19: The Unitary EU Patent System
Edited by Justine Pila and Christopher Wadlow

Volume 20: The EU Charter of Fundamental Rights as a Binding Instrument: Five Years Old and Growing
Edited by Sybe de Vries, Ulf Bernitz and Stephen Weatherill

Volume 21: The Images of the Consumer in EU Law: Legislation, Free Movement and Competition Law
Edited by Dorota Leczykiewicz and Stephen Weatherill

Passing Wealth on Death

Will-Substitutes in Comparative Perspective

Edited by
Alexandra Braun
and
Anne Röthel

·HART·
PUBLISHING
OXFORD AND PORTLAND, OREGON
2016

Hart Publishing
An imprint of Bloomsbury Publishing plc

Hart Publishing Ltd
Kemp House
Chawley Park
Cumnor Hill
Oxford OX2 9PH
UK

Bloomsbury Publishing Plc
50 Bedford Square
London
WC1B 3DP
UK

www.hartpub.co.uk
www.bloomsbury.com

Published in North America (US and Canada) by
Hart Publishing
c/o International Specialized Book Services
920 NE 58th Avenue, Suite 300
Portland, OR 97213-3786
USA

www.isbs.com

HART PUBLISHING, the Hart/Stag logo, BLOOMSBURY and the Diana logo are trademarks of Bloomsbury Publishing Plc

First published 2016

British Library Cataloguing-in-Publication Data
A catalogue record for this book is available from the British Library.

ISBN: HB: 978-1-84946-698-1
ePDF: 978-1-50990-736-6
ePub: 978-1-50990-735-9

Library of Congress Cataloging-in-Publication Data

Names: Braun, Alexandra, editor. | Röthel, Anne, editor.

Title: Passing wealth on death : will-substitutes in comparative perspective / edited by Alexandra Braun and Anne Röthel.

Description: Oxford ; Portland, Or. : Hart Publishing, An imprint of Bloomsbury Publishing Plc, 2016. | Series: Studies of the Oxford institute of European and comparative law ; v. 22 | Includes papers presented at a conference held 27 and 28 March 2015 at Lady Margaret Hall in Oxford. | Includes bibliographical references and index.

Identifiers: LCCN 2016011349 (print) | LCCN 2016011741 (ebook) | ISBN 9781849466981 (hardback : alk. paper) | ISBN 9781509907359 (Epub)

Subjects: LCSH: Inheritance and succession—Congresses. | Estate planning—Congresses.

Classification: LCC K805.A6 P37 2016 (print) | LCC K805.A6 (ebook) | DDC 346.05/2—dc23

LC record available at http://lccn.loc.gov/2016011349

Series: Studies of the Oxford Institute of European and Comparative Law, volume 22

Typeset by Compuscript Ltd, Shannon
Printed and bound in Great Britain by
TJ International Ltd, Padstow, Cornwall

TABLE OF CONTENTS

Part II: Overarching Perspectives

LIST OF CONTRIBUTORS

Reinhard Bork is Professor of Civil Procedure and General Procedural Law at the University of Hamburg.

Alexandra Braun is Associate Professor of Law at the University of Oxford and Fellow and Tutor in Law at Lady Margaret Hall, University of Oxford.

Angela Campbell is Associate Professor at the Faculty of Law at McGill University and Associate Provost (Policies, Procedures and Equity) at McGill University.

Daniel Carr is Lecturer in Private Law at the University of Edinburgh.

Gregor Christandl is Assistant Professor at the Institute for Italian Law at the University of Innsbruck.

Anatol Dutta is Professor of Law, Chair of Civil Law, Private International Law and Comparative Law at the University of Regensburg.

Thomas P Gallanis is Associate Dean for Research, N William Hines Chair in Law, and Professor of History at the University of Iowa.

Jonathan Herring is Professor of Law at the University of Oxford and Fellow and Tutor in Law at Exeter College, University of Oxford.

Dominique Jakob is Full Professor of Private Law and Director of the Center for Foundation Law at the University of Zürich.

Susanne Kalss is Professor at the Institute for Civil and Corporate Law at the Vienna University of Economics and Business.

Paul Matthews is Visiting Professor at the Dickson Poon School of Law, King's College London, and Master of the High Court, Chancery Division.

Nicola Peart is Professor of Law at the University of Otago.

Cécile Pérès is Professor of Private Law at the Université Panthéon-Assas (Paris II).

Anne Röthel is Professor of Law, Chair of Civil Law, European and International Private Law at the Bucerius Law School in Hamburg.

Lionel Smith is Sir William C Macdonald Professor of Law at the Faculty of Law at McGill University, and Professor of Private Law at the Dickson Poon School of Law, King's College London.

Prue Vines is Professor of Law at the University of New South Wales.

LIST OF ABBREVIATIONS

ABGB	Allgemeines Bürgerliches Gesetzbuch (*Austrian Civil Code*)
ABI	Association of British Insurers
AC	Appeal Cases (UK)
AcP	Archiv für die civilistische Praxis
ACT	Australian Capital Territory
act	Actualité
ACWS	All Canada Weekly Summaries
al	alternative
AILR	Australian Indigenous Law Reporter
All ER	All England Law Reports
All ER (Comm)	All England Law Reports (Commercial Cases)
ALR	Australian Law Reports
ALRI	Alberta Law Reform Institute
Art/art/Arts/arts	Article/article/Articles/articles
Aus	Australia
BBl	Bundesblatt (*Swiss Federal Gazette*)
BCCA	British Columbia Court of Appeal (*Canada*)
Beav	Beavan's Rolls Court Reports
BGB	Bürgerliches Gesetzbuch (*German Civil Code*)
BGE	Entscheidungen des Schweizerischen Bundesgerichtes: Amtliches Sammlung, Arrêts du Tribunal Federal Suisse: Recueil Officiel (*Official collection of the decisions of the Swiss Federal Court*)
BGer	Bundesgerichtsentscheide (*Decisions of the Federal Supreme Court of Switzerland*)
BGH	Bundesgerichtshof (*German Federal Supreme Court*)
BGHZ	Sammlung der Entscheidungen des Bundesgerichtshofs in Zivilsachen *(Decisions of the German Federal Supreme Court in civil law matters)*

Bk	Book
Bli NS	Bligh's House of Lords Reports, New Series
BT-Drs	Bundestags-Drucksache (*Publication by the German Federal Parliament*)
BV	Bundesverfassung (*Swiss Federal Constitution*)
BVerfG	Bundesverfassungsgericht (*German Federal Constitutional Court*)
BVerfGE	Sammlung der Entscheidungen des Bundesverfassungsgerichts (*Collection of the decisions of the German Federal Constitutional Court*)
BVG	Berufliches Vorsorge Gesetz (*Swiss Federal Law on Occupational Retirement, Survivors' and Disability Persion Plans*)
BVV 3	Verordnung über die steuerliche Abzugsberechtigung für Beiträge an anerkannte Vorsorgeformen (*Swiss Ordinance on the Tax Deductibility of Contributions to Recognized Forms of Benefit*)
BW	Burgerlijk Wetboek (*Dutch Civil Code*)
C	Communication from the Commission
CA	California
CA	Canada
CA	Court of Appeal
CanLII	Canadian Legal Information Institute
Cass	Corte Suprema di Cassazione (*Italian Supreme Court*)
Cass	Cour de Cassation (*French Supreme Court*)
Cass ch mixte	Chambres mixte de la Cour de Cassation (*French Supreme Court, divisional court*)
Cass civ	Chambres civiles de la Cour de Cassation (*French Court of Cassation, civil divisions*)
Cass com	Chambre commerciale de la Cour de Cassation (*French Court of Cassation, commercial division*)
CBR	Canadian Bankruptcy Reports
C Civ	Code civil (*French Civil Code*)
C Civ	Codice civile (*Italian Civil Code*)
C Civ	Código civil (*Spanish Civil Code*)
CCQ	Civil Code of Quebec (*Canada*)
CE	Conseil d'Etat (*French Council of State*)

cf	compare
Ch D	Chancery Division
CHF	Schweizer Franken (*Swiss franc*)
Ch/ch	Chancery Division
ch/chs	chapter/chapters
Ch App	Law Reports, Chancery Appeal Cases
CJ	Chief Justice
CLR	Commonwealth Law Reports (Australia)
cl/cls	clause/clauses
cols	columns
COM	European Commission documents
Con Constit	Conseil constitutionnel (*Constitutional Council, France*)
Cour const Belge	Cour constitutionnelle Belge (*Belgian Constitutional Court*)
COVIP	Commissione di vigilanza sui fondi pensione (*Italian Supervisory Commission for Pension Funds*)
cp	compare
CQLR	Compilation of Quebec Laws and Regulations
CRI	Corporate Rescue and Insolvency
Cr & Ph	Craig & Phillips' Chancery Reports
CS	Québec Cour Supérieure (*Quebec Superior Court*)
CSOH	Scotland Court of Session, Outer House
Cth	Commonwealth of Australia
D	Dunlop, Bell & Murray's Reports, Session Cases
D	Digest
DB	Der Betrieb
déc	décision (*French court decision*)
Dir	Directive
div	division
DLR	Dominion Law Reports
DM	Deutsche Mark
DMC	*donatio mortis causa*
doctr	doctrine
EBRI	Employee Benefit Research Institute
EC	European Community

edn	edition
EIR	European Insolvency Regulation
EQ	Equity Cases
ER	The English Reports
ERISA	Employee Retirement Income Security Act of 1974 (*US*)
esp	especially
ETPJ	Estates, Trusts & Pensions Journal
ETR	Estates & Trusts Reports
Eurostat	Statistical Office of the European Union
EWHC	High Court (England and Wales)
EWCA Civ	Court of Appeal, Civil Division (England and Wales)
F	Fraser's Court of Session Cases
F 2d	Federal Reporter, Second Series
Fam	Law Reports, Family Division
Fam Law	Family Law
FLR	Family Law Reports
FamRZ	Zeitschrift für das gesamte Familienrecht
FATF	Financial Action Task Force (on Money Laundering)
FCA	Federal Court of Appeal (*Canada*)
FC	Family Court of New Zealand
FCR	Family Court Reports
FEGLIA	Federal Employee's Group Life Insurance Act of 1954 (*US*)
FL-IPRG	Gesetz über das internationale Privatrecht (*Liechtenstein Private International Law*)
FL-OGH	Oberster Gerichtshof (*Liechtenstein Supreme Court*)
FRNZ	Family Reports of New Zealand
FS	Festschrift
GAAR	General Anti-Abuse Rule (*UK*)
GmbHR	GmbH-Rundschau
GS	Gedächtnisschrift
GWD	Greens Weekly Digest
Hare	Hare's Reports
HC	High Court
HCA	High Court of Australia

HGB	Handelsgesetzbuch (*German Commercial Code*)
HL	House of Lords (*UK*)
HLC	Clark & Finnelly's House of Lords Reports
HMRC	Her Majesty's Revenue and Customs (*UK*)
HTC	Hague Trusts Convention
IA	Insolvency Act 1986 (*UK*)
ICR	International Corporate Rescue
IHT	Inheritance Tax
InsO	Insolvenzordnung (*German Insolvency Code*)
I(PFD) Act	Inheritance (Provision for Family and Dependents) Act 1975 (*England and Wales*)
IPRG	Bundesgesetz über das Internationale Privatrecht (*Swiss Federal Code on Private International Law*)
IR	Irish Reports
IRA	Individual Retirement Account
ISTAT	Istituto Nazionale di Statistica (*Italian National Institute of Statistics*)
Iul D	Julian Digest
J	Judge
JA	Justice of Appeal
JCLS	Journal of Corporate Law Studies
JE	Jurisprudence-Express
Kay	Kay's Vice Chancellors' Reports
KB	Kings Bench Division
KG	Kammergericht (*Berlin, German Regional Appeal Court*)
KTS	Zeitschrift für Insolvenzrecht
L	Loi (*French law*)
Law Com	Law Commission
LC	Lord Chancellor
LES	Liechtensteinische Entscheidungssammlung (*Collection of the decisions of the Liechtenstein courts*)
LG	Landgericht (*German Regional Court*)
LGBl	Liechtensteinisches Landesgesetzblatt (*Liechtenstein Journal of Laws*)
LGDJ	Librairie générale de droit et de jurisprudence

lit	sub-paragraph
LJ	Lord Justice
LJQB	Law Journal Reports, Queen's Bench
LPA	Law of Property Act 1925 (*England and Wales*)
LPartG	Lebenspartnerschaftsgesetz (*German Law on Civil Partnership*)
LR	Law Reports
LR QB	Law Reports, Queens Bench Division
LT	Law Times
M	Macpherson's Session Cases
Mac & G	Macnaghten & Gordon's Chancery Reports
Macq	Macqueen's Scottish Appeal Cases
Man	Manitoba
MCA	Matrimonial Causes Act 1973 (*England and Wales*)
MD	Maryland
MN	Minnesota
Mor	Morison's Dictionary of Decisions
MWPA	Married Women's Property Act 1882 (*England, Wales and (Northern) Ireland*)
NBER	National Bureau of Economic Research
NE	North Eastern Reporter
NE 2d	North Eastern Reporter, Second Series
NEST	National Employment Savings Trust
Nfld & PEIR	Newfoundland and Prince Edward Island Reports
NJW	Neue Juristische Wochenschrift
NJW-RR	Neue Juristische Wochenschrift—Rechtsprechungs-Report Zivilrecht
no	number
NSW	New South Wales
NSW Trustee & Guardian	New South Wales Trustee and Guardian
NSWCA	New South Wales Court of Appeal (*Australia*)
NSWSC	New South Wales Supreme Court (*Australia*)
NT	Northern Territory
NW 2d	North Western Reporter, Second Series

NY	New York
NZ	New Zealand
NZ	Österreichische Notariatszeitung
NZCA	New Zealand Court of Appeal
NZFC	New Zealand Family Court
NZHC	New Zealand High Court
NZFLR	New Zealand Family Law Reports
NZLC	New Zealand Law Commission
NZLR	New Zealand Law Reports
NZSC	New Zealand Supreme Court
OECD	Organisation for Economic Co-operation and Development
OFT	Office of Fair Trading
Ohio Rev Code	Ohio Revised Code
OGH	Oberster Gerichtshof (*Austrian Supreme Court*)
OJ	Official Journal of the European Union
OLG	Oberlandesgericht (*German Regional Court of Appeal*)
OLGE	Rechtsprechung der Oberlandesgerichte auf dem Gebiet des Zivilrechts (*Collection of Decisions of the German Regional Courts of Appeal in Private Law Matters*)
OLR	Ontario Law Reports
OLRC	Ontario Law Reform Commission
Ont	Ontario
ONCA	Ontario Court of Appeal
ONSC	Ontario Supreme Court
OR	Obligationenrecht (*Swiss Code of Obligations*)
OR	Ontario Reports
P	The Law Reports: Probate Division (England and Wales)
PC	Privy Council
PCB	Private Client Business
PD	Law Reports: Probate, Divorce and Admiralty Division
PEICA	Prince Edward Island Court of Appeal (*Canada*)
PGR	Personen- und Gesellschaftsrecht (*Liechtenstein Person and Companies Act*)
POD	Payable-on-Death
PRA (NZ)	Property (Relationships) Act 1976 (*New Zealand*)

Prec Ch	Precedents in Chancery
PREFON	Caisse nationale de prévoyance de la fonction publique
pt	Part (of statute)
P Wms	Peere Williams's Reports
P	Pacific Reporter
P 2d	Pacific Reporter, Second Series
QBD/QB	Queen's Bench Division
QCCA	Court of Appeal of Quebec
Qld	Queensland
Qd R	Queensland Reports
QPC	Question prioritaire de constitutionnalité (*French anterior constitutional review*)
QPP	Quebec Pension Plan
R	Rettie, Crawford & Melville, Session Cases
Reg/reg	Regulation/regulation
Req	Chambre de Requêtes de la Cour de Cassation (*Chamber of Petitions of the French Court of Cassation*)
RESP	Registered Education Savings Plan
revd	reversed
RG	Reichsgericht (*Imperial Supreme Court, Germany*)
RGZ	Sammlung der Entscheidungen des Reichsgerichts in Zivilsachen (*Collection of Decisions of the German Imperial Court in Private Law Matters*)
RRIF	Registered Retirement Income Fund
RRSP	Registered Retirement Savings Plan
RSA	Revised Statutes of Alberta (*Canada*)
RSC	Revised Statutes of Canada
RSBC	Revised Statutes of British Columbia (*Canada*)
RSNB	Revised Statutes of New Brunswick (*Canada*)
RSNu	Revised Statutes of Nunavut (*Canada*)
RSNWT	Revised Statutes of Northwest Territories (*Canada*)
RSO	Revised Statutes of Ontario (*Canada*)
RSPEI	Revised Statutes of Prince Edward Island (*Canada*)
RSY	Revised Statutes of Yukon (*Canada*)

S	Shaw's Session Cases
SA	South Australia
SBC	Statutes of British Columbia (*Canada*)
SCt	Supreme Court Reporter
SCTA	Superannuation Complaints Tribunal of Australia
SC	Supreme Court/Session Cases
SC (HL)	Session Cases, House of Lords
SCC	Supreme Court of Canada
SCCA	Supreme Court of Canada Rulings on Applications for Leave to Appeal and Other Motions
sch	schedule (of statute)
SchlT AG	Schlusstitel Aktiengesellschaft (*Final Title AG*)
SchlT ZGB	Schlusstitel Zivilgesetzbuch (*Final Title Swiss Civil Code*)
SCR	Supreme Court Reports
SGB VI	Sozialgesetzbuch VI: Gesetzliche Rentenversicherung (*German Social Law Code, Book VI: Statutory Pension Insurance*)
SJ	La Semaine Judiciaire
SLPQ	Scottish Law & Practice Quarterly
SLT	Scots Law Times
SLT (News)	Scots Law Times, News Section
SLT (Sh Ct)	Scots Law Times, Sheriff Court Reports
SLT (Lyon Ct)	Scots Law Times, Lyon Court Reports
SME	Small and Medium Enterprises
SMSF	Self-Managed Superannuation Fund
SO	Statutes of Ontario (*Canada*)
So 2d	Southern Reporter, Second Series
SP	Scottish Parliament
SR	Systematische Sammlung des Bundesrechts (*Systematic Collection of Swiss Federal Law*)
SR (NSW)	New South Wales State Reports
s/ss	section/sections
SS	Statutes of Saskatchewan (*Canada*)
STC (SCD)	Simon's Tax Cases, Special Commissioners' Decisions

Supp	Supplement
SW 2d	South Western Reporter, Second Series
SW 3d	South Western Reporter, Third Series
Tas	Tasmania
TC	Tax Cases
Temp LQ	Temple Law Quarterly
TFSA	Tax-Free Savings Account
TOD	Transfer-on-Death
trans	translation
Treas Reg	Treasury Regulation
UK	United Kingdom
UKHL	United Kingdom House of Lords
UKPC	United Kingdom Privy Council
UKSC	United Kingdom Supreme Court
UPC	Uniform Probate Code (*US*)
US	United States of America
US	United States Reports
USC	United States Code
UTC	Uniform Trust Code
ÜBest GmbH	Übergangsbestimmungen Gesellschaft mit beschränkter Haftung (*Transitional Provisions regulating the GmbH*)
VersR	Versicherungsrecht
Ves Sen	Vesey Senior's Chancery Reports
Vic	Victoria
vol	volume
VVG	Versicherungsvertragsgesetz (*German Insurance Contract Act*)
WA	Western Australia
WL	Westlaw
WLR	Western Law Reporter (*Canada*)
WLR	Weekly Law Reports
WN	Weekly Notes
W & S	Wilson & Shaw's Appeal Cases, House of Lords
WTLR	Wills & Trust Law Reports

WTO	World Trade Organization
ZEV	Zeitschrift für Erbrecht und Vermögensnachfolge
ZfS	Zeitschrift für Schadensrecht
ZGB	Schweizerisches Zivilgesetzbuch (*Swiss Civil Code*)
ZIP	Zeitschrift für Wirtschaftsrecht
ZPO	Zivilprozessordnung (*German Civil Procedure Code*)

Introduction

ALEXANDRA BRAUN AND ANNE RÖTHEL

I. Scope and Focus of the Volume

A considerable amount of wealth is currently being passed on death outside the traditional sphere of rules which regulate the transfer of wealth on death. This is primarily due to two reasons. First, 'anticipated succession' whereby wealth is transmitted during a person's lifetime in anticipation and in advance of a future succession; and, secondly, the transfer of wealth on death through mechanisms other than wills or intestacy rules. As a result, a significant proportion of wealth transmission is no longer governed by the rules of succession. This development calls into question the scope and the role of succession law, as well as its underlying policies.

This book deals with the second of these developments, ie, with the way in which wealth is being passed on death through mechanisms that operate as functional equivalents to a will. These include, for example, life insurance, various pensions and retirement plans, bank and savings accounts, trusts, foundations, forms of joint ownership with right of survivorship etc. In the US, these mechanisms have been grouped under the legal category of 'will-substitutes' and have captured the attention of legal scholars, legal practitioners, and lawmakers alike. This has led to considerable literature in the field, as well as to regulatory interventions.[1] Consequently, the area is generally well researched in the US.

By contrast, relatively little is known about developments in other jurisdictions where the transfer of wealth on death other than by will or intestacy has often failed to attract much academic interest. This was the motivation behind the international conference which was convened on 27 and 28 March 2015 at Lady Margaret Hall in Oxford, the proceedings of which are published in this volume. The aim of the conference was to advance the understanding of the scope

[1] In the US, the phenomenon has developed especially throughout the 20th century. See JH Langbein, 'Major Reforms of the Property Restatement and the Uniform Probate Code: Reformation, Harmless Error, and Nonprobate Transfers' (2012) 38 *American College of Trust and Estate Counsel Law Journal* 1. The publication of NF Dacey, *How to Avoid Probate!* (New York, Crown, 1965) seems to have accelerated developments in the US. This is suggested by SE Sterk and MB Leslie, 'Accidental Inheritance: Retirement Accounts and the Hidden Law of Succession' (2014) 89 *New York University Law Review* 165, 167, and DJ Feder and RH Sitkoff, 'Revocable Trusts and Incapacity Planning: More than Just a Will Substitute' (2016) 24 *Elder Law Journal* (forthcoming).

of the proliferation of 'will-substitutes' and to obtain a better picture of the types of mechanisms employed in practice. It was also to shed light on the underlying rationale of will-substitutes, to establish and promote a scholarly debate across a number of different jurisdictions, and to generate comparative knowledge, which has so far been unavailable. The contributions contained in this volume are thus designed to enhance the emerging interest in the comparative study of succession law.[2]

Before we explain the structure of this book, it is useful to reflect on the origin and meaning of the term 'will-substitutes' so as to gain a better understanding of the scope and focus of this volume.

II. The Origins and Meaning of the Term 'Will-Substitutes'

The term 'will-substitutes' was coined in the American context where it takes a very specific meaning. In the 1930s Thomas Atkinson dedicated a chapter of his *Handbook of the Laws of Wills* to will-substitutes, examining devices that were used to obviate the execution of a will or the judicial administration of a person's estate.[3] Although several other American authors have since studied 'will-substitutes', or devices that 'substitute the will',[4] the term seems to have gained greater international attention following its use by John Langbein in an article published in 1984, in which he examined the reasons for their proliferation.[5] For Langbein, will-substitutes are 'non-probate wills', ie, instruments that transfer wealth on death but that do not have to comply with the formalities prescribed for wills, and that pass wealth outside the traditional US probate procedures.

Langbein is one of the drafters of the *Restatement (Third) of Property, Wills and Other Donative Transfers*, and it is therefore no surprise that one of its sections is dedicated to will-substitutes.[6] At the heart of the definition included in the

[2] See, for instance, the two volumes in the series *Comparative Succession Law* published by OUP and edited by KGC Reid, MJ De Waal and R Zimmermann.

[3] TE Atkinson, *Handbook of the Laws of Wills*, vol 1 (St Paul MN, West Publishing Co, 1937) ch 4.

[4] CW Leaphart, 'The Trust as a Substitute for a Will' (1930) 78 *University of Pennsylvania Law Review* 626; WJ Bowe, *Estate Planning and Taxation*, vol 1 (Buffalo NY, Dennis, 1957) ch VI; LM Jones, 'The Use of Joint Bank Accounts as Substitute for Testamentary Disposition of Property' (1955) 17 *University of Pittsburgh Law Review* 42; LW Schraeder, 'Bank Deposits as Will Substitutes in Missouri' (1963) 28 *Missouri Law Review* 482; ME Meyer, 'The Revocable Trust as a Will Substitute—A Coming of Age' (1967) 39 *University of Colorado Law Review* 180.

[5] JH Langbein, 'The Nonprobate Revolution and the Future of the Law of Succession' (1984) 97 *Harvard Law Review* 1108.

[6] *Restatement Third of Property: Wills and Other Donative Transfers* § 7.1(a) (Philadelphia, American Law Institute, 2003). The text of the section is reproduced in ch 1 below, p 10. *The Restatement (Second) of Property (Donative Transfers)* of 1983 addressed will-substitutes briefly in vol 4 at section 32.4, entitled 'Document of Transfer as a Substitute for a Will'.

Restatement is the fact that the transfer on death takes place *outside probate*. In other words, the transfer does not involve a probate court, which ascertains the validity of the will and oversees the administration of the estate. Thus, the definition in the *Restatement* is coupled with the procedural aspect of estate administration in the US, and the connecting factor of the various instruments employed is the absence of state control.

However, it is clear that will-substitutes do not just play a role in legal systems that have a formal probate procedure governing the transfer of wealth. Will-substitutes are part of the reality of many jurisdictions, irrespective of the technical process through which wealth is transferred on death. Hence, this book adopts a broader conception of 'will-substitutes', which does not centre on the procedural aspects of the transfer. In this volume, the term is intended to refer to all types of instruments or mechanisms that are functionally equivalent to wills in that they can be used to identify the beneficiary of wealth to be passed with effect on death.[7] Such instruments are usually intentional and revocable up until death, leaving the disponer with substantial control over the assets during his or her lifetime.[8] But, even where the instrument does not present all of these features, it can still serve functions similar to those of a will.[9] However, instruments that operate entirely during lifetime (ie, instances of anticipated succession referred to earlier), or that bind the transferor already during his or her lifetime, do not in principle fall within the scope of this volume.[10]

III. Will-Substitutes: Not a New Phenomenon or Challenge

Unlike what one might expect, will-substitutes are not a new phenomenon.[11] The will has never been the only instrument used to pass wealth on death. In fact, though representing the main instrument used during Roman times, wills fell into disuse after the fall of the Roman Empire and only became popular again during

[7] The will can also have other functions such as appointing an executor or a guardian of one's children, but the focus in this book is on the will as a mode for the distribution of wealth on death.

[8] For this reason, most authors have not included in their discussions benefits that pass by way of matrimonial property regimes, as the transfer usually takes place automatically. This is different from certain marital property arrangements or agreements that can be used to benefit a spouse. For France, see C Pérès, ch 7 below II.A.iii, who defines them, however, as 'impure' will-substitutes. For Germany, see A Dutta in ch 8 below VI.B.

[9] Such as, for instance, partnership clauses, which are not freely revocable, or the New Zealand relationship property entitlement claims which are not technically speaking 'dispositions'.

[10] This is the reason why this volume does not include, for instance, a discussion of inheritance contracts (*Erbverträge*), common in German, Austrian and Swiss law.

[11] Langbein, 'Major Reforms of the Property Restatement and the Uniform Probate Code', above n 1, 10 f.

the twelfth century, when the will experienced a sort of renaissance.[12] Thus, at least in certain periods of history, other instruments have prevailed over the will. What is more, the will has not always had the scope it has now. In both common and civil law jurisdictions, certain assets could not be disposed of through wills.[13] Also, some of the mechanisms discussed in this volume have been around for centuries, for example, gifts *mortis causa*, the trust, and joint tenancies.[14]

It has always been difficult to characterise those instruments that allow for a transfer of wealth on death within the structure of private law.[15] In this respect it is interesting to note that Roman lawyers had employed the term '*mortis causa capio*' to refer to modes of acquisition on death other than by inheritance or legacy.[16] In other words, the term indicated that those transfers took effect on death but that they did not have a specific action, and therefore did not have a specific name.[17] These included, for instance, the *donatio mortis causa*,[18] which by the time of the classical period was increasingly compared with legacies.[19]

IV. Will-Substitutes: Difficulties and Open Questions

In many ways, today's lawyers face the same problems and uncertainties that Roman lawyers faced. In fact, one of the principal problems that will-substitutes create, from the perspective of a succession lawyer, is to determine where will-substitutes fit on the map and which area of law they should fall under, for example, whether they should be treated as *inter vivos* instruments or rather as testamentary dispositions that belong within the realm of succession law.

[12] G Rossi, 'Il testamento nel medioevo fra dottrina giuridica e prassi' in MC Rossi (ed), *Margini di libertà: testamenti femminili nel medioevo. Atti del convegno internazionale, Verona, 23–25 ottobre 2008* (Verona, Cierre Edizioni, 2010) 45, 53; S Werkmüller 'Rechtsgeschäfte auf den Todesfall in den deutschen Rechten des Mittelalters' in *Actes à cause de mort* (Brussels, De Boeck Université, 1993) 257, 260; E Besta, *Le successioni nella storia del diritto italiano* (Milan, Giuffrè, 1961) 147 ff.

[13] In England, land could not be disposed of by will until the mid-16th century. See J Baker, *The Oxford History of the Law of England: Volume VI 1483–1558* (Oxford, OUP, 2003) ch 35; R Kerridge, 'Testamentary Formalities in England and Wales' in KGC Reid, MJ De Waal and R Zimmermann (eds), *Comparative Succession Law, volume 1. Testamentary Formalities* (Oxford, OUP, 2011) 305, 308 ff. For details about medieval law, and in particular Germanic law, see K Gottschalk, 'Erbe und Recht. Die Übertragung von Eigentum in der frühen Neuzeit' in S Willer, S Weigel and B Jussen (eds), *Erbe. Übertragungskonzepte zwischen Natur und Kultur* (Berlin, Suhrkamp Verlag, 2013) 85, 99.

[14] See ch 3 below, fn 8.

[15] For an overview of the discussion in Germany, see M Harder, *Zuwendungen unter Lebenden auf den Todesfall* (Berlin, Duncker & Humblot, 1968).

[16] M Kaser, *Das Römische Privatrecht*, vol 2 (Munich, CH Beck, 1975) 564 ff; H Lange and K Kuchinke, *Erbrecht*, 5th edn (Munich, CH Beck, 2001) 740 f.

[17] D 39.6.31 pr.

[18] E Schlagintweit, 'Die Erwerbung auf den Todesfall (*mortis causa capio*) nach römischem Recht' (1863) 6 *Jahrbücher für die Dogmatik des heutigen römischen und deutschen Privatrechts* 318; E Böcking, *Römisches Privatrecht: Institutionen des römischen Civilrechts*, 2nd edn (Bonn, M Cohen, 1862) 290 ff.

[19] F Schulz, *Classical Roman Law* (Oxford, Clarendon Press, 1954) 332; Kaser, above n 16, 564.

This matters not just in the context of the formalities applicable to wills, but also in relation to a number of default rules which regulate wills, including rules on: the automatic revocation of wills in case of remarriage or divorce; unworthiness and forfeiture of the beneficiary; lapse; the construction of wills etc. In addition, it is unclear whether and to what extent these mechanisms should be exempted from the application of those succession rules that are aimed at protecting the interests of third parties, such as creditors and family members and dependants.

There are indeed difficulties with drawing a clear line between lifetime and *mortis causa* dispositions.[20] This is confirmed by the European Succession Regulation (Brussels IV), which came into force in August 2015.[21] Alongside instruments that operate a transfer *otherwise than by succession*, the Regulation recognises the category of 'Disposition of Property upon Death (DoPuD)', which includes not just wills and joint wills, but also agreements as to succession, and only these fall within the scope of the Regulation.

Thus, will-substitutes raise a number of questions that are not only relevant for their practical implications, but which are also interesting from a theoretical point of view. In fact, because will-substitutes can operate largely outside the scope of current succession rules, they raise questions about the role of the will and also the purpose of succession law as a whole. Their proliferation raises doubts about the functioning and the scope of succession law and about its underlying principles and policies. For these reasons, the contributions in this volume do not explore merely the many instruments that are used to pass wealth on death across a number of jurisdictions, but also consider wider questions about the impact that these developments have on the coherence of succession law, as well as on its boundaries and its scope.

V. Structure of the Book

This book is divided into two parts. Part one contains contributions from common law, mixed legal and civil law jurisdictions, which explore will-substitutes within a particular legal system (chapters one to nine). These chapters aim to clarify which instruments serve as a means of passing wealth on death, the rationale that lies behind their use, and how they are regulated within the respective jurisdiction, ie, which mandatory or default provisions are applied to them. Their objective is also to shed light on other questions which consider the overall attitude towards

[20] For an attempt to establish a set of criteria that distinguish testamentary dispositions from lifetime ones, see K Muscheler, *Erbrecht* (Tübingen, Mohr Siebeck, 2010) 61 f.

[21] Regulation (EU) 650/2012 of the European Parliament and of the Council of 4 July 2012 on jurisdiction, applicable law, recognition and enforcement of decisions and acceptance and enforcement of authentic instruments in matters of succession and on the creation of a European Certificate of Succession [2012] OJ L201/107.

will-substitutes such as: are will-substitutes perceived as accepted expressions of the private autonomy of a person or are they rather seen with suspicion? Is the approach of individual systems towards will-substitutes coherent or is there need for further academic research and/or future law reform?

The starting point for this section is the developments in the US, where a 'non-probate revolution' has taken place over the course of the past century,[22] and where, as we have seen, the term 'will-substitute' was coined. One of the aims of this volume is to ascertain whether, and to what extent, a similar 'revolution' has taken place elsewhere. This includes the question of whether the issues that have arisen in other jurisdictions are the same as those that have emerged in the US, and whether the legal discourse has developed in a similar manner. Given the differences between the jurisdictions examined in this volume, and the lack of common structures and existing doctrinal approaches in this field of law, we have refrained from establishing a rigid questionnaire but have invited our contributors to identify the aspects and developments that they regard as most striking or important.

Alongside contributions that examine developments in specific jurisdictions, in part two, the book also features contributions that explore the concept of will-substitutes from a variety of different perspectives, for example, those of company owners (chapter ten), international investors (chapter eleven), third parties such as creditors (chapters twelve to thirteen), and family members and dependants (chapters fourteen to fifteen), who are affected by transfers of wealth that take place outside the realm of succession law. The picture that the authors have provided demonstrates the complexity and colourfulness of this area of law and we would like to thank them for their efforts in exploring these aspects.

We would further like to thank the Institute of European and Comparative Law in Oxford, and in particular its Administrator, Ms Jenny Dix, for her invaluable support in organising the conference. Our thanks also go to our own home institutions, Lady Margaret Hall and the Bucerius Law School, and last but not least to our funders, the John Fell Fund of the University of Oxford, the British Academy, and the Deutsche Forschungsgemeinschaft, who have so generously sponsored the research, the event, as well as the editorial work, that has led to this volume. Last but not least, we would like to thank Mr Philipp Poitiers, and especially Dr Johanna Croon, for their invaluable assistance in the editing process of this volume.

[22] Langbein, 'The Nonprobate Revolution', above n 5.

Part I

Will-Substitutes from the Perspective of Individual Jurisdictions

1

Will-Substitutes: A US Perspective

THOMAS P GALLANIS*

This chapter aims to introduce the phenomenon of will-substitutes in the US to a transnational readership. The chapter consists of six principal parts. After this brief introduction, part I lays a foundation by defining the terms of art 'will-substitute' and 'nonprobate transfer', by locating the law(s) governing will-substitutes within the federal-state structure of the US, and by explaining the reasons why in the US will-substitutes are often used. Part II surveys the principal types of will-substitute used in the US: revocable trust instruments, life insurance beneficiary designations, pension and retirement account beneficiary designations, multiple-party and payable-on-death (POD) bank account registrations, transfer-on-death (TOD) registrations of securities or automobiles, deeds creating joint tenancies and tenancies by the entirety in land, and TOD deeds of land. Part II also briefly discusses gifts *causa mortis*. Part III explains the distinction between 'pure' and 'imperfect' will-substitutes. The former fully replicate the essential features of a will; the latter do not. Part III also explains why will-substitutes are valid under US law even though they need not comply with the formalities required for a testamentary transfer. Part IV explores the rights of third parties in assets transferred at death by a will-substitute. These third parties include taxing authorities, the decedent's creditors and the decedent's surviving spouse and children. Part V explores a dominant trend in US succession law: the harmonisation of the default rules governing wills and will-substitutes. Part VI then explores a counter-trend: the federal pre-emption of state succession law, particularly relating to pension plans and life insurance. A brief conclusion follows.

* I should disclose that I served as an Associate Reporter for the *Restatement Third of Trusts*, as a member of the Consultative Group for the *Restatement Third of Property: Wills and Other Donative Transfers* and as the Reporter for the Uniform Real Property Transfer on Death Act. I currently serve as executive director of the Uniform Law Commission's Joint Editorial Board for Uniform Trust and Estate Acts, which is the official body monitoring and advising on all uniform laws in the fields of trusts and succession. In this chapter, however, I am speaking in my individual capacity only. Portions of this chapter draw on TP Gallanis, *Family Property Law: Cases and Materials on Wills, Trusts, and Estates*, 6th edn (St Paul MN, Foundation Press, 2014). It is a pleasure to thank my students Robert Fitzgerald, Adrian Kowalski, Daniel McGrath and Maximilian Traut for research assistance, and the University of Iowa College of Law for research support.

I. Foundational Matters: Terms of Art, the US Federal-State Structure, and Reasons for Will-Substitute Popularity

The traditional way to transmit property at death is by writing a valid will. The court-supervised process of determining whether a will is valid is called 'probate', from the Latin *probare*, meaning 'to prove'. The court in which this occurs is typically called a 'probate court'. The same court also oversees a related process: the administration of the decedent's estate. The relationship between 'probate' and 'administration' is so close that, in informal usage, the two terms are used synonymously.

Yet there are ways to transmit property at death that need not involve a court process. Rather than using a will, the owner of property can instead use a 'will-substitute' to arrange for a 'nonprobate transfer'. Put simply, a nonprobate transfer occurs outside probate; it does not require any court process. The owner of property merely designates one or more beneficiaries to receive the property at the owner's death. A formal definition of a will-substitute appears in the *Restatement Third of Property*, which defines a will-substitute as

> an arrangement respecting property or contract rights that is established during the donor's life, under which (1) the right to possession or enjoyment of the property or to a contractual payment shifts outside of probate to the donee at the donor's death; and (2) substantial lifetime rights of dominion, control, possession, or enjoyment are retained by the donor.[1]

One example of a will-substitute is a life insurance beneficiary designation. The owner of the life insurance policy can designate a beneficiary to receive the proceeds on the owner's death. The proceeds are paid directly from the insurance company to the beneficiary, without involving a probate court.

The laws governing will-substitutes in the US are primarily state, not federal, laws. (We will encounter an important exception in part VI.) The laws of succession and trusts, the law of property, the law of the family, the law of insurance (including life insurance), even the law of debtor and creditor: these are all areas of state law. This means that each of the 50 states, plus the District of Columbia, has its own law on point. Having so many jurisdictions within the US makes it

[1] *Restatement Third of Property: Wills and Other Donative Transfers* § 7.1(a) (Philadelphia, American Law Institute, 2003). No definition of 'will-substitute' appears in the Uniform Probate Code (UPC). The UPC frequently uses the term 'nonprobate transfer' but defines it only in § 6-102(a). That section concerns the liability of nonprobate transferees for creditor claims and for statutory allowances to the decedent's surviving spouse and children. Because the section is specifically about liability, its definition of 'nonprobate transfer' is deliberately non-comprehensive, excluding joint tenancies of land. See UPC § 6-102(a) and the accompanying Comment.

complicated to generalise about 'the US law' of will-substitutes. Any general statement may not be true for each of these 51 jurisdictions.

This chapter focuses predominantly but not exclusively on the uniform laws promulgated by the Uniform Law Commission.[2] The Commission has been particularly active in the fields of succession and trusts, most notably with the Uniform Probate Code (UPC) and the Uniform Trust Code (UTC). There are more than 25 uniform acts in the area of succession or trusts.[3] Some of these acts have been adopted by many state legislatures while others have been adopted by a smaller number of state legislatures. Yet even the acts that have not been widely adopted have been influential. An example is the UPC. The UPC, or an amended version of it, has been enacted in 17 states plus the US Virgin Islands.[4] The influence of the UPC is far greater than this number suggests because many additional states have enacted parts of the UPC without adopting it entirely.

The point for present purposes is this: the law of will-substitutes is primarily state law, and this law varies among the many jurisdictions within the US. One can speak of 'majority' or 'uniform' approaches but these will not necessarily be universal.

Another topic about which it is hard to generalise is the reasons why a particular individual might elect to use a will-substitute. In many instances, will-substitutes are cheaper, quicker and easier to create than wills. For instance, when starting a new job, one can readily complete standard forms naming a beneficiary for an employer-sponsored pension account and life insurance policy. Similarly, when opening a bank account, one can readily complete the bank's form to register the account in joint ownership or to name a pay-on-death beneficiary. Completing these forms is faster and easier than writing a will and is essentially costless. Not all will-substitutes are so straightforward, however. The preparation of a revocable trust instrument is typically more complicated than the preparation of a will.

A second reason why will-substitutes can be popular is that they avoid probate, which is a public,[5] court-supervised process.[6] As John Langbein wrote in a seminal article on 'The Nonprobate Revolution and the Future of the Law of Succession':

> The probate system has earned a lamentable reputation for expense, delay, clumsiness, makework, and worse. In various jurisdictions, especially the dozen-odd that have

[2] For background on uniform laws in the US, including the UPC, see TP Gallanis, 'Trusts and Estates: Teaching Uniform Law' (2014) 58 *St Louis University Law Journal* 671. See also the website of the Uniform Law Commission, www.uniformlaws.org. That website has the full text of each uniform law and explains where each law has been enacted.

[3] See the acts listed in Gallanis, 'Trusts and Estates', above n 2, 674–75, to which now must be added the Uniform Fiduciary Access to Digital Assets Act, approved in 2014 and revised in 2015, and the Uniform Trust Decanting Act, approved in 2015.

[4] See www.uniformlaws.org/Act.aspx?title=Probate Code.

[5] For discussion, see FH Foster, 'Trust Privacy' (2008) 93 *Cornell Law Review* 555 (examining privacy's costs as well as its benefits).

[6] For a critique of probate in one US jurisdiction, see JH Langbein, 'The Scandal of Connecticut's Probate Courts', available at www.law.yale.edu/faculty/1766.htm (containing the advice 'Don't Die in Connecticut').

> adopted or imitated the simplified procedures of the Uniform Probate Code of 1969 ('UPC'), the intensity of hostility to probate may have abated a little. There are, however, intrinsic limits to the potential of probate reform. As Richard Wellman, the principal draftsman of the UPC, forthrightly declared: 'The assumption that administration of an estate requires a judicial proceeding is as doubtful as it is costly'. Because the Anglo-American procedural tradition is preoccupied with adversarial and litigational values, the decision to organize any function as a judicial proceeding is inconsistent with the interests that ordinary people regard as paramount when they think about the transmission of their property at death: dispatch, simplicity, inexpensiveness, privacy. As long as probate reform still calls for probate, it will not go far enough for the tastes of many transferors, who view probate as little more than a tax imposed for the benefit of court functionaries and lawyers.[7]

Will-substitutes function to pass property at death without being subject to the probate process required for wills. Will-substitutes are sometimes referred to as probate-avoidance devices, or as nonprobate wills. They do not, of course, eliminate the desirability of having a will. Some will-substitutes are asset-specific (life insurance, previously mentioned, is an example), so a will remains necessary for the decedent's other property. Also, a will is helpful as a backstop even for property affected by a will-substitute, in case the decedent outlives the designated beneficiary.

A third reason why some individuals may choose to use a will-substitute is that the rights of creditors and surviving spouses and children are, depending on the jurisdiction and on the will-substitute, more restricted in property passing by will-substitute than in property passing by will. I shall have more to say about this in part IV. This differential, however, typically does not apply to taxing authorities, as we shall see in part IV. Will-substitutes are subject to transfer taxation.

II. Principal Types of Will-Substitute

In the US, will-substitutes take seven principal forms: (1) revocable trust instruments; (2) life insurance beneficiary designations; (3) pension and retirement account beneficiary designations; (4) multiple-party and POD bank account registrations; (5) TOD registrations of securities or automobiles; (6) deeds creating joint tenancies and tenancies by the entirety in land; and (7) TOD deeds of land. Also meriting mention are gifts *causa mortis* (8).

[7] JH Langbein, 'The Nonprobate Revolution and the Future of the Law of Succession' (1984) 97 *Harvard Law Review* 1108, 1116–17. For a new empirical study arguing instead that 'court oversight adds more value and costs far less than assumed', see D Horton, 'In Partial Defense of Probate: Evidence from Alameda County, California' (2015) 103 *Georgetown Law Journal* 605.

A. Revocable Trust Instruments[8]

A trust is revocable if the person creating the trust (the settlor) retains the power to revoke it. Under modern law (eg, UTC § 602), the settlor is presumed to have retained the power to revoke or amend the trust unless the trust instrument expressly provides otherwise. Revocable trusts are commonly used as will-substitutes. In such an arrangement, the settlor typically retains not only the power to revoke or amend the trust but also the lifetime right to the trust's income and, in many instances, discretionary access to the trust's corpus. After the settlor dies, the assets remaining in the trust can be used for the benefit of—or, depending on the terms of the trust, be distributed directly to—the remainder beneficiaries. No court process is needed.

B. Life Insurance Beneficiary Designations[9]

A life insurance policy is a contract between an insurer and a policyholder. The contract promises to pay a specified sum (the proceeds) if a specified person (the insured, who may but need not be the policyholder) dies during the policy's term. The policyholder owns the policy and its associated rights, including the right to name the beneficiary or beneficiaries to whom the proceeds will be paid if the insured dies during the term. The payment of the proceeds to the beneficiary can be structured in many ways; these include a single lump-sum payment, a series of payments made over a fixed period, or a series of payments annuitised over the lifetime(s) of one or more beneficiaries. The payment option is selected by the policyholder or, failing that, by the beneficiary. Life insurance is straightforwardly a will-substitute. If the insured dies during the term of the policy, the proceeds are paid directly from the insurer to the beneficiary. No court process is required.

[8] Data on the number or asset size of revocable trusts are hard to obtain because US law does not require *inter vivos* trusts to be recorded. However, institutional trustees that are part of the US Federal Reserve System must make annual reports to federal regulators. These reports indicate that, at the end of 2011, 'roughly $860 billion [was] held in about 780,000 private and charitable trust accounts'. J Dukeminier and R Sitkoff, *Wills, Trusts, and Estates*, 9th edn (New York, Wolters Kluwer, 2013) 393.

[9] According to the *2014 Life Insurance Fact Book* published by the American Council of Life Insurers, in 2013 the 850 life insurers operating in the US had over 274 million life insurance policies in force. These policies represent roughly $19.6 trillion of protection in force. Of this amount, roughly $8.2 trillion was provided through group insurance policies (usually provided by employers or professional associations) and $11.4 trillion was provided in individual policies. The average face value of an individual life insurance policy in 2013 was $165,000. The *Fact Book* is available at www.acli.com/Tools/Industry%20Facts/Life%20Insurers%20Fact%20Book/Pages/Default.aspx.

C. Pension and Retirement Account Beneficiary Designations[10]

A pension plan account arises from a contract between a plan sponsor and a plan participant. Many pension plans are employer sponsored, with the employees as the participants. Employer-sponsored plans are either defined benefit plans or, more commonly, defined contribution plans. A defined benefit plan entitles the participant to a retirement benefit according to a predetermined formula, such as an annual income in retirement determined by the participant's average salary while working multiplied by the number of years with the employer. In a defined contribution plan, in contrast, the employer makes a specified contribution each pay period—in many instances, the employee also contributes—and then the funds available at retirement are determined by the investment performance of the account, with the investment choices under the employee's control. In addition to employer-sponsored plans, there are also other vehicles for retirement savings, most notably the individual retirement account (known as an IRA).

Once the participant retires, the participant controls the amount and timing of distributions from the pension or other retirement account, subject to certain rules on minimum required distributions that apply once the participant reaches the age of 70.5 years. Funds remaining in the account at the participant's death are distributed to the beneficiaries as designated by the participant or, if no designation was made, to the beneficiaries as defined by the account's governing documents. The distributions occur without any court process and can be structured in various forms such as a lump-sum payment or annuity.

D. Multiple-Party and Payable-On-Death Bank Account Registrations[11]

Bank and other financial intermediary accounts are frequently registered in the names of more than one person. These accounts generally take one of four forms: joint accounts, trust accounts (so-called 'Totten' trusts), POD accounts, or agency accounts. These forms do not necessarily reveal the depositor's purpose in creating the account. The depositor may intend to confer on the other party beneficial lifetime rights or survivorship rights or both. For example, if Alice deposits funds in a bank account registered jointly in the names of 'Alice or Bill', Alice may have

[10] In 2013, 51.3% of all workers in the US worked for an employer or union sponsoring a retirement plan; of these, 40.8% participated in the plan. EBRI, EBRI Issue Brief no 405 (October 2014) 1, available at www.ebri.org/pdf/briefspdf/EBRI_IB_405_Oct14.RetPart.pdf.

In 2013, private-sector employer-sponsored plans held about $8.1 trillion, and IRAs held about $7.1 trillion. EBRI, EBRI Issue Brief no 414 (May 2015) 31, available at www.ebri.org/pdf/briefspdf/EBRI_IB_414.May15.IRAs.pdf.

[11] I know of no data on the number or value of bank accounts with multiple parties or pay-on-death beneficiary designations.

used the joint form for any one of three different purposes: (1) to give Alice and Bill lifetime rights to withdraw funds for their personal benefit, with the survivor receiving funds remaining in the account upon the death of the first to die (akin to joint tenancy); (2) to give Bill the legal power to draw from the account for Alice's benefit but not Bill's and no survivorship right (an agency account, in which Bill acts as Alice's agent); or (3) to give Bill the right to any funds remaining in the account at Alice's death but no lifetime rights or powers (the equivalent of a Totten trust or a POD account).

The Totten trust is created when a person deposits funds in a bank account in his or her name 'in trust for' another person. The depositor typically retains exclusive control of the account until death, when any remaining funds pass to the beneficiary. These accounts are functionally equivalent to a will, except that no court process is required. The Totten trust takes its name from the leading New York case—*Matter of Totten*[12]—validating the arrangement. The *Restatement Third of Trusts*, the *Restatement Third of Property*, and the UPC all recognise the validity of Totten trusts.[13]

Like Totten trusts, joint bank accounts contain a survivorship feature. The balance in the account at the death of a depositor shifts to the surviving account holder(s) without going through probate. Joint bank accounts are widely accepted as will-substitutes throughout the US. It is worth noting, however, that (except in a very few states) the funds in a joint bank account are not owned in joint tenancy (or tenancy by the entirety, if between spouses). That is to say, a deposit into such an account does not transfer an undivided interest therein to the other account holder(s). Rather, each account holder owns his or her own contributions to the account.[14] If one account holder withdraws an amount in excess of his or her contributions, the other account holder(s) can force that excess to be returned.[15]

POD accounts are created when a depositor registers the account in his or her name 'payable on death' to another person. Unlike joint accounts, the form of the POD account discloses the depositor's intention to transfer ownership of the account only at the depositor's death. This difference has led most courts to treat joint and POD accounts differently. In the absence of validating legislation, POD accounts are generally held by courts to be testamentary, invalidating the

[12] *Matter of Totten*, 71 NE 748 (New York CA 1904).

[13] *Restatement Third of Trusts* § 26 (Philadelphia, American Law Institute, 2003); *Restatement Third of Property* §7.1 Comment i; UPC § 6-201(8)(ii), § 6-212.

[14] eg *Enright v Lehmann*, 735 NW 2d 326 (Minnesota Supreme Court 2007), holding that, of the funds in a joint account, a creditor may only garnish the funds contributed by the debtor, unless the creditor proves by clear and convincing evidence that the depositor(s) of the other funds intended to confer them on the debtor.

[15] This right is routinely waived by inaction, possibly triggering federal gift tax consequences when the statute of limitations expires. See Treas Reg § 25.2511-1(h)(4); *Estate of Lang v Commissioner*, 613 F 2d 770 (United States CA for the Ninth Circuit 1980). Consequently, as between the co-account holders, a deposit into a joint bank account is revocable; no federal gift tax consequences are triggered because the tax law treats the deposit as an 'incomplete' gift.

attempted transfer of ownership on the depositor's death.[16] POD accounts have fared much better in the legislatures. The UPC and non-uniform legislation in many states validate POD accounts without requiring compliance with the formalities required of wills.[17] The *Restatement Third of Property* also recognises the validity of POD accounts.[18]

E. Transfer-On-Death Registrations of Securities or Automobiles[19]

When Article VI of the UPC was revised in 1989, provisions were added authorising what was then a new form of ownership of investment securities: TOD registration. As the prefatory note to Article VI explains,

> [t]he purpose of … the revised article is to allow the owner of securities to register the title in transfer-on-death (TOD) form … The legislation enables an issuer, transfer agent, broker, or other such intermediary to transfer the securities directly to the designated transferee on the owner's death.[20]

The legislation enables securities to be registered with the same kind of TOD or POD provisions as a bank account. Some states have carried TOD registration further, extending it to automobiles.[21]

F. Deeds Creating Joint Tenancies and Tenancies by the Entirety in Land[22]

Joint tenancy is a concurrent estate in land held by multiple persons who share the 'four unities': (1) unity of time: the persons receive their interests in the land at the same moment; (2) unity of title: the persons receive their interests from the same source, meaning the same deed or will; (3) unity of interest: the persons receive the same type of interest, for example, a fee simple absolute or a life estate; and (4) unity of possession: each person has the same right to possess the land. Tenancy by the entirety is a concurrent estate existing only between spouses. At common law, it was said that tenancy by the entirety required five unities: the four unities of joint tenancy plus a fifth unity—unity of person. (The common

[16] For discussion, see WM McGovern, 'The Payable on Death Account and Other Will Substitutes' (1972) 67 *Northwestern University Law Review* 7.

[17] eg UPC § 6-212(b)(2).

[18] *Restatement Third of Property* § 7.1 Comment g.

[19] I know of no data on the number or value of securities or automobiles registered in TOD form.

[20] UPC, Prefatory Note to Art VI. See also R Wellman, 'Transfer-On-Death Securities Registration: A New Title Form' (1987) 21 *Georgia Law Review* 789.

[21] Arizona, Arkansas, California, Connecticut, Delaware, Illinois, Indiana, Kansas, Missouri, Nebraska, Nevada, Ohio, Vermont, Virginia.

[22] I know of no data on the number or value of parcels of land held in joint tenancy or tenancy by the entirety.

law viewed a husband and wife as one person.) An important feature of joint tenancy and tenancy by the entirety is that the tenants have a right of survivorship (*ius accrescendi*). When one joint tenant dies survived by one or more, or when one tenant by the entirety dies survived by the other, the decedent's interest in the land passes automatically and outside probate to the survivor(s); the interest does not pass to the decedent's devisees or heirs.

G. Transfer-On-Death Deeds of Land[23]

TOD beneficiary designations are not limited to personalty such as securities or automobiles. Within the US, 26 jurisdictions authorise TOD deeds of interests in land. Fourteen of these jurisdictions do so because they have enacted the Uniform Real Property Transfer on Death Act.[24] The other 12 jurisdictions have statutes predating or differing from the uniform Act.[25] Under either set of statutes, an

[23] No comprehensive data on TOD deeds are available. Some counties in some states have made it possible to search online for the number of TOD deeds recorded in that county in a given year. By way of illustration, here are data from Jackson County (population 674,158 in the 2010 census) in the State of Missouri (the earliest state to authorise TOD deeds):

Year	TOD deeds recorded in that year	Year	TOD deeds recorded in that year
1989	3	2003	2,171
1990	68	2004	2,294
1991	125	2005	2,276
1992	117	2006	2,283
1993	125	2007	2,222
1994	1,669	2008	2,124
1995	1,751	2009	2,179
1996	1,863	2010	2,121
1997	1,916	2011	2,252
1998	1,994	2012	2,364
1999	1,964	2013	2,429
2000	2,115	2014	2,887
2001	2,004	2015	2,943
2002	2,190		

This information is available through a search engine on the website of the Jackson County Recorder of Deeds: http://records.jacksongov.org/RealEstate/SearchEntry.

[24] Alaska, District of Columbia, Hawaii, Illinois, Nebraska, Nevada, New Mexico, North Dakota, Oregon, South Dakota, Texas, Virginia, Washington, West Virginia. See www.uniformlaws.org/LegislativeFactSheet.aspx?title=Real Property Transfer on Death Act.

[25] Arizona, Arkansas, Colorado, Indiana, Kansas, Minnesota, Missouri, Montana, Ohio, Oklahoma, Wisconsin, Wyoming.

individual owning an interest in land may designate one or more primary TOD beneficiaries and one or more contingent TOD beneficiaries. While the owner is alive, the beneficiaries have no interest in the land. At the owner's death, the property interest passes outside probate to the primary beneficiaries who survive the owner or, if none survives the owner, to the contingent beneficiaries who survive the owner. The transfer is not testamentary, hence need not comply with the formalities for wills.

H. Gifts *Causa Mortis*

A brief word is appropriate about gifts *causa mortis*, which are authorised by US law but are infrequently used. Any gift requires at least three essential elements: (1) intention of the donor to make a gift; (2) transfer of the property from the donor to the donee; and (3) acceptance of the gift by the donee. In addition to these required elements, a gift *causa mortis* has two other important preconditions. First, the subject of the gift must be personalty, not realty; real property cannot be transferred by gift *causa mortis*. Second, the donor must have an objectively reasonable expectation of his or her own *imminent* death and must in fact die from the expected event. If the donor survives the event, the gift *causa mortis* is automatically revoked. If the donor's fear of death is unreasonable or if the expected event is not imminent, the gift *causa mortis* is ineffective. Thus, for example, a gift *causa mortis* made by a patient being carried into a hospital room for surgery would be upheld,[26] but a gift *causa mortis* by a soldier departing the next day for battle would be rejected.

III. 'Pure' Versus 'Imperfect' Will-Substitutes; Validity of Will-Substitutes

John Langbein's seminal article on the 'Nonprobate Revolution' introduced a distinction between 'pure' and 'imperfect' will-substitutes. A pure will-substitute, like a will, is ambulatory and revocable; it 'reserves to the owner complete lifetime dominion, including the power to name and to change beneficiaries until death'.[27] Beneficiary designations for life insurance policies, pension and retirement accounts and POD bank accounts are examples of pure will-substitutes. In contrast, an imperfect will-substitute effectuates a transfer at death but also a transfer *inter vivos*. An example of an imperfect will-substitute is joint tenancy. If Adam buys land and arranges for it to be titled in the name of 'Adam and Eve as joint

[26] *Coley v Walker*, 680 So 2d 352 (Alabama Court of Civil Appeals 1996).

[27] Langbein, The Nonprobate Revolution', above n 7, 1109.

tenants and not as tenants in common', Adam has created a will-substitute. Under the right of survivorship (*ius accrescendi*) inherent in a joint tenancy, Adam's interest in the land will pass outside probate to Eve when Adam dies. However, the arrangement is not ambulatory, because Eve has present rights in the land. Nor is the arrangement necessarily fully revocable. Adam can remove Eve's right of survivorship by severing one or more of the unities of the joint tenancy, thereby transforming the joint tenancy into a tenancy in common. Adam can also obtain a judicial partition of the land, typically dividing it into two parcels; one would be owned by Adam, one by Eve. But unless a resulting trust is declared,[28] Adam cannot regain full ownership of the entire original parcel of land; Eve's interest in the land remains hers. For these reasons, the transfer from Adam to Eve in joint tenancy is an imperfect will-substitute.

Under traditional law, a transfer of property intended to occur at the owner's death is a testamentary transfer and must be effectuated by a valid will.[29] To be valid, a will typically must be signed by the testator (or by another person on the testator's behalf) and attested by witnesses.[30] These requirements do not apply, however, if the transfer is nontestamentary.

The beneficiary designations in will-substitutes do not and need not comply with the requirements for wills. This is because will-substitutes are deemed to be nontestamentary. In some instances, this conclusion has been reached by judicial decision, with the court holding that the will-substitute arrangement satisfies the so-called 'present interest' test. As explained in the *Restatement Third of Property*:

> The traditional explanation for why a will-substitute is not a will is that a will-substitute transfers ownership during life—it effects a *present* transfer of a *nonpossessory future* interest or contract right, the time of possession or enjoyment being postponed until the donor's death.[31]

The present transfer test has been rightly critiqued by John Langbein as a legal fiction:

> The odor of legal fiction hangs heavily over the present-[transfer] test. We see courts straining to reach right results for wrong reasons and insisting that will-like transfers possess gift-like incidents. Courts have used such doctrinal ruses to validate not only the revocable inter vivos trust, but other will substitutes as well ... What is the difference between the revocable and ambulatory interest created by a will, and a vested but defeasible interest in life insurance or pension proceeds? None at all, except for the form of words.[32]

[28] On which, see *Scott and Ascher on Trusts*, 6th edn (New York, Wolters Kluwer, 2009) ch 43. See esp ibid at 2935, observing that some states, including New York, have enacted statutes abolishing the purchase money resulting trust of land.

[29] A rare exception is the gift *causa mortis*.

[30] In 2008, UPC § 2-502(a)(3)(B) introduced notarisation as a substitute for attestation.

[31] *Restatement Third of Property* § 7.1 Comment b.

[32] Langbein, 'The Nonprobate Revolution', above n 7, 1128.

It is a legal fiction employed by the courts,[33] and a useful one.[34] More recently, will-substitutes have been validated as nontestamentary by statute. One such statute is UPC § 6-101, which provides in pertinent part:

> A provision for a nonprobate transfer on death in an insurance policy, contract of employment, bond, mortgage, promissory note, certificated or uncertificated security, account agreement, custodial agreement, deposit agreement, compensation plan, pension plan, individual retirement plan, employee benefit plan, trust, conveyance, deed of gift, marital property agreement, or other written instrument of a similar nature is nontestamentary.

IV. Rights of Third Parties: Taxing Authorities, Creditors and the Surviving Spouse and Children

A. Taxing Authorities

Property passing from the decedent at death is subject to estate taxation.[35] The core statutory provision of federal estate taxation is Internal Revenue Code § 2033, which subjects to tax 'the value of all property to the extent of the interest therein of the decedent at the time of his death'.[36] This provision makes the decedent's probate estate subject to estate taxation. It also applies to property owned by the decedent at death for which the decedent arranged a TOD or pay-on-death beneficiary designation. Congress soon recognised, however, that measures had to be taken to subject other will-substitutes to estate taxation; otherwise, the other will-substitutes could be used as tax avoidance devices. Many of the statutory provisions of federal estate taxation beyond § 2033 are devoted to the purpose of taxing property transferred by will-substitutes, such as life insurance,[37] joint tenancies

[33] A leading case is *Farkas v Williams*, 125 NE 2d 600 (Illinois Supreme Court 1955).

[34] After a court in Ohio invalidated a revocable trust in *Mathias v Fantine*, 1990 WL 21446 (Ohio App 5 Dist), the Ohio General Assembly swiftly reversed the decision by legislation. See Ohio Rev Code § 5804.02(E) (originally numbered as § 1335.01(C)):

A trust is not invalid because a person, including but not limited to, the creator of the trust, is or may become the sole trustee and the sole holder of the present beneficial enjoyment of the corpus of the trust, provided that one or more other persons hold a vested, contingent, or expectant interest relative to the enjoyment of the corpus of the trust upon the cessation of the present beneficial enjoyment. A merger of the legal and equitable titles to the corpus of such a trust shall not be considered as occurring in its creator, and, notwithstanding any contrary provision of Chapter 2107 of the Revised Code, the trust shall not be considered to be a testamentary trust that must comply with that chapter in order for its corpus to be legally distributed to other beneficiaries in accordance with the provisions of the trust upon the cessation of the present beneficial enjoyment.

[35] In 2015, the federal estate tax exemption is $5.43 million per person, and the highest federal estate tax rate is 40%.

[36] 26 USC § 2033.

[37] 26 USC § 2042(2).

and joint accounts,[38] pension or retirement account death benefits,[39] and revocable trusts.[40] Even irrevocable trusts with a retained life estate are subject to tax.[41]

B. Creditors

One of the core functions of probate is creditor protection: the decedent's debts are paid from the decedent's estate before the remaining estate assets are transferred to the decedent's devisees or heirs. Under traditional law, creditor claims were made against the probate estate only, not against property passing by will-substitute. For example, the traditional rule was that a settlor's power to revoke a revocable trust did not subject the trust to claims of the settlor's creditors unless the settlor was also a trust beneficiary.[42] Modern US law takes the opposite approach with respect to revocable trusts. The power to revoke a revocable trust is considered an ownership-equivalent power, making the assets in the trust subject to claims of the settlor's creditors. This modern approach is endorsed by the *Restatement Third of Trusts* and codified in the UTC.[43] With respect to will-substitutes other than revocable trusts, however, the law in the US is more in line with the traditional approach; most states deny creditors of the decedent's estate access to most other forms of will-substitute.[44] Only a small number of states have enacted provisions equivalent to UPC § 6-102(b), which provides that 'a transferee of a nonprobate transfer is subject to liability to any probate estate of the decedent for allowed claims against decedent's probate estate … to the extent the estate is insufficient to satisfy those claims'.

C. The Surviving Spouse and Children

Freedom of disposition is a hallmark of the US law of succession.[45] The decedent's spouse is the only relative favoured by a protection against intentional disinheritance.[46] In a minority of states, this protection takes the form of a

[38] 26 USC § 2040.

[39] 26 USC § 2039.

[40] 26 USC § 2038(a)(1).

[41] 26 USC § 2036(a)(1).

[42] *Restatement Second of Trusts* § 330 Comment o (Philadelphia, American Law Institute, 1959).

[43] *Restatement Third of Trusts* § 25 Comment e; UTC § 505.

[44] EH Gagliardi, 'Remembering the Creditor at Death: Aligning Probate and Nonprobate Transfers' (2007) 41 *Real Property, Probate and Trust Journal* 819.

[45] RH Sitkoff, 'Trusts and Estates: Implementing Freedom of Disposition' (2014) 58 *St Louis University Law Journal* 643.

[46] This statement requires some qualification. If there is no surviving spouse, the decedent's surviving children (especially if they are minor or dependent children) may be entitled to some statutory allowances. See, eg UPC §§ 2-402 to 2-404. These are chargeable only against the probate estate unless the state has enacted a statute akin to UPC § 6-102, discussed in the prior paragraph.

community property regime. In the majority of states, where the 'separate property' rather than community property regime prevails, the surviving spouse has a statutory claim to a portion of the decedent's estate.[47] These statutes provide the spouse with a forced share. Because the forced share is expressed as an option that the surviving spouse can elect or let lapse during the administration of the decedent's estate, the forced share is typically called the elective share.

Traditional elective share statutes apply to the assets in the decedent's probate estate. This is changing, but not swiftly or completely. One of the most troublesome issues regarding elective share law is the extent to which the elective share statutes can fail to extend to will-substitutes. An elective share is of little value to a surviving spouse if it applies only or primarily to the decedent's probate estate, because the decedent could use one or more will-substitutes to implement a dispositive plan effectively disinheriting the surviving spouse. Many courts, using different approaches, have responded by working to preserve the effectiveness of the statutory elective share. The most common of these approaches is known as the illusory transfer test. The leading case adopting the illusory transfer test was the New York case of *Newman v Dore*.[48] In that case, the testator executed trust agreements by which he transferred all his real and personal property to his trustees. The trust agreements were executed three days before his death and when cross-actions for dissolution of his marriage were pending. The terms of the trusts reserved to the testator the right to the income for life, the power to revoke the trusts and the power to control the trustees in all aspects of the trusts' administration; the testator's spouse received no beneficial interest in the trusts. She challenged the validity of the transfers to the trustees. The Court found that the trusts were illusory and therefore part of the testator's estate for purposes of his widow's rights. Judicial doctrines such as the illusory transfer test remain important in states that have not amended their elective share statutes to extend to will-substitutes.

Today, many states have amended their elective share statutes to apply to a specified list of will-substitutes. The concept of providing in the statute a list of will-substitutes to be subjected to the surviving spouse's elective share was pioneered by legislation in New York and Pennsylvania and adopted by the UPC. This approach resolves the problem that arises under conventional elective share statutes, illustrated by *Newman v Dore*, of shifting to the courts the burden of deciding whether and under what circumstances will-substitutes are subject to the elective share. The elective share provisions of the current version of the UPC aim to reach all property owned or owned in substance by the decedent, whether passing through or outside probate.[49]

[47] Except in Georgia.

[48] *Newman v Dore*, 9 NE 2d 966 (New York CA 1937).

[49] UPC §§ 2-201 to 2-214. For discussion, see L Waggoner, 'The Multiple-Marriage Society and Spousal Rights under the Revised Uniform Probate Code' (1991) 76 *Iowa Law Review* 223; L Waggoner, 'The Uniform Probate Code's Elective Share: Time for a Reassessment' (2003) 37 *Real Property, Probate and Trust Journal* 1.

V. Major Trend: Harmonisation of Default Law

A distinction is often made in the law of succession between mandatory rules and default rules.[50] Mandatory rules apply irrespective of the donor's intention. The traditional Rule Against Perpetuities, for example, is a mandatory rule. Default rules, on the other hand, are intent-effectuating and yield to the donor's expression of a contrary intention. The rules of intestacy are default rules; a donor who does not want them to apply can circumvent them by writing a valid will.

The formal requirements for a valid will—typically writing, signature and attestation—are mandatory rules. They apply to all testamentary transfers. They do not apply to valid will-substitutes which, as we have seen, are considered to be nontestamentary.

Formal requirements aside, most of the rules of wills law are default rules. An important question is whether the default rules of wills law should apply to will-substitutes. In his seminal article on the 'Nonprobate Revolution', John Langbein answered this question in the affirmative: 'The subsidiary rules are the product of centuries of legal experience in attempting to discern transferors' wishes and suppress litigation. These rules should be treated as presumptively correct for will-substitutes as well as for wills'.[51] The same position is taken by the *Restatement Third of Property*:

> Although a will-substitute need not be executed in compliance with the statutory formalities required for a will, such an arrangement is, to the extent appropriate, subject to substantive restrictions on testation and to rules of construction and other rules applicable to testamentary dispositions.[52]

A major trend in US succession law is the harmonisation of the default rules applying to wills and to will-substitutes. Three examples illustrate the point: (1) revocation on divorce; (2) simultaneous or near simultaneous death; and (3) antilapse.

A. Revocation on Divorce

Under traditional statutes, the testator's divorce revokes any provisions in the testator's will benefiting the testator's former spouse, unless the will provides to the contrary. In the language of the original version of the UPC: 'If after executing a will the testator is divorced or his marriage annulled, the divorce or annulment

[50] For the distinction, see TP Gallanis, 'Default Rules, Mandatory Rules, and the Movement for Same-Sex Equality' (1999) 60 *Ohio State Law Journal* 1513, 1515. For further elaboration, see TP Gallanis, 'The Trustee's Duty to Inform' (2007) 85 *North Carolina Law Review* 1595, 1617–19.

[51] Langbein, 'The Nonprobate Revolution', above n 7, 1136–37.

[52] *Restatement Third of Property* § 7.2.

revokes any disposition or appointment of property made by the will to the former spouse … unless the will expressly provides otherwise'.[53] The modern trend, exemplified by the current version of the UPC, is to extend the revocation on divorce rule to will-substitutes. The current UPC provides:

> Except as provided by the express terms of a governing instrument …, the divorce or annulment of a marriage … revokes any revocable disposition or appointment of property made by a divorced individual to his [or her] former spouse in a governing instrument.[54]

The term 'governing instrument' is defined in the UPC to encompass wills and will-substitutes alike:

> 'Governing instrument' means a deed, will, trust, insurance or annuity policy, account with POD designation, security registered in beneficiary form (TOD), transfer on death (TOD) deed, pension, profitsharing, retirement, or similar benefit plan, instrument creating or exercising a power of appointment or a power of attorney, or a dispositive, appointive, or nominative instrument of any similar type.

B. Simultaneous or Near Simultaneous Death

The law of succession requires the devisees or heirs of a decedent to survive the decedent in order to be able to succeed to the decedent's property. What happens if a devisee or heir dies with the decedent in a common disaster? How would a court determine who survived whom?[55] The position at common law was that the question was not to be answered by the use of a presumption. Instead, the question was an issue of fact to be resolved in each instance. In 1940, the Uniform Law Commission promulgated the Uniform Simultaneous Death Act, which provided:

> Where the title to property or the devolution thereof depends upon priority of death and there is no sufficient evidence that the persons have died otherwise than simultaneously, the property of each person shall be disposed of as if he had survived.[56]

This 'no sufficient evidence rule' works well when the order of deaths is unknown, but when the deaths occur in an ascertainable and rapid succession, the rule reaches the undesirable result that the decedent's property passes through the estate of the dead devisee or heir.[57] In response, the Uniform Law Commission promulgated in

[53] UPC (pre-1990) § 2-508.

[54] UPC § 2-804(b)(1)(A).

[55] For discussion, see TP Gallanis, 'Death by Disaster: Anglo-American Presumptions, 1766–2006' in R Helmholz and W Sellar (eds), *The Law of Presumptions: Essays in Comparative Legal History* (Berlin, Duncker & Humblot, 2009).

[56] Uniform Simultaneous Death Act (1940) § 1.

[57] For an example, see *Janus v Tarasewicz*, 482 NE 2d 418 (Illinois Appellate Court 1985).

1991 and amended in 1993 a Revised Uniform Simultaneous Death Act[58] (to bring it in line with the provisions of the UPC).[59] The Revised Act provides that

> if the title to property, the devolution of property, [or] the right to elect an interest in property … depends upon an individual's survivorship of the death of another individual, an individual who is not established by clear and convincing evidence to have survived the other individual by 120 hours is deemed to have predeceased the other individual.[60]

The Uniform Simultaneous Death Act contained provisions extending its 'no sufficient evidence' rule to life insurance[61] and to joint tenancy and tenancy by the entirety.[62] The Revised Act extends its 120-hour requirement of survival to all provisions of survivorship in a 'governing instrument'[63] and to all property co-owned 'with right of survivorship'.[64]

C. Antilapse

In the law of wills, if a devisee fails to survive the testator, the devise fails—in technical parlance, it 'lapses'. What happens to a lapsed devise? In the absence of an expressly designated alternative taker or an applicable antilapse statute—discussed in the next paragraph—a lapsed devise devolves as follows. If lapse occurs in a provision other than the will's residuary clause, a lapsed devise of personal property passes to the decedent's residuary devisees. (Under early common law, this rule was not followed for land. However, many states have enacted legislation that causes real as well as personal property to pass under the residuary clause. A few statutes, however, preserve the common law rule for land.) If lapse occurs in the will's residuary clause—the residuary clause is in favour of one person, or is in favour of more than one person and does not create a class gift—the conventional view is that the death of a residuary devisee causes the share intended for the deceased devisee to pass by intestacy.[65] This is known as the 'no-residue-of-a-residue rule'. Some judicial decisions have rejected the no-residue-of-a-residue rule and have held that the lapsed share passes to any

[58] The Revised Uniform Simultaneous Death Act has been enacted in 12 states plus the District of Columbia. See www.uniformlaws.org/Act.aspx?title=Simultaneous Death Act.

[59] UPC § 2-702. For discussion, see E Halbach and L Waggoner, 'The UPC's New Survivorship and Antilapse Provisions' (1992) 55 *Albany Law Review* 1091, 1094–99.

[60] Uniform Simultaneous Death Act (1993) § 2.

[61] Uniform Simultaneous Death Act (1940, as amended 1953) § 5.

[62] ibid, § 3.

[63] Uniform Simultaneous Death Act (1993) § 3.

[64] ibid, § 4.

[65] eg *Estate of Levy*, 415 P 2d 1006 (Oklahoma Supreme Court 1966); *Estate of McFarland*, 167 SW 3d 299 (Tennessee Supreme Court 2005); *Swearingen v Giles*, 565 SW 2d 574 (Texas Court of Civil Appeals 1978); *Estate of Mory*, 139 NW 2d 623 (Wisconsin Supreme Court 1966).

residuary devisees who survive the decedent.[66] The *Restatement Third of Property* is aligned with this position.[67]

Almost all jurisdictions in the US do not follow the common law rules of lapse. Instead, the jurisdictions have enacted antilapse statutes.[68] The 'antilapse' label, however, is misdescriptive. Antilapse statutes typically do not reverse the common law rule of lapse. In other words, they do not eliminate the requirement of survival so that devised property passes to the estates of predeceasing devisees. Instead, antilapse statutes leave the requirement of survival intact and then provide a statutory substitute gift, usually to the devisee's descendants who survive the testator. In the language of UPC § 2-603:

> If a devisee fails to survive the testator and is a grandparent, a descendant of a grandparent, or a stepchild of either the testator or the donor of a power of appointment exercised by the testator's will, the following apply:
>
> (1) … if the devise is not in the form of a class gift and the deceased devisee leaves surviving descendants, a substitute gift is created in the devisee's surviving descendants. …
>
> (2) … if the devise is in the form of a class gift other than … [a multiple-generation class gift, such as 'descendants' or 'heirs'], a substitute gift is created in the surviving descendants of any deceased devisee.

Antilapse statutes typically apply only to wills. This is true of the antilapse provisions of the UPC prior to 1990, and it remains true of almost all of the antilapse statutes in states that have not adopted the UPC as revised in 1990. As so revised,[69] the UPC extends antilapse-type protection to future interests in trusts[70] and to 'beneficiary designations',[71] a term referring to 'a governing instrument naming a beneficiary of a … nonprobate transfer at death'.[72]

VI. Counter-Trend: Federal Pre-Emption of State Succession Law

The US law of succession is traditionally state, not federal, law. However, some federal statutes—primarily the Employee Retirement Income Security Act of 1974

[66] eg *Estate of Jackson*, 471 P 2d 278 (Arizona Supreme Court 1970); *Corbett v Skaggs*, 207 P 819 (Kansas Supreme Court 1922); *Niemann v Zacharias*, 176 NW 2d 671 (Nebraska Supreme Court 1970); *Frolich Estate*, 295 A 2d 448 (New Hampshire Supreme Court 1972); *Commerce Nat'l Bank v Browning*, 107 NE 2d 120 (Ohio Supreme Court 1952); *Slack Trust*, 220 A 2d 472 (Vermont Supreme Court 1966).

[67] *Restatement Third of Property* § 5.5 Comment o.

[68] For a state-by-state compilation, see *Restatement Third of Property* Statutory Note to § 5.5.

[69] For discussion, see Halbach and Waggoner, above n 59, 1099–147.

[70] UPC § 2-707. For discussion, see L Waggoner, 'The Uniform Probate Code Extends Antilapse-Type Protection to Poorly Drafted Trusts' (1996) 94 *Michigan Law Review* 2309.

[71] UPC § 2-706.

[72] UPC § 1-201(4).

(ERISA), which governs employee benefits such as employer-sponsored pensions and life insurance—are being interpreted by the US Supreme Court so as to make it impossible for state legislatures or state courts to complete the unification of the default rules of wills and of will-substitutes.

Section 514(a) of ERISA provides that the provisions of Titles I and IV of ERISA 'shall supersede any and all State laws insofar as they may now or hereafter relate to any [ERISA-governed] employee benefit plan'.[73] The words 'relate to' are broad, and the US Supreme Court has interpreted them very broadly.

In 2001 in *Egelhoff v Egelhoff*,[74] the US Supreme Court was faced with a typical revocation-on-divorce scenario. David Egelhoff designated his wife, Donna, as the beneficiary of his pension benefits and life insurance proceeds. David and Donna later divorced. Two months after the divorce, David died in a car accident, not having changed his beneficiary designations. David's children from a prior marriage argued that the State of Washington's revocation-on-divorce statute—which, like UPC § 2-804, extends the revocation-on-divorce rule to non-probate mechanisms—revoked the designations benefiting Donna. A divided US Supreme Court disagreed, holding that the state statute was pre-empted because the life insurance policy and pension plan were ERISA-governed.[75]

In response to the danger of federal preemption of state wealth transfer law, the Uniform Law Commission inserted the following provision into the UPC's revocation-on-divorce statute and into other UPC provisions that might be the subject of preemption:

> If this section or any part of this section is preempted by federal law with respect to a payment, an item of property, or any other benefit covered by this section, a former spouse, relative of the former spouse, or any other person who, not for value, received a payment, item of property, or any other benefit to which that person is not entitled under this section is obligated to return that payment, item of property, or benefit, or is personally liable for the amount of the payment or the value of the item of property or benefit, to the person who would have been entitled to it were this section or part of this section not preempted.[76]

This provision imposes a post-distribution constructive trust for the purpose of remedying unjust enrichment. As the Official Comment explains:

> This provision respects ERISA's concern that federal law govern the administration of the plan, while still preventing unjust enrichment that would result if an unintended beneficiary were to receive the pension benefits. Federal law has no interest in working a broader disruption of state probate and nonprobate transfer law than is required in the interest of smooth administration of pension and employee benefit plans.[77]

[73] 29 USC § 1144(a).

[74] *Egelhoff v Egelhoff*, 532 US 141 (2001).

[75] For a critique, see TP Gallanis, 'ERISA and the Law of Succession' (2004) 65 *Ohio State Law Journal* 185.

[76] UPC § 2-804(h)(2). See also UPC § 2-110 (elective share), § 2-702 (survival by 120 hours), § 2-706 (antilapse), § 2-803 (slayer rule).

[77] Comment to UPC § 2-804(h)(2).

In 2013, the US Supreme Court decided *Hillman v Maretta*,[78] another standard revocation-on-divorce case. Warren Hillman named his wife, Judy, as the beneficiary of a life insurance policy governed by FEGLIA (the Federal Employees' Group Life Insurance Act of 1954), which has a preemption provision similar to ERISA's. The couple later divorced; Warren married Jacqueline; then Warren died without having revised his beneficiary designation. The plan administrator paid the proceeds to Judy as the named beneficiary. Jacqueline agreed that the state's revocation-on-divorce rule was pre-empted but sued Judy for the proceeds under the state's version of subsection (h)(2), the statutory constructive trust remedy. In *Hillman*, the Court unanimously decided that the statutory constructive trust remedy was pre-empted.

In January 2014, the Uniform Law Commission revised the Official Comment to UPC § 2-804 (the revocation-on-divorce provision) in response to *Hillman*:

> The Court's decision in *Hillman* has many unfortunate consequences. First, the decision frustrates the dominant purpose of wealth transfer law, which is to implement the transferor's intention. The result in *Hillman*, that the decedent's ex-spouse remained entitled to the proceeds of the decedent's life insurance policy purchased through a program established by FEGLIA, frustrates the decedent's intention. Second, the *Hillman* decision ignores the decades-long trend of unifying the law governing probate and nonprobate transfers. The revocation-on-divorce rule has long been a part of probate law (see, eg pre-1990 Section 2-508). In 1990, this section extended the rule of revocation on divorce to nonprobate transfers. Third, the decision in *Hillman* fosters a division between state- and federally-regulated nonprobate mechanisms. If the decedent in *Hillman* had purchased a life insurance policy individually, rather than through the FEGLIA program, the policy would have been governed by the Virginia counterpart of this section.[79]

VII. Conclusion

The US law of succession is in the midst of transition. The laws governing wills and will-substitutes have been harmonised to a great extent, but not fully. Not all of the default rules of wills law have been extended to will-substitutes, even in the UPC.[80] The rights of creditors in assets transferred by will-substitute remain inadequately protected as, in many jurisdictions, do the elective share rights of the decedent's surviving spouse. Moreover, recent scholarship urges improvements

[78] *Hillman v Maretta*, 133 S Ct 1943 (2013).

[79] Comment to UPC § 2-804(h)(2). For critiques of *Hillman*, see JH Langbein, 'Destructive Federal Preemption of State Wealth Transfer Law in Beneficiary Designation Cases: *Hillman* Doubles Down on *Egelhoff*' (2014) 67 *Vanderbilt Law Review* 1665; L Waggoner, 'The Creeping Federalization of Wealth-Transfer Law' (2014) 67 *Vanderbilt Law Review* 1635, 1639–46.

[80] See, eg UPC § 2-606, applying the doctrine of 'ademption by extinction' only to wills.

to will-substitute beneficiary-designation forms in order better to effectuate the donors' dispositive wishes.[81] Much remains to be done.

Whether, and if so when, the project of harmonisation can be completed is unclear. The US Supreme Court's rulings on ERISA pre-emption are at least a temporary obstacle,[82] as is the resistance encountered in state legislatures when one or another lobbying interest feels threatened by law reform.[83]

The leap forward came in 1990 with the revisions to the UPC, drafted primarily by Lawrence Waggoner, who also served as the Reporter for the *Restatement Third of Property: Wills and Other Donative Transfers*. Joining him in both projects was John Langbein. As they explained in 2003 in the Restatement,

> will substitutes have proliferated and become alternative means of passing property at death … This Restatement (along with the Restatement Third, Trusts, the Revised Uniform Probate Code, and the Uniform Trust Code) moves toward the policy of unifying the law of wills and will substitutes.[84]

Further movement towards that policy now depends on my generation and the generations following. Whatever we accomplish rests on the foundation built by Waggoner and Langbein. In the words of Newton, '[i]f I have seen further it is by standing on [th]e sho[u]lders of Giants'.[85]

[81] SE Sterk and MB Leslie, 'Accidental Inheritance: Retirement Accounts and the Hidden Law of Succession' (2014) 89 *New York University Law Review* 165.

[82] For a solution, see Gallanis, 'ERISA and the Law of Succession', above n 75, 196–97.

[83] On the efforts of the American Council of Life Insurers to exempt life insurance from the surviving spouse's elective share, see L Waggoner, G Alexander, ML Fellows and TP Gallanis, *Family Property Law: Cases and Materials on Wills, Trusts, and Future Interests*, 3rd edn (New York, Foundation Press, 2002) 611–15.

[84] *Restatement Third of Property* § 7.2 Comment a.

[85] Letter from Isaac Newton to Robert Hooke, 5 February 1675/76, in H Turnbull (ed), *The Correspondence of Isaac Newton, Vol 1: 1661–1675* (Cambridge, CUP [for the Royal Society], 1959) 416.

2

Will-Substitutes in Canada

ANGELA CAMPBELL*

While the number of Canadians who use will-substitutes is unknown, it is clear that they are widely deployed for the purposes of estate planning. This chapter explains the essence of various will-substitute instruments in common law Canada and in the civil law province of Quebec. It proceeds to explain the key rationales driving the creation of will-substitutes from a Canadian perspective. The final part of this chapter centres on the potential policy issues and concerns that these instruments engender.

A preliminary, definitional word is in order prior to engaging with the substance of this chapter. In this work, a 'will-substitute' denotes an instrument that transfers property from a donor to a beneficiary at the time of the former's death. In this respect, a will-substitute is much like a will; both instruments allow an individual to dictate how her or his assets will be disposed of upon death. However, unlike a will, a will-substitute usually also entails the donor's loss of control over the property in question while she or he is still alive. The will-substitute is hence unlike a will in this respect; in the case of a will, the testator retains ownership and control over assets named in that instrument until her or his death. Moreover, testamentary dispositions (ie, dispositions made by a will) remain revocable up until the time of a testator's death. By contrast, the grantor of a will-substitute may not retain a right of revocation in relation to the designation of the beneficiary of that instrument.[1]

I. Types of Will-Substitute

The present section addresses the various categories of will-substitute in Canadian common law and Quebec civil law. It explains the rules in place to govern wealth

* The author is grateful for research and editing assistance from Beth Mountford, and for support received from the *Chambre des Notaires du Québec*, the Foundation for Legal Research and the McGill Faculty of Law.

[1] AH Oosterhoff, *Oosterhoff on Wills and Successions*, 7th edn (Toronto, Carswell, 2011) 112–13.

transfer through these vehicles. The sections of this chapter that follow engage in a more analytic discussion of will-substitutes, endeavouring to highlight the factors that drive decisions underlying the creation of will-substitutes and the potential pitfalls of these instruments.

The present discussion leaves aside revocable living trusts. These are less popular in Canada as will-substitutes than they are in the US, given the relatively high rate at which income from living (as opposed to testamentary) trusts is taxed in Canada.[2] Moreover, assets that move in or out of Canadian trusts are treated as dispositions such that value increases at the time of asset disposition are subject to tax. Two exceptions are the alter ego trust and the joint partner trust, which are not subject to tax on capital gains. These are more appealing estate planning vehicles in Canada and merit attention in this context. Both of these types of trust have, however, been aptly explained elsewhere.[3]

A. Gifts

i. Canadian Common Law

A gift in Canadian law is not entirely distinct from a bequest made by a will. Wills are themselves juridical instruments that effectuate the gratuitous transfer of wealth. The obvious distinction, however, between the gift and the bequest is the time at which the transfer of the object occurs. *Inter vivos* gifts involve the immediate disposition of an asset to the donee, whereas the bequest by will gives rise to proper transfer only once the testator dies and her or his estate opens.

A gift has testamentary implications in that it decreases the size of an estate and thus reduces probate fees and the scope of assets available to estate creditors. For the purposes of the present discussion, however, such dispositions are generally irrelevant, as they do not meet the requirements of a will-substitute. More precisely, an *inter vivos* gift typically involves the immediate transfer of the asset or benefit to the donee during the donor's lifetime, which is unlike a will-substitute where the asset or benefit is transferred at the time of death.

More pertinent to the discussion is the *donatio mortis causa*, also known as a 'death bed gift'. Such a gift must be one of personal property, made with a view to the donor's death, and made conditional upon the donor's death from an illness existing at the time the donation is made.[4] Furthermore, the subject matter of the gift must be adequately delivered to the donee at the time of donation.[5] Although the gift takes effect upon delivery, its absolute effect occurs upon the death of the

[2] M Pasternak, 'Estate Planning for Canadians' (*Investopedia*), www.investopedia.com/articles/retirement/08/estate-planning-canadians-canada.asp.

[3] MJ Rochwerg and LA Hemmings, 'Will Substitutes in Canada' (2008) 28 *Estates, Trusts & Pensions Journal* 50, 52–54.

[4] ibid, 113; R Spenceley, *Probate Planning Through Will Substitutes* (North York, CCH Canadian Limited, 2000) 42–43.

[5] Oosterhoff, above n 1, 113.

donor.[6] Thus, the gift is revocable until the donor's death.[7] With the exception of Ontario, Prince Edward Island, the Yukon, the Northwest Territories and Nunavut, the *donatio mortis causa* does not form part of the estate of the deceased and is therefore not subject to probate fees.[8]

ii. Quebec Civil Law

In the civil law of Quebec, a gift that divests the donor of her or his property on the condition of her or his death, and which takes place only at that time, is also termed a gift *mortis causa*.[9] Such a gift is null unless it is made by marriage or civil union contract or unless it may be upheld as a legacy.[10] The donees of gifts *mortis causa* are limited to a donor's future spouse, actual spouse and their respective and common children, born or yet unborn.[11] A gift *mortis causa* that meets the conditions of validity in Quebec civil law is revocable. Yet a donor may stipulate that such a gift is irrevocable, in which case the donor may not dispose gratuitously of the property by will or by an *inter vivos* act without the donee's consent and the consent of other interested persons, unless the disposition consists of 'property of little value or customary presents'. The donor can, however, alienate the property in question by onerous title, given the donor's ongoing rights in the property that form the object of a gift *mortis causa* that has been stipulated as irrevocable.[12]

Gifts *mortis causa* do not form part of the succession in Quebec. Yet, because the province does not charge probate fees there is limited incentive to use these devices for estate planning. As indicated, they are typically formed at the time of marriage or civil union celebration and often thought of as gifts in consideration of the marriage or union. It is not surprising then, that a divorce causes a gift *mortis causa* made to a spouse in consideration of marriage to lapse.[13]

B. Joint Interests

i. Canadian Common Law

Under Canadian common law, property that is owned in joint tenancy is transferred directly to a surviving joint tenant.[14] As such, the share of the deceased joint

[6] ibid.

[7] ibid, 114.

[8] Succession Law Reform Act, RSO 1990, c S 26, s 72 (Succession Law Reform Act); Dependants of a Deceased Person Relief Act, RSPEI 1988, c D-7, s 19 (Dependants of a Deceased Person Relief Act); Dependants Relief Act, RSNWT 1988, c D-4, s 19 (Dependants Relief Act (NWT)); Dependants Relief Act, RSNu 1988, c D-4, s 19 (Dependants Relief Act (Nu)); Dependants Relief Act, RSY 2002, c 56, s 20 (Dependants Relief Act (Y)).

[9] Art 1808 Civil Code of Québec (CCQ).

[10] Art 1819 CCQ.

[11] Art 1840 CCQ.

[12] Art 1841 CCQ.

[13] Art 519 CCQ. See the discussion in *Droit de Famille-3200* JE 99-216 (CS).

[14] See also ch 1 above, p 16 f and chs 3, 4 and 5 below, p 60, p 88 f, p 112 f in this volume.

tenant does not devolve to her or his estate.[15] Accordingly, joint tenancy may be an attractive financial and estate planning tool because the right of survivorship allows ownership of an asset to bypass the estate and transfer directly to a surviving joint tenant.[16] This has the effect of deferring the probate process and taxation of the property until the death of the surviving joint tenant. It further shields the property in question from seizure by creditors of the estate of the deceased joint tenant.[17]

In Ontario, Prince Edward Island, the Yukon, the Northwest Territories and Nunavut, the value of property the deceased owned in joint tenancy is included when calculating the net value of the estate in dependants' relief claims.[18] This allows dependent creditors to access the value of assets the deceased held in joint tenancy. That being said, the asset itself is shielded from the probate process and from the claims of creditors. Thus, even in these provinces and territories, joint tenancy remains an attractive planning tool, allowing for the relatively simple administration of the property during the first joint tenant's life as well as after her or his death.

a. Presumption of Advancement and Presumption of Resulting Trust

Joint investment accounts are a particularly attractive option when a transferor intends for the survivor to keep the entirety of assets in the account upon her or his death.[19] Normally, the principles of joint tenancy apply to such accounts. However, more complex issues arise where an account holder makes a donative transfer of assets in the account to another individual so as to create a joint tenancy. The outcome of such a transfer will depend on the intentions of the transferor and the relationship between the transferor and the transferee.

Ordinarily this type of donative transfer gives rise to a presumption of resulting trust such that if the transferor predeceases the transferee, the latter is presumed to hold the assets in the joint account in trust for the transferor's estate. By contrast, a presumption of advancement (gift) has conventionally applied in Canadian common law where a father transferred property voluntarily to his child or took property jointly in his name and the child's. This exception allowed

[15] MJ Rochwerg and LA Hemmings, 'Trusts, Trustees, Trusteeships III: Use of Trusts as Will Substitutes' (*Miller Thomson LLP*, 23 September 2008), www.millerthomson.com/assets/files/article_attachments/Use_of_Trusts_as_Will_Substitutes_Trusts_Trustees_Trusteeships_III.pdf; See, eg Estates Administration Act, RSO 1990, c E 22, s 2.

[16] Rochwerg and Hemmings, 'Trusts, Trustees, Trusteeships III', above n 15.

[17] ibid.

[18] Succession Law Reform Act, above n 8, s 72(1)(d); Dependants of a Deceased Person Relief Act, above n 8, s 19; Dependants Relief Act (NWT), above n 8, s 19; Dependants Relief Act (Nu), above n 8, s 19; Dependants Relief Act (Y), above n 8, s 20.

[19] S Mallin, 'Estate Planning—Will Substitutes' (*Lorne Steinberg Wealth Management*, April 2013), www.steinbergwealth.com/uploads/64946/Financial%20Planning/Financial%20Planning%20-%20Estate%20Planning%20_2_.pdf.

the transferee to benefit from the survivorship rule of joint tenancy, taking the benefit of the assets in the account rather than holding these in trust for the deceased joint tenant's estate. Recently, courts extended this presumption of advancement to situations in which a mother gratuitously disposed of property to a child, or held property jointly with a child.[20] Matrimonial property law reform in Canada in the 1970s and 1980s replaced a comparable rebuttable presumption of advancement, which arose when a husband gratuitously transferred property to his wife or placed property jointly in his own name and his spouse's. Even today, funds on deposit in both spouses' names are deemed to be held in joint tenancy.[21]

However, the Supreme Court's decision in *Pecore v Pecore* re-established the presumption of resulting trust—displacing the presumption of advancement—in cases of a parent's gratuitous transfer of assets into joint accounts held with adult children.[22] In rationalising this shift, the Supreme Court emphasised the principal aim of the presumption of advancement, in relation to children, as upholding the parental obligation of support. Yet this presumption is not compelling where adult children are concerned, given that they are often financially independent. Rather than intending to bestow the benefit of the full assets held in joint accounts on their adult children, elderly parents often name those children as joint tenants on bank accounts for the sake of convenience, to have the child assist with the financial management of their affairs. A court is hence to presume that a parent who sets up joint accounts with an adult child did so with a view to having the transferee aid in managing her or his affairs. A transferee may rebut this presumption with proof, on a balance of probabilities, of the parent's intention to gift the assets in the joint account to her or his child.

Joint accounts thus remain effective vehicles for the nontestamentary transfer of property, even when just one of the people named on the account makes deposits and thus a presumption of resulting trust arises. In those cases, legal title to the assets in the account remains with the surviving account holder, yet that person holds the property on trust for the estate and thus does not enjoy the beneficial interest in the property. This instrument remains revocable in that the transferor, during her or his lifetime, has the ability to make withdrawals on the account and can effectively deplete the account in this manner.[23] Any intention to gift the assets in the joint account to the joint tenant, where the latter is not a minor child of the donor, must be made explicit so as to ensure the rebuttal of the presumption of resulting trust that would otherwise apply.

[20] Oosterhoff, above n 1, 116 and 117; see *Dagle v Dagle* (1990), 70 DLR (4th) 201 (PEICA), 81 Nfld & PEIR 245.

[21] ibid. See also: Family Law Act, RSO 1990, c F 3T, s 4.

[22] *Pecore v Pecore* [2007] 1 SCR 795, 2007 SCC 17; see also: *Madsen Estate v Saylor* [2007] 1 SCR 838, 2007 SCC 18.

[23] *Edwards v Bradley* (1956), 2 DLR (2d) 382 (ONCA); revd [1957] SCR 599.

b. Joint Fixed Assets

Joint tenancy in relation to real property is an efficient way to transfer ownership to the surviving joint tenant. This can be especially attractive for spouses in relation to a family residence. Title is transferred to the surviving joint tenant via a survivorship grant application with a minimal fee without having the move through the estate and, in some provinces, this process avoids the probate process.[24]

Within Canadian common law jurisdictions, unless a deed of property specifies otherwise, joint title is taken by a tenancy in common, not joint tenancy.[25] In contrast to joint tenancy, property owned under a tenancy in common vests a specific portion of the property in each tenant in common. That is, when one tenant in common dies, her or his share devolves to her or his estate and is dealt with by will.[26] Tenancy in common is not advantageous from a tax avoidance perspective; however, it is beneficial for ensuring that the property passes to its intended beneficiary.[27] For example, if a husband and wife are tenants in common of a family vacation home, the husband may leave his interest in the home to his children by will. When the husband dies the wife will remain the owner of her interest in the home and the husband's interest will pass to his children.

ii. Quebec Civil Law

The right of survivorship does not exist in Quebec. Property that is owned in undivided co-ownership (ie, shared ownership) does not transfer to the surviving co-owner on the death of the first co-owner. Instead, the deceased's undivided interest in the property devolves to her or his estate.

Under Quebec civil law, particular rules of public order exist to preserve the rights of married or civil union spouses in assets that are considered by law to form part of the 'family patrimony'. These assets include: the family residence(s) and their furnishings; family vehicles; benefits acquired in a pension plan or registered retirement savings plan during the union; and earnings registered during the union under a pension plan. Assets in the family patrimony are deemed to belong to both spouses, regardless of who is registered as their owner. The family patrimony is partitioned when the union formally dissolves or on the death of a spouse. As such, an individual may not, by will or by will-substitute, dispose of her or his spouse's interests in the family patrimony.[28]

[24] Mallin, above n 19.
[25] eg Conveyancing and Law of Property Act, RSO 1990, c C 34, s 13.
[26] Mallin, above n 19.
[27] ibid.
[28] Arts 414 ff CCQ.

C. Life Insurance

i. Canadian Common Law

A majority of Canadians own life insurance; while reliable statistics on this matter are difficult to obtain, media reports suggest that between approximately one-half to two-thirds of Canadians' lives are insured.[29] Life insurance is a contract under which an insurer undertakes to pay insurance benefits on the death or on the occurrence of a specified event. Life insurance provides a tax-free cash payment to an insured's named beneficiaries upon death.[30] This can be advantageous insofar as it provides named beneficiaries with access to liquidity relatively quickly, which can aid in covering end-of-life expenses such as debts or funeral costs.[31]

An insured has the right to designate a beneficiary of the life insurance in the contract of insurance, by designation, or by will.[32] Even if the designation of the beneficiary is testamentary, the benefits remain exempt from probate and do not form part of the estate.[33] The beneficiary may be more than one person or it may be the estate of the insured.[34] In some provinces, if the estate is named as insurance beneficiary, insurance proceeds will form part of the estate and thus will be subject to probate fees and the claims of creditors.[35] Otherwise, insurance proceeds will not form part of the insured's estate and will instead pass directly to the named beneficiary.[36] In this latter situation, the insurance proceeds generally are shielded from claims advanced by creditors of the estate.[37] This being said, the immunity of insurance proceeds may be compromised by legislation that integrates the value of insurance proceeds within the estate's overall value in the context of dependants' relief claims. In Ontario, Prince Edward Island, the Yukon, the Northwest Territories and Nunavut, life insurance policies form part of the settlor's estate for the purpose of calculating the value of the estate in assessing dependants' relief claims.[38]

[29] Investment Executive, 'One-Third of Canadians Don't Have Life Insurance: Survey' (Investment Executive, 24 November 2010), www.investmentexecutive.com/-/news-55908; M Johne, 'Peace-of-Mind Can, Indeed be Bought' (*Globe and Mail*), www.v1.theglobeandmail.com/partners/free/lifestages/article_08.html.

[30] Ontario Securities Commission, 'Life Insurance Basics' (Ontario Securities Commission), www.getsmarteraboutmoney.ca/en/managing-your-money/investing/personal-insurance/Pages/Life-insurance-basics.aspx#.VVd1QVzrPqU.

[31] ibid.

[32] Insurance Act, RSO 1980, c 218, s 190, 192 (Insurance Act).

[33] Spenceley, above n 4, 86.

[34] Insurance Act, above n 32, s 190.

[35] Oosterhoff, above n 1, 120.

[36] See, eg Insurance Act, above n 32, s 196(1), which provides that when insurance monies become payable, this benefit 'is not part of the estate of the insured and is not subject to the claims of the creditors of the insured'.

[37] Oosterhoff, above n 1, 120.

[38] Succession Law Reform Act, above n 8, s 72(1)(d); Dependants of a Deceased Person Relief Act, above n 8, s 19; Dependants Relief Act (NWT), above n 8, s 19; Dependants Relief Act (Nu), above n 8, s 19; Dependants Relief Act (Y), above n 8, s 20.

Moreover, there is some authority to suggest that insurance proceeds are not exempt from seizure under Canada's federal Income Tax Act to settle tax amounts owed by the deceased.[39]

Beneficiary designations in life insurance policies are not binding on the policyholder and can be amended unless these designations were stipulated as irrevocable. Where an irrevocable designation has been made, the beneficiary's consent is generally required to revoke the original designation. These principles may differ where the insured purports to make an irrevocable beneficiary designation by a will rather than through the insurance contract.[40]

ii. Quebec Civil Law

The Civil Code of Quebec outlines the rules pertaining to the payment of life insurance in Quebec.[41] Life insurance may be payable to the policyholder, the participant, or a specified beneficiary.[42] The designation of a beneficiary is made in the policy or in another written document, which can be in the form of a will.[43] If there is no clear beneficiary designation or if the insurance is payable to the policyholder's succession, assigns, liquidators, heirs or other legal representatives, the insurance benefits form part of the succession and are subject to seizure.[44] In contrast, sums payable to a designated beneficiary do not form part of the succession of the insured, and named beneficiaries are thus not responsible for the debts of the succession.[45] This point is underscored by the rule exempting insurance proceeds paid to a designated beneficiary who is the insured's married or civil union spouse, ascendant, or descendant from seizure until the beneficiary receives the sum insured.[46]

As in common law jurisdictions, life insurance beneficiary designations are generally revocable under Quebec civil law, unless the insured stipulated an irrevocable designation in a document other than a will.[47] Where the insured names her or his married or civil union spouse as the beneficiary, that designation will be irrevocable by operation of law unless the insured stipulated otherwise.[48] Further, as is true of gifts *mortis causa*, divorce or the dissolution of a civil union causes a spousal designation as a beneficiary or a subrogated policyholder to lapse.[49]

[39] Oosterhoff, above n 1, 121.

[40] See, eg insurance legislation in Ontario: Insurance Act, above n 32, ss 190(1), (2), 191; and in British Columbia: Insurance Act, RSBC 2012, c 1, ss 59(1), (2), 60.

[41] Arts 2445 ff CCQ.

[42] Art 2445 CCQ.

[43] Art 2446 CCQ.

[44] Art 2456 CCQ para 1; see, eg *Robichaud (Succession)*, JE 96-1513 (CS) [*Robichaud (Succession)*].

[45] Art 2455 CCQ; see, eg *Labranche c Hébert*, JE 95-1900 (CS).

[46] Art 2457 CCQ; see also art 2444 CCQ.

[47] Art 2449 CCQ.

[48] Art 2449 CCQ.

[49] Art 2459(2) CCQ.

D. Pension Plans

There are different types of pension plan in Canada. Private plans are usually employer sponsored with the employer, and sometimes the employer and employee together, making contributions during the pension holder's employment. Public plans are those sponsored by the federal and provincial or territorial governments, and these provide benefits when a person retires. A third category of plan is developed from an individual's personal savings through a government-registered account. These registered plans are incentivised by tax advantages. Each of these types of pension plan is explained in turn here.

i. Canadian Common Law

a. Private Pension Plans

Statistics Canada reports that, as of 2012, 38.4 per cent of Canadian workers in the public and private sectors (not including the national armed forces) held registered private pension plans.[50] These plans provide for vesting and locking-in of pension benefits after a designated period of employment and attainment of a certain age.[51] Pension benefits are generally payable in the form of a life annuity that begins upon retirement. The annuity may be guaranteed for a number of years and made payable to the employee's surviving spouse, estate, or a named beneficiary.

In several provinces, when an individual dies before pension benefits are paid, the benefits are payable to her or his surviving spouse, subject to certain restrictions.[52] Similarly, when an individual has a spouse at the time pension payments commence, the pension is a joint pension that is payable during the joint lives of the pension holder and her or his spouse.[53] After the death of either the pension holder or the spouse, the pension is payable to the survivor for life subject to certain restrictions; the pension remains payable even if the surviving spouse remarries.[54]

An individual may also designate a beneficiary for her or his pension plan.[55] A designated beneficiary has the right to enforce payment of the benefit.[56] In some provinces, benefits designated to a beneficiary pass directly to the named

[50] Statistics Canada, 'Percentage of Labour Force and Employees Covered by a Registered Pension Plan (RPP)' (Statistics Canada, 29 April 2011), www.statcan.gc.ca/tables-tableaux/sum-som/l01/cst01/labor26a-eng.htm. See also: Statistics Canada, 'Pension Plans in Canada, as of January 1, 2013' (Statistics Canada, 28 August 2014), www.statcan.gc.ca/daily-quotidien/140828/dq140828d-eng.htm.

[51] Oosterhoff, above n 1, 123.

[52] Pension Benefits Act, RSO 1990, c P 8, s 48; Pension Benefits Standard Act, RSBC 1996, c 352, s 34.

[53] Pension Benefits Standard Act, RSBC 1996, c 352, s 35.

[54] ibid, s 35 f.

[55] Wills, Estates and Successions Act, SBC 2009 c 13, s 85 (Wills, Estates and Successions Act); Wills and Succession Act, SA 2010, c W-12.2, s 71.

[56] Wills, Estates and Successions Act, RSBC 1996, c 352, s 93.

beneficiary and therefore do not form part of the estate.[57] This allows the pension proceeds to bypass the probate process. Pensions are thus generally exempt from seizure by creditors.[58] However, in Ontario for example, pension and other retirement plans are included in calculating the net value of an estate in connection with dependants' relief claims.[59]

Although a pension that passes directly to a surviving spouse or named beneficiary does not form part of the deceased's estate, case law in Canada is inconclusive as to whether proceeds designated to a surviving spouse or named beneficiary are testamentary or lifetime dispositions. Some decisions have considered such designations to be testamentary in nature, which would expose pension beneficiaries to the claims of estate creditors. Others have come to the opposite conclusion. At least one author maintains that the classification of pension designations as testamentary is incorrect, and that the beneficiaries of such designations should be protected from estate creditors, save for circumstances where the pension beneficiary is the estate itself.[60] In Ontario this position appears to have been adopted by the Court of Appeal for the province in a decision confirming that proceeds paid under a private pension to a beneficiary were shielded from claims advanced by creditors of the pension holder's estate.[61]

b. Canada Pension Plan

The Canadian Pension Plan is a public insurance scheme for Canadian workers outside Quebec who are over the age of 18 and earn an annual income in excess of $3,500.[62] When a pension holder dies, a lump-sum death benefit is paid to her or his estate.[63] Additionally, a survivor's pension may be paid to the contributor's surviving legal or common law spouse.[64] Children's benefits will also be payable to dependent children on a monthly basis.[65]

ii. Quebec Pension Plan

The Quebec Pension Plan (QPP) is a compulsory public insurance plan that exists for persons of full age working in Quebec with an annual income that surpasses

[57] ibid, s 95.
[58] Pension Benefits Act, RSO 1990, c P 8, s 66(1).
[59] Succession Law Reform Act, above n 8, s 72(1)(g).
[60] Oosterhoff, above n 1, 124.
[61] *Amherst Crane Rentals Ltd v Perring*, (2004) 241 DLR (4th) 176 (ONCA), 50 CBR (4th) 1 (hereafter: *Amherst Crane Rentals Ltd*).
[62] Government of Canada, 'Contributions to the Canada Pension Plan' (Government of Canada, 20 May 2014), www.servicecanada.gc.ca/eng/services/pensions/cpp/contributions/index.shtml.
[63] Government of Canada, 'Death Benefit' (Government of Canada, 22 May 2014), www.servicecanada.gc.ca/eng/services/pensions/cpp/death-benefit.shtml.
[64] Government of Canada, 'Survivor's Pension' (Government of Canada, 1 November 2013), www.servicecanada.gc.ca/eng/services/pensions/cpp/survivor-pension.shtml.
[65] Government of Canada, 'Benefits for Children under 25' (Government of Canada, 6 August 2013), www.servicecanada.gc.ca/eng/services/pensions/cpp/child.shtml.

$3,500.[66] When a pensioner dies a death benefit will be awarded to her or his estate provided she or he has made all required contributions to the QPP.[67] Subject to certain restrictions the surviving married, civil union, or de facto spouse may be entitled to a surviving spouse's pension.[68] Quebec law states that the death benefit and the survivor spouse's pension are not considered to derive from the deceased pensioner's succession, suggesting that these funds bypass the estate of the deceased.[69]

E. Registered Plans

i. Registered Retirement Savings Plans and Registered Retirement Income Funds

The Canada Revenue Agency defines a registered retirement savings plan (RRSP) as 'an arrangement between an individual and an issuer (an insurance company, a trust company or a bank) under which retirement income commences at maturity'.[70] RRSPs are thus privately owned accounts registered with the state, which accrue from personal contributions. These contributions are tax deductible to the payor and earnings within the plan are exempt from taxes, although RRSP payments are taxable on receipt. RRSPs are widely held in Canada, with nearly 60 per cent of Canadians having contributed to this type of retirement savings plan.[71]

A registered retirement income fund (RRIF) is an arrangement between an individual and a carrier, such as an insurance company, a trust company or a bank, that is registered by the Canada Revenue Agency.[72] An individual initially transfers property to the carrier, which then pays that individual a yearly sum on retirement, starting the year following the one of the RRIF plan's establishment.[73] RRIF earnings are tax free; however, the sums paid out are taxable on receipt.[74]

[66] Régie des rentes Québec, 'The Quebec Pension Plan' (Régie des rentes Québec), www.rrq.gouv.qc.ca/en/programmes/regime_rentes/Pages/regime_rentes.aspx.

[67] Act Respecting the Quebec Pension Plan, CQLR c R-9, s 128. See also Régie des rentes Québec, 'The Death Benefit' (Régie des rentes Québec), www.rrq.gouv.qc.ca/en/deces/deces_conjoint/autres_rentes/Pages/prestation_deces.aspx.

[68] Régie des rentes Québec, 'The Quebec Pension Plan', above n 66.

[69] Act Respecting the Quebec Pension Plan, above n 67, s 146.

[70] Canada Revenue Agency, 'About Registered Retirement Savings Plan and Registered Retirement Investment Funds' (Canada Revenue Agency, 10 May 2013), www.cra-arc.gc.ca/tx/rgstrd/rrsprrif-reerferr/bt-eng.html.

[71] CBC News, '59% of Canadians Say They Contributed to RRSP, RBC Poll Suggests' (CBC News, 5 February 2014), www.cbc.ca/news/business/59-of-canadians-say-they-contributed-to-rrsp-rbc-poll-suggests-1.2524237.

[72] Canada Revenue Agency, 'Registered Retirement Investment Fund' (Canada Revenue Agency, 17 February 2014), www.cra-arc.gc.ca/tx/ndvdls/tpcs/rrif-ferr/menu-eng.html.

[73] ibid.

[74] ibid.

RRSPs and RRIFs devolve to an individual's estate upon death; subsequently, the sum of a RRSP or RRIF will be included in the deceased's final income tax return and subject to the calculation of probate fees. However, an individual may designate a beneficiary of her or his RRSP or RRIF.[75] In some provinces a RRSP or RRIF with a designated beneficiary does not devolve to the deceased's estate; and therefore, is not included in the deceased's final tax return or the calculation of probate fees. The RRSP or RRIF is transferred to the designated beneficiary and taxes are payable by the beneficiary in the year in which the funds are withdrawn from the account.

There has been considerable instability over time within Canadian jurisprudence as to whether the proceeds of registered savings plans form part of the deceased's estate or whether these should be paid directly to named beneficiaries, bypassing the estate and remaining shielded from potential claims of creditors. Initially, courts suggested that these benefits formed part of the estate and did not benefit from creditor protection.[76] Subsequently, a line of jurisprudence suggested that RRSP or RRIF benefits designated to beneficiaries would be available to creditors only if all other estate assets were exhausted but failed to meet creditors' claims.[77] Most recently, the Ontario Court of Appeal has held that proceeds in a RRSP vest in the designated beneficiary after the plan owner's death and do not move into the owner's estate. As such, plan benefits are not vulnerable to claims advanced by estate creditors.[78] Provinces other than Ontario may take a different approach to this issue given that each jurisdiction will have distinct legislative provisions governing beneficiary designations.

ii. Registered Education Savings Plans

A registered education savings plan (RESP) is a savings account that provides estate planning benefits such as tax deferral opportunities.[79] A RESP can also bypass the probate process if the RESP subscriber names a successor subscriber by will.[80] A RESP with a named successor subscriber will pass to the successor subscriber upon the death of the sole subscriber. Upon this transfer the successor subscriber will be responsible for making payments to the RESP, and the beneficiaries of the RESP will continue to benefit.

If no successor subscriber is named, it is likely that the RESP will be terminated. Upon termination all contributions to the RESP will be refunded to the estate of the subscriber and all Canada Education Savings Grants will be refunded to the

[75] Income Tax Act, RSC 1985, c 1 (5th Supp), s 69(1).
[76] *Canadian Imperial Bank of Commerce v Besharah*, (1989) 68 OR (2d) 443, 58 DLR (4th) 705.
[77] *Banting v Saunders Estate*, 2000 CanLII 22834 (ONSC).
[78] *Amherst Crane Rentals Ltd*, above n 61, leave to appeal to SCC refused, [2004] SCCA no 430.
[79] Mallin, above n 19.
[80] ibid.

government.[81] The estate must pay income tax and probate fees on the refunded sum; additionally, if certain conditions are met the estate may be charged a penalty fee.[82] Moreover, when the sole subscriber of a RESP dies without naming a successor subscriber, the beneficiaries of the RESP are prevented from receiving their intended benefits.

iii. Tax-Free Savings Accounts

A tax-free savings account (TFSA) allows Canadians over the age of 18 to save tax free throughout their lifetime.[83] An individual may contribute to her or his TFSA up to the yearly limit plus any unused contributions or withdrawn amounts from the previous year.[84] A TFSA without a successor holder or designated beneficiary devolves to the deceased holder's estate and is distributed in accordance with the terms of her or his will.[85]

In provinces and territories that recognise the TFSA beneficiary designation, the holder of a TFSA may designate a successor holder. Upon the death of the TFSA holder, all rights and interests in the account will be transferred to the successor holder.[86] A TFSA that is transferred to a successor holder bypasses the probate process and is not subject to taxes on the deceased holder's income tax return.[87] The successor holder may make tax-free withdrawals from the TFSA; she or he may also make contributions subject to her or his yearly limits.[88]

The holder of a TFSA may designate a beneficiary of the account, such as surviving spouses or common law partners, children and qualified donees.[89] If there is no successor holder, the TFSA ceases to exist upon the death of the holder and the property in the TFSA is transferred to the designated beneficiaries.[90] The designated beneficiaries need not pay tax on payments made out of the TFSA provided the total payments do not exceed the fair market value of all the property held in the TFSA at the time of the holder's death.[91]

[81] F Gradley, 'RESPs and Estate Implications' (*Advisor*, 12 May 2009), www.advisor.ca/tax/estate-planning/resps-and-estate-implications-2745.

[82] ibid.

[83] Canada Revenue Agency, 'Tax-Free Savings Account' (Canada Revenue Agency, 24 February 2014), www.cra-arc.gc.ca/tx/ndvdls/tpcs/tfsa-celi/menu-eng.html.

[84] ibid.

[85] Canada Revenue Agency, 'Successor Holder' (Canada Revenue Agency, 14 February 2014), www.cra-arc.gc.ca/tx/ndvdls/tpcs/tfsa-celi/dth/sccrhldr-eng.html.

[86] ibid.

[87] ibid.

[88] ibid.

[89] Canada Revenue Agency, 'Designated Beneficiaries' (Canada Revenue Agency, 14 February 2014), www.cra-arc.gc.ca/tx/ndvdls/tpcs/tfsa-celi/dth/srvr-eng.html.

[90] ibid.

[91] ibid.

II. Rationale for and Concerns Surrounding Will-Substitutes

A. Rationales Underlying Will-Substitutes

Estates practitioners in common law Canada will point to tax advantages as a key motivator underlying the creation of will-substitutes. This is true even though no Canadian jurisdiction presently levies an inheritance tax on estates. Instead, probate fees and estate-related taxes relate to the costs associated with estate administration and with deemed dispositions triggered by the transfer of the deceased's property from the estate to a beneficiary. Indeed, the Supreme Court of Canada has held that probate 'fees' do constitute a tax, but a tax that each province and territory has legitimate authority to implement.[92]

All provinces across Canada except Quebec levy taxes for the administration of estates, although Quebec's rules of procedure do include a tariff of just over $100 for probating wills or obtaining letters of verification.[93] Estate administration taxes apply regardless of whether the deceased died with a valid will or intestate. As in many other jurisdictions, estate taxes and fees in Canada are determined by the size of the estate. This area is subject to the governance of the provinces and territories, and thus the formula in place for determining the scope of estate administration taxes will vary from one jurisdiction to the next. Ontario, for example, has quite a simple formula, whereby estates with a net value of $0 to $50,000 will be taxed at $5 per $1000, whereas estates valued at more than $50,000 are taxed at $250, plus $15 per $10,000 in excess of $50,000. In Alberta, the Northwest Territories and Nunavut, estate taxes range from $25 to $400 maximum, with a scale that escalates according to the net worth of the estate.

In jurisdictions like Ontario, where there is no ceiling on the tax that may be imposed on estates, there may be a real incentive to reduce the size of an estate that holds significant wealth. By diminishing assets within the estate, the corresponding taxes and fees exacted upon that estate when it opens are also reduced. Hence, estate planners will look to the possibility of transferring assets through will-substitutes that benefit from a tax shelter when assets transfer to beneficiaries. A clear example is property that transfers to a survivor joint tenant. The proceeds of life insurance are also exempt from taxation when they pass to the beneficiary.

Aside from tax issues, will-substitutes can form attractive estate planning devices for their relative simplicity of operation, as compared with the schemes in place for administering wills or intestate successions. The process of probate or will verification occurs through an application to the court in the jurisdiction where

[92] *Re Eurig Estate* [1998] 2 SCR 565, [1998] SCJ no 72; see also Spenceley, above n 4, 10–11.

[93] Tariff of Court Costs in Civil Matters and Court Office Fees, CQLR c T-16, r 9, s 17.

the deceased resided.[94] Once granted, probate registers the authenticity of the will and vests the estate executor with the authority to administer the estate assets. The time required for probate will depend on the nature of the estate. Where the will and its assets are simple, probate will be a relatively rapid and straightforward affair. Yet estates are often complex, causing the probate process to become time-consuming, cumbersome and expensive. This will be the case, for example, if the deceased had assets in diverse jurisdictions or had prepared multiple documents that might constitute testamentary instruments. Matters may also be complicated if a will is believed to exist but cannot be found; if a will was made in another jurisdiction and thus raises conflict of law questions; if no suitable executor or estate trustee is appointed or identifiable; if the will is contested; or if assets in the estate must be sold to meet the claims of creditors or the entitlements of the heirs or beneficiaries. These challenges can be especially arduous for family members who survive the deceased and require ready access to the estate's fixed or liquid assets, or who were economically dependent on the deceased during the latter's lifetime. A key benefit of will-substitutes thus lies in the relative ease with which property passes to a beneficiary.

A further rationale that may underlie the creation of will-substitutes relates to their ability to put assets beyond the reach of state regimes for protecting creditors of the estate. The issue of creditor interests in will-substitutes in Canada is addressed elsewhere in this collection,[95] and thus will not be explored in depth here, although part of the discussion below considers questions concerning the extent to which will-substitutes may defeat the claims of dependants who are creditors of an estate.

A final motivator underlying the creation of will-substitutes may relate to an estate planner's privacy concerns. Wills become public pursuant to probate as does, in some jurisdictions, an itemised inventory of assets in the estate. In contrast, will-substitutes remain private documents even after a grant of property to the beneficiary has taken place. Thus, if an individual wishes to preserve the confidentiality of a disposition of property, will-substitutes will foster this objective with far greater certainty than is true for testamentary dispositions. Interestingly, this point has been made indirectly in connection with the *post-mortem* transfer of secret or sacred knowledge within indigenous populations in postcolonial jurisdictions. Passing such knowledge by will is problematic because of the publicity that this entails. At the same time, will-substitutes, as they are conventionally understood, are not ideal for this purpose either, given that intellectual property in the form of cultural knowledge is not typically the object of a will-substitute instrument. Consequently, secret or half-secret trusts have been proposed as viable options for the distribution of such property.[96]

[94] Note that in Quebec probate is required for holograph wills and wills made before witnesses, but not for notarial wills. See art 772 CCQ.

[95] See ch 12 below.

[96] P Vines, 'Consequences of Intestacy for Indigenous People in Australia: The Passing of Property and Burial Rights' (2004) 8 *Australian Indigenous Law Reporter* 406, 414.

B. Concerns Related to Will-Substitutes

Preoccupations articulated in relation to will-substitutes circulate around two key themes. The first relates to the fact that will-substitutes need not adhere to the formal requirements of will-making, whereas the second addresses concerns about individuals' use of will-substitutes to defeat the otherwise legitimate claims that family members dependent on a deceased would have against the latter's estate. A closer inspection of legislative regimes governing estates in Canada suggests that there may be less cause for disquiet in regard to these concerns than one might initially believe.

Will-substitutes are not subject to the requirements of wills set up by statute in regard to their formal validity. This may prompt concerns that will-substitutes can be too readily made, and thus lack the gravitas of formation with which will writing is commonly associated. Wills are said to be characterised by an *animo testandi*, ie, by the intention of making fixed and final dispositions in relation to the distribution of property after death. The language of the will thus cannot be ambiguous as to intention, nor can it be precatory. Instead, the will must be framed in decisive and directive terms, reflective of an intention of finality in regard to the distribution of the testator's assets on death.[97]

Having said this, statutory provisions do not prescribe mandatory scripts for wills. Instead, discerning a testator's intention is a matter of judicial interpretation and discretion, based on legal principles. When it comes to the formal requirements of wills, nowhere in Canada does a statute stipulate the terminology or language that a will must include. Rather, formal validity for wills can be easily achieved. All jurisdictions across Canada recognise the holograph will, which requires nothing more than a document expressing testamentary intentions written entirely and signed in the testator's own hand.[98]

Canadian legislation also recognises wills made before witnesses. This form of a will increases its solemnity but remains uncomplicated in its most basic iteration. It requires the testator's signature or attestation of signature before two witnesses who in turn sign the document. Although this is a more formalised type of will, in both the common law provinces and in civil law Quebec, it need not include the involvement of a solicitor or notary.[99]

The absence of complex requirements to create a formally valid will suggests that a concern about the exemption of will-substitutes from these requirements may be misplaced. Moreover, the institutes included within will-substitutes have, themselves, their own formal requirements, such as gifts *mortis causa* and contracts for life insurance. Courts will interpret and assess the validity of these instruments

[97] *Bennett v Toronto General Trusts Corporation* [1958] SCR 392, 14 DLR (2d) 1; *Molinari v Winfrey* [1961] SCR 91.

[98] Succession Law Reform Act, above n 8, s 6; art 726 CCQ.

[99] ibid, s 4; arts 727 ff CCQ.

against legal rules governing formal validity.[100] Thus, the distinct requirements for will-substitutes as to form should not necessarily be a cause for deep concern among estates specialists.

As indicated, the capacity for will-substitutes to move the assets of a deceased person beyond the reach of the latter's dependants may also be viewed as inequitable or problematic. Succession law across Canada centres on the principle of testamentary freedom. In Canadian common law jurisdictions and in Quebec civil law alike, an individual is free to plan her or his estate as she or he wishes, and there is no forced heirship regime in place in any province or territory that would reserve a portion of an estate for the deceased's spouse, children or other relatives.

Yet while a testator is free to leave assets in an estate by will to whomever she or he wishes, legislative mechanisms are in place in each jurisdiction that allow for an aggrieved dependant to bring a claim against an estate where she or he can establish that the testator failed to fulfil alimentary obligations to the applicant. In the common law, these obligations can be moral or legal in nature.[101] Such claims are termed dependants' relief or wills variation applications.[102]

The size of the estate subject to such applications will weigh heavily in judicial analyses in their regard. As such, vigorous use of will-substitutes could theoretically wield a significant impact on the entitlements of dependent family members. Notably, if the deceased significantly reduced the value of her or his estate by disposing of assets via will-substitutes during her or his lifetime, those assets could not—barring an express legislative provision to the contrary—be considered in the valuation of the estate for the purposes of assessing dependants' relief or wills variation claims.

In an effort to attenuate the risk of creditors of alimentary support removing, *post mortem*, their assets from the reach of dependent family members, some provinces have established statutory regimes that allow courts to include assets transferred by will-substitutes within estate valuation, in the context of dependants' relief or wills variation claims.[103]

Ontario law thus distinctly provides that transactions via will-substitutes—such as: gifts *mortis causa*; deposit accounts that the deceased held in trust; joint accounts and property held in joint tenancy; life insurance proceeds from group insurance or policies the deceased owned; and amounts paid to designated beneficiaries through pension or retirement savings plans—are included in the net estate and are thus subject to charge on dependants' relief claims.[104]

[100] See *Robichaud (Succession)*, above n 44.

[101] See *Tataryn v Tataryn Estate* [1994] 2 SCR 807 and *Cummings v Cummings*, 2004 CanLII 9339 (ONCA). But see the limited reading afforded to the notion of a moral obligation in the recent decision of the Ontario CA in *Verch Estate v Weckwerth*, 2014 ONCA 338 (CanLII).

[102] Succession Law Reform Act, above n 8, ss 57 ff; Wills, Estates and Successions Act, above n 55, s 60.

[103] Oosterhoff, above n 1, 902; See ch 12 below, p 254.

[104] Succession Law Reform Act, above n 8, s 72.

Accordingly, in assessing a common law spouse's claim for dependants' relief, the Ontario Superior Court included the estate assets as well as a spousal RRSP, life insurance proceeds, and a pension death benefit in the valuation of the deceased's estate.[105]

Not all jurisdictions create such provisions to protect dependent creditors. In Quebec, for example, creditors of alimentary support are entitled to claim a financial contribution from a succession.[106] In assessing such claims, courts are directed to consider the assets in the succession, which may have been reduced through dispositions made during the deceased's lifetime via will-substitutes.[107] At the same time, the Civil Code indicates that where a spouse or child claims support, a court may include within the succession *inter vivos* 'liberalities'—which are defined as gratuitous dispositions[108]—that the deceased made during the three years preceding her or his death, as well as liberalities that take effect at the time of death.[109] This provision, while less explicit than that in place within Ontario's successions legislation, creates a mechanism that allows for the inclusion of gratuitous dispositions made via will-substitutes within the assets of the estate. Its effects are therefore potentially as wide-ranging as those of relevant Ontario law. Such protective legislation, which retrieves the value of dispositions made by will-substitutes or other vehicles, can offset concerns about protecting dependants whose entitlements might otherwise be decreased through transfers that would reduce an estate's net worth.

III. Conclusion

This chapter sets out the various forms that will-substitutes may take in Canada, and the manner in which these are governed by law. It offers an overview of the regulation of will-substitutes under Canadian common law and Quebec civil law. The particular will-substitutes considered here are: gifts, notably, the *donatio mortis causa*/*mortis causa* gift; joint interests in property; life insurance; pension plans; and registered savings plans.

The chapter describes these instruments and the manner in which these can be used to shield and transfer wealth. It then examines the dominant rationales underlying the creation of will-substitutes in Canada, including: avoidance of estate taxation; the relative simplicity and rapidity of the operation of will-substitutes;

[105] *Quinn v Carrigan*, 2014 ONSC 5682, 244 ACWS (3d) 749.

[106] Art 684 CCQ.

[107] Art 686 CCQ.

[108] F Allard, M-F Bich, J-M Brisson, É Charpentier, P-A Crépeau, M Devinat, Y Emerich, P Forget, N Kasirer (eds), *Private Law Dictionary and Bilingual Lexicons: Obligations* (Montreal, Éditions Yvon Blais, 2003) 185.

[109] Art 687 CCQ.

protection from estate creditors; and the preservation of privacy in relation to wealth transfer.

Finally, this chapter considers some of the potential policy concerns and objections that may be raised in relation to will-substitutes in Canada. The discussion here also demonstrates, however, that disquiet over will-substitutes need not be pronounced. First, preoccupations over formal validity must be considered in view of the fact that wills are not necessarily difficult to create, nor are legal professionals necessarily involved in their drafting. Will-substitutes are themselves governed by particular formal requirements that courts will use to assess their validity. Second, concerns about moving a deceased person's assets beyond the reach of her or his creditors are attenuated by dependants' relief or wills variation legislation that allows certain assets to be included in the calculation of an estate's net value for the purposes of evaluating claims for alimentary support brought against the estate.

Future research on will-substitutes in Canada will be worthwhile. Such work would stand to illuminate the extent to which these instruments are deployed as a mode of estate planning. Insights gleaned from such research could counterbalance concerns about the relative low rate of will making in Canada,[110] demonstrating how will-substitutes might complement wills as a mode of planning for the management of one's assets after death. The value of such work will be particularly useful if it can probe at relationships between demographic factors and will- or will-substitute-making, investigating whether an individual's social or economic context affects her or his propensity to engage in estate planning either via testamentary or nontestamentary instruments.

[110] The rate of will-making among Canadians is just under 50%. See Lawyers' Professional Indemnity Company (LawPRO), 'Survey: More Than Half of Canadians Do Not Have a Signed Will' (*LawPRO*, 7 May 2012), www.lawpro.ca/news/pdf/Wills-POAsurvey.pdf.

3

Will-Substitutes in England and Wales

ALEXANDRA BRAUN*

I. Introduction

Will-substitutes, that is to say mechanisms that are functionally equivalent to wills, are very common in the US, where much of the wealth is transferred on death by means other than wills, and thus outside traditional probate procedures. This has led some authors to speak of a 'non-probate revolution'.[1] The phenomenon has not only attracted widespread interest among legal scholars, but has also led to responses by both the drafters of the Uniform Probate Code (UPC) and the *Restatement Third of Property*, who have tried to accommodate will-substitutes within the law of donative transfers and to harmonise substantive laws governing wills and will-substitutes.[2]

Given similarities in the structure of their succession laws and the administration of estates, one might expect that developments in England and Wales are similar.[3] The purpose of this chapter is to investigate whether this is the case, and to provide an assessment of the transfer of wealth on death in England by means other than by will or intestacy. It will emerge that, by comparison with the US, on this side of the Atlantic, legal scholars, as well as law reformers, have paid relatively

* The author is grateful to the John Fell Fund for funding research assistance for this chapter, and to the Alexander von Humboldt Foundation for providing funding for a sabbatical leave during which parts of this chapter were written. The author further thanks Victoria Coleman for her invaluable assistance with the research, and Gregor Christandl, Jan Peter Schmidt, Lionel Smith and Anne Röthel for helpful comments on an earlier draft.

[1] JH Langbein, 'The Nonprobate Revolution and the Future of the Law of Succession' (1984) 97 *Harvard Law Review* 1108.

[2] JH Langbein, 'Major Reforms of the Property Restatement and the Uniform Probate Code: Reformation, Harmless Error, and Nonprobate Transfers' (2012) 38 *American College of Trust and Estate Counsel Law Journal* 1; GMP McCouch, 'Probate Law Reform and Nonprobate Transfers' (2008) 62 *University of Miami Law Review* 757; GMP McCouch, 'Will Substitutes under the Revised Uniform Probate Code' (1993) 58 *Brooklyn Law Review* 1123. More recently, MB Leslie and SE Sterk, 'Revisiting the Revolution: Reintegrating the Wealth Transmission System' (2015) 56 *Boston College Law Review* 61 and ch 1 above, p 9.

[3] When reference is made to England in this chapter, this refers to England and Wales.

little attention to the phenomenon and the effect of the use of will-substitutes.[4] This might suggest that will-substitutes do not play an important role in practice. This, however, is not the case. Even though in England one cannot quite speak of a 'non-probate revolution', the will does not represent the only mechanism by which people transfer wealth on death.[5] Despite the fact that the rate of testation in England is probably higher than in several other European countries,[6] testators in England are often members of a private pension scheme, have set up a trust, hold property in joint names, or have stipulated a life insurance policy.[7] Thus, wills are complemented by other means of passing benefits on death. What is more, some of the mechanisms used have been in place for quite some time.[8] That said, in recent decades, the transfer of wealth through instruments functionally equivalent to wills seems to have gained a new economic importance, due, especially, to investments in life insurance policies and private pension schemes.

Among the will-substitutes most commonly used in the US are revocable trusts, life insurance, pension accounts as well as various types of pay-on-death (POD) accounts.[9] In England, the picture is somewhat different. Wills aside, most wealth appears to be transferred on death through private pension schemes, life insurance, as well as survivorship operating on death of a joint tenant. Some of the 'mass-will-substitutes' found in the US, such as transfer-on-death (TOD)

[4] An exception is JG Miller, *The Machinery of Succession*, 2nd edn (Aldershot, Dartmouth Publishing Co Ltd, 1996) 1. See also R Kerridge and AHR Brierley, *Parry and Kerridge: The Law of Succession*, 12th edn (London, Sweet & Maxwell, 2009) 1–5; and C Sawyer and M Spero, *Succession, Wills and Probate*, 3rd edn (London, Routledge, 2015) ch 2.

[5] J Finch, L Hayes, J Masson, J Mason and L Wallis, *Wills, Inheritance, and Families* (Oxford, Clarendon Press, 1996) 32 and 37: 'Thus, taking the total picture of the transmission of property, it is clear that wills play a relatively small role in quantitative terms'.

[6] For comparative figures see KGC Reid, MJ De Waal, and R Zimmermann (eds), *Comparative Succession Law, volume 2. Intestate Succession* (Oxford, OUP, 2015) 444. The latest figures from the English Judicial and Court Statistics of 2012 reveal that 41% of the people who died in 2012 left a will: *Court Statistics Quarterly* January to March 2013, www.gov.uk/government/uploads/system/uploads/attachment_data/file/207804/court-stats-q1-2013.pdf. The percentage seems to have remained more or less stable over the years. However, according to R Kerridge, 'Intestate Succession in England and Wales' in ibid, 323, 332, 'almost 85% of those in respect of whose estate grants of probate or letters of administration were taken out actually died leaving valid wills'.

[7] The term 'life insurance' is used so as to include both life assurance and life insurance policies.

[8] One example is trusts, which were developed partly in order to cater for shortcomings in the succession law of the time. See Langbein, 'Major Reforms of the Property Restatement and the Uniform Probate Code', above n 2, 10–11. The *donatio mortis causa* too developed in order to avoid the technicalities of testamentary law. CV Margrave-Jones, *Mellows: The Law of Succession*, 5th rev edn (London, Butterworths Law, 1993) 520. And, by the 14th century, the common law had already fully developed the distinction between a tenancy in common and a joint tenancy, the latter allowing for the operation of the *ius accrescendi*, which was apparently related to a desire to overcome the technical problems of the conveyance and to avoid feudal dues. F Pollock and FW Maitland, *History of English Law*, vol 2, 2nd edn (1898) 20.

[9] Langbein, 'Major Reforms of the Property Restatement and the Uniform Probate Code', above n 2, 10; McCouch, 'Will Substitutes under the Revised Uniform Probate Code' above n 2; Leslie and Sterk, above n 2, and ch 1 above, p 12. There is no agreement, however, as to which instrument is most relevant from an economic perspective.

registrations of securities or automobiles, POD bank accounts, or TOD deeds,[10] are not available here. Although revocable trusts are popular elsewhere,[11] in England, they do not seem to be as common. Perhaps this is partly due to their tax treatment, as well as the fact that there is a great deal of uncertainty as to how far settlors can reserve powers to themselves.[12]

This chapter explores some of the most common mechanisms used in England,[13] the rationale behind their use, as well as how the law deals with them and the consequences that arise from their proliferation. In doing so, it considers will-substitutes from different perspectives, including those of creditors and family members and dependants. It argues that the current state of the law in England is unsatisfactory and that it is time for a proper discussion involving non-probate transfers and their relationship with current succession laws.

II. Principal Types of Will-Substitute

A. Private Pension Schemes

As is the case in the US,[14] in England, private pension schemes are a common mechanism for passing wealth on death. Together with homes, pensions often represent the most significant financial asset of a household.[15] Although the primary function of private pension schemes is to accumulate and invest savings so as to pre-empt the risk of insufficient or inadequate income on retirement, they can also lead to a payment of benefits on death of the member. The type of death

[10] On the latter see, SN Gary, 'Transfer-on-Death Deeds: The Non-Probate Revolution Continues' (2006) *Real Property, Probate and Trust Journal* 529. In Canada they are not used either. See ch 12 below, p 257.

[11] KD Schenkel, 'The Trust-As-Will Portmanteau: Trill or Spork?' (2013) *Quinnipiac Probate Law Journal* 40.

[12] See C McKenzie, 'Having and Eating the Cake: A Global Survey of Settlor Reserved Power Trusts: Part 1' (2007) 5 *Private Client Business* 336, 339 who also shows that revocable trusts are common in offshore jurisdictions. See ch 11 below, p 238. As to the Canadian context, see ch 12 below, p 255.

[13] This chapter will not explore the use of contracts to make wills, automatic accruer clauses in partnerships, or statutory succession in residential or agricultural tenancy.

[14] According to SE Sterk and MB Leslie, 'Accidental Inheritance: Retirement Accounts and the Hidden Law of Succession' (2014) 89 *New York University Law Review* 165, in the US, individuals hold more than nine trillion dollars in employer-sponsored defined contribution plans and individual retirement accounts (IRAs). In England, in 2012, £2,405bn was invested in private pension funds. This represents an 8% increase from £2,230bn in 2011: see Association of British Insurers (ABI), 'Funds held in Life and Pension products in 2012', Data Bulletin November 2013, www.abi.org.uk/Insurance-and-savings/Industry-data/~/media/DBDADF2BB9CD4C8B88419CD2B9E37D5E.ashx, 2.

[15] In 2012/14, aggregate total wealth of all private households in Great Britain was £11.1 trillion, and private pension wealth accounted for 40%. In 2008/10, 2010/12 and 2012/14 private pension wealth accounted for the largest share of aggregate total wealth. See Office for National Statistics, 'Total Wealth, Wealth in Great Britain 2012–14', http://webarchive.nationalarchives.gov.uk/20160105160709/http://www.ons.gov.uk/ons/dcp171776_428631.pdf, ch 2. In this sense also the Law Commission's report on *Intestacy and Family Provision Claims on Death* (Law Com No 331, 2011) para 7.99.

benefit varies considerably depending on the pension scheme and on whether the member dies before or after retirement.

i. Benefits in Case of Death in Service

Where the member dies before retirement, pension schemes usually provide death benefits either in the form of a lump-sum payment, a dependant's pension, or a combination of both. Generally speaking, dependant's pensions may be paid to a spouse, civil partner, cohabitant, child or other dependant of the deceased.[16] In most schemes the benefit automatically goes to the spouse or to a dependant, or, if there is no spouse or dependant within the category defined by the scheme, the pension goes to the estate, is absorbed into the fund or refunded.

In principle, lump-sum benefits can be paid to a wider category of people, though this depends on the scheme. Quite often potential beneficiaries include the member's personal representatives, spouses, civil partners, relatives, nominees, those benefiting under a will, anyone financially dependent on the member, a charity, or a trust.[17] The scheme's rules usually allow the member to nominate the beneficiary of the lump-sum payment. However, irrespective of whether or not the scheme is contract or trust based, such nominations are not usually binding on the scheme administrators or trustees who, in the exercise of their discretion, can nominate someone else.[18]

ii. Benefits in Case of Death after Retirement

Where the member dies after retirement, depending on the scheme, some death benefits may be payable in the form of a guaranteed pension. In this case, if the member dies before the end of the guaranteed period, any remaining payments will be paid to his or her estate, to be distributed according to the will or intestacy rules. Defined benefits schemes will often pay a proportion of the pension that the member was receiving when he or she died to his or her spouse or children.

Until recently, when a member of a defined contribution scheme retired, he could take up to 25 per cent of the pension pot, as a lump sum tax free; the remainder if taken as a lump sum was subject to onerous tax charges. Depending on the scheme, the effect of pension legislation was that the member had to invest the remaining 75 per cent by purchasing either a 'compulsory purchase annuity', a 'drawdown pension' or a combination of both. Since April 2015, everyone with a defined contribution pension fund who is aged 55 or over has complete freedom

[16] s 167 and sch 28, para 15 of the Finance Act 2004.

[17] On the latter option, see G Thomas, 'Trust of Death Benefits Under Occupational Pension Schemes—Deep Waters for Advisers: Part 1' (1995) *Private Client Business* 133.

[18] Depending on whether or not the scheme is trust or contract based, distribution takes place through trustees or scheme administrators. When reference to trustees is made, this chapter intends to refer to both.

to access the whole of their pension fund as a lump sum, regardless of the size of the fund, though only the first 25 per cent will be tax free. Thus, members are no longer forced to invest the money in an annuity or a drawdown pension, though those options will still be available and most people will probably continue to invest in them.[19]

Where upon retirement the member has invested the pension pot in a drawdown pension or an annuity, more benefits may be payable on death. Through an annuity, the member can provide for dependants by purchasing a guaranteed term annuity, a joint life annuity, or both. In the former, the insurance company will make the payments for a guaranteed period, even if the member dies, while in the latter the payment is made for the life of the beneficiary. In the case of drawdown pensions, death benefits can be provided in the form of a drawdown pension, a lump-sum payment or an annuity. In addition, since 2006, member value protection annuities are also available, providing a return of any unpaid capital on death as a lump sum.

Thus, pensions offer a variety of different possible ways of passing wealth on death of the member and often the amount of money passed is not insignificant.[20] For instance, in occupational pension schemes, the lump sum is normally calculated as a multiple of the member's yearly earning at the time of death, or a multiple of four times the yearly salary or greater. Most personal pensions will pay the full value of the pension fund, so that the amount can be considerable. In some instances both a lump sum and a dependant's pension, of up to two-thirds of the member's prospective pension plus return of member's contributions with interest, is payable.[21] NEST (National Employment Savings Trust) pension schemes only pay out a lump sum equal to the value of the member's pension account if the member dies before retirement. It is then paid to the person nominated by the member, as the nomination is binding.

iii. The Distribution of Death Benefits

We have seen that most pension schemes allow the member to nominate the beneficiary of the death benefit. These nominations are normally required to be

[19] In the past, lifetime annuities were often best suited to those with a smaller pension fund. See C Hayes, R Newman and F Lagerberg (eds), *Tolley's Tax Guide 2012–13* (London, Tolley Publishing, 2012) 341 and Pensions Policy Institute, 'Briefing Note No 61', December 2011, www.pensionspolicyinstitute.org.uk/briefing-notes/briefing-note-61-the-implications-of-ending-the-effective-requirement-to-annuitise-by-age-75. As to the impact of the abolition of any requirement to take out an annuity, see ABI, 'UK Insurance Key Facts 2014 publication', www.abi.org.uk/~/media/Files/Documents/Publications/Public/2014/Key%20Facts/ABI%20Key%20Facts%202014.pdf, 12. Tax changes are discussed below at section IV.C.

[20] In determination *Hawkins* (PO-2753) the lump sum amounted to £51,559; in *Childs-Hopkins* (K00663) to £96,000; in *Wheeler* (PO-267) to £150,053; and in *Tompkins* (J00510) to £562,600.

[21] For details, see Office for National Statistics, 'OPSS Annual Report 2011', www.ons.gov.uk/ons/rel/pensions/occupational-pension-scheme-survey-annual-report/2011-annual-report/index.html, chs 5 and 6.

in writing and signed by the member, and are generally revocable according to the rules of the respective scheme, but cannot be expressed in a will. As noted above, in many cases nominations are not binding on the trustees, which is why they are frequently referred to as letters of wishes. In other words, unlike in other common law jurisdictions,[22] the distribution is left to the discretion of the trustees.

When deciding who will receive a benefit, trustees must act in accordance with the scheme and take into consideration not just the nominee(s) chosen by the member, but all potential beneficiaries, as defined by the scheme. However, in most cases they will simply abide by the nomination, unless the member's circumstances have changed after the nomination was made.[23] Inevitably, this can lead to situations where complaints are brought to the Pensions Ombudsman questioning the manner in which the discretion was exercised.[24] There are, however, also pension schemes in which nominations are binding, as is the case with NEST nominations, in which case the trustees will pay the person nominated by the member.[25]

The reason why most private pension schemes provide trustees with discretion to choose the beneficiary of the lump-sum death benefit is to avoid any risk of the payment being treated as part of the member's estate for the purposes of inheritance tax.[26] Although non-binding nominations are less like wills, pensions still allow for a transfer of wealth on death, though as determined by the trustees. Where they are binding, they are clearly a will-substitute.

B. Statutory Nominations

A mechanism, often mentioned in succession textbooks, is statutory nominations, which represent a non-probate testamentary instrument provided by the legislature.[27] Initially, the purpose behind these nominations was to grant poorer members of society the possibility of transferring funds or investments held by certain bodies,[28] such as industrial and provident societies, friendly societies and

[22] In Canada and in the US, beneficiary designations are binding. See ch 2 above, p 39 and ch 1 above, p 14. In Australia, it depends on the scheme. For further details, see A Braun 'Pension Death Benefits: Opportunities and Pitfalls' in B Häcker and C Mitchell (eds), *Current Issues in Succession Law* (Oxford, Hart Publishing, 2016) ch 10.

[23] ibid, 247.

[24] ibid, 252.

[25] Recent changes to the HMRC Manual indicate that any nomination that is binding triggers inheritance tax (IHT), irrespective of who is the beneficiary. See the HMRC guidance, 'IHTM17052 (Pensions: IHT charges: general power over death benefits)', www.hmrc.gov.uk/manuals/ihtmanual/ihtm17052.htm.

[26] D Pollard, *The Law of Pension Trusts* (Oxford, OUP, 2013) 137; R Kerridge, 'Testamentary Formalities in England and Wales' in KGC Reid, MJ De Waal and R Zimmermann (eds), *Comparative Succession Law, volume 1. Testamentary Formalities* (Oxford, OUP, 2011) 305, 307; Miller, *The Machinery of Succession*, above n 4, 335.

[27] *In re Barnes* [1940] Ch 267, 272–73.

[28] Lord Mersey in *Eccles Provident Industrial Co-operative Society Ltd v Griffiths* [1912] AC 483, 490.

trade unions, outside probate rules, by using a written nomination, rather than a will, which must be signed in writing before two witnesses.[29] Although, at some point in the past some schemes allowed statutory nominations for relatively large sums,[30] nowadays, they are only permitted for small sums of up to £5,000,[31] which is probably one of the reasons why they are no longer as common in practice.[32]

Unlike most pension nominations, statutory nominations are binding on the administrators of the scheme. In this sense, they are closer to wills, although unlike wills,[33] statutory nominations can be validly made at the age of 16, and are expressly excluded from having to comply with formality requirements set out in section 9 of the Wills Act 1837. That said, the various statutes regulating such nominations usually require writing, and in many cases it must be attested by one or more witnesses, so that the differences in form are not as significant as they initially appear. In fact, where a statutory nomination complies with the formality requirements for wills, it may be proved as a will.[34]

People can (and often) dispose of such investments by will instead of by statutory nomination,[35] something that is not usually possible in the context of pensions. This allows testators to change their minds by simply revoking the will or by varying it through a codicil, though in this instance the advantages of a non-probate transfer are of course lost. However, a nomination made under a statutory provision takes precedence over a will, whether the will is made before,[36] or after the nomination.[37] Thus, once a statutory nomination is made, it may be revoked by a notice complying with the formalities for such a nomination, but it cannot be revoked by a will or codicil.[38]

C. Life Insurance

Unlike pension schemes, which are primarily designed to provide for retirement, an important rationale behind life insurance has traditionally been to transfer

[29] s 23 of the Industrial Provident Societies Act 1965; s 66 of the Friendly Societies Act 1974; s 17 of the Trade Union and Labour Relations (Consolidation) Act 1992; and sch 3 para 1(2) of the Trade Union (Nominations) Regulations 1977 (SI 1977/789) and the Trade Union (Nominations) (Amendment) Regulations 1984 (SI 1984/1290).

[30] Until 1981, National Savings Certificates and deposits in the National Savings Bank up to £100,000 could be passed outside probate.

[31] Miller, above n 4, 112.

[32] In fact, National Savings Certificates and savings in the National Savings Bank pass under a nomination only if made before 1 May 1981. See Kerridge and Brierley, above n 4, 4. For details about their operation, see A Samuels, 'Nominations in Favour of a Deceased to Take Effect on Death' (1967) 31 *Conveyancer & Property Lawyer* 85.

[33] An exception is made for minor soldiers in actual military service or by minor seamen at sea: s 11 of the Wills Act 1837.

[34] *Re Baxter's Goods* [1903] P 12.

[35] Kerridge and Brierley, above n 4, 5.

[36] *Eccles Provident Industrial Co-operative Society Ltd v Griffiths*, above n 28.

[37] *Bennet v Slater* [1899] 1 QB 45.

[38] Kerridge and Brierley, above n 4, 5; Margrave-Jones, above n 8, 362.

wealth and liquidity on death, particularly following the premature death of the policyholder.[39] However, life insurance has also been increasingly regarded as a saving device, and in many cases this factor will be as important as the protection it affords. In other words, the transfer of benefits on death may not always be at the forefront of the mind of a person who takes out a life insurance policy.

Be that as it may, the proceeds of insurance policies often form an important means of providing for the family of a deceased person. In 2013, the average pay-out on a term life insurance policy was £51,500 and total claim pay-outs were £1.3 billion. The average claim payment for whole life insurance was £10,300 and the total payment amounted to £449 million.[40] Although life insurance represents an important financial asset, funds held in insurer-administered life business fell in 2010 by 37 per cent to £150 billion, the lowest level since 1992, and have not really recovered since then.[41] The reasons for this fall in popularity may include reduced benefits, as well as the risk that the insurance company may not pay out,[42] or that a person may become unable to continue payments.

As is the case with pension schemes, there are different types of life insurance policies, all of which result in different consequences for creditors and dependants, as well as different tax implications. Among these, only 'own life for the benefit of another' policies operate as will-substitutes. Since the Contracts (Rights of Third Parties) Act was passed in 1999, a trust is no longer necessary for a beneficiary of such a life insurance policy to have a direct claim.[43] Nevertheless, it is still advisable to include policies in trusts, as this is a way of avoiding inheritance tax. Tax considerations aside, if there is a trust, the proceeds are paid directly to the beneficiary without entering the deceased's estate, and in principle, they are not available to the deceased's creditors,[44] nor do they fall into the 'net estate' for the purposes of the Inheritance (Provision for Family and Dependants) Act 1975 (I(PFD) Act), unless the court invokes the anti-avoidance provision in section 10(7).[45]

An express declaration of trust is not necessary where the policy falls under section 11 of the Married Women's Property Act 1882 (MWPA). This provision

[39] Miller, above n 4, 311.

[40] ABI, 'News Release 27 May 2014', www.abi.org.uk/News/News-releases/2014/05/270-families-helped-every-day-by-Life-Critical-Illness-Income-Protection-insurance-payouts-2013: '270 families helped every day by Life, Critical Illness and Income Protection insurance payouts in 2013'.

[41] See ABI, 'Funds held in Life and Pension products in 2012', above n 14, 6, figure 5.

[42] Research from Aegon in June 2013 shows that among the barriers are: the expenses; the complexity of the schemes; and the concern that money would not be paid out. Aegon Press Release 2013, www.aegon.com/en/Home/Investors/News/Press-Releases/: 'Aegon UK Research Identifies the Barrier to buying protection'. However, statistics provided by the ABI for 2013 indicate that 98.4% of term life insurance policies and 99.9% of whole life insurance claims were paid. ABI, '270 families helped every day by Life, Critical Illness and Income Protection insurance payouts in 2013', above n 40. These statistics represent 90% of the market.

[43] For an account of the law prior to the 1999 Act, see Miller, *The Machinery of Succession*, above n 4, 316.

[44] See below at section III.D.

[45] For more details, see below at section III.E, and ch 14 below, p 299.

states that where a policy of assurance is effected by a person on his own life and expressed to be for the benefit of his wife and children or any of them, or by a woman on her own life and expressed to be for the benefit of her husband or children or any of them, this creates a trust in favour of the beneficiaries named in the policy.[46] Where the MWPA does not apply, it is possible to declare a trust or to assign the policy to trustees to hold on trust for certain beneficiaries.

On the other hand, where there is no trust, the payment is payable to the personal representative, the money goes to the estate and is distributed according to the will or intestacy rules. It is, therefore, available to creditors and dependants and also subject to inheritance tax.

D. Holding Property in Joint Names

i. Introduction

As is the case in other common law jurisdictions, under English law, where title to property is held in joint names (as opposed to tenancy in common) survivorship operates on death of one of the joint tenants. It follows, that the deceased's title extinguishes and automatically vests in the surviving joint tenant who becomes absolutely entitled to the property. Survivorship operates such that absolute title is acquired outside probate procedures and thus directly. The right of survivorship can be removed through severance, though this cannot take place through a will.

Even though the legal title may be held in joint names and pass through survivorship on death of one of the tenants, it does not necessarily follow that the survivor is beneficially entitled to the property such that he may hold it on trust for the deceased's estate. This depends on how and why the joint tenancy was established but the reasons for holding property jointly vary, the benefit of survivorship being just one of them.[47] In principle, where a person gratuitously acquires or transfers property into the name of another person or into joint names, and there is lack of evidence of the intention of the purchaser/transferor, a presumption of a resulting trust operates, whereby the surviving tenant holds the legal title on trust for the estate of the first to die. This presumption can be rebutted, for instance, through proof of an intention to make a gift to the transferee. A gift is presumed, where the transfer is made by a husband to his wife or by a father to his children or someone standing in *loco parentis*.[48] However, pursuant to section 199 of the Equality Act 2010, this presumption of advancement will be

[46] This applies also to civil partners, s 70 of the Civil Partnership Act 2004.

[47] According to CK Wehringer, 'Joint Ownership—No Substitute for a Will' (1967) 39 *New York State Bar Journal* 301, joint ownership is not an adequate substitute to a properly drawn will.

[48] The presumption can be rebutted however: *Simpson v Simpson* (*The Times* 11 June 1988). For differences with Canada, see ch 12 below, p 34.

abolished, though at the moment it is not clear when this legislative change will come into effect.[49]

All types of property can be held jointly, including land, bank accounts, life insurance and annuities, bonds, and shares. This chapter will only focus on land and on bank accounts, as these are a very common will-substitute.

ii. Joint Tenancy of Land

In England, joint tenancy is an important way of holding, and thus of passing real property on death, partly due to the dramatic rise in levels of home ownership and of house prices over the course of the past decades. Data obtained directly from the Land Registry reveals that the amount of land registered to joint proprietors has increased over the past 10 years, as have the applications to transfer title on the death of a joint proprietor, except for a drop in 2013. Husbands and wives often hold property, and in particular their home, as joint tenants[50] and, judging from case law, it is not uncommon for parents to purchase or to transfer the property into joint names with one of their children.

As noted above, when a joint tenant dies, the surviving tenants become immediately entitled to the whole. For the purposes of the land register, the change in title is registered upon provision of a death certificate, a grant of probate, or a letter of administration.[51] No fee is payable and there is no need for a lawyer to be involved, which means that the surviving tenant acquires absolute title quite quickly and at almost no cost.

Given that the parameters of the operation of presumed resulting trusts in the case of gratuitous transfers of land are uncertain, it is more likely that a joint tenant will obtain a beneficial title in the real property.[52]

iii. Joint Bank Accounts

Unlike in the US, in England, banks do not provide 'account-specific wills' in the form of POD bank accounts.[53] Nonetheless, it is not uncommon for people to

[49] It has recently been doubted whether it ever existed. W Swadling, 'Legislation in Vain' in A Burrows, D Johnston and R Zimmermann (eds), *Judge and Jurist. Essays in Memory of Lord Rodger of Earlsferry* (Oxford, OUP, 2013) 655.

[50] According to Roger Kerridge, 80% of married couples hold their property as joint tenants: Kerridge, 'Intestate Succession in England and Wales', above n 6.

[51] www.landregistry.gov.uk/public/guides/public-guide-9.

[52] In this sense, see L Tucker, N Le Poidevin and J Brightwell, *Lewin on Trusts*, 19th edn (London, Sweet & Maxwell, 2014) 9–015 who refer to the uncertain effect of s 60(3) of the Law of Property Act 1925 (LPA) and of the HL decision in *Stack v Dowden* [2007] UKHL 17. This does not, however, hold true of cases of purchase in joint names.

[53] For a detailed discussion see WM McGovern, 'The Payable on Death Account and Other Will Substitutes' (1972) 67 *Northwestern University Law Review* 7, 9. In Canada too they are not common, see ch 12 below, p 257.

transfer bank accounts into joint names with the intention that the surviving holder should benefit on death of the other.

There are few statistics on the number of joint bank accounts in the UK. Recent estimates show that there are more than 76 million personal current accounts held with banks in the UK and that the number is rising.[54] Data from the Office of Fair Trading suggest that for 28 per cent of UK adults the main current account is a joint account.[55] The proportion has risen to 30 per cent for households with a combined income of between £20,000 and £40,000 and to 36 per cent for households with a combined income above £40,000.[56]

As noted above, although bank accounts may be held in joint names, this does not necessarily mean that on the death of one of the joint tenants, the survivor will enjoy the beneficial interest, especially if the intention of the transferor is unclear.[57] There are many reasons for establishing or transferring accounts into joint names and the desire to benefit the other tenant on death through survivorship may not necessarily be the only one. A common motive for transferring an account into joint names is, in fact, administrative convenience.[58]

Married couples normally hold bank accounts jointly to allow both parties to draw on the other's funds in the account, as well as to benefit one another on death.[59] There are, however, also cases in which an elderly person transfers an account into the name of a child, or a niece or nephew, with the intention that the transferee can undertake withdrawals or payments on their behalf, and assist with shopping, paying bills and other tasks.[60] Where that is the case it can be difficult to determine whether the survivor was meant to benefit from the account on death or rather to hold it on trust for the estate, an issue that may lead to litigation.[61]

In the absence of a clear intention, and unless the presumption of advancement applies, a resulting trust usually operates such that the transferee holds the account

[54] Office of Fair Trading, 'Review of the Personal Current Account Market (2013)', Report no OFT1005rev, webarchive.nationalarchives.gov.uk/20140402142426/http:/www.oft.gov.uk/shared_oft/reports/financial_products/OFT1005rev, 26, 27. This estimate was based on information provided to the OFT by banks.

[55] ibid, Annex C table 9/1.

[56] ibid, Annex C table 9/3.

[57] In the US too, joint bank accounts give rise to problems. See G Eddington, 'Survivorship Rights in Joint Bank Accounts: A Misbegotten Presumption of Intent' (2014) 15 *Marquette Elder's Advisor* 175.

[58] Reasons of administrative convenience were found in *Marshal v Crutwell* (1875) LR 20 EQ 328; *Lloyd v Pughe* (1872) 8 Ch App 88; and *Hoddinott v Hoddinott* (1949) 2 KB 406. For a discussion, see NA Clayton, 'Joint Accounts and Reasons of Convenience' (1989) 4 *Journal of International Banking Law & Regulation* 146.

[59] JE Todd and LM Jones, *Matrimonial Property* (London, HMSO, 1972) report that 21% of married couples interviewed had a joint account. See also K Rowlingson and S McKay, *Attitude to Inheritance in England* (Bristol, The Policy Press, 2005) 66, who reveal that 71% of those interviewed had ownership (including joint ownership) in the form of savings and investments in bank accounts or building societies.

[60] Langbein, 'The Nonprobate Revolution', above n 1, 1112.

[61] The complications that can arise if the intention is not clear are illustrated in the recent decision in *Drakeford v Cotton* [2012] EWHC 1414 (Ch).

on trust for the transferor and later for his or her estate.[62] This presumption can be rebutted,[63] where the transferor clearly intended to make an immediate gift to the transferee, so that both can make withdrawals during their lifetime and in their own interest, or to make a gift on death.[64] In such instances, the gift to the transferee has been described as 'an immediate gift of a fluctuating and defeasible asset consisting of the chose in action for the time being constituting the balance in the bank account'.[65]

Where an intention to benefit the transferee on death is found, it is questionable whether the transaction is of a testamentary nature, thus requiring the formalities of a will, an aspect that will be discussed later.[66] In fact, in practice, the transfer of a bank account into joint names usually requires only the filling in of a form, and some banks allow for applications to be made online or over the phone.

E. The *Donatio Mortis Causa*

One way of benefiting someone on death, other than by will, is by way of a *donatio mortis causa*. This is probably one of the oldest will-substitutes available in England. The doctrine was introduced into English law through the ecclesiastical courts and it became prominent after the Statute of Frauds of 1677 abolished nuncupative wills.[67] Although the modern relevance of the *donatio mortis causa* is debatable, recent case law shows that the device is still in use today.[68]

The *donatio mortis causa* consists of a revocable gift made during a person's lifetime, in contemplation of the donor's impending death, but which takes effect only on his death.[69] Given that the *donatio mortis causa* takes effect on death and remains revocable until then, it is in many ways similar to a will. It does not, however, require the formalities imposed on wills. Further, the subject matter of the gift must be delivered to the donee during the donor's lifetime,[70] and the donor must be considering the probability of death in the near future and not just sometime

[62] According to Tucker et al, above n 52, para 9-87, a motive of convenience will not in general be inferred where cheques are drawn regularly by the provider of the money to the exclusion of the other holder; also it is more difficult in cases of a deposit account than in the case of a current account.

[63] The presumption was rebutted in *Aroso v Coutts & Co* [2002] 1 All ER (Comm) 241; [2001] WTLR 797, though not in *Sillett v Meek* [2007] EWHC 1169 (Ch); [2009] WTLR 1065.

[64] Such an intention to benefit the nephew only on death of the aunt was found in *Young v Sealey* [1949] Ch 278.

[65] *Re Figgis* [1969] 1 Ch 123, 149; see references in *Sillars v Inland Revenue Commissioners* [2004] STC (SCD) 180; [2004] WTLR 591.

[66] See below at section IV.D.

[67] A Borkowski, *Textbook on Succession*, 2nd edn (Oxford, OUP, 2002) 320.

[68] *Vallee v Birchwood* [2014] Ch 271 (Ch) and *King v Chiltern Dog Rescue* [2016] Ch 221 (CA).

[69] Margrave-Jones, above n 8, 10, 520–21. For a complete account, see A Borkowski, *Deathbed Gifts: The Law of donatio mortis causa* (Oxford, Blackstone Press, 1999).

[70] Delivery of the actual subject matter of the gift is not essential where the donee is given the means of obtaining that subject matter, such as a key to a box or title deeds concerning land.

in the future, and for a specific reason.[71] Thus, its scope is restricted. Although until recently, only tangible property was capable of forming the subject matter of a *donatio mortis causa*,[72] since the decision of the Court of Appeal in *Sen v Headley*, in England, land can also become the subject matter of a valid *donatio mortis causa*.[73]

The *donatio mortis causa* is revocable until the donor's death, by express revocation or by resuming the property,[74] but cannot be revoked by a subsequent will.[75] Where the donor recovers from the illness or survives the event from which he had contemplated death, revocation is automatic.[76]

III. The Reach of Provisions Regulating Succession

A. Introduction

For the purposes of formalities, in the US, will-substitutes are treated as non-testamentary.[77] However, in many other respects they are considered as functionally equivalent to wills, and default provisions applicable to wills are therefore frequently extended. The same applies to many of the provisions aimed at protecting the interests of third parties, though the approach is not yet uniform.[78] Unlike in the US, in England, there has never been a comprehensive debate about how to treat instruments that allow for a transfer of wealth on death outside probate, and whether or not the law of wills should apply to them. As a consequence, the state of the law is often equivocal and the approach frequently piecemeal.

B. Formality Requirements for Wills

As noted above, the *donatio mortis causa* is generally seen as a form of testamentary disposition that does not have to comply with the formalities prescribed by section 9 of the Wills Act 1837.[79] For this reason, it is sometimes described as an

[71] *King v Chiltern Dog Rescue*, above n 68. The CA held that *Vallee v Birchwood*, above n 68, had been wrongly decided.

[72] This was said *obiter* by the House of Lords in *Duffield v Elwes* (1827) 1 Bli NS 497.

[73] *Sen v Headley* [1991] Ch 425. For a discussion of the different position in Australia and New Zealand see ch 5 below, p 108. On whether or not it is possible to use a DMC in relation to registered land, see N Roberts, 'Donationes mortis causa in a Dematerialised World' (2013) *Conveyancer & Property Lawyer* 113.

[74] Kerridge and Brierley, above n 4, 125.

[75] *Jones v Selby* (1710) Prec Ch 300, 303.

[76] *Staniland v Willott* (1850) 3 Mac & G 664.

[77] Ch 1 above, p 23.

[78] Ch 1 above, pp 20 ff.

[79] It requires, however, delivery of the gifted property.

anomaly or as having an 'amphibious' nature[80] and, more recently, suggestions have been made that it ought to be kept within its proper bounds, so as 'not to allow [the *donatio mortis causa*] to be used as a device in order to validate ineffective gifts'.[81] Statutory nominations also represent an exception, though introduced by statutory law. However, as noted above, both mechanisms operate in a limited context and have specific requirements.[82]

In England, courts have addressed the question of the applicability of section 9 of the Wills Act 1837, in relation to pension scheme nominations and joint bank accounts, and in both contexts have come to the conclusion that the Act was not applicable.

In the case of pension schemes, the only two decisions addressing the question have focused principally on the type of control that the deceased exercised over the money invested in the scheme during his or her lifetime, and thus on whether or not he could assign his rights under the scheme.[83] Although in both cases the pension nominations were seen to present certain testamentary characteristics, they were considered to fall outside the scope of the said provision.[84] The Privy Council suggested, however, that where the interest of the member of the scheme is absolute and indefeasible, the nomination would be captured by the Wills Act.[85] Nevertheless, given that nowadays nominations are often mere letters of wishes that do not bind trustees, the problem no longer carries the same relevance.

The issue of whether section 9 of the Wills Act applies has also arisen in relation to joint bank accounts. The only English case in which the question has been discussed is *Young v Sealey*,[86] where Romer J concluded that, even though the intention was for the transferee to benefit only on death of the transferor, the disposition was not invalid by reason of failure to comply with the requirements of the Wills Act.[87] Romer J was sympathetic towards the position of earlier Canadian and Irish cases, in which such bank accounts were regarded as testamentary.[88]

[80] *Sen v Headley*, above n 73, 647; *Re Beaumont* [1902] 1 Ch 889, 892.

[81] Jackson LJ in *King v Chiltern Dog Rescue*, above n 68, [52].

[82] See above section II.B.

[83] *Re Danish Bacon Co Ltd Staff Pension Fund Trusts* [1971] 1 WLR 248 and *Baird v Baird* [1990] 2 AC 578 (PC). JR Martyn, S Bridge and M Oldham, *Theobald on Wills*, 16th edn (London, Sweet & Maxwell, 2001) 25.

[84] For a critical discussion of the arguments employed by the courts see Braun, above n 22, pp 239–44, and WJ Chappenden, 'Non-Statutory Nominations' (1972) *Journal of Business Law* 20.

[85] This is why the PC in *Baird v Baird*, above n 83, distinguished the Canadian Supreme Court decision in *Re MacInnes* [1935] 1 DLR 401. *Theobald on Wills*, above n 83, 25. For details, see Braun, above n 22, 241.

[86] *Young v Sealey*, above n 64.

[87] MC Cullity, 'Joint Bank Accounts with Volunteers' (1969) 85 *Law Quarterly Review* 530, 542 seems to think that Romer J clearly preferred the view that the transaction was testamentary but did not feel confident enough to reach that conclusion.

[88] Case law across common law jurisdictions is conflicting. Although there was a trend in some common law jurisdictions to regard joint bank accounts as testamentary (see the Canadian cases *Hill v Hill* (1904) 8 OLR 710 and *Larondeau v Larondeau* [1954] 4 DLR 24, and the Irish case *Owens v Greene* [1932] IR 225 which was, however, overruled in *Lynch v Burke and Allied Irish Banks plc* [1995]

However, he was of the view that it was difficult to take the same approach at first instance, especially as it would have defeated the deceased's express intention, and as he was unsure as to whether there were any unreported cases on the issue.[89]

C. Other Provisions Applicable to Wills

Formality requirements aside, it is unclear whether and to what extent other rules applicable to wills, such as those concerning capacity, revocation of wills, lapse, forfeiture, undue influence or the interpretation and rectification of wills, are applicable to will-substitutes. The current state of the law would appear to be incoherent on this point.

We know that, as is the case with wills, some statutory nominations are revoked by a subsequent marriage of the nominator,[90] but it is not clear what happens where property is transferred by other means. A MWPA trust of a life insurance policy is not automatically invalidated by the divorce of a married couple and the same holds true of an express trust.[91] A divorce or remarriage does not per se affect a joint tenancy or a gift made *mortis causa*. As far as pension nominations are concerned, the fact that many of them are not binding means that even if the scheme rules are silent, trustees can simply pay out to another beneficiary, though they do not have to. In fact, it may well happen that the trustees decide, even against the express intention of the member of the scheme, that the former spouse will take a benefit under the pension.[92] But what happens when the nomination is binding? There is no clear answer.

It is also uncertain whether the rules on lapse extend to these mechanisms. Statutory nominations fail if the nominee predeceases the nominator,[93] and the same is true in the case of a *donatio mortis causa*,[94] but what about other types of will-substitute? While some pension schemes allow for more than one nominee to be nominated and generally advise members to establish an order of preference, where the nomination is binding and there is only one nominee who predeceases the member, the question poses itself. That said, where the nomination is remitted to the discretion of the trustees, they can take into account changing circumstances.

2 IR 159), more recent decisions were in favour of treating them as non-testamentary, finding a voluntary settlement with a reserved life interest and power of revocation (*Re Reid* (1921) 64 DLR 243 and *Russell v Scott* (1936) 55 CLR 440). For a useful analysis of the case law, see JG Miller, 'Joint Bank Accounts as Testamentary Dispositions' (1992) 6 *Trust Law International* 57.

[89] *Young v Sealey*, above n 64, 295. Romer J did not, however, find there to be a trust.

[90] Miller, above n 4, 117, fn 99, and Margrave-Jones, above n 8, 362. See s 66(7) of the Friendly Societies Act 1974.

[91] R Surridge, B Murphy and J Noleen, *Houseman's Law of Life Assurance*, 14th edn (London, Bloomsbury Professional, 2011) para 12.53.

[92] Braun, above n 22, 248.

[93] *In re Barnes*, above n 27, 274.

[94] Kerridge and Brierley, above n 4, 126.

Insurance policies too may require the holder to select a contingent, and where the policy is held on trust, the problem does not arise.

Finally, it is uncertain to what extent forfeiture rules operating in case of unlawful killing apply to will-substitutes, as there is little authority on the point.[95] In the case of a joint tenancy, forfeiture would seem to lead to a severance of the joint tenancy, and thus a tenancy in common.[96] Forfeiture rules also seem to apply to life insurance,[97] and pensions,[98] so that the person committing a crime against the deceased cannot benefit,[99] but case law is scarce and not always authoritative.

D. Protecting the Interests of Creditors

Most of the mechanisms discussed in this chapter operate such that a direct transfer to the beneficiary occurs and the property does not, therefore, fall within the estate.[100] It follows that, in principle, creditors cannot satisfy their credit against this property. This is certainly the case for pension death benefits, which are generally unavailable, irrespective of whether or not the estate is insolvent, unless payment is made to the estate. Similarly, wealth transferred through statutory nominations is also unavailable to creditors.[101]

Life insurance policies of a person's own life for the benefit of another are available to creditors, so long as they are not held on trust which, as noted above, is advisable for a number of reasons. That said, where there is a trust, should the policyholder become bankrupt, the protection depends on the nature of the trust. If a non-statutory trust is created at an undervalue, and the policyholder becomes bankrupt within two years, the courts can ignore the existence of the trust and use the assets to pay the bankrupt's creditors. Full protection from bankruptcy only exists when a non-statutory trust has been in force for at least five years.[102]

[95] I Williams, 'How Does the Common Law Forfeiture Rule Work?' in B Häcker and C Mitchell (eds), *Current Issues in Succession Law* (Oxford, Hart Publishing, 2016) 51, who favours a forfeiture rule that works in an intellectually coherent manner.

[96] *Re K* [1985] Ch 85 (Ch) 100, 100. For the position under Australian and New Zealand law see ch 5 above, p 129.

[97] *Cleaver v Mutual Reserve Fund Life Association* [1892] 1 QB 147 (CA). The trust had become incapable of being performed and the insurance money formed part of the estate of the insured.

[98] *Glover v Staffordshire Police Authority* [2006] EWCA 2141 (Admin). See I Greenstreet, 'Murder Most Horrid and Other Crimes and Misdemeanours—What Crimes do you have to Commit to Lose your Pension?' (2002) 93 *British Pension Lawyer* 15, 16 ff.

[99] The Forfeiture Act 1982 also applies to the *donatio mortis causa*: s 2(1)(a)(iii).

[100] For details about the protection of creditors in English law, see ch 13 below, pp 271 ff.

[101] In *Bennet v Slater* [1899] 1 QB 45 it was suggested that if the member happened to die insolvent, his executor or administrator might recover the money so paid from the nominee, but this was rejected by the court. The creditor might, however, act against the nominee. See Miller, *The Machinery of Succession*, above n 4, 113.

[102] ss 339, 423 and 341 of the Insolvency Act 1986. See also Surridge et al, above n 91, para 12.15, and P Hamilton, *Life Assurance Law and Practice* (London, FT Law & Tax, 1995) para A5.7.

If bankruptcy occurs between two and five years, protection will be available, provided that the policyholder was solvent at the time he created the trust. Where the trust is effected under the MWPA, protection of the policy proceeds on bankruptcy is available from the start, unless the creditors can show that the policy was taken out with the intention to defraud them, in which case they would be able to obtain the premiums paid.[103] After the creditor's claims have been satisfied, any amount left over is held for the beneficiaries.

Conversely, property transferred through a *donatio mortis causa* is liable for the payment of debts if all other assets are exhausted.[104] For jointly held property, survivorship is automatic so that, in principle, the deceased's interest in the joint tenancy does not form part of their estate and is not therefore available to creditors.[105] In relation to estates that are insolvent, however, the law has recently changed.[106] For insolvency administration orders presented after the commencement of the Insolvency Act 2000, a trustee in bankruptcy may make an application to court and apply for an order requiring the surviving joint tenant to pay to the trustee an amount not exceeding that which would restore the trustee's position to what it would have been had the deceased been determined bankrupt immediately before his death. Unless the circumstances are exceptional, the court must assume that the interests of the deceased's creditors outweigh all other considerations.[107]

Thus, the rights of creditors are not always equally protected under each mechanism, an issue that also arises in the US.[108] A further problem is that, due to the fact that property is passed on death through different mechanisms and the transfer is fragmented, a creditor may have to deal with several beneficiaries and not just the personal representative.

E. Protecting the Interests of Family Members and Dependants

As is explained elsewhere in this volume,[109] in England, a dependant may present an application to court for a discretionary order for maintenance out of the estate of the deceased,[110] to be brought within six months of the date when the grant of

[103] s 11 of the MWPA and s 423 of the Insolvency Act 1986. *Holt v Everall* (1876) 2 Ch D 666. See also ch 13 below, p 273.

[104] Kerridge and Brierley, above n 4, 509; Miller, above n 4, 291. Critical of this view is S Warnock-Smith '"Donationes Mortis Causa" and the Payment of Debts' (1978) *Conveyancer & Property Lawyer* 130. In the case of secret trusts, creditors would still seem to be able to get their hands on the estate, as the deficiency must be borne rateably by the part bound by the trust. *Re Maddock* [1902] 2 Ch 220.

[105] s 3(4) of the Administration of Estates Act 1925. Kerridge and Brierley, above n 4, 475. However, the interest of the deceased as an equitable tenant in common does devolve to the personal representative.

[106] s 12(1) of the Insolvency Act 2000, which has inserted a new s 421A into the Insolvency Act 1986.

[107] s 421A (3) of the Insolvency Act 2000. For details see, esp Kerridge and Brierley, above n 4, 539–40.

[108] Ch 1 above, p 21.

[109] See ch 14 below, p 285.

[110] Inheritance (Provision for Family and Dependants) Act 1975.

representation was taken out.[111] This may not be effective, however, where little or nothing is left in the estate.

Since 1975, the scope of such discretionary orders has been extended so as to include wealth transmitted through a *donatio mortis causa*,[112] statutory nominations[113] and property the deceased owned jointly, be that real or personal property.[114] Conversely, death benefits under pension schemes are not, in principle, subject to such court orders,[115] unless the member's estate is entitled to payment of any death benefits. This is somewhat surprising considering the fact that pension death benefits can sometimes be of considerable value and that, in the case of divorce or dissolution of a civil partnership, pension sharing is now possible.[116]

In its recent intestacy report, the English Law Commission considered making pension benefits (including both lump-sum payments and dependant's pensions) available to family members, but then decided not to recommend changes, even though the present law can cause hardship in individual cases, and despite the fact that just over half of the consultees favoured reform (and only one-quarter opposed reform). The decision was based on the argument that 'only 50 per cent of the over 65 population have a pension and most of these pensions are worth less than £20,000'.[117] Whether these figures are accurate is questionable, particularly in light of the discussion above.[118] Be that as it may, it would seem that the Law Commission's real concern was to avoid courts overriding the discretion vested in pension trustees.[119] However, not all pension schemes confer a discretionary power on the trustees and the nomination may be binding on them.

Life insurance benefits too seem to be outside the reach of courts. Although in the past, the Law Commission had considered recommending the extension

[111] s 4 of the I(PFD) Act. In its recent report on Intestacy, the Law Commission suggested courts should be granted the power to extend this time limit. Law Com No 331, above n 15, paras 7.83 and 7.96.

[112] s 8(2) of the I(PFD) Act. The change was recommended by the Law Commission in the *Second Report on Family Property: Family Provision on Death* (Law Com No 61, 1974) para 136.

[113] See s 8(1) of the I(PFD) Act.

[114] s 9(4) of the I(PFD) Act. See *Re Crawford* [1983] 4 FLR 273 (lump sum paid into a joint account). For some examples involving real property jointly held see: *Kourkey v Lusher* (1982) 12 Fam Law 86 in which the claim was rejected. It was granted in *Powell v Osbourne* [1993] 1 FLR 1001 (CA); *Jessop v Jessop* [1992] 1 FLR 591 and *Dingmar v Dingmar* [2007] Ch 109. Interesting also *Lim (An infant) v Walia* [2014] EWCA Civ 1076; [2014] WLR (D) 339.

[115] Unless a nomination is made pursuant to an 'enactment'. See *Goenka v Goenka* [2014] EWHC 2966 (Ch).

[116] R Ellison and M Rae, *Family Breakdown and Pensions*, 2nd edn (London, Butterworths, 2001) 50; D Salter and R Bamber (ed), *Pensions and Insurance on Family Breakdown*, 2nd edn (Bristol, Family Law, 1999) 133 ff.

[117] Law Com No 331, above n 15, para 7.108. Critical of the position of the Law Commission already prior to the latest report, RD Oughton, *Tyler's Family Provision*, 2nd edn (Abingdon, Professional Books, 1984) 232.

[118] See above at section II.A.

[119] Law Com No 331, above n 15, para 7.119. It is interesting to note that already in the Working Paper No 42 on *Family Law: Family Property Law* (1971), the Law Commission had asked for views as to whether courts should be given the power to substitute their own discretion for that of the trustees of a pension fund (see para 3.71) but it accepted that the case for interference had not been made out. See Law Com No 61, above n 112, para 213.

of powers of avoidance to benefits payable under insurance policies,[120] the 1975 I(PFD) Act limited it to the amount of the premium.[121] If premiums are made less than six years before the death of the deceased, an order may be granted requiring the beneficiary of the proceeds of the policy to pay a sum of money as an order under section 2 of the I(PFD) Act.

Thus, in England, dependants will not be able to access pension death benefits or insurance proceeds through the family provision legislation. Given the amount of wealth invested in such financial instruments, this seems problematic.[122] However, litigation under the I(PFD) Act is expensive so that it may not always be desirable to bring a claim. Nevertheless, '[t]he court can take account of benefits derived from a pension fund in assessing the resources available to claimants and to other beneficiaries of the estate'.[123]

IV. Rationale Behind the Use of Will-Substitutes

A. Changes in the Investment of Wealth

It is difficult to provide an accurate account of the reasons underlying the choice of how wealth is passed on death, as there is little empirical data available. The motives can vary depending on the type of will-substitute used and sometimes there may be more than one reason underpinning a particular choice. Much, therefore, is speculative. Nevertheless, some information can be gleaned from an examination of the advantages and disadvantages of the most popular devices, both from the perspective of the deceased and the potential beneficiary.

When exploring the rationale behind the proliferation of will-substitutes, one needs to bear in mind that, the *donatio mortis causa* aside, the distribution of wealth on death is not necessarily the primary objective of the mechanisms discussed in this chapter. For instance, the objective of pension schemes is mainly to provide for the retirement of the member. Life insurance, too, is often perceived as a valuable saving device, and only secondarily as a way to benefit someone on death. As noted above, the decision to transfer property into joint names may also be motivated by reasons of administrative convenience.[124] To some extent, therefore,

[120] Law Com No 42, 1971, above n 119, para 3.71. See also Law Com No 61, above n 112, paras 203–05.

[121] This is possible on the basis of s 10(7) of the I(PFD) Act. See ch 14 below, p 299.

[122] See also ch 14 below, p 302.

[123] Law Com No 331, above n 15, para 7.74. See also *Tolley's Pension Law*, Issue 85, D3-84. s 3(1) of the I(PFD) Act requires the court to consider the 'financial resources and financial needs' of any applicant or beneficiary, which will include the destination of any pension benefit. See, for instance, *P v G (Family Provision: Relevance of Divorce Provision)* [2004] EWHC 2944 (Fam), [2006] 1 FLR 431. Also, a court order may well influence the decision of the trustees of the pension scheme.

[124] See above at section II.D.iii.

the transmission of benefits on death may be an auxiliary or additional motive or even just a useful by-product of the arrangement. In fact, many of these mechanisms can do more than a will.[125] Also, generally speaking, pension death benefits and life insurance proceeds can only be allocated in accordance with the provisions of the respective schemes, ie, through nominations. This means that, at least in England, it may not even be open to a testator to use a will in order to dispose of such benefits and proceeds.

It follows, that the phenomenon discussed in this chapter is partly the result of changes in the way we hold and invest wealth. Given that it is now common to invest in financial assets, it is inevitable that we dispose of the wealth so invested in ways foreseen by the individual financial providers, rather than by a will. In fact, many of these mechanisms represent a method of passing wealth that is restricted to the type of asset that the particular financial intermediary happens to offer. This means that, at least in England, will-substitutes cannot be understood merely as a means of avoiding the traditional modes of transfer and the rules, whether procedural or substantive, applicable to wills, especially where using the will is not even an option.[126]

B. Avoiding Some of the Effects of Probate

It is well known that in the US, the most commonly cited reason for the proliferation of will-substitutes is the desire to avoid probate and supervised administration, so as to reduce fees and delays in the administration of the estate and to preserve privacy.[127] In England, the desire to circumvent probate procedure does not seem to feature so prominently among persons' motivations.[128] This is most likely due to differences in the probate procedure on both sides of the Atlantic. In fact, the English system of administration of estates involves minimum court interference with the personal representative and does not require participation of a legal practitioner, which makes it generally less expensive.[129]

That said, even in England, time may be a factor in preferring a non-probate transfer. Although for the majority of people (62 per cent) the probate process

[125] See ch 11 below, p 232.

[126] See also ch 4 below, pp 81 ff.

[127] Langbein, 'The Nonprobate Revolution', above n 1, 1116; Leslie and Sterk, above n 2, 287, who speak of an obsession with avoiding probate. Langbein also reports of occasional corruption in probate courts: JH Langbein, 'Substantial Compliance with the Wills Act' (1975) 88 *Harvard Law Review* 489, 504.

[128] Miller, *The Machinery of Succession*, above n 4, 111, 291. The same seems to be true of Canada: see ch 2 above, pp 44 ff and ch 12 below, p 525.

[129] Research carried out by YouGov indicates that the average cost of gaining professional help with probate is £2,500: see 'The use of probate and estate administration services', January 2012, www.legalservicesboard.org.uk/Projects/reviewing_the_scope_of_regulation/yougov_research.pdf, 5. Furthermore, the fee payable to the Probate Service is £45, and where the value of the estate is £5,000 or less, no charge is made.

would seem to be complete within six months,[130] personal representatives cannot be compelled to distribute the estate before the expiration of one year from the death.[131] Also, since an application under the I(PFD) Act can be made up to six months after the grant, where a claim is likely, distribution will not normally be made within this period. Conversely, non-probate transfers often lead to a direct and, therefore, speedier transfer, providing the survivor with immediate resources. This is certainly true of life insurance, of property held jointly, as well as of *donationes mortis causa*, but not necessarily true of pensions.

Another effect of probate is that the will becomes public. Hence, if a person prefers to keep the identity of the beneficiary confidential, it might be best to resort, for instance, to a life insurance policy or a joint bank account.[132]

Finally, as is well known, a function of probate is to protect creditors. As noted above, pension schemes and, to some extent, life insurance policies shelter assets from creditors on death. Even so, whether this is an incentive for using them is doubtful, though from the perspective of the member and the nominee, it is certainly a helpful side effect. In any case, the existence of a lifetime cap allowance for pension schemes reduces the likelihood that a member will invest all of his wealth in a private pension scheme.[133] As for life insurance policies, payments are only protected if the policy is held on trust and it is unclear how often that is the case. And payments under statutory nominations are only of limited value.

C. Tax Advantages

Unlike in the US, where tax avoidance is not the main rationale for the popularity of non-probate mechanisms,[134] in England, tax mitigation is a primary concern for estate planners and testators. In the UK, if the estate (including any assets held in trust and gifts made within seven years of death) is valued over the current inheritance tax threshold of £325,000,[135] inheritance tax is generally payable at 40 per cent,[136] though dispositions in favour of a spouse or civil partner with a permanent home in the UK are not taxed. A person whose estate exceeds the

[130] ibid, 52.

[131] s 44 of the Administration of Estates Act 1925.

[132] Or a secret trust. J Jaconelli, 'Wills as Public Documents—Privacy and Property Rights' (2012) *Cambridge Law Journal* 147; R Meager, 'Secret Trusts—Do They Have a Future?' (2003) *Conveyancer & Property Lawyer* 203. Of the view that secrecy may be a reason for setting up a joint account is R Keane, *Equity and the Law of Trusts in the Republic of Ireland*, 2nd edn (Haywards Heath, Bloomsbury Professional Ltd, 2011) para 12.09.

[133] For details see Braun, above n 22, 236.

[134] See ch 1 above, p 20. In the US, will-substitutes are subject to estate tax. However, in 2015, the US federal estate tax exemption amount is $5.43 million.

[135] Married couples and civil partners are entitled to double the allowance, passing on assets to their children or other relations worth up to £650,000 before a tax charge is triggered. It should be noted that the current government has announced an increase in the threshold to £500,000 per person. The move, which was outlined in the Conservative Manifesto, will be effective as of 6 April 2017.

[136] Or at 36% if the estate qualifies for a reduced rate as a result of a charitable donation.

threshold may, therefore, have an incentive to search for alternative means of transferring their wealth.

In England, private pension schemes are generally considered a tax-sheltered savings vehicle.[137] Contributions into the fund receive tax relief, and there is no capital gains or income tax on the funds in the scheme. Prior to the 2015 pension changes, a deceased member's defined contribution pension could be paid out as a lump sum tax free if the member died before the age of 75 and before he had touched his pension pot. Otherwise, if the member was over the age of 75 when he died, or had already started to take benefits from his pension pot, it was taxed at 55 per cent. This 55 per cent tax charge was abolished with effect from 6 April 2015. Under the new legislation,[138] the question as to whether or not tax is payable on a lump sum depends only on the age of the member when he or she dies. If the member dies before the age of 75, his or her beneficiary can take the whole pot as a tax-free lump sum, or use it to provide a regular pension through a flexi-access drawdown arrangement or annuity, which is tax free. If the member dies after the age of 75, the beneficiary can take the whole pot as a lump sum, but will be taxed at 45 per cent (although the government is expected to review this).[139] With effect from 6 April 2016, if the defined contribution pot is used to provide a pension (through a drawdown arrangement or by purchasing an annuity), it will be taxed at the beneficiary's income tax rate. If they choose to take regular smaller lump sums, they too will be taxed as income. There are, therefore, considerable tax advantages to taking out a pension, though this does not apply to the new NEST scheme.[140]

Life insurance held on trust is also seen as a tax saving device.[141] They can help to avoid inheritance tax, as they prevent the life insurance proceeds from potentially pushing the value of the estate over the tax threshold.[142] By contrast, benefits transferred through statutory nominations form part of the nominator's estate for the purposes of inheritance tax. As for property transferred through a *donatio mortis causa*, it would seem that the personal representative can reclaim the tax from the donee if the estate has insufficient assets to pay the tax.[143]

[137] Research carried out for the savings and investment company 'Standard Life' reveals that almost 2 out of 5 of UK adults (39%) are aware of the tax efficiency of pensions, with an increase of 10% compared with 2012. Standard Life, 'Consumers becoming more switched on to tax benefits of pensions', Article of 6 May 2013, ukgroup.standardlife.com/content/news/new_articles/2013/060513 TaxBenefitsOfPensions.xml.

[138] These changes do not apply to defined benefits schemes.

[139] The Government has launched a consultation as to whether there is a case for reforming pensions tax relief. CM 9102 entitled 'Strengthening the incentive to save: a consultation on pensions tax relief', 8 July 2015.

[140] NEST Adviser News, April 2013, www.nestpensions.org.uk/schemeweb/NestWeb/includes/public/docs/NEST-adviser-news-april-2013,PDF.pdf, 3.

[141] For details about the tax regime, see J Lowe, *Giving and Inheriting* (London, Which? Books, 2011) 134.

[142] *Houseman's Law of Life Assurance*, above n 91, para 15.25.

[143] Margrave-Jones, above n 8, 535. However, *Simon's Taxes*, binder 8, part 10.112 seems to indicate the contrary. See also C Whitehouse and L King, *A Modern Approach to Wills, Administration and Estate Planning (with Precedents)*, 3rd edn (Bristol, Jordan Publishing Limited, 2015) 90, para 3.28.

Transferring real property into joint names does not in and of itself avoid the imposition of inheritance tax. If the deceased person owned property jointly with a person who is not their spouse or civil partner, inheritance tax may be payable on their share of the joint property. This will be the case if the total value of their estate or property is higher than the threshold mentioned earlier, or where the transfer was not intended to be a gift but motivated by reasons of convenience.[144] As for joint bank accounts, the tax treatment varies: it depends on the beneficial interests in the account, which in turn depend on the intention of the account holders,[145] which is, as noted above, often difficult to ascertain.[146] Thus, although tax considerations may have fuelled the interest in some mechanisms, such considerations are not applicable to all mechanisms.

D. Other Potential Reasons

Tax considerations aside, there are other potential reasons why people may choose modes of transfer on death other than wills. For instance, although it is arguable that the formalities required for wills (ie, signed, in writing and witnessed by two adults) are not too burdensome,[147] it may be desirable to use a less formal mode, such as a *donatio mortis causa* or a statutory nomination, especially since English courts have been stringent in their interpretation of formality requirements, with only slight deviances resulting in wills declared void.[148] It is, therefore, possible to assume that some testators may intend to minimise the risk of litigation and to prevent their testamentary dispositions from being contested on grounds of lack of formality (lack of undue execution), as well as lack of capacity or want of knowledge and approval, or on the basis of forgery or undue influence.[149] It is indeed often more difficult to contest some of the dispositions carried out through the mechanisms discussed in this chapter.[150] That said, generally speaking, the avoidance of formality requirements does not seem to play a major role.

Another reason, or at least a helpful consequence of using a pension scheme or a life insurance policy to transfer wealth on death, could be to shelter assets from

[144] For details about bank accounts, see L King, 'Joint Bank Accounts and Inheritance Tax' (2013) 3 *Private Client Business* 97. Where a single account was transferred into joint names, the personal representatives often argue that there was a tenancy in common so as not to pay tax over the whole account.

[145] ibid.

[146] See above section II.D.iii.

[147] s 9 of the Wills Act 1837.

[148] Kerridge, 'Testamentary Formalities in England and Wales', above n 26, 326.

[149] That there is no shortage of probate disputes, see P Reed, 'Capacity and Want of Knowledge and Approval' in B Häcker and C Mitchell (eds), *Current Issues in Succession Law* (Oxford, Hart Publishing, 2016) 169.

[150] However, a *donatio mortis causa* may be set aside for fraud or undue influence. See Miller, *The Machinery of Succession*, above n 4, 291.

claims under the I(PFD) Act. Whether this represents an incentive is doubtful, at least in the case of pensions, which are generally motivated by different considerations.

V. Problems and Perils of the Current State of the Law

The developments examined in this chapter show that in England, testators enjoy considerable freedom in exercising their private autonomy on death, and, in particular, in the choice of instruments they want to use. Though, in principle, this is to be welcomed, it sometimes comes at a price for the deceased, third parties and the legal system more generally: for instance, where the freedom undermines the functions of probate or the operation of substantive rules. We have already noted that some mechanisms, such as life insurance and pension plans, allow the deceased to shield property from claims of creditors and dependants.[151] Although there may be public policy considerations for treating wealth in a pension scheme or life insurance differently from wealth transferred by other means,[152] these considerations are rarely spelt out clearly and the lack of a principled approach can lead to potential injustices. A transfer of wealth on death outside the realm of succession law can also have consequences for the deceased's wishes and the functioning of the administration of the estate more generally.

A. Defeating the Intention of the Deceased

Some of these mechanisms discussed entail the risk that the wealth a person has accumulated is not distributed according to their wishes. For example, in respect of pension death benefits, sometimes the distribution can even go against the wishes expressed by the member.[153] And, as we noted earlier, in the case of joint bank accounts, the intention of the deceased is often difficult to ascertain—a risk that does not seem to exist with POD bank accounts common in the US—and the surviving tenant may end up holding the property on trust for the estate. These outcomes come into tension with one of the cardinal principles of the law of succession, namely that succession law is to fulfil the intention of the deceased.[154]

[151] See above at section III.D. Langbein, 'The Nonprobate Revolution', above n 1, 1125: '[T]he nonprobate system disperses assets widely and facilitates transfer without creditors' knowledge'.

[152] For the position in Canada see ch 12 below, p 264. Interestingly, in *Cairnes (Deceased), Re* [1983] 4 FLR 225; (1982) 12 Fam Law 177, 230 counsel for the plaintiff argued that public policy demands that as many of these [pension] funds nominated should fall into the net provided by the 1975 Act.

[153] For details see Braun, above n 22, 247 ff.

[154] Langbein, 'The Nonprobate Revolution', above n 1, 1136–37. See also ch 1 above, p 29.

Another aspect, caused by the absence of a formal probate procedure for these mechanisms, is that there is no court assessment of whether the disposition reflects the genuine intention of the deceased. This means that, in principle, it will be more difficult to contest the beneficiary designation, especially where the decision is made by a trustee. Although this may be in the interest of the deceased, who may well have chosen the device for that particular reason, there is a risk that he or she was unduly influenced. In other words, some of these mechanisms lack intent-effectuating doctrines, such that testamentary freedom may be undermined to some extent.[155]

There is also room for mistakes due to a lack of transparency of the rules, and a lack of uniform and standardised procedural requirements for certain instruments.[156] Indeed, the products offered by pensions and life insurance providers are often very different, as are the rules concerning the nomination or revocation of beneficiaries. What is more, the interaction between these rules and the rules for wills is often uncertain, and as a result, there is potential for litigation.[157]

B. Increasing the Complexity of Estate Planning and the Administration of the Estate

There is little doubt that the proliferation of different mechanisms for the transfer of wealth renders estate planning more difficult and complex.[158] Since each mechanism is governed by different rules and the tax implications vary considerably, it is hard to manage the planning without external help.[159] This may ultimately increase costs for the testator.

The administration of the estate by the personal representative too may become more complicated. Even though some of the assets transferred do not qualify as probate assets, they count as part of the participant's taxable estate. In fact, the personal representative must complete forms that pose questions about the deceased's assets, including pensions, joint accounts and insurance policies, so as to allow HMRC to determine what will be included in the estate for tax purposes.[160]

155 ML Leslie, 'Frustration of Intent in the Wealth Transmission Process' (2014) 4(2) *Onati Socio-Legal Series* 283, 302. Also, some pension schemes limit the choice of members. For details see Braun, above n 22, 237.

156 Braun, above n 22, 237.

157 For details concerning the interaction of pension nominations and wills see Braun, above n 22, 255. As for Canada, see ch 12 below, p 263.

158 KD Schenkel, 'Testamentary Fragmentation and the Diminishing Role of the Will: An Argument for Revival' (2008) 41 *Creighton Law Review* 155.

159 See, however, Langbein, 'Major Reforms of the Property Restatement and the Uniform Probate Code', above n 2, 16, according to whom '[f]or better or worse, and in my view it is worse, non-probate all too often means non-lawyer'.

160 Personal representatives have to fill in either a full Inheritance Tax Account IHT 400, or an IHT205 and/or an IHT 207 form, if the estate is an excepted estate.

Also, some of the wealth transferred outside probate is available to pay debts.[161] The extent to which personal representatives will be aware of these dispositions is unclear, and some benefits may remain unclaimed.[162] Finally, the work of the courts too might be rendered more arduous, for instance, in the context of applications under the family provision legislation.

VI. Conclusion

According to John Langbein, in the US, the states have been playing an important hand in encouraging the growth of the non-probate system.[163] From a review of the few decisions regarding the applicability of section 9 of the Wills Act to pension scheme nominations and joint bank accounts, it would seem that, in England, courts have taken a favourable view towards alternative modes of transfer of wealth on death.[164] This is mirrored by recent changes to the tax regime of defined contribution pension schemes, indicating that the British Government supports the transfer of wealth on death through pension schemes.

Nevertheless, unlike in the US, in England, law reformers have shown little interest in the developments in this area and the mechanisms discussed in this chapter are not usually examined from the perspective of succession law, or as part of a more general phenomenon of transfers outside probate. Legislative interventions in this context have so far been piecemeal and there has been no attempt to integrate non-probate mechanisms into succession law in a more systematic manner, as is the case in the US.[165] This does not necessarily mean that England ought to follow the American example and create two separate but parallel systems: a non-probate system existing alongside the probate one.[166] However, at the moment, the problem in England is that it is still unclear where will-substitutes fit on the map of legal transfers, ie, whether they belong to lifetime or *mortis causa* transactions.

This inertia might be explained by the fact that so far, relatively few cases have reached the courts, and the phenomenon has not attained the economic

[161] See above at section III.D.

[162] £400 million is the amount of unpaid money in life assurance and pension schemes. See Unclaimed Assets Register, www.uar.co.uk/.

[163] Langbein, 'Major Reforms of the Property Restatement and the Uniform Probate Code', above n 2, 15.

[164] See above at section III.B.

[165] While English law has statutory provisions in place for statutory nominations of modest value, it does not regulate nominations in pension schemes, which can be of considerable value. See Braun, above n 22, 233–4.

[166] See the criticism by Schenkel, 'Testamentary Fragmentation and the Diminishing Role of the Will', above n 158, 179.

significance it has in the US, where the financial industries seem to have been far more creative in developing new instruments.[167] Also, as some of these devices straddle the boundaries between lifetime and *mortis causa* dispositions, and given the fact that most of them are so different in nature, any decision as to whether or not to treat them like wills and to apply relative provisions by analogy must be taken with great care. Nonetheless, these arguments cannot justify the lack of attention this area has hitherto received in this country, both from legal scholars and law reformers. It is, therefore, to be hoped that when considering reform of the law of wills, the English Law Commission will take the opportunity to also consider will-substitutes.[168]

[167] Though see the array of mechanisms discussed by Paul Matthews in ch 11 below.

[168] The Law Commission's announcement that it will work on wills from 2016 does not explicitly mention whether it will also investigate the extent to which the law of wills is to be applied to functionally similar dispositions taking effect on death.

4

Will-Substitutes in Scotland

DANIEL CARR*

I. Introduction

The modern law of succession in Scotland is under-researched. There are books,[1] but there is no detailed modern monograph. Such a full treatment is awaited. Even less consideration has been given to the concept of will-substitutes as a class of devices and instruments, though some books do address the subject.[2] Scots law recognises a number of will-substitute devices, and has done so in various guises for some time, and, in particular, the main devices have been developed since at least the mid-nineteenth century. However, because the topic has never been treated together in anything like the detail that has occurred in the US,[3] for example, there are a number of problems with the various devices and how they fit into the policy decisions and doctrinal structures underpinning them. In some cases the individual instruments are themselves unclear, while in other cases the individual devices are quite well understood on their own, but the implications of those devices for the broader law of succession and how they fit together is considerably more problematic. The very fact that will-substitutes have not been considered in great detail might suggest that they are underused, and in individual

* My thanks to Alexandra Braun and Anne Röthel for the invitation to participate in this fascinating project and for their generous hosting. I would also like to thank George Gretton for helpful comments on my draft paper, my research assistant Jenny Hamilton and Johanna Croon for her editorial assistance. Any and all errors are mine alone.

[1] The main up-to-date practitioner's text is EM Scobbie, *Currie on Confirmation of Executors*, 9th edn (Edinburgh, W Green, 2011); more accessible accounts are H Hiram, *The Scots Law of Succession*, 2nd edn (Haywards Heath, Tottel, 2007); DR Macdonald, *Succession*, 3rd edn (Edinburgh, W Green, 2001); GL Gretton and AJM Steven, *Property, Trusts and Succession*, 2nd edn (Haywards Heath, Bloomsbury Professional, 2013).

[2] Hiram, above n 1, Macdonald, above n 1 and Scobbie, above n 1. Only Macdonald describes the devices together as will-substitutes: Macdonald, above n 1, ch 5. See also GL Gretton, 'Quaedam Meditationes Caledoniae: The Property/Succession Borderland' (2014) 3 *European Property Law Journal* 109.

[3] See ch 1 above.

instances, as will become apparent, this seems to be true. A number of the devices that will be considered seem to have been common in the nineteenth century, but have since become rare (or non-existent) in the reported cases. However, that is not to say that they do not remain competent. The reasons that some of these devices have fallen into disuse are likely to be many and complex, reacting to and mirroring societal change and changes in the law. Furthermore, it is hard to make assertions about the usage of the various will-substitute devices because there is virtually no empirical data concerning their use. A further consideration is the extent to which such devices are *necessary*. There has never been the surge of hostility[4]—one might even say hysteria—in respect of the confirmation of estates (the Scottish equivalent of probate) that seems to have captured the popular imagination in the US since the 1960s.[5] It is perhaps speculative to suggest that this has been so because the Scottish confirmation system works efficiently, but that certainly seems to be a possibility.[6] Another possibility is a deeper societal difference based upon individual liberty and a more individualised juridification of society in general, yet that is also a speculative suggestion. There seem to be as many 'homemade will' templates online for Scottish testators as anywhere else. On the other hand, there is certainly an ideological flavour to characterising the will-substitute revolution in America as a competition between an essentially privatised system of inheritance via will-substitutes against the state's public probate system.[7] Indeed, the rise of will-substitutes and their perceived advantages in the US has been about more than simple dissatisfaction (justified or otherwise) with the efficiency of the probate procedures in America.

In the present chapter I consider a selection of will-substitutes which have the potential to be used in Scotland. The coverage is not exhaustive, and in particular does not consider will-substitutes which are common elsewhere, such as the revocable (or irrevocable) trust.[8] Likewise, the chapter does not consider instruments which might be used as will-substitutes which are available in Scotland, but which are almost never used (or are endangered, such as the *donatio mortis causa*) or are not easily characterised as will-substitutes.

[4] See ME Meyer, 'The Revocable Trust as a Will Substitute—A Coming of Age' (1967) 39 *University of Colorado Law Review* 180, 181.

[5] It seems that a popular book, NF Dacey, *How to Avoid Probate!* (New York, Crown, 1965), was important in developing the popular view of probate, or at least captured the zeitgeist.

[6] In the febrile US context a leading scholar pointed to England as an example of how probate should work: WF Fratcher, *Probate can be Quick and Cheap: Trusts and Estates in England* (New York, Pageant Press, 1968).

[7] RH Sitkoff, 'Trusts and Estates: Implementing Freedom of Disposition' (2013) 58 *St Louis University Law Journal* 643, 654.

[8] On which see ch 3 above as well as ch 5 below, II.C. and III.

II. Will-Substitutes: What Are They and Why Have Them?

A. General

While in Scotland the primary means of disposing of property on death is by a will, it seems that this is no longer so in the US. One leading commentator has gone so far as to say that trusts—the will-substitute *par excellence*—have 'eclipsed wills as the preferred vehicle for implementing a donor's freedom of disposition'.[9] Indeed, the prevalence of will-substitutes in the US has reached the stage that a policy question has arisen about the extent to which the classic doctrines of wills such as the classic primary question of formalities and more subtle 'secondary rules'[10] ought to be extended to will-substitutes.[11] Furthermore, with the increased proliferation and sophistication of will-substitute instruments[12] comes a concomitant increase in complexity, which has implications for estate planning and transaction costs.[13]

B. Control

One of the key things that a 'successful' will-substitute will seek to do is to maintain the desirable functions of a testament—control over assets by a person who wishes to arrange for their disposal on death, and the related idea of revocability: the idea that wills are ambulatory and do not become final until death. The leading instrument here is often thought to be the revocable trust, but it suffers from fragility, too. No doubt there are disputes about wills, but so too are there disputes about revocable trusts, especially those that do the work of a will.[14] Likewise, it can

[9] Sitkoff, above n 7, 652. See also DM English, 'The Impact of Uniform Laws on the Teaching of Trusts and Estates' (2014) 58 *St Louis University Law Journal* 689; GMP McCouch, 'Will Substitutes under the Revised Uniform Probate Code' (1993) 58 *Brooklyn Law Review* 1123.

[10] Such as interactions with forced heirship, rules of construction, 'antilapse' rules, presumptions of death, and express or implied revocation by divorce or subsequently born children: I refer to these below, section II.D.

[11] JH Langbein, 'Major Reforms of the Property Restatement and the Uniform Probate Code: Reformation, Harmless Error, and Nonprobate Transfers' (2012) 38 *American College of Trust and Estate Counsel Law Journal* 1; GMP McCouch, 'A Comment on Unification' (2008–09) 43 *Real Property, Trust and Estate Law Journal* 499. See also ch 1 above.

[12] See the list in ML Kaufmann, 'Should the Dead Hand Tighten its Grasp?: An Analysis of the Superwill' (1988) *University of Illinois Law Review* 1019.

[13] KD Schenkel, 'Testamentary Fragmentation and the Diminishing Role of the Will: An Argument for Revival' (2008) 41 *Creighton Law Review* 155.

[14] BES Fogel, 'Trust Me? Estate Planning with Revocable Trusts' (2014) 58 *St Louis University Law Journal* 805, 812.

be difficult to ensure that all the property of the deceased is actually encompassed in the trust fund, hence the necessary development of the so-called 'pour over' will which operates to mop up any property which is not in the trust fund and transfer it into the trust upon death. So it is rare that a trust will be able to do *all* of the work that a will can. Yet, in addition to maintaining the desirable elements of a will, a successful will-substitute must also achieve things that probate cannot. One such factor is the maintenance of privacy—probate is a public process administered by a court, and is therefore a matter of public record. Will-substitutes, in theory, can remain private;[15] yet, like in any dispute, if litigation occurs the terms of the 'private' instrument could emerge in court anyway.[16] This is a manifestation of the broader idea of a 'privatised' law of succession, which in turn poses questions about the extent to which such a system would allow sidestepping of public law rules and public offices like guardians for adults with legal capacity, and the extent to which it will allow sidestepping of creditors and rights of forced heirship creditors. A related question concerns choice of law clauses—it seems easier to insert a contractual choice of law clause in a number of will-substitutes than in a testament (if that is possible at all).[17]

C. Efficiency

Further justifications for will-substitutes are the ease with which some devices allow 'transfers' to be carried out with fewer formalities and less involvement from lawyers and courts. The attraction of such simplified procedures includes minimising distress and administrative burdens at what can be a very difficult time. More broadly, it is likely that broader claims to economic efficiency based on reduced transaction costs etc can be made. Likewise, mechanisms designed to be more efficient and simpler than will-substitutes will often allow the beneficiary of the instrument to realise the substantive benefits more quickly than under standard probate procedures. Expediting the enjoyment of the subject of the instrument might be extremely important where, for example, the deceased had dependants without income or the remaining household incomes are stretched. So in Scotland the executors of the estate must wait six months before distributing the estate, which is a not insubstantial amount of time. An example of a will-substitute designed to take advantage of simplicity and speed would be to use a joint bank

[15] FH Foster, 'Trust Privacy' (2008) 93 *Cornell Law Review* 555; FH Foster, 'Privacy and the Elusive Quest for Uniformity in the Law of Trusts' (2006) 38 *Arizona State Law Journal* 713.

[16] Fogel, above n 14, 816.

[17] See some of the literature dealing with the somewhat analogous position of trusts: L Luttermann, 'Jurisdiction Clauses in Trust Instruments—Creating Certainty or Muddying the Water?' (2011) 17 *Trusts & Trustees* 293; P Matthews, 'What is a Trust Jurisdiction Clause?' (2003) 7 *Jersey Law Review* 232.

account[18] or joint tenancy[19] and, in some US states, the idea of such an account creating a 'Totten trust'. As we will see, similar attempts have been advanced in Scotland, though with mixed and inconclusive results.

D. Formalities and Adjectival Law

Will-substitutes also seek to evade the formalities associated with testaments, especially in jurisdictions with relatively arduous requirements. Similarly, there can be differential capacity requirements for different legal acts, and some will-substitutes could be more (or less) generously treated.[20] The argument is straightforward: a will-substitute is not a will and therefore need not comply with the formalities required of a will. In Scotland the formalities required for a testament are minimal but writing is required, which is not the case for many will-substitutes dealing with non-heritable property. A particular issue arises about the rules concerning the amendment of a will by a representative, which can make a will-substitute attractive. In some jurisdictions it is not possible for a guardian to rectify or amend a testament,[21] but it is possible to alter another type of instrument which might constitute a will-substitute, which in turn might provide a desirable degree of flexibility or an unacceptable elision of rules designed to protect individuals.[22] Judicial decisions about guardian recommendations occur in Scotland and they also demonstrate a reticence about amending testaments.[23] Furthermore, as mentioned above,[24] other technical questions related to formalities, interpretation and doctrines of implied revocation are important. Whether a clean bifurcation exists between applying such doctrines to testaments and refusing to do so in relation to will-substitutes is an important question for a jurisdiction. In Scotland, it is not clear if recent English authority suggesting that wills should be interpreted in the same way as contracts will be followed,[25] though it

[18] G Eddington, 'Survivorship Rights in Joint Bank Accounts: A Misbegotten Presumption of Intent' (2014) 15 *Marquette Elders' Advisor* 175.

[19] NW Hines, 'Joint Tenancies in Iowa Today' (2013) 98 *Iowa Law Review* 1233.

[20] R Whitman, 'Capacity for Lifetime and Estate Planning' (2013) 117 *Pennsylvania State Law Review* 1061.

[21] In Scotland it is currently not possible to amend a testament at all, though there are alternative procedures: *Marley v Rawlings* [2015] AC 157 [87 ff] (Lord Hodge). Reform of the rules for some wills seems likely: SP Bill 75 Succession (Scotland) Bill [as introduced] Session 4 (2015) ss 3–4.

[22] RC Brashier, 'The Ghostwritten Will' (2013) 93 *Boston University Law Review* 1803, 1824; RC Brashier, 'Policy, Perspective, and the Proxy Will' (2009) 61 *South Carolina Law Review* 63.

[23] *T Applicant* 2005 SLT (Sh Ct) 97; *G Applicant* 2009 SLT (Sh Ct) 122; *H Applicant* 2011 SLT (Sh Ct) 178; *Guardian of P* 2012 GWD 39-771.

[24] See above n 10.

[25] In *Marley v Rawlings* [2015] AC 157 the UKSC held that construction and interpretation of wills is not entirely different from construction in contract law, and it will be interesting to see how the lower courts in Scotland (and England!) interpret this as a new departure in interpretation; on this see *In Re Huntley* [2014] EWHC 547 (Ch); *Burnard v Burnard* [2014] EWHC 340 (Ch); *In Re Freud* [2014] EWHC 2577 (Ch). Lord Hodge's remarks about Scottish law did not touch upon the interpretation point.

is submitted that it probably will be.[26] Scottish law currently recognises a presumption of the implied revocation of testaments where a child is subsequently born,[27] but does not apply such a presumption to testaments following divorce.[28] However, the Scottish Government[29] proposes to reverse the current law so that testamentary writings are presumed to be revoked upon divorce.[30] It is not clear if the existing or proposed rules would be applied to any or all will-substitutes capable of revocation.[31] Another open question is the applicability of the unworthy heir rule[32] to will-substitutes, though there is authority which suggests that the rule applies to will-substitutes.[33]

E. Autonomy Beyond Traditional Property Law

Do will-substitutes allow greater potential to capture 'future interests' in a way that the snapshotting of the estate on death by probate does not? Will-substitutes elsewhere are arguably not as limited with regard to the need to demonstrate that something is property. It seems that for a will to control the descent of a thing it must be a *res* susceptible to ownership.[34] Will-substitutes are not necessarily so limited, and, therefore, could be used to address problematic categories of things such as frozen eggs or sperm.[35] Furthermore, not only are will-substitutes less

[26] The Scottish courts gratefully adopted and applied the leading contractual interpretation cases *Chartbrook Ltd v Persimmon Homes Ltd* [2009] AC 1101 and *Rainy Sky SA v Kookmin Bank* [2011] 1 WLR 2900: see, eg *Luminar Lava Ignite Ltd v Mama Group plc* 2010 SC 310 [41] (Lord Hodge). One might argue that the law of succession is sufficiently different in Scotland to justify a different approach, but the current flow of authority suggests that view will not be adopted.

[27] The *conditio si testator sine liberis decesserit*, see *Greenan v Courtney* 2007 SLT 355; *Stevenson's Trs v Stevenson* 1932 SC 657. RRM Paisley, 'The Mechanics of Operation of the *conditio si testator sine liberis decesserit* in Scots Law' (2014) 3 *Juridical Review* 187; RRM Paisley, 'The Roman and Civilian Origins of the conditio si testator sine liberis decesserit in Scots Law' (2015) 19 *Edinburgh Law Review* 1.

[28] *Henderson's JF v Henderson* 1930 SLT 743; *Couper's JF v Valentine* 1976 SC 63; *cf* English law here Wills Act 1837, s 18A, and *In Re Sinclair (decd)* [1985] Ch 446.

[29] Scottish Government, *Consultation on Technical Issues to Succession* (2014) ch 3 paras 13–17.

[30] SP Bill 75 Succession (Scotland) Bill as introduced Session 4 (2015), s 1.

[31] See, eg SN Gary, 'Applying Revocation-on-Divorce Statutes to Will Substitutes' (2004) 18 *Quinnipiac Probate Law Journal* 83.

[32] *Hunter's Excrs Petrs* 1992 SC 474; *Tannock v Tannock* 2013 SLT (Sh Ct) 57; *Cross Petr* 1987 SLT 384; *Gilchrist Petr* 1990 SLT 494. See generally J MacLeod and R Zimmermann, 'Unworthiness to Inherit, Public Policy, Forfeiture: The Scottish Story' (2013) 87 *Tulane Law Review* 741; R Zimmermann, '"Nemo ex suo delicto meliorem suam condicionem facere potest" Kränkungen der Testierfreiheit des Erblassers—englisches im Vergleich zum kontinentaleuropäischen Recht' in S Grundmann, B Haar, H Merkt, P Mülbert and M Wellenhofer (eds), *FS für Klaus Hopt*, vol 1 (Berlin, De Gruyter, 2010) 269; R Kerridge, 'Visiting the Sins of the Fathers on their Children' (2001) 117 *Law Quarterly Review* 371; N Peart, 'Reforming the Forfeiture Rule: Comparing New Zealand, England and Australia' (2002) 31 *Common Law World Review* 1.

[33] *Burns v Secretary of State for Social Services* 1985 SC 143. *cf Paterson Petr* 1986 SLT 121; *McCreight v West Lothian Council* 2009 SC 258.

[34] D Horton, 'Indescendability' (2014) 102 *California Law Review* 543.

[35] EN McQuain, 'Inheritance of Frozen Reproductive Material' (2013) 40 *Ohio Northern University Law Review* 301.

rigid, the fact that much modern wealth is tied up in financial products 'invites' the use of will-substitutes.[36] It is not clear if Scottish law is sufficiently flexible to accommodate will-substitutes which encompass property interests better than testamentary succession, though the law of obligations might be able to carry out similar functions.

F. Creditors' Interests[37]

Other important factors related to the efficacy and uses of will-substitutes in Scotland are the rules governing creditors' interests. Generally the rules of testate succession require creditors'[38] claims to be satisfied by the estate before forced heirship creditors and legatees under a testament, while the forced heirship holders take precedence over the legatees. The potential for will-substitutes to prejudice the rights of creditors is real. A will-substitute might prevent a *res* or interest forming part of the deceased's estate by carrying it directly to someone outwith the normal rules of testate succession, and in so doing bypasses the rights of creditors and forced heirship holders. Alternatively, even if the *res* does form part of the confirmed estate, a will-substitute which generates an obligation creates a concomitant creditor who will rank among the other creditors; but such will-substitutes can be framed as 'debts' upon the estate so that they will take precedence over forced heirship rights and testamentary provisions. Furthermore, that supercharged effect might, conceivably, be achieved with *less* formality than the traditional testament that is being subordinated to the informal will-substitute. Much of the difficulty here is compounded by Scottish law's recognition of 'succession contracts' and is considered below.[39]

III. Joint Accounts

A. Desirability as a Will-Substitute

It is trite law that a standard bank account is a contractual relationship between bank and customer—in particular it is not ordinarily impressed with a fiduciary or proprietary dimension—which is conceptualised as a loan from the

[36] Langbein, above n 11, 12.

[37] An important topic is not addressed in this chapter: taxation. The use of will-substitutes to evade taxation is likely to be a prime objective, though the extent to which this is realistic is questionable.

[38] 'Creditor' here means someone with a right but not a legatee or someone with a forced heirship right.

[39] See below at section VIII.

customer to the bank.[40] Once created the contract makes the depositor a creditor of a debt owed by the debtor bank, which, ordinarily, is to be repaid as and when demanded.[41] One well-known potential will-substitute is the 'joint bank account'. The basic idea is straightforward enough: two or more people open a joint bank account in joint names and are (normally) given joint authorisation rights with respect to the account. The efficacy of such an arrangement as a will-substitute is the potential to have the survivor simply become the sole account holder upon the death of the other account holder without resort to any further juridical acts. Such an arrangement would also avoid awaiting the confirmation of executors and the six-month delay which they observe before distributing the estate, while allowing flexible usage of the funds in the account by both parties during life. Another desirable element for many would be the well-known duty of confidentiality owed by a bank to the account holder.[42]

B. Juristic Basis

The question is whether such an arrangement can be created so as to operate as an effective will-substitute in this manner. An important distinction must be made between the ministerial authority to administer the account and the substantive 'ownership' of the debt which constitutes the value of the 'funds in' the account.[43] Often a joint account will give each holder the authority to act alone in relation to the full value of the account, but that does not necessarily denote sole 'ownership' of those funds. Indeed, it seems that normally the position will be that there is presumed to be joint 'ownership' of the contents of the bank account, even if a 'survivorship' clause is included.[44] It might be, however, that the terms of the account reflect and embody the substantive ownership of the funds—a manifestation of the account holder's intentions when depositing funds into the account. Furthermore, even if the surviving account holder is unable to retain the deceased's share in a question with his executors, that does not mean that the bank is not obliged to pay the fund to the survivor in accordance with its contractual obligation.[45] Thus, the survivor may uplift the funds in a ministerial capacity but will be susceptible to a claim by the executors or other legatees.

Alternative approaches might be to declare an express trust over the contents of the bank account,[46] or, considerably less certainly, to argue that the terms of

[40] *Foley v Hill* (1848) 2 HLC 28; 9 ER 1002; *Ross v Lord Advocate* 1986 SC (HL) 70.

[41] See *Macdonald v North of Scotland Bank Ltd* 1942 SC 369, 375 (Lord Justice-Clerk (Cooper)).

[42] *Tournier v National Provincial and Union Bank of England* 1924 1 KB 461.

[43] *Bank of Scotland v Robertson* (1870) 8 M 391; *Allan's Exr v Union Bank of Scotland* 1909 SC 206.

[44] *Bank of Scotland*, above n 43.

[45] *The Union Bank of Scotland Ltd v Campbell* (1898) 6 SLT 196.

[46] See *Graham's Trs v Gillies* 1956 SC 437.

such an account might create a 'Quistclose trust'.[47] Conceptualisations based on donation *mortis causa*[48] or trusts could protect the funds in the account from creditors. The account's constitutive arrangements might also be construed as creating a contractual right or *jus quaesitum tertio* in favour of the surviving account holder,[49] which in turn could be considered a debt of the deceased's estate that, although it might need administrative involvement from the deceased's executor depending on its terms, would formally take priority over legal rights and other legacies.[50] Much, indeed one might say everything, will depend upon the terms on which the account holders and bank entered into the underlying contract creating the account. In that vein, there is an outside possibility which hinges upon the understanding of joint and common property in Scotland—if it is possible to expressly create joint property, outwith the traditional categories of trusts and unincorporated associations, then the account could be constituted as joint property.[51] When one account holder dies her indistinct and unseverable share of the joint property account would accrue (or accresce) to the survivor by force of law alone: the deceased's interest would cease to exist as an asset in her patrimony.

Finally, another alternative mechanism, which has been considered in relation to bank accounts, has been the special destination.[52] A succession of cases have denied that a special destination can be created over 'a deposit receipt', most of them preferring to analyse mention of a survivor in this context as being a question of donation.[53] It seems that these authorities remain the law and will prevent a modern bank account from being the subject of a special destination.[54] However, that does not mean that an alternative arrangement based upon the mechanisms discussed above is ruled out.

Much of this account is speculative and derived from logical application of existing principles of Scots private law—few have been tested, and it is perhaps unlikely that a solicitor would (perhaps could) recommend to a person that they use their estate as the test case. However, it is worth remarking that a person's bank

[47] GL Gretton, 'Scotland' in W Swadling (ed), *The Quistclose Trust: Critical Essays* (Oxford, Hart Publishing, 2004).

[48] Although donations *mortis causa* could be vulnerable to reduction as gratuitous alienations at common law or under the Bankruptcy (Scotland) Act 1985, s 34.

[49] Such arrangements might be described as 'nominations', perhaps by analogy with pensions etc.

[50] See the discussion of 'succession contracts' below at section VIII.

[51] See the discussion of 'common property' below at section IV.

[52] See below at section V.

[53] *Cuthill v Burns* (1862) 24 D 849, 857 (Lord Benholme); *Watt's Trs v Mackenzie* (1869) 7 M 930, 933–34 (Lord Neaves); *Miller v Miller* (1874) 1 R 1107, 1110 (Lord Neaves); *Crosbie's Trs v Wright* (1880) 7 R 823; *Jamieson v McLeod* (1880) 7 R 1131; *Blyth v Curle* (1885) 12 R 674, 679 (Lord President (Inglis)); *Macdonald v Macdonald* (1889) 16 R 758; *Dinwoodie's Excr v Carruther's Excr* (1895) 23 R 234, 238 (Lord Young), 239 (Lord Trayner); *Morrison v Forbes* (1890) 17 R 958; *Macfarlane's Trs v Miller* (1898) 25 R 1201; *Rose v Cameron's Excr* (1901) 3 F 337.

[54] *McCarthy's Exrs v McCafferty* 2000 GWD 14-549. See J Kerrigan, 'Special Destinations—Survivorship and Bank Accounts Revisited' 2011 SLT (News) 5; MC Meston, 'Survivorship Destinations and Bank Accounts' (1996) *Scottish Law & Practice Quarterly* 315.

account is likely to be among the highest value assets a person has alongside her house and pension, and so developing innovation along these lines might not be impossible.

IV. Forms of Co-Ownership

The law in Scotland recognises two forms of co-ownership whereby two or more persons hold an ownership interest over a single piece of property: (1) common property and (2) joint property. Common property gives each owner extensive rights of use and each owner has an ownership interest which is a distinct *pro indiviso* share of the property, which, in turn, can be alienated or will devolve to heirs upon death. Joint property is conceptually different.[55] Joint property exists where more than one person is the owner of property; but, crucially, unlike common property, the several owners do not have a distinct share that can be alienated or bequeathed. Therefore, upon death (or in other circumstances of ceasing to be joint owner) the indistinct interest of the deceased individual ceases[56] and the survivors remain owners of the whole. These are general rules of common property in Scotland.[57] The current state of the law seems to suggest that it is *not* possible to stipulate that the co-ownership interest of two or more persons who are not trustees or members of an unincorporated association are 'joint', as opposed to 'common', owners of a single piece of property. This severely limits the extent to which setting up a co-ownership holding of property can be used as an effective will-substitute—the main attraction of such an arrangement relies upon the *jus accrescendi* of joint ownership carrying the deceased joint owner's interest to the survivor, and it seems that in Scottish law that is only available for trustees and members of an unincorporated association.

Nevertheless, the position is not clear beyond all doubt. It is not completely clear that there really is a '*numerus clausus*' of joint property interests, and the leading modern authority suggests that if a contractual nexus between the co-owners, or some other relationship beyond co-ownership per se exists between them, then it might be possible to consider the situation to be joint property.[58] Yet, and to complicate matters still further, it is not clear if that connection needs to be one which is known and recognised in specific situations (eg, trusts, partnerships, unincorporated associations etc) or whether ad hoc arrangements in specific cases

[55] See chs 1, 2 and 3 above, p 16 f, p 33 f and p 60 in this volume.

[56] An alternative conceptualisation would be to say that the interest reverts to the remainder; but it does not add to the analysis or the rights held by the survivors.

[57] They apply to moveable and heritable property; though cases on moveable property are rare, they do arise, see *Lawson v Leith & Newcastle Steam-Packet Co* (1850) 13 D 175 (a ship); *Murray v Johnstone* (1896) 23 R 981 (a trophy).

[58] *Banff Burgh Council v Ruthin Castle Ltd* 1944 SC 36, 68 (Lord Justice-Clerk (Cooper)).

could create joint property. It is perhaps telling that a husband and wife seem *not* to be considered to be joint owners, and it is difficult to imagine a better-established relationship or connection between co-owners.

All that said, Scottish law does have an alternative mechanism to achieve a similar result—a 'special destination'. Special destinations are considered in detail in the next section; however, it is useful here to mention that the conceptual basis of a special destination is somewhat different from joint ownership. A special destination creates a situation whereby the interest of one person is carried by operation of law at the death of one party to the survivor; yet, the Scottish sources are clear that a special destination is *not* predicated upon a relationship of joint property.[59] It is only upon death that a special destination takes effect (automatically)[60] to transfer that share to the survivor.

V. Special Destinations

A. Introduction

Special destinations are one of the main types of will-substitute known to Scots law. A destination is an inherent condition attached to the ownership of a piece of property. As such, a special destination is not a testamentary writing (a will), but it can have testamentary effect because it can determine to whom title will pass upon the death of the institute. In other words, a special destination can transfer an ownership interest held by one person (the 'institute') to an identified person (the 'substitute') upon the death of the institute. This transfer occurs separately from the provisions of a will, and outwith the concomitant confirmation of the testamentary estate and involvement of an executor.[61] The closest analogy in the common law tradition is a joint tenancy, but they are conceptually distinct in important ways.[62] The most common type of property that is subject to a special destination is corporeal heritable property (land, broadly speaking), but special destinations can also regulate incorporeal heritable property,[63] incorporeal moveable and corporeal moveable property.

[59] *Steele v Caldwell* 1979 SLT 228, 231–32 (Lord Ordinary (Allanbridge)); *Smith v Mackintosh* 1988 SLT 453, 457 (Lord Ordinary (Sutherland)).

[60] *Povey v Povey* 2014 SLT 643 [21] (Lord Ordinary (Doherty)).

[61] For a historical and comparative treatment see: GL Gretton, 'Fideicommissary Substitutions: Scots Law in Historical and Comparative Perspective' in KGC Reid, MJ de Waal and R Zimmermann (eds), *Exploring the Law of Succession* (Edinburgh, EUP, 2007).

[62] See above at section V.

[63] eg *Oliphant of the Ilk* 2004 SLT (Lyon Ct) 14, 15.

B. Heritable Property

i. Creation

Special destinations can arise in a number of contexts, but the most common situation is where a 'survivorship destination' is inserted into a conveyance of heritable property in favour of two or more purchasers who are purchasing the property with a view to becoming common proprietors. The survivorship destination provides that upon the death of one common owner her *pro indiviso* share will be transferred to the survivor(s) by virtue of the special destination—no further steps are required.[64] The arrangement is a common one for married couples who purchase a house in common. Because the destination is inserted into the conveyance this must be done by the transferor at the request of those who are seeking the creation of the special destination in their favour. A less common situation in which a special destination is encountered is where an executor gives effect to a substitutive destination-over when transferring property in accordance with a testamentary legacy; however, because destinations-over are destinations contained in testamentary writings and this situation is rare, no more will be said about it here.[65]

ii. Evacuation (Revocation)

If a special destination has been created a further question arises about the means by which it can be 'evacuated' (broadly speaking this means revoked) or evaded. The extent to which special destinations are amenable to such revocation or evasion has implications for their efficacy and attractiveness as will-substitutes. If the substitute who is to receive under the special destination predeceases the institute then the special destination is at an end: there is no substitute, and her estate does not take the benefit of the destination. Furthermore, the institute can dispose of her *pro indiviso* share *inter vivos*: the institute is the owner and can transfer her share to another. If the institute does transfer her share then upon her death there is no property interest that can be carried by the special destination; indeed, one variant of this approach involves executing a conveyance to the institute himself (with the concurrence of the substitute) minus the destination in order to purge the destination.[66] In accordance with first principles of law, a substitute can renounce the special destination.[67] By statute a divorce[68] or dissolution of a civil partnership[69] will evacuate a survivorship destination between spouses or

[64] *Povey*, above n 60.
[65] See generally GL Gretton and KGC Reid, *Conveyancing*, 4th edn (Edinburgh, W Green, 2011) ch 26.
[66] See ibid, ch 26, para 20 judicially approved in *Povey*, above n 60, [24] (Lord Ordinary (Doherty)).
[67] *Povey*, above n 60, [24] (Lord Ordinary (Doherty)).
[68] Family Law (Scotland) Act 2006, s 19.
[69] Civil Partnership Act 2004, s 124A.

civil partners in relation to heritable property.[70] Currently special destinations are more vulnerable than testamentary provisions in this situation because divorce does not automatically revoke testamentary provisions, though proposed reforms will bring consistency.[71]

Perhaps the most intellectually difficult route to an effective evacuation is by means of a contradictory legacy by the institute.[72] Two elements are required: (1) the *power* to evacuate the destination, and (2) any purported evacuation must comply with formalities requirements. Answering the question whether the institute has the power to evacuate begins with investigating the conveyance which created the destination—was an express clause included which bestowed the power to evacuate?[73] If there is no express clause governing the power to evacuate, as is often the case, then resort must be had to a series of presumptions.[74] There is presumed to be no power to evacuate where there is a marriage contract, a clause of return, where both parties contributed to the price, and perhaps where the destination was created pursuant to a direction in a will or trust;[75] outwith these situations there is presumed to be a power to evacuate the destination.[76] These presumptions against having a 'power' to evacuate the destination are really manifested examples of the general rules about irrevocability, especially where there are 'contractual' arrangements akin to those discussed below under the heading of 'Succession Contracts'.[77] The presumption concerning the joint contribution to the purchase price[78] is the most important as it encompasses many situations of common ownership and, in particular, in the case of a married couple. If a power to evacuate exists it is still necessary to demonstrate that the evacuation is specific and complies with the requisite formalities.[79]

[70] *Willson v Willson* 2009 FLR 18 [16] (Lord Ordinary (Drummond Young)).

[71] See text to n 30.

[72] ie the institute changes her mind and leaves her share, which is subject to the special destination to a third party by the terms of her will.

[73] See the model clause and explanation provided by Gretton and Reid, above n 65, ch 26, para 7.

[74] ibid, ch 26, para 16.

[75] The basis of this presumption seems to flow from the idea that by accepting a gift, which is subject to a special destination, the institute takes the gift subject to an enforceable condition in the form of the special destination, and, therefore, is unable to evacuate the special destination by legacy because the conditional acceptance of the gift operates as a restraint: *Renouf's Trs v Haining* 1919 SC 497, 507 (Lord Dundas); *Taylor's Exrs v Brunton* 1939 SC 444, 447 (Lord President (Normand)), 448 (Lord Moncrieff); *Brown's Trs v Brown* 1943 SC 488, 492 (Lord Justice-Clerk (Cooper)), 494 (Lord Mackay), 496 (Lord Wark). Of course a difficulty here is that the tenor of these decisions is that any accepted gift of property subject to a special destination can be seen as subject to a condition (the destination), and, therefore, is not capable of evacuation. In other words, the special destination is self-protective because it constitutes a condition that prevents evacuation.

[76] Gretton and Reid, above n 65, ch 26, para 16.

[77] See below at section VIII. See *Shand's Trs v Shand's Trs* 1966 SC 178, 185 (Lord Wheatley), 186 (Lord Walker).

[78] *Perrett's Trs v Perrett* 1909 SC 522. The decision was expressly revisited in a later case, and a suggestion that the decision in *Perrett* was 'a bastard child lacking precedent, principle and legitimacy' was rejected: *Shand's Trs*, above n 77, 184 (Lord Justice-Clerk (Grant)).

[79] Succession (Scotland) Act 1964, s 30.

iii. *Efficacy as Will-Substitute*

During the institute's life his or her distinct *pro indiviso* share operates like any other, and so creditors can attack it. The question which was, at least at one time, more doubtful was whether creditor's rights transmitted against the interest once it vested in the substitute when the destination became effective on the institute's death. One first instance decision held that an institute's creditors could not pursue the substitute who received the interest by virtue of a special destination;[80] however, the decision has been overruled and it is established that creditors can proceed against the institute's share (only).[81] That diminished the attractiveness of a special destination as a will-substitute to avoid creditors. However, the special destination does carry out the transfer of the institute's interest to the substitute automatically. However, it has been observed that because confirmation will often be required on the rest of the estate the actual strength of this apparent advantage is questionable in most cases.[82] Furthermore, the law relating to special destinations has been the subject of criticism. The effect of a special destination is not always clear to the parties involved and can come as an unwelcome surprise. Furthermore, 'evacuating' a special destination is more difficult than revoking a legacy in a testament which might achieve a similar result.

C. Beyond Heritable Property

i. *Written Documents and Title*

It is possible to create a special destination over moveable property.[83] Uncertainty exists with regard to documents of title, bonds and other financial instruments; it seems the analysis of each instrument must focus on 'the nature and effect of the documents themselves, and on whether they are sufficient, *proprio vigore*, as operative destinations, to give a right to the persons named in them'.[84] Often, as with the discussion of co-ownership above,[85] the operation of such 'destinations' is considered alongside the rules relating to donation, and donation *mortis causa* in particular. There is a body of authority which suggests that a special destination can be inserted into stock certificates,[86] bonds,[87]

[80] *Barclay's Bank Ltd v McGreish* 1983 SLT 344. The decision was criticised: M Morton, 'Special Destinations as Testamentary Instructions' (1984) SLT (News) 133; JM Halliday, 'Special Destinations' (1984) SLT (News) 180; GL Gretton, 'Death and Debt' (1984) SLT (News) 299.

[81] *Fleming's Tr v Fleming* 2000 SC 206, 207–08 (Lord Sutherland).

[82] Gretton and Reid, above n 65, ch 26, para 6.

[83] *Connell's Trs v Connell* (1886) 13 R 1175.

[84] ibid, 1182 (Lord Adam).

[85] See above at section IV.

[86] *Connell's Trs*, above n 83, 1184 (Lord Adam); *Oliver v Oliver's Trs* 1915 2 SLT 262; *Taylor's Exrs*, above n 75.

[87] *Walker's Trs v Walker* (1878) 5 R 965; *Lang's Trs v Lang* (1885) 12 R 1265; *Connell's Trs*, above n 83, 1184 (Lord Adam); *Paterson's JF v Paterson's Trs* (1897) 24 R 499.

debenture bonds,[88] documents creating an annuity,[89] and certificates of debt.[90] On the other hand, a deposit receipt payable to the deceased or the survivor will *not* create an effective destination unless it can be shown that it constituted a donation *mortis causa*.[91] It seems that the overarching principle is that a destination will be competent and effective where the document 'forms the title to the sum contained in it'.[92]

ii. Not Testamentary Writings

It has been judicially observed that special destinations in this context (though the point must be a general one) are *not* testamentary writings, and, therefore, will not be revoked by a standard revocation of testamentary writings in a testament.[93] The contrary opinion has also been expressed.[94] It is perhaps open to question whether this is a manifestation of the rule that a general testamentary provision does not evacuate a special destination;[95] or, alternatively, if it is a related but different exercise which suggests that because special destinations are not testamentary writings they are not comprehended by a standard revocation clause at all or have an obligational character.[96] Furthermore, if not a testamentary writing then the requisite formalities for a special destination here might be different. However, given that apparent rule for recognising a destination as valid requires a document which is determinative of 'title' to the destination it seems that writing will be necessary even though heritable property is not involved.[97]

iii. Scope of Future Use

The application of special destinations to financial instruments and documents of title has not always been enthusiastically embraced.[98] Most of the leading cases

[88] *Buchanan v Porteous* (1879) 7 R 211, 214 (Lord Justice-Clerk (Moncrieff)), 214–215 (Lord Gifford).

[89] *Connell's Trs*, above n 83, 1184 (Lord Adam).

[90] *Walker's Trs*, above n 87; *Connell's Trs*, above n 83.

[91] *Connell's Trs*, above n 83, 1185–86 (Lord Adam); *Macdonald v Macdonald*, above n 53; *Penman's Trs v Penman* (1896) 4 SLT 67, 68 (Lord Ordinary (Kincairney)); *Paterson's JF*, above n 87, 508 (Lord McLaren); *Macfarlane's Trs*, above n 53; *Sillars v McAlpine* (1907) 15 SLT 365; *Macpherson's Excrx v Mackay* 1932 SC 505.

[92] *Connell's Trs*, above n 83, 1184 (Lord Adam); although cp Lord Shand's compelling dissenting opinion (1186) in favour of giving effect to the deposit-receipt destination.

[93] *Connell's Trs*, above n 83, 1183 (Lord Adam); *Paterson's JF*, above n 87.

[94] *Brydon's Curator Bonis v Brydon's Trs* (1898) 25 R 708, 713–14 (Lord McLaren); *Lockhart Petr* 1922 SLT 556, 561–62 (Lord Skerrington); *Turnbull's Trs v Robertson* 1911 SC 1288, 1294 (Lord Kinnear).

[95] See *Walker's Trs*, above n 87, 969 (Lord President (Inglis)), 970 (Lord Deas).

[96] See *Murray's Excrs v Geekie* 1929 SC 633, 637–38 (Lord President (Clyde)), 647 (Lord Blackburn).

[97] See *Colenso's Excr v Davidson* 1930 SLT 359.

[98] *Macdonald v Macdonald*, above n 53, 766 (Lord Young); *Paterson's JF*, above n 87, 508 (Lord McLaren), 511 (Lord Kinnear); *Brydon's Curator Bonis*, above n 94, 713 (Lord McLaren); *Macfarlane's Trs*, above n 53, 1212 (Lord McLaren).

were decided in the nineteenth century and early-twentieth century; therefore it is hard to know to what extent such special destinations are still used. That is perhaps surprising given the efficacy with which a number of different documents of title can be transferred. Likewise, the age of the decisions makes it unclear how they would be interpreted in an age where new forms of documentary title have emerged. It seems that nominations also do some of the work of such special destinations.

VI. Life Assurance

Another form of common will-substitute is a policy of life assurance. The structure of the policy, and in particular to whom it is payable, will be material when considering whether the device operates as a fully fledged will-substitute or not. If the policy funds are payable to the deceased or to his executors, on the event of his death or someone else's, then the policy does not operate as a will-substitute which avoids the executory process, though it is an instrument that has effect upon death. The funds are simply added to the deceased's estate for distribution by the executors, and, furthermore, they are subject to claims for legal rights.[99] Alternatively, if the policy of life assurance was taken out by the deceased on his own life or upon another whose life he had an insurable interest in, and payable to another, then the funds are payable to that identified person.[100] A historic difficulty arose in this situation where a husband took out a policy for the benefit of his wife where he was insolvent, because the arrangement was viewed as revocable gift, and his creditors could revoke such a gift and divest the wife of her interest.[101] In order to remedy this state of affairs the Married Women's Policies of Assurance (Scotland) Act 1880 was passed in order to allow a husband to make an irrevocable gift to his wife which would be beyond the reach of creditors (the *jus mariti* meant that any other gifts to the wife that were not in trust would belong to the husband, and hence be within the reach of creditors). The 1880 Act did two things: (1) it allowed a married woman to effect a policy of life assurance, on her own life or that of her husband, the benefit of which was vested separately and entirely in her;[102] and (2) where a husband (now either spouse or a civil partner) effected a life assurance policy, on his own life,[103] in favour of his wife or children, that policy was deemed

[99] *Muirhead v Muirhead's Factor* (1867) 6 M 95.

[100] *Smith v Kerr* (1869) 7 M 863; *Coulson's Trs v Coulson* (1901) 3 F 1041.

[101] See, eg *Craig v Galloway* (1860) 22 D 1211, revd (1861) 4 Macq 267.

[102] Married Women's Policies of Assurance (Scotland) Act 1880, s 1.

[103] Innovations on the basic model of life assurance are permissible: *Chrystal's Trs v Chrystal* 1912 SC 1003; *Walker's Trs v Lord Advocate* 1955 SC (HL) 74; *Barclay's Tr v IRC* 1975 SC (HL) 1; *Will v IRC* 1981 SC (HL) 44.

a trust in their favour.[104] Furthermore, the person in whose favour the policy was effected is immediately vested with the beneficial interest upon the creation of the policy,[105] because the trust is created by force of section 2 of the 1880 Act.[106] Concomitantly, the husband's interest is limited by the trust to that of a trustee.[107] Nevertheless, the constitution of that statutory trust is contingent upon the subsistence of the marriage (at least policies in favour of spouses, probably not those in favour of children): the dissolution of the marriage by divorce could end the trust.[108] Therefore, the trust can be conceived as irrevocable, though it ends in the event of divorce.[109] The court will attempt to return to the *status quo ante*, as it would in the case of a failure of any trust, such as giving the surrender value of the policy to the husband.[110]

It is also possible for someone else to take out a policy on the deceased's life, provided she has the requisite insurable interest, such as a spouse or civil partner,[111] and the policy payable to the spouse who has taken out the policy on the deceased's life. Such a policy will be payable directly to the nominate beneficiary without falling into the deceased's estate. However, this is less a case of will-substitution and need not be pursued further here.

VII. Nominations

A. Statutory Nominations

It is possible to avoid executory administration under a testament by nominating a person to take certain benefits directly as a nominee. Many such nominations are statutory nominations.[112] The relevant legislation is UK legislation, and therefore the rules are the same as in England.[113] Broadly speaking, legislation allows

[104] Married Women's Policies of Assurance (Scotland) Act 1880, s 2.

[105] *Stewart v Hodge* (1901) 8 SLT 436, 438 (Lord Ordinary (Stormonth Darling)).

[106] The importance of this provision is that it removed the need to demonstrate delivery of the policy, which had prevented such arrangements taking effect in the past: *Scottish Provident Institution v Jarvie's Trs* (1887) 14 R 411.

[107] The powers of trusteeship here have been equated to those of a standard trustee by statute: Married Women's Policies of Assurance (Amendment) (Scotland) Act 1980, s 2.

[108] *Wallace v Wallace* 1916 1 SLT 163, 166 (Lord Anderson). The exact basis of the cessation of the trust is perhaps unclear: at one point it is said 'all beneficial interest in the trust has been forfeited by her' (166); but later it is said 'the trust purposes have failed, as the pursuer has now no wife to benefit' (ibid). Because the divorce was prompted by the wife's desertion, it might be that the reference to forfeiture is not meant as renunciation or in a technical sense.

[109] 'I do not regard the trust constituted by the policy as irrevocable, but only so during the subsistence of the marriage', *Wallace v Wallace*, above n 108, 166 (Lord Anderson).

[110] ibid.

[111] See Scobbie, above n 1, ch 10, para 143.

[112] See ibid, ch 13, paras 4–7; R Kerridge and AHR Brierley, *Parry and Kerridge: The Law of Succession*, 12th edn (London, Sweet & Maxwell, 2009) ch 1, para 6.

[113] See ch 3 above II.B.

someone to be nominated to receive a payment of invested funds directly from designated institutions in accordance with rules specific to that institutional holding. A number of miscellaneous specific enactments providing for such payments by nomination are governed by the Administration of Estates (Small Payments) Act 1965, which stipulates that such direct payments can only be made up to an amount as designated by statutory instrument: the current limit is £5,000.[114] Important examples of such statutes providing for nominations include funds held by building societies, national savings bank accounts, national savings certificates, industrial and provident societies, trade unions, premium savings bonds, government stock and various public sector pension schemes.[115]

B. Death in Service Nominations

Beyond the so-called 'statutory' nominations, capped at £5,000, it is also possible to nominate someone to receive a payment in lieu of accrued pension entitlements: otherwise known as 'death in employment or service' payments. The particulars of the nomination and payment will be governed by the particular scheme. The exact nature of the nomination might be uncertain, and, in particular, the question whether it is properly to be understood as a testamentary writing has implications for formalities and revocation.[116]

i. Revocation and Formalities

The Privy Council has held that such a nomination was *not* a testamentary writing and more akin to a power of appointment, but that the matter will always be one of interpreting the particular terms of any scheme.[117] English case law has reached a similar conclusion;[118] whereas Canadian case law has reached the opposite conclusion.[119] Scottish authority is unclear and arguably contradictory, even allowing for interpretation of specific schemes. In one case a nomination was revoked by a later testament on the basis that the nomination did not settle the entitlement to the funds and was simply an administrative measure.[120] A different case suggested that a nomination was a testamentary writing, and, therefore, in the absence of compliance with statutory formalities it had 'no force or effect in law'.[121] It is true that in one case it was observed that a nomination had 'testamentary effect' insofar as the deceased could not be said to have died intestate, but it also acknowledged

114 Administration of Estates (Small Payments) (Increase of Limit) Order 1984/539.
115 See the references in Scobbie, above n 1, ch 13, para 7.
116 See above at section II.D.
117 *Baird v Baird* [1990] 2 AC 548 (PC, Trinidad and Tobago).
118 *Re Danish Bacon Co Ltd Staff Pension Fund Trusts* [1971] 1 WLR 248.
119 *Re MacInnes* [1935] 1 DLR 401; see ch 12 below II.E.
120 *Young v Waterson* 1918 SC 9.
121 *Morton v French* 1908 SC 171, 173.

that the nomination did not comply with the requisite formalities needed to execute a valid will.[122] While in yet another case it was held that a nomination was not revoked by marriage or the subsequent birth of a child, and, in fact, the nomination was an *inter vivos* gift of the future debt to the nominee and was therefore not susceptible to any claims by forced heirship holders of legal rights.[123] Yet, in later cases a nomination was considered to be a special destination.[124] This multitude of analyses poses questions about revocability in particular. A special destination can only be revoked (technically it is 'evacuated') with precision, whereas a testamentary writing can be revoked by a general revocation clause.[125] Of course, if a nomination were not considered to be a testamentary writing at all then such a revocation would be invalid. Similarly, testamentary writings are subject to some presumptions of revocation (subsequent child born,[126] no divorce)[127] unlike special destinations; though, to complicate matters further, a special destination will be evacuated by divorce (unlike a testamentary writing).[128] If a nomination is seen in obligational terms—ie, it is seen as a gift or promise (contract being unlikely, but it could conceivably be contractually due)—then it is irrevocable.

ii. Creditors' Rights

There is some uncertainty regarding the authority about whether legal rights will be available with regard to funds paid under a nomination.[129] In one case it was held that a gratuity paid to the deceased's executors was subject to legal rights;[130] however, it seems clear that the particular wording of the statute which provided that the 'Treasury may grant to his legal personal representatives a gratuity'[131] implied that, because payment was to be made to the executors, this addition should be added to the estate for distribution, and was therefore subject to legal rights claims. In another case where a husband paid into an annuity scheme, which was payable to his wife upon his death, the annuity was not subject to legal rights on the simple basis that the right to the annuity payment was never a part of the husband's estate and was payable to the widow alone.[132] The latter authority

[122] *Gill v Gill* 1938 SC 65, 71 (Lord Fleming).

[123] *Campbell v Campbell* 1917 1 SLT 339. The decision also alludes to the idea of a succession contract: see below at section VIII.

[124] *Ford's Tr v Ford* 1940 SC 426, 431 (Lord President (Normand)); *Clark's Exrs v Macauley* 1961 SLT 109.

[125] See above at section V.B.ii.

[126] The so-called rule of the *conditio si testator sine liberis decesserit.*

[127] See above at text to nn 27–31.

[128] See above at section V.B.ii.

[129] *cf Lim v Walia* [2015] 2 WLR 583; *Goenka v Goenka* [2014] EWHC 2966 (Ch); *Dingmar v Dingmar* [2006] EWCA Civ 942.

[130] *Beveridge v Beveridge's Excrx* 1938 SC 160.

[131] Superannuation Act 1909, s 2(1).

[132] *Craigie's Trs v Craigie* (1904) 6 F 343. Though *cf McFarlane v McFarlane's Trs* (1906) 13 SLT 751 where the annuities were considered to be *donationes mortis causa* and hence, under the law at the time, revocable at the instance of the husband and were so revoked by his testament if she should claim

seems to represent the general rule, the former being concerned with the particular wording of the statute, and has been followed in relation to a nomination with regard to a benevolent society.[133]

VIII. Succession Obligations[134]

A. Introduction

A person might attempt to distribute her estate by way of a succession contract or *pactum successorium*. A succession *contract* is a contract whereby two people have agreed—hence it is necessarily a bilateral and *inter vivos* juridical act—that one of them will leave the other property by virtue of the contract. The contract might provide for the distribution of the property itself, or it might purport to impose an obligation to execute a testamentary writing in favour of the contract creditor.[135] The law's insistence upon testamentary formalities explains why most legal systems are suspicious at best about succession contracts purporting to distribute property per se. But many systems recognise the validity of a contract obliging the debtor to execute adequate testamentary provisions to satisfy the terms of the contract. Such contracts are valid in some common law jurisdictions such as Australia[136] and England.[137] They are also valid in Scotland,[138] and the debtor's *jus testamenti* can be restricted by contract.[139] A distinction can be drawn between positive and negative obligations under such a contract. A person might agree not to alter or revoke an existing testamentary writing, thereby creating an obligation not to do something; alternatively, an obligation may be constituted which requires the debtor to take positive action to create or alter an existing testamentary writing.[140]

her legal rights. However, a later case seems to state that where gifts are unrevoked at the time of the deceased's death they *do not* form part of the estate for the purposes of assessing legal rights: *Hutton's Trs v Hutton's Trs* 1916 SC 86 (Full Bench, 13 judges).

[133] *Struthers v Marshall* (1904) 12 SLT 736.

[134] Most of the discussion is of contracts, but much of the discussion is applicable to other forms of obligation, notably promises.

[135] See *De Lathouwer v Anderson* [2007] CSOH 54, 2007 SLT 437 [7] (Lord Ordinary (Emslie)).

[136] *Schaefer v Schuhmann* [1972] AC 572 (PC, Aus). However, while such contracts are valid, they will not necessarily oust a court's power to order a discretionary distribution of the deceased's estate to dependants: *Dillon v Public Trustee of New Zealand* [1941] AC 294 (PC, NZ); *Barnes v Barnes* [2003] HCA 9, (2003) 214 CLR 169; *Re Brown* (1955) 219 LT 129. See also ch 5 below III.F.

[137] Kerridge and Brierley, above n 112, ch 6, paras 1 ff.

[138] J Dalrymple, 1st Viscount of Stair, *The Institutions of the Law of Scotland*, 2nd edn (1693) III. 8. 28 and 33.

[139] *Rollo's Trs v Rollo* 1940 SC 578, 584 (Lord Moncrieff).

[140] *Johnston v Goodlet* (1868) 6 M 1067, 1072 (Lord Justice-Clerk (Patton)).

B. Formalities

Proving rights under such contracts has in many ways been more difficult than recognising their validity as legal devices in the abstract. If the contract relates to land then it must be in writing.[141] There is authority which suggests that such contracts relating to any kind of property might need to be in writing;[142] but this matter is less clear,[143] and, it is suggested, should follow the general law of proof for contracts *or* promises.[144] On the other hand, the apparent rule that writing will be required seems to have a strong basis in policy: allowing such contracts to be proven in the absence of writing 'supersedes' the law of testamentary formalities,[145] and hence the judicial hostility to such unwritten contracts.[146] It is perhaps unclear how far the courts today would insist upon writing (outwith the context of heritable property) on the basis of that policy justification given the changes to the law of proof and formalities in relation to testamentary writings, contracts and promises which have occurred since many of these leading cases were decided.[147] Strict insistence upon writing would obviously significantly undermine the extent to which such arrangements would operate as effective will-substitutes when the formalities relating to testamentary writings are so generous today. Nevertheless, written contracts in that context might fill some gaps in the rare situation where there is a will but it is invalid.[148] Another possibility is that unwritten contracts might fare better in situations of intestacy, though different questions might arise about the extent to which executors are bound by such undertakings.

Contracts providing for the execution or preservation of a testamentary writing are not in themselves testamentary writings, and, therefore, will not necessarily be revoked by the standard revocation clause of some testaments.[149] Indeed, more generally, such revocation clauses must be interpreted carefully and will not necessarily revoke specific testamentary legacies either.[150]

141 Requirements of Writing (Scotland) Act 1995, s 1(2)(a)(i). The rules at common law are similar: *Khosprowpour v MacKay* [2014] CSOH 175; *McEleveen v McQuillan's Excrx* 1997 SLT (Sh Ct) 46.

142 *Edmonston v Bruce* (1861) 23 D 995.

143 The report in *Edmonston*, above n 142, speaks of a contract, but subsequent authority (*Smith v Oliver (no 1)* 1911 SC 103, 111 (Lord President (Dunedin))) has suggested that the case was concerned not with contract, but rather with the law of promise, which, in turn, would explain the suggestion that writing would be necessary.

144 *Smith v Oliver*, above n 143, 110 (Lord President (Dunedin)).

145 *Johnston*, above n 140, 1072 (Lord Justice-Clerk (Patton)).

146 *Hallett v Ryrie* (1907) 15 SLT 367, 368–69 (Lord Ordinary (Salvesen)).

147 Primarily the Requirements of Writing (Scotland) Act 1995.

148 Little formality is required to execute a valid will in Scotland—'subscription' by the testator is all that is required: Requirements of Writing (Scotland) Act 1995, s 2.

149 *De Lathouwer*, above n 135, [9] (Lord Ordinary (Emslie)); *Montgomerie's Trs v Alexander's Trs* 1911 SC 856.

150 *Clark's Excr v Clark* 1943 SC 216.

It might be that personal bar or *rei interventus* will constitute an enforceable obligation to execute a testamentary writing generally, and, in particular, might create such obligations in relation to the land in the absence of writing.[151]

C. Remedies

Even if a succession contract has been recognised by the court, questions of enforceability loom large. In Scots law specific implement is, it is sometimes said,[152] the 'primary' remedy for breach of contract, though that is probably to put matters too highly.[153] Nevertheless, specific implement can be claimed by right,[154] subject to the court's discretion to deny the remedy *in exceptional cases.*[155] Can a court order someone to alter—or even create—a testament in accordance with a contractual obligation? In the leading case[156] the court reserved its opinion whether specific implement would be available; yet, there were suggestions the court would be less inclined to order specific implement in this context than in others.[157] On the other hand, if, as recent case law seems to suggest,[158] the court will only refuse specific implement *exceptionally* where a very cogent reason makes implement inconvenient and unjust, the focus being on the inconvenience and injustice that the performing party might suffer,[159] it is at least questionable whether executors—who would have to perform any such decree—would suffer any 'injustice'. This posits a somewhat counterintuitive hypothetical: it might be easier to enforce a succession obligation by waiting for the debtor to die and then seek decree of specific implement against an executor than it would be to seek to specifically enforce the same obligation against the debtor in life. In any event, whatever the position with regard to specific implement, it seems well settled that damages are available for breach of such obligations.[160]

If a succession obligation has been duly constituted there seems no reason in principle why interdict should not be available as a remedy to, say, prevent an alteration of an existing testament; however, interdict is itself a remedy which is

[151] *Khosprowpour*, above n 141, [23] (Lord Ordinary (Turnbull)).

[152] TB Smith, *A Short Commentary on the Law of Scotland* (Edinburgh, W Green, 1962) 854.

[153] WW McBryde, *The Law of Contract in Scotland*, 3rd edn (Edinburgh, W Green, 2007) ch 23, para 8.

[154] *Highland and Universal Properties Ltd v Safeway* 2000 SC 297, 300–01 (Lord President (Rodger)).

[155] *Whyte and Mackay Ltd v Capstone International Inc* 2011 SC 221 [23] (Lord Hardie).

[156] *Rollo's Trs*, above n 139.

[157] ibid, 584–85 (Lord Moncrieff). In *De Lathouwer*, above n 135, the pursuer sought specific implement if the arrangement could be shown to be a *testamentary writing* (which it was not); the alternative case, based on breach of a contractual undertaking to test, sought only damages, which might suggest further reticence about claiming specific implement.

[158] See above nn 154 and 155.

[159] *Highland and Universal Properties Ltd*, above n 154, 300 (Lord President (Rodger)).

[160] *De Lathouwer*, above n 135.

subject to discretionary control,[161] and it is at least doubtful that the court would interdict a person from exercising his power to revoke a testament on pain of imprisonment for contempt, rather than order an award of damages. Likewise, the fact that interdict is preventive[162] and prohibitive makes it less useful in this context given the ease with which a testament might be altered. It might be more appropriate to seek to interdict the executor of the deceased from a course of action, such as disposing of a disputed piece of property, and seek reduction or partial reduction of the testament.

D. Revocation: Void or Voidable?

The authorities disclose a somewhat curious suggestion that by entering into a succession contract a testator makes his will irrevocable[163] and unalterable.[164] On one view such an interpretation would render interdict superfluous. However, it is difficult to see what *exactly* is meant by saying that the will is irrevocable: does this mean that the will *cannot* be altered or that it *ought* not to be altered? This poses questions about the extent of testamentary freedom, in particular the idea that all is ambulatory until the death of the testator.[165] Later authority suggests that a testament is always revocable until death; indeed it has been said that a clause within a testament purporting to make it irrevocable will not be effective.[166] One rationalisation of this line of authority would be that the clause within a testament is itself ambulatory as a testamentary writing, whereas a succession obligation constituted outwith a testament does not suffer from the same infirmity. A deeper conceptualisation might be that the document constituting the will itself can be altered, but its effects cannot; though it is not clear what that distinction would add. Intriguingly, there is authority which suggests that once a succession contract has been entered into any later contradictory deeds are 'ineffectual',[167] which suggests that such subsequent deeds which are inconsistent with an antecedent succession obligation are void. It is difficult to see how this can be so.[168]

[161] *Grahame v Magistrates of Kirkcaldy* (1882) 9 R (HL) 91, 91–92 (Lord Watson); *Ben Nevis Distillery (Fort William) Ltd v North British Aluminium Co* 1948 SC 592, 598 (Lord President (Cooper)).

[162] *Church Commissioners for England v Abbey National Plc* 1994 SC 651, 659–60 (Lord President (Hope)).

[163] In *Paterson v Paterson* (1893) 20 R 484, 487 the Lord Ordinary stated: '[The] authorities appear to establish that an *inter vivos* agreement to make a testament or grant a legacy will bar revocation of a will or legacy made in implement of it'. However, the interlocutor pronounced (486) speaks of reduction and so it is not clear if the later settlement in breach of the antecedent agreement was void or required to be deprived of any effect.

[164] W Forbes, *The Institutes of the Law of Scotland* (1722, 2012 reprint) 358.

[165] J Erskine, *An Institute of the Law of Scotland* (1773) III. 9. 5; Lord Kames, *Principles of Equity*, vol 1, 3rd edn (1778) 195.

[166] GJ Bell, *Principles of the Law of Scotland*, 4th edn (1839) § 1864; *Dougall v Dougall* (1789) Mor 15949.

[167] Stair, above n 138, III. 8. 33.

[168] Matters are different, if the argument is that an unconditional transfer has occurred, as opposed to an agreement about such a transfer or another form of obligation, because the transferor no longer

Another source suggests that the effect of such a contract is the same as a 'deed of gift delivered *in liege poustie*',[169] which suggests that the obligation is better characterised not as a legacy but as an *inter vivos* donation, but that approach does not provide much assistance with regard to the ability of the obligor to alter the terms of any subsequent testament in breach of that obligation.[170] Other secondary sources suggesting that an offending testament 'may be set aside' perhaps suggest it is voidable.[171]

E. Offside Goals

A recent case has confirmed the possibility of relying upon the 'offside-goals rule' in Scots law where there is an existing succession contract.[172] The 'offside-goals rule'[173] is that a personal right to receive a real right[174] held by a person cannot be prejudiced later by someone taking a subsequent real right if that later person knew of the pre-existing personal right or took the subsequent right gratuitously.[175] The title of the bad faith or gratuitous grantee is voidable at the instance of the person holding the antecedent personal right. The application of the rule in the context of a succession contract suggests that the debtor in such an arrangement's subsequent actions, which are incompatible with the underlying succession obligation, will create voidable titles in those who receive in bad faith or gratuitously. In most succession cases, as in *Wheeldon*,[176] it will be the gratuitousness limb of the 'offside-goals rule' that will render transfers (and deeds) voidable and susceptible to reduction,[177] because legatees under the subsequent inconsistent testament will rarely be onerous.

has *power* to act in a manner contrary to the initial grant: cp *Turnbull v Tawse* (1825) 1 W & S 80 (HL) with *Murison v Dick* (1854) 16 D 529 (IH). In *Curdy v Boyd* (1775) Mor 15946 it seems that the decision of the Court rested upon the ground that Curdy had effected a completed transfer, which could not be revoked by subsequent writings, and the observation 'besides, that *pacta de successione viventis* are valid by our law' seems to be *obiter*.

[169] Erskine, above n 165, III. 9. 6. '*Liege poustie*' being the term for someone in good health, as opposed to someone labouring under a sickness, which might attract the limitations of the law of the deathbed.

[170] It might be seen as a completed donation, which would take the subject of the donation outwith the estate (or patrimony) of the deceased, but this arguably conflates an obligation and a transfer of property.

[171] CN Fraser, 'Wills and Succession' in JL Wark (ed), *Encyclopaedia of the Laws of Scotland*, vol 15 (Edinburgh, W Green, 1933) para 1354.

[172] *Wheeldon's Excr v Spence's Excr* 2014 GWD 15-267. See also *Paterson*, above n 163.

[173] *Rodger (Buildings) Ltd v Fawdry* 1950 SC 483, 501 (Lord Justice-Clerk (Thomson)).

[174] *Wallace v Simmers* 1960 SC 255. *cf Advice Centre for Mortgages Ltd v McNicoll* 2006 SLT 591; *Gibson v Royal Bank of Scotland* 2009 SLT 444.

[175] The rule is itself controversial, its parameters contested.

[176] *Wheeldon*, above n 172.

[177] ibid, [20–24] (Lord Ordinary (McEwan)).

F. Ranking: Creditors, Forced Heirship and Legatees

A crucial question about such obligations is classificatory: are they debts, which will be deducted from the whole estate before distribution, or are they rights postponed to other claimants, such as children or spouses claiming 'legal rights'[178] or other legatees? One old case suggests such an obligation would be treated as a legacy,[179] and hence only falling due from the 'dead's part',[180] rather than as a debt which would be payable from the whole estate; but the report is far from clear.[181] The answer to this question is important for obvious reasons. The starting point for any enquiry must be an examination of the specific terms of the extra-testamentary obligation and any testament.[182] It is not easy to explain why a duly constituted obligation subsequently breached and triggering an award of damages should not be a simple debt, payable from the whole estate. Much the same can be said of the alternative remedy of specific implement if so ordered. Yet, allowing such claims on those terms would obviously prejudice other claimants, including those entitled to legal rights. It would be odd that a properly executed testament could not defeat legal rights, but that an obligation constituted by a contract or promise would have the potential to do so. Such unwelcome consequences might explain the courts' reticence to recognise the *actual constitution* of such arrangements in actual cases, while opining that they are valid in the abstract. One possible approach would be to follow the Commonwealth authority that such obligations do not necessarily prejudice dependants' discretionary awards from the courts.[183] Indeed, on one view, the fixed share entitlements of 'legal rights' have a stronger doctrinal claim to protection than the discretionary awards available under statutes.

By the same token, there is a potentially circular difficulty when it comes to distinguishing between one of these obligations and a legacy. Traditionally, the constitution of legacies has been conceptually distinct from the execution of a testament in that a legacy can be created outwith a testament.[184] A legacy created outside a testament is termed a 'codicil',[185] and is subject to the same formalities as a full testament.[186] But we have already seen that older Scottish authority

[178] The somewhat confusing name given to forced heirship rights in Scotland: children (or 'the issue') are entitled to the 'bairn's part' or '*legitim*', while surviving spouses are entitled to claim his *jus reliciti* or her *jus relictae*; statutory provisions exist giving similar rights to civil partners.

[179] '[O]bligement to leave a legacy, which was found an effectual legacy without further solemnity': Stair, above n 138, III. 8. 33.

[180] The part of the estate, which the deceased can transfer by testament, which is insulated from the claims of those with forced heirship rights in testate succession.

[181] *Houston v Houston* (1631) Mor 8049. See Stair, above n 138, III. 8. 33; Forbes, above n 164, 358.

[182] *cf Duguid v Caddall's Trs* (1831) 9 S 844, 846 n.

[183] See above, n 136.

[184] Erskine, above n 165, III. 9. 6.

[185] ibid.

[186] Requirements of Writing (Scotland) Act 1995, s 1(2)(c).

held that a contract to leave a legacy was treated as having created an effectual legacy.[187] There is authority suggesting that a prima facie testamentary writing will be treated as such and the onus is on the person claiming otherwise to demonstrate it is not a testamentary writing, but the authority is perhaps weaker than may first appear.[188]

IX. Conclusion

Scottish law recognises a number of different types of will-substitute, and the effectiveness of the various devices as will-substitutes can be variable. It is striking that few, if any, of these instruments can be said to represent clearly settled law. Furthermore, although there is scope for will-substitutes to be used in Scotland, many of the doctrines that could be used have fallen into disuse or were never really clearly expressed and utilised. It is not clear that there is any appetite to dust down existing mechanisms or develop new ones; likewise, those mechanisms that seem a little unclear seem more likely to be abandoned than developed or refined. Indeed, the potential uncertainty about the effect of a number of the more common will-substitutes is not encouraging. In particular, nominations under private or public pension and investment arrangements are under-theorised in Scotland (as elsewhere) and different conceptualisations could have markedly different results. Ultimately the effectiveness of will-substitutes will be determined according to the nascent and incomplete criteria and purposes outlined at the beginning of this chapter. It seems clear that there are Scottish will-substitutes which *could* meet many of those criteria, though whether anyone wants them is questionable. It might be a job for the jurist to market the potential solutions.

The topic raises deep questions about the entire law of succession and what objectives it should pursue. The relative lack of interest and use of will-substitutes as a coherent organising category in Scotland means that as a system it is far away from undertaking the second level question which the US appears to have reached—will-substitutes are so common that they no longer operate outside the traditional succession structures; rather the structures have been altered to accommodate and regulate them.[189] In Scotland the absence of that level of use leaves

[187] *Houston*, above n 181. The effect is rather like that of the equitable maxim: Equity looks on that as done which ought to be done; except here the legacy could be constituted in favour of someone who would be termed 'a volunteer' by English equity. Lord Kames cites the following principle: 'Equity holds a deed to be granted where it ought to be granted', *Principles of Equity*, vol 2, 3rd edn (1778) 501.

[188] *Sim v Sim* 1915 2 SLT 201, 203 (Lord Ordinary (Ormidale)). Lord Ormidale cited *Stoddart v Grant* (1852) 1 Macq 163 (HL); (1852) 15 D (HL) 23 as authority for this proposition, indeed the headnote of Macqueen's report of *Stoddart* makes the same claim. However, so far as I can see, Lord Truro's speech in the House of Lords (not reproduced in Dunlop's report) does not make this point.

[189] See ch 1 above.

will-substitutes a somewhat untouched subject as a matter of systematising the different mechanisms. In turn, the absence of systemic appreciation means that there is no overarching regulation: should, for example, the rules about implied revocation and the unworthy heir which are applicable to testamentary writings be applied to will-substitutes? Likewise, the lack of a systemic approach to will-substitutes explains why many of the mechanisms have an uncertain fit within the broader law of succession. An example of this is the succession contract, which might be interpreted in such a way as to defeat a testament and forced heirship creditors. I suspect that if there were an explosion of will-substitutes, especially less familiar ones, the courts would be tempted to lean on the rules relating to testaments in an attempt to maintain the overall policy choices already embedded within the existing law of succession, but that is rather speculative. As is often the case where the law is uncertain, the situation in Scotland can be seen as unfortunate and inconsistent, dangerous even; or, the Scottish position might be seen as pregnant with opportunity for some juristic entrepreneurship.

5

Will-Substitutes in New Zealand and Australia

NICOLA PEART* AND PRUE VINES

I. Introduction

Australia and New Zealand are often bracketed together, for good reason. They are both British colonies, settled in the late-eighteenth and early-nineteenth centuries.[1] They are geographically proximate at the bottom of the world and, when Australia became a federal state in 1900, New Zealand considered joining the federation.[2] Both colonies inherited English common law and looked to Britain for guidance in the development of their laws.[3] They inherited the British system of land tenure, with its doctrine of estates in land and the Crown being the ultimate owner of the land. But they did not have separate courts for common law, equity and ecclesiastical matters. A single court was established in each of the colonies with general jurisdiction.[4]

* I am grateful to Andrew Snoddy JD, Research Assistant, Faculty of Law, University of Otago for his assistance in locating historical material for this paper.

[1] Colonisation of Australia began in 1788 with the settlement of New South Wales as a penal colony: JM Bennett and Alex Castles, *A Source Book of Australian Legal History* (Sydney, Law Book Co, 1979) 1–5. New Zealand was annexed to New South Wales in 1839 and became a separate colony in 1841 following the signing of the Treaty of Waitangi in 1840 between the chiefs of the indigenous Maori tribes and the British Crown: see P Joseph, *Constitutional and Administrative Law in New Zealand* (Wellington, Brookers, 2007) 138.

[2] The Commonwealth of Australia Constitution Act 1900 (UK) established Australia as a federal state comprising New South Wales, Queensland, Victoria, Tasmania, South Australia and Western Australia. The Constitution made provision for New Zealand to join the Commonwealth of Australia, but a Royal Commission recommended against it, citing loss of legislative and financial independence and socio-economic and political differences: see *Report of the Royal Commission on Federation* (Wellington, 1901).

[3] The reception of English succession law in Australia and New Zealand is outlined in N Peart and P Vines, 'Intestate Succession Law in Australia and New Zealand' in KGC Reid, MJ de Waal and R Zimmermann (eds), *Comparative Succession Law, volume 2. Intestate Succession* (Oxford, OUP, 2015) 349.

[4] R Croucher and P Vines, *Succession: Families, Property and Death*, 4th edn (Australia, LexisNexis Butterworths, 2013) 1.44. In New Zealand the Supreme Court Ordinance of 1844 gave the Supreme Court of New Zealand general jurisdiction.

Both Australia and New Zealand have high rates of testation at about 50 per cent of people dying.[5] Yet, will-substitutes are widely used in both countries, albeit in different ways and for different reasons. While succession and estate law is similar in Australia and New Zealand, different social and fiscal legislation is responsible for different forms of will-substitute.

Aside from joint tenancies and life insurance payments, which are common in both countries, the distinctive will-substitutes in New Zealand are the relationship property entitlement that surviving spouses, civil union partners and de facto partners (cohabitants) can claim on death under the Property (Relationships) Act 1976 (PRA (NZ)) and *inter vivos* trusts, which are widely used in New Zealand, inter alia, to avoid family provision and relationship property claims. Although they are settled *inter vivos*, in practice they operate as will-substitutes in New Zealand, because the settlor is able to benefit from the trust assets in much the same way as before the settlement. Pension schemes are less likely to operate as a will-substitute in New Zealand than in Australia, where the compulsory superannuation scheme is the most significant will-substitute. Joint tenancies and trusts are also common in Australia, but their effectiveness as a will-substitute may be constrained by notional estate provisions to protect family members from loss of support following the death of their spouse, partner or parent.[6]

Donationes mortis causa are not a common means of transmitting property on death in either country and, unlike England, they have not yet been upheld in respect of land.[7] Constructive trusts[8] and, in New Zealand, the Law Reform (Testamentary Promises) Act 1949 (NZ)[9] make it largely unnecessary to argue the existence of a *donatio mortis causa*.[10] Contracts to leave property by will are

[5] The 2013 survey by Newspoll for the NSW Trustee & Guardian showed a testation rate of 59% in New South Wales. In 2012, 79% of Queenslanders over the age of 35 and 98% of those over 70 had a current will. In New Zealand between 2012 and 2014 there were between 29,568 and 31,963 deaths per year and between 14,896 and 15,583 wills admitted to probate or annexed to letters of administration, a testation rate of just over 50%.

[6] The Uniform Succession Law, which was the product of co-operation of all the States and Territories through their Law Reform Commissions, includes notional estate provisions, but so far New South Wales is the only State to adopt them: Succession Act 2006.

[7] *Wilson v Paniani* [1996] 3 NZLR 378. In *Hobbes v NSW Trustee & Guardian* [2014] NSWSC 570 the Court referred to *Sen v Headley* [1991] Ch 425, but did not have to decide the matter because the indicia of title had not been provided. For England see ch 3 above, p 63 and for the US ch 1 above, p 18.

[8] In Australia unconscionability is the basis for imposing a constructive trust, *Baumgartner v Baumgartner* (1987) 1 FLR 915; 164 CLR 137 (HCA). In New Zealand a constructive trust is imposed if the legal owner and the applicant had a reasonable expectation that the beneficial ownership of the real and/or personal property would be shared because of the direct or indirect contributions made by the applicant to the property in question, *Lankow v Rose* [1995] 1 NZLR 277 (CA).

[9] The Law Reform (Testamentary Promises) Act 1949 (NZ) empowers the court to enforce a deceased person's promise to make testamentary provision for the applicant as a reward for the applicant's services to the deceased; *Samuels v Atkinson* [2010] NZFLR 980 (CA) enforcing a promise of shares; *Byrne v Bishop* (2001) 20 FRNZ 609 (CA) enforcing a promise of farms.

[10] See, eg *Hayward v Giordani* [1983] NZLR 140 (CA) where a constructive trust was imposed against the trustees of the estate of the deceased to give effect to a common intention that the home be equally shared by the deceased and her partner.

perhaps more common, especially in Australia where until recently they were seen as an effective means of removing property from the estate. But they no longer necessarily take priority over family provision claims and are thus not a reliable will-substitute.[11]

II. New Zealand

New Zealanders commonly use joint tenancies and life insurance policies as will-substitutes to provide for a surviving spouse or partner or for children. In the context of second relationships, a life insurance policy may be intended to provide for children of an earlier relationship or to protect the interests of the surviving spouse of a second marriage. However, as explained in the next two sections, these arrangements are vulnerable to claims under the PRA (NZ).

A. Property Entitlements of Surviving Spouses and Partners

Unlike England and Australia, New Zealand has given surviving spouses, and more recently de facto partners (cohabitants), the right to claim their relationship property entitlement on death as well as on separation. On death, this claim determines the parties' respective property entitlements prior to the application of succession law to the deceased estate. It was first introduced for spouses by the Matrimonial Property Act 1963 (NZ).[12] Under that Act the division of property was at the discretion of the court and based on the spouses' respective contributions to the property in dispute.[13] The focus on contributions to the property usually meant that the parties' assets were unequally divided, with the primary income earner, normally the husband, generally taking the larger share.[14] Domestic and other non-monetary contributions, usually provided by the wife, carried less weight and their attribution to the acquisition, enhancement, or retention of non-domestic assets was not appreciated.[15]

[11] *Barns v Barns* [2003] HCA 9; 214 CLR 169; 196 ALR 65; *Hamilton v Hamilton* [2003] NZFLR 883; *Bristow v Smith* [2013] NZHC 2866. For Scotland see ch 4 above.

[12] Both the surviving spouse and the estate had the right to apply for an order dividing the parties' matrimonial property after death. Applications by the estate were often made to reduce the estate below the level where estate duty was payable, as in *Re Mora* [1988] 1 NZLR 214 (CA).

[13] Matrimonial Property Act 1963 (NZ), ss 5 and 6.

[14] M Henaghan and N Peart, 'Relationship Property Appeals in the New Zealand Court of Appeal 1958–2008– The Elusiveness of Equality' in R Bigwood (ed), *The Permanent New Zealand Court of Appeal* (Oxford, Hart Publishing, 2009) 99.

[15] eg *E v E* [1971] NZLR 859 (CA); *Haldane v Haldane* [1975] 1 NZLR 672 (CA). The new Act did not persuade the courts to adopt a presumption of equal sharing in applications under the Matrimonial Property Act 1963 (NZ): see *Re Mora*, above n 12, 217 and *Slater v Lowes* (1993) 10 FRNZ 286, 297.

Dissatisfaction with the courts' failure to appreciate the value and importance of non-monetary contributions to a marriage persuaded Parliament to adopt a new Matrimonial Property Act in 1976 in which marriage was characterised as a partnership to which both spouses were presumed to contribute equally, albeit in different ways. The Act introduced a community property regime based on a presumption of equal sharing[16] of the couple's 'matrimonial property': the family home and family chattels, whenever they were acquired, and any property acquired during or for the benefit of the marriage other than property acquired by gift, inheritance or distribution from a trust settled by a third party.[17] But this new regime applied only on separation.[18] The old Matrimonial Property Act 1963 (NZ) with its property-based contributions and old fashioned attitudes to domestic contributions continued in force[19] until the 1976 Act was amended in 2001 to apply on death as well.[20]

De facto partners were included at the same time and given the same rights as married couples, if the partners had lived together as a couple for at least three years.[21] The Act was renamed the Property (Relationships) Act 1976 (NZ) (PRA (NZ)) to take account of the inclusion of de facto relationships.[22] Matrimonial property is now called 'relationship property', and is still defined to capture the family home and chattels as well as the property produced by the partnership. Several other aspects of the regime have been changed, mostly to strengthen the equal sharing regime.[23] It applies unless the parties have formally contracted out of the Act.[24]

The right to claim arises only when the marriage, and now the de facto relationship or civil union, ends because the parties have separated or one of them has died.[25] During the relationship each party is free to deal with their own assets

[16] Equal sharing did not apply if the marriage was of less than three years' duration, Matrimonial Property Act 1976 (NZ), s 13. Domestic property was not equally shared, if extraordinary circumstances existed that made equal sharing repugnant to justice (s 14) and, in the case of non-domestic matrimonial property, if the contribution of one spouse was clearly greater than that of the other spouse (s 15).

[17] Matrimonial Property Act 1976 (NZ), ss 8–10.

[18] ibid, s 25(2).

[19] ibid, s 57(4).

[20] Property (Relationships) Amendment Act 2001 (NZ), which added Part VIII to deal with relationships ending on death.

[21] PRA (NZ), ss 4, 4C, 14A and 85. The definition of a de facto relationship is in s 2D. Civil union partners were included in 2005, Property (Relationships) Amendment Act 2005 (NZ).

[22] Following the adoption of the Civil Union Act (NZ) in 2004, the PRA (NZ) was amended to include civil union partners on the same basis as spouses, Property (Relationships) Amendment Act 2005 (NZ). Civil unions have the equivalent status to marriage and can be entered by same sex and heterosexual couples.

[23] eg the distinction between the exceptions to equal sharing for domestic and non-domestic property referred to in n 16 above was removed. In relationships of three or more years duration all relationship property is divided equally unless extraordinary circumstances exist that make equal sharing repugnant to justice, PRA (NZ), s 13. This is a notoriously difficult standard to meet.

[24] Matrimonial Property Act 1976 (NZ), s 21 and PRA (NZ), s 21.

[25] PRA (NZ), s 25.

as they wish.[26] Hence, the current regime is referred to as a 'deferred community property' regime. It applies on death at the election of the surviving spouse or partner. If the survivor wishes to proceed under the Act, he or she must elect 'option A'.[27] If the survivor chooses not to proceed under the Act or fails to make a choice, 'option B' applies.[28] In that case the surviving spouse or partner retains the property he or she owns, takes any jointly owned assets by survivorship and inherits such provision as is available under the deceased's will or the intestacy rules. The usual reason for a surviving spouse or partner to apply for a division of relationship property is where the deceased owned most of the couple's assets and the deceased's will is vulnerable to family provision claims from other family members, such as the deceased's children from an earlier relationship.[29]

If the surviving spouse or partner elects to apply for a division of relationship property, the effect is to vest in the survivor and in the estate of the deceased their respective shares of the relationship property. Property is thus transmitted to the surviving spouse or partner on death of the other spouse or partner, outside the will. Prior to the abolition of estate duty in 1993,[30] any property vested in the surviving spouse under the Matrimonial Property Act 1963 (NZ) did not form part of the dutiable estate.[31] Under the PRA (NZ), the application for division takes priority over any inheritance rights or family provision claims.[32] Electing to proceed under the Act thus operates as a will-substitute.

The consequence of applying for division is that the surviving spouse or partner forfeits whatever provision would have been available under the deceased's will or the intestacy rules, unless the deceased expressed a contrary intention in his or her will or the court reinstates the inheritance to avoid injustice.[33] Anecdotal evidence suggests that few testators include a contrary intention clause in their will, either out of ignorance or because they reject the likelihood of such a claim. The court is also rarely asked to reinstate the inheritance.[34] If the relationship property entitlement is inadequate, the surviving spouse or partner may in addition make an

[26] ibid, s 19. The court may prevent a disposition if it is satisfied that the disposition is intended to defeat the rights of one of the parties under the Act, PRA (NZ), s 43. Under s 44 the court has the power to set aside a disposition that was made to defeat the rights of a party under the Act.

[27] PRA (NZ), s 61. The election must be made by completing a prescribed notice of election after receiving legal advice about the effect and implications of the choice, PRA (NZ), s 65. The election must be made within six months of death or grant of administration, whichever is the later, PRA (NZ), s 62.

[28] PRA (NZ), s 68. The choice of option is irrevocable. However, the surviving spouse may apply to the court to set aside the choice of option under certain circumstances: PRA (NZ), s 69.

[29] *Flathaug v Weaver* [2003] NZFLR 730 (CA).

[30] The Estate Duty Abolition Act 1993 (NZ) retained estate duty only for persons dying before 17 December 1992 and the Estate Duty Repeal Act 1999 (NZ) repealed estate duty.

[31] Estate and Gift Duties Act 1968 (NZ), s 75A; *Re Mora*, above n 12.

[32] PRA (NZ), s 78.

[33] ibid, ss 76 and 77.

[34] *B v Adams* (2005) 25 FRNZ 778 (FC) and *OPS v Estate LNS* FC Blenheim FAM-2004-006-302 303, 18 February 2005 are rare examples.

application under the Family Protection Act 1955 (NZ) for further provision from the estate.[35]

B. Joint Tenancies and Family Provision

Couples commonly arrange to hold their homes and bank accounts as joint tenants. On the death of the first spouse or partner, the jointly owned assets are transmitted to the surviving spouse or partner, bypassing the estate of the deceased spouse or partner. The surviving spouse or partner might receive the bulk of the couple's assets this way, in which case he or she is unlikely to apply for a division of relationship property under the PRA (NZ). However, other family members, in particular children of a deceased's former relationship, may override this choice by calling on the personal representative of the deceased to apply for a division of relationship property to recover the deceased's relationship property entitlement for the estate.[36] Such an application normally has the effect of severing any joint tenancies and preventing the surviving spouse or partner from taking other assets by survivorship, such as the benefit of a life insurance policy.[37] Those assets are included in the pool of relationship property and divided between the survivor and the estate.

Unlike the surviving spouse or partner, the personal representative cannot apply for a division as of right. Leave is required, which the court may only grant if refusing leave would cause serious injustice.[38] In *Public Trust v Whyman* the Court of Appeal held that leave should be granted whenever a meritorious claim would otherwise be defeated.[39] In that case the purpose of pursuing a relationship property claim was to enable the deceased's children, aged 12 and 14, to receive financial support from their father's estate. After an acrimonious divorce the children's father and his new partner deliberately settled their property as joint tenancies to prevent his children from receiving anything from their father's estate. While this was a particularly deserving case to force a severance of the joint tenancy, there have been other cases where the persons for whose benefit the application for division was sought were neither dependent on the deceased, nor in financial need.[40]

[35] PRA (NZ), s 57; eg *De Muth v Lee* [2005] NZFLR 281.

[36] PRA (NZ), s 88(2).

[37] *De Muth v Lee*, above n 35 (joint bank account); *Crotty v Williams* FC Hamilton FAM-2002-19-1082; FP19/271/03, 29 August 2005 (jointly owned family home). PRA (NZ), s 83 gives the court discretion not to classify jointly owned assets as relationship property; *B v Adams*, above n 34, where the couple's holiday home and family chattels were classified as the widow's separate property.

[38] PRA (NZ), s 88(2).

[39] *Public Trust v Whyman* [2005] 2 NZLR 696 (CA).

[40] *Horne v Public Trust* HC Nelson CIV-2010-442-44, 4 May 2010 (leave declined); *Morgan v Public Trust* HC Auckland CIV-2006-404-3636, 20 November 2006 (leave granted); *Public Trust v Relph* [2009] 2 NZLR 819 (HC) (leave granted). In *H v T* HC Christchurch CIV-2006-409-2615, 5 June 2007 the Court granted leave to the personal representative of the murdered wife to prevent her killer husband from retaining all of the couple's relationship property.

The Family Protection Act 1955 (NZ) empowers the court to order such provision out of the estate as it thinks fit if the deceased has not made adequate provision for the claimant's 'proper maintenance and support'.[41] The deceased's spouse or partner, children and grandchildren (regardless of age), as well as step-children and parents subject to certain conditions, are eligible to make a family protection claim.[42] Financial need is not a requirement. Adult, financially independent children commonly succeed if the deceased has failed to recognise the importance of the parent–child relationship.[43] In *Williams v Aucutt* the Court of Appeal explained what was meant by 'proper maintenance and support':

> 'Support' is an additional and wider term than 'maintenance'. In using the composite expression, and requiring 'proper' maintenance and support, the legislation recognises that a broader approach is required and the authorities referred to establish that moral and ethical considerations are to be taken into account in determining the scope of the duty. 'Support' is used in its wider dictionary sense of 'sustaining, providing comfort'. A child's path through life is supported not simply by financial provision to meet economic needs and contingencies but also by recognition of belonging to the family and of having been an important part of the overall life of the deceased. Just what provision will constitute proper support in this latter respect is a matter of judgment in all the circumstances of the particular case. It may take the form of lifetime gifts or a bequest of family possessions precious to its members and often part of the family history. And where there is no economic need it may also be met by a legacy of a moderate amount. On the other hand, where the estate comprises the accumulation of the family assets and is more than sufficient to meet other needs, provision so small as to leave a justifiable sense of exclusion from participation in the family estate might not amount to proper support for a family member.[44]

If a child has a meritorious claim based on this test, which would be unenforceable because the deceased's surviving spouse or partner owns all the assets or acquired them by survivorship, the court is likely to grant leave for a division of relationship property to recover property for the estate to satisfy the child's family

[41] Family Protection Act 1955 (NZ), s 4. New Zealand was the first country in the common law world to give the courts power to override the terms of a will, Testator's Family Maintenance Act 1900 (NZ). The rationale for the introduction of this Act was to prevent dependence on the state, see 1900 New Zealand Parliamentary Debates, vol 111, cols 503–04. But within a decade, in *Re Allardice* [1910] 29 NZLR 959, the wording of the Act was construed more liberally to encompass a breach of moral duty in which destitution was not a prerequisite.

[42] Family Protection Act 1955 (NZ), s 3. Stepchildren are eligible only if they were being maintained by the deceased immediately before the deceased died, s 3(d). A parent is eligible if he or she was being maintained by the deceased immediately before death or if the deceased leaves no surviving spouse, partner or child of his or her marriage, civil union or de facto relationship, s 3(1A).

[43] *Williams v Aucutt* [2000] NZFLR 532 (CA) is New Zealand's leading case on this point. The deceased had left 5% of her $950,000 estate to the applicant daughter and 95% to her other daughter because the applicant daughter was financially well positioned whereas the other daughter was dependent on the state for support. The CA doubled the provision for the applicant to recognise the special bond between parent and child.

[44] *Williams v Aucutt* [2000] NZFLR 532, [52].

protection claim.[45] Joint tenancies between couples are thus not always a secure will-substitute in New Zealand. But, where the joint tenants are not a couple, such as a parent and child, there is nothing in the Family Protection Act (NZ) to force a severance of the joint tenancy. Nor does the court have power to include such property in the deceased estate on a notional basis for family provision purposes.[46] The survivorship rule applies regardless of the adverse effect it may have on the financial needs of the deceased's family members.

C. Trusts

The risk of claims under the PRA (NZ), both on separation and on death, and the vulnerability of estates to claims under the Family Protection Act (NZ) are common reasons for property owners in New Zealand to transfer their major assets, including their home, into a discretionary trust during their lifetime.[47] The courts' liberal approach to family protection claims and the unpredictability of awards is of particular concern to property owners wishing to favour some family members over others, such as preferring the second spouse over the children of a former marriage or differentiating between children. Trusts allow property owners to control the destination and distribution of their assets after death without court interference. Property transferred into trust cannot be clawed back into the settlor's estate to satisfy family protection claims, not even if the trust was settled to defeat such claims.[48] Unlike some jurisdictions in Australia, New Zealand courts have no power to designate a notional estate for purposes of making family provision orders.[49] The PRA (NZ) does have a claw-back mechanism, but only for dispositions that were made with the intention of defeating the relationship

[45] *Re Williams* [2004] 2 NZLR 132 (HC), where the Court declined leave to apply for a division because no serious injustice would result, if the daughter from the deceased's earlier marriage could not enforce her family protection award as she was not in financial need, was criticised by the CA in *Public Trust v Whyman*, above n 39 both in terms of the test applied and the outcome. See also *Morgan v Public Trust*, above n 40 and *Public Trust v Relph*, above n 40.

[46] See, eg *Morgan v Bohm* [2013] NSWSC 145 and the discussion below.

[47] The 2013 census showed an increase in homes held in trust from 12.3% in 2006 to 14.8% in 2013, Statistics New Zealand. The census does not collect data on whether the home is held as a joint tenancy.

[48] See, eg *Beaven v Beaven* [2015] NZFC 611, where the parents arranged with one of their sons to transfer the remainder of their farm to a trust for his and their benefit to protect it from challenge by their other four children after the parents' death.

[49] New South Wales introduced the concept of a notional estate into its Family Protection Act in 1982. As part of the Uniform Succession Law Project by the Australian jurisdictions, the Queensland Law Reform Commission produced a report recommending that notional estate provisions be included in all jurisdictions; National Committee for Uniform Succession Laws, *Family Provision: Supplementary Report to the Standing Committee of Attorneys General*, Report 58 (July 2004). See further Croucher and Vines, above n 4, 15.26–15.31.

property rights of the claimant spouse or partner.[50] Trusts are therefore a very effective mechanism to avoid such claims.

Technically, of course, an *inter vivos* trust is not a will-substitute because it takes effect during the settlor's lifetime, not on the settlor's death. In practice, however, family trusts in New Zealand operate as will-substitutes. It is common for owners to settle their major assets on a discretionary trust of which they are the trustees as well as the primary beneficiaries. They control the trust through their trusteeship or by retaining the power to appoint and remove trustees. In their capacity as trustee they have the power to distribute income and capital to themselves as primary discretionary beneficiaries. But unless and until they do so, discretionary beneficiaries can hold themselves out as not beneficially owning any of the trust assets. They merely have a hope or expectation that the trustees will exercise their discretion in their favour.[51] By controlling the trust the settlors are able to enjoy all of the benefits of the assets they have transferred into trust. They treat the trust assets as if they still fully own them, often in complete disregard of their fiduciary duties. They do not hold trustee meetings; they do not pass resolutions; they may not even have financial accounts or a separate bank account for the trust. Unless the trust has income earning assets, they will not be required to file a tax return for the trust. There is often nothing to alert an outsider to a change in property ownership. The home will still be in the settlors' names if there is no independent trustee. The settlors still live in it pursuant to a right of occupation granted by themselves as trustees and they make all the decisions in relation to the home. Provided there was a genuine intention to create a trust, as there usually is, poor administration will not result in a finding that the trust is a sham.[52] When the settlors die, the trust assets become available to the next generation of beneficiaries, outside the estate.

In many countries trusts have tax implications, particularly a trust that allows the settlor to control the trust for his or her own benefit. Fiscally the settlor may be treated as still owning the assets held in such a trust. But in New Zealand settling or holding property on trust is now largely fiscally neutral.[53] There is no capital gains tax or stamp duty, so the cost of transferring assets into trust is low. The top personal tax rate and the trustee tax rate are both set at 33 per cent.[54] Since the

[50] PRA (NZ), s 44 allows the court to set aside a disposition of property intended to defeat the relationship property rights of a spouse or partner, provided the recipient received the property otherwise than in good faith and for valuable consideration; *Gray v Gray* [2013] NZHC 2890; *SMW v MC* [2013] NZHC 396, [2014] NZFLR 71.

[51] *Hunt v Muollo* [2003] 2 NZLR 322 (CA) and *Johns v Johns* [2004] 3 NZLR 202 (CA); *Nation v Nation* [2005] 3 NZLR 46 (CA); *Kain v Hutton* [2008] 3 NZLR 589 (SC).

[52] *Official Assignee v Wilson* [2008] 3 NZLR 45; *Clayton v Clayton* [2015] NZCA 30.

[53] S Tomlinson and G Tubb, 'Tax Planning and Trusts—Drawing the Line' presented at the New Zealand CLE Ltd Conference, *Trusts Conference 2015* (Auckland and Wellington, 2015) 141.

[54] That was not the case between 2000 and 2010, when the top personal tax rate was 39% and the trustee tax rate 33%; Income Tax Act 1994 (NZ), sch 1A, cls 4 and 9 and sch 1B, as amended in 1999, established the misalignment between the personal and trustee tax rates. The two tax rates were aligned with effect from 1 October 2010, Income Tax Act 2007 (NZ), sch 1, as amended in 2010. Tax avoidance

abolition of estate duty in 1993, settlors can continue to benefit from the property they settled on trust without those assets being included in their notional estate on death. Furthermore, since the abolition of gift duty in 2011, property owners have been able to divest themselves of all their assets in one go.[55] They can therefore transfer the bulk of their assets into trust and yet continue to benefit from the assets through the trust as if nothing had changed. Given that fiscal environment, there is an obvious attraction in having a trust. There is no register of trusts in New Zealand, but estimates based on filed tax returns and the types of property commonly transferred into trust suggest that there may be more than 400,000 trusts in New Zealand.[56] In a population of 4.5 million, this number of trusts puts New Zealand at a much higher rate of trusts per head of population than Australia, England or Canada.[57] That said, it is unclear how many of these are discretionary trusts of the type described above.

Succession planning and protection of assets from claims by creditors, spouses and partners, and family provision obligations are common reasons for settling property on trust.[58] Legitimate claimants have relatively few remedies. Creditors can rely on the Property Law Act 2007 (NZ) and the Insolvency Act 2006 (NZ) to set aside dispositions to trusts, but they are time limited unless the dispositions were made with the intention to defeat creditors' rights.[59] Spouses and partners

was identified as an issue and anti-avoidance measures were adopted, which were used to prosecute people using trusts for income splitting purposes, *Penny and Hooper v Commissioner of Inland Revenue* [2011] NZSC 85, [2012] 1 NZLR 433. Also, the ability to use trusts to divert income to minor beneficiaries, who were on a lower tax rate, was significantly curtailed in 2001 when such income was taxed at a flat rate of 33%, Income Tax Act 1994 (NZ), s HH 3A, as amended by the Taxation (Beneficiary Income of Minors, Services-Related Payments and Remedial Matters) Act 2001 (NZ).

[55] Taxation (Tax Administration and Remedial Matters) Act 2011 (NZ), s 245 repealed gift duty for gifts made on or after 1 October 2011. Prior to the abolition of gift duty, owners commonly structured a settlement on trust as a sale with a debt back to the settlors, which was then forgiven in annual instalments of $27,000, the maximum amount that could be gifted without incurring gift duty. It slowed down the alienation of assets, frequently leaving a debt owing to the estate against which a family protection claim could be made, see M Littlewood, 'The History of Death Duties and Gift Duty in New Zealand' (2012) 18 *New Zealand Journal of Taxation Law and Policy* 66 explores the reasons for introducing, modifying and eventually repealing these taxes.

[56] Tax returns filed in respect of estates and trusts in New Zealand increased from 145,900 in March 2001 to 247,700 in March 2010. It dropped down to 238,700 in 2012 and rose again to 240,300 in 2013. Anecdotal evidence suggests that many trusts do not have to file tax returns because they hold only non-income earning assets, such as the family home and holiday home.

[57] See New Zealand Law Commission, *Review of the Law of Trusts—Some Issues with the Use of Trusts in New Zealand* (NZLC IP20, 2010) 7, where the comparatively high use of trusts in New Zealand is discussed.

[58] Eligibility for asset and means-tested state support has also been a common reason for owners divesting themselves of property to a discretionary trust. However, the rigorous use of statutory powers to look through trusts is removing this justification for having a trust, B Patterson, 'Residential Care Subsidies—Problems and Puzzles' and 'Commentary' on this paper by T Donnelly, Senior Solicitor Ministry of Social Development, presented at the New Zealand Law Society CLE Ltd Conference, 'Trusts—Best Practice in 2013' (Wellington and Auckland, 2013) 133 and 159 respectively.

[59] Property Law Act 2007 (NZ), s 348 and Insolvency Act 2006 (NZ), sub-pt 7, 'Irregular transactions before adjudication'.

can also apply to have dispositions set aside if they can show that the dispositions were made to defeat their relationship property rights.[60] In the absence of such evidence, trust assets are generally safe from claims under the PRA (NZ).[61] That Act applies only to property that the parties beneficially own according to the general law.[62] Family provision claimants are also limited to the assets beneficially owned by the deceased at the time of death. Trusts are therefore a very effective mechanism to control the disposition of property after the settlor's death and hence a popular will-substitute.

Trusts are also commonly used to hold land of the indigenous Maori people. Land is of special significance to Maori people.[63] It is seen as providing a spiritual link to their ancestors, which limits their rights in scope and time. Traditionally, only those persons with an ancestral connection to the land could be given use of it, which tended to preclude its permanent alienation. After New Zealand was colonised, Maori customary rights to land were converted into common law title to facilitate alienation to the settlers. Most Maori land is now freehold. To accommodate customary rights and the interests of the many descendants with an ancestral connection to the land, the Te Ture Whenua Maori Act 1993 (NZ) established special Maori land trusts under the supervision of the Maori Land Court.[64] These trusts prevent individual owners from leaving their land to some family members to the exclusion of others. Their purpose is to retain the land for the benefit of all the descendants and, where possible, to facilitate economic use of the land.

[60] PRA (NZ), s 44.

[61] However, if the parties were married or in a civil union and the trust was an ante-nuptial or post-nuptial settlement, the court may make orders in respect of the trust under the Family Proceedings Act 1980, s 182 to give effect to the parties' reasonable expectations of the trust when it was settled; *Ward v Ward* [2010] 2 NZLR 31 (SC).

[62] PRA (NZ), s 2 defines 'owner' as 'the person who, apart from this Act, is the beneficial owner of the property under any enactment or rule of common law or equity'. 'Property' is defined as including real and personal property, any estate or interest in such property, any debt or chose in action and any other right or interest. Although ownership is defined by reference to the general law, the courts have pursued a range of unconventional arguments to access trust assets to prevent trusts undermining the social policy of the equal sharing regime, see N Peart, M Henaghan and G Kelly, 'Trusts and Relationship Property in New Zealand' (2011) 17 *Trusts & Trustees* 866. The most recent example is *Clayton v Clayton*, above n 52, where the CA held that the husband's power to add and remove beneficiaries was property and equated to the value of the trust assets. The Supreme Court has granted leave to appeal this ruling, *Clayton v Clayton* [2015] NZSC 84.

[63] J Ruru, 'Implications for Maori' in N Peart, M Briggs and M Henaghan (eds), *Relationship Property on Death* (Wellington, Brookers, 2004) ch 16.

[64] The Ture Whenua Maori Act 1993 (NZ) established five types of trust, each with a distinctive purpose. The most common trust is the Ahu Whenua trust, the purpose of which is to promote the use and administration of the land in the interests of the Maori landowners. It often has a commercial purpose. The Whenua trust enables the whanau (family) to bring together their interests in land for the benefit of themselves and their descendants.

D. Pensions

New Zealand has a state funded superannuation scheme governed by the New Zealand Superannuation and Retirement Income Act 2001 (NZ). It entitles all New Zealand citizens or permanent residents to a pension from the age of 65, provided they normally live in New Zealand and have done so for at least 10 years after reaching the age of 20. At least five of those 10 years must have been after their fiftieth birthday.[65] While the entitlement is universal, the fortnightly rate depends on the recipient's other income and whether they are single and living alone or married or in a de facto relationship.[66] As everyone is personally entitled to New Zealand Superannuation, nobody derives any benefit on the death of another. Payment simply ceases when a superannuant dies. If the deceased had a spouse or partner who was also receiving New Zealand Superannuation, he or she continues to do so, but at the rate of a single person. This pension scheme therefore does not operate as a will-substitute.

New Zealand Superannuation is the sole or primary source of income for 60 per cent of people over the age of 65.[67] It is based on the average after-tax wage, which is not particularly generous.[68] Income earners are thus encouraged to save for their retirement. To that end Parliament introduced KiwiSaver in 2007, a voluntary retirement savings scheme for all employees, which requires employers to make contributions and gives members tax credits and, until May 2015, a $1,000 tax-free start-up contribution to new members.[69] In 2013 this scheme had 2.2 million members, which is almost half the population.[70] KiwiSaver is not a will-substitute either, because on death the contributors' savings are paid into their estate.[71]

There are other pension schemes that do operate as will-substitutes. Several schemes pay death benefits directly to the contributor's surviving spouse or partner and minor children, giving the member no power to nominate an alternative beneficiary.[72] However, some schemes do allow the member to surrender up to

[65] New Zealand Superannuation and Retirement Income Act 2001 (NZ), ss 7 and 8.

[66] The rates are set out in the New Zealand Superannuation and Retirement Income Act 2001 (NZ), sch 1.

[67] For 40% of the population it is the sole source of retirement income and for 20% it constitutes 80% of their income, see Commission for Financial Literacy and Retirement Income, *Focusing on the Future—Report to Government of the 2013 Review of Retirement Income Policies* (Wellington, 2013) 27.

[68] The weekly amount payable to a couple is currently 66% of the average wage after tax. In addition, the state provides free or heavily subsidised health and disability services, subsidised housing for those unable to afford to house themselves, a no-fault accident compensation scheme for personal injuries, default support for residential care as well as other subsidies for the elderly, see Commission for Financial Literacy and Retirement Income, above n 67, 20–24.

[69] KiwiSaver Act 2006 (NZ), s 3. The Government's $1000 tax-free contribution for new members of KiwiSaver was abolished on 21 May 2015.

[70] Commission for Financial Literacy and Retirement Income, above n 67, 62.

[71] KiwiSaver Act 2006 (NZ), sch 1, cl 9.

[72] eg the Government Superannuation Fund Act 1956 (NZ), s 45 entitles the surviving spouse or partner to receive an annuity of half the retiring allowance that the contributor was receiving prior to death or payment of the contributor's contributions less any amount received by the contributor prior

half of their annual pension in exchange for a lifetime annuity to be paid to a designated person.[73] The annuity is calculated on an actuarial basis to avoid any increase or decrease in the fund's liabilities. The member's decision to surrender is irrevocable once the first payment has been made to the designated person. On the death of that person, the payment ceases. The member's pension is not then increased by virtue of the death of the designated person.

E. Life Insurance

A life insurance policy will operate as a will-substitute if it is expressed to be for the benefit of the insured's spouse, partner, or children, or the spouses or partners of the insured's children. On the death of the insured the money payable will not form part of the estate or be subject to the deceased's debts, unless the policy was effected and the premiums were paid to defraud creditors.[74]

The insured's intention of providing for a designated beneficiary may be defeated if his or her surviving spouse or partner elects to apply for a division of relationship property under the PRA (NZ). Such proportion of the policy as is attributable to the relationship is then classified as relationship property and subject to division, unless the court decides otherwise.[75] That would also be the case if the estate were granted leave to apply for a division to recover assets for the estate to meet entitlements or family provision claims by other family members.

III. Australia

The social and fiscal environment in Australia is very different from New Zealand. While neither country has estate duty or gift duty, the fiscal and social policies of Australia generate different incentives for will-substitutes. Stamp duty and capital gains tax, for example, are a significant disincentive for settling property on trust, and the compulsory superannuation regime means that most adults use will-substitutes in the form of nominations.

to death. Section 47 mandates the authority administering the fund to pay an allowance to each child of the deceased who is under the age of 16. The authority has discretion to (continue to) pay an allowance to a child of the deceased contributor to assist with the child's education until the child reaches the age of 18. It may also continue paying an allowance to a physically or mentally disabled child of the deceased contributor for such period as it thinks fit. See also the National Provident Act 1950 (NZ) and the National Provident Restructuring Act 1990 (NZ).

[73] Government Superannuation Fund Act 1956 (NZ), s 91B.

[74] Life Insurance Act 1908 (NZ), s 75A.

[75] PRA (NZ), s 8 as modified by s 83 for relationships ending on death.

A. Property Entitlements Under the Family Law Act 1975 (Cth)

Unlike New Zealand, the property adjustment regime in Australia's Family Law Act 1975 (Cth) for spouses and partners whose relationship has ended does not apply on death.[76] The regime is similar to England's Matrimonial Causes Act 1973 except that it also applies to de facto partners. It gives the court discretion to adjust property between the parties and takes account of all of the parties' financial resources, including any benefit that either of them may derive from trusts.[77]

B. Joint Tenancies

As in New Zealand, joint tenancies of real property are common in Australia. They have become the major way for couples to own their home in Australia. This, combined with the prevalence of superannuation, means that for many Australians a will is of far less significance than it was in the past. The majority of their wealth is held in these two ways.[78] Couples also often have joint bank accounts. The funds pass by survivorship unless there is evidence that the survivor holds the funds on a resulting trust for the estate.[79]

C. Trusts

Inter vivos trusts are a less attractive property structure in Australia than in New Zealand. Australia has capital gains tax and stamp duty, which makes the transfer of assets into trust more expensive. The earlier preferential treatment of distributions to minors (one of the major drivers of investment in discretionary trusts) ended in 2011 and they can no longer apply the low income tax offset to their unearned income. Nonetheless, trusts remain a significant estate planning vehicle in Australia, partly because of their ability to endure beyond the death of the settlor, providing continuity and stability.

[76] Family Law Act 1975 (Cth), s 4(1) where 'breakdown' is defined to exclude a marriage or de facto relationship that ends by reason of death.

[77] ibid, s 79(4) and s 75(2)(b). See also *Kennon v Spry* [2008] HCA 56; 251 ALR 257 where the High Court of Australia held that the definition of property included the assets held in a discretionary trust settled by Dr Spry for the benefit of his wife and children.

[78] The common law presumption that property owned by couples is held as joint tenants has been statutorily reversed in New South Wales and Queensland, see Conveyancing Act 1919 (NSW), s 26(1) and Land Titles Act 1994 (Qld), s 56.

[79] *Russell v Scott* (1936) 55 CLR 440.

The Commonwealth Government has also provided for a special disability trust for people who have a severe disability or medical condition.[80] This type of trust can be *inter vivos* or testamentary. There are very specific requirements for such a trust. They can only have one beneficiary; he or she must be over 16 years of age with a disability that would qualify them for Disability Support Pension or equivalent; if they have a carer, the carer must qualify for Carer Payment or Carer Allowance; or the beneficiary must be living in a government-funded institution with a disability that prevents working for more than seven hours a week. It is also possible to set up a trust for a child under 16 years who meets similar requirements.

The aim of the trust is to provide accommodation and other care needs of the beneficiary. That must be its primary purpose. The beneficiary cannot contribute compensation money to the trust, nor can the beneficiary contribute other property unless he or she received it by will no more than three years before transferring it to the trust. Any other person can give to the trust. The advantage of such a trust is that it allows the beneficiary to continue to be eligible for means-tested income support which otherwise the payments might prevent. Whether these are will-substitutes is complex, since they may operate within a will or *inter vivos*. They are mentioned here because their terms are dictated by statute so that the intention of Parliament is substituted for that of the testator, and because they contemplate operation on and after death.

D. Superannuation and Superannuation Death Benefits

Australia has a compulsory superannuation scheme that applies to all employed persons. This scheme provides for a pension or lump sum on retirement or a death benefit that will pass to a person within the requirements of the legislation and the deed of the trust. Very often a person's major asset will be their interest in a superannuation fund. It is not part of their estate unless it has been specifically directed to the executor.[81] As superannuation is compulsory and employers are required to make a contribution from the employee's salary to the fund of 9.5 per cent (rising to 12 per cent in 2025), this is a significant part of most Australians' wealth. Benefits paid from superannuation funds are taxed less than other funds, and lump sum and pension benefits drawn on from the age of 60 are tax free at present. A member's superannuation death benefit must always be

[80] Social Security Act 1991 (Cth), pt 3.18A (ss 1209 ff) and the Veteran's Entitlements Act 1986 (Cth), pt 3B div 11B (ss 1209 ff).

[81] Superannuation Industry (Supervision) Act 1993 (Cth) sets up a compulsory retirement fund for each person. The superannuation death benefit is paid by the trustees of the fund either to a dependent beneficiary at their discretion (usually on the basis of a nomination by the deceased), or to the nominee in the case of a binding nomination. It is protected from all debts except funeral and testamentary expenses.

paid on death, making nominations a significant will-substitute. Where the person receiving the death benefit is a dependant, for example, a spouse or a child under 18 years old,[82] the whole amount is tax free. Where a non-dependant receives the death benefit, the tax payable will be less than is normally paid on income because there is usually a tax-free component calculated by reference to the source of the income to the fund.

The superannuation industry in Australia is in two parts. For employees a range of industry-based superannuation funds exist. However, it is also possible for people to have a self-managed superannuation fund (SMSF). The differences between industry superannuation funds and self-managed superannuation funds are sometimes great. One major difference is that SMSFs do not have access to the Superannuation Complaints Tribunal of Australia.

A significant will-substitute in Australia, therefore, is the nomination that may be made by the superannuant.[83] Both industry superannuation funds and SMSFs can provide for binding or non-binding nominations. Binding nominations allow a person to nominate the legal personal representative or a dependant or dependants of the member to receive the death benefit.[84] Of course, if the death benefit is paid to the legal personal representative it will become part of the estate. 'Dependant' is defined as including 'the spouse of the person, any child of the person and any person with whom the person has an interdependency relationship'.[85] Unless the binding nomination is repeated it lapses after three years or less if the rules of the fund stipulate a shorter time. Where a binding nomination lapses, it becomes a simple nomination and the trustee's discretion to appoint the death benefit reappears. When the trustee's discretion is exercised, members of industry superannuation funds or their dependants may contest the distribution. They are sometimes successful. The tribunal then sets aside the trustee's decision and substitutes its own decision.[86] The tribunal can also scrutinise the validity of a binding nomination and may substitute its own decision if it so decides.

E. Life Insurance, Superannuation and Protection from Debt

Because of compulsory superannuation, which often has death benefits incorporated, free-standing life insurance is relatively rare in Australia.

[82] Superannuation Industry (Supervision) Act 1993 (Cth), s 10.

[83] Superannuation Industry (Supervision) Act 1993 (Cth) (effective from 31 May 1999), s 59(1A).

[84] Superannuation Industry (Supervision) Regulations 1994 (Cth), reg 6.17A(7).

[85] Superannuation Industry (Supervision) Act 1993 (Cth), s 10.

[86] See, eg *D14-15/191* [2015] SCTA 47 where the deceased died without making a nomination and the trustee decided to pay the entire death benefit to the surviving de facto spouse. The Tribunal held that the four-year-old son of the deceased and the de facto partner and the deceased's mother were also dependants and decided that the benefits should be paid 50% to the de facto spouse and 50% on trust for the son to be held by two trustees, one of whom being the de facto spouse.

A benefit of life insurance in Australia, and a reason which might make it attractive as a will-substitute, is that life insurance and death benefits in superannuation are statutorily protected from debt.[87] This means that it can make sense to nominate primary family members as beneficiaries of life insurance or death benefits, while leaving others to take by will, because the estate is not protected from debt. This is complicated by the fact that the protection from debt does not include funeral and testamentary expenses.[88] Such policies nonetheless have special status. *Donationes mortis causa* are in principle available for payment of debts when the estate is insolvent, although this seems to be rare in practice.[89]

F. Contracts for Passing of Property on Death

For many years in Australia it was received wisdom that making a contract to pass property on death in order to avoid the property passing by will, or a contract to leave certain property by will, was effective in removing the property from the estate.[90] If the contract was valid, then once the testator had died, the will did not apply to the subject matter of the contract, because in equity it had become the property of the promisee. Estates were planned on this basis from the 1970s until 2003, in particular as a way of avoiding family provision. In 2003, the High Court of Australia decided in *Barns v Barns* that such contracts should always be read as subject to the family provision legislation.[91] In that case the testator died, leaving his wife and two children. The testator and his wife made mutual wills (regarded as the contract in this case), which provided that the farm would go to the survivor of them, and then to the son, excluding the daughter. They were of the view that she had been provided for already. The High Court, by majority, reversed the decision of the Supreme Court of South Australia that the contract took the farm out of the reach of the family provision legislation (South Australia had no notional estate provisions in its family provision legislation). The High Court took the view that the obligation to make a will under the contract should always be read as subject to the family provision legislation. This ruling brought the High Court of Australia into line with New Zealand.[92] In jurisdictions without notional estate provisions, a contract to leave property by will or to pass property on death must now always be read subject to the family provision legislation so that the promise cannot be more than 'I promise to leave whatever is left after a family provision claim'.[93]

[87] Life Insurance Act 1995 (Cth), s 205; Superannuation Act 1992 (Cth).
[88] *Re McCallum* (1907) 7 SR (NSW) 523.
[89] *Smith v Casen* (1718) 1 P Wms 406; *Re Korvine's Trusts* [1921] 1 Ch 343.
[90] *Schaeffer v Schumann* [1972] AC 572 (PC).
[91] *Barns v Barns* (2003) 214 CLR 169.
[92] *Dillon v Public Trustee of New Zealand* [1941] AC 294 (PC).
[93] In New Zealand, contracts to leave property by will do not necessarily take priority over either family provision or testamentary promises claims, *Hamilton v Hamilton*, above n 11; *Bristow v Smith*, above n 11.

G. Family Provision and the Notional Estate

As in New Zealand, all Australian jurisdictions allow certain eligible people[94] to apply for provision from the estate if adequate provision has not been made for them by will or intestacy rules.[95] However, the Australian courts are less likely to make a family provision award solely to recognise the family bond.[96] In the absence of financial need or dependence, an adult financially independent child must generally have some special need or special moral claim to warrant judicial interference with the terms of a deceased parent's will.

Nonetheless, the importance of family provision is such that the Uniform Succession Law and New South Wales have adopted notional estate provisions to protect the interests of family provision claimants. These provisions allow the subject matter of a transaction made before death to be clawed back so that a family provision claim can be made. The notional estate provisions are an intersecting set of provisions, which use the motive of the transaction, the lack of full valuable consideration and the timing before death as reasons to set aside the transaction and make the property available for a family provision claim.

The 'prescribed transactions' targeted by the legislation are widely defined, and include both acts and omissions. The failure to sever a joint tenancy,[97] the failure to make a nomination or to amend a trust deed,[98] and the payment of a death benefit by a trustee where the superannuant did nothing[99] may all form part of the notional estate, along with the more obvious entry into a contract or deed or trust. To activate the provisions, there must also be a failure to give full valuable consideration. The failure to sever a joint tenancy has been a difficult issue, but it is clear that mere retention is not enough to create the valuable consideration required for this purpose.[100]

The mental state of the testator and the timing of the transaction also affect the way the court determines notional estate. If the other requirements are met and

[94] In New South Wales, eligible claimants are first the spouse (including de facto and same-sex partners) and children. People outside these categories are eligible in New South Wales if they were ever dependent on the deceased and either were a grandchild or a member of the deceased's household. A person may also be eligible if they were living with the deceased at the time of death and either that person or the deceased provided, without pay, the other with domestic support and personal care. This latter category does not include a spouse or de facto spouse but could include another relative such as a sibling or a friend. The categories of eligible people are slightly different in other jurisdictions, Victoria having the broadest eligibility requirement, that the person be one 'for whom the deceased had responsibility to make provision'; Administration and Probate Act 1958 (Vic), s 91.

[95] Family Provision Act 1969 (ACT); Family Provision Act 1970 (NT); Succession Act 2006 (NSW) ch 4; Succession Act 1981 (Qld) s 41 Inheritance (Family Provision) Act 1972 (SA); Administration and Probate Act 1958 (Vic) pt IV; Testator's Family Maintenance Act 1912 (Tas); Family Provision Act 1972 (WA).

[96] Croucher and Vines, above n 4, ch 15.

[97] Succession Act 2006 (NSW), s 76(2)(b).

[98] *Large v Higham (no 2)* [2010] NSWSC 560.

[99] Succession Act 2006 (NSW), s 76(2)(e).

[100] *Cetejovic v Cetejovic* [2007] NSWCA 33.

the testator entered into the transaction between three years and one year before death with the intention of defeating family provision, or one year before death where the moral obligation of the testator to the plaintiff outweighed the moral obligation of the testator to enter into the transaction, or on death, the court can make a notional estate order. As such an order extinguishes the right of the other party to the transaction in most cases; the court must consider this in deciding whether to make the designating order.

A recent case illustrates the potential reach of notional estate provisions.[101] A man died in Victoria, leaving an estate valued at over $50 million. By a long chain of ownership of companies within companies, the deceased was a director of a number of corporations in New South Wales that owned real property. The deceased's mistress and child (who had already been given $5.7 million by the will) brought an action under New South Wales law claiming that the deceased's failure to exercise a direction to distribute the property to them was a prescribed transaction under the Act. The claim failed, but only because the deceased as a director was regarded as not having sufficient control over the assets to dispose of the real estate, even though he could have exercised control over income and capital. However, the latter were held to be situated in Victoria and could not be included in the notional estate.

II. Enduring and Irrevocable Powers of Attorney

An enduring power of attorney and an irrevocable power of attorney can have effect as will-substitutes in Australia.[102] In an enduring power of attorney the appointor chooses a person to act for them when they lose capacity and this continues until death.[103] An irrevocable power of attorney lasts beyond death. It arises where the power is expressed to be irrevocable and there is consideration.[104]

The enduring power of attorney cannot be used to make a will; but the transactions of the enduring attorney may alter the effect of a will (therefore being a form of will-substitute), where the attorney exercises the power to sell property which was the subject matter of a gift in the will. It thus causes an ademption of the gift. As this disadvantages the beneficiary of the will, the courts have made an exception where there was an authorised sale by the attorney, the testator had no capacity, the court was satisfied that the testator would have wanted the beneficiary to have the

[101] *Hitchcock v Pratt* [2010] NSWSC 1508.

[102] Powers of attorney are governed by common law and legislation. Powers of Attorney legislation in the Australian jurisdictions includes Powers of Attorney Act 2006 (ACT); Powers of Attorney Act 1998 (Qld); Powers of Attorney Act 2003 (NSW); Powers of Attorney Act (NT); Powers of Attorney and Agency Act 1984 (SA); Guardianship and Administration Act 1990 (WA); Powers of Attorney Act 2000 (Tas); Instruments Act 1958 (Vic).

[103] Powers of Attorney Act 2003 (NSW).

[104] ibid, s 15.

proceeds of sale and the proceeds could be identified with certainty.[105] However, the New South Wales Court of Appeal rejected this approach.[106] This problem has now been statutorily resolved in New South Wales and Tasmania.[107] Where there is an ademption of a testamentary gift by the sale of the subject matter of the gift, the testamentary beneficiary becomes entitled to an equivalent interest in any surplus money or other property arising from the sale. This exception to the normal rule on ademption has only been held to apply to enduring powers of attorney, not to irrevocable powers of attorney. In South Australia and Tasmania, the court is given the power to make an order to ensure that no beneficiary in such circumstances is disproportionately advantaged or disadvantaged.[108]

I. Applications to the Public Trustee to Have Estate Distributed According to Aboriginal Customary Law

The transmission of property on death of Australia's Indigenous people has necessitated the development of special rules to accommodate their cultural practices and expectations. Wills are very uncommon among the Indigenous people and the general intestacy rules do not reflect their laws and customs.[109] Provision has therefore been made in the Northern Territory, New South Wales and Tasmania[110] for the family of an Aboriginal person who dies intestate to apply to the Public Trustee to have the estate distributed according to customary law. Northern Territory's Administration and Probate Act, for instance, provides for a document to be drawn up that is 'accompanied by a plan of distribution of the intestate estate prepared in accordance with the traditions of the community or group to which the intestate Aboriginal belonged'.[111] As there are over 600 Indigenous language groups and 300 'nations' in Australia, with widely differing cultural ideas about use of land and notions of kinship, it is impossible to develop a single set of succession rules for Indigenous people. A court approved distribution plan provides the necessary flexibility to accommodate the particular customs and practices of the deceased person and his or her family. This system is an important response to the difficulties faced by Indigenous people in Australia whose needs were not being met by the general law of succession.

In some respects a court sanctioned distribution plan may not be regarded as a will-substitute because it concerns distribution of an estate, the plan is not drawn up by the deceased, and the distribution plan is made after death. On the other

105 *Re Viertel* [1997] 1 Qd R 110.
106 *RL v NSW Trustee & Guardian* [2012] NSWCA 39.
107 Powers of Attorney Act 2003 (NSW), s 22.
108 Powers of Attorney and Agency Act 1984 (SA), s 11A; Powers of Attorney Act 2000 (Tas), s 32AH.
109 Peart and Vines, above n 3.
110 Succession Act 2006 (NSW), pt 4.4; Administration Act (NT), div 4A; Intestacy Act (2010) (Tas), pt 4.
111 Administration and Probate Act (NT), s 71B.

hand, it is a mode of transmission of property on death that does not conform to the general succession rules and is subject to court approval.

IV. Rationale for the Use of Will-Substitutes

The reasons why people in Australia and New Zealand choose to use will-substitutes as a means of holding and transmitting property on death are many and varied. In some cases the transfer on death may not even be the sole or primary factor. Pension schemes are primarily intended to provide for the contributor's retirement, but the death benefits for a spouse or nominee are likely to be an additional reason for joining a scheme, whether it is optional, as in New Zealand, or compulsory, as in Australia. The settling of a trust may also be motivated by factors other than passing property on death. Protecting assets against claims by creditors or spouses or partners on separation may be the primary reason, but preserving the assets for the next generation is often a secondary motive.

Tax is always a relevant factor, whether negatively or positively. Even in New Zealand, where trusts and pensions are now largely fiscally neutral, tax considerations still play a prominent role in the use of will-substitutes. On the other hand, the avoidance of estate duty is no longer a reason for finding alternative ways of passing property on death in either Australia or New Zealand. Both countries abolished estate duty in the latter part of the last century.[112]

As in England,[113] and in contrast to the US,[114] probate avoidance and estate administration do not appear to feature as motivating factors for will-substitutes. Obtaining probate of a will or a grant of administration is a straightforward process in most cases and not particularly expensive.[115] Besides, given the high testation rate in both Australia and New Zealand, it seems that will-substitutes do not fully replace the need for a will.

The primary rationale for using will-substitutes in New Zealand seems to be a desire on the part of owners to control the destination of their property without interference from other family members or the state. Trusts are a particularly effective device for that purpose. On the settlor's death, a trust offers an almost

[112] Estate duty was abolished in Australia in the 1970s, see Succession and Gift Duties Abolition Act 1976 (Qld); Estate Duty Assessment (Amendment) Act 1978 (Cth); Stamp Duties (Amendment) Act 1975 (Further Amendment) Act 1980 (NSW); Deceased Person's Estates Duties (no 2) Act 1978 (Tas); Gift Duty Tax Amendment Act 1979 (SA); Probate Duty Act 1980 (Vic); Death Duty Act Amendment Act 1978 (WA). New Zealand abolished estate duty in 1993, Estate Duty Abolition Act 1993 (NZ).

[113] See ch 3 above IV.A. and B.

[114] See ch 1 above, p 11 f.

[115] In New Zealand, probate applications are handled centrally through the High Court Registry in Wellington. The filing fee is $200; High Court Fees Regulations 2013. Unless there are complications, probate is usually granted within about six weeks. Australian processes are similar, being carried out through the registry of the Supreme Court in each state or territory.

cast iron protection against claims by family members, even by those in need of financial support. Only the PRA (NZ) provides an opportunity to recover assets that were disposed of to defeat the rights of a spouse or partner under the Act.[116] But establishing the required intent places a heavy onus on the applicant spouse or partner.

Australia is different in that regard. Its notional estate provisions prevent will-substitutes from defeating meritorious family provision claims. Nonetheless, the desire to control property distribution after death remains an important reason for having trusts and joint tenancies in Australia.

V. The Effect of Will-Substitutes on Succession Law

Despite the widespread use of will-substitutes to pass property on death, the major issue of current concern about their effect on succession law is the extent to which they undermine a testator's moral duty to provide for his or her family.[117] In Australia the notional estate provisions are intended to prevent testators from evading their responsibilities. Capital gains tax and stamp duty also help to mitigate the use of will-substitutes and hence their adverse effect on family provision.

Neither of those constraints operates in New Zealand. Aside from a *donatio mortis causa*, the subject matter of which is treated as part of the estate for purposes of a claim under the Family Protection Act 1955,[118] will-substitutes are immune to family protection claims.[119] There is no provision in the Act to recover property alienated *inter vivos*, whether or not the alienation was for value or intended to defeat claimants' rights. Nor does the Act allow the court to include transactions as part of a notional estate against which family protection claims can be made. By means of will-substitutes owners have absolute freedom to dispose of their assets on death. The repeal of gift duty and the absence of capital gains tax and stamp duty mean that in New Zealand there is no constraint on the freedom to put property beyond the reach of the Family Protection Act. Given that New Zealand

[116] PRA (NZ), s 44.

[117] Prior to the abolition of estate duty, the application of the survivorship rule to a joint bank account could be construed as a testamentary disposition, if the evidence showed that there was no intention to give the survivor a beneficial interest in the account's funds during the joint lifetime of the parties; *Edgar v Commissioner of Inland Revenue* [1978] 1 NZLR 590 (HC).

[118] Family Protection Act 1955 (NZ), s 2(5).

[119] *Re Thompson* [1933] NZLR s 59. The funds in a joint bank account are part of the estate, if the survivor was not intended to have a beneficial interest in the funds during the joint lifetime of the parties. More commonly, there is evidence of an intention to confer beneficial ownership on the survivor, as in *Re Brownlee* [1990] 3 NZLR 243, where the presumption of advancement also applied. WM Patterson, *Law of Family Protection and Testamentary Promises*, 4th edn (Wellington, LexisNexis NZ, 2013) 5.3–5.6. See ch 3 above III.E.

was the first country in the common law world to introduce this type of constraint on testamentary freedom, it seems ironic that it should now have reverted to the common law position prior to the introduction of family provision legislation in 1900, especially in relation to children. Spouses and partners do at least have the protection of the PRA (NZ).

Lack of compliance with the formal requirements for making a will poses no particular concern in Australia or New Zealand, because their legislatures have given the courts the power to validate non-compliant documents if the court is satisfied that they express the deceased's testamentary wishes.[120] Similarly, marriage is less likely to revoke a prior will now that the court can look at a broader range of circumstances to determine whether the will was made in contemplation of marriage and should therefore be upheld.[121] Besides, many couples live together in a de facto relationship prior to marriage and are subject to the same proprietary consequences as married couples.[122] The revocation on marriage of wills made during a couple's preceding de facto relationship does not sit well with a relatively seamless transition from a de facto to a marital relationship. Trusts and joint tenancies may provide better protection and greater certainty for such couples than the intestacy rules.

The forfeiture rule that prevents killers from benefiting financially from their victim's death does apply to some will-substitutes. At common law in Australia the killer of a joint tenant holds the survivorship share on a constructive trust in favour of another appointed by the court.[123] In New Zealand the Succession (Homicide) Act 2007 deprives a killer of any non-probate assets of the victim that would have passed to the killer, such as *donationes mortis causa* and joint tenancies.[124] A joint tenancy devolves as if it were a tenancy in common in equal shares and any other non-probate assets are distributed as if the killer had predeceased the victim.[125] The Act applies only to intentional and reckless killings, not to killings caused by a negligent act or omission, infanticide, assisted suicide, or killing as part of a suicide pact.[126] The Act replaces the rules of law, equity and public policy.[127]

[120] Wills Act (ACT), s 11A; Succession Act 2006 (NSW), s 8; Wills Act 2000 (NT), s 10; Succession Act 1981 (Qld), s 18; Wills Act 1936 (SA), s 12(2); Wills Act 2008 (Tas), s 10; Wills Act 1997 (Vic), s 9; Wills Act 1970 (WA), s 32; Wills Act 2007 (NZ), s 14.

[121] Wills Act 1968 (ACT), s 20(3); Wills Act 2000 (NT), s 14(3); Succession Act 2006 (NSW), s 12(3); Succession Act 1981 (Qld), s 14(3)(a); Wills Act 1936 (SA), s 20(2); Wills Act 1997 (Vic), s 13(3)(a); Wills Act 2008 (Tas), s 16(a); Wills Act 1970 (WA), s 14(1)(a); Wills Act 2007 (NZ), s 18.

[122] Family Law Act 1975 (Cth); PRA (NZ). For purposes of the PRA (NZ) a de facto relationship that immediately precedes a marriage is deemed to be part of the marriage; PRA (NZ), s 2B.

[123] *Re Thorp* (1961) 80 WN (NSW) 61; *Rasmanis v Jurewitsch* (1968) 70 SR (NSW) 407. See ch 3 above, p 66.

[124] Succession (Homicide) Act 2007 (NZ), ss 4 and 8(1).

[125] ibid, s 8.

[126] ibid, s 4 definition of homicide.

[127] ibid, s 5.

So, there is no discretion to depart from the forfeiture rule, either to avoid its application or to apply it to excluded killings. This is in contrast to Australia where there is some discretion to modify the rule in cases of less culpable killings, both under statute and common law[128] But there is no consistent approach and no universal endorsement that the rule should not apply to certain killings.[129]

VI. Conclusion

There has been a 'non-probate revolution' in Australia and New Zealand in response to social and fiscal incentives. Trusts, joint tenancies and pensions are pre-eminent in the range of will-substitutes in both countries. The desire to retain greater control over the destination of property explains the wide use of trusts and joint tenancies, while the cost of funding the retirement of an ageing population is driving the increase in pension schemes. Except for family provision, there is little concern that will-substitutes sidestep succession law. While some Australian jurisdictions have taken steps to curtail the adverse effects of will-substitutes on family provision claims, New Zealand is unlikely to address that issue until dependent family members once again look to the state for support, as they did prior to the enactment of family provision legislation in 1900.

[128] Forfeiture Act 1995 (ACT) and Forfeiture Act 1995 (NSW) and see n 129 below for common law cases.

[129] In *Re Keitley* [1992] 1 VR 583 (where the wife shot her husband after years of abuse) and *Permanent Trustee Co v Freedom from Hunger Campaign* (1991) 25 NSWLR 140 (where the husband killed his terminally ill wife and then himself) the killers were allowed to inherit, while in *Troja v Troja* (1994) 33 NSWLR 269 the Court held that the rule should be strictly applied.

6

Will-Substitutes in Italy

GREGOR CHRISTANDL

I. In Search of Alternative Modes of Succession

A. Will-Substitutes in Italian Legal Scholarship

According to recent statistical data, the percentage of Italians making wills is extremely low. Only about 16 per cent of all estates declared in 2009 were distributed according to a will.[1] Considering that, under Italian law, wills and intestate succession[2] (Art 457 para 1 Codice Civile, hereafter C Civ) are the only two permissible means of transferring property upon death (*mortis causa*), it follows that more than four estates out of five are settled according to the rules of intestacy. Contrary to several other continental legal systems,[3] the Italian legal system strictly prohibits inheritance contracts as a device for transferring property on death (Art 458 C Civ). Stimulated by foreign developments, especially the studies on anticipated succession in Germany and the revision of the prohibition of succession pacts in France, Italian legal scholars started to explore the boundaries of the prohibition of succession pacts in the early 1980s.[4] Their objective was

[1] In exact numbers, 15.78% of all declared successions in Italy in 2009 were governed by a will. See Società, notai e AACC insieme per successioni tutelate, www.movimentoconsumatori.it/news.asp?id=4604.

[2] On intestacy rules under Italian law, see A Braun, 'Intestate Succession in Italy' in KJC Reid, MJ de Waal and R Zimmermann (eds), *Comparative Succession Law, volume 2. Intestate Succession* (Oxford, OUP, 2015) 67.

[3] See, eg Germany: §§ 2274–2302 BGB; Switzerland: Arts 512–15 ZGB; Austria: § 602 ABGB (limited to spouses). For a comparative study on increasing autonomy in succession law even in France, Belgium and Italy see A Braun, 'Towards a Greater Autonomy of Testators and Heirs' (2012) *Zeitschrift für Europäisches Privatrecht* 461.

[4] Legal practitioners, by contrast, became interested in the topic only at a later stage and have not tried to apply the results of the theoretical discussion in practice, presumably due to the unpredictable risk of violating the prohibition of succession pacts.

to uncover alternative instruments to a will that allow an individual to pass on property to the next generation without following intestacy rules.[5]

Their research resulted in an abundant variety of devices known as *istituti alternativi al testamento*,[6] *successioni anomale per contratto*,[7] or *fenomeni parasuccessori*,[8] which can roughly be divided into two main categories. The first category of *negozi transmorte* comprises devices functioning on the basis of a lifetime transfer, which becomes final only on death and remains freely revocable until that moment. The second category of devices, called *negozi post mortem*, consists of *inter vivos* transfers, which are immediately final and thus irrevocable, but which take effect only upon the transferor's death.[9] These latter arrangements fall into the category of instruments of anticipated succession and, as such, fall outside the scope of this volume.

Italian literature sometimes refers to a further distinction between 'perfect' and 'imperfect' will-substitutes.[10] However, this distinction, which suggests that some devices are wills in all but name and thus fulfil the same functions as wills, is not convincing. It is claimed here that such perfect will-substitutes do not exist because they would not present sufficient advantages that would set them apart from wills.

B. The Italian Background: The Prohibition of Succession Pacts

As already mentioned, any exploration of alternative devices to wills under Italian law needs to deal with the ban on succession pacts as per Article 458 C Civ.[11]

[5] Literature on will-substitutes in Italian law is abundant. For a bibliography, see M Ieva, 'Art 458' in F Delfini and V Cuffaro (eds), *Commentario del Codice civile—Delle Successioni—I: Artt 456–564* (Turin, UTET, 2009) 51 ff. For an overview of the topic see A Braun, 'Testamentary Formalities in Italy' in KJC Reid, MJ de Waal and R Zimmermann (eds), *Comparative Succession Law, volume 1. Testamentary Formalities* (Oxford, OUP, 2011) 122–24. The first in-depth analysis was carried out by A Palazzo, *Autonomia contrattuale e successioni anomale* (Naples, Jovene, 1983) 1 ff; a more recent monograph on the topic was published by M Ieva, *I fenomeni a rilevanza successoria* (Naples, Jovene, 2008); see also A Palazzo, *Testamento e istituti alternativi* (Padua, Cedam, 2008) 241–535.

[6] Palazzo, *Autonomia contrattuale e successioni anomale*, above n 5, 1 ff.

[7] ibid, 6.

[8] M Ieva, 'I fenomeni c.d. parasuccessori' (1988) *Rivista notarile* 1139; M Ieva, 'Successione—X Fenomeni parasuccessori' in *Enciclopedia giuridica Treccani* (2002); M Ieva, *I fenomeni a rilevanza successoria* (Naples, Jovene, 2008).

[9] Such arrangements are in particular onerous lifetime gifts as well as conditional lifetime gifts. See Ieva, 'Successione', above n 8, 9 f.

[10] ibid, 9.

[11] Art 458 C Civ—Prohibition of succession pacts: 'Except for what is provided for in Arts 768bis ff, any agreement by which someone disposes of his own estate is void. Any act by which someone disposes of or renounces to the claims that he may acquire with regard to a future succession is equally void'. (Art 458 C Civ—Divieto di patti successori: 'Fatto salvo quanto disposto dagli articoli 768bis e seguenti, è nulla ogni convenzione con cui taluno dispone della propria successione. È del pari nullo ogni atto col quale taluno dispone dei diritti che gli possono spettare su una successione non ancora aperta, o rinunzia ai medesimi'.)

Under this provision, all binding agreements by which a person disposes of his succession are void. Italian law therefore prohibits any agreements that transfer rights or obligations to one or more persons upon the death of a living person (*patti istitutivi*).[12]

The rationale of this prohibition, which can be traced back to Roman law,[13] and which was received by way of the French Civil Code has never been clear. While in French law, the prohibition mainly served to avoid the unequal treatment of heirs, and was never applied particularly strictly, in Italy the prohibition of succession pacts has traditionally been justified as serving the need to protect the free will of the testator.[14] According to this reasoning, the testator should not be allowed to become bound by the terms of a *mortis causa* disposition because any decision about the transfer of property on death should be based on the testator's own will alone, and not that of anybody else. Thus, the testator needs to remain free to change his will at any time until his last breath. In addition, the prohibition serves to shield the testator from any danger posed by those who would benefit from an earlier death of the testator (*votum captandae mortis, pactum corvinium*).[15] However, none of these reasons have ever been convincing,[16] leading some people to explain the prohibition of succession pacts as simply being a policy choice made by the legislature.[17] There have been many powerful voices calling for the abolition of this prohibition,[18] but none have been successful so far. The recently introduced

[12] Agreements concerning rights that someone expects with regard to another person's future succession (*patti dispositive*) and agreements by which someone renounces to future rights deriving from another person's succession (*patti rinunciativi*) are equally prohibited and thus void. L Balestra and M Martino, 'I patti successori' in G Bonilini (ed), *Trattato di diritto delle successioni e donazioni*, vol 1 (Milan, Giuffrè, 2009) 72–81; G Bonilini, *Manuale di diritto ereditario e delle donazioni*, 6th edn (Turin, UTET, 2013) 22–25.

[13] Under Roman law, succession pacts by which the deceased instituted the other party or a third party as an heir or promised to institute the other party or a third person as an heir were void. Diocl C 8,38,4; Iul D 45,1,61. By contrast, donations *mortis causa*, by which only single assets were transferred on death, were allowed. For a detailed analysis see G Vismara, *La storia dei patti successori*, vol I (1941) 74–108; see also M Kaser and R Knütel, *Römisches Privatrecht*, 20th edn (Munich, Beck, 2014) § 65 para 23.

[14] Cass 15 July 1983, no 4827, (1984) *Rivista del notariato* 245; C Gangi, *La successione testamentaria nel vigente diritto italiano*, vol 1 (Milan, Giuffrè, 1964) 40; Balestra and Martino, above n 12, 122; G Capozzi, *Successioni e donazioni*, vol 1, 3rd edn (Milan, Giuffrè, 2009) 40; FM Gazzoni, 'Patti successori: conferma di una erosione' (2001) *Rivista del notariato* 232, 234. MV De Giorgi, 'Patto successorio' in *Enciclopedia del diritto* (1997) 533 f, who considers this reason insufficient, given that many legal systems recognise the validity of succession pacts.

[15] Bonilini, above n 12, 24; Gangi, above n 14, 40.

[16] G Zanchi, 'Percorsi del diritto ereditario attuale e prospettive di riforma del divieto dei patti successori' (2013), www.juscivile.it/contributi/33%20-%20GIULIANO%20ZANCHI.pdf, 700, 725–29.

[17] Balestra and Martino, above n 12, 121 f; Zanchi, above n 16, 733. It is obvious, however, that this is no explanation at all, for policy choices are based on certain reasons, which in the case of the prohibition of succession pacts remain unknown.

[18] A Palazzo, *Testamento e istituti alternativi* (Padua, Cedam, 2008) 466 f; M Ieva, 'Divieto di patti successori e tutela dei legittimari' in S delle Monache (ed), *Tradizione e modernità nel diritto successorio* (Padua, Cedam, 2007) 297–302; R Lenzi, 'Il problema dei patti successori tra diritto vigente e prospettive di riforma' (1988) *Rivista del notariato* 1209, 1248; P Rescigno, 'Le possibili riforme del diritto ereditario' (2012) *Giurisprudenza italiana* 1941. On a law proposal for abolition of Art 458 C Civ, see Zanchi, above n 16, 761.

patto di famiglia concerning the transfer of businesses from one generation to the next does not constitute an exception to the prohibition of *patti istitutivi*, as it regularly constitutes a lifetime transfer.[19]

With specific regard to will-substitutes, the prohibition of succession pacts means that devices falling under its scope of application may not be used. But which devices qualify as succession pacts under Italian law? Because there is no consensus on which agreements fall under the prohibition, answering this question is a difficult task. According to the prevailing view, the prohibition applies to any contractual transfer of property whose main cause is death, and should therefore not apply in cases where death is only an accessory element (condition, term).[20] It bans any agreements that seek to exclusively regulate relationships and situations arising at the time of death,[21] based on the fact that such agreements lack any lifetime effects. The typical feature of an agreement *mortis causa* is that both the object of the disposition and the beneficiary are determined only at the time of death.[22] Thus, the object of the disposition is determined by what remains in terms of quantity and quality at the time of death (*quod superest*), while the beneficiary is considered insofar as he or she is alive at the time when death occurs.[23] So, for example, where a donation contains a clause according to which it shall take effect if the beneficiary survives the donator and only with regard to those assets which will be left at the time of death (*donatio de residuo si praemoriar*), both requirements for a *mortis causa* disposition are met. Such a donation is therefore void as it serves the primary function of disposing of property for the time after death, which under Italian law is reserved to a will or the rules on intestacy. By contrast, where the donation refers to a specific object, but takes effect only where the beneficiary survives the donator (*donatio si praemoriar*), it is commonly considered to be valid, since the object is fixed immediately, both in its quality and quantity at the time of the donation, and is therefore defined independently of the moment of death.[24]

[19] It does, however, constitute an exception to *patti rinunziativi*, by which the forced heirs waive their rights regarding a future succession in exchange for lifetime compensation. For more details on the *patto di famiglia* and its nature see Braun, 'Towards a Greater Autonomy of Testators and Heirs', above n 3, 472.

[20] Cass 24 April 1987, no 4053, (1990) *Rivista di diritto civile* II, 91; FA Moncalvo, 'I negozi transmorte' in G Bonilini (ed), *Trattato di diritto delle successioni e donazioni*, vol 1 (Milan, Giuffrè, 2009) 195 f.

[21] G Giampiccolo, 'Atto "mortis causa"' in *Enciclopedia del diritto* (1958) 232; Moncalvo, above n 20, 196.

[22] Giampiccolo, 'Atto "mortis causa"', above n 21, 233. But see Balestra and Martino, above n 12, 94–103.

[23] Giampiccolo, 'Atto "mortis causa"', above n 21, 233.

[24] Even though this is the view shared by most authors and courts (Cass 9 May 2000 (2001) *Rivista del notariato* 227), there are some voices which do not follow this distinction, considering even a donation *si praemoriar* as a prohibited succession pact. CM Bianca, *Diritto civile: 2 la famiglia le successioni*, 3rd edn (Milan, Giuffrè, 2001) 494; Cass 24 April 1987, no 4053, (1990) *Rivista di diritto civile* II, 91.

II. General Characteristics of Will-Substitutes

A. Immediate Effect and Revocability

Unlike wills, which take effect at the time of death of the testator, will-substitutes *(negozi transmorte)* are immediately effective. This means that the claim or interest passes to the beneficiary at the time of the disposition, while death is only the condition upon which the transfer of the claim or interest becomes final. Notwithstanding their immediate effect, will-substitutes remain revocable until the disposing party's death. Once revoked, the disposition is removed with retroactive effect.[25]

B. Will-Substitutes as Indirect Gifts and Applicable Rules

Will-substitutes are typically part of a contractual arrangement in which the transferee is the beneficiary of a gratuitous lifetime transfer. They are therefore effective independently of whether the beneficiary disclaims the inheritance left by the disposing party or turns out to be unworthy to inherit under succession law. Yet some rules of succession law do apply to will-substitutes, for example, those extended to indirect gifts by Article 809 C Civ. Gratuitous transfers made by will-substitute are thus subject to the hotchpot rule (*collazione*), with the exception of transfers made in recognition of services or according to usage, and those made for purposes of maintenance, education, health or marriage (Arts 770, 742 C Civ). According to the hotchpot rule, which prescribes the combining of lifetime gifts and the estate in order to achieve equal division among certain heirs, the beneficiary of the will-substitute is required to surrender what he has acquired by way of direct or indirect lifetime gifts or accept that his share of inheritance is reduced accordingly. This rule, however, applies only to the spouse or a child of the disposing party, who together with the surviving spouse and the disposing party's siblings or children participates in the distribution of the estate under intestacy rules or under a will. Hence, if a father dies leaving two children, the child who received a lifetime gift will be required to reduce his intestacy or testamentary share accordingly and consequently receive less from the estate in order to ensure equal division among the children.[26]

[25] Palazzo, *Autonomia contrattuale e successioni anomale*, above n 5, 57; A Palazzo, *Le successioni*, vol 1, 2nd edn (Milan, Giuffrè, 2000) 49–f; Ieva, 'Successione', above n 8, 2; MR Marella, 'Il divieto dei patti successori e le alternative convenzionali al testamento' (1991) 7 *Nuova giurisprudenza civile commentata* 91, 93 f.

[26] eg if the deceased leaves two children an estate of 300 and made an indirect gift of 100 to one child during their lifetime, an equal distribution of the assets requires that both children receive 200 each. This is achieved by reducing the intestacy or testamentary share (150) of the child who received the lifetime gift by 50, so that he only takes 100 from the estate.

Gratuitous transfers by means of will-substitute constitute indirect gifts (Art 809 C Civ) and are therefore subject to the claw-back claims of forced heirs (*legittimari*). In order to protect forced heirs against any intention on the part of the deceased to defeat their inviolable claims, any assets transferred gratuitously during lifetime (no matter when) are taken into account to determine the basis on which the claims of the forced heirs are calculated. If the assets of the estate are insufficient to satisfy the claims of the forced heirs, the direct or indirect lifetime gifts must be recovered and returned to the estate, starting from the most recent one and reaching back to all previous ones, until the claims of all forced heirs are satisfied. The forced heirs' claims are of particular practical importance because they comprise up to three-quarters of the deceased's patrimony (= estate and lifetime gratuitous transfers) in cases where the deceased is survived by two children and a spouse (Art 542 para 2 C Civ).

C. Stipulations in Favour of Third Parties

The will-substitute form most commonly availed of under Italian law is the contract in favour of a third party, whereby a third party is the intended beneficiary in a contract between a promisee (the future deceased) and a promisor. According to Article 1411 C Civ, a contract in favour of a third party is valid if the promisee has an interest in the contract, even if that interest is merely of a moral or emotional nature.[27] The promisee may, for example, simply wish to make a gift to the beneficiary. At the time of the stipulation, the beneficiary acquires a conditional right, which means that the claim or interest passes immediately, but may be waived by the beneficiary or revoked by the promisee as long as the beneficiary has not accepted the benefit vis-a-vis both the promisee and the promisor (Art 1411 C Civ).

With regard to will-substitutes, Article 1412 C Civ is of particular importance. According to this provision, the contracting parties may agree that the transfer of the material benefit to the beneficiary should become final only when the promisee dies. Until then, the promisee may revoke the beneficiary's claim at any time, also by will, irrespective of whether the beneficiary has formally accepted the transfer.[28] Stipulations in favour of a third party in the event of death are considered paradigmatic will-substitutes under Italian law because, while the claim or interest passes immediately, it only becomes final when the promisee dies. The promisee therefore reserves a right of revocation until the moment of death. There is general agreement that this form of third-party contract is appropriate for

[27] A Zaccaria, 'Art 1411' in G Cian and A Trabucchi (eds), *Commentario breve al codice civile*, 11th edn (Padua, Cedam, 2014) para VII.

[28] Exceptionally, such a benefit to be performed on death may become irrevocable even before, if the promisee declares in writing that he waives his right of revocation (Art 1412 C Civ).

ownership and other rights *in rem*,[29] as it allows a promisee to transfer an interest in land to a beneficiary while ensuring that this transfer will only become final on the promisee's death.[30]

Comparing these stipulations with wills raises the question of whether such contracts allow the promisee to nominate the beneficiary at a later stage or even to nominate a different beneficiary after having revoked the transfer. While there is a specific provision relating to life insurance contracts (Art 1920 C Civ) that allows this expressly, there are no such provisions relating to contracts in favour of third parties in general. According to the prevailing view, however, the promisee may, at any later stage, nominate a beneficiary or amend a nomination already made.[31]

III. Third-Party Contracts

Third-party contracts, as mentioned above, are the most common form of will-substitute. This section will deal with the instruments usually discussed under this heading. Particular attention will be devoted to those third-party contracts that are of particular practical importance, such as life insurance contracts, private pension schemes and succession clauses in partnership agreements.

A. Life Insurance Contracts

Because Italians commonly use life insurance contracts as savings instruments,[32] the life insurance sector in Italy is of considerable economic importance.[33] The rules governing the transfer of wealth on death in this sector are therefore highly relevant to the transfer of wealth on death in general. Life insurance contracts typically contain nominations of a third-party beneficiary who receives the proceeds of the policy in the event of the insured party's death (Art 1920 C Civ).

[29] Cass 17 July 1982, no 3050, (1982) *Vita notarile* 1225; Cass 1 February 2003, no 18321, (2004) *Rivista del notariato* 1228; Palazzo, *Autonomia contrattuale e successioni anomale*, above n 5, 123; Zaccaria, above n 27, para V.

[30] The beneficiary would thus acquire the right *in rem* only at the time of death of the promisee. See Palazzo, *Autonomia contrattuale e successioni anomale*, above n 5, 130.

[31] Moncalvo, above n 20, 204; against M Ieva, *I fenomeni a rilevanza successoria* (Naples, Jovene, 2008) 32 f, according to whom esp with regard to rights *in rem* a later designation would create too much uncertainty for the traffic.

[32] This is expressly recognised by Cass 26 June 2000, no 8676, (2000) *Giustizia civile Massimario* 1405 (saving device for social security).

[33] In 2013, the technical provisions in this sector amounted to €453,080 million. ANIA, *L'assicurazione italiana 2013–2014* (2014) 107 (www.ania.it/export/sites/default/it/pubblicazioni/rapporti-annuali/2014/LAssicurazione-italiana-2013–2014.pdf). See, however, M Rossetti, *Il diritto delle assicurazioni*, vol 3 (Padua, CEDAM, 2013) 811–15, who points out that Italy has the lowest number of life insurance policies per inhabitant (0.2) among industrialised nations.

This nomination may be made in the insurance contract itself or by a separate and later declaration to be communicated in writing to the insurer. It may even be contained in a later will made by the insured.[34] In any case, the nominated third party immediately acquires a conditional claim to receive the proceeds of the policy from the insurer on the insured party's death, provided that the insured party does not revoke the nomination prior to his death (Art 1921 C Civ).[35] The claim to the proceeds thus passes outside the estate on the basis of the insurance contract, meaning that the rules of succession law do not generally apply to this transfer.[36] The beneficiary may therefore disclaim the insured party's inheritance without losing the benefits under the insurance contract.[37] This can be advantageous, especially if the estate is insolvent. Moreover, the provision on unworthiness to inherit (Art 463 C Civ) does not apply to life insurance benefits.[38] In order to fill this gap, the rules on life insurance contracts contain a similar rule.[39]

Transfers of wealth under life insurance contracts are typically gratuitous transfers (Art 809 C Civ), and as such do remain subject to some of the rules of succession law. For example, where the beneficiary participates in the distribution of the insured party's estate the benefits received from the life insurance contract need to be taken into account when determining the shares among brothers, sisters and the surviving spouse (hotchpot rule, *collazione*, Art 741 C Civ).[40] So if one of several siblings received life insurance benefits from his late father, his share under intestacy or under a will is reduced proportionally in order to ensure fair distribution of the estate among the closest family members. However, the deceased may exclude the application of the hotchpot rule, in which case he would still be bound to respect the inviolable claims of the forced heirs (*successione necessaria*), which are calculated taking into account the total amount of premiums paid to the insurance company without capital gains (Art 1923 para 2 C Civ).

[34] Even where the nomination is contained in a will, the transfer remains a lifetime disposition that is not subject to succession law, for the beneficiary acquires the right directly from the insurance contract, independently of where the designation is contained (insurance contract, will or separate document). Moncalvo, above n 20, 207; Palazzo, *Testamento e istituti alternativi*, above n 18, 466 f (the will being only a 'vehicle' containing the designation).

[35] As a rule, nominations in insurance contracts are revocable. However, the insured may exceptionally waive his right of revocation in writing. In this case, the waiver takes effect as soon as the beneficiary has accepted the benefit vis-a-vis the insured party. Both the waiver of the right of revocation and the acceptance by the beneficiary need to be communicated to the insurer in writing (Art 1921 C Civ).

[36] Cass 23 March 2006, no 6531, (2006) *Giustizia civile Massimario* 9; Cass 14 May 1996, no 4484, (1997) *Giustizia civile* I, 167. This is true also where the designation made by the insured refers to the heirs under a will or the heirs under intestacy rules.

[37] G Fanelli, 'Assicurazione sulla vita' in A Azara and E Eula (eds), *Novissimo Digesto Italiano*, vol 1, 2nd edn (Turin, UTET, 1957) 1378, 1398.

[38] For an application by analogy A Zoppini, 'Contributo allo studio delle disposizioni testamentarie "in forma indiretta"' (1998) 52 *Rivista trimestrale di diritto e procedura civile* 1077, 1102–05.

[39] If the beneficiary attempts to take the insured party's life, Art 1922 C Civ excludes the beneficiary from the benefits under the life insurance contract. For inconsistencies, see below section VI.C.

[40] Except where the proceeds of the insurance were granted in recognition of services or according to usage, for maintenance, education, health or marriage (Art 742 C Civ).

The transfer of wealth under a life insurance contract has one important advantage over the transfer of wealth under a will: the benefits transferred by a life insurance contract enjoy the special privilege of being protected against the claims of both the insured's and the beneficiary's creditors (Art 1923 C Civ). There is, however, no consensus as to the reasons for this privilege.[41] The courts justify it by referring to the social security function of life insurance contracts.[42] According to this reasoning, the benefits are protected against the claims of the beneficiary's creditors even after liquidation.[43] Others have explained this privilege as having to do with insurance companies' need for protection against the hassle of possible claims brought by creditors of the insured or the beneficiary. On the basis of this explanation, however, the benefits would not enjoy any protection against the claims of the beneficiary's creditors beyond the time of liquidation.[44]

It has been claimed that life insurance contracts with a third-party beneficiary can serve to ensure the maintenance of the surviving partner in unmarried relationships. Under Italian law, partners in cohabitation do not have any succession rights with regard to each other. Thus, the surviving partner could be nominated as the beneficiary of a life insurance policy, while the insured partner may waive his right of revocation.[45] However, where the right of revocation is waived, we are no longer dealing with a will-substitute, but with an irrevocable lifetime gift, which takes effect on death and thus constitutes a device of anticipated succession.

B. Complementary Private Pension Plans

Complementary pension schemes were introduced in Italy in the early 1990s,[46] at a time when the public pension system, clearly weakened as a result of demographic change, was in need of privately funded schemes to support it.[47] In June 2014, about 6.3 million people (6.2 million in December 2013) were members of a complementary pension scheme in Italy, with the capital invested in such schemes totalling €121 billion (€116.4 billion in December 2013).[48] The continuous rise

[41] For a discussion of the different views see L Buttaro, 'Assicurazione sulla vita' in *Enciclopedia del diritto*, vol 3 (1958) 608, 653 f.

[42] Cass Sezioni Unite 31 March 2008, no 8271, (2009) *Giustizia civile* I, 2489; S Barison and M Gagliardi, *Il Codice Civile—Commentario: Dell'assicurazione sulla vita Artt. 1919–1927* (Milan, Giuffrè, 2013) 105–08.

[43] Cass Sezioni Unite 31 March 2008, no 8271, (2009) *Giustizia civile* I, 2489. P Corrias, 'Art 1923' in G Volpe Putzolu (ed), *Commentario breve al diritto delle assicurazioni* (Padua, Cedam, 2010) 139. For criticism see Rossetti, above n 33, 835 f, 866.

[44] Buttaro, above n 41, 652.

[45] Moncalvo, above n 20, 207 f.

[46] Law no 421 of 23 October 1992, Art 3, para 1 lit v; D Lgs no 124 of 21 April 1993, replaced by D Lgs no 252 of 5 December 2005—Disciplina delle forme pensionistiche complementari.

[47] For an overview on Italian pension reform see L Ferruz Agudo and M Alda García, 'Pension Reform in Italy: Description and Evaluation' (2011) 16 *Pensions* 96–106.

[48] COVIP, *La previdenza complementare—principali dati statistici, secondo trimestre 2014*, www.covip.it/?cat=37.

of both the number of members and the invested assets attests to the economic importance of these plans, also with regard to the transfer of wealth on death.

According to Article 14 paragraph 3 D Lgs no 252/2005, the intestate or testate heirs[49] or other beneficiaries nominated by the member of a private pension plan, who dies before retirement receive the benefits from the pension fund. If there are no heirs and no nominated beneficiaries, the benefits go to the fund, except where the fund is held by a private insurance company. In this case, the entire amount is assigned to social purposes to be determined by the Italian Ministry of Welfare. Originally, the law did not grant pension plan members the right to designate beneficiaries. Thus, in the absence of a surviving spouse, the children and the parents were the beneficiaries, provided that they were maintained by the pension plan member. If none of these persons were surviving, the assets were withdrawn by the fund, even if the pension plan member had other surviving relatives (brothers, sisters, nephews and nieces, uncles, aunts, etc). In order to obviate likely grounds of unconstitutionality,[50] this rule was revised in 1999.[51]

The issue of what happens to a pension fund member's benefits in the event of his death before retirement, ie, whether the transfer of such benefits to the heirs or nominated beneficiaries passes through the estate of the pension fund member, is not entirely clear.[52] In its guidelines of 2008, the Italian Supervisory Commission for Pension Funds (COVIP)[53] supported by the Italian tax agency[54] ruled that such benefits should not become part of the estate.[55] Besides having important tax implications,[56] this means that the benefits go directly to the beneficiaries without passing through the estate of the deceased. The beneficiaries therefore do not have to accept the inheritance in order to benefit from the pension fund,[57] and are

[49] These are the beneficiaries (spouse, children and other descendants, parents and other ascendants, siblings, other relatives within the sixth degree), who inherit under intestacy rules or those persons who inherit under a will.

[50] MA Procopio, *Fondi pensione e TFR. Profili giuridici e disciplina tributaria* (Milan, IPSOA, 2008) 127, fn 193. On these doubts see G De Nova, *Il contratto—dal contratto atipico al contratto alieno* (Padua, Cedam, 2011) 107 f.

[51] Law no 144 of 17 May 1999, Art 58 para 8 lit c.

[52] M Pallini, 'La "mobilità tra le forme pensionistiche complementari"' (2007) 30 *Nuova giurisprudenza civile commentata* 803 f, who favours the view that benefits from pension funds going to third parties are subject to succession law in order to ensure full protection of forced heirs. This view is shared by G Levi, 'I fondi pensione nel lavoro privato' in G Amoroso, V Di Cerbo and A Maresca (eds), *Diritto del lavoro*, vol 1, 3rd edn (Milan, Giuffrè, 2009) 2457, 2522.

[53] COVIP, *Orientamenti interpretativi in merito all'articolo 14, comma 3 del decreto legislativo n 252/2005*, www.covip.it/wp-content/uploads/D080715_01.pdf. See also G Zampini, 'Trasferimento e riscatto delle posizioni individuali' in M Cinelli (ed), *La previdenza complementare* (Milan, Giuffrè, 2010) 566.

[54] Circolare dell'Agenzia delle Entrate 18 dicembre 2007, no 70/E.

[55] Against, G Santoro Passarelli, *Il trattamento di fine rapporto* (Milan, Giuffrè, 2009) 156.

[56] As a part of the estate, the benefits would be taxed according to the inheritance tax (4% for spouse and ascendants and descendants with an amount of exemption of €1,000,000). As pension plan benefits, however, they are subject to a tax of 15% (which after 15 years of membership in a pension plan is reduced by 0.3% for every additional year of membership until it reaches the minimum of 9%). For an overview, see www.cooperlavoro.it/diritti-e-prestazioni/105/.

[57] COVIP, *Riscatto per premorienza*, October 2009, www.covip.it/?cat=98.

furthermore not subject to the rules on unworthiness to inherit. Moreover, the process of nominating a beneficiary is not subject to any special formal requirements other than the requirement to inform the pension fund of the beneficiary in writing. This nomination can be changed at any time before retirement, and can most probably also be changed by will (applying Arts 1412 and 1920 C Civ here). Where several beneficiaries are nominated, the shares of each beneficiary are determined according to the pension fund member's wishes.

Where a pension fund member dies after retirement, the question of whether his survivors receive any payments from the remaining pension fund money will depend on the fund,[58] and the scheme chosen by the deceased at the time of retirement (Art 11 para 5 D Lgs no 252/2005). If the pension fund member, upon retiring, chooses a scheme that includes benefits for a third party after his death, he will receive significantly lower periodical payments during his life, depending also on the life expectancy of the third-party beneficiary. The costs of this option can deter pension fund members from choosing such schemes, so that any investments in their name remaining in the fund after their death are kept by the pension fund.

A number of questions regarding pension fund nominations are still left unanswered by legal literature. It has not yet been discussed whether nominations may be made irrevocable, like nominations in life insurance contracts, and whether Article 1922 C Civ (exclusion for attempting the life of the insured) could be applied by analogy to nominations in pension funds. It is also unclear whether the privilege of protection against the claims of the creditors of the nominated beneficiary apply (Art 1923 para 1 C Civ).[59] Similarly, it is not clear whether the whole proceeds including the returns or only the total payments (as in Art 1923 para 2 C Civ) are taken into account for determining the shares of the forced heirs.

C. Clauses in Partnerships and Corporations

The structure of the Italian business economy is characterised by a particularly high number of small and medium-sized businesses. In most of these partnerships and corporations, one or more closely connected families hold the power to nominate the governing bodies of the company.[60] In order to ensure the intergenerational

[58] Pension funds are not required to provide for any benefit in favour of third parties where the pension fund member dies after retirement. Art 11 para 5 D Lgs no 252/2005 only refers to the possibility of assigning the remaining benefits to the beneficiaries 'for the better protection of the pension fund member'.

[59] Art 11 para 10 D Lgs no 252/2005 shields only the pension money from claims of the pension fund member's creditors.

[60] F Scaglione, 'Patti sociali' in A Palazzo and A Sassi (eds), *Trattato della successione e dei negozi successori: 2. Negozi successori anticipatori* (Turin, UTET, 2012) 652.

continuity of these family run businesses, various contractual clauses have been developed.[61] The clauses most frequently used in practice are:

1. Clauses guaranteeing that the heirs of the deceased partner take his position in a partnership (continuation clauses, *clausole di continuazione*).
2. Clauses that prevent the transfer of the shares to the heirs of the partner and ensure that the shares of the deceased accrue to the remaining partners or shareholders (*clausole di consolidazione*).
3. Clauses that require the approval of the other partners before the family members or other persons take the position of the deceased in the partnership.
4. Clauses that establish an option in favour of the other partners or shareholders to buy the shares from the heirs.
5. Clauses that assign a right of pre-emption in favour of the partners or shareholders if the heirs decide to sell the shares.

Among all these clauses, optional continuation clauses (*clausole di continuazione facoltativa*) and consolidation clauses (*clausole di consolidazione*) come closest to the definition of a will-substitute.[62] These clauses are very special will-substitutes in the sense that they allow someone to dispose of shares in a way that would not be possible in a will.

Partners can use continuation clauses to ensure that their respective heirs under a will or under intestacy rules take their position in the partnership after their death. These clauses involve that the surviving partners make the corresponding promise of this option to the deceased partner's heirs. According to the prevailing view among legal scholars, these clauses constitute third-party contracts. The partners have the power to unilaterally revoke the clause in a will. After such revocation, the default rule (Art 2284 C Civ) applies, according to which the surviving partners are free to decide on what happens with the deceased partner's shares. They may liquidate them to the heirs, dissolve the partnership altogether or continue the partnership with the heirs.

Consolidation clauses prevent the shares from falling into the estate of the deceased by ensuring that they accrue in favour of the surviving partners as soon as one of the partners dies. Here again, the same effect could not be achieved by a will, as a will cannot regulate the transfer of shares in partnerships. In exchange for the accrual, the surviving partners promise to liquidate the shares in favour of the heirs of the deceased. These clauses, which are fairly common in practice, are seen by some authors as void, as they constitute violations of the prohibition of succession pacts,[63] and as they involve defining the object and the beneficiaries of

[61] See further ch 10 below V.

[62] Scaglione, above n 60, 661.

[63] In favour of the invalidity under Art 458 C Civ, see: Ieva, *I fenomeni a rilevanza successoria*, above n 31, 67, who points out that these clauses meet both requirements for *mortis causa* dispositions (transfer only at death and only to the extent of what remains). Against this view: Palazzo, *Autonomia contrattuale e successioni anomale*, above n 5, 172 on the grounds that these consolidation clauses treat death just like any cause of termination of the position as partner or shareholder.

the clauses only at the time of the partner's death. However, the Italian Supreme Court has confirmed the validity of these clauses,[64] provided that they guarantee compensation in favour of the heirs in exchange for the accrual. In order to serve as a real will-substitute, a right of revocation could be granted to the partners in the form of a right of withdrawal from the partnership under the conditions, which the partners consider essential for the accrual in favour of the surviving partners.[65] As a means of avoiding inheritance tax, consolidation clauses have long enjoyed widespread use. In an attempt to prevent these tax avoidance practices, a tax law reform changed the rules by including these transfers in the taxable estate.[66]

With regard to corporations (joint-stock companies and limited companies), transferability of shares on death can be restricted in that it can be made dependent on the approval of the governing bodies of the company (*clausole di gradimento*, Arts 2355bis, 2469 C Civ), or in that the company or the shareholders can be assigned a right of pre-emption.[67] If the transfer of shares to heirs is made subject to approval, then the company may either accept the heirs as new shareholders or reject them. If it rejects them, the company itself or the shareholders will buy the deceased shareholder's shares (Art 2357 C Civ), liquidating their value to the heirs. These clauses limit the transferability of shares inherited by shareholders' heirs,[68] by allowing the surviving shareholders to decide whether they want the heirs to become company shareholders or whether they want to liquidate the shares in question in order to keep the heirs outside the corporation. The clauses cannot, however, be understood as will-substitutes in a strict sense, as they do not provide for revocability with regard to the right of pre-emption of the fellow shareholders.

D. Other Devices in Favour of Third Parties

i. Life Annuities in Favour of Third Parties

A further device under Italian law by which a person can provide for the maintenance of survivors after his death is the life annuity contract in favour of a third party (*rendita vitalizia a favore di terzi*). In this type of contract (Arts 1872, 1875 C Civ), one party makes an immediate transfer of personal or real property or of other assets, while the other party promises to make periodical payments in favour of the beneficiary for as long as the beneficiary, another person, or a group of other persons lives (Art 1873 C Civ).[69] Hence, A may transfer real property to

[64] Cass 16 April 1975, no 1434, (1976) *Giurisprudenza italiana* I, 1, 591.

[65] Scaglione, above n 60, 685; Palazzo, *Testamento e istituti alternativi*, above n 18, 481.

[66] GF Campobasso, *Diritto commerciale 2 Diritto delle società*, 8th edn (Turin, UTET, 2012) 111; Ieva, *I fenomeni a rilevanza successoria*, above n 31, 70.

[67] Scaglione, above n 60, 695–700.

[68] Cass 12 February 2010, no 3345, (2010) *Giustizia civile* 1895.

[69] Palazzo, *Autonomia contrattuale e successioni anomale*, above n 5, 93–96; Ieva, *I fenomeni a rilevanza successoria*, above n 31, 44–48.

B, who in exchange promises to make regular payments (annuities) of money or other fungibles in favour of A's partner starting after the death of A and for as long as the partner lives. According to the general rule on stipulations in favour of third parties, the promisee may revoke the benefit until his death. Thus, if A separates from his partner after concluding a life annuity contract, he may revoke the stipulation (Art 1412 C Civ) and designate a different beneficiary. This device protects the beneficiary against possible claw-back claims by forced heirs only where the beneficiary is a close relative (spouse or child, not a companion) of the deceased, and only with regard to the level of assets required for his maintenance (Arts 809, 742 C Civ).[70]

ii. Maintenance Contracts in Favour of Third Parties

Where the promisee intends to provide the beneficiary not with regular payments but with board and lodging, clothes, moral and material assistance provided by the promisor, he may decide to conclude a maintenance contract in favour of third parties (*contratto di mantenimento, vitalizio assistenziale a favore di terzo*).[71] This type of contract is applicable, for example, in cases where a parent wants to make sure that a handicapped child continues to be provided for after that parent's death. It involves the promisee transferring with immediate effect real or personal property or assets to the promisor, who in exchange promises to provide all the necessary moral and material assistance to the beneficiary, from the time of the promisee's death to the time of the beneficiary's death. This atypical[72] contract form is considered a perfect substitute for so-called maintenance bequests (*legato di alimenti*, Art 660 C Civ) in a will. Just like such bequests, it gives the promisee the power to revoke the benefit in favour of the third party until the time of his death (Art 1412 C Civ).[73] One problematic aspect of this contract form, however, is that it ends if the promisor dies, because the promisor's obligation to provide moral and material assistance to the beneficiary is of a strictly personal nature.[74] On the other hand, because the maintenance contract is an onerous contract, it can serve to deprive any forced heirs of their legitimate shares.[75] For example, if A transfers his house to a friend in exchange for that friend's promise to provide moral and material assistance to A's companion, A's children cannot challenge the

[70] Ieva, *I fenomeni a rilevanza successoria*, above n 31, 176.

[71] Commissione Studi Civilistici, *Contratto di mantenimento a favore del terzo 'post mortem'*, www.notarlex.it/studi/successioni/Studio_4089.pdf.

[72] Cass 19 July 2011, no 15848, (2011) *Giustizia civile Massimario* 1085; Cass 25 March 2013, no 7479, (2013) *Giustizia civile Massimario* 321.

[73] Ieva, *I fenomeni a rilevanza successoria*, above n 31, 51.

[74] D Riccio, 'Le rendite vitalizie' in M Bessone (ed), *Trattato di diritto privato*, vol 14 (Turin, Giappichelli, 2005) 321, 360; M Sala, 'Contratti atipici vitalizi a titolo oneroso e risoluzione per inadempimento'(1993) 43 *Giustizia civile* 1054, 1057; Commissione, above n 71.

[75] M Paradiso, 'Vitalizi alimentari, alea e risoluzione per inadempimento' in *Studi in onore di Nicolò Lipari*, vol 2 (Milan, Giuffrè, 2008) 2109, 2124.

house transfer by filing a claw-back claim because, under a maintenance contract, the transferee's obligation depends on uncertain events.[76] In order to prevent this type of contract from being abused, the law requires that there must be a certain degree of proportionality between the value of the real property transferred and the possible costs of the assistance to be provided. If the courts establish that there was disproportion between the value of the real property transferred and the foreseeable value of the assistance at the time the contract was concluded (*sproporzione originaria tra le prestazioni*), then they may assume that the transferor was trying to simulate a donation and may therefore allow the forced heirs to bring claw-back claims against the transfer.[77]

iii. Fiduciary Contracts

It is generally accepted, although not without reservation, that an asset may be transferred to a fiduciary who is then bound to transfer the asset to the beneficiary or to a third party upon a certain event.[78] In the context of will-substitutes, a person may decide to transfer real property to a fiduciary who is then obliged to transfer that property to a third party upon the transferor's death. While at least one court has deemed this legal arrangement as being in conflict with the prohibition of succession pacts,[79] authors generally hold the contrary view. They tend to hold that the transfer occurs *inter vivos* and that the object of the transfer is determined independently of the moment of death.[80] But while it is certainly true that the transfer is immediate and thus occurs prior to the death of the transferor, it is not unreasonable to assume that this transfer form is sometimes used to evade the prohibition of succession pacts. This aspect aside, however, there are numerous downsides to using fiduciary contracts as will-substitutes: one of these is that the fiduciary is obligated to transfer ownership to the beneficiary only upon the transferor's death. If contrary to his obligation he decides instead to transfer the ownership to another person, only damages are available in favour of the beneficiary. Further disadvantages include the fact that the assets are not protected

[76] It is unclear whether the transferor will ever be in need of assistance and it is also unclear for how long the transferee will need assistance.

[77] Cass 25 March 2013, no 7479, (2013) *Giustizia civile Massimario* 321. In this case, the father of two sons had transferred his only piece of land to his son and his spouse in exchange for moral and material assistance. After the father's death, the second son claimed that the maintenance contract was a simulated donation, considering in particular that the father had already been 85 years old at the time of contract conclusion and that the possible value of the assistance had been out of proportion with regard to the value of the transferred piece of land. The Supreme Court ordered a retrial, the main objective of which was to determine the value of the piece of land, stating that in the event of a disproportion, a simulated donation can be presumed. See also Cass 11 July 1994, no 6532, (1994) *Giustizia civile Massimario* 949.

[78] For an overview see PM Putti, 'Negozio fiduciario' in *Digesto delle discipline privatistiche—Sezione civile*, 2nd aggiornamento (Turin, UTET, 2003), 911–27.

[79] See A Palazzo, *Le successioni*, vol 1, 2nd edn (Milan, Giuffrè, 2000) 56, referring to Tribunale di Milano 18 April 1974.

[80] See ibid 57; Ieva, *I fenomeni a rilevanza successoria*, above n 31, 58.

against any creditors the fiduciary may have,[81] and that a fiduciary contract requires two separate transfers, each of which is subject to taxation. All these aspects make fiduciary contracts particularly unattractive as will-substitutes.[82]

iv. Bank Deposits in Favour of Third Parties

Whether a bank deposit in favour of third parties is a valid alternative to a will or is in conflict with the prohibition of succession pacts is the object of debate. Where the deposit follows the rules on third-party contracts, it is certainly valid.[83] According to Article 1412 C Civ, the money placed in the bank account is assigned to the beneficiary with immediate effect, but will be accessible (paid to the beneficiary) only after the depositor's death, while the depositor keeps a right of revocation until his death.[84] Under the law on the prevention of money laundering, bank deposits in favour of third parties require the respective beneficiary to be identified.[85] And although transferred outside succession law, the fact that they constitute indirect donations (Art 809 C Civ) makes them subject to claims from forced heirs. They are therefore taken into account under the hotchpot rule, which serves to determine the shares to be allocated to the depositor's spouse, brothers and sisters (*collazione*). Where the depositor reserves his right to make withdrawals until his death, he is considered to show merely the intention to transfer what remains on the account at the time of his death (*quod superest*). Considering that, under Italian law, the transfer of remaining assets on death can only be effected via a will, a contract that allows such withdrawals is deemed to violate the prohibition of inheritance pacts (Art 458 C Civ) and is therefore void.[86]

[81] M Lupoi, 'Trusts in Italy as a Living Comparative Law Laboratory' (2013) 19 *Trusts & Trustees* 302, 305.

[82] Ieva, *I fenomeni a rilevanza successoria*, above n 31, 58.

[83] For an ample discussion of the reasons against and in favour of the validity of such bank deposits in favour of third parties: S Tondo, 'Note sul "trust": comparazione con una nostra prassi bancaria' (1993) *Rivista del notariato* I, 53–65.

[84] F Angeloni, *Commentario del Codice civile Scialoja-Branca: Del contratto a favore di terzi Art 1411–1413* (Bologna, Zanichelli, 2004) 302; C Caccavale, 'Contratto e successioni' in V Roppo (ed), *Trattato del contratto*, vol 6 (Milan, Giuffrè, 2006) 519; Moncalvo, above n 20, 209; F Giorgianni and CM Tardivo, *Manuale di diritto bancario*, 2nd edn (Milan, Giuffrè, 2009) 448.

[85] D Lgs no 231 of 21 November 2007, Art 18 lit b = Art 8 lit b Dir 2005/60/EC on the prevention of the use of the financial system for the purpose of money laundering and terrorist financing. F Maimeri and R Perri, 'Art 1834' in E Gabrielli and D Valentino (eds), *Commentario del Codice civile: Dei singoli contratti artt 1803–1860* (Turin, UTET, 2011) 349.

[86] Palazzo, *Autonomia contrattuale e successioni anomale*, above n 5, 109–11; Moncalvo, above n 20, 210; Ieva, *I fenomeni a rilevanza successoria*, above n 31, 80 f. Such a contract was, however, considered to be valid by Tribunale di Catania 5 March 1958 (1961) *Banca, borsa e titoli di credito* II, 311. On this decision, see Palazzo, *Autonomia contrattuale e successioni anomale*, above n 5, 109. For its validity also G Molle, *I contratti bancari*, 4th edn (Milan, Giuffrè, 1981) 163, who distinguishes between a clause where the beneficiary receives something depending on future acts of the promisor (*de eo quod superit*) and a clause where the beneficiary receives what remains at the time of death of the promisor, considering the contract void only in the latter case. This distinction is not convincing.

v. Mandate Post Mortem

At least in abstract terms, a mandate contract could constitute a will-substitute. Take for example the scenario of a grandmother directing her lawyer to hand over jewellery or money to her granddaughter upon the grandmother's death (*mandato post mortem*). While mandate contracts generally lapse when the mandator dies (Art 1722 no 4 C Civ), they can remain in effect beyond the mandator's lifetime if he had expressed his wish that the mandate be executed only once he is deceased.[87] Yet, such a mandate *mortis causa*, by which an individual intends to transfer an asset of the estate outside succession law, conflicts with the prohibition of succession pacts. According to the courts, a mandate by which the deceased orders the mandatary to transfer something that has not been transferred during lifetime to a third party is void for violation of the prohibition of succession pacts according to Article 458 C Civ. By contrast, where the mandate involves handing over something that has already been transferred to the third party, the contract is valid (*mandatum post mortem exequendum*).[88] This interpretation is in line with the general definition of a disposition *mortis causa*,[89] where the transfer occurs only at the time of the disposing party's death and only with regard to what is left at the time of his death (*id quod superest*). Where an individual puts money into a savings account in favour of his partner and orders the bank to hand the passbook over to the partner once he dies, we are dealing with a mandate *post mortem exequendum*. In this case, the transfer to the beneficiary is immediate and the handing over of the passbook to the beneficiary is simply a material act, which does not imply any transfer of assets. The same can be said for donations where the donator donates an asset with immediate effect but reserves the right to use it until his death. If a mandatary is ordered to hand over the asset to the beneficiary after the mandator's death, the mandate is considered a material act concerning a transfer that had already been completed during the deceased's lifetime, and is therefore not seen to violate the prohibition of succession pacts. Under Italian law, therefore, a mandate contract cannot serve as a will-substitute, but can serve as an accessory contract that allows a will-substitute to work effectively (eg, bank deposit in favour of third parties which orders the bank to hand over the savings book to the beneficiary).

[87] Death of the mandator as a cause of extinction of the mandate is considered a default rule by the prevailing view. A Finessi, 'Art 1728' in G Cian and A Trabucchi (eds), *Commentario breve al codice civile*, 11th edn (Padua, Cedam, 2014) ch 12, para 6.

[88] Cass 4 October 1962, no 2804, (1963) *Foro italiano* I, 49–53, where the mandator ordered his spouse to hand over savings books to his eight grandchildren after his death.

[89] See above, nn 21 f.

IV. Trusts and Similar Devices

A. Trusts

Since Italy ratified the Hague Convention of 1 July 1985 on the law applicable to trusts and their recognition in 1989,[90] Italian practitioners have started to make use of so-called domestic trusts for the transfer of wealth on death. Domestic trusts *(trusts interni)*, a notion coined by one of the leading Italian scholars on trust law, Maurizio Lupoi, are trusts whose elements are entirely located in Italy (Italian settlor, Italian trustee, Italian beneficiaries, assets in Italy), while the only foreign element is the law chosen by the settlor to govern the trust.[91] After a long debate on the admissibility of such domestic trusts under the Hague Convention, there is now common agreement that domestic trusts ruled by foreign law are to be recognised in Italy.[92] For succession purposes, a trust may be used to skip one generation with regard to the transfer of a family-owned business or with regard to family assets, so that the first generation will enjoy only the income of the business or the assets, while the second generation will receive the business or the assets.[93] In order to serve as a will-substitute and not as a form of anticipated succession, such a trust would need to be arranged in such a way as to reserve in the hands of the settlor the power to change the beneficiaries of the trust or to cancel the trust altogether.[94] However, because such living revocable trusts are susceptible to attack on several grounds, they are not common in Italian practice.[95] Revocable trusts can, for example, be considered sham trusts and thus be declared void.[96] A recent decision by the Tribunale di Reggio Emilia in a bankruptcy proceeding declared a trust unrecognisable under the Hague Convention based on the fact that it gave the settlor unlimited power to change the terms of the trust.[97] Other

[90] Law no 364 of 16 October 1989, in force from 1 January 1992.

[91] Lupoi, 'Trusts in Italy', above n 81, 303.

[92] On the debate regarding the compatibility of these trusts with Italian law and their use in practice see A Braun, 'Italy: The Trust Interno' in D Hayton (ed), *The International Trust*, 3rd edn (London, Jordan Publishing, 2011) 787–817.

[93] Lupoi, 'Trusts in Italy', above n 81, 306.

[94] A Palazzo and A Sassi, *Trattato della successione e dei negozi successori: 2. Negozi successori anticipatori* (Turin, UTET, 2012) 528; Zoppini, 'Contributo allo studio delle disposizioni testamentarie "in forma indiretta"', above n 38, 1114.

[95] Braun, 'Italy: The Trust Interno', above n 92, 796; S Bartoli and D Muritano, *Le clausole dei trusts interni* (Turin, UTET, 2008) 225. Beyond the reasons indicated above, this may be due to the fact that most of the time the law of England or the law of Jersey is chosen to be applied to the trust interno. Braun, 'Italy: The Trust Interno', above n 92, 795. English law allows revocability only as an exception to the general rule of irrevocability, while Jersey changed its law in 2006, introducing the power to revoke in s 40(1) of the Trusts (Jersey) Law.

[96] The opinions expressed in the literature on this point differ. For the validity of a clause by which the settlor reserves the right to change the beneficiaries, see Bartoli and Muritano, above n 95, 32–39; S Bartoli, *Trust e atto di destinazione nel diritto di famiglia e delle persone* (Milan, Giuffrè, 2011) 354–57.

[97] Tribunale Reggio Emilia 21 October 2014, Giurisprudenza locale—Modena 2014.

problems of such trusts include the fact that they may conflict with the prohibition of succession pacts[98] and that, used as an alternative to a will, they can interfere with the rules on forced heirship and can thus—in line with Article 15 lit c of the Hague Convention—be subject to claw-back claims brought by forced heirs.[99]

B. Separation of Assets According to Article 2645ter C Civ

Article 2645ter C Civ, introduced in 2006,[100] allows immoveable and registered moveable property (vehicles, aeroplanes and ships) to be dedicated to a purpose 'worthy of protection under the legal system'[101] (Art 1322 para 2 C Civ), for the benefit of persons with a disability, of public administration institutions or of other institutions and individuals,[102] who are not the disposing party.[103] The effect of separating registered real or personal property,[104] and assigning it to a certain purpose is that, even though ownership is not necessarily transferred,[105] the assets are separated from the disposing party's other assets, and that once the deed of separation is registered, it will take effect also with regard to third parties. Dedicating assets to a certain purpose reduces the liability pool for the creditors of the disposing party and therefore limits general liability with regard to all present and future assets (Art 2740 C Civ). In order to be valid, such an act must be

[98] R Montinaro, 'Successione mortis causa, pactum fiduciae e trust' in G Bonilini (ed), *Trattato di diritto delle successioni e donazioni*, vol 1 (Milan, Giuffrè, 2009) 251, 267–71.

[99] In a recent case brought before the Italian Supreme Court, the settlor's daughter born out of an extra-matrimonial relationship filed a claim to declare the invalidity of a trust her father had established prior to his death, which transferred his assets to trustees located both in the UK and Switzerland, thus depriving her of her forced share. The Italian Supreme Court, however, had only to decide on the question of whether Italian courts had jurisdiction with regard to this case, since the deed contained a jurisdiction clause. These clauses are considered to be without effects with regard to third parties. See Cass Sezioni Unite 20 June 2014, no 14041, unpublished.

[100] Law no 51 of 23 June 2006, Art 39bis.

[101] How exactly this 'interest worthy of protection under the legal system' is to be understood, is unclear. It is generally held that while the legal system does not allow assets to be separated in order to protect them from creditors, it does allow assets to be protected in order to dedicate them to a certain cause (eg, the maintenance of a relative, the maintenance of a castle etc). In any case, it is always a case by case decision whether the interest of the parties is worthy to be protected. On the notion see R Lenzi, 'Atto di destinazione' in *Enciclopedia del diritto*, Annali V (2012) 52, 68–72; R Dicillo, 'Atti e vincoli di destinazione' in *Digesto delle discipline privatistiche—sezione civile*, 3rd aggiornamento (Turin, UTET, 2007) 151, 164 f.

[102] At first sight, this list is misleading as it seems to limit the availability of this instrument with regard to certain beneficiaries. However, everybody, both legal entities of all kind and natural persons, may be beneficiaries under an act of separation of assets for a certain purpose.

[103] Lenzi, 'Atto di destinazione', above n 101, 67.

[104] It is debated whether only registered property with a special system of publicity may be the object of similar acts of separation. See Dicillo, above n 101, 160; A Zoppini and L Nonne, 'Fondazioni e trust quali strumenti della successione ereditaria' in P Rescigno and M Ieva (eds), *Trattato breve delle successioni e donazioni*, 2nd edn (Padua, Cedam, 2010) 147, 174. On the different views, see Bartoli, above n 96, 136–52.

[105] The assets dedicated to a specific purpose may also remain with the disposing party. Lenzi, 'Atto di destinazione', above n 101, 60.

adopted in the form of a notarial document and may not be established for longer than 90 years, or longer than the beneficiary's lifetime where the beneficiary is a natural person. In order to serve as a will-substitute, the disposing party would need to reserve the right to control the terms of the separated assets. However, according to the prevailing view, such an enduring power to control and revoke the disposition (eg, in order to change the beneficiaries) is contrary to the scope of this device under Article 2645ter C Civ and thus not permitted.[106] However, drawing on the rules of revocable trusts, some other authors tend to allow free revocability.[107]

V. Family Pacts

In 2006, the Italian legislature finally responded to the repeated recommendation of the European Commission to offer procedures that are more suitable for the intergenerational transfer of small and medium-sized businesses.[108] Thus, the so called family pact (*patto di famiglia*) was introduced in Articles 768bis-octies C Civ.[109] This instrument allows the owners of a business or of shares in a company to transfer the business or the shares to one or more descendants during lifetime with the consent of the other forced heirs.[110] Even though the assignment typically takes immediate effect and is thus an instrument of anticipated succession,[111] it may exceptionally come with the characteristics of a will-substitute. In fact, it has been pointed out that nothing in the provisions expressly excludes the parties to the family pact from postponing the effects of the assignment with regard to the moment of death.[112] In addition, according to Article 768septies no 2 C Civ, the assignor may, by express declaration in the contract, reserve himself a

[106] ibid, 79; Dicillo, above n 101, 167; Zoppini and Nonne, above n 104, 174.

[107] Bartoli, above n 96, 356, who points out, however, that just as with revocable trusts there is a certain risk that such an act of separation of assets may be considered a sham and thus be void.

[108] Commission Recommendation of 7 December 1994 on the transfer of small and medium-sized enterprises (94/1069/EC); Commission Communication of 28 March 1998 on the transfer of small and medium-sized enterprises (98/C 93/02); Commission Communication of 14 March 2006: 'Transfer of Businesses—Continuity through a new beginning' (COM 2006/117).

[109] Law no 55 of 14 February 2006.

[110] Braun, 'Testamentary Formalities in Italy', above n 5, 124; for a detailed analysis see Braun, 'Towards a Greater Autonomy of Testators and Heirs', above n 3, 470–73.

[111] A Zoppini, 'Profili sistematici della successione "anticipata"' (2007) 53 *Rivista di diritto civile* II 273, 289; G Amadio, 'Profili funzionali del patto di famiglia' (2007) 53 *Rivista di diritto civile* II 345, 351; Palazzo and Sassi, above n 94, 734.

[112] In the sense of a time limit (when I die; *cum moriar*) or of a suspensive condition (if I die frist; *si praemoriar*): S Delle Monache, 'Funzione, contenuto ed effetti del patto di famiglia' in A Zaccaria (ed), *Tradizione e modernità nel diritto successorio* (Padua, Cedam, 2007) 328; G Sicchiero, 'La causa del patto di famiglia' (2006) 22 *Contratto e impresa* 1261, 1272. For a detailed analysis on this point see M Ieva, 'Patto di famiglia' in *Enciclopedia del diritto*, Annali VI (2013) 634, 646 ff.

right to terminate the contract at his free will. The family pact can therefore serve as a will-substitute. It must be mentioned, however, that such an arrangement runs contrary to the policy goals pursued by the legislature of ensuring the stable and reliable transfer of businesses to the next generation during the lifetime of the owner.[113]

VI. Tensions with General Policy Goals of Succession Law

A. Prohibition of Succession Pacts and Forced Heirship

It has already been mentioned that will-substitutes are in tension with the prohibition of succession pacts. This prohibition partly serves the purpose of protecting those close relatives of the deceased who are forced heirs,[114] making it easier to ensure that the rights of the forced heirs are respected. For example, a contract by which one party transfers what remains at the time of his death to someone who in exchange provides some lifetime service would be valid in the absence of the prohibition, and executing it would reduce the pool of assets used to calculate the share of the forced heirs. Succession pacts are thus perceived as a potential risk to the protection of the claims of forced heirs. The same can be said with regard to devices that serve as will-substitutes, because they may make it difficult for forced heirs to see their expectations fulfilled. The main reason for this is that, like donations, will-substitutes create asset transfers outside succession law. It is therefore more difficult for the closest relatives to discover all the possible paths that the assets of the deceased might have taken during his lifetime. Consider, for example, a bank deposit in favour of a third party where the bank took the mandate *post mortem exequendum* to hand over the disposing party's savings book to the beneficiary after the disposing party's death. In such circumstances, this indirect gift might remain unknown to the forced heirs. Furthermore, because will-substitutes regularly constitute indirect donations, they make it more difficult for forced heirs to define the exact basis on which their share is to be determined. In addition, depending on the arrangement chosen by the deceased, they can also make it particularly difficult to identify the person

[113] A Palazzo, 'Il patto di famiglia tra tradizione e rinnovamento del diritto privato' (2007) 53 *Rivista di diritto civile* II 261, 270; A Pischetola and G Corasantini, 'Il patto di famiglia' in F Preite (ed), *Atti notarili: Diritto comunitario e internazionale*, vol 4 (Turin, UTET, 2011) 1793; Ieva, *I fenomeni a rilevanza successoria*, above n 31, 198 f.

[114] Ieva, 'Successione', above n 8, 3; M Ieva, 'Divieto dei patti successori e tutela dei legittimari' (2005) 49 *Rivista del notariato* 933, 935.

against whom a claw-back claim may be brought. This is especially true for trusts, where it is unclear whether the action of the forced heirs is to be brought against the trustee or against the beneficiaries.[115]

B. Will Formalities

The general requirement for a specific written form of wills[116] does not appear to be in great tension with will-substitutes, for most of the arrangements mentioned above require some written document signed by the disposing party. So, for example, the nomination of a beneficiary in a life insurance contract requires a written statement (Art 1920 C Civ). The same is true for the nomination of a beneficiary under a private pension scheme, where the Italian Supervisory Commission for Pension Funds provides a special form to be completed by the insured. With regard to arrangements involving real property, the written form is always required (Art 1350 C Civ). So, for example, when a maintenance contract is concluded, the transfer of real property in exchange for the service to be provided needs to be adopted in writing. The same goes for trusts and fiduciary agreements, as well as for consolidation clauses and other continuation clauses in partnership contracts. In most cases, therefore, the basic formalities required for will-substitutes do not substantially deviate from the formal requirements for wills.

C. Unworthiness to Inherit

The rules on unworthiness to inherit do not apply to will-substitutes. Hence, if the beneficiary of a transfer by will-substitute threatened the life of or even killed the disposing party, or interfered with his free will, his eligibility to receive the transfer would not be affected by the regulations concerning unworthiness to inherit (Art 463 C Civ). This can give rise to problematic situations. For example, if the transferee kills the transferor and beneficiary in a maintenance contract, no consequences arise as to the validity of the transfer. Only life insurance contracts offer a special provision designed to fill the gap. Life insurance contracts stipulate that if the beneficiary threatens the life of the disposing party, he will lose the right to receive the benefits according to Article 1922 C Civ. The same applies where the beneficiary intentionally takes the life of the disposing party (Art 1900 C Civ). In this latter case, however, the prevailing view is that not only is the beneficiary deprived of the right to receive the benefits, but also the heirs. This means that the

[115] M Lupoi, *Istituzioni del diritto dei trust e degli affidamenti fiduciari* (Padua, Cedam, 2008) 83 f, who expresses the pious wish that Italian practice does not apply the trust in order to prejudice the position of the forced heirs. Ieva, 'Successione', above n 8, 14; Zoppini and Nonne, above n 104, 164 f; Montinaro, above n 98, 286–91.

[116] On will formalities in Italian law see Braun, 'Testamentary Formalities in Italy', above n 5, 126–41.

insurance company is released on the grounds that a risk triggered intentionally[117] cannot be insured.[118] Private pension schemes do not contain any similar rules on unworthiness. Here, if the beneficiary kills the pension fund member, he will remain eligible to receive the benefits, unless the heirs decide to revoke the indirect donation on the basis of ingratitude (Arts 809, 801 C Civ). This disparateness could be avoided by extending the provision on unworthiness by analogy to the beneficiaries of a private pension scheme.

D. Rules on Revocation

The revocation rules applicable to wills, especially those governing nominations of third-party beneficiaries in life insurance contracts, harbour potential for tension.[119] What happens, for instance, if a will containing a nomination for a life insurance contract is revoked by a later will? Does this generic revocation include all dispositions of the previous will (Art 680 C Civ) or does the nomination need to be revoked separately? And what should happen in cases where the revocation of a will containing the nomination is itself revoked (revocation of revocation)? Does Article 681 C Civ apply, allowing the original nomination to revive? And can a nomination contained in the insurance contract be revoked by a generic nomination of an heir in a later will?

According to the prevailing view, the nomination of a beneficiary in a life insurance contract contained in a will should be classified as a lifetime disposition.[120] Thus, one could argue that a revocation of a previous *mortis causa* disposition (ie, a will) does not necessarily include the lifetime disposition (ie, nomination of third party) contained in the revoked will. Similarly, one could argue that a later generic will, which does not refer to the life insurance benefits, cannot revoke a previous nomination made in the life insurance contract. Indeed, some hold that a designation or revocation of a life insurance nomination is valid even if the will in which it is contained is invalid on the grounds of formalities.[121]

[117] A special rule applies to suicides, where according to Art 1927 C Civ, the insurance company does not have to pay if suicide is committed within two years after the life insurance contract had been signed.

[118] L Bugiolacchi, 'L'assicurazione sulla vita a favore di terzo' in G Alpa (ed), *Le assicurazioni private*, vol 3 (Turin, UTET, 2006) 2556, 2599. Many authors have criticised this contradictory view. See Buttaro, above n 41, 662; N Gasperoni, 'Assicurazione: III Assicurazione sulla vita' in *Enciclopedia Giuridica Treccani* (1994) 14; Rossetti, above n 33, 865.

[119] The same problems arise with regard to nominations in private pension schemes if one allows these nominations and their revocation to be made in a will.

[120] Fanelli, above n 37, 1399; Buttaro, above n 41, 658; Gasperoni, above n 118, 12, Rossetti, above n 33, 854; Bugiolacchi, 'Assicurazione sulla vita e nuova designazione del benficiario' (2004) *Responsabilità civile e previdenza* 833–36; Palazzo, *Testamento e istituti alternativi*, above n 18, 357 ff. Against G Giampiccolo, *Il contenuto atipico del testamento* (Milan, Giuffrè, 1954) 306; clearly followed by Palazzo, *Autonomia contrattuale e successioni anomale*, above n 5, 87 ff, who later changed his view.

[121] Buttaro, above n 41, 658; Rossetti, above n 33, 854; Palazzo, *Testamento e istituti alternativi*, above n 18, 353; against Gasperoni, above n 118, 13.

This view supports the principle that nominating life insurance beneficiaries in a will should be a purely autonomous act.

In a recent case, the Tribunale di Palermo[122] had to decide whether a generic disposition in a will ('all real and personal property including money and other financial assets shall go to my spouse') could be interpreted as a revocation of the previous nomination of the 'intestate heirs' as beneficiaries contained in the life insurance contract. It held that contrary to the general opinion a nomination in a will had to be considered an atypical *mortis causa* disposition and was thus subject to the rules of interpretation for wills. As a consequence, the previous nomination in the contract was considered to have been revoked. While this result was not subject to criticism, the fact that the reasoning behind it had classified the nomination as a *mortis causa* disposition was. It was argued that the same conclusion could have been reached by claiming that, notwithstanding their lifetime character, nominations of life insurance beneficiaries in a will are regularly so intertwined with *mortis causa* dispositions that they are subject to the rules of interpretation of wills. As a consequence, what counts is the real intention of the deceased.[123]

However, this answer is not entirely satisfactory. For example, it generally does not serve to solve cases where a lack of corresponding information in a will makes the task of reconstructing the (real) intention of the deceased impracticable. Moreover, it does not tell us whether the rules on revocation apply where, in the absence of an express revocation and thus in the absence of a clear intention, only those dispositions are considered to be revoked which are incompatible with the previous ones (Art 682 C Civ).

It seems fair that the application of the rule of revocation for incompatibility (Art 682 C Civ) is extended to all cases where doubts concerning the real intention of the deceased remain. This will regularly have the effect that previous nominations in a life insurance contract or will are not affected by a later will, as long as the will does not contain any express revocation or reference to the insurance money. So, for example, if the deceased names his daughter as the beneficiary in an insurance contract or will and later makes a new will instituting his spouse as his universal heir, without mentioning the insurance money, the nomination is not incompatible[124] with the disposition in the will and can therefore not be considered to have been revoked.[125] So, unless the will gives some clear indications regarding the true intention of the deceased, prior nominations (whether contained in a will or not) should remain in effect. This should hold true even where the circumstances that may have triggered the nomination have changed

[122] Tribunale Palermo 22 January 2003 (2004) *Responsabilità civile e previdenza* 823 ff.

[123] Bugiolacchi, 'Assicurazione sulla vita e nuova designazione del benficiario', above n 120, 839.

[124] Indeed, the relationship between a nomination and the institution of a universal heir is the same as the relationship between a bequest (*legato*) and the institution of a universal heir, where no question of compatibility arises.

[125] Against without explanation Rossetti, above n 33, 860, who considers a nomination in a will to be revoked if a later will is made without nomination.

(eg, divorce or separation from the beneficiary of the life insurance contract). Indeed, in the absence of a clear intention expressed by the deceased (and in the absence of a legal presumption to the contrary even for wills), we simply do not know whether the deceased might not have wanted to hold on to the original nomination in the life insurance contract for a different reason. In case of doubt, the nomination therefore stands.

VII. For a New Discussion on Will-Substitutes in Italy

There is an abundance of literature on will-substitutes in Italian law. Yet it seems that this literature has always stood in marked contrast with the practical relevance of many of the aforementioned alternative devices for the transfer of wealth on death. Indeed, the primary goal of the mainly theoretical discussion on will-substitutes in Italy has always been to show that there are some routes around the prohibition of succession pacts. Practitioners, however, not least because of the unpredictable currents of case law, have continued to fear the risks of an infringement, steering as far away from them as possible. This explains why the mostly dogmatic debate on contractual will-substitutes in Italy has lacked any substantial progress over the years.[126]

This is not to say, however, that Italian law does not have functioning will-substitutes. Quite the contrary; some instruments expressly regulated by law, like nominations of third-party beneficiaries in life insurance contracts and in complementary pension schemes, are certainly of considerable practical importance. In particular, nominations in life insurance contracts by which a certain part of one's assets can be shielded against the creditors of the insured and the beneficiary, offer considerable advantages over a transfer by will, and thus constitute important will-substitutes. Yet, as we have seen, in the absence of any coordination with the rules on succession law, some serious tensions can arise, especially with regard to unworthiness to inherit and to the rules on the revocation of wills.

In light of recent inheritance tax reforms, taxation aspects are not usually a reason for choosing will-substitutes,[127] nor is avoiding probate an issue under Italian law.[128] In Italy, the need for will-substitutes has often been explained by

[126] Indeed, most texts produced on this topic by the main contributors to the debate on will-substitutes are simply republished over and over without substantial changes, a fact that makes the lack of progress and the sterility of the discussion immediately obvious.

[127] Ieva, *I fenomeni a rilevanza successoria*, above n 31, 2–3.

[128] Avoiding probate is indicated as one of the main reasons for choosing a will-substitute in the US, where the concept was coined by John Langbein, 'The Nonprobate Revolution and the Future of the Law of Succession' (1984) 97 *Harvard Law Review* 1108, 1116. There is no probate proceeding under Italian law that a will-substitute would help to avoid.

claiming that the law of wills does not differentiate between different types of assets and therefore falls short of meeting the diverse needs that result from the increasing degree of asset complexity, for example, the complexity of business transfers.[129] Another reason for making use of will-substitutes was said to lie in the need to provide maintenance for those who are not members of the inner family circle or to protect and preserve for certain assets.[130] However, most of the contractual devices discussed as will-substitutes in Italian legal scholarship are unsuited to meet these needs. This is particularly true with regard to the intergenerational transfer of businesses.

For a successful intergenerational transfer of a business, will-substitutes as unilateral revocable acts are insufficient. What is needed are stable and thus irrevocable contractual arrangements between the old and the young generation, where all interested parties cooperate to find the best solution for the continuation of the company and for the members of the family. For that purpose, the Italian legislature introduced the family pact, a contractual arrangement between the owner of a business, the descendant(s) continuing the business and the closest family members.[131] But the many downsides to this instrument, for example its strong protection of forced heirship and the fact that it encumbers the descendants with the task of liquidating the shares to the other family members, have so far prevented its success. Considering that 99 per cent of Italian businesses are SMEs[132] and that more than 70 per cent of these businesses are family run,[133] it seems obvious that Italian succession law needs a reform that eliminates the prohibition of succession pacts and significantly reduces the protection of forced heirs. Only in this way can a successful intergenerational transfer of businesses be achieved. Particularly with regard to the transfer of companies on death, a will as a unilateral act is certainly inadequate to ensure a successful continuation of an entire business, as is a revocable will-substitute. By contrast, devices of anticipated succession seem to be more suited and are more frequently used in practice, but the disposing party is not always prepared to give away his assets irrevocably during his lifetime. Clauses in partnership or corporation agreements cannot solve the problem.

Will-substitutes also have serious disadvantages when it comes to the need to provide for somebody (eg, non-married partners, handicapped children with special needs, close friends in need) after one's death. First, will-substitutes, like

[129] See, eg Palazzo, *Autonomia contrattuale e successioni anomale*, above n 5, 3; Marella, above n 25, 94; Lenzi, 'Il problema dei patti successori tra diritto vigente e prospettive di riforma', above n 18, 1212; Zanchi, above n 16, 744.

[130] Palazzo, *Autonomia contrattuale e successioni anomale*, above n 6, 62–156; Ieva, *I fenomeni a rilevanza successoria*, above n 31, 11–15.

[131] ISTAT, 'Rapporto annuale 2013, Ch 2, Il sistema delle imprese italiane: competitività e potenziale di crescita', www.istat.it/en/files/2013/05/cap2.pdf, 65.

[132] Eurostat, *Key figures on European business with a special feature on SMEs* (Luxembourg, 2011) 12.

[133] ISTAT, *Rapporto annuale 2013, Chapter 2 Il sistema delle imprese italiane: competitività e potenziale di crescita*, www.istat.it/en/files/2013/05/cap2.pdf, 65.

bequests, are indirect donations and as such are typically subject to the claw-back claims of forced heirs.[134] Second, they do not offer any better protection to the beneficiary in need of maintenance, for they are just as unstable (revocable) as wills. Third, and contrary to wills, they require an immediate (though revocable) transfer of assets, which might make them less attractive for the disposing party than a bequest in a will. Fourth, will-substitutes are constantly exposed to the danger of being caught by the trap of succession pacts,[135] and fifth, will-substitutes as indirect donations are subject to the same taxation as direct donations and transfers under a will.[136]

It follows that most of the devices discussed on a theoretical level in Italy cannot solve the problems they were intended for. The discussion on will-substitutes therefore needs to be restarted. The future debate should be less concerned with the description of devices that may not be in conflict with the prohibition of succession pacts and focus more on those devices that are relevant in practice. The lack of coordination between will-substitutes used in practice and the general rules of succession law gives rise to many questions that need to be studied more closely.

[134] Maintenance expenses for handicapped children are not subject to claims of forced heirs (Arts 809 and 742 C Civ).

[135] A Zoppini, 'Contributo allo studio delle disposizioni testamentarie "in forma indiretta"', above n 38, 1087.

[136] *Memento pratico—Famiglia e patrimonio* (Ipsoa—Francis Lefebvre, 2014) 6603–09.

7

Will-Substitutes in France

CÉCILE PÉRÈS

I. Hard Conditions for Will-Substitutes

At first sight, French law does not provide the most propitious setting for will-substitutes. There are several reasons for this. First, French law rests upon the principle known as *succession to the person*, by which successors acquire the deceased's property, rights, interests and liabilities as of the time of death. The deceased's estate is merged with the estates of the heirs, who can then manage it as their own. Consequently, the heirs' powers are unlimited, but so is their liability,[1] with the result that, in principle, they are answerable for the estate's liabilities above and beyond the assets they receive. Under French law, succession is also extrajudicial in character, so that, usually, the settlement of a succession will not give rise to court proceedings. However, the emergence of will-substitutes seems closely bound to the competing system known as *succession to property*, found in common law jurisdictions. Under this system, an administrator verifies the proper title of claimants in the succession, manages the succession and liquidates the liabilities in such a way that the heirs collect only the outstanding balance.[2] Research in the US regularly establishes a connection between the success of will-substitutes and the desire to avoid probate,[3] itself considered unnecessary, lengthy and too costly.[4]

[1] F Terré, Y Lequette and S Gaudemet, *Droit civil, Les successions, Les libéralités*, 4th edn (Paris, Dalloz, 2014) no 785. The law of 23 June 2006 reforming successions and gifts departed from the principle of succession to the person by creating the posthumous-effect mandate, allowing the future decedent to appoint an agent tasked with administering all or part of the estate included in the succession in place of the heirs. It is governed by arts 812 ff of the Civil Code. On this point, see esp C Brenner, 'La gestion de la succession' (2006) *Dalloz* 2559.

[2] On differences between systems, see generally YH Leleu, *La transmission de la succession en droit comparé* (Brussels, Bruylant, 1996).

[3] This is very clear in JH Langbein, 'The Nonprobate Revolution and the Future of the Law of Succession' (1984) 97 *Harvard Law Review* 1108. The shift against probate in the US was captured by the publication of the bestseller by NF Dacey, *How to Avoid Probate* (New York, Crown, 1965). See also GMP McCouch, 'Will Substitutes under the Revised Uniform Probate Code' (1993) 58 *Brook Law Review* 1123 ff.

[4] Langbein, above n 3, 1116–17. Probate in the US costs on average 1.5% of the value of the estate, sometimes more in some states: J Talpis, 'Succession Substitutes' (2011) 356 *Recueil des cours de l'Académie de droit international de La Haye* 9–238, esp 22 fn 5.

In contrast, the extrajudicial character of succession under French law renders such avoidance strategies pointless in this respect.

Second, succession is designed to be universal in scope. It is the *only* legal mechanism for passing on property upon death. Succession may be statutory (intestate) or voluntary (testate), depending on whether the decedent has named an heir in a will. Statutory succession may itself subject property to variable rules of transmission, which at times take account of not just the closeness of the tie with the deceased, but also the origin or nature of the property, in what are termed anomalous (or abnormal) successions. These contrast with regular successions that are subject to the principle known as the *unity of succession*.[5] But the transmission and acquisition of property upon death is invariably effected by succession. There is no alternative.

Third, under French law, succession is subject in part to rules of public policy that delimit the scope of individual testamentary intentions. In particular, the deceased may have freely disposed of his property by way of gifts, but within the limits, when there are forced heirs,[6] of the free portion.[7] If the limit is exceeded, gifts made by the deceased are subject to claw-back in part or in full. Thus, it can be readily understood that French law looks to thwart any attempts to remove property from the ambit of succession and the forced portion and to transfer it *post mortem* by some other means, and the consistency of French law depends on this. To compound this restrictive effort, as a matter of public policy, in principle the Civil Code prohibits any agreements regarding the succession of a living person on pain of nullity.[8] In some cases, this rule has been used to void transfer operations that might otherwise resemble will-substitutes.[9]

Lastly, the Civil Code formally prohibits the making of gifts other than by donation or a will.[10] Anyone wishing to dispose 'gratuitously of all or of part of his

[5] A principle which was formally enshrined by the drafters of the Civil Code of 1804 (former art 732: 'The law considers neither the nature nor the origin of property in settling succession') but vanished from the Code with the enactment of the law of 3 December 2001. In favour of the continuation of the principle in positive law, see Y Lequette, 'La règle de l'unité de la succession après la loi du 3 décembre 2001: continuité ou rupture?' in *Mélanges Ph Simler* (Paris, Dalloz–Litec, 2006) 172 ff.

[6] Forced heirs (*héritiers réservataires*) are issue, in proportions that vary with the number of children (arts 913 and 913-1 C Civ) and, if there are no issue, the surviving spouse is forced heir of one-quarter of the estate (art 914-1 C Civ).

[7] Art 912 C Civ: 'The reserved portion is that part of the assets and rights of the succession whose devolution, free of charges, legislation assures to certain heirs, called forced heirs, provided they are called to the succession and provided they accept it. The disposable portion is that part of the assets and rights of the succession that is not reserved by legislation and of which the deceased can freely dispose by liberalities'. (This as well as all subsequent translations of French provisions are taken from Légifrance, www.legifrance.gouv.fr/Traductions/en-English/Legifrance-translations.)

[8] Art 722 C Civ: 'Agreements having the purpose of creating rights or renouncing rights to all or part of a succession not yet opened or of an asset forming a part of it are effective only in the cases in which they are authorised by legislation'. Italian Law also prohibits these succession pacts under the influence of Roman Law: see ch 6 above I.B.

[9] On the accretion clause, see below section II.A.iv.

[10] Art 893 al 2 C Civ: 'A liberality may be accomplished only by donation inter vivos or by testament'.

property, or his rights for another's benefit',[11] must necessarily do so either by a gift *inter vivos* or by a will *mortis causa*. Again there is no alternative method. However, because of the dangers for the donor who depletes his estate without reciprocal consideration, gifts are subject to particular formal rules for their validity. It is true that a distinction has to be drawn on this point. For wills, the form requirements laid down by statute[12] are absolute and may not be avoided. A legal instrument cannot be a will unless it satisfies the requisite testamentary forms,[13] while the unilateral instrument by which a person disposes of his property upon death is necessarily a will. Any other purported disposition in the form of a will-substitute therefore appears impossible.[14] For lifetime gifts, the position is quite different as far as form requirements are concerned. A donation[15] must be executed before a notary or otherwise it will be declared void.[16] But this solemn requirement, which holds only for what are termed 'ostensible gifts', has long brooked numerous exceptions.[17] In particular, it is generally accepted that certain instruments considered to be neutral,[18] such as a payment, an acknowledgement of debt, a clause waiving or conferring a right with respect to a third party, may be accepted as donations, even if not made before a notary. Such donations are termed 'indirect'. It is further accepted that donations may be disguised to take on the appearance of instruments for valuable consideration by dint of some pretence. Such donations are valid and are essentially treated as gifts. However, precisely because they are recaptured by the succession law, and because they require a lifetime transfer through which the donor immediately and irrevocably divests himself of the asset, they are not true alternatives to succession.

For all of these reasons, French law appears from the outset to be less amenable than other legal systems, and particularly common law jurisdictions, to the development of will-substitutes, in the sense—assuming the concept has been

[11] By the definition of gift (liberality) in art 893 al 1er C Civ.

[12] Besides privileged testaments, four forms of will are provided for and regulated by law: holograph, officially-recorded, secret (art 969 C Civ) and international wills.

[13] Terré, Lequette and Gaudemet, above n 1, no 406 remarking (371, fn 2) that 'legacies cannot be granted by way of indirect or hand-to-hand gifts. And while a disguised legacy may be made, it will have to have been made in the form of a will (*Nancy, 14 juill. 1875, DP 1876.2.177, S. 1876. 2.232; Caen 30 mai 1888 sous Req. 27 mai 1889, S. 1889. 1. 426)*'.

[14] French law has no equivalent to s 6-102 of the Revised Uniform Probate Code (UPC), by which the testamentary nature of will-substitutes can be excluded so they can escape nullity while at the same time subjecting various (esp fiscal) aspects of them to the rules applicable to wills.

[15] Which art 894 of the C Civ defines as 'an act by which the donor divests himself now and irrevocably of the thing donated in favour of the donee, who accepts it'.

[16] Art 931 C Civ: 'All acts containing a donation inter vivos shall be executed before notaries, in the ordinary form of contracts; and the notaries shall retain an original of them, on pain of nullity'.

[17] This concerns indirect donations, disguised donations (which presuppose some subterfuge) and hand-to-hand gifts (which rely on the tradition of the thing given). They became valid through a movement to put an end to gift giving in solemn form dating from pre-revolutionary law. See J-F Montredon, *La désolennisation des libéralités*, preface B Teyssié, vol 209 (Paris, LGDJ, Bibliothèque de droit privé, 1987); M Nicod, 'Le formalisme en droit des libéralités' (PhD thesis, University of Paris XII, 1996).

[18] That is to say different from gratuitous instruments and instruments for consideration.

properly understood here[19]—of legal devices ensuring the voluntary and freely revocable transfer of property upon death outside the usual channels of the law of succession. Will-substitutes do not form a legal category identified as such under French law. Accordingly, French legal literature on will-substitutes is essentially about comparative law, through the study of North American estate planning techniques,[20] and international private laws concerning the determination of the law governing such legal tools in an international context.[21]

Under these circumstances, it is all the more remarkable that French law, which seems so adequately armed to counter any will-substitute, actually allows them to thrive. In looking for the principal forms of will-substitute under French law, it will be seen that in certain instances, property may be passed upon death while escaping the application of conventional rules governing succession. But the rationale of succession law, which is strained by these exceptional mechanisms, is never far distant: it is not easily expunged and it is always prone to realigning these elements with the law of succession.

The issue will therefore be addressed in two stages. After highlighting the main manifestations of will-substitutes in French law (section I), we shall examine the limits that French law imposes upon them (section II).

II. Manifestations of Will-Substitutes

Upon reflection, French law has quite a large number of devices by which property or a right may be passed on death other than in the customary way under the law of succession. These may be reminiscent of will-substitutes, but more often than not, the peculiarities of such devices, compared with the provisions of a will, explain why the property or right in question escapes from the regular settlement of an estate. These devices will be examined first, after which we will be in a position to focus on the mechanisms that seem to correspond most closely to will-substitutes, and that prompt lively debate.

Let us look first at 'imperfect' (subsection A) and then at 'pure' (subsection B) will-substitutes.

[19] On the terminological difficulty of finding an expression referring to an identical reality in common law and continental law systems, see Talpis, above n 4, 24 f.

[20] See, esp M Goré, 'Estate Planning: quelques aspects de l'anticipation successorale en droit américain' in *Le droit privé français à la fin du XXe siècle, Etudes offertes à P Catala* (Paris, Litec, 2001) 383 ff. On the techniques of anticipated succession in an international context, see G Soudey, *L'Estate Planning—Optimisation civile et fiscale d'une succession internationale*, preface by Y Lequette (Paris, LexisNexis, 2011); M Revillard, *Stratégie de transmission d'un patrimoine international* (Paris, Defrénois-Lextenso éd, 2009); E Fongaro, 'L'anticipation successorale à l'épreuve du "règlement successions"' (2014) 2 *Journal du droit international (Clunet)*, doctr 5.

[21] See, esp E Bendelac, 'Le transfert de biens au décès autrement que par succession en droit international privé' (PhD thesis, University of Paris II, 2014). On trusts in French private international law, see also S Godechot, *L'articulation du trust et du droit des successions*, preface by Y Lequette (Paris, Editions Panthéon-Assas, 2004). For a recent, close study of private international law see Talpis, above n 4, who uses the broader idea of succession substitutes detached from its American origins.

A. Imperfect Will-Substitutes

A number of legal mechanisms may resemble will-substitutes without actually or entirely constituting them, in that they are imperfect forms of substitute. This category is itself highly diverse.[22] In some instances, the difference from pure will-substitutes is glaringly obvious; in others it is more subtle and we are almost dealing with a disposition *mortis causa*. In other words, there is subtle shading within the range of will-substitutes.

i. Inter Vivos *Transfers?*

At times the transfer is *inter vivos* and irrevocable. For example, a donation of legal (bare) ownership while retaining a life interest (usufruct),[23] is a favourite way of providing for a future succession, which entitles the donor to continue to use and enjoy the property. Such donations benefit from advantageous tax arrangements, since the conveyancing duties are levied on the value of the legal ownership alone. When the donor dies, the life interest lapses and no new taxation is levied. But the donor, for all that he remains the beneficial owner, irrevocably and presently transfers legal ownership. The transfer of that title is therefore firm and final: it is effected *inter vivos* and not *mortis causa*,[24] meaning that it cannot be held to express the donor's last wishes.[25]

ii. Pay-As-You-Go Retirement Schemes

At times the choice of beneficiary and the rules applicable are determined entirely by the law with no involvement of the decedent's wishes, which again curbs any analysis of them as will-substitutes, albeit for other reasons. This is the case, for example, of the widow(er)'s pension entitlement that the Social Security Code[26]

[22] *cf* Talpis, above n 4, 46 ff, who distinguishes between 'pure succession substitutes' (which are in fact testamentary in nature and fully revocable, such as the designation of the beneficiary in a life insurance policy); 'imperfect succession substitutes' (which are not of a testamentary nature because they give rise to a right for the beneficiary during the donor's lifetime—eg, an acquisition under a joint tenancy, an accretion clause or an irrevocable trust *inter vivos*—even if the transfer only occurs on death); and 'functional succession substitutes' (lumping into a residual category the mechanisms for effecting transfers on death otherwise than by succession but not meeting the criteria of the previous two categories, such as the right of reversion for retirement pensions, matrimonial advantages or bare ownership donations that reserve usufructus).

[23] Art 949 C Civ: 'A donor is allowed to reserve for his benefit or to dispose of, for the benefit of another, the enjoyment or the usufruct of the movable or immovable property donated'.

[24] Particularly because the special irrevocability of donations (associated with art 894 C Civ) prohibits the donor from including in the donation a unilateral option of breaking it off and taking back the property donated. For a critique of the special irrevocability of donations, see esp W Dross, 'L'irrévocabilité spéciale des donations existe-t-elle?' (2011) *Revue trimestrielle de droit civil* 25 ff.

[25] On the notion of the instrument *mortis causa* as having as its subject matter an item of the future succession by contrast with the instrument *inter vivos* pertaining to a current item of his estate, see esp C Bahurel, 'Les volontés des morts. Vouloir pour le temps où l'on ne sera plus' (PhD thesis, University of Paris II, 2012) no 343 ff.

[26] Arts L 353-1 ff.

grants to the surviving spouse under the French statutory pay-as-you-go retirement pension scheme,[27] on the terms and conditions it lays down.[28] The reversionary right, which the surviving spouse acquires upon the death of the spouse, is distinct from the lifetime entitlement to the retirement pension that by inference was extinguished with the death of the insured.[29] Under all these aspects, there is no will-substitute.

iii. Marital Property Arrangements

At other times, the features of the will-substitute appear slightly more definite but remain imperfect. A particular example here is the enrichment of spouses under marital property arrangements. Under French law, a matrimonial advantage is a profit of a pecuniary nature that a spouse may derive from marital property arrangements and that he or she would not enjoy under the statutory matrimonial arrangement of community of acquisitions (*communauté réduite aux acquêts*). The arrangement is therefore contractual in nature and presupposes a (pre)nuptial settlement. This is the case, for example, with universal common property with a clause attributing all the common property to the surviving spouse. This combination is often chosen by elderly couples when changing their marital property arrangements. It is intended as a way for spouses to organise their succession in advance, instead of making a gift. Such a clause means that all of the spouses' property is common property.[30] Upon death of the first to die, the common property vests in the survivor, with the effect of voiding the estate of all its substance. The success of this legal arrangement has long been explained on grounds of taxation. In principle, matrimonial advantages are not held to be gifts,[31] but rather instruments for valuable consideration.[32] They are therefore not subject to duties on gratuitous transfers. But this fiscal advantage, compared with gifts *mortis causa* and intestate succession, disappeared with the enactment of the law of 21 August 2007, in that since then the surviving spouse has been exempted from paying death transfer duties.[33]

[27] And not the surviving partner (nor a fortiori an unmarried partner): Con Constit, déc no 2011-155 QPC, 29 July 2011, (2011) *Revue trimestrielle de droit civil* 748 observations J Hauser; CE, 18 June 2010, no 315076, (2010) *Revue trimestrielle de droit civil* 764 observations J Hauser; Cass civ (2e) 23 January 2014, no 13-11362, (2014) *Dalloz* 968 note L Andrieu (2014) *Actualité juridique Famille* 197 observations H Roberge.

[28] Particularly of age and means.

[29] M Grimaldi, *Droit civil, Successions*, 6th edn (Paris, Litec, 2001) no 66, fn 219.

[30] Or almost: Art 1526 C Civ.

[31] Except where there is a child not born within the marriage, so as to protect its forced share (*réserve héréditaire*). In this case, the matrimonial advantage is treated as a gift and the child may act against the step-parent to reduce excessive matrimonial advantages that eat into the provision (art 1527 al 2 C Civ).

[32] The question prompted doctrinal discussion but was decided directly by law (art 1527 al 1er C Civ).

[33] Art 796-O bis Code général des impôts.

In any event, enrichments under marital property arrangements are not true will-substitutes. Some do not take effect upon dissolution of the marriage but in the course of the marriage, which excludes any idea of a transfer *post mortem*. This is, for instance, the case with a straightforward universal shared property arrangement without attribution to the surviving spouse,[34] which is also fully effective in the event of divorce. It is true, though, that matrimonial advantages whose effects are deferred on dissolution of the marriage until the death of either spouse,[35] escape from conventional succession rules. Because in principle it is not considered to be a gift, the matrimonial advantage is not reintegrated into the estate for the purposes of identifying a possible infringement of the forced shares. It therefore enables the enrichment of one of the spouses upon death of the other without the property so acquired becoming part of the deceased's estate. Yet even under this assumption, there are restrictions on characterising such arrangements as true will-substitutes. First, the beneficiaries' freedom of choice is restricted, in that by inference a matrimonial advantage can be granted to the spouse alone.[36] Next and most importantly, the matrimonial advantage does not arise from a unilateral instrument *mortis causa*, but rather from an agreement *inter vivos*. It is not because the effects of an instrument can be deferred until death that the instrument is a will. The fact is that the matrimonial advantage cannot be freely revoked by the spouse who has bestowed it on his or her partner, and who acquires it in the lifetime of the donor upon entering into the (pre)nuptial agreement.

iv. Tontine *or Accretion Clauses*

An identical restriction is found with the *tontine* or accretion clause, by which the deceased's interests vest in the survivor. This is a clause whereby two people acquire property together while stipulating that on the death of either, the property is to be deemed the sole property of the survivor. The clause is often stipulated for cohabitants or for spouses with separate property. It was long highly advantageous in fiscal terms, in that it was not subject to gratuitous transfer duties. This was particularly beneficial for unmarried couples, who could thereby escape from a 60 per cent tax rate on the value of the property transferred. But since 1980 the

[34] Such a universal community has full effect if the spouses divorce (art 265 al 1er C Civ). However, paragraph 3 of the same article allows what is called an alternative liquidation clause to be stipulated, providing in the marriage contract for a return to the statutory community if the common property arrangement is dissolved by divorce.

[35] Since these advantages are revoked as of right in the event of divorce (art 265 al 2 C Civ).

[36] Partners who have entered into a civil partnership agreement may opt not for the statutory regime of separation of property but for the contractual undivided property regime provided for by law (art 515-5-1 C Civ). It is generally held that the list of property that art 515-5-2 C Civ formally excludes from this contractual undivided property is mandatory. The partners therefore cannot agree to a universal undivided property arrangement. The reason given is that the law has not provided here for an equivalent, for the benefit of stepchildren, of the action to deduct excessive matrimonial advantages granted by art 1527 al 3 C Civ against the surviving partner.

fiscal advantage of the clause has practically vanished.[37] The *tontine* arrangement is treated as a gift for tax purposes. Its legal nature has, however, changed. Initially, France's supreme civil law court, the Cour de cassation, construed the *tontine* as an agreement on the succession of a living person and declared it void.[38] Then in the late 1950s,[39] the Cour de cassation departed from its own precedent, and ever since has accepted a *tontine* agreement as valid on the following grounds. The Court holds that each purchaser is the owner of the property on the double condition subsequent of one of them dying first, and the condition precedent of the other surviving.[40] As the condition produces a retroactive effect, the predeceased 'has therefore never been the owner of the property whereas the survivor has always been the owner, even if he or she had no way of knowing it'.[41] The Cour de cassation infers from this that the acquisition of property with such a clause is not a gift but rather a contract involving uncertainty for valuable consideration,[42] the contingency residing in the parties' uncertainty regarding the order in which they will die. The property therefore passes without entering the estate of the deceased, and thus escapes both the hotchpot rule and the forced portion. Additionally, the predeceased's creditors have no claim over the property since it is deemed their debtor was never the owner.[43] Again, the *tontine* contains certain features of a will-substitute: it is clearly intended to affect the law of succession, its effects only become operative upon death—albeit they operate retroactively to the date of acquisition—and the donor can freely choose the beneficiary. But it cannot be viewed entirely as an alternative form of testamentary disposition: it is an agreement *inter vivos* that cannot be freely revoked unilaterally. To compound this, the Cour de cassation holds that in the presence of such a clause, joint ownership rules under ordinary law are not applicable. Thus, the *tontine* arrangement is not joint ownership[44] because ultimately there has only ever been a single

[37] Art 754-A Code général des impôts. By way of exception, the law provides that the accretion clause is not subject to gratuitous transfer duties when the property acquired under the *tontine* arrangement is the main common residence of the purchasers and its overall value (not revised since 1980) is less than €76,000 (which is very rare).

[38] Cass, req, 24 January 1928, (1928) 1 *Dalloz périodique* 157, (1928) *Revue trimestrielle de droit civil* 458 observations R Savatier, (1929) 1 *Sirey* 137 note H Vialleton. In principle, succession pacts are banned under French Law, see above section I.

[39] Cass civ, 3 February 1959, (1960) *Dalloz* 592 note E de la Marnière, (1960) *La semaine juridique édition générale* 11823 note P Voirin, (1960) *Revue trimestrielle de droit civil* 692 observations R Savatier; Cass ch mixte, 27 November 1970, (1971) *Dalloz* 81 conclusion Lindon. See also G Morin, 'La clause d'accroissement' (1971) *Dalloz*, Chronique 55.

[40] This analysis is criticised in academic writing, see below n 98.

[41] Cass civ 1re, 14 December 2004, (2005) *Defrénois* 617 observations R Libchaber.

[42] See also Cass civ 1re, 14 December 2004, *Bulletin civil des arrêts de la Cour de cassation* I, no 313, (2005) *Defrénois* 617 observations R Libchaber, (2005) *Revue des contrats* 693 observations A Bénabent. As the clause is subject to French law when the real property acquired is located in France, it often seems to be specified by aliens purchasing property in France, see Talpis, above n 4, 123.

[43] Cass civ, 1re, 18 November 1997, *Bulletin civil des arrêts de la Cour de cassation* I, no 214.

[44] Cass civ 1re, 9 November 2011, no 10-21710, *Bulletin civil des arrêts de la Cour de cassation* I, no 199, (2012) *Defrénois* 343 note N Leblond, (2012) *Revue trimestrielle de droit civil* 95 observations J Hauser, (2012) *Revue des contrats* 445 observations R Libchaber adjudicating that the accretion clause excludes undivided ownership but not undivided usufruct to infer that the spouse who, on the court's

owner. Accordingly, for so long as they are alive, the clause holders are prisoners of the *tontine*, and anyone wishing to exit from the arrangement and individually reach a share-out[45] cannot do so if the other refuses.[46] This can cause serious difficulties, particularly if a couple breaks up. Put otherwise, although the *tontine* arrangement does indeed transfer property upon death other than through the law of succession to a freely chosen beneficiary, its irrevocable character and its status with respect to the law of property mean that it cannot be viewed as a testamentary disposition.

Let us now see whether French law provides pure forms of will-substitute.

B. Pure Will-Substitutes: Life Insurance

Under French law, life insurance is the purest form of will-substitute. To appreciate the magnitude of this phenomenon, it must first be underlined that life insurance is the favourite French form of saving, playing the role private pension plans fulfil in other jurisdictions. In France, private pension plans do not exist in a general sense[47] because of the importance of the pay-as-you-go system mentioned earlier.[48] There have been several attempts to introduce private pension plans,[49] which so far have failed for ideological and political reasons. However, the Bank of France reports that financial investments in life insurance at the end of June 2014 stood at €1,841 billion.[50] It is estimated that over 60 per cent of households in France hold a life insurance policy.[51] What makes this form of investment so attractive is its good performance in terms of yield,[52] as well as the tax advantages

decision, has exclusive usufruct of the property owes compensation for occupying it to the joint title holder of the usufructus. More recently, see also Cass civ 1re, 17 December 2013, no 12-15453, (2014) *Revue des contrats* 425 observations S Pellet.

45 The individual right to share-out follows from the ordinary law of undivided property (art 815 C Civ).

46 On this astonishing situation, see esp C Grimaldi, 'Mystérieuse tontine' in *Mélanges G Champenois* (Paris, Defrénois, 2012) 417 ff. Exclusion of the individual right to share-out is explained in that, when both purchasers were alive, there was true joint ownership and not two concurrent individual rights of ownership juxtaposed.

47 There actually exist some pension schemes, but their access is limited to a small number of people. The most important one is the PREFON (the personal pension scheme in the public service sector) that has been established for civil servants. It is an optional scheme, sustained exclusively by members' contributions and deductable from income tax. An annuity is paid up to the death of a member, who can opt for conveyance of the annuity towards another beneficiary in case of his death (*réversion*).

48 See above section II.A.ii.

49 eg: Proposition to ameliorate the social protection of salaries and to create retirement funds, Ordinary session of the Senate 1998–99, no 187.

50 The financial newspaper *Les Echos* (2 September 2014) reports that the net intake under life insurance schemes came to €3.9 billion in July, the highest for four years. This record rise can be explained by the lower returns on regulated savings products (esp the *livret A*).

51 According to a study by the French statistics office, Insee, '*L'assurance vie en 2010*', www.insee.fr/fr/themes/document.asp?ref_id=ip1361.

52 Even if the yield is lower than in the past. Moreover, a downturn in the remuneration on life insurance is currently announced.

it offers, even though today the tax breaks are less of an incentive than they were in the past.[53] Ever since the major statute on insurance was passed on 13 July 1930, life insurance has fallen outside the scope of succession law. The difficulty stems from the fact that this derogation scheme was introduced for life insurance contracts that no longer bear any relation to the savings products on which today's insurance companies thrive.

To understand this, it must briefly be recalled that life insurance has changed substantially since the 1980s.[54] Classically, life insurance is a providential operation essentially in the form of insurance in the event of death. The insured contracts with an insurer to cover his close family, and particularly any underage children, against falling into need if he or she were to die prematurely. In this classic form, the insurance contract is a matter of chance for each party: 'if the contingency does not occur, the premiums will be irredeemable; if the contingency arises, the amount paid out may be far higher than the premiums paid'.[55] In the presence of such a contingency, the insurance contract is a contract for good and valuable consideration, the chance nature of the event precluding any characterisation of it as a gift. This is compounded by the fact that life insurance is traditionally analysed as a form of contract conferring a right on a third party.[56] The insured as contractor has the insurer as promisor agree to pay upon death an amount of money for the benefit of a third party named by the insured. However, in a contract conferring a right on a third party, the right of the beneficiary with respect to the promisor arises directly; it is not transferred via the insured's estate, who has only depleted his wealth by the amount of the premiums paid. Technically, the contract conferring a right on a third party and the three-way nature of the operation[57] rule out the idea of a transfer of wealth between the insured and the beneficiary. The 1930 statute made allowance for these specific features, particularly with respect to the law of succession, in two ways. First, pursuant to article L 132-12 of the Insurance Code, upon the insured's death, the capital paid out by the insurer is not part of the estate, and the beneficiary alone is deemed to have been entitled to it as of the

[53] In relation to death transfer duties alone, they vary with the date the life insurance policy was taken out and the age of the insured at the time paid out. For pay-outs before the age of 70 years, no transfer duty is owed up to €152,500 and above that, the amount levied is 20% on the taxable net share of each beneficiary up to €700,000, and 31.25% beyond that.

[54] For detailed historical developments on life insurance policies, see esp C Béguin, 'Les contrats d'assurance sur la vie et le droit patrimonial de la famille' (PhD thesis, University of Paris II, 2011).

[55] F Terré and Y Lequette, *Les grands arrêts de la jurisprudence civile*, vol 1, 12th edn(Paris, Dalloz, 2007) no 132, 744.

[56] Art 1121 C Civ: 'One may likewise stipulate for the benefit of a third party when such is the condition for a stipulation that one makes for oneself or for a donation which one makes to another. He who made that stipulation may no longer revoke it if the third party has declared that he wishes to take advantage of it'. The *stipulation pour autrui* is defined as an agreement by which one of the parties (the stipulator) has the other (the promisor) promise to perform a service for the benefit of a third party (the beneficiary).

[57] On the approximation that can be made in this respect between life insurance and the lifetime trust but also on the differences between them, see Godechot, above n 21, no 330.

date of the contract, regardless of the date on which the contract was accepted. Second, pursuant to article L 132-13 of the same Code, neither the capital nor the premiums paid are subject to hotchpot or reduction for infringement of the forced share. The underlying rationale of the law of succession is set aside. Likewise, the customary rights of recovery of the insured's creditors are set aside.[58] Beyond the allowance for the technical specificities of the classic life insurance contract, this preferential treatment can be explained on policy grounds, that is to say the intention to provide an incentive for providential operations that are socially useful, especially when they mean that the insured's dependent children are not left uncared for, in the event of the insured's early demise.

However, over the last 30 years or so, the forms of life insurance have diversified greatly. So-called modern forms have emerged alongside the classical ones. They themselves are varied and refined, but share the common feature of being not providential but rather investment operations. Further, it is these modern forms that explain the French fad for life insurance. They are in particular what are termed 'mixed' life insurance policies by which

> the insurer undertakes to pay to the insured, if alive at the term of the contract, or, should he or she die before then, to the designated beneficiary, a capital sum which, in either case, shall be equal to the amount of the accumulated premiums, plus financial interest and less management charges.[59]

The rule of the game is that 'the guaranteed capital will necessarily be paid out by the insurer, but it will represent only the savings value attained as of the day it is paid out'.[60] The question then is whether to apply to such investment products the exemptions provided for by the Insurance Code for providential operations. This question has sparked considerable controversy in French legal scholarship,[61] which came to a head over whether these modern forms of life insurance constitute aleatory contracts. At loggerheads are, on one side, insurers and their defenders who have tried to show that these savings products are genuine insurance contracts, and on the other side, specialists of family law and the law of succession who

[58] Art L 132-14 states that, in principle, '[t]he contracting party's creditors may not claim the capital or annuity insured in favour of a specific beneficiary. The contracting party's creditors shall be solely entitled to the reimbursement of their premiums, in the case specified in the second paragraph of Art L 132-13, pursuant either to Art 1167 of the Civil Code or Arts L 621-107 and L 621-008 of the Commercial Code'. This exception concerns the case of manifestly excessive premiums compared with the insured's resources (see section III.A.iii).

[59] M Grimaldi, 'L'assurance-vie et le droit des successions' (2001) *Defrénois*, 3 ff, esp no 2.

[60] ibid.

[61] Among very many references, see J-L Aubert, 'L'aléa et l'assurance sur la vie' in *Mélanges H Groutel* (Paris, Litec, 2006) 13 ff; J Aulagnier, 'L'assurance-vie est-elle toujours un contrat d'assurance?' (1996) *Droit et patrimoine* 43; M Grimaldi, 'Réflexions sur l'assurance-vie et le droit patrimonial de la famille' (1994) *Defrénois* 737 ff; Grimaldi, 'L'assurance-vie et le droit des successions', above n 59, 3 ff; J Kullmann, 'Contrats d'assurance sur la vie: la chance de gain ou de perte' (1996) *Dalloz* Chronique 25; H Lécuyer, 'Assurance vie, libéralité et droit des successions' (1998) *Droit de la famille* Chronique 7; V Heuzé, 'Un monstre et son régime: le contrat commutatif d'assurance sur la vie' in *Mélanges J Bigot* (Paris, LGDJ, 2010) 193 ff. See also Béguin, above n 54.

have argued the contrary. The Cour de cassation adjudicated the issue in four decisions rendered together on 23 November 2004.[62] The Court decided that life insurance contracts are chance-event contracts, even when they perform pure investment operations, on the grounds that 'life insurance contracts, the effects of which depend on the duration of human life, involve a factor of chance'.[63] These decisions were heavily criticised.[64] Not every contract the effects of which depend on human lifespan is for that reason an aleatory contract. If that were so, all agreements entered into with mere mortals and not performed immediately would be aleatory contracts![65] A chance requires something more in that the uncertainty has to affect the very balance of the agreement.[66] This 'deliberate violation of the categories' of civil contract law means that the savings so invested escape from all the rules of the law governing successions and gifts: it suffices therefore 'to invest substantial amounts in life insurance to remove them from the legitimate entitlements of one's heirs and deprive them of their forced share'.[67] In fact there is no upper limit as to the amount that can be invested. This is compounded by the fact that the solution chosen for life insurance is not entirely consistent with respect to that followed by French case law when dealing with a common law trust. In particular,

> when a person domiciled in France dies, after having established a lifetime trust abroad effecting a gift *mortis causa*, the property passed on by the trust is, when there are forced heirs, subject to reduction in the event it infringes the forced portion.[68] Yet, the operation so effected is remarkably similar to investment insurance policies, which are exempt from that same reduction. In both instances, we are dealing with operations designed to manage and pass on savings through some third party, the trustee in one instance, the insurance company in the other. In both cases, the human lifespan influences the naming of the beneficiary.[69]

[62] Cass ch mixte, 23 November 2004, *Bulletin des arrêts de la chambre mixte de la Cour de cassation*, no 4 (4 arrêts); *Grands arrêts de la jurisprudence civile*, 12th edn (Paris, Dalloz, 2007) no 132 observations F Terré and Y Lequette; (2005) *Dalloz* 1905 note B Beignier; (2005) *Defrénois* 607 observations J-L Aubert; (2005) *La semaine juridique édition générale* 187 no 13 observations R Le Guidec; (2005) *Revue des contrats* 297 observations A Bénabent; (2005) *Revue trimestrielle de droit civil* 434 observations M Grimaldi.

[63] ibid.

[64] However, in favour of characterisation as a contingent contract, see J Ghestin, 'La Cour de cassation s'est prononcée contre la requalification des contrats d'assurance vie en contrats de capitalisation' (2005) *Revue la semaine juridique édition générale* 111.

[65] Bénabent, above n 62.

[66] Y-M Laithier, 'Aléa et théorie générale du contrat' in Association Henri Capitant (ed), *L'aléa* (Paris, Dalloz, 2011) 7 ff, esp 15: 'It is true that the subscriber loses the amount paid in premiums if he dies and there is therefore uncertainty as to the beneficiary of the service. But the economic balance of the contract is not affected by this uncertainty. The risk of loss is not matched by a chance of gain for the subscriber. If he lives long enough, he gains nothing more than what he paid in minus the management charges. And if he dies, the loss, assuming there is a loss, does not entail the corresponding enrichment of the insurer'.

[67] Terré and Lequette, above n 55, no 8, 747.

[68] Cass civ 1re, 20 February 1996, (1996) *Dalloz* 390 and chronique by Y Lequette, 231.

[69] Terré and Lequette, above n 55, no 8, 747 f.

The divergence in treatment between the trust, established abroad and regulated by foreign law, which is subjected to successions and gifts rules, and the life insurance taken out in France and subject to French law, which escapes these rules, is inconsistent.

From a narrow legal perspective, there is nothing to justify this exclusion from the succession. In truth, there were economic reasons for the Cour de cassation's solution. These economic reasons do not transpire directly from reading the Cour de cassation's decisions, as the exclusively legal statement of the Court confined itself to raising the contingent character of the contracts. But those economic considerations were weighty indeed. The fact of the matter is that the Cour de cassation made its adjudication in light of a memorandum submitted by the Ministry of Economy and Finance, as well as memorandums from the French Insurers Federation and the notaries' governing body, the Conseil supérieur du notariat. At the time, those documents cautioned against a major risk of destabilisation and a loss of confidence in a sector that was crucial for France's economy and public finances.[70] Economics won the day. Yet, the Cour de cassation could have rendered an incentive decision, ie, it could have revealed their true legal nature and clawed back into the estate the amounts it now allowed to be transferred, so as to ensure they did not infringe the forced portion. And for its part, the legislature could have reassured economic actors and savers by exempting such transfers from the duties levied on gifts. But ultimately the Cour de cassation lacked the resolve. By contrast, the Belgian Constitutional Court ruled the statute on life insurance unconstitutional, where it led to differences in treatment of the forced heirs, depending on whether or not they were beneficiaries of a life insurance policy.[71] Since then a priority issue of constitutionality was raised in France in much the same terms, but the Cour de cassation, deeming it unreasonable, declined to forward it to the Conseil constitutionnel,[72] just as it refused to countenance any arguments based on a contradiction with the European law of human rights.[73]

[70] According to these documents, recharacterising life insurance policies as capitalisation contracts 'would deeply affect the strategies of providence, saving and estate transfer for which mixed life insurance policies provide a simple and highly effective tool for millions of French people. Given the amounts at stake and the highly reassuring image of life insurance, such an upheaval would not only entail systemic risks for the Paris marketplace but would not fail to spark a far-reaching and lasting crisis of confidence among savers with respect to the whole statutory and fiscal regime put in place by the State around saving and providence products', quoted by Terré and Lequette, above n 55, no 9, 748, who add (749): '[T]o put things more bluntly, the funds invested in this kind of contract are invested massively in government bonds, so that any measure that might dissuade individuals from subscribing to such contracts could endanger the public finances'.

[71] Cour const Belge, 26 June 2008, arrêt no 98/2008, (2008) *Revue trimestrielle de droit civil* 526 observations M Grimaldi.

[72] Cass civ 2e, 19 October 2011, no 11-40063.

[73] Cass civ 1re, 19 March 2014, no 13-12076, *Bulletin civil des arrêts de la Cour de cassation* I, no 52, (2014) *La semaine juridique édition notariale* 1338 note P Pierre. No change in legislation on life insurance is contemplated: a ministerial reply of spring 2014 excludes any reform of the subject (on the reply, see F Perrotin, *Les Petites Affiches*, 3 December 2014, 4).

In any event, what must be noted here is that in the case of life insurance, we are dealing with a genuine will-substitute.[74] The beneficiary is freely chosen by the donor. True, the third party must accept the benefit of the contract, but he or she is not contractually bound to the insured. Moreover, the insurer pays the planned amount to the beneficiary after the insured's demise. It is therefore a transfer upon death. But above all, this time the designation of the beneficiary can be freely revoked by the insured up until death. As long as the third party has not accepted the benefit of the insurance,[75] the insured making the contract for another's benefit is entitled and is *alone* entitled to revoke it.[76] He or she can therefore freely change beneficiaries. Lastly, if the insured outlives the contract, it is to him or her that the insurer pays out the insured amount at term. And while the contract runs, the insured usually has the option of redemption, ie, the possibility to ask the insurer for immediate payment before maturity. Should the insured, however, die, the amounts paid by the insurer to the beneficiary from the premiums paid in by the insured are fully exempted from the application of succession law and the rules on the forced portion.[77]

Nevertheless, circumvention of succession rules through will-substitutes is not allowed without restrictions, as will now be examined.

III. The Barriers to Will-Substitutes

The transfer of property upon death outside succession rules does considerable violence to the conventional rules applicable to the transfer of wealth, and sometimes for no good reason, as has been seen. This is why the rationale of succession is always quick to powerfully reassert itself.

These limits imposed on will-substitutes are varied. Some consist in the reintegration of the property into the estate and in returning to the standard rules

[74] See Talpis, above n 4, 71 ff, who characterises it as a pure succession substitute.

[75] If the beneficiary accepts and the subscriber 'accepts that acceptance' (on this surprising figure, see C Grimaldi, 'L'"acceptation de l'acceptation" d'un contrat d'assurance-vie' (2008) *Defrénois* 1645), the subscriber can no longer exercise the redemption option. The amount paid on the contract by the subscribers is therefore irrevocable since it cannot be redeemed.

[76] Art L 132-9 al 2 Code des assurances: 'As long as there has been no acceptance, the person making the provision shall be solely entitled to revoke said provision, and as a consequence his creditors or legal representatives may not exercise such right during his lifetime. When a guardianship has been opened with respect to the person making the provision, revocation may only be made with the authorization of the judge of guardianships or the family council if formed'.

[77] The standard clause proposed by insurers generally designates as the beneficiary 'my life partner, failing that my children born or to be born, in equal shares among them, living or represented, failing that my statutory heirs according to the rules of succession'. When the life insurance benefits the surviving life partner, the sums acquired escape from any liquidation operations concerning forced shares (*réserve héréditaire*). If there is no surviving life partner, the standard clause finally complies with the ranking of heirs provided for by the law of succession. But it is always possible to customise the clause and designate the beneficiary(ies) otherwise.

for the transfer of wealth on death. Others more modestly aim to apply to will-substitutes rules inspired by the law of succession, but without subjecting the property transferred to the standard set of succession rules. Succession is therefore on some occasions a source of reintegration of the property into the estate (subsection A), and on others a source of inspiration for the rules applicable to the property (subsection B).

A. Property Clawed Back into the Estate

Exemption from succession by recourse to will-substitutes (be they perfect or imperfect) runs up against limits. These limits vary in that some are mandatory, while others are voluntary.

In some instances, the law or the courts require that property transferred by means of will-substitutes be reintegrated into the deceased's estate. The aim is to protect the statutory heirs, and in particular the forced heirs. These are safety valves that apply not just to pure will-substitutes, which are testamentary in nature, but also to most imperfect will-substitutes, which are not strictly testamentary, but which can be used to transfer property upon death outside the usual channels of succession. Three such restrictions can be evoked, all of which are mandatory.

i. Limits to Matrimonial Advantages

The first limit is specific to matrimonial advantages between spouses and is intended to protect children who are not issues of the two spouses in the context of stepfamilies. It is a protective measure for modern-day Cinderellas, so to speak. In principle, as seen, these matrimonial advantages are treated as instruments for valid consideration and not as gifts between spouses. By way of exception, the position is different when stepchildren are involved. This is because, unless there is a will, they do not inherit from their step-parents and thus may see the property of their own parent, as transferred by (pre)nuptial agreement, escape their claim. In this case, matrimonial advantages are treated as gifts,[78] and if they infringe the forced share of the offspring in question, they are deemed excessive[79] and must be reduced,[80] on request of the stepchild, to the proportion of the wealth that the

[78] Under art 1527 al 2 C Civ.

[79] On how to calculate an excessive matrimonial advantage, see Cass civ 1re, 19 December 2012, *Bulletin civil des arrêts de la Cour de cassation* I, no 269, (2013) *Defrénois* 1154 observations G Champenois.

[80] No equivalent measure has been provided with the civil partnership agreement. This is why it is proposed (but the question is still debated) to consider that partners, who have opted to subject their property not to the statutory regime of separation of property but to contractual indivision, cannot bring back into the undivided property arrangement property that the law (art 515-5-2 C Civ) formally excludes from its ambit.

deceased could have disposed of by way of gift to his or her partner.[81] There is no need to prove the predeceased partner's intention to make a gift. It is sufficient that there is a stepchild and that the matrimonial advantage is excessive.

ii. *Limits to* Tontine *or Accretion Clauses and Life Insurance Constructions*

The second limit concerns the *tontine* or accretion clause, and life insurance contracts. It relates to situations where there is no identifiable chance event. Where that is the case, the contract is characterised as a gift and the wealth passed on is subject to the standard rules of the law of succession. For the *tontine*, the Cour de cassation has had the opportunity to recharacterise the accretion clause as a gift in a matter in which the age and health of the purchaser, who alone had paid for the purchase of property, meant that he was likely to die first.[82] The difficulty arose from the fact that, to recharacterise the clause as a gift, and thereby subject it to the rules of succession, the Cour de cassation made two separate findings: first, the fact that the predeceased purchaser had paid for the property exclusively and second, his age and state of health at the time of purchase. Nevertheless, in an earlier decision the Cour de cassation had concluded that the mere fact that a purchaser had paid for the purchase alone was insufficient grounds to deny the contingent character of the clause.[83] Thus, it remains unclear whether the exclusive nature of the payment is sufficient for the operation to be clawed back into the normal course of succession. The Cour de cassation will have to clarify its case law on this point. For life insurance, the courts are willing to recharacterise a life insurance contract as an indirect gift when the circumstances in which the beneficiary is designated betray the present and irrevocable wish of the insured to deplete his fortune for the beneficiary and deprive him of the possibility of exercising the redemption option. Such was the case, for example, in a matter where a man who knew he was ill had taken out life insurance for 82 per cent of his wealth, and three days before his death had made his partner the beneficiary of the contract.[84] These are residual hypotheses of contract subscription or beneficiary designation *in articulo mortis*. It is worth noticing that in practice such litigation does not concern forced heirship alone. In many cases, recharacterisation as an indirect donation is sought by the tax authorities, for gratuitous transfer duties (tax litigation), or by central or

[81] That is up to the available share between spouses laid down by art 1094-1 C Civ.

[82] Cass civ 1re, 10 May 2007, *Bulletin civil des arrêts de la Cour de cassation* I, no 173, (2007) *Dalloz* 2134 observations M Nicod, (2007) *Revue des contrats* 1165 observations A Bénabent.

[83] Cass civ 1re, 14 December 2004, above n 42.

[84] Cass ch mixte, 21 December 2007, *Bulletin civil des arrêts de la Cour de cassation* no 13, (2008) *La semaine juridique édition générale* 10029 note L Mayaux, (2008) *Dalloz* 1314 note F Douet, (2008) *Revue trimestrielle de droit civil* 137 observations M Grimaldi. See also Cass com, 26 October 2010, no 09-70927: a man with cancer had taken out three contracts two weeks after his worsened state of health had led him to discontinue his occupational activity.

local government, so as to recover from the estate the welfare support granted to the deceased at the end of his life (welfare litigation).[85]

iii. Limits to Excessive Life Insurance Premiums

The third limit is peculiar to life insurance. It concerns manifestly excessive premiums. Article L 132-13 of the Insurance Code provides that the sums paid as premiums by the insured under the insurance policy escape from the rules on claw-back and reduction for infringement of the forced portion. But the law states an exception for premiums that are manifestly excessive with respect to the insured's financial capacity. If the premium paid was manifestly excessive, the amount is reintegrated into the estate. Thus, the idea of a manifestly excessive premium requires definition. The Cour de cassation has laid down a few guidelines. For the Court, the manifestly excessive character of the premiums is appraised at the time of payment, and in light of the age and financial and family circumstances of the insured and the usefulness of the contract to him or her.[86] However, there is much litigation on the question and in practice it is difficult to determine in advance whether or not one is dealing with manifestly excessive premiums. The concept remains blurred and the courts have notably broad powers of determination. But as things stand, the manifestly excessive premium is the forced heirs' most effective weapon against life insurance.[87]

iv. Voluntary Claw-Back

Lastly, it should be emphasised that the reintegration into the estate of the property transferred is not always an imposed requirement. It may also be wished by the future deceased. The Cour de cassation made such a finding in a notable decision of 8 July 2010,[88] stating that a party signing a life insurance contract may wish to include the insured capital in his estate and pass it to one of his heirs, in the form of a legacy. In other words, the will-substitute may turn into a testamentary disposition by wish of the deceased. The Cour de cassation thus accepts that the personal wishes of the insured of an insurance agreement may impede the theoretical solution it itself enshrined in 2004. This is a very opportune

[85] These claims for recouping welfare support are based on art L 132-8 of the Code de l'action sociale et des familles. They come within the jurisdiction of the administrative tribunals. On these claims, see esp P Potentier, 'La récupération de l'aide sociale' (2006) *Defrénois* 773 ff.

[86] eg Cass civ 1re, 4 July 2007, *Bulletin civil des arrêts de la Cour de cassation* I, no 258; 28 June 2012, no 11-14662; 19 March 2014, no 13-12076, (2014) *La semaine juridique édition notariale* 1338 note P Pierre.

[87] Although it is acknowledged that the premiums paid are manifestly excessive, the precise consequences are debated. Some decisions order all premiums to be recaptured by the estate, others only the proportion that was excessive. The law makes no fiscal arrangements for excessive premiums.

[88] Bulletin civil des arrêts de la Cour de cassation, I, no 170, (2011) *Revue trimestrielle de droit civil* 167 observations M Grimaldi, (2010) *Revue générale de droit des assurances* 1128 observations L Mayaux.

solution,[89] even though it has been challenged.[90] It allows someone who has put his assets into a life insurance policy to include them in his estate when arranging for their bequeathal. In practice, the amounts thus passed on to the heirs are taken into account in the context of the liquidation of the estate. The will-substitute no longer excludes succession arrangements but combines them without, it seems, entailing any loss of tax benefits related to life insurance.[91]

Under all these hypotheses, it can be seen that will-substitutes are defeated and the property transferred is brought back into the estate and passed on under the conventional succession rule. In a slightly different way, the law of succession is also sometimes a source of inspiration for specific rules applicable to will-substitutes.

B. Rules Inspired by the Law of Succession

The law of succession is a source of inspiration for rules on will-substitutes. As such it serves as a benchmark, which shows that these mechanisms are closely bound together. The plainest illustration is life insurance. The law provides that the life insurance contract ceases to operate for a beneficiary convicted of wilfully killing the insured. In the case of a mere attempt to kill, the victim who took out the insurance is entitled to revoke beneficiary designation, even if the beneficiary had already accepted the contract made for his or her benefit.[92] It is a matter of denying the criminal any profit he may derive from his crime. The approach is the same as that which makes it possible to find the statutory heir undeserving when he has made or attempted to make an attack on the deceased's life,[93] and deny him his rights under the law of succession or the mechanism that, under identical circumstances, revokes gifts made to a dishonest recipient.[94]

However, the assimilation of will-substitutes into the rules applicable to successions is far from perfect. It remains limited to life insurance. In fact, the

[89] eg the spouse who has had children from a previous marriage may designate the spouse as beneficiary of a life insurance policy and provide in a testamentary provision that the capital paid by the insurer shall be included in the quarter of the succession to which the surviving spouse is entitled as statutory heir. On this example and others, see observations Grimaldi, above n 88.

[90] Doubt has been cast on the feasibility and the risk, in fiscal terms, of gratuitous transfer duties being applied on successions and not the more favourable life insurance regime (see esp Mayaux, above n 88, observations on Cass civ 1re, 8 July 2010; D Faucher, 'Bénéficiaire d'un contrat d'assurance-vie demandant au notaire de l'intégrer à la succession', note on Cass com, 10 December 2013 (2014) *La semaine juridique édition notariale* act 120; F Douet, 'Retour sur l'intégration volontaire de l'assurance-vie dans la succession' (2014) *La semaine juridique édition notariale* act 178). But see M Leroy and M Iwanesko, 'L'intégration volontaire de l'assurance-vie dans la succession' (2013) *Revue de la semaine juridique édition notariale* 1263; M Leroy and F Fruleux, 'Successions: analyse raisonnée en faveur de l'intégration volontaire de l'assurance vie dans les opérations liquidatives' (2014) *Droit fiscal* 215.

[91] But this is much debated and remains uncertain (see the reference, above n 88).

[92] Art L 132-24 Code des assurances.

[93] The causes of unworthiness are provided for in arts 726 and 727 C Civ.

[94] This is called revocation of gifts for 'cause of ingratitude'. It is provided for by arts 955 (donations) and 1046 (legacies) C Civ.

Cour de cassation decided that the matrimonial advantage granted to spouses is not called into question when one of the spouses murders the other. In the case in question, the (pre)nuptial agreement contained a clause attributing all of the universal community to the surviving spouse. The Cour de cassation found that the surviving spouse, who was sentenced to 10 years' imprisonment for murder, could not be denied this matrimonial advantage.[95] The solution is technically sound: a matrimonial advantage is neither part of the succession nor a gift. Therefore, it is not subject to the rules of unworthiness, or the rules concerning the revocation of gifts for ingratitude. But the result is repugnant to common sense and morals. However, the same holds for *tontines*, as the Cour de cassation adjudicated in a decision of 5 December 2012,[96] dealing with a case in which an unmarried partner killed himself after having ended his partner's life. Litigation ensued between the respective heirs of the victim and the murderer. The Cour de cassation found that the *tontine* should be performed and that the murderer should be considered the sole owner of the property that he had acquired with the victim.[97] Again the solution can be explained on technical grounds, albeit criticised,[98] that rely on the fiction that under the *tontine* the survivor is supposed to have always been the owner of the property and 'therefore was so already before having eliminated' the predeceased.[99] True, there does remain the possibility of suing the criminal for wrongdoing and obtaining by way of damages some form of restitution of the value of a portion of the wealth acquired.[100]

[95] Cass civ 1re, 7 April 1998, *Bulletin civil des arrêts de la Cour de cassation* I, no 146, (1998) *Revue trimestrielle de droit civil* 457 observations B Vareille.

[96] Cass civ 1re, 5 December 2012, *Bulletin civil des arrêtes de la Cour de cassation* III, no 181, (2013) *Revue des contrats* 945 observations M Latina, 994 observations A Bénabent and 1021 observations C Goldie-Genicon.

[97] The applicants in the appeal to the Cour de cassation relied on art 1178 C Civ on conditions. According to the article, '[a] condition is considered fulfilled when the debtor who is bound by such condition prevents it from being fulfilled'. In the case in point, it was a matter of considering that the party to the *tontine* who committed the murder prevented the condition of the victim surviving from being fulfilled. The analysis assumed it would also be accepted that, in the *tontine* arrangement, each is the owner of a share of the property on the condition subsequent that he predeceases and of the other share on the condition precedent that he survives. But the Cour de cassation dismissed the appeal finding that 'there was not in the relations between the parties one who owed a duty and one who was owed a duty and that article 1178 of the Civil code did not apply'.

[98] See, esp F Zénati, 'Propriété et droits réels' (1995) *Revue trimestrielle de droit civil* 149, 151 who regrets that the analysis in terms of accretion in the narrow sense (occurring without retroactive effect on the death of one of the owners) was abandoned. For a critique of the instrumentalisation of the concept of the condition in the case of the *tontine* arrangement, see M Latina, *Essai sur la condition en droit des contrats*, vol 505 (Paris, LGDJ, Bibliothèque de droit privé, 2007) no 122 ff. And, returning to another analysis by which each party to the *tontine* owns a share of the property on the condition subsequent that he predeceases and of another share on the condition precedent that he survives, see Grimaldi, 'Mystérieuse tontine', above n 46.

[99] Hauser, observations, above n 44.

[100] This is what happened in the case that gave rise to the decision of 5 December 2012. The victim's heirs were awarded damages of half the market price of the property purchased under the *tontine* arrangement. For an analysis in terms of contingency, see (2013) *Revue des contrats* 994 observations A Bénabent arguing that when the contingency vanishes in the course of the contract (here by murder), the contract (here the *tontine* clause) lapses and cannot have effect. In the case in point, this amounts to liquidating the property by considering there were two owners.

IV. Conclusion

It is suggested that the legal contortions to remove property from the natural ambit of succession reach their limits here. More broadly, for will-substitutes, the current state of French law ultimately proves hardly satisfactory. Psychologists might say that French law is in denial. Officially, will-substitutes have no standing as such, and therefore we bend over backwards in an endeavour to explain, sometimes wholly unconvincingly, that certain property may be transferred on death by competing techniques, and in alternative to the law of succession. It might be possible to muddle through with this to some extent, if the wealth thus transferred outside succession were not so substantial. But life insurance indicates the opposite. Comparative analysis of will-substitutes may enable us to say whether this state of denial is liable to be lasting or whether given time and step by step, legal systems will ultimately overcome it.[101]

[101] In the US, the UPC now submits transfers under probate and non-probate procedures to rules that are broadly similar on many points. Property transferred outside the probate procedure is even recaptured by the estate (eg, the interesting arrangement of the augmented estate of the surviving spouse, which is composed of property transferred by will-substitutes and provides a basis for inheritance tax assessment of the surviving spouse (s 2.203)).

8

Will-Substitutes in Germany

ANATOL DUTTA

I. Introduction

In German law, the expression 'will-substitutes' is neither a term of art nor a general concept discussed in legal doctrine and literature. However, the idea that a testator intentionally transfers wealth upon death outside testate or intestate succession—as it is stipulated in the fifth book of the German Civil Code, the *Bürgerliches Gesetzbuch* (BGB)—is not unknown to German law. If one bears in mind the common denominator of will-substitutes—the aim of the testator to substitute and to avoid the preconditions or consequences in terms of transfers under succession law—there are, on a very abstract level, at least four possible implications of German succession law which can be avoided with will-substitutes. In addition, I would like to mention a fifth example, which at first sight falls outside the pattern by not avoiding, but rather by allowing the application of succession law to certain assets—assets which cannot be transferred under 'pure' succession law. I am referring to the last item of my chapter, to partnership shares.

For the purposes of this project, will-substitutes are restricted to *intentional* transfers. Transfers upon death by operation of law, even if they are not subject to succession law mechanisms, are not included in the scope of this chapter. In Germany, such transfers concern, for example, rights of the surviving spouse based on the default matrimonial property regime,[1] special succession in land used for

[1] See § 1371(2) and (3) BGB, which allow the surviving spouse to opt for a participation in the gains accrued during the marriage outside succession law; if the surviving party does not opt for a '*rechnerischer Zugewinnausgleich*', the '*pauschalierter Zugewinnausgleich*' (see § 1371(1) BGB) compensates him or her for the accrued gains with an increase of the intestacy share (§ 1931 BGB) by another quarter, which is payable as a lump sum. However, see below section VI.B with regard to marital agreements as will-substitutes.

agriculture,[2] the rights and duties stemming from tenancy agreements[3] and rights to current payments of public benefits.[4] These transfers take effect without (and partly even against) the intention of the testator and, hence, are not intended to avoid certain implications of transfers under succession law.

II. Pensions

Before assessing the five types of will-substitute in German law, I would like to make a preliminary remark on pensions, which appear to be one of the main examples for will-substitutes in other jurisdictions.[5] Under German law, the transfer of pension rights as such—provided that those rights are transferable at all—does not require the use of will-substitutes. For most Germans, the statutory pension scheme remains the basis of the retirement provision. However, upon death of the insured, the pension rights expire[6] and cannot be transferred by operation of law. Rather, secondary pension rights might directly originate *ex lege*—without any transfer—in certain family members of the deceased, as is the case for the statutory widow's and orphan's pension.[7] Other publicly subsidised pension schemes, such as the recently introduced '*Riesterrente*', only survive the death of the insured person if the pension rights are transferred—within or outside succession law—to certain close dependants of the deceased, in particular to the surviving spouse.[8] However, this does not mean that pension rights have nothing to do with will-substitutes. Sometimes, rights to private pensions are transferred by contracts in favour of a third person and take effect upon death. These contracts are a form of will-substitute and will subsequently be discussed (below section III.C); but this will-substitute—ie, contracts in favour of a third person—is also used for the transfer of other financial assets. Therefore, it is not restricted to private pensions.

[2] Due to historic reasons, the special regimes for the succession in agricultural land are laid down in several legal instruments: partly, in the *Höfeordnung* (for the former British zone), partly in the *Anerbengesetze* of the German Länder (*badisches Hofgütergesetz*, *hessische Landgüterordnung* and *rheinland-pfälzische Höfeordnung*), and partly in federal law (§§ 13 ff of the *Grundstückverkehrsgesetz*).

[3] The surviving spouse, registered partner, children or other close dependants have the right to continue the tenancy agreement of the deceased with the landlord, see §§ 563, 563a BGB.

[4] See § 56 of the Social Law Code, Bk I: General Part, the *Sozialgesetzbuch I: Allgemeiner Teil*, which stipulates that certain public benefits are directly transferred to the surviving spouse, registered partner, children or other close dependants without being part of the estate.

[5] See chs 1, 2, 3, 5 and 6 above, p 14, p 39 ff, p 53 ff, p 118 f, p 121 f, p 139 ff in this volume.

[6] See § 102(5) of the Social Law Code, Bk VI: Statutory Pension Insurance, the *Sozialgesetzbuch VI: Gesetzliche Rentenversicherung* (SGB VI).

[7] Which is regulated in §§ 46 ff SGB VI.

[8] See for details § 93 of the Income Tax Act, the *Einkommensteuergesetz*, which provides that the public subsidies for the '*Riesterrente*' have to be returned if the pension rights are transferred to a non-qualified person.

III. Avoiding the Special Provisions on Testamentary Dispositions

A first example of will-substitutes in German law relates to the special provisions on testamentary dispositions, which the testator aims to avoid. These are mainly the provisions on wills (*Testamente*), but also on joint wills of spouses or registered partners (*gemeinschaftliche Testamente*), and succession agreements (*Erbverträge*), as the three general instruments for the expression of testamentary freedom under German law.

A. Testamentary Dispositions Under German Law

In Germany—as in almost all legal systems—such testamentary dispositions are subject to special provisions, which derogate from the general provisions governing other expressions of party autonomy (eg, contracts or gifts). In particular, testamentary dispositions must comply with certain formalities in order to safeguard that the testator duly documents his or her intention, and in order to prevent disputes between the potential beneficiaries.[9] In principle, these testamentary formalities are not difficult to fulfil. The BGB (see §§ 2231 No 2, 2247 BGB) allows a holograph will. This will has to be drawn up single-handedly and has to be signed by the testator. Unlike in other jurisdictions, no witnesses are required. The same formalities apply to joint wills, but with the difference that the holograph form only has to be observed by one of the spouses or registered partners if both testators sign the joint will (see § 2267 BGB). However, the testator or, as in joint wills, the testators can avail themselves of the notarial form by establishing a public will (*öffentliches Testament*), see §§ 2231 No 1, 2232 BGB. The formal requirements for succession agreements are stricter. Here, the holograph form does not suffice; succession agreements between the testator and the other parties have to be notarised (see § 2276 BGB).

Apart from those formal requirements, other special provisions for wills concern the capacity of the testator to testate (§ 2229 BGB), the exclusion of a representation of the testator and restrictions on a power of appointment granted by the testator to third persons regarding the designation of the heirs (§§ 2064 f, § 2274 BGB). Furthermore, the binding effects of testamentary dispositions are governed by special regulations. They allow the testator to revoke wills at his or her discretion (§§ 2253 ff BGB); the revocation of joint wills and succession agreements is limited (§§ 2271 f, §§ 2289 ff BGB). Additionally, German law provides for special provisions on the avoidance of testamentary dispositions if mistakes have occurred, if the testator erred or if the testator was threatened when testating

[9] See BGH 9 April 1981, BGHZ 80, 242, 246.

(§§ 2078 ff, §§ 2281 ff BGB). Finally, German succession law contains a wide range of statutory rules on the interpretation of testamentary dispositions based on the presumed intention of the testator. For example, § 2069 BGB provides the following. If the testator selects one of his or her descendants to be an heir, and that descendant does not become an heir (eg, because he or she predeceases the testator), the descendants of the testator's descendants become testate heirs to the same extent that they would have inherited from the predeceased descendant under intestate succession.

A further group of special provisions relates to the possible content of testamentary provisions. There is a kind of *numerus clausus* of matters, which can be the object of a testamentary disposition. This notably applies to the modalities by which the estate is transferred upon death to the beneficiaries of the testamentary disposition. Under German law, the testator can select the beneficiary to be his or her testate heir (§§ 1937, 1941 BGB), who then directly and automatically becomes the owner of the estate upon death (see for details below sections IV.A and VII.B). Furthermore, the beneficiary can be nominated in the testamentary disposition as a legatee receiving a right *in personam* against the heirs regarding only a certain object in the estate (§ 1939 BGB). Finally, the testator can favour the beneficiary in his or her testamentary disposition by obliging the heirs or legatees to transfer certain assets to the beneficiary based upon a condition. German succession law technically knows two different kinds of condition: an *Auflage*, which obliges the heirs or legatees, without giving the beneficiary a right to claim performance (see § 1940 BGB), or a *Potestativbedingung*, which suspends the effects of a testamentary disposition if an uncertain event occurs or does not occur (§ 158, §§ 2074 f BGB), for example, the performance by the heirs or legatees towards the beneficiary of that condition.

B. Lifetime Gifts upon Death as Will-Substitutes?

On first sight, a lifetime gift upon death—ie, the promise of a gift, which is based on a lifetime contract (see § 518(1)1 BGB) and which becomes effective upon the death of the donor under the condition that the donee survives the donor—could be a rather simple form of will-substitute that could be used to avoid the special provisions for testamentary dispositions. Of course, German succession law is aware of the danger that the special provisions of succession law could be easily circumvented by such gifts as will-substitutes. A rather famous provision of the BGB—§ 2301(1)1 BGB—states that such lifetime gifts upon death have to comply with the requirements for testamentary dispositions ('*Auf ein Schenkungsversprechen, welches unter der Bedingung erteilt wird, dass der Beschenkte den Schenker überlebt, finden die Vorschriften über Verfügungen von Todes wegen Anwendung*'). Hence, lifetime gifts upon death cannot be used as will-substitutes under German law, as they would be treated like a will.

The statutory consequences of § 2301(1)1 BGB—namely that the special provisions on testamentary dispositions apply to such gifts—is, at least in the prevailing opinion, understood as a reference to the special requirements for succession agreements, and not as a reference to those for wills or joint wills,[10] meaning that a notarial act is required. Lifetime gifts upon death are based, as already mentioned, on a contract. Thus, the provisions governing succession agreements are regarded as the most appropriate regime for such gifts among the special provisions on testamentary dispositions. The provisions for lifetime gifts only apply if the lifetime gift upon death is effected during the lifetime of the donor (see § 2301(2) BGB).

C. Contracts in Favour of a Third Party Taking Effect upon Death as Will-Substitutes

However, not all lifetime gifts upon death are covered by the evasion clause in § 2301 BGB. In particular, there is one situation where, according to German case law, wealth can be transferred by gifts taking effect upon death of the donor without being subject to the special requirements for testamentary dispositions: I am referring to the transfer of assets by a contract in favour of a third party taking effect upon death. According to § 331(1) BGB, a *Vertrag zugunsten Dritter*, a contract in favour of a third party, can provide that the third-party beneficiary shall be able to claim performance from the promisor upon the death of the promisee. For example, such a contract in favour of a third party can be concluded with a bank as the promisor, which shall transfer the savings or securities to a certain account of the beneficiary upon the death of the promisee. A parallel provision can be found in § 159(2) of the German Insurance Contract Act, the *Versicherungsvertragsgesetz* (VVG), for one of the most important contracts in favour of a third party taking effect upon death, namely life insurance contracts. Both provisions, § 331(1) BGB as well as § 159(2) VVG, which clarify that such contracts in favour of a third party vest rights in the third-party beneficiary upon death of the promisee, only govern the relationship between the promisor and the promisee (the so-called *Deckungsverhältnis*). They are silent on the relationship between the promisee, the party to the contract and the third party beneficiary (the so-called *Valutaverhältnis*). The basis—the *causa*—for the benefits flowing from the promisee to the beneficiary upon death within the *Valutaverhältnis* will, in most cases, be a gift taking effect once the promisee dies. Hence, the promisee acts at the same time as a donor and the beneficiary as a donee. During the lifetime of the donee, the donative contract on the gift can be concluded between the promisee-donor on the one side, and the beneficiary-donee on the other, as a promise of a gift by the promisee-donor.[11] It can, however, also be concluded after the death of the donor. German courts

[10] See, eg R Kanzleiter in *von Staudingers Kommentar zum Bürgerlichen Gesetzbuch* (Berlin, De Gruyter, 2006) § 2301 BGB para 3; for a different view see, eg H-J Musielak in F Säcker, R Rixecker, H Oetker and B Limperg (eds), *Münchner Kommentar zum Bürgerlichen Gesetzbuch*, 6th edn (Munich, Beck, 2012) § 2301 BGB para 13.

[11] See BGH 19 October 1983, (1984) *Neue Juristische Wochenschrift* 480, 481.

quite generously interpret such a contract in favour of a third party taking effect upon death of the promisee as an offer for a gift which is accepted by the donee by simply receiving performance by the promisor,[12] for example, the bank or insurer.

If the evasion clause in § 2301(1) BGB was applicable to such transfers, the gift between the promisee-donor and the beneficiary-donee would have to meet the requirements of a testamentary disposition (which, as a general rule, will not be the case, especially, if § 2301(1) BGB is read as a reference to the provisions on succession agreements, see section III.B). Therefore, the German courts consistently held that § 2301 BGB shall neither apply to the *Deckungsverhältnis*, the relationship between promisor and promisee, nor to the *Valutaverhältnis*, the relationship between donor and donee in the event of a contract in favour of a third party taking effect upon death of the promisee-donor.[13] On the one hand, this view is mainly based on § 331(1) BGB and § 159(2) VVG, which stress that such transfers are not subject to the special provisions on testamentary dispositions and, on the other hand, on the belief of the German population that such transfers can be effected outside the requirements of succession law. The German Federal Court of Justice—almost using will-substitute terminology—speaks of such contracts in favour of a third person taking effect upon death as instruments which the testator can choose 'instead of testamentary dispositions'.[14] However, such indirect transfers by contracts in favour of third parties are not entirely outside the domain of succession law. They are—as far as they are based on a gift—subject to the forced heirship regime[15] which does not only apply to testamentary dispositions violating the compulsory share of family members of the testator (see §§ 2303 ff BGB), but also allows for a restoration of gifts and, in some cases, even a claw-back from the donee (§§ 2325 ff BGB).[16]

IV. Avoiding 'Probate'

A. The Absence of Probate in German Succession Law

In the US, the 'will-substitute' discussion focused, in particular, on the aim of the testator to avoid probate.[17] German law does not provide for a comparable

[12] See BGH 29 January 1964, BGHZ 41, 95; BGH 26 November 1975, BGHZ 66, 8; BGH 30 October 1974, (1975) *Neue Juristische Wochenschrift* 382; BGH 19 October 1983, (1984) *Neue Juristische Wochenschrift* 480.

[13] See BGH 26 November 1975, BGHZ 66, 8; see the decision of the Imperial Court in RG 8 February 1923, RGZ 106, 2.

[14] BGH 19 October 1983, (1984) *Neue Juristische Wochenschrift* 480, 481.

[15] See, eg BGH 28 April 2010, BGHZ 185, 252.

[16] See for more details ch 15 below, p 304 ff.

[17] JH Langbein, 'The Nonprobate Revolution and the Future of the Law of Succession' (1984) 97 *Harvard Law Review* 1108. See ch 1 above, p 11 f.

special probate procedure. Rather, the heirs—testate or intestate—automatically and directly receive upon death of the deceased (*Grundsatz des Vonselbsterwerbs*, the principle of automatic and direct transfer to the heirs) the estate as a whole (*Grundsatz der Universalsukzession*, the principle of universal succession). Both principles are explicitly stated in § 1922(1) BGB (*'Mit dem Tode einer Person (Erbfall) geht deren Vermögen (Erbschaft) als Ganzes auf eine oder mehrere andere Personen (Erben) über'*). Hence, there is—at first sight—no need to avoid any succession formalities with will-substitutes.

However, on closer inspection, the transfer of the estate under German succession law can also entail difficulties, which a testator might try to avoid. For example, in the event of testate succession, a will can be challenged by third parties and, hence, court proceedings similar to probate proceedings might be necessary in order to establish the transfer under succession law (although, at least theoretically, it happens by operation of law).

B. Postmortal and Transmortal Mandates as Will-Substitutes

Postmortal or transmortal mandates are mandates which survive the death of the principal and allow an agent to act for or against the estate, ie, the heirs, irrespective of the validity of the will and, hence, any 'probate' proceedings. They can function as will-substitutes which, to a certain extent, avoid succession law proceedings. A mandate given by the principal during lifetime does not cease with the death of the principal. This is confirmed by the interpretation rules in §§ 168 sentence 1, 672, 675 BGB and also by special rules for certain types of mandate, notably in § 52(3) of the German Commercial Code, the *Handelsgesetzbuch* (HGB), and § 86 of the German Civil Procedure Code, the *Zivilprozessordnung* (ZPO). The agent can administrate the estate on the basis of the mandate, and also, if covered by the scope of the mandate, make gifts to third persons.

Such postmortal or transmortal mandates are widely accepted by German courts[18] and are not subject to the special provisions for testamentary dispositions. § 2301(1) BGB (see above section III.B.) does not apply,[19] even if the agent has a power to make gifts, and hence the testator as the principal, similar to an *inter vivos* gift upon death, does not suffer any economic loss during lifetime because he or she can revoke the mandate. A rather formalistic argument is often raised against the application of § 2301(1) BGB. It is claimed that, in contrast to cases of lifetime gifts upon death, the testator (as the principal) does not become a party to the gift, but rather the heirs (as successors of the deceased), which are represented by an

[18] See BGH 18 April 1969, (1969) *Neue Juristische Wochenschrift* 1245, 1246; BGH 18 May 1988, (1988) *Neue Juristische Wochenschrift* 2731.

[19] See BGH 18 June 1962, (1962) *Neue Juristische Wochenschrift* 1718; BGH 18 April 1969, (1969) *Neue Juristische Wochenschrift* 1245; BGH 23 February 1983, BGHZ 87, 19; BGH 12 November 1986, BGHZ 99, 97; BGH 18 May 1988, (1988) *Neue Juristische Wochenschrift* 2731.

agent on the basis of the postmortal or transmortal mandate. In this respect, postmortal or transmortal mandates can also be characterised as will-substitutes. They can be used to avoid the special provisions for testamentary dispositions and are similar to contracts in favour of a third party taking effect upon death (see above section III.C). Furthermore, postmortal or transmortal mandates are not seen as instruments for the circumvention of the special provisions on testamentary executors,[20] which can only be appointed by a testamentary disposition under German law (see §§ 2197 ff BGB). The main difference between a postmortal or transmortal mandate on the one hand, and testamentary execution on the other, concerns the legal position of the agent: so long as the mandate can be revoked (also by the heirs), the position of the agent is not comparable to that of a testamentary executor, which can only be dismissed on certain grounds (see § 2227 BGB).

V. Avoiding the Rules Against Perpetuities

A third area where will-substitutes can be used in German law concerns the tying up of the estate for future generations.

A. Restrictions on Tying Up the Estate

Under German succession law, a testator can preserve the estate only to a limited extent. Mechanisms under succession law to perpetuate the estate are, for example, subsequent succession or substitutions (*Vor- und Nacherbschaft* according to §§ 2100 ff BGB), permanent testamentary execution (*Dauervollstreckung* according to § 2209 BGB) or the exclusion of the heirs' right to divide the estate (*Ausschluss der Auseinandersetzung* according to § 2044(1)1 BGB). In the same way as the English rule against perpetuities, German succession law limits these mechanisms—at least approximately speaking—to the subsequent generation after the testator (see § 2109, § 2210, § 2044(2) BGB).

B. Private or Family Foundations as Will-Substitutes

However, those 'German rules against perpetuities'[21] which are limited to transfers under succession law can be circumvented by private or family foundations.

[20] See BGH 18 June 1962, (1962) *Neue Juristische Wochenschrift* 1718.

[21] See, eg W Reimann, who qualifies these time limits as 'Die "rules against perpetuities" im deutschen Erbrecht' (2007) *Neue Juristische Wochenschrift* 3034.

By establishing a foundation according to §§ 80 ff BGB, the settlor creates a legal person (*rechtsfähige Stiftung*). This legal person can serve as the legal owner of the estate which is to be preserved for a certain purpose. Although the settlor loses formal ownership of the property transferred to the foundation, he or she can retain economic control of the property, for example, as an organ of the foundation. In the settlement of the foundation, the settlor is able to appoint himself or herself as the only member of the foundation's board.[22] Furthermore, the settlor can be among the beneficiaries of the foundation. Once the settlor dies, the assets owned by the foundation are not legally transferred, but stay within the foundation, which is not subject to a rule against perpetuities, unlike in other jurisdictions such as Austria. However, economically, the benefits of the property will now be attributed to other persons as organs or beneficiaries of the foundation.[23] Hence, at least factually, a transfer of wealth is effected outside the boundaries of succession law.

Of course, such an indirect transfer presupposes that the foundation can be established for private purposes, rather than being restricted to charitable purposes. Otherwise, the foundation could not be regarded as a will-substitute for private transfers. The admissibility of private and family foundations was debated for a long time in Germany.[24] Today it is widely accepted that such foundations with private purposes can be established,[25] unlike in other systems, for example, in Swiss law.[26]

Private foundations are not only a mechanism to avoid the rules of German succession law against perpetuities. They can even be used to oust succession law as a whole. For future generations, the property of the foundation is no longer subject to succession law. Rather, the economic advantages of the property held by the foundation are used for the benefit of society as a whole on the terms of the settlement of the foundation. The property tied up in the foundation is subject to the 'private succession law' created by the settlor when establishing the foundation and defining its purposes. It constitutes a privately created succession regime and has to be limited by the legislature if the succession law model of the state is to serve a meaningful purpose for society, the economy and families rather than being at the disposal of an individual.[27] This danger, however, does not apply to the

[22] See, eg R Hüttemann and P Rawert in *von Staudingers Kommentar zum Bürgerlichen Gesetzbuch* (Berlin, De Gruyter, 2011) § 86 BGB para 8.

[23] *cf* eg A Röthel, 'Vermögenswidmung durch Stiften oder Vererben: Konkurrenz oder Konkordanz?' in H Kohl, F Kübler, C Ott and K Schmidt (eds), *GS für Rainer Walz* (Cologne, Heymann, 2008) 617, 622 ff, who stresses the succession nature of foundations regarding the estate of the settlor.

[24] See, esp the critical view of D Reuter in F Säcker, R Rixecker, H Oetker and B Limperg (eds), *Münchner Kommentar zum Bürgerlichen Gesetzbuch*, 6th edn (Munich, Beck, 2012) §§ 80, 81 BGB para 96 ff.

[25] See, eg J Ellenberger in *Palandt, Bürgerliches Gesetzbuch*, 74th edn (Munich, Beck, 2015) § 80 BGB para 8.

[26] See ch 9 below III.

[27] See, for details, A Dutta, *Warum Erbrecht?—Das Vermögensrecht des Generationenwechsels in funktionaler Betrachtung* (Tübingen, Mohr Siebeck, 2014).

immediate succession after the settlor. Rather, the establishment of a foundation only allows the settlor to deviate from the succession law rules against perpetuities for his or her succession. In all other respects, the establishment of a foundation is treated as a gratuitous transfer of the settlor, subject especially to forced heirship rights,[28] which not only apply to testamentary dispositions, but also, as already mentioned, to gifts (see above section III.C).

VI. Avoiding Forced Heirship of Descendants and Ascendants

There are will-substitutes which can, at least to a certain extent, be used even to control forced inheritance rights—notably those of the descendants and ascendants of the testator, or those in favour of the surviving spouse.

A. The Position of the Surviving Spouse in German Succession Law

In particular, the strong position of the children in German succession law can endanger the position of the surviving spouse. The testator cannot transfer the entire estate to the surviving spouse as the sole testamentary beneficiary, if the testator is survived by children or parents, who are also among the forced heirs under German law (see § 2303 BGB). This even applies to mutual wills, such as the so-called '*Berliner Testament*', a testamentary instrument quite common in Germany. With this instrument the spouses assign the estate of the predeceased spouse first to the surviving spouse and later, upon death or remarriage of the survivor, to the children, with binding effect on the survivor (§§ 2271(2), 2270(2) BGB), who is even not free, at his or her own discretion, to dispose of the inherited assets *inter vivos*.[29] For purposes of forced heirship, such testamentary arrangements are regarded as constituting an exclusion of the children after the death of the predeceasing spouse. Thus, they trigger forced inheritance rights of the children against the surviving spouse as the sole testamentary heir.[30] Beyond

[28] See KG 19 December 1902, OLGE 6, 330, 331; RG 30 April 1903, RGZ 54, 399, 400 ff; LG Baden-Baden 31 July 1998, (1999) *Zeitschrift für Erbrecht und Vermögensnachfolge* 152, 152 ff; OLG Karlsruhe 9 December 2003, (2004) *Zeitschrift für Erbrecht und Vermögensnachfolge* 470, 471. *cf* also BGH 10 December 2003, BGHZ 157, 178, 185 ff.

[29] § 2287(1) BGB by analogy, see BGH 23 September 1981, BGHZ 82, 274, 276 ff.

[30] If the arrangement is carried out by subsequent succession (*Vor- und Nacherbschaft*) with the surviving spouse being the first heir and the children the subsequent heirs ('*Trennungslösung*'), § 2306(2) BGB gives the children the right to reject their testamentary position and to claim their forced heirship rights after the death of the predeceased spouse. However, if the arrangement is carried out by a sole

these constraints on dispositions upon death in favour of the surviving spouse, *inter vivos* transactions between spouses are even more restricted than transfers to other family members; the limitation period for a restoration or claw-back of spousal transfers does not commence prior to the dissolution of the marriage (see § 2325(3)3 BGB). Yet in practice, it appears that, at least the common children, rarely exercise their forced inheritance rights where the interests of the surviving spouse—their father or mother—are endangered.[31]

B. Marital Agreements as Will-Substitutes

One should, however, not overlook matrimonial property law, which enables the spouses to considerably improve the position of the survivor by marital agreement. German matrimonial property law allows spouses to protect the respective survivor against forced inheritance rights of other family members. Although rarely agreed upon today outside rural areas in Bavaria, spouses may establish a continued community of property (*fortgesetzte Gütergemeinschaft*), which maintains the entire property of the spouses in the hands of the survivor during his or her lifetime.[32] Even the forced heirship provisions for gifts *inter vivos* do not apply.[33] Hence, a marital agreement establishing such a continued community of property could, with regard to forced heirship, be characterised as a will-substitute avoiding the consequences of a testamentary disposition in favour of the surviving spouse. The functions of ownership are transferred to the surviving spouse outside succession law.

VII. Allowing the Application of Succession Law to Certain Assets

As already indicated, the final—fifth—group of will-substitutes can be located slightly outside the pattern. These instruments are not used in order to avoid certain implications of succession law. Rather, one of their main aims is to subject certain

heirship position of the surviving spouse and the children will be mere heirs of the surviving spouse ('*Einheitslösung*'), § 2303(1)1 BGB applies because the children are excluded from the estate of the predeceased spouse, although they indirectly benefit from that estate as heirs of the surviving spouse, § 2269 BGB contains a presumption for the '*Einheitslösung*' if it is unclear which legal construction was chosen by the spouses.

[31] See, eg H Klingelhöffer, 'Ist unser Erbrecht noch zeitgemäß?' (2010) *Zeitschrift für Erbrecht und Vermögensnachfolge* 385, 386.

[32] §§ 1483 ff BGB.

[33] See BGH 27 November 1991, BGHZ 116, 178 (*cf*, however, also RG 22 November 1915, RGZ 87, 301).

assets—shares in partnerships—to succession law at all. Hence, they broaden the scope of succession law and the scope of the effects of testamentary dispositions, maybe in a manner quite similar to the one described in other contributions to this volume. At the same time, however, these substitutes also modify the succession process in order to avoid friction between succession law and company law.

A. The Default Succession Rules as to Partnership Shares

Regarding partnerships, mainly the *Gesellschaft bürgerlichen Rechts*,[34] the *offene Handelsgesellschaft*[35] and the *Kommanditgesellschaft*,[36] which still play an important role in terms of small and medium-sized businesses in Germany, in the German *Mittelstand*, the default rules dealing with the death of a partner endanger the continuation of the partnership. In terms of the *Gesellschaft bürgerlichen Rechts*, the default rules prescribe that the partnership is dissolved upon death of one of the partners unless the partnership agreement provides otherwise (see § 727(1) BGB). However, difficulties for the partnership arise under the default rules (see § 131(3)1 no 1 HGB) even if the partnership survives the death of the partner. This is the case of a *Gesellschaft bürgerlichen Rechts* (if there is a continuation clause in the partnership agreement) or of an *offene Handelsgesellschaft* or *Kommanditgesellschaft*. The death of the partner does not dissolve the partnership, but only terminates the membership of the deceased partner (or his or her heirs respectively). The share of the dead partner is—quite similar to a joint ownership under common law—accrued to the other partners (see § 738(1)1 BGB in conjunction with § 105(3) HGB). However, and this might endanger the future of the partnership, the dead partner (or his or her heirs respectively) has to be compensated for the loss of the share; he or she can claim the value of the assets he or she hypothetically would have received if the partnership had been dissolved (see § 738(1)2 BGB). Hence, the partnership is burdened with cash debts and liquidity will be diminished.

B. Succession Arrangements in Private–Partnership Agreements as Will-Substitutes

In order to safeguard the future of the partnership, the partnership agreement can influence the default mechanisms operating in the event of a partner's death.

[34] The *Gesellschaft bürgerlichen Rechts*, the general partnership, is regulated in §§ 705 ff BGB.

[35] The *offene Handelsgesellschaft*, the commercial partnership, is regulated in §§ 105 ff HGB; if there are no special provisions, the rules on the *Gesellschaft bürgerlichen Rechts* apply.

[36] The *Kommanditgesellschaft*, the commercial partnership with a limited liability of some of the partners (the so-called *Kommanditisten*) but an unlimited liability of at least one of the partners (the so-called *Komplementär*), is regulated in §§ 161 ff HGB; if there are no special provisions, the rules on the *offene Handelsgesellschaft* and the *Gesellschaft bürgerlichen Rechts* apply.

These rules have mainly been developed by the Federal Court of Justice.[37] According to its case law, the partners can include a succession clause (*Nachfolgeklausel*) in their partnership agreement, which provides that the partnership shares are inheritable—an option which, in the meantime, has also been recognised by the legislature (*cf* § 139(1) and § 131(3) HGB). However, this solution requires that the successor becomes an heir of the dead partner under succession law. If that is not the case, the share can only be 'transferred' indirectly by a so-called accession clause (*Eintrittsklausel*), which grants the potentially succeeding partner a right towards the other partners to accede to the partnership as a third party.[38]

Do these succession arrangements in partnership agreements operate as will-substitutes? At first sight, only a transfer by accession clause (*Eintrittsklausel*) circumvents succession law, quite similar to transfers by contracts in favour of third parties taking effect on death (see above section III.C). Succession clauses (*Nachfolgeklauseln*) in partnership agreements, as already mentioned, only seem to widen the scope of succession law as they convert the partnership share into an inheritable asset. However, succession clauses also modify the succession process for those shares in order to avoid certain technicalities of succession law, which could endanger the continuation of the partnership. As already mentioned, under German law (see above section IV.A), the whole of the estate—including an inheritable partnership share—is directly transferred to the heirs. Such a transfer does not cause problems if there is only one heir. Furthermore, this heir, as the sole heir, directly receives the partnership share among other assets and thus also succeeds within the partnership. However, problems would arise if the principle of universal succession applies and the dead partner is survived by more than one heir. In such a case, a community of heirs, an *Erbengemeinschaft*, would hold the partnership share. However, the liability of the heirs within the *Erbengemeinschaft* is, in principle, limited to the estate[39]—a limitation which would contradict the unlimited liability of partners in a German partnership.[40] Additionally, the rules on the management and the representation within the community of heirs, deviate from those of partnerships—a fact which could incapacitate the management of the partnership. Hence, the German courts came to the conclusion that an *Erbengemeinschaft* cannot hold a partnership share—not even temporarily. Instead, the inheritable share is divided between the heirs directly after the death of the partner on the basis of the succession clause in the partnership agreement. Therefore, it does not fall to the *Erbengemeinschaft*. This result has also been recognised by the

[37] BGH 22 November 1956, BGHZ 22, 186; BGH 21 December 1970, BGHZ 55, 267; BGH 20 April 1972, BGHZ 58, 316; BGH 10 February 1977, BGHZ 68, 225; BGH 4 May 1983, (1983) *Neue Juristische Wochenschrift* 2376; BGH 30 April 1984, BGHZ 91, 132; BGH 14 May 1986, BGHZ 98, 48; BGH 3 July 1989, BGHZ 108, 187; BGH 10 January 1996, (1996) *Neue Juristische Wochenschrift* 1284; BGH 9 November 1998, (1999) *Neue Juristische Wochenschrift* 571.

[38] See BGH 10 February 1977, BGHZ 68, 225; BGH 29 September 1977, (1978) *Neue Juristische Wochenschrift* 264.

[39] See §§ 1967 ff and §§ 2058 ff BGB.

[40] See § 128 HGB, which is not only applicable to the partners of a *offene Handelsgesellschaft* and the partners with unlimited liability within a *Kommanditgesellschaft*, but which is also applicable, by analogy, to a *Gesellschaft bürgerlichen Rechts*.

legislature (*cf* § 139(1) HGB). The courts even go a step further in that the partners are free to declare in their agreement that the share of one of the partners shall only be inheritable in favour of certain heirs of the respective partner. If the partners agree on such a *qualifizierte Nachfolgeklausel*, a qualified succession clause, the share is directly transferred to the nominated heir as a succeeding partner. However, the will-substitute character of such arrangements mainly concerns the technicalities of the succession process, which is adjusted to the needs of the partnership. This is the only aspect where partnership law takes precedence over succession law. For all other remaining aspects of succession law, German courts treat the share as if it belonged to the estate, for example, in terms of the distribution of the estate among the heirs[41] or in terms of calculating forced heirship.[42] Here, the will-substitute character has no negative function to oust certain preconditions or consequences of a will under succession law, but has the positive function of allowing the transfer of a certain asset, which could not be performed under classic succession law.

Just for the sake of completeness: other arrangements in the articles of association of companies or in partnership agreements which simply safeguard that the share is transferred to a certain person in the event of a shareholder's or partner's death are not included in the scope of this chapter. This applies at least to the extent that the shareholder or partner could have reached the same result with a testamentary disposition. For example, such arrangements regarding a private limited company, a *Gesellschaft mit beschränkter Haftung*, can be implemented by a cession clause, a *Abtretungsklausel*, which obliges the heirs of the shareholder (and, hence, an heir as a succeeding party to the articles of association) to assign the share to a certain person.[43] Alternatively, a transfer authorisation clause, an *Übertragungsermächtigungsklausel*, which empowers the remaining shareholders to transfer the share to a third person, can be used.[44] All these arrangements only serve the purpose of safeguarding the interests of the other shareholders or partners, by preventing the share being transferred freely. Therefore, they are not will-substitutes but rather mechanisms to control the testamentary freedom of a third person regarding a certain asset.

VIII. Conclusion

This short survey has shown that German law has no general doctrine or common purpose governing will-substitutes. The examples mentioned are in common use.

[41] See BGH 22 November 1956, BGHZ 22, 186, 197; BGH 10 February 1977, BGHZ 68, 225, 238.

[42] See BGH 10 February 1977, BGHZ 68, 225, 238 ff; *cf* also BGH 14 May 1986, BGHZ 98, 48, 50 ff; BGH 3 July 1989, BGHZ 108, 187, 192 ff.

[43] See RG 25 March 1943, Deutsches Recht 1943, 812; OLG Celle 24 July 1958, (1959) *GmbH-Rundschau* 113; BGH 5 November 1984, BGHZ 92, 386, 390; *cf* also RG 8 October 1912, RGZ 80, 175, 178 ff.

[44] See BGH 20 June 1983, (1983) *Neue Juristische Wochenschrift* 2880, 2881.

Unfortunately, reliable data on the exact amount of the wealth transferred by such will-substitutes in Germany is unavailable; with regard to life insurance, the German insurance industry reports that approximately €4 billion have been paid after deaths in 2013[45]—a rather low figure compared with the €230 billion which are estimated to have been transferred in the same period under succession law. Nevertheless, from my perspective as a succession lawyer, will-substitutes should be regarded with some suspicion, the more so, as these instruments only operate if the testator makes arrangements—limiting the benefits of those substitutes to testators with legal counsel. Hence, it is no surprise that six years ago, one of our hosts, Anne Röthel, in her comprehensive opinion for the 68th *Deutsche Juristentag*—the biannual meeting of the German Jurists Association—advocated the reintegration into succession law of at least two of the will-substitutes mentioned in my chapter: contracts in favour of third parties taking effect upon death and succession clauses in partnership agreements.[46]

[45] See Gesamtverband der Deutschen Versicherungswirtschaft, *Die deutsche Lebensversicherung in Zahlen (2014)*, www.gdv.de/wp-content/uploads/2014/07/GDV-Lebensversicherung-in-Zahlen-2014.pdf, 22.

[46] A Röthel, *Ist unser Erbrecht noch zeitgemäß?* (Munich, Beck, 2010) A 3, 40 f and 43 ff.

9

Will-Substitutes in Switzerland and Liechtenstein

DOMINIQUE JAKOB*

'Will-substitutes' is a term developed under common law, whose meaning is therefore necessarily subject to adaptation when applied in a 'continental' legal environment. With regard to Swiss and—where of particular interest—Liechtenstein law, this chapter intends to present where the legal framework for using will-substitutes diverges from common law (section I) and which legal tools have emerged from this specific environment. While foundations (sections III and IV), trusts (section V) and life insurance (section VI) will be canvassed in greater detail, some less prominent 'substitutes' will only be briefly mentioned (section II). Variation in form between common and continental law, however, does not imply disparity in purpose. On the contrary, the following analysis will show that appropriate estate planning can also achieve typical will-substitute goals under Swiss and Liechtenstein law.

I. *Eo Ipso* Succession and the Need for Will-Substitutes

Neither Switzerland nor Liechtenstein know a full-blown, common law style probate process.[1] The Swiss legal tradition follows the German model, where the estate vests in the heirs, ie, the legal successors to the *de cujus*, by operation of law and without the intervention of the court or an administrator (arts 537, 560 of the

* The author wishes to thank his assistants Claude Humbel, Deborah Kappeler and Dr Peter Picht for their invaluable assistance in drafting this chapter.

[1] For a general overview on the probate process, see P Wendel, *Wills, Trusts, and Estates* (New York, Aspen Publishers, 2010) 6 ff, for the juxtaposition of the European approach of universal succession see ibid, 10.

Swiss Civil Code, the *Schweizerisches Zivilgesetzbuch* (ZGB)).[2,3] Administration of the estate may occur, but only in specific cases such as where the testator has named an executor (so-called *Willensvollstrecker*, see arts 517 ff ZGB).[4] In Liechtenstein, which adopted the Austrian General Civil Code, the *Allgemeines Bürgerliches Gesetzbuch* (ABGB)[5] in the early-nineteenth century, the estate does not automatically vest in the heirs, but instead is at rest (so-called '*hereditas iacens*') until the heir(s) formally accept it, pursuant to §§ 799 ff ABGB, and the court devolves it according to § 819 ABGB. Thus, the system in Liechtenstein resembles more closely a common law probate process rather than the Swiss system of *eo ipso* succession, as it requires positive action by various parties in order for the estate to pass from the *de cujus* to the heirs.

Against this background, under both Liechtenstein and particularly Swiss law, there is less reason to use will-substitutes in order to avoid a probate process. Accordingly, wills are of comparably higher importance. Nevertheless, both Switzerland and Liechtenstein know several constellations where the idea of a wealth transferral *outside* the classical inheritance system can be appealing. First, without the need to rely on the inheritance system, the wealth distribution becomes more predictable and controllable, as a monitored step by step transfer of the assets is possible. Second, dissipation of the assets can be avoided. If, for instance, a testator has one Picasso and six daughters, it will be an almost insurmountable task to retain the painting in the family, should it fall under the regular inheritance process. Third, perhaps the central reason for employing a will-substitute in practice is the aim of avoiding or at least mitigating the cogent rules on forced succession. In Switzerland, these rules are extremely strict with, for example, the children's statutory share amounting to three-quarters of the estate.[6] Finally, but no less significant, tax planning is an important driver for the use of will-substitutes.

II. Principal Will-Substitutes in Switzerland and Liechtenstein

The principal types of will-substitute used in Switzerland and Liechtenstein are foundations, trusts and life insurance. In addition, Swiss law offers several other instruments that could be employed to transfer wealth upon death outside inheritance law.

[2] Swiss Civil Code of 10 December 1907 (SR 210).

[3] U Bürgi in A Büchler and D Jakob (eds), *Kurzkommentar ZGB, Schweizerisches Zivilgesetzbuch* (Basel, Helbing Lichtenhahn, 2012) art 560 para 5 f. German law is explained in ch 8 above.

[4] H Grüninger in A Büchler and D Jakob (eds), *Kurzkommentar ZGB, Schweizerisches Zivilgesetzbuch* (Basel, Helbing Lichtenhahn, 2012) arts 517/518 paras 1 ff.

[5] General Civil Code of 1 June 1811, LGBl 1967 no 34; it was enacted in Liechtenstein on 18 February 1812.

[6] See art 417 para 1 ZGB.

Marital property law[7] transfers wealth from the decedent to the surviving spouse before,[8] and, in general, without the intervention of succession law.[9] However, since the division of marital property and the inheritance procedure are closely intertwined, thorough estate planning has to take their reciprocal effects into consideration.[10]

One, albeit controversial[11] option of the bequeather, is to establish a joint account (a so-called *compte joint*),[12] which incorporates a clause (so-called *Erbenausschlussklausel*) that entitles the surviving tenant to dispose of all the assets and to exclude the heirs from becoming a party to the joint account contract (between the bank and the joint creditors). However, where the transaction is qualified as a *donatio mortis causa* pursuant to article 245 paragraph 2 of the Swiss Code of Obligations, the *Obligationenrecht* (OR),[13] inheritance rules apply and the remaining creditors have to respect the forced share of the heirs.[14]

Another possibility for the *de cujus* to influence his estate after death is to grant a power of appointment which takes or maintains effect *post mortem*. As the authorised representative has to safeguard the interests of the heirs,[15] however, the scope of action remains very limited.

Finally, wealth can be passed upon death by way of succession in shares to partnerships through a continuation clause (so-called *Fortsetzungsklausel*) that

[7] For a general overview on the Swiss matrimonial law, see H Hausheer, T Geiser and R Aebi-Müller, *Das Familienrecht des Schweizerischen Zivilgesetzbuches*, 4th edn (Bern, Stämpfli, 2010) paras 12.02 ff.

[8] The expression 'before' is here not one of time, but rather refers to the order in which the rules of matrimonial property law and succession law are to be applied.

[9] Pursuant to art 204 para 1 ZGB, the marital property regime is dissolved on the death of a spouse (or on the implementation of a different regime).

[10] Rules on statutory shares, for instance, can also be enforceable against prenuptial contracts, see art 216 paras 1 and 2 ZGB; for a good overview of this intensely discussed topic, see P Bornhauser, *Der Ehe- und Erbvertrag, Dogmatische Grundlage für die Praxis* (Zurich, Schulthess, 2012) paras 84 ff.

[11] See E Huggenberger, 'Vertragsbeziehungen und AGB' in P Abegg, A Geissbühler, K Haefeli and E Huggenberger (eds), *Schweizerisches Bankenrecht, Handbuch für Finanzfachleute*, 3rd edn (Zurich, Schulthess, 2012) 68; the discussion regarding the legality of 'survivorship clauses' has been raging for decades, see, eg the dispute between E Wolf, 'Die Berechtigungen am Compte joint nach dem Tode eines Kontoinhabers' (1971) 67 *Schweizerische Juristen-Zeitung* 349 ff and P Früh, 'Erbenausschlussklausel beim "Compte joint"' (1972) 68 *Schweizerische Juristen-Zeitung* 137 ff; the Swiss Federal Court has admitted survivorship clauses *in dicta* in BGE 94 II 167, in recent decisions it was silent on the matter, see BGer 5P.17/2002 of 12 February 2002.

[12] NP Vogt and S Liniger, 'The Survivor Takes All: Joint Tenancy-ähnliche Rechtsfiguren im schweizerischen Recht' in HC von der Crone, P Forstmoser, RH Weber and R Zäch (eds), *FS für Dieter Zobl zum 60. Geburtstag* (Zurich, Schulthess, 2004) 323; Huggenberger, above n 11, 57; D Rochat and P Fischer, 'Compte joint et clause d'exclusion des héritiers: de la difficulté de servir plusierurs maîtres' (2012) *successio 2012* 240/241 f.

[13] Law of Obligations of 30 March 1911 (SR 220).

[14] See C Huguenin, *Obligationenrecht, Allgemeiner und Besonderer Teil*, 2nd edn (Zurich, Schulthess, 2014) para 2862 f.

[15] R Watter in H Honsell, NP Vogt and W Wiegand, *Basler Kommentar, Obligationenrecht I, Art 1-529 OR*, 5th edn (Basel, Helbing Lichtenhahn, 2011) art 35 paras 7 ff; Huguenin, above n 14, para 1085.

takes effect on the withdrawal or death of one of the partners.[16] However, the devil once again lies in the detail and in certain constellations such a clause might be qualified as a disposition *mortis causa* that in turn would have to fulfil the relevant formal requirements and respect the rules on statutory portions.[17]

III. Foundations: Switzerland

A. Nature and Legal Framework

Switzerland follows a classical foundation model whereby a foundation is an independent legal entity created through the destination of assets to a particular purpose (art 80 ZGB).[18] This can happen either *inter vivos* or by way of a will (art 81 ZGB).[19] A Swiss foundation will result in a definitive separation of assets, as the foundation is *irrevocable* and the founder loses control over the assets that have to serve the purpose of the foundation in accordance with the original intention of the founder. At least in theory, the founder retains no more influence on the foundation and its assets than any other third party.[20] The fact that the founder cannot distribute the assets to the beneficiaries or his heirs may at first sight counter-indicate the use of a foundation as a will-substitute. However, prudent drafting and planning can preserve a degree of influence to the founder, and after his death to the heirs. As an example, the founder can retain the competence to modify the foundation purpose (art 86a ZGB). Furthermore, he can secure himself or a family member a position on the foundation board or another organ and thus reserve some influence for the family. Hence, even the classical Swiss foundation can be modelled so as to serve as a will-substitute. Moreover, even though with

[16] A Meier-Hayoz and P Forstmoser, *Schweizerisches Gesellschaftsrecht mit Einbezug des künftigen Rechnungslegungsrechts und der Aktienrechtsrevision*, 11th edn (Bern, Stämpfli, 2012) § 12 paras 94 ff; D Staehelin in H Honsell, NP Vogt and R Watter, *Basler Kommentar, Obligationenrecht II, Arts 530–964 OR, Arts 1–6 SchlT AG, Arts 1–11 ÜBest GmbH*, 4th edn (Basel, Helbing Lichtenhahn, 2012) art 545/546 para 12.

[17] Staehelin in Honsell, Vogt and Watter, above n 16, art 545/546 paras 9, 12. See chs 6 and 8 above III.C and VII.B.

[18] D Jakob in A Büchler and D Jakob (eds), *Kurzkommentar ZGB, Schweizerisches Zivilgesetzbuch* (Basel, Helbing Lichtenhahn, 2012) art 80 para 2 f; for the different possible purposes, see H Grüninger in H Honsell, NP Vogt and T Geiser (eds), *Basler Kommentar, Zivilgesetzbuch I, Art 1-456 ZGB*, 5th edn (Basel, Helbing Lichtenhahn, 2014) art 80 paras 12 ff; for a categorisation of the different types of foundation see D Jakob, *Schutz der Stiftung, Die Stiftung und ihre Rechtsverhältnisse im Widerstreit der Interessen* (Tübingen, Mohr Siebeck, 2006) 72 ff.

[19] For further details, see Grüninger in Honsell, Vogt and Geiser (eds), above n 18, art 81 paras 1 ff; Jakob in Büchler and Jakob (eds), above n 18, art 81 paras 1 ff.

[20] For a deepened analysis of the relationship between the founder and the foundation see Jakob, *Schutz der Stiftung*, above n 18, 103 ff; for the situation in Switzerland see Grüninger in Honsell, Vogt and Geiser (eds), above n 18, art 80 para 6; D Jakob, 'Ein Stiftungsbegriff für die Schweiz' (2013) 132 *Zeitschrift für Schweizerisches Recht* 185, 253 f.

a foundation an infinite perpetuation can be achieved, this is not a prerequisite for the establishment of a foundation. The trend rather goes in the direction of schemes that permit possible distribution of all foundation assets to the beneficiaries. Time-limited foundations (so-called *Stiftungen auf Zeit*) and spend-down foundations (so-called *Verbrauchsstiftungen*) are nowadays firmly established under Swiss law.[21]

B. Types of Will-Substituting Foundations and their Issues

If one looks at the various types of Swiss foundation,[22] one can distinguish between ordinary or 'classic' foundations and family foundations. The most important classic foundation is the charitable foundation, which is not a typical will-substitute, but can also serve estate planning purposes. As Switzerland is home to over 13,000 classic foundations with combined assets of some 100 billion Swiss Francs, this type of foundation is not only the most important one in the foundation sector, but also of significant relevance to the Swiss economy.[23]

Compared with charitable foundations, private purpose foundations come closer to the will-substitute concept. One example is the so-called company or corporate foundation that may receive and hold the shares of a corporation and thus aims at preserving a business that would otherwise be jeopardised by the succession process.[24] Since the Swiss Federal Court clarified that a Swiss foundation may serve as a holding foundation pursuing economic goals,[25] Switzerland is able to provide an attractive model for entrepreneurs seeking to preserve their life's work and to channel the assets via estate planning. However, this model entails certain legal and economic concerns, as a foundation created solely to perpetuate its own assets might be illicit (so-called *Selbstzweckstiftung*).[26] Furthermore, if the shares are the only assets of the foundation, insufficient diversification inconsistent with the modern portfolio theory might present a conceivable risk.[27] Another drawback is that such holding-structures are relatively inflexible and might encounter difficulties when it comes to adapting to economic needs

[21] See Jakob in Büchler and Jakob (eds), above n 18, art 80 para 5.

[22] Jakob in Büchler and Jakob (eds), above n 18, pre-arts 80–89a paras 7 ff.

[23] For further reference, see Grüninger in Honsell, Vogt and Geiser (eds), above n 18, pre-arts 80–89a para 1; B Eckhardt, D Jakob and G von Schnurbein, *Der Schweizer Stiftungsreport 2014* (Basel and Zürich, 2014) 4.

[24] For further detail, see Grüninger in Honsell, Vogt and Geiser (eds), above n 18, pre-arts 80–89a paras 15 ff; Jakob in Büchler and Jakob (eds), above n 18, pre-arts 80–89a paras 9 ff.

[25] See BGE 127 III 337 E 2.c f.

[26] Jakob in Büchler and Jakob (eds), above n 18, art 80 para 3.

[27] The diversification principle is one of the key principles when it comes to the investment of foundation assets, as confirmed in BGE 124 III 97 E 2.a by the Swiss Federal Court; see L Krauss, 'Vermögensanlagen und Anlagevorschriften für klassische Stiftungen' in YA Moor, D Dubach, L Krauss, M Brandenberger and D Roos (eds), *Vermögensanlagen von Pensionskassen und klassischen Stiftungen* (Bern, Stämpfli, 2010) 41, 64 ff.

and possible changes in the relevant market.[28] Lastly, being a classic foundation, the company foundation is subject to public supervision by a state authority (art 84 para 1 ZGB), a fact that may deter prospective founders.

Company foundation purposes can be mixed with family, charitable or other purposes. Such a mixed foundation is not only permitted, but is even a traditional foundation model in Switzerland. Several important Swiss companies are held by foundations with a mixed purpose structure. Here, too, specific concerns arise. Due to the combination and parallel perpetuation of multiple, potentially highly diverse interests, problems might occur after the death of the patriarch, since in the second or third generation these interests may increasingly drift apart. Accordingly, in a second phase—unless planned accurately—these structures may lead to problems and at times a collapse may only be prevented through the exit of one of the stakeholders.[29]

C. Family Foundations in Switzerland

A special regime applies to family foundations, ie, foundations with family members of the founder as beneficiaries.[30] This type may, prima facie, even be seen as the prototypical inheritance foundation, since the assets are intended to be passed on to the heirs or beneficiaries. Indeed, family foundations enjoy some attractive privileges, as there is no ongoing public supervision (art 87 ZGB) and no mandatory registration in the commercial register.[31] However, family foundations suffer from one major impediment. According to the 'notorious' article 335 paragraph 1 ZGB, family foundations in Switzerland are only permitted 'in order to meet the costs of raising, endowing, or supporting family members or for similar purposes'.[32] This provision has been interpreted in such a way that payments on a regular basis without further preconditions are not permitted, and hence no family maintenance or enjoyment foundations are admissible under Swiss law.[33] Even though for decades the majority of scholars and practitioners have been consistently critical of this interpretation, it has so far been upheld

[28] Meier-Hayoz and Forstmoser, above n 16, § 23 paras 12 ff take a very critical position.

[29] For a legal perspective on the intertwining of family matters with charitable foundations, see T Wüstemann, 'Familienpartizipation und gemeinnützige Stiftungen—rechtliche Herausforderungen und Chancen im nationalen und internationalen Kontext' in D Jakob (ed), *Stiftung und Familie* (Basel, Helbing Lichtenhahn, 2015) 25, 29 ff.

[30] See Jakob in Büchler and Jakob (eds), above n 18, art 87 para 4; art 335 paras 1 ff.

[31] The latter privilege has now been abolished: From 1 January 2016 all types of foundation have to be registered; see the new art 52 ZGB and art 6b para 2bis SchlT ZGB. This important amendment results from the effort of the Swiss Parliament to comply with the recommendations of the FATF, see the 'Bundesgesetz zur Umsetzung der 2012 revidierten Empfehlungen der Groupe d'action financière' of 12 December 2014, BBl 2014, 9689.

[32] For further reference on family foundations, see Grüninger in Honsell, Vogt and Geiser (eds), above n 18, art 335 paras 6 ff; Jakob in Büchler and Jakob (eds), above n 18, art 87 para 4; art 335 paras 1 ff.

[33] See again Grüninger in Honsell, Vogt and Geiser (eds), above n 18, art 335 paras 6 ff; Jakob in Büchler and Jakob (eds), above n 18, art 87 para 4; art 335 paras 1 ff.

by Swiss courts.[34] Thus, the family foundation would have the potential to serve as a valuable instrument of 'private succession law',[35] but the overly narrow interpretation of Swiss courts is a considerable impediment.

D. Foundation and Inheritance Law: Core Overlaps

However, all the above-mentioned matters face one specific obstacle, namely the way the rules on forced heirship react to the establishment of a foundation.[36] If assets are transferred to a third party such as a foundation *inter vivos*, the value of these assets will be included in the calculation of the share of the forced heirs. In cases where the testator has exceeded his testamentary freedom, an abatement claim, ie, a claim aimed at granting the compulsory portion to those entitled to it, may be brought against the foundation when the assets were transferred either (i) within five years prior to the death of the founder[37] *or* (ii) with an abusive intention.[38] In these cases, those heirs who do not receive the full value of their forced heirship entitlement may sue the foundation to have the disposition abated to the permitted amount. Accordingly, even though foundations can function well as will-substitutes, forced heirship rules might lead to an abatement claim against the foundation, at least in cases where the founder happens to die within five years of its establishment.

Hence, from the viewpoint of the founder, it is advisable to persuade the forced heirs to waive their legal shares. This, of course, is another challenging task, which might more easily be achieved if the waiving heirs receive an inducement, such as a substantial payment, membership of the foundation council, or the position of foundation beneficiaries.[39]

[34] In detail, *cf* Jakob, 'Ein Stiftungsbegriff für die Schweiz', above n 20, 323; D Jakob, 'Freiheit durch Governance—Die Zukunft des Schweizer Stiftungsrechts mit besonderem Blick auf die Familienstiftung' in D Jakob (ed), *Stiftung und Familie* (Basel, Helbing Lichtenhahn, 2015) 61, 71 ff; see also G Studen, 'Die Familienstiftung und der gesellschaftliche Wertekanon im Wandel der Zeiten' in D Jakob (ed), *Stiftung und Familie* (Basel, Helbing Lichtenhahn, 2015) 89 ff.

[35] Expression coined by A Dutta, *Warum Erbrecht?—Das Vermögensrecht des Generationenwechsels in funktionaler Betrachtung* (Tübingen, Mohr Siebeck, 2014) 78, 79 ff; further ch 8 above V.B.

[36] This flows from the fact that under certain circumstances, *inter vivos* gifts could be added to the estate; see Grüninger in Büchler and Jakob (eds), above n 4, art 475 paras 2 ff; art 527 paras 4 ff; D Staehelin in H Honsell, NP Vogt and T Geiser (eds), *Basler Kommentar, Zivilgesetzbuch II, Art 457-977 ZGB, Art 1-61 SchlT ZGB*, 4th edn (Basel, Helbing Lichtenhahn, 2011) art 475 paras 1 ff; R Forni and G Piatti in H Honsell, NP Vogt and T Geiser (eds), *Basler Kommentar, Zivilgesetzbuch II, Art 457-977 ZGB, Art 1-61 SchlT ZGB*, 4th edn (Basel, Helbing Lichtenhahn, 2011) art 527 paras 7 ff.

[37] Grüninger in Büchler and Jakob (eds), above n 4, art 527 para 5; Forni and Piatti, above n 36, art 527 paras 7 ff.

[38] Grüninger in Büchler and Jakob (eds), above n 4, art 527 para 6; Forni and Piatti, above n 36, art 527 paras 10 ff.

[39] This entails risks for both parties, as usually the waiving party does not exactly know how large their legal share will be, see H Lange and K Kuchinke, *Erbrecht*, 5th edn (Munich, Beck, 2001) 169; Jakob, *Schutz der Stiftung*, above n 18, 287; D Jakob, 'Die Haftung der Stiftung als Erbin oder als "Beschenkte"' in R Hüttemann, P Rawert, K Schmidt and B Weitemeyer (eds), *Non Profit Law Yearbook 2007* (Cologne, Carl Heymann, 2008) 113, 122.

IV. Foundations: Liechtenstein

A. Types of Family Foundation in Liechtenstein

As we have seen, Swiss family foundations face severe constraints. As a reaction, many Swiss (and other international) clients opt for the establishment of a foundation in other jurisdictions, such as the Principality of Liechtenstein.[40] One of the main categories of private foundation under the laws of Liechtenstein is the family foundation.[41] There are two forms of family foundation under the Liechtenstein Persons and Companies Act, the *Personen- und Gesellschaftsrecht* (PGR):[42] First, the so-called 'pure' family foundation under article 552 § 2 paragraph 4 no 1 PGR, and second, the so-called 'mixed' family foundation pursuant to article 552 § 2 paragraph 4 no 2 PGR. The former is limited to similar purposes to those allowed under article 335 of the ZGB. Hence, in Liechtenstein, as in Switzerland, 'pure' family foundations may not unconditionally distribute assets to the beneficiaries, but rather such distributions must be linked to the specific purposes of a 'pure' family foundation.[43] As opposed to Switzerland, in Liechtenstein, however, such an unconditional distribution of assets to beneficiaries becomes possible when a 'mixed' family foundation is employed.[44] According to article 552 § 2 paragraph 4 no 2 PGR, a 'mixed' family foundation must predominantly pursue the purposes of 'pure' family foundations, but it can also pursue charitable purposes or other private (such as unconditional maintenance or enjoyment) purposes. If unconditional payments predominate, the foundation is still admissible as an ordinary private foundation (but without specific family foundation privileges).[45] As shown above, the private foundation under the PGR—in contrast to the Swiss family foundation—allows the unconditional distribution of assets to its beneficiaries. Thus, it is an interesting device that may be employed in order to transfer wealth to the next generation outside the inheritance law context.

[40] The foundation law of Liechtenstein was completely revised on 28 June 2008 and entered into force on 1 April 2009, *Gesetz vom 26 Juni 2008 über die Abänderung des Personen- und Gesellschaftsrechts*, LGBl 2008 no 220, which amended the Law on Persons and Companies of 20 January 1926, LGBl 1926 no 4.

[41] D Jakob, *Die Liechtensteinische Stiftung, Eine strukturelle Darstellung des Stiftungsrechts nach der Totalrevision vom 26 Juni 2008* (Vaduz, Liechtenstein, 2009) paras 114 ff.

[42] Law on Persons and Companies of 20 January 1926, LGBl 1926 no 4.

[43] Such as the 'defrayal of costs of upbringing or education, provision for or support of members of one or more families or similar family interests'. For the conditions of the latter see R Quaderer, *Die Rechtstellung der Anwartschaftsberechtigten bei der liechtensteinischen Familienstiftung* (Schaan, GMG Juris, 1999) 64. Furthermore, see Jakob, *Die Liechtensteinische Stiftung*, above n 41, para 116 f.

[44] Jakob, *Die Liechtensteinische Stiftung*, above n 41, para 116 f.

[45] Quaderer, above n 43, 66; H Bösch, *Liechtensteinisches Stiftungsrecht* (Bern, Stämpfli, 2005) 275; Jakob, *Die Liechtensteinische Stiftung*, above n 41, paras 116 ff. This nuance remains relevant under the reformed foundation law of Liechtenstein: A 'normal' private foundation loses certain special advantages—such as bankruptcy privileges for beneficiaries—exclusively granted to 'pure' family foundations.

B. Family Foundations: Key Differences from Swiss Law

In a nutshell, the attractiveness of the Liechtenstein foundation is due to a variety of reasons. First and foremost, foundations that partially or exclusively serve the maintenance of their beneficiaries are permitted under Liechtenstein law.[46] In addition, the Liechtenstein foundation has some quite special features. In particular, the founder himself can be one, or even the sole beneficiary of the foundation. Furthermore, he can reserve tight control and extensive rights in the statutes,[47] such as the right to change the purpose of the foundation or to revoke it.[48] The possibility of having the foundation established by a fiduciary is another advantage, since it enhances privacy.

Moreover, under Liechtenstein law, there is a stronger protection against interference by succession rules, as the ABGB provides for a two-year abatement period (§ 785 para 3 ABGB), compared with a five-year period in Switzerland and a 10-year period in Germany.[49] Under § 29 paragraph 5 of the Liechtenstein Private International Law, the *Gesetz über das internationale Privatrecht* (FL-IPRG),[50] the two-year period will even prevail over the normally applicable inheritance law if a case is ruled by a Liechtenstein court. Liechtenstein's private international law is thus designed to foster 'asset protection' for foundations.

All these features suggest that the Liechtenstein family foundation is a suitable will-substitute. However, estate planners always have to take account of the international environment, an environment which has recently become increasingly hostile towards Liechtenstein (or other private) foundations. Therefore, quite a number of settlors have seen their foundation structures collapse under the attention of foreign judges.

C. Liechtenstein (Family) Foundation: An Internationally Viable Instrument?

This increasingly hostile international legal environment is due to the very success of Liechtenstein foundations on the one hand, and a number of individual cases of misuse on the other. Because Liechtenstein foundations are highly flexible and attractive instruments, other jurisdictions may be reluctant to (fully) acknowledge them, regarding them as potentially violating the respective mandatory law.

[46] This stands in sharp contrast to the somewhat deadlocked legal situation in Switzerland, see Jakob, *Die Liechtensteinische Stiftung*, above n 41, paras 44 f, 114 ff.

[47] ibid, paras 247 ff.

[48] ibid.

[49] For Switzerland, see above section III.D; for Germany, see § 2325 para 3 *Bürgerliches Gesetzbuch* and ch 8 above V.B.

[50] Code on Private International Law of 19 September 1996, LGBl 1996 no 194, in its version after the revision of the foundation law in 2009.

In Switzerland, Liechtenstein foundations can be relatively sure of recognition. In a pivotal decision of 2009, the Swiss Federal Court ruled that article 335 ZGB[51] is no *loi d'application immédiate*, ie, no overriding mandatory provision under Swiss international private law, and accordingly will not prevail over applicable Liechtenstein law.[52] Thus, any family foundation duly established under the laws of Liechtenstein will be recognised by Swiss courts pursuant to article 154 of the Swiss Federal Code on Private International Law, the *Bundesgesetz über das Internationale Privatrecht* (IPRG),[53] even though it contains maintenance or enjoyment foundation features. In Germany, however, Liechtenstein foundations encounter increasingly adverse conditions, at least when instances of tax evasion are involved or in cases where the founder retains a controlling position. In those cases, there is a tendency for German courts to 'pierce the veil' of the foundation, ie, to refuse recognition on the grounds either of some form of sham doctrine or of the domestic *ordre public*.[54]

The German cases, in particular, teach a very important lesson, namely that estate planning has to be constantly aware of relevant connections to other jurisdictions (domicile of heirs, property) which might treat a will-substitute less favourably than its jurisdiction of establishment. A second lesson can be added: that a founder has to accept that the more flexibility and control he retains, the weaker will be the protection of his assets. Limitation periods for abatement actions, for instance, might not run where, from an economic point of view, the founder has not truly separated himself from the earmarked assets. Hence, the potential claims of forced heirs remain valid.[55] From a tax perspective, assets that are still effectively

[51] *cf* above section III.C.

[52] BGE 135 III 614, 618 f E 4.3; in BGE 102 II 136, the Swiss Federal Court held that foreign rules on the compulsory portion that differ from those applicable in Switzerland do not conflict with the Swiss *ordre public*.

[53] Federal Code on Private International Law of 18 December 1987 (SR 291).

[54] Thus, German courts have refused to recognise foundations in the context of presumed tax avoidance, even though German law recognises foreign foundations in principle; see OLG Stuttgart 5 U 40/09 of 29 June 2009, OLG Düsseldorf 22 U 126/06 of 30 April 2010 and the criticism in D Jakob and M Uhl, 'Die liechtensteinische Familienstiftung im (Durch-)Blick ausländischer Rechtsprechung' (2012) 5 *Praxis des Internationalen Privat- und Verfahrensrechts* 451 ff, with a critical view also on the decision of the Austrian Supreme Court OGH 30b 1/10h of 26 May 2010; D Jakob and G Studen, 'Die liechtensteinische Stiftung in der aktuellen deutschen Zivilrechtsprechung' (2011) *Zeitschrift für das Recht der Non Profit Organisationen* 4 ff; both articles demonstrate that after Liechtenstein's foundation law reform a *general* suspicion towards Liechtenstein foundations seems no longer appropriate.

[55] According to the so-called *Vermögensopfertheorie*, a complete separation of the assets of the foundation from those of the founder is required for the abatement period to commence (since Liechtenstein adopted the Austrian *Allgemeines Bürgerliches Gesetzbuch*, a referral to the Austrian literature and even to its jurisprudence may prove useful in those cases); see Bösch, above n 45, 712 ff; N Arnold, *Privatstiftungsgesetz Kommentar*, 3rd edn (Vienna, LexisNexis Publishers, 2013) Introduction para 23b with further references; Jakob, *Die Liechtensteinische Stiftung*, above n 41, para 243, para 686 f with further references; as a general reference see Jakob, 'Die Haftung der Stiftung als Erbin oder als "Beschenkte"', above n 39, 113, 120 ff; for the jurisprudence, see Liechtenstein Supreme Court, FL-OGH 03 CG.2011.93 of 7 December 2012, E 9.2.18 ff, (2013) *Zeitschrift für Stiftungswesen* 54 ff, which followed the jurisprudence of the Austrian Supreme Court, see OGH of 5 June 2007, 10 Ob 45/07, (2007) *Zeitschrift für Stiftungswesen* 86.

controlled by the founder will also not be treated as economically separate from his fortune. As a result, the foundation will be treated as 'transparent' and taxed accordingly. A prospective founder's choice between 'asset protection' and 'control' can be quite difficult. If he fails to sufficiently release control, the foundation assets may be abated or otherwise afflicted. If, on the other hand, the founder devolves too much control, his foundation may cease to be an effective will-substitute in that he may be unable to direct its asset distribution policy in a reliable manner. One way out of this predicament could be for the founder to retain a right to revoke the foundation, but with another person as ultimate beneficiary.[56] This way the founder could retain a certain influence while the separation of assets would nevertheless be effected.[57]

In sum, if structured correctly, a Liechtenstein foundation can be used as an effective will-substitute. Yet, it is vital for the founder or his estate planner to examine recognition of the structure in all potentially affected jurisdictions.

V. Trusts in Switzerland and Liechtenstein

A. Switzerland

Trusts are not uncommon in the Swiss legal landscape and Switzerland has a prospering trust industry. This may strike some as surprising given that Switzerland has no trust law of its own and there is no such thing as a 'Swiss law of trusts'. However, the prosperity of the Swiss trust sector can be explained by the fact that Switzerland is not only an important international financial centre, but has also ratified the Hague Trusts Convention (HTC),[58] which obliges Switzerland to recognise foreign trusts and to apply to them the law under which they were created.[59] This means that in Switzerland *foreign law* trusts can potentially be used as *Swiss* will-substitutes. Such use generates an overlap with Swiss domestic

[56] For the legal situation in Austria, see Arnold, above n 55, Introduction para 23b.

[57] Jakob, *Die Liechtensteinische Stiftung*, above n 41, para 687.

[58] Convention on the Law Applicable to Trusts and on their Recognition concluded 1 July 1985. In Switzerland, it entered into force on 1 July 2007 (SR 0.221.371).

[59] See the Dispatch on the Convention on the Law Applicable to Trusts: 'HTÜ, Botschaft zur Genehmigung und Umsetzung des Haager Übereinkommens über das auf Trusts anzuwendende Recht und über ihre Anerkennung vom 2.12.2005' BBl 2006 551, 562 ff. Previously, Swiss scholars, courts and practitioners tried to fit the trust into known Swiss legal institutions, see R Gassmann in M Amstutz, P Breitschmid, A Furrer, D Girsberger, C Huguenin, M Müller-Chen, V Roberto, A Rumo-Jungo, A Schnyder and HR Trüeb (eds), *Handkommentar zum Schweizer Privatrecht* (Zürich, Schulthess, 2007) Art 149a paras 1 ff; M Seiler, *Trust und Treuhand im Schweizerischen Recht unter besonderer Berücksichtigung der Rechtsstellung des Trustees* (Zürich, Schulthess, 2005); D Jakob and P Picht, 'Der trust in der Schweizer Nachlassplanung und Vermögensgestaltung—Materiellrechtliche und internationalprivatrechtliche Aspekte der Ratifikation des HTÜ' (2010) *Aktuelle Juristische Praxis* 855, 856; BGE 96 II 79; BGer 4C 94/2005 of 14 September 2005.

inheritance law, as the system of the HTC strives to comply with domestic law (*cf* art 15 HTC). At the risk of oversimplification, it might be stated that the rules of forced heirship, abatement and inheritance in general apply to a foreign trust in much the same way as they would to a Swiss or foreign foundation.[60] One important difference remains, however. Lacking a respective legal tradition, Swiss courts seem to feel far less confident when dealing with cases involving trusts than they do when tackling foundation cases. A prominent example of this effect is the case of *Rybolovlev v Rybolovleva*.[61]

Shortly before his divorce, the Russian billionaire Dimitri Rybolovlev transferred a billion-dollar fortune into two irrevocable discretionary Cyprus trusts.[62] Subsequently, his wife Elena claimed part of that fortune in the course of divorce proceedings in a Geneva court, which actually pierced the veil of the trusts and froze the assets in an interim measure, pursuant to article 178 ZGB.[63] In doing so, the Geneva court completely ignored the HTC and the applicable Cyprus trust law, solving the case by applying exclusively Swiss domestic law. Notwithstanding sharp criticism from both national and international scholars, the Swiss Federal Supreme Court upheld the decision as 'non-arbitrary' and therefore compliant with Swiss federal law.[64] Prima facie, these judgments may draw a fairly discouraging picture for trusts in Switzerland. However, in *Rybolovlev* a bad case truly produced bad law, since the establishment of the two Cyprus trusts was a blatant attempt to evade marital property rules, and Dimitri Rybolovlev retained an overly strong influence on the trusts.[65] Furthermore, the court's piercing of the veil—at least at the level of the Swiss Federal Supreme Court—was limited to interim measures, where specific private international law principles come into play.[66] In 2014, however, the lower court rendered its main decision,[67] in which Elena was adjudicated the highest divorce claim ever awarded in Switzerland (over four billion dollars). Since the decision as yet remains unpublished and the higher court has recently overruled that decision,[68] there is scope for speculation and

[60] That is the reason why heirs should be involved whenever planning a trust in Switzerland, see Jakob and Picht, above n 59, 870.

[61] The decisions in the main proceedings were not published. The decisions in the interim procedures can be found as follows: Cour de Justice du Canton de Genève of 4 March 2010, C/29642/2008; Swiss Federal Supreme Court of 26 April 2012, BGer 5A 259/2010. For an overview of the fairly complex Rybolovlev case, see D Jakob, D Dardel and M Uhl, *Verein—Stiftung—Trust, Entwicklungen 2012* (Bern, Stämpfli, 2013) 175 ff.

[62] ibid, 175 f.

[63] Cour de Justice du Canton de Genève of 4 March 2010, arrêt C/29642/2008.

[64] Swiss Federal Court of 26 April 2012, BGer 5A 259/2010, E 9.

[65] ibid, E 7.

[66] Jakob, Dardel and Uhl, above n 61, 177.

[67] Unpublished.

[68] See the decision of the Cour de Justice du Canton de Genève of 5 June 2015 (unpublished) in which the Court acknowledges the establishment of the trusts and reduces the amount for the divorce claim drastically (an estimated CHF 564 million) reasoned by the fact that it did not take into account the increase in value after the disputed assets were transferred to the trust. It has been announced, however, that an appeal has been filed to the Swiss Federal Supreme Court.

hope that the Swiss courts will develop a more systematic approach to trust cases in the future.

B. Liechtenstein

Liechtenstein is one of the very few civil law countries[69] that actually has its own national trust law,[70] albeit with a somewhat contractual trait.[71] Liechtenstein trusts are notably successful in the national context. However, the international acceptance of the Liechtenstein trust is at least as problematic as that of the Liechtenstein foundation, and might be even more uncertain in countries such as Germany which generally do not recognise trusts.

VI. Pension Plans and Life Insurance in Switzerland

A. Will-Substitutes and the Swiss Social Security System

Pursuant to articles 111 ff of the Swiss Federal Constitution, the *Bundesverfassung* (BV),[72] the Swiss social security system is based on three pillars.[73]

The first pillar is constituted by the old-age, survivors' and disability insurance scheme. It is a general, compulsory insurance, and according to article 112

[69] As another example, San Marino introduced a trust law in 2010 (Trust Law of 1 March 2010 no 42, last modified through decree no 98 of 25 July 2013); for further reference, see A Vicari, 'Country Reports: San Marino' (2012) 18 *The Columbia Journal of European Law Online* 81 ff (available at www.cjel.net/wp-content/uploads/2012/03/countryreport_sanmarino81-92.pdf). Furthermore, Hungary introduced a trust law in its 2014 reform of the Civil Code (Act V of 2013 of 15 March 2014 regarding the regulation of the Hungarian trust). For further reference, see Dentons Budapest Newsletter, 'Die Stiftung im neuen Bürgerlichen Gesetzbuch' of 2 January 2014; Dentons Budapest Newsletter, 'Die Treuhandschaft im neuen Bürgerlichen Gesetzbuch' of 13 February 2013, both available at www.dentons.com.

[70] F Schurr, 'Liechtensteinische Vermögensstrukturen für Familienvermögen im heutigen Umfeld' in D Jakob (ed), *Stiftung und Familie* (Basel, Helbing Lichtenhahn, 2015) 111 ff; G Meier and O Schmidt, 'Liechtenstein' in A Kaplan, *Trusts in Prime Jurisdictions*, 3rd edn (London, Globe Law and Business, 2010) 275 ff; Jakob, *Die Liechtensteinische Stiftung*, above n 41, paras 72 ff, also for a brief overview on the main features of the Liechtenstein trust. Next to the trust, Liechtenstein also knows so-called trust enterprises, which were introduced to the PGR in 1928 (art 932a § 1-170 PGR).

[71] Meier and Schmidt, above n 70, 279.

[72] Federal Constitution of the Swiss Confederation of 18 April 1999, as of 9 February 2014 (SR 101).

[73] For a general overview, see T Locher, *Grundriss des Sozialversicherungsrechts*, 3rd edn (Bern, Stämpfli, 2003) § 1 paras 33 ff; P Bornhauser, 'Zusammenspiel erbrechtlicher und sonstiger durch den Tod ausgelöster Ansprüche' (2005) *Jusletter* of 10 January 2005, paras 5 ff; R Aebi-Müller, 'Die drei Säulen der Vorsorge und ihr Verhältnis zum Güter- und Erbrecht des ZGB' (2009) *successio* 7 ff.

paragraph 2(b) of the Federal Constitution, it aims to cover basic living expenses.[74] Survivor benefits under the first pillar undoubtedly fall outside the inheritance law system, neither forming part of the estate nor qualifying as potential abatement actions since they are not part of the statutory share calculations.[75] However, the first pillar is characterised by a pay-as-you-go system—ie, a system where the collected pension contributions are used immediately to cover the running costs of pensions—and consequently there is no room for a private transferral of wealth or even estate planning under this pillar.[76]

The occupational pension scheme pursuant to article 113 of the Federal Law on Occupational Retirement, Survivors' and Disability Pension Plans, the *Berufliches Vorsorge Gesetz* (BVG)[77] forms the second pillar, which aims at enabling the policyholder to maintain his standard of living after retirement (art 113 para 2 lit a BV). This scheme is divided into a compulsory (pillar 2a) and a non-compulsory (pillar 2b) part. Under the former, every employee with an annual salary exceeding a certain sum[78] has to be insured under an occupational pension scheme with a minimal amount, whereas the latter comprises policies that exceed this legal minimum.[79] The benefits flowing from the compulsory occupational pension scheme under pillar 2a remain entirely outside the scope of inheritance law,[80] since pillar 2a is a compulsory public law institution whose protective purpose may not be impaired by inheritance law interference.[81] Opinions differ concerning the non-compulsory occupational pension scheme under pillar 2b. The prevailing legal scholarship, however, and (at least in principle) the Swiss Federal Court

[74] For further detail, see Aebi-Müller, 'Die drei Säulen der Vorsorge und ihr Verhältnis zum Güter- und Erbrecht des ZGB', above n 73, 7 f; Bornhauser, 'Zusammenspiel erbrechtlicher und sonstiger durch den Tod ausgelöster Ansprüche', above n 73, para 5 f.

[75] Staehelin in Honsell, Vogt and Geiser (eds), above n 36, art 476, paras 16, 18; T Koller, 'Familien- und Erbrecht und Vorsorge' (1997) *recht*, Studienheft no 4, 22 f; JN Druey, *Grundriss des Erbrechts* (Bern, Stämpfli, 2002) § 13 para 27.

[76] For the pay-as-you-go system see Aebi-Müller, 'Die drei Säulen der Vorsorge und ihr Verhältnis zum Güter- und Erbrecht des ZGB', above n 73, 7.

[77] Federal Law on Occupational Retirement, Survivors' and Disability Pension Plans of 25 June 1982, as of 1 January 2014 (SR 831.40).

[78] This threshold is regularly adjusted in line with inflation; in 2015, it amounted to CHF 21.150, *cf* www.bsv.admin.ch/kmu/ratgeber/00848/00851/index.html?lang=de.

[79] Aebi-Müller, 'Die drei Säulen der Vorsorge und ihr Verhältnis zum Güter- und Erbrecht des ZGB', above n 73, 8; Bornhauser, 'Zusammenspiel erbrechtlicher und sonstiger durch den Tod ausgelöster Ansprüche', above n 73, paras 7 ff.

[80] BGE 129 III 305 E 2; Druey, above n 75, § 13 para 27; Aebi-Müller, 'Die drei Säulen der Vorsorge und ihr Verhältnis zum Güter- und Erbrecht des ZGB', above n 73, 20; Staehelin in Honsell, Vogt and Geiser (eds), above n 36, art 476 para 17; P Tuor, B Schnyder, J Schmid and A Rumo-Jungo, *Das Schweizerische Zivilgesetzbuch*, 13th edn (Zurich, Schulthess Juristische Medien, 2009) § 68 para 29; P Izzo, *Lebensversicherungsansprüche und –anwartschaften bei der güter- und erbrechtlichen Auseinandersetzung (unter Berücksichtigung der beruflichen Vorsorge)* (Freiburg, Universitätsverlag, 1999) 313 ff; R Aebi-Müller, *Die optimale Begünstigung des überlebenden Ehegatten—Güter-, erb-, obligationen- und versicherungsrechtliche Vorkehren unter Berücksichtigung des Steuerrechts*, 2nd edn (Bern, Stämpfli, 2007) para 03.46.

[81] For further detail, *cf* Aebi-Müller, 'Die drei Säulen der Vorsorge und ihr Verhältnis zum Güter- und Erbrecht des ZGB', above n 73, 20.

are inclined to qualify the entire second pillar as a unique legal institute under public law and to exclude it from the rules of inheritance law. For estate planning purposes, however, it has to be clarified that in the vast majority of cases, the employees are bound to a pension institution by signing an employment contract. They can rarely influence the arrangement of the occupational pension scheme regarding either the compulsory or the non-compulsory component.[82]

The third pillar consists of additional individual provisions which are entirely optional. It is composed of two distinct parts: on the one hand, the tied voluntary pension (pillar 3a) and on the other, the flexible voluntary pension (pillar 3b). Together, pillars 3a and 3b aim to reduce possible financial gaps left by the other two pillars in order to ensure maintenance of the previous living standard after retirement.[83] Pillar 3a originates in article 82 paragraph 1 BVG and the Ordinance on the Tax Deductibility of Contributions to Recognized Forms of Benefit, the *Verordnung über die steuerliche Abzugsberechtigung für Beiträge an anerkannte Vorsorgeformen* (BVV 3)[84] that allow a tax deduction for certain bound voluntary insurance, including certain types of life insurance. Its major advantage over pillar 2b, ie, the non-compulsory occupational pension scheme, is the absence of factual constraints on taking out insurance in a prescribed way and on determining the beneficiaries of the insurance.[85] Pillar 3b consists of all the investments that fail to fulfil the requirements of BVV 3. Certain life insurance might also fall within this category. In the third pillar marital property law and inheritance law can come to full application.[86]

B. Life Insurance[87]

Private insurance in the third pillar that are paid to a third party upon the demise of the decedent and policyholder have to be taken into consideration

[82] ibid, 20; Izzo, *Lebensversicherungsansprüche und –anwartschaften bei der güter- und erbrechtlichen Auseinandersetzung*, above n 80, 313 f; M Trigo Trindade, 'Prévoyance professionelle, divorce et succession' (2000) *Semaine Judiciaire* 505; Aebi-Müller, *Die optimale Begünstigung des überlebenden Ehegatten*, above n 80, para 03.49; for the jurisprudence of the Swiss Federal Court, see BGE 129 III 305 E 2.3, 2.7; BGE 130 I 205 E 8.

[83] Bornhauser, 'Zusammenspiel erbrechtlicher und sonstiger durch den Tod ausgelöster Ansprüche', above n 73, paras 30 ff.

[84] Ordinance on the Tax Deductibility of Contributions to Recognized Forms of Benefit (BVV 3) of 13 November 1985, as of 1 January 2009 (SR 831.461.3).

[85] Aebi-Müller, 'Die drei Säulen der Vorsorge und ihr Verhältnis zum Güter- und Erbrecht des ZGB', above n 73, 22 f.

[86] Aebi-Müller, *Die optimale Begünstigung des überlebenden Ehegatten*, above n 80, paras 09.63 ff; Aebi-Müller, 'Die drei Säulen der Vorsorge und ihr Verhältnis zum Güter- und Erbrecht des ZGB', above n 73, 13.

[87] Life insurance has a central role in Switzerland, with just under CHF 30 billion life insurance payout in 2013, see www.bfs.admin.ch/bfs/portal/de/index/themen/12/05/blank/kennzahlen/ges_praemienein.html.

in the settlement of the estate.[88] This is mainly due to the fact that in the tied voluntary insurance there is no link to an employment contract, hence the policy taker is free to choose whether he or she wishes to take out insurance.[89] However, the beneficiary of such a contract under pillar 3a receives the insurance payment directly pursuant to article 78 of the Federal Law on Insurance Contracts, the *Versicherungsvertragsgesetz* (VVG),[90] which is why the payment does not fall within the estate[91] and can function as a will-substitute. As this creates opportunities to circumvent the rules of succession law, articles 476 and 529 ZGB specifically protect statutory heirs and the compulsory portion to which they are entitled. Pursuant to these provisions, the surrender value of the life insurance has to be included in the calculation of the statutory share. Importantly, only insurance with a surrender value fall under article 476 ZGB, such as whole life insurance and mixed insurance, but not endowment insurance.[92] Insurance under pillar 3b may be included in the estate if the insurance is received on the basis of a disposition of property upon death. They do not fall within the estate if a third person receives the insurance as a beneficiary under an insurance contract. In principle, however, and similarly to pillar 3a, only the surrender value of the insurance falls into the computation basis for the compulsory share pursuant to articles 476 and 529 ZGB.[93]

In sum, while with regard to pension funds the room for manoeuvre is highly restricted and estate planning proves exceedingly difficult, life insurance can indeed be employed as will-substitutes. Care has to be taken, however, in order to avoid them falling within the estate and thus under the inheritance process.

VII. Concluding Remarks

The absence of a full-blown probate process creates a specific environment for will-substitutes in Switzerland and Liechtenstein. Will-substitutes do not really

[88] W Zumbrunn, 'Private Lebensversicherungen in der Erbteilungspraxis' (2006) *Aktuelle Juristische Praxis* 1207.

[89] Aebi-Müller, 'Die drei Säulen der Vorsorge und ihr Verhältnis zum Güter- und Erbrecht des ZGB', above n 73, 22 f.

[90] Federal Law on Insurance Contracts of 2 April 1908 as of 1 January 2011 (SR 221.229.1)

[91] Zumbrunn, above n 88, 1207; Aebi-Müller, 'Die drei Säulen der Vorsorge und ihr Verhältnis zum Güter- und Erbrecht des ZGB', above n 73, 23; Druey, above n 75, § 13 para 30; P Izzo, 'Assurances- Vie et LPP: Droit des successions et régimes matrimoniaux' (2002) *La Semaine Judiciaire* 107.

[92] Thus the consequences under succession law vary according to the insurance policy, for more detail see S Plattner, 'Erbrecht und Versicherungen, Die Lebensversicherungen der Säule 3a und 3b als Instrument der Nachlassplanung und Nachlassteilung' in J Schmid (ed), *Nachlassplanung und Nachlassteilung* (Zürich, Schulthess, 2014) 220 ff; see also Staehelin in Honsell, Vogt and Geiser (eds), above n 36, art 476 paras 23 ff.

[93] Details are still controversial, for further reference see Plattner, above n 92, 220 ff; Staehelin in Honsell, Vogt and Geiser (eds), above n 36, art 476 para 10.

serve as 'substitutes', but rather as additional instruments to pass on wealth upon death. As has been seen, such instruments can nonetheless present attractive estate planning options provided clear limitations, such as forced share provisions, and legal risks are taken into account. On an international level in particular, certain Swiss and Liechtenstein will-substitutes are increasingly subject to criticism. Structures which were state-of-the-art 10 years ago may cause problems today. More than ever, estate planners have to be aware of the broader picture, including national as well as international limitations, in order to avoid civil and tax liability. For this reason a cross-border dialogue between scholars and practitioners from a range of jurisdictions such as that at the 'Oxford Conference on Will-Substitutes' of March 2015, on which this publication is based, is most valuable.

In view of the fruitful and at times controversial discussion at the conference, the author would like to close with an additional remark. Core questions remain regarding what a will-substitute actually is and how international inheritance law reacts to this type of legal instrument. In the author's view, a will-substitute, without particular relevance to the term itself, is an instrument for passing on assets *outside* inheritance law. Inheritance law and other provisions such as insolvency law may accept, restrict or otherwise impact such transfer, depending on the decisions legislature takes in the involved jurisdictions. From this perspective, however, employing will-substitutes should not be regarded as an 'evasion' of cogent inheritance rules, but rather as the legitimate use of instruments granted by law in an overall estate planning context. This insight strongly advocates the switch from a 'negative' avoidance-based approach to a 'constructive' one. In a constructive perspective, will-substitutes have the potential of passing *more than just property* from one generation to another. Foundations in particular are apt to acquire a separate and genuine function: they can, for instance, transmit the specific traditions or the identity of a family (eg, in the form of a *family foundation*) or serve as a tool for sharing family values and strengthening family governance (eg, in terms of a *charitable foundation* set up by a family as an intergenerational joint family project). Accordingly, it would seem worthwhile, in future research and discussion, to accentuate this underdeveloped perspective.[94]

[94] See D Jakob (ed), *Stiftung und Familie* (Basel, Helbing Lichtenhahn, 2015), a volume based on a conference dealing primarily with these important issues.

Part II

Overarching Perspectives

10

Will-Substitutes from the Perspective of Business Owners

SUSANNE KALSS

I. Interfaces Between Company and Succession Law

The lifetime of human beings is limited. This is a difference between natural persons and entities with legal personality. The death of a natural person triggers succession law mechanisms. It follows that succession law is only applicable to companies when they are held by natural persons, and not by legal entities such as companies or foundations.

Succession law is closely linked to the issue of private ownership of businesses and the private ownership of shares in businesses. It is also connected to the issue of private arrangements governing succession upon the entrepreneur's or shareholder's death.

Inheritance of company shares or of corporate assets is currently characterised by specific features. However, several fundamental considerations support the idea of a distinct procedure for the treatment of corporate assets when these are transferred via succession. The company itself or its shares should not be simply equated with other assets. These fundamental considerations are applicable from the perspective of company and corporation law for cases where succession is governed by wills, intestacy or contractual arrangements. Therefore, it is possible, and can make sense, to use company law mechanisms to regulate the succession in the company or its shares, which take effect parallel to traditional forms of succession mechanism, or may even circumvent them.

Four material aspects ought to be mentioned here to clarify the special techniques of the transfer of corporate assets:

1. Succession law is the law governing *inheritance* and *distribution* of assets on death of a person – company law is the law governing the *organisation* and *continuation* of a company.
2. Ownership of corporate shares not only involves assets but also property rights and control rights.

3. Corporate succession not only affects the heirs and potential by-passed heirs, ie, children neglected by the testator and therefore excluded from the inheritance, but also several other groups of persons.
4. Corporate property differs from other property; it constitutes special property.

A. Tasks of Succession Law and Company Law

Company law and succession law do not form a hierarchical relationship. Neither succession law nor company law takes precedence over the other field of law.[1] Rather, they coexist with equal rank. They are also used for the performance of distinct regulatory tasks:[2] the law of succession has the *function of distributing and transferring assets*. It determines who is entitled to the testator's property.[3] By contrast, company law governs which rights, relationships and memberships (if at all) can be passed on in accordance with the law and the company articles.[4] The object of company law is to ensure efficient shareholder cooperation and the continued existence of the business, as well as to govern the legal relationships among its members, and that between the company and third parties. It ensures effective cooperation and balance of interests.[5]

i. Distribution and Equality

Succession law is the law of distribution. Its distributive effect is apparent in intestacy rules, pursuant to which the family, whose members are divided into circles of relationships or *parentelae*, is typically invoked as the fundamental statutory model. Family members belonging to the same generation are usually treated equally, which causes the distributive effect. For example, if the longer living parent is survived by three children, according to Austrian law and the law of many other jurisdictions, each child inherits a proportional share, that is one-third of the estate. Dispositive intestacy rules provide that each family member of the same generation should ultimately inherit the same amount. Succession law makes no distinction in terms of age, qualifications or individual interests in the transferred

[1] M Schauer, 'Nachfolge im Recht der Personengesellschaften' in M Gruber, S Kalss, K Müller and M Schauer (eds), *Erbrecht und Vermögensnachfolge* (Vienna, Springer, 2010) § 31 para 2, 988, 990 f; M Schauer, *Rechtsprobleme der erbrechtlichen Nachfolge bei Personengesellschaften* (Vienna, Verlag Österreich, 1999) 399 f; H Wiedemann, 'Zum Stand der Vererbungslehre in der Personengesellschaft' in U Hübner and W Ebke (eds), *FS Großfeld* (Heidelberg, Verlag Recht und Wirtschaft, 1999) 1309, 1310.

[2] S Kalss, 'Unternehmensnachfolge in Kapitalgesellschaften' in M Gruber, S Kalss, K Müller and M Schauer (eds), *Erbrecht und Vermögensnachfolge* (Vienna, Springer, 2010) § 32 para 2, 1033, 1036.

[3] Schauer, 'Nachfolge im Recht der Personengesellschaften', above n 1, § 31 para 2, 991; Wiedemann, above n 1, 1310 f.

[4] Schauer, 'Nachfolge im Recht der Personengesellschaften', above n 1, § 31 para 2, 991; S Kalss and S Probst, *Familienunternehmen: Geschäfts- und zivilrechtliche Fragen* (Vienna, Manz, 2013) no 20/8.

[5] S Kalss, C Nowotny and M Schauer, *Österreichisches Gesellschaftsrecht* (Vienna, Manz, 2008) no 1/3; C Windbichler, *Gesellschaftsrecht* (Munich, Beck, 2013) 1 f.

property. Often, however, talents and interest are not distributed equally among all heirs; in particular, this applies to corporate property.

ii. Reserved Portion

This distributive effect is particularly apparent in the provisions determining which requirements must be fulfilled in order for a person to be entitled to a reserved portion. The testator's descendants are typically entitled to a reserved portion, regardless of any mention in the will, as many civil law jurisdictions provide for forced heirship.[6] Under Austrian law, and the law in many other European legal systems, the testator's descendants and spouse have a mandatory right to at least half the estate. For instance, in Germany, the Netherlands, Poland, Switzerland, Greece and Austria, the marital spouse and the children receive half of the estate. The special nature of this portion lies in the fact that it often consists of a right to money, the sum of which is a proportionate share as measured in comparison to the estate in its entirety and to the position of testate heirs. In order to make this money available, and to enable the heir to satisfy this debt, enterprises or shares must often be sold. While the enterprise or company is not directly affected, the corporate property is often the testator's only property, or at least the only material property, forcing the heir to take recourse to this corporate property. The distribution of dividends is usually insufficient for this purpose.

Frequently, entire enterprises, or at least a stake in them, must be sold in order to facilitate payment of the reserved portion. In other cases, enterprises distribute substantial special dividends to enable an heir of the deceased shareholder to actually satisfy his obligations arising under succession law.

While company law is generally aimed at the continued existence and efficient functioning of the company, succession law has a *restricted transfer function* with distributive effect. This contrast gives rise to constant tensions between succession law and company law. Given the fact that these conflicting legal influences and the distribution can jeopardise the existence of the company (problems concerning finance and personnel), company law is applied in order to secure the financial basis of the company, the qualification of the personnel and the manageability of the enterprise. This is achieved by restricting the distributive effect of succession law, whether by direct transfer to certain persons or other mechanisms fulfilling the same function.

iii. Communities of Heirs

The existence of communities of heirs such as the community of heirs (*Erbengemeinschaft*) under the German Civil Code (*Bürgerliches Gesetzbuch*) as

[6] S Kalss, 'The Interaction Between Company Law and the Law of Succession – A Comparative Perspective' in S Kalss (ed), *Company Law and the Law of Succession – General Report* (Heidelberg, Springer, 2015) fn 58.

well as the joint ownership community (*Miteigentumsgemeinschaft*) under the Austrian Civil Code (*Allgemeines Bürgerliches Gesetzbuch*, hereafter ABGB) is an important consequence of the principle of distributive equality. Both are characterised by the fact that a legal act of just one member of the community (eg, filing for an action for annulment or partition) can lead to its dissolution.

The joint ownership extends to physical objects, as well as rights, such as shares or other company memberships. Successors are obliged to jointly exercise their shareholder or partnership rights. In order to do so, they must find a way to agree upon various measures and to establish a common position. The law requires unanimity for important measures, which means that individual members are in a position to block one another. As a result, the entire community becomes unstable and is permanently exposed to the risk of paralysed and decreasing companies.

The community of heirs, as known by German law, exists with regard to each physical object, provided that the inheritance is not partitioned. Partition would lead to the annulment of the community of heirs and can be sought by each co-heir before or after the property is transferred to the heirs. However, prior to the transfer, it is not effective *in rem*. In the same way as a community of joint ownership is divided, under Austrian law an inheritance is partitioned, pursuant to § 841 ABGB, either by an agreement on inheritance partition (*Erbteilungsübereinkommen*) or, if no agreement is reached, by an action for partition (*Erbteilungsklage*) and a subsequent judgment.

B. Ownership Involves Controlling Rights and Property Rights

There are two central aspects, which need to be clearly distinguished, in the context of owning an enterprise or corporate shares. These two aspects of ownership involve property rights and also rights of control and influence,[7] which may be exercised or held by different people. Consequently, they may also be transferred and allocated separately on death of the owner. Even though these two aspects can – and must – be distinguished, it must be emphasised that they influence one another. The larger the extent of the influence that can be exerted by an individual shareholder (eg, through double-voting rights or shareholder agreements), the higher the value and the price of the share.

Property rights over enterprises or corporate shares include the ownership of a stake and the benefit derived from added value. Moreover, this ownership also entitles to dividends, a right to settlement in the event of transfer, the option to merge the company or to change its legal form, as well as the yields generated by selling the share. Rights of control or influence, that is to say the option of exercising power in a company and over its assets, include the right to vote at

[7] A Dutta, *Warum Erbrecht? – Das Vermögensrecht des Generationenwechsels in funktionaler Betrachtung* (Tübingen, Mohr Siebeck, 2014) 32 ff.

shareholder meetings (general meeting or assembly), as well as managerial positions or incumbency in the supervisory board, such as the supervisory committee of an enterprise.

As property rights and control rights can be separated, they may also be transferred separately in the event of legal succession upon the holder's death. The separate, but nonetheless proportionate, transfer of these different components of the share in the corporate property secures participation of all successors in the company as provided for by succession law. This means that two things can be guaranteed: on the one hand, the succession law principle of distribution and, on the other, the concentration of decision-making processes within a company to safeguard efficient management, as intended by company law. Property rights as well as the rights of control and influence at the shareholder meeting, or the entitlement to positions in certain executive bodies of the company, can be allocated to specific heirs or legal successors. Separating rights of control and influence is often the key mechanism for the implementation of legal succession in an enterprise in a manner that is conducive to securing the corporate need for a concentration of influence and efficient management. As a rule, only the invocation of succession law and the acceptance of the inheritance with its subsequent takeover are necessary for the transfer of property rights. In many cases, the allocation and takeover of control rights require specific suitability, ability and qualifications for managing the enterprise and exercising control in a manner which guarantees sustainable success.[8] Apart from the person's individual qualifications, it is necessary to ensure that the decision-making processes are managed efficiently so that this efficiency is reflected at the operative management level, as well as at the supervisory and ownership levels.

C. Divergent Interests

Succession to corporate property affects primarily the legal successors and the bypassed heirs. However, several additional groups of people are also affected. The following interests may be at stake after the death of a shareholder or owner:[9]

- The *testator's* interest in preserving his testamentary freedom and the ability to freely dispose of his own property, including shares.
- The interest of the heir(s) in receiving and freely disposing of the inherited property.
- The interest of those entitled to reserved portions in receiving a certain part of the net inheritance value.

[8] *cf* Kalss and Probst, above n 4, 672 ff.

[9] Kalss and Probst, above n 4, 655; Schauer, 'Nachfolge im Recht der Personengesellschaften', above n 1, § 31 paras 1 ff, 989 ff.

- The interest of the other shareholders in being able to acquire the share of the deceased party, or at least being able to influence the selection of any new shareholder(s), if they wish to continue the company either alone or with new shareholders.
- The interest of the business in efficient and decisive management processes and administration; this applies also to the managers of the company as well as to the employees of the company.

The other shareholders have an interest in knowing and influencing who replaces the deceased shareholder, ie, with whom and with how many new shareholders they will have to collaborate in the future. The company itself, represented by the management and by the employees, is directly affected. Both groups are interested in the continued existence of the company under reasonable and feasible conditions. The public, in turn, is interested in the continuing existence of the company, as it guarantees employment, which in turn generates profits in the region and value in the country. Thus, the public has a financial interest in the (feasible) continuation of the company in the event of succession, which means that the interests of the deceased party's heirs and bypassed heirs must balance against those of the public. This is a situation that affects a large number of people and can entail significant consequences.

D. Corporate Property as Special Property

'Property' is not 'property'. Rather, there are various types of property, ranging from money and jewellery, real estate, a picture or art collection, to companies. These different types of property necessitate the development of corresponding means and justifications for their transfer. The following illustrates the difference between a sum of money and corporate property:

- Corporate property (ie, companies or corresponding corporate stakes in companies) differs from other property in that its value is more *volatile*, in the sense that it is easily susceptible to rapid changes.[10] This is a marked difference from a sum of money, for example, which only changes due to inflation, etc.
- The value of an enterprise that has been fragmented among heirs is often diminished in comparison to the value of the original enterprise in its undivided state. While a sum of money maintains its original total sum upon division (30 + 30 + 30 = 90), this is not necessarily applicable to the division of corporate property. Typically, the value depends on the entire enterprise. Divisions and split-offs can increase value, but not typically as a consequence of distribution.

[10] B Dauner-Lieb, *Unternehmen in Sondervermögen* (Tübingen, Mohr Siebeck, 1998) 29 f.

- The *market environment* gives rise to almost daily fluctuations of the value of corporate property. A possible example is the loss of buyer segments due to the employment of more efficient technologies, the earlier recognition of new trends and the prompt implementation of a new business model by another enterprise.
- Ultimately, the value of an individual enterprise depends materially on the way it is managed, and on the entrepreneurial performance of the owner.[11]

The continued operation of the enterprise also involves substantial entrepreneurial risks, including the risk of total loss or that of a material part of the inherited assets upon takeover. Once the transfer of the sum has been effected, the recipient of a reserved portion in cash is no longer exposed to this risk, which puts him in a privileged position vis-a-vis the heir of the company. He is entitled to a sum of money either immediately or soon after the death of the testator, without being exposed either to the risk of fluctuation in value, or in company earnings. Thus, the notion of compensating this risk would support a different and special succession rule as regards corporate property.

Given the various distinct features of enterprises, it is desirable and sometimes necessary to explore alternative procedures for the transfer of corporate assets. In particular, this is true for the transfer of corporate assets organised as companies. These transfer procedures may be governed by the general rules of succession law or may lie outside the bounds of succession law.

II. Special Rules for Agricultural Enterprises

In Poland, Germany and Austria there are special rules for corporate succession in farming and forestry enterprises.[12] The justification for establishing special rules in this sector is macroeconomic in nature and founded upon the need to protect the public interest. The existence of farming and forestry enterprises ought not to be jeopardised by distribution, especially as a certain size is essential in order to secure the feasibility of the enterprise. At the same time, it ought to be facilitated and ensured that only the most qualified successor obtains and continues the farming enterprise, which is essential to safeguard its existence and the production of food. Therefore, the distribution of such farming or forestry enterprises and the subsequent creation of many sub-enterprises are to be avoided:

- Since the applicable legal rules aim to prevent erosion of the substance of commercial farming and forestry enterprises, they impose substantial limits

[11] H Fleischer, 'Unternehmensbewertung im Personengesellschafts- und GmbH-Recht' in H Fleischer and R Hüttemann (eds), *Rechtshandbuch Unternehmensbewertung* (Cologne, Otto Schmidt, 2015) 707, 728 f.

[12] Kalss, 'The Interaction Between Company Law and the Law of Succession', above n 6, fn 303.

on the entitlement to a reserved portion. As a consequence, a forced heir does not receive half or another portion of the estate, but a share that, measured against the generated earnings, is certain to pose no risk to the sustained continuation of the enterprise.

— The continued existence and the efficient management of the farming or forestry enterprise are secured by the rule that the person with the best qualifications and training prevails as heir over other potential candidates. The principal factor is not the age of the heir, but the desire to secure a feasible amount of functioning farming and forestry enterprises in order to supply the public with food.[13]
— Finally, the application of the special succession law rule to cases where the enterprise is continued for another 10 years serves as an incentive for long-term commitment; if it is sold prior to the expiry of 10 years, the division of the proceeds of the sale is governed by general succession law rules.

III. Private Replication of these Rules

The macroeconomic importance of appropriate rules for corporate succession is not limited to farming and forestry enterprises. For instance, an empirical study for Austria shows that some 6,800 corporate successions take place each year.[14] Therefore, a value of macroeconomic proportions is certainly at issue when it comes to the continued existence or the discontinuation of these enterprises. It is not only farming and forestry enterprises that have significant macroeconomic value. Enterprises generally offer jobs, create value and are therefore extremely important for securing the livelihood of the population. Hence, there is a macroeconomic interest in securing the existence of such enterprises and in ensuring that they do not fragment when distribution occurs, as provided for under the rules of intestacy or forced heirship. The continuation of the enterprise means creation of value for larger regional units and society at large. Above all, the jobs dependent on the enterprise can be preserved, not only in economically strong regions and in urban areas, but also in regions where employment opportunities are scarce. The importance of enterprises in such regions is all the greater in macroeconomic terms.

In practice, appropriate solutions balance the interests of all involved parties (the entrepreneur, the person handing over the enterprise, his children and the

[13] S Probst, 'Anerben- und Höferecht' in M Gruber, S Kalss, K Müller and M Schauer (eds), *Erbrecht und Vermögensnachfolge* (Vienna, Springer, 2010) 113, 114 ff.

[14] KMU Austria, *Übergabepotenzial in Österreich, Studie im Auftrag der Wirtschaftskammer Österreich* (2014).

enterprise itself). They are based on an assessment of these interests in compliance with the applicable law, and are usually implemented through contractual arrangements between these parties.

These arrangements are aimed not just at securing the existence of the enterprise, and its affordability for the entrepreneur, who continues the enterprise, but also at providing an appropriate financial settlement for those entitled to a reserved portion. It is also vital to ensure that the parents who pass on the enterprise are supported and cared for. In practice, therefore, arrangements often provide solutions to these needs. Nonetheless, a statutory rule is desirable and advisable to regulate cases where there is no will or contractual arrangement, and accidents or other unforeseen events have occurred.

The notion of special rules and the justification of special succession rules for farming and forestry enterprises can also be applied to other business sectors. The techniques are: concentrating the inheritance in the hands of one suitable successor, and determining the reserved portions on the basis of the earnings of the enterprise, and the extent to which it is affordable for the company to provide the portion from its corporate earnings. Thus, from a legal policy perspective it would certainly be reasonable not only to provide greater private autonomy, but also to establish a special set of rules applicable to all companies.[15] From a modern perspective, this is not only legitimate in order to secure farming and forestry enterprises, but should also apply to service enterprises, for instance, in the tourism sector or in industrial manufacturing. In any case, the existence of enterprises should be secured in order to preserve economic strength in the macroeconomic interest. Laws should make it possible to concentrate the inheritance in the hands of one person. In the case of corporate succession, the reserved portions should be determined on the basis of the earnings of the last 10 years, instead of on the basis of the market value of the whole company at the time of the testator's death. If the earnings are unexpectedly higher, then there should be a duty to pay where the enterprise is sold for a higher price within 10 years after the inheritance. If a higher value of the enterprise is subsequently established, the heirs who had received a sum can once again participate in the profits. This model would provide incentives and would also secure the continued existence of the enterprise in order to continue creating value within the family, the workforce of the enterprise and its business partners. Succession law aside, tax law provisions must also be considered. For example, reserved portions bequeathed by an entrepreneur should be recognised as business expenses, whereas the entitlement to reserved portions should be taxed at half the rate of other incomes in order to balance the interests involved.

[15] S Probst quoted in S Kalss, 'Überlegungen zur Gestaltung der Unternehmensrechtsnachfolge im Zuge der laufenden Erbrechtsreform' (2015) *Österreichische Notariatszeitung* 50, 52.

IV. Succession Law Arrangements Already Possible Under Applicable Law

Under Austrian law and also under the law of other jurisdictions, it is already sometimes possible to find suitable arrangements. It must be borne in mind that company law rules usually require unanimity on the part of the shareholders for their amendment, whereas last wills and testaments can be made by the testator alone and can be unilaterally changed at any time prior to his death. Thus, succession law offers greater freedom for the individual to organise his affairs.

First, one very important area of flexibility in succession law is the ability to nominate, either by will or by anticipated succession, a single person as the corporate successor. In doing so, it is possible to secure efficient corporate management and continuance tailored to this one person. Many laws of succession allow for a delayed payment in cash of reserved portions for several years.[16] The option of being able to grant other assets *in lieu*, particularly shares in the enterprise that only grant dividend rights, but no influence (eg, preferred shares without voting rights, profit participation rights (*Genussrechte*), sub-shares or other rights based on the earnings of the enterprise), is even more important. In this respect, it is necessary to make both contractual and company law arrangements in order to effect a supplementary or necessary succession law transfer of assets as intended. The future Austrian law of succession allows participation rights (*Genussrechte*), silent partnerships or other stakes in companies without rights of influence – precisely for the purpose of securing efficient decision-making structures in enterprises.[17] Dutch law makes it possible to issue special certificates to satisfy reserved-portion rights.[18] The shareholders need to remember to harmonise the rules governing the company's articles and succession law dispositions (wills or contractual arrangements).

V. Possible Company Law Arrangements

A. Partnerships

The assessment of the special nature of corporate assets, the macroeconomic justification for special rules, and the effectiveness of private arrangements show

[16] See P Barth and U Pesendorfer, *Erbrechtsreform 2015* (Vienna, Manz, 2015) 101 quoting paras 766 ff ABGB.

[17] S Kalss and C Cach, 'Unternehmensnachfolge "neu"—Was bringt die Erbrechtsreform 2015?' (2015) *Steuer- und Wirtschaftskartei* 659, 675 ff.

[18] W Burgerhart and L Verstappen, 'Company Succession in the Netherlands' in S Kalss (ed), *Company Law and the Law of Succession* (Heidelberg, Springer, 2015) 347.

that company law offers a tradition of specific and legally recognised private arrangements, which can be employed for the organisation of succession within an enterprise. Furthermore, it seems to be the case that will-substitutes play a much more significant role in the company law context than in scenarios involving other types of assets. For instance, German and Austrian company law governing partnerships already offer a broad array of methods and means to decide on material issues in the context of corporate succession.

In this context it is important to distinguish between (a) gaining the status of partner and (b) the entitlement to be compensated. In any case, there are company law options which are aimed at excluding heirs or particular legal successors from becoming members of the partnership. In other words, they are refused succession to the real corporate value of the enterprise, or a share therein, and are instead granted compensation. Sometimes, there are even more far-reaching company law options that actually reduce this compensation or exclude it, by prohibiting the settlement in favour of the other partners, and at the expense of the heirs.[19]

In the following, specific company law options are presented. The statutory starting point is the dissolution of the partnership with the possibility of continuing the business with the heirs. The partnership articles must therefore provide for any arrangement.

A *continuation clause* sets forth that, upon the death of one of the partners, the other partners to the partnership can continue the business, without it being dissolved.[20] The heirs of the deceased partner are neither entitled nor obligated to take his place. *In lieu* of a share in the partnership, the entitlement to compensation is inherited. Due to the continuation clause, the partners can therefore prevent unwanted or unsuitable people from entering the partnership. Thus, certain people are excluded by company law from taking a share in the business, while nevertheless maintaining entitlement to compensation for the value under succession law. This entitlement applies to intestate as well as forced heirs. Therefore, there is a risk related to capital flow in favour of the heirs of the deceased partner. In principle, the right to compensation must be estimated based on the value of the enterprise, and the deceased partner's share should be calculated on this basis as one proportionate part of the whole. According to this mechanism, the substance or the value of the earnings is material for the calculation of the real value, not the book value.[21]

It is also admissible to combine a *continuation clause* with a *settlement exclusion clause*. Contractual arrangements based on this combination are also binding on the heirs; for instance, a book value clause, which is an evaluation method

[19] See on this Kalss and Probst, above n 4, 662; Schauer, 'Nachfolge im Recht der Personengesellschaften', above n 1, § 31 paras 10, 990 f, 999 ff; M Schauer, *Rechtsprobleme der erbrechtlichen Nachfolge in Personengesellschaften* (Vienna, Österreich, 1999) 84.

[20] See chs 6 and 8 above.

[21] Kalss and Probst, above n 4, 662; Schauer, 'Nachfolge im Recht der Personengesellschaften', above n 1, 1002; on the aspect of the proportionate part of the whole: Fleischer, above n 11, 728 f.

provided for by company law. However, the right of an heir to compensation can by excluded by the articles of the partnership. Such a clause is admissible because the heir's interests play no role from a company law perspective. The testator may freely dispose over his property during his lifetime. The continuation clause with exclusion of settlement must apply mutually among all partners. Therefore, this is a donative transaction involving a money interest. It is effective vis-a-vis all partners and their heirs. Hence, not only can the continued existence of the partnership be secured by employing a continuation clause which favours the other partners and prohibits other undesired partners from entering the partnership, the financial substance of the partnership can also be fully secured in favour of the other partners.

A *successor clause* is a provision in the partnership articles, according to which the partnership remains undissolved upon the death of one of the partners, but instead continues with the heirs of the deceased partner. This means that the legal consequence of dissolution is inhibited and the flow of assets (due to the right to compensation) is prevented. However, this can give rise to the problem that a simple successor clause allows each heir to enter the partnership; thus, undesired and unsuitable heirs could also become partners. Merely their status as heirs is decisive. Preventive measures can and should be taken in the form of corresponding provisions in the partnership articles, for example, by cancelling certain management or representation rights, or by admitting only one statutory heir. However, it is also admissible to include a termination clause to get rid of partners (*Hinauskündigungsklausel*), which accords the other partners the right to terminate the membership of the heir(s) within a certain time, or if certain circumstances occur.[22]

The *qualified successor clause* is a rule in the partnership articles which provides that only individuals who fulfil certain requirements can be admitted as partners. The partnership articles can even name a particular person or determine specific qualification criteria, such as prior education and family membership. The qualified successor clause ensures that people also approved of by the other partners take the place of the deceased. Nevertheless, the new partners and successors must have the status of heirs, guaranteeing the interplay between company law and succession law rules.[23]

An *entry clause* in the partnership articles grants a third party the right to take the place of a deceased partner within the partnership upon the death of such a partner. This right of the third party is based on the partnership articles, not on succession law. The right of entry offers the entitled party a particularly strong position since it is admissible regardless of succession. The partnership and the other partners are dependent on the decision of the entitled party when such company law arrangements occur. Thus, in the interests of the continued existence of

[22] Kalss and Probst, above n 4, 736.

[23] Schauer, 'Nachfolge im Recht der Personengesellschaften', above n 1, 1018; Kalss and Probst, above n 4, 664.

the partnership, and in order to secure the interests of the other partners, as well as to strengthen the position of the partners, a contractual clause is always to be construed as a successor clause, and not as an entry clause. If the entitled party decides to refrain from entering, the planned corporate succession is frustrated. Therefore, drafting an entry clause must be considered carefully. Moreover, if the entry right is not exercised by the entitled party, the settlement amount must be paid out by the partnership in favour of the deceased partner's estate. The legal position of those entitled to a reserved portion is thus dependent on the occurrence of an entry clause. First, depending on whether the entitled party enters the partnership and, second, when he desists from entering the partnership, on how the settlement amount is calculated. From a company law perspective, the entry clause only makes sense if previously known candidates are to be admitted into the partnership, and the continued existence of the partnership can be secured. The material difference between an entry clause and a successor clause is that the entry based on the entry clause depends solely on the partnership articles and is generally independent from succession law.[24] The party entitled to enter acquires the right to membership upon the death of the deceased partner not by inheritance under succession law, and thus not on the basis of a title under succession law, but directly from the other partners on the basis of the contractual provision.[25] By contrast, the successor clause requires that there really is a legal successor, and that certain persons, whether on the basis of intestacy rules or testamentary succession, do in fact succeed. Specifically, if a person ultimately cannot assume the position of an heir, due to a successor clause, its succession law effect, namely the *ex lege* transfer of rights to the named successor, cannot ensue from the devolution of the property.

This shows that, depending on the choice of clause, and its wording in the partnership articles, company law and succession law interact in different ways. Company law can completely set aside the succession law transfer of property or can be coordinated with succession law dispositions, depending on the specific contractual provisions.

B. Corporate Law

Within the field of corporate law, pre-formed contractual arrangements are less comprehensive. In contrast to the law on partnerships, it is impossible to provide in advance in the company articles that an heir is prohibited from participating, but that the relevant share is to fall directly to other shareholders or third parties. Within the field of corporate law, the interface between company and succession

[24] Schauer, 'Nachfolge im Recht der Personengesellschaften', above n 1, 1022; Schauer, *Rechtsprobleme der erbrechtlichen Nachfolge in Personengesellschaften*, above n 19, 618 f.

[25] M Schauer, *Rechtsprobleme der erbrechtlichen Nachfolge bei Personenhandelsgesellschaften* (Vienna, Österreich, 1999) c 630.

law is even clearer. It is also possible within the field of corporate law to make comprehensive arrangements in order to replicate mechanisms in the company articles similar to those of partnerships. This is true especially when combined with a corresponding clause in the company articles, ie, a clause setting out a duty of the heir to transfer the share to the other shareholders or a third person as soon as he has acquired it *de lege* by universal succession or another form of succession law inheritance. At the same time, the share price can also be significantly reduced through inheritance. Finally, the heir does not acquire membership in the company or only acquires temporary membership. Under corporate law, it is also possible for the compensation of value to be substantially reduced. Depending on the specific provision, this contractual rule not only affects the position of the direct heir and temporary shareholder, but also the legal position of the bypassed children and legal successors of the deceased shareholder, because their reserved portions are also determined by the whole assets—including the shares—of the deceased. While this means that under the law of corporations the transfer cannot be solely governed by the company articles, the combination of succession law transfer and company law duty to transfer, along with corresponding valuation rules, accomplishes the same function.

VI. Summary

The special nature of corporate property justifies separate rules that secure the efficient continuation of the company and the existence of the enterprise. In companies there arise various interests, the enterprise's value is quite volatile and very difficult to measure; often it is not feasible to divide the assets without destroying their value. The necessity for long-term value creation forms the core of the macroeconomic argument and reflects the public interest in a special rule for corporate succession. According to applicable law, extensive private provisions can be included in the company articles, ensuring that only certain persons can become members of the company; additionally, it is possible to materially determine and to reduce amounts of the compensation, which in turn entails a reduction of reserved portions. Therefore, the provisions in the company articles can substantially affect and materially influence the freedom of testamentary disposition. The articles of the company are not will-substitutes in the strict sense, but they share the feature that they can be applied to avoid the mechanisms of the general rules of succession law.

11

Will-Substitutes from the Perspective of (International) Investors

PAUL MATTHEWS

I. Introduction

An enduring *leitmotiv* in modern legal scholarship is the appearance of law and legal issues in novels and plays. Sometimes it is done to make a serious, social or political point. Sometimes it is just part of the story, which may be about lawyers, or structured around a legal process. And sometimes it is merely for comic effect.[1] A historical curiosity is that in the past, when (say) property law was way more complex than it is now, authors who were not lawyers still managed to handle sophisticated points of law accurately, and, moreover, evidently could expect their audiences to appreciate this too. English lawyers see this, for example, in much of the work of William Shakespeare,[2] Jane Austen,[3] Charles Dickens[4] and Anthony Trollope.[5] In modern times, by comparison, the law in literature is often misstated, even invented, and readers are treated to all kinds of strange ideas that could never have been or be the law in practice.[6]

A favourite legal institution of nineteenth-century writers in English was the *tontine*, invented in France in the seventeenth century by the Neapolitan banker Lorenzo di Tonti. '*The Wrong Box*', a great comic novel by Robert Louis Stevenson and Lloyd Osbourne, was published in 1889. Bryan Forbes made a successful film

[1] eg G à Beckett, *The Comic Blackstone* (London, 1846).

[2] eg W Shakespeare, *The Merchant of Venice* (London, 1600).

[3] eg J Austen, *Pride and Prejudice* (London, T Egerton, 1813); see also G Treitel, 'Jane Austen and the Law' (1984) 100 *Law Quarterly Review* 549.

[4] eg C Dickens, *The Pickwick Papers* (London, Chapman and Hall, 1836–37); C Dickens, *Bleak House* (London, Bradbury and Evans, 1852–53).

[5] eg A Trollope, *Orley Farm* (London, Chapman and Hall, 1861–62).

[6] See, eg JK Jerome, *Stage-Land: Curious Habits and Customs of its Individuals* (London, Chatto & Windus, 1889).

of it in 1966, starring more vintage British actors and comedians than you can shake a stick at. The plot of the book and the film was very simple. In the early-nineteenth century, the fathers of a group of young boys at school each put up £1,000, the total sum to go to the boy who lives longest. Towards the end of the century there were only two left, two elderly brothers who hated each other, and each wanted to scoop the pool so as to be able to benefit his own descendants. All sorts of mayhem ensued, up to and including murder. Typically in such stories, as indeed here, the *tontine* is of the capital and accrued interest. In practice *tontines* in England (to the extent that they were lawful)[7] were of income rather than capital.

My point is that, although will-substitutes may not always feature largely in legal textbooks, and lawyers may not always be able to tell you the rules applying to them, they still play a part in popular culture. Like fairies and paper money, people *believe* that they exist, and so they do. This has parallels elsewhere in law. For example, a generation ago Claude Witz convincingly demonstrated[8] that the contract-like institution of the *fiducie* (from the *fiducia* of the Roman law) survived the abolition of the *ancien régime* in French law and the introduction of the Code Civil, in which it is not mentioned. It is still used as such in Belgium, where (unlike France) there has been no legislation to put it on a statutory footing. And—going further afield—the Chinese still use the ancient customary property law idea of *dian* today, although all the old law was abolished during the time of Chairman Mao, and it does not appear in the new property and commercial legislation desired by Deng Xiaoping and enacted in the last 30 years.[9] Good ideas last, whatever the lawyers say.

II. Will-Substitutes

In the conference that gave occasion to this publication, we were considering the impact of will-substitutes. We think of them nowadays as means of transferring property rights. In early Roman law, however, the main function of the institution of an heir was not the transmission of property rights at all. It was to nominate a person to carry out important religious and social functions.[10] Property was a later development. But although in the modern law wills are used for the appointment

[7] See below section IV.D.

[8] C Witz, *La fiducie en droit privé français* (Economica, Paris, 1981).

[9] B Ling, 'Civil Law' in C Wang and X Zhang (eds), *Introduction to Chinese Law* (Hong Kong/Singapore, Sweet & Maxwell Asia, 1997) 171–73; L Chen, '100 years of Chinese Property Law' in L Chen and CH van Rhee (eds), *Towards a Chinese Civil Code* (Leiden, Nijhoff, 2012) 101–03.

[10] B Nicholas, *An Introduction to Roman Law* (Oxford, Clarendon Press, 1962) 237; W Buckland, *A Text-Book of Roman Law*, 3rd edn (Cambridge, CUP, 1962) 283; A Watson, *Roman Private Law* (Edinburgh, Edinburgh University Press, 1971) 93; JAC Thomas, *Textbook of Roman Law* (Amsterdam, North Holland Publishing Co, 1976) 479.

of executors and guardians of children, and instructions for the disposal of the body, among other functions, their main function relates to property rights. So when we speak here of will-substitutes, we are speaking of substitutes for this role alone, and not for the others.

The role assigned to me is to look at these will-substitutes from the point of view of the investor, especially the *international* investor. Now, investors are strange people. They acquire property rights, but generally speaking do not seek to enjoy the property *in specie*. Indeed, the property may not be capable of being so enjoyed. This is especially true of intangibles such as intellectual property rights, and company shares. Even if it can be enjoyed *in specie*, instead they look to turn such enjoyment into money. They look to the financial return on the capital invested. So their concern is not with the *enjoyment* of the physical thing, but with the *value* flowing from it. It may be an income stream, or it may be a capital gain, or it may be both, but it is the *financial value* of the thing, expressed in either form, that matters. Never mind the quality, feel the *income* (or gain).

An investor in one sense is rather like a psychologist. When I was young, and we were all much more naive and less politically correct than we are now, a jokey—but now rather suspect—definition of a psychologist was a person who, when a pretty girl entered the room, *looked at all the other people*. So, too, an investor is not interested so much in his or her own gratification. Instead an investor is interested in how much everyone else is prepared to pay for theirs. Value to you is not what *you* will pay to enjoy a good, but what *they* will.

Investors interested in will-substitutes are broadly of three kinds. First, there is the investor who wishes to pass on his accumulated wealth on death, but for some reason not by means of a will. Second, there is the investor who uses a will-substitute as an investment vehicle because it presents certain characteristics which are in themselves useful or desirable; absence of tax or regulatory burdens are prominent examples. Third, there is the investor who seeks to invest in *someone else's* will-substitute.

The first category is not really about investors at all. It is just that the person wanting to pass on wealth has accumulated it by investment. It could just as easily have been someone who earned money from hard work or inherited it and now wants to dispose of it on death. There is nothing special about the investor in this case. The general rules about will-substitutes apply. The second category is different. The will-substitute is used not so much for its (undoubted) ability to pass on wealth to others, but because it is a useful form in which to make the investment. This is particularly true of certain types of trust. The third category is different again. Here the investor did not chose to create the will-substitute, but either takes it over from the creator or his successor, or obtains some interest in it, in order to make the investment. In other words, the third situation is purely motivated by investment considerations, whereas the second may be motivated by others as well. So the substance of this chapter is directed to the second and third situations.

Will-substitutes are usually more sophisticated institutions than wills themselves. This is generally because they achieve an object which is the main object of a will to achieve (to transmit property rights on death), but at the same time do other things which have nothing as such to do with wills. The sophistication is partly due to the legal structure concerned, but also to investment considerations. Thus, in order for will-substitutes to work effectively, there is a need for at least three things. First, there must be a high quality and stable legal system. Second, there must be clarity about the facts of each case, as most financial investments are based on taking a perceived risk. Third, there must be some sort of financial services industry, supplying expert services such as actuaries (to assess risk accurately), agents to sell and buy the financial products which form will-substitutes, and an educated populace prepared to buy and use them.

III. International Investors

Now, I need to say something about international investors. First, nowadays we live in a global economy, and with the benefit of modern technology we can know things more quickly and extensively from all over the world than our ancestors could ever have hoped to do. So the global market place is a very real one. Second, investors now have the choice of investing directly from their own countries, or of investing from elsewhere.

'Elsewhere' in this context has a double meaning. Many investors are based in jurisdictions different from those in which they were born or grew up. Many more, however, staying at home, incorporate companies or form trusts in such jurisdictions. When we talk about international investors, we need to distinguish 'offshore' from 'onshore'. In what follows, everything that is not offshore is onshore. Obviously.

A. Offshore

What does 'offshore' mean? First, it has to do with the supply of *services* (usually financial) which could be supplied to a client or recipient in his or her own territory of residence or of business, but which are supplied from another territory because it is advantageous to that person in some way to do so. Second, it has to do with the fact that the majority (usually the overwhelming majority) of such services from a given jurisdiction are exported from that jurisdiction to an onshore jurisdiction. The offshore jurisdiction does not use that volume of services for its domestic purposes. So, for example, we would not normally regard the UK as an offshore jurisdiction.

But this is subject to two qualifications. The first is that one could give a different answer to that question in respect of some discrete areas of UK financial service activity, for example, foreign exchange services. The second qualification is that the foreign consumer may not care whether those services come from the UK or from Jersey, as long as it is not from his or her own country. To that consumer, both may be offshore.

Moreover, the fact that a particular state is offshore today does not mean that it will be offshore tomorrow. These things change over time. In the 1950s Jamaica was, almost accidentally, an offshore jurisdiction, because of double tax treaty advantages. But, for political and other reasons, all of this was brought to an end in the 1960s, and nobody nowadays would regard Jamaica as an 'offshore' jurisdiction. Conversely, Madeira was not historically an offshore jurisdiction, merely a rather sleepy backwater, forming part of Portugal. Today, however, it is marketing itself aggressively, not only as a tourist destination but also as an 'offshore centre'.

In the past, the services supplied by 'offshore' were—as a general rule—not of the same quality as those supplied 'onshore'. In onshore jurisdictions, people were better trained and had better resources. But people wanted such services from offshore for another reason, ie, because additional value was given to the recipient of the services by the fact of the place of supply: *abroad*. A person based in an onshore jurisdiction could export some or all of his or her economic interests without physically leaving the onshore home. Instead, his or her *money* would leave the country. Almost certainly, in one form or another, it would come back again too, to be enjoyed later on. Money would be routed temporarily through another place. It was a form of 'money tourism'. The importance of trusts as a vehicle for these things to happen—especially for international investors—cannot be overestimated.

The point was so as to be able to avoid otherwise applicable rules onshore. Of course, you could avoid applicable rules simply by lying, and saying that you did not have any money, improving your chances of non-detection by depositing the money confidentially with a bank in an offshore jurisdiction as well. In the past, offshore jurisdictions did not really care very much whether people told the truth back home. But the world has shrunk, and, as we know—and care more—what our neighbours are doing, standards have changed.

These days the idea, at a minimum at least, is not to *evade* any of the onshore rules, but to structure transactions as to *avoid* those rules. The difference may be simply illustrated. If I have a job, and earn a salary, I have an obligation to report it and pay tax on it. If I fail to report it, or lie about my salary, and thereby do not pay tax (or not the whole of it), I *evade* the tax that I am legally liable for. If on the other hand I give up my job, so that I no longer have the salary at all, I *avoid* the tax, because in the changed circumstances which I have brought about the rules no longer apply and I am no longer legally liable for it. A homely test is, could you tell the truth and still not have to pay?

Generally speaking,[11] merely investing abroad will not enable you to *avoid* an unwelcome legal consequence. For that, you need a different legal structure.[12] At best, foreign investment may help you to lie, and thereby *evade* the consequence of the domestic rule. Thus, many persons have made deposits in offshore bank accounts and failed to declare the interest. This is tax evasion.

Politicians may openly *wish* that no one avoided any rules, and indeed structured their transactions so as to pay the maximum tax possible, but they know that that is simply pie in the sky. Human nature does not work like that. And, despite the development of various principles designed to prevent the most egregious examples of non-economic effect tax avoidance exercises from having impact on tax liability,[13] and the enactment of specific anti-avoidance rules in the UK tax code,[14] and now a general anti-abuse rule (GAAR),[15] it is still the law—at least in the UK—that no taxpayer is *obliged* so to organise his or her affairs so as to pay the maximum tax possible,[16] even if attempts at tax avoidance hardly demonstrate good citizenship.[17] The existence of trusts in the common law world, with their infinite variety, and the ability to create proprietary interests tailored to particular fact situations lends itself to this kind of planning. But even in the civil law world the imposition of tax—or the availability of reliefs—in specified situations is a well-known instrument of policy, and decisions taken there can be as much tax driven as in the common law countries.

The onshore rules which are sought to be avoided in this way are not just tax rules, either. They are often rules of other kinds, including rules of a regulatory nature,[18] rules relating to creditor protection[19] (including insolvency rules),[20]

[11] In the past, however, when tax systems were less sophisticated, examples existed of mere investments abroad, which were tax efficient. One such was the use of Jersey *rentes* (a kind of rentcharge over Jersey land, which counted as a foreign immoveable) to avoid UK estate duty: see P Matthews and J Mowbray, 'Trust Law' in P Bailhache (ed), *A Celebration of Autonomy* (St Helier, Jersey Law Review Ltd, 2005).

[12] Though the existence of, eg, duty-free allowances in many countries does sometimes permit a traveller abroad to purchase goods (= invest) there and bring them home free of domestic taxes.

[13] See, eg *WT Ramsay Ltd v Inland Revenue Commissioners* [1982] AC 300.

[14] See, eg Finance Act 2003, s 75A; Taxes Consolidation Act 1997, s 811.

[15] Finance Act 2013, pt 5, sch 43.

[16] *Attorney-General v Duke of Richmond and Gordon* [1909] AC 466, 475; *Commissioner of Stamp Duties v Byrnes* [1911] AC 386, 392; *Levene v Inland Revenue Commissioners* [1928] AC 217, 226–27; *Ayrshire Pullman Motor Services v Inland Revenue Commissioners* [1929] 14 TC 745, 763; see also *Helvering v Gregory*, 69 F 2d 809, 810 (1934).

[17] *Latilla v Inland Revenue Commissioners* [1943] AC 377, 381 (Lord Simon LC).

[18] eg rules about the consolidation of balance sheets in company law.

[19] See, eg P Matthews, 'The Asset Protection Trust: Holy Grail, or Wholly Useless?' (1995) 6 *King's College Law Journal* 62, and (1996) 6 *Offshore Tax Planning Review* 57; P Matthews, 'Asset Protection Trusts in English Law' in F Schurr (ed), *Trusts in the Principality of Liechtenstein and Similar Jurisdictions* (Baden-Baden, Nomos, 2014).

[20] On seeking to apply English law to German debtors, see, eg *Sparkasse Hilden Ratingen Velbert v Benk* [2012] EWHC 2432 (Ch); *Sparkasse Bremen AG v Armutcu* [2012] EWHC 4026 (Ch).

rules relating to marital support and provision on separation or divorce,[21] and rules relating to inheritance and succession, including (i) rules requiring estates to be subject to probate,[22] and (ii) rules allocating fixed rights or shares to or in a deceased's estate to close relatives (so-called 'forced heirship')[23] and the family provision legislation.[24] All of these may be capable of being avoided if transactions are structured through offshore jurisdictions.

These attempts to encourage onshore people to put their money offshore are well known, and are the subject of criticism in a series of increasingly strident publications in the popular press.[25] But similar techniques may also be employed *inside* onshore jurisdictions, or groups of onshore jurisdictions, such as the US and the European Union. Typically, such trading blocs have rules requiring free movement of goods and services within the bloc, and the creation of some kind of 'single market' with minimal compliance requirements and no additional taxation. So some states within the bloc will try to attract business to their jurisdiction by undercutting the tax or regulatory burdens, or even technical rules, prevalent in the other states.

States such as Delaware and Wyoming in the US have been doing this for years, but in the European Union this has also been true of places such as Ireland, Luxembourg, Austria and Madeira. It is better known than it was, though less well known than it might be, that the UK remains a tax haven to certain privileged groups of people, in particular those who are not *domiciled* in any part of the UK, but may be *resident* there.[26] All these states are trying effectively to sell, and make money out of, their presence inside the trading bloc and their 'rights' to the free movements of goods and services.

Nor is it just *inside* trading blocs, or just in relation to tax and regulation, that such competition exists. In OECD terms, the US is a tax haven for non-US people. For example, US bank interest paid to and gains on US quoted stocks and shares made by non-US investors are not taxed. Sometimes this goes too far. Some years ago, the US was ordered by the World Trade Organization to remove the tax

[21] See, eg P Matthews, 'The Impact on Onshore and Offshore Trusts of English Matrimonial Litigation' (2006) 10 *Jersey Law Review* 27; P Matthews in M Harper, D Goodman, P Hamlin, P Matthews, P Burgess, P Fudakowska and E Gale (eds), *International Trust and Divorce Litigation*, 2nd edn (Bristol, Jordans, 2013) ch 9.

[22] So producing often unwelcome publicity. See ch 1 above, p 11 f.

[23] See, eg P Matthews, 'Imperative Inheritance Law, Comparative Law—United Kingdom' in C Castelein, R Foqué and A Verbeke (eds), *Imperative inheritance law in a late-modern society* (Antwerp, Intersentia, 2009).

[24] In England and Wales, it is easily avoidable, as the family provision legislation applies only to persons dying domiciled in England and Wales. The French or German domiciliary who dies leaving a house in London has in effect complete freedom of testation in respect of it, as the succession is governed by the *lex rei sitae* (English law) but *without* the family provision rules grafted on top.

[25] See, eg N Shaxson, *Treasure Islands: Tax Havens and the Men who Stole the World* (London, The Bodley Head, 2011).

[26] The so-called 'non-dom' rule has been much criticised, and the UK Government Budget of July 2015 has made proposals to rein in its effect, but only by 2017.

advantages given to 'foreign sales corporations', a means by which the US Treasury subsidised US exports.[27] And witness the intense competition among certain European countries to attract international arbitration work,[28] or e-commerce, by providing modern, up to the minute legislation and other facilities. Globalisation is presenting new challenges to us all.

But, whatever the rules may be, onshore regimes fight back against offshore ones with anti-avoidance rules, and against tax-competing onshore regimes (and offshore ones too) with political campaigns. In relation to tax, for example, anti-avoidance rules in the UK have a long history, dating back to the Finance Act 1936. After some 80 years of legislating to close loopholes and shut off avoidance techniques, the UK tax system has arrived at a point where, for most UK residents, it is often better to *import* trusts rather than to export them, in the sense that the tax regime applicable to offshore trusts is harsher in many cases than that applicable to domestic trusts. So if you have a domestic trust, you have no incentive to export it. And if you have an offshore trust, you have an incentive to repatriate it.[29]

In addition 'offshore' is regularly attacked at a political level by high-tax or bureaucratically centralised jurisdictions, especially France. Under the control of these countries, international organisations such as the OECD have attacked on different fronts. A relatively narrow target has been the potential instability of some parts of the underdeveloped offshore banking system. The Financial Stability Forum was established in 1999, following a G-7 initiative. In its *Report of the Working Group on Offshore Centres*,[30] offshore centres were classified according to the quality of banking supervision, adherence to international standards and international co-operation. No rating of any *onshore* jurisdictions was included in the report, although the risk of a global banking collapse is more likely to result from instability there (the so-called 'Herstatt' problem).[31]

Another, slightly wider, target has been the recirculation in financial systems of the proceeds of crime: 'money laundering'. The Financial Action Task Force (FATF)[32] (set up by the G-7, under the OECD, in 1989) has tried to encourage, cajole and threaten countries, offshore and onshore, to introduce anti-money laundering legislation. Conspiracy theorists see the drive to greater information exchange (ie, with onshore jurisdictions) as a necessary first step in destroying the low-tax autonomy of offshore jurisdictions. After all, half the world's money laundering is estimated to take place *inside the US*, but the FATF's *Review to Identify*

[27] See WTO Appellate Body Report of 10 February 2000, available at www.wto.org/wto/dispute/distab.htm.

[28] eg the (UK) Arbitration Act 1996.

[29] On migration of trusts generally, see P Matthews, *Trusts: Migration and change of proper law* (London, Key Haven Publications, 1997).

[30] 5 April 2000, established by the Financial Stability Forum.

[31] Although there are now European Union rules on banking stability.

[32] See www.fatf-gafi.org.

Non-Cooperative Countries or Territories,[33] included neither that country nor any other 'onshore' jurisdiction.

A third form of attack, again by the OECD, has been to seek greater transparency in tax matters. This will enable high-tax jurisdictions to extend the territorial scope of their own fiscal imposts more effectively. One aspect of this has been to try to distinguish so-called 'harmful' tax competition (in their eyes, very bad) from ordinary 'tax competition' (ie, *onshore*; also—in their eyes at least—very bad, but they prefer not to say so openly until offshore has been neutered; divide and rule is alive and well). The original 1998 stance of the OECD was heavily criticised, and has since been modified. It now no longer suggests that offshore centres must impose income tax. It has limited its initiative to 'tax evasion and illegal tax avoidance' (*sic*). It also accepts the desirability of a level playing field among offshore centres.

The UK Government (which is responsible for the foreign relations of many of those jurisdictions, because they are British colonies or dependencies) some years ago began a programme of 'checking up' on the British offshore systems in place, to see if they matched what it rather grandly called 'world standards'.[34] I had the privilege of assisting some of these jurisdictions with this process. There is a certain irony here, as, in the case of the newer offshore centres, it was the UK Government that had originally encouraged them—indeed in some cases subsidised them—to lessen their economic dependence on Britain, by *becoming* offshore finance centres. But what it means in practice is that the UK, instead of standing up for its colonies and dependencies and the Commonwealth (and ignoring its dogged defence of its *own* right to set its own taxes and regulatory standards competitively vis-a-vis other European states), can look its OECD partners in the face and blandly assert that it is doing its best to solve the problem.

B. Other Abroad

But not everywhere is 'offshore'. Some jurisdictions are merely 'abroad'. Not our country, but not pejoratively offshore, either. There are a surprisingly large number of countries in the world where there is no tax and where there are few restrictions on lifetime transfers to third parties. Many of these countries are Arab or Muslim states, particularly in the Middle East. Even if there *are* tax or other regulatory burdens for some people in such countries, they may not apply to, say, members of the ruling royal family. And such families may be considerably

[33] 22 June 2000; see www.oecd.org/fatf.

[34] The supposition is that these have long existed, and are agreed by all. The reality is that it has just invented them, and they are not agreed at all; but this is, after all, politics: see D Mitchell in M Grundy (ed), *OFC Report 2001: Report of Offshore Financial Centres and Services* (London, Campden Publishing, 2001).

extended. As a result, some people from these countries may be very interested in investment in onshore countries, but only in tax-neutral ways via offshore ones (because their local law imposes no tax, and the target jurisdiction permits non-residents or non-domiciliaries to escape the local tax net).

IV. Will-Substitutes Offshore and Abroad

The general law, especially that relating to succession, is not fundamentally different offshore. Offshore jurisdictions are also local jurisdictions for the people who live there. They have their own legal systems, common law or civil law, or sometimes other systems of law. They have will-substitutes, just like other systems of the same kind. So in common law offshore jurisdictions, they will have trusts, for example. In civil law offshore jurisdictions, they will have usufructs, and so on. And investors and others from elsewhere can make use of such will-substitutes. What makes them especially attractive is not that the will-substitutes available in offshore jurisdictions are more sophisticated (usually it is the opposite), but that they are *offshore*. So we need to consider what such international investors, faced with the possibility of creating will-substitutes, might actually do.

A. Trusts

Trusts are probably the most pervasive will-substitutes in the common law world. And because they are so protean, and can be modelled just as the settlor wishes, to serve the exact purpose required, they come—from a civilian point of view, at least—in a bewildering range of shapes and sizes. Now, the kind of trust that best suits an investor is usually a bare trust, where the trustee has no duty towards the beneficiary except to keep the trust property safe and to transfer it as the beneficiary may require (including to the beneficiary) on demand.[35] This gives the investor certainty while taking advantage of the fact that it is the trustee and not the beneficiary that is the legal owner. In today's world of dematerialised securities, held through organisations such as Euroclear, such a trust can be extremely useful, indeed sometimes even essential. Unfortunately, the one kind of trust that is *not* a will-substitute is the bare trust. When the absolutely-entitled beneficiary dies, someone else steps into the beneficiary's shoes. But it is the law of *succession* and not the law of *trusts* that tells us who that person is.

However, there are lots of other kinds of trust which *are* will-substitutes, or at least have will-substitute effects. All life interest trusts fall into this category. These

[35] See, eg *Saunders v Vautier* (1841) 4 Beav 115, Cr & Ph 240; *Hardoon v Belilios* [1901] AC 118; *Stephenson v Barclays Bank Trust Co Ltd* [1975] 1 All ER 625; P Matthews, 'All About Bare Trusts' (2005) *Private Client Business* 266, 339.

include the so-called 'thin' trust, where property is held by a trustee for a beneficiary (often the settlor) for life, with power for the beneficiary to appoint capital to himself, and subject thereto on trust for such person or persons as the beneficiary may appoint.[36] If the power of appointment permits (and usually it does), the appointment can be revocable. This is not itself tax efficient, but it preserves flexibility. (A less aggressive version—'semi-skimmed', if you like—makes the power to appoint capital subject to the trustee's consent, or even confers it directly on the trustee. Either way it is not within the beneficiary's unfettered control.)

In these life interest trusts, when the beneficiary dies, the capital passes by virtue of the provisions in the trust, and not of the law of succession. This can be used by an investor who for any reason (tax, confidentiality, incapacity, etc) does not want to be the 100 per cent owner of an acquired asset, but does desire still to have the benefit of it during life and then to make the choice as to who benefits from it after death. Note that the beneficiary's rights under a trust of this kind *not created* by an investor *can still be bought* by one, who would then step into the beneficiary's shoes. (This gives rise to all sorts of other problems, with which we are not now concerned.)

Even where the trust is just a plain vanilla life interest trust, investors may still be interested. In the past trusts—whatever their provisions as to beneficiaries—were used as trading vehicles in many countries (among them Australia and parts of the US) because they were less heavily taxed than incorporated businesses. These were the so-called trading trusts.[37] You still find them occasionally today, though usually this is because there is some other advantage than tax involved. It might be that the local law has a particularly troublesome law of ultra vires for corporations, or there is too much publicity given to the activities of companies, and too much disclosure of financial information required of them.

But investors may be interested in life interest trusts for another reason. There is the possibility of an investor buying the life interest for a capital sum. On the one hand, the life tenant may prefer capital to income. On the other, the investor may be willing to gamble that the beneficiary will die earlier than his age and health would suggest, and so the investor will turn a handsome profit. Reversionary societies specialise in this kind of business. It is something like life assurance in reverse. If you do enough of this kind of business—just like life assurance—it ceases to be so much of a gamble overall, and becomes another branch of actuarial science.

Indeed, in the past this became so popular that nineteenth-century draftsmen had to work out how to *prevent* prodigal life tenants from selling their income rights so as to raise capital for gambling, or drink, or other vices. As we know, in

[36] This is in substance a more formal version of what in the US is called a Totten trust, see ch 1 above, p 15.

[37] See, eg D Hayton, P Matthews and C Mitchell (eds), *Underhill and Hayton on the Law of Trusts and Trustees*, 18th edn (London, Lexis Nexis, 2010) paras 1.120–21.

America they just changed the law to make certain life interest inalienable (the so-called 'spendthrift' trust). But in England they came up with the 'protective' trust, where the beneficiary's life interest under the trust is limited to come to an end in the event that the life tenant attempts to sell or mortgage it.[38] The only limit here is public policy. A settlor cannot create a protective life interest trust with himself as the protected life tenant and hope to avoid the effect of bankruptcy on the settled assets.[39]

It can be done the other way round, too. Where the remainderman has need of money, he can sell his interest, which may be vested, or—more likely with aristocratic family trusts—contingent. He acquires money today, instead of an inheritance (maybe) tomorrow. It is another version of the bird in the hand being worth two in the bush.

An example, which could easily have been something written by PG Wodehouse, but is in fact from real life, is that of the Seventh Duke of Leinster, the premier duke, marquess and earl in the peerage of Ireland. As a young man, Lord Edward FitzGerald was addicted to gambling, and he also defied his family to marry a chorus girl (nicknamed 'the Pink Pyjama Girl'). However, as the youngest of the fifth duke's three sons, he had no real expectation of taking the settled estates under the family trusts. Cut off from his family, and with a wife to support, he needed money, and so sold his reversionary rights for a comparatively small sum. Unfortunately, the middle brother was killed in the First World War, and the eldest (the sixth duke) went mad, and died young in an asylum. Thus, on the death of his father in 1922, Lord Edward succeeded to the senior family title, but with no entitlement to the family estates, and ended up living in a two-room flat in Pimlico, where he died in 1976.[40]

So, as the purchaser of the reversion found out in that case, there is money to be made. The investor may specialise in buying up reversions and (if he buys enough) will find that he can price his business properly and make money overall, just like life assurers.

Another kind of trust which is much in vogue offshore is the revocable trust.[41] Here someone, usually the settlor, has a power of revocation. If it is exercised, the complex trusts disappear, and the trust property is held on trust for the settlor. Its attraction largely stems from tax issues. A revocable trust can be a so-called 'grantor' trust,[42] and so avoid unwelcome tax charges arising under US law on the creation and operation of a non-grantor trust. US tax and trust lawyers are thus rather conditioned towards creating grantor rather than non-grantor trusts.

[38] See the Trustee Act 1925, s 33, and eg Hayton, Matthews and Mitchell (eds), above n 37, paras 11.68–77.

[39] *Re Burroughs-Fowler* [1916] 2 Ch 151.

[40] The current holder of the title is the 9th Duke, his grandson.

[41] See, eg C McKenzie, 'Having and Eating the Cake: A Global Survey of Settlor Reserved Power Trusts: Part 1' (2007) 5 *Private Client Business* 336, 428.

[42] The word commonly used in the US for 'settlor' is 'grantor'. In English law 'grantor' refers to the person who grants *any* property right or interest, and thus goes much wider than 'settlor'.

Unfortunately, in UK tax law the impact is the other way round: a revocable trust attracts tax charges (both income and capital) which an irrevocable one may not, and so UK tax and trust lawyers generally have the opposite conditioning. So long as the settlor (and his or her spouse) is excluded from enjoying the trust property in the future, it strictly does not matter if other powers (eg, to direct the investment of the trust fund[43] or to consent to the exercise of power by the trustee) are reserved to the settlor.

Yet revocable trusts are of little interest to us here. An investor in a trust—particularly an international investor—is unlikely to be prepared to invest in any trust where the settlor retains the power to revoke it, because it makes the whole structure precarious. Who would pay to invest in a trust structure that can have the rug pulled out from underneath it at any moment?

Discretionary trusts[44] may also be seen as will-substitutes, but in the UK they are heavily taxed and so increasingly unpopular. In any event, an investor would not be interested in acquiring the discretionary interest of a beneficiary, for the same reasons of precariousness which make revocable trusts unattractive.

If the trust—of whatever nature—is offshore, the investor can avoid important burdens, such as taxation, but also engagement with onshore regulatory bodies. Offshore regulators are usually more sensitive to the need not to scare away foreign investors. If the trust is *onshore*, on the other hand, it is not the end of the world. There are still opportunities to invest. But the tax and regulatory burdens will almost certainly be heavier. Some problems may be mitigated if the trust holds 100 per cent of the shares in an underlying private company, which in turn holds the investment portfolio.

B. Usufruct and Bare Ownership

Although civil law systems do not have trusts, they all have the idea of the usufruct and bare ownership.[45] This dismemberment or fragmentation of property into two real rights allows civil lawyers to keep faith with the Roman law idea of *dominium*.[46] This is that *in principle* (and subject to the limited number—the so-called *numerus clausus*—of limited lesser real rights) there should be *one* person with *all* the rights in a thing, the owner, the person with the highest real right of all, *ownership*.

[43] See *Vestey's Executors v IRC* [1949] 1 All ER 1108, HL.

[44] *cf* ch 5 above II.C and III.C.

[45] See, eg M Amos and F Walton, *Introduction to French Law*, 3rd edn (Oxford, Clarendron Press, 1967) 118–19; J Bell, S Boyron and S Whitaker, *Principles of French Law* (Oxford, OUP, 1998) 298 f; EJ Cohn, *Manual of German Law*, vol 1 (London, BIICL, 1968) para 440; J Zekoll and M Reimann (eds), *Introduction to German Law*, 2nd edn (The Hague, Kluwer Law International, 2005) 242 f; S Durand, *L'usufruit successif* (Paris, Defrénois, 2006).

[46] Buckland, above n 10, 186–89; Thomas, above n 10, 133–35.

Usufruct and bare ownership are similar, in *functional* terms at least, to the life interest trust, though of course without the trustee. To some extent they amount to a will-substitute too, though, as the usufruct model is largely immutable, and comes in only one flavour, it is a much less flexible one than the trust. But the same actuarial calculations can be made about the likely lifespan of usufructuaries, and therefore about the value of the bare ownership. Consequently an investor may well be interested in buying the bare ownership of a valuable asset, subject to a usufruct, or the usufruct of a valuable asset which he can rent out for an income. But unless the investor buys a lot of them there is still a significant risk involved.

Generally speaking, however, an international investor will not see such great advantages in investing in a civil law country with all the tax and publicity that that entails. So any investment will be based on purely economic criteria, and will normally be effected through a vehicle that conceals the true economic owner's identity. If the anti-money-laundering rules get in the way, by requiring the disclosure of too much publicity, that is frequently the end of the story. It is not that the investor is a money launderer. It is just that privacy is valued more highly than economic return. The investor goes somewhere else.

C. Foundations

The foundation is a legal institution by which a person divides his patrimony into two parts, retaining one but with the other creating an independent and separate fund (usually with legal personality) dedicated to a particular purpose or purposes.[47] In its original limited forms it was confined to public or charitable purposes.[48] But in some legal systems[49] it may be used for private purposes too. In such cases a foundation may be drafted so as to achieve more or less whatever a trust may achieve. But it is rare to find a system which allows the transfer to third parties of the founder's reserved rights (where such rights are lawful in the first place) or of the rights conferred upon beneficiaries. So the usefulness of the foundation for international investors is limited.

[47] See, eg K Neuhoff and U Pavel (eds), *Trusts and Foundations in Europe, A Comparative Survey* (London, Bedford Square Press, 1971); F Noseda, 'The International Foundation Scene in Trepidation' (2009) *Private Client Business* 109; F Noseda, 'The Foundations (Jersey) Law 2010—A Civilian Perspective' (2010) 14 *Jersey and Guernsey Law Review* 48.

[48] See, eg art 18 of the French *Loi du 23 juillet 1987*: 'Foundation refers to the act by which one or more persons, physical or legal, decide irrevocably to devote assets, rights or resources to the carrying out of a non-profit-making project of public interest'.

[49] eg Liechtenstein, Panama, the Netherlands. See UE Ramati, *Liechtenstein's Uncertain Foundations* (Dublin, Hazlemore Ltd Tax Publications, 1993) and E Ferrer-Morgan, *The Private Foundation under Panamanian Law* (Panama, Morgan and Morgan, 1995) as well as ch 9 above IV. A.

D. *Tontines*[50]

I have already mentioned *tontines*. Considering that they were invented by an Italian in France in the 1750s, there are a lot more of them in English law than you might think. Indeed, proposals for *tontines* as serious investments were presented to the English Parliament in the late-seventeenth century.[51] And not many people know that the famous company law case of *Foss v Harbottle*,[52] on derivative actions, is actually based on a property development *tontine* concerning the Victoria Park Company in Manchester.

It is sometimes asserted that *tontines* were forbidden in English law by the Life Assurance Act 1774.[53] This is not in fact correct. That Act does not mention *tontines* by name, let alone forbid them.[54] What it does forbid is the making of insurance on the lives of persons in which the insured *has no interest*. This critical phrase is not defined. Case law thereafter raised and decided numerous points on the question of insurable interest.[55] Whether a person has an insurable interest in the life of another person is therefore not a straightforward question at all.

Tontines in French law[56] are not common, because they go against the French desire to keep property in the family.[57] That is, in your own family, by which is meant your own bloodline. But they are possible. And paradoxically, in modern times many British buyers of French houses have opted for the *tontine* as a means of replicating the most important feature of English joint tenancy, to which they are of course accustomed, that is, *survivorship*.

But the *clause tontine* in a French conveyance does not give *both* co-owners a co-extensive interest in the property. Instead, it retrospectively[58] attributes the entire ownership of the property from the beginning *to the survivor* of the acquirers. You just do not know, until the death of the first to die, which of them that is. The one who dies first does not give up his or her interest in the property to the other, by release, accretion or otherwise. On the contrary, he or she never had

[50] See, eg A Lange, J List and M Price, 'Using Tontines to Finance Public Goods: Back to the Future?' (2004) NBER Working Paper no 10958, December 2004.

[51] 'A Proposal for a Yearly Increase of Wealth, by Subscriptions to advance Money upon Lives', and 'Proposals for the Increase of Trade … pursuant to the Votes of Parliament the 15th of December 1692'.

[52] *Foss v Harbottle* (1843) 2 Hare 461.

[53] 14 Geo 3, c 48.

[54] There were a large number of *tontines* floated in the 1790s, and indeed in modern times the Insurance Companies Act 1982 by s 1 and sch 1 provided that class V of 'long-term business' is 'Tontines'.

[55] See, eg M Clarke, *The Law of Insurance Contracts*, 3rd edn (London, LLP, 1997) ch 3; R Merkin, 'Life and Accident Assurance' in R Merkin (ed), *Colinvaux's Law of Insurance*, 10th edn (London, Sweet & Maxwell, 2014) ch 18.

[56] See H Dyson, *French Property and Inheritance Law* (Oxford, OUP, 2003) 154–58.

[57] See ch 7 above, p 160.

[58] Art 1179 C Civ.

an interest in the first place.[59] It is rather like a special destination in Scots law,[60] although the latter is a wider concept.[61]

So every purchase *en tontine* in French law is a speculation of a kind. Hence the French themselves, being so attached to their land, do not use it very much for the purchase of, say, family homes. What I buy goes to my children, not to my surviving spouse. A gambling investor might buy the rights of one of the *tontine* 'co-owners', but if you back the wrong horse you will lose your money.

I am not aware of a great market for international investors using *tontines*. The trouble is that no one operating through an offshore vehicle, trust or company, or even foundation, would really want to come onto the radar screen of an onshore civil law country's authorities. And especially not France. So any market is likely to keep discreetly out of sight.

E. Joint Tenancies

Joint tenancy is one of the great mysteries of English law. Co-ownership as a practical idea is obvious, even though it is conceptually inconvenient for the Roman law principle of *dominium*. (Indeed the purist reforming draftsmen of the *Code Napoléon* of 1804 conferred the right on any co-owner to put an end to the *indivision*,[62] so that French people could not effectively contract to maintain co-ownership between themselves.)[63] But the idea that a person could be a co-owner, and yet not have something to pass on to an heir is not easy to grasp. Nor is the idea that *each* joint tenant owns the whole property. Indeed, the survivorship idea was so fundamental to joint tenancy that, at common law, corporations (which could not die) could not be joint tenants.[64] Although joint tenancy is most often met with in relation to land, it can apply to chattels too, and of course applies to choses in action, for example joint bank accounts.[65]

As an idea, joint tenancy is brilliant when it comes to trusts and trustees. You might have thought that the draftsmen of the 1925 legislation in England must have invented it, instead of simply picking up and pressing into service something that had been part of English law for centuries. What better form of co-ownership

[59] See Dyson, above n 56, 154.

[60] J Sinclair, *Handbook of Conveyancing Practice in Scotland* (London, Butterworths, 1986) para 9.5(b); T Guthrie, *Scottish Property Law*, 2nd edn (Haywards Heath, Tottel, 2005); GL Gretton and AJM Steven, *Property, Trusts and Succession*, 2nd edn (Haywards Heath, Bloomsbury Professional, 2013) paras 29.8–10.

[61] See ch 4 above V.

[62] Art 815 C Civ.

[63] This was reformed by laws of 1976 and 2006.

[64] *Law Guarantee & Trust Society Ltd v Bank of England* (1890) 24 QBD 406, 411; the rule was reversed by the Bodies Corporate (Joint Tenancies) Act 1899; see *Re Thompson's ST* [1905] 1 Ch 229.

[65] See ch 3 above II.D.iii.

could there be for a trustee than one which says that, while you are alive, you are a legal owner but that, when you die survived by at least one co-trustee, you disappear and all your property rights simply evaporate, so that the surviving trustees can carry on holding all the trust property for the beneficiaries without the need to consider the position of your heirs? In England the 1925 legislation made significant reforms to the use of joint tenancies, but other common law countries have not necessarily done the same.[66]

Joint tenancy is also very useful from the point of view of persons beneficially entitled to property. For example, a couple may buy a house together, but not make wills.[67] On the death of one, if the house is owned by them as beneficial joint tenants, the survivor will take the whole, outside the rules of succession. And because the beneficial joint tenancy can be easily—and unilaterally—turned into a tenancy in common in equity (the process of 'severance'), the joint tenants who fall out can protect their heirs' position with a simple step. Moreover, there is no need for any publicity, as the creditors and heirs of a deceased joint tenant are not prejudiced by doing so.

There is no joint tenancy in French law, though of course, as we have already noticed, there is the *clause tontine*. In matrimonial property contracts there is also the *clause d'attribution intégrale*, by which matrimonial property vests in the survivor of a married couple. (This has tax advantages over other forms of transmission.) German law has the *Gesamthand*, where no joint owner can dispose of his own interest separately, and none holds any defined part of the whole. For example, this is used in the concept of the partnership. Perhaps more surprising is that both Jersey and Guernsey law know not only ownership of land in common, but also *joint* ownership, where the distinguishing feature is survivorship, just like joint tenancy. No one is quite sure where that came from. It is probably just another example of a legal transplant from England to the Channel Islands.

The joint tenancy is useful for different types of investor. First, there are investors who want to pass on their wealth to another person (with whom they become joint tenants) but wish to benefit from it in the meantime. Second, there are investors who (whether for tax mitigation, anonymity or other reasons) want to invest behind a trust, but do not want to run the risk of a single trustee embezzling the funds. So there will be a plurality of trustees, holding as joint tenants. Third, investors can (at least in theory) speculate on their own lives by buying in joint tenancy with one another. But it should be noted that an investor cannot buy the interest of an existing single joint tenant as a speculation. This is because the sale itself causes a severance, and so what the investor actually obtains is a tenancy in common, and there is no speculation on the life of the first to die.

[66] eg Canada, US. In some US states even tenancies by entireties still exist; see, eg O Phipps, 'Tenancy by Entireties' (1951) 25 *Temple Law Quarterly* 24; R Huber, 'Creditors; Rights in Tenancies by the Entireties' (1960) 1 *Boston College Law Review* 197; *United States v 1500 Lincoln Avenue*, 949 F 2d 73 (3d Cir 1991); *In re Chinosorn*, 2000 WL 46074; ch 1 above II.F.

[67] Where (as is common) the house accounts for the bulk of the wealth of the deceased, using a joint tenancy to pass it to the surviving joint tenant takes away most of the incentive to make a will at all.

There is nothing really to prevent an international investor from using joint tenancies for investment opportunities in the UK. The non-domiciliary provisions of the UK tax code provide enough opportunity for the transactions to be carried out in a tax-neutral way.

F. Life Assurance Policies

Life assurance policies are a form of contract, by which usually a series of regular payments are (though sometimes a single lump sum premium is) paid to an insurer with a view to paying a capital sum on a certain death occurring. Typically we refer to life *assurance* rather than life *insurance*. The difference is that—in the classical form of life assurance at least—the contingency is in fact certain to happen at some time, and so is not in fact a contingency at all. The only thing that is not certain is the *date* of death.

Because policies once created can be held on (*inter vivos*) trust for others, but the substantive trust property (the insurance monies) are paid out only on death, life assurance is a well-known form of will-substitute.[68] Indeed, in some countries with weak historical and cultural support for capital investment markets (like France) or an overbearing state that abuses its position to offer marginally higher interest rates to small savers than the commercial market can (like France)[69] it is one of the most important forms of long-term saving, as well as a means of providing, outside a will, for those whom you do not want the rest of your family to know about. (It is hardly surprising that, although France has railed mightily against trusts as vehicles of money-laundering *par excellence*, it has said *nothing* about the use of life assurance for the same purpose.) In England there is even a statutory trust of life assurance policies in certain cases.[70]

From the point of view of the insurers, the risks inherent in individual contracts are mitigated, and indeed should disappear, if each contract is priced on an actuarial basis, and there are enough of them to even out the ups and downs of individual cases. In the past many life assurance companies have been run on a mutual basis, ie, that they are in effect owned by their policyholders. But this is not actually necessary. A life insurance company can be run as an ordinary business, via a company limited by shares, which are traded among the public. So a person may invest in life assurance just by buying shares in a life assurance company.

In addition there is—and has been for centuries—a market in second-hand life assurance policies. Here there is much more of a speculation involved. The purchasing investor having worked out the likely expectancy of the life assured buys the existing policy, preferably fully paid up, so that there is nothing more to pay by way of premium, for a price representing the value of the sum assured, discounted

[68] See ch 3 above, p 58.
[69] See ch 7 above, p 167.
[70] See the Married Women's Property Act 1882, s 11. See ch 3 above, p 58 f.

for immediate payment, and then hopes that the life assured dies sooner rather than later than the actuarial expectancy would indicate.

Again, an international investor would probably have an offshore vehicle—almost certainly corporate rather than a trust, though maybe a company *owned by a trust* in an appropriate case—for the purposes of any investments of this kind. In itself the company is not normally a will-substitute, because the shares in the company will pass on the death of their holder to the person designated by the applicable succession rules, rather than to a person designated by the company's memorandum or articles of association. The company is used because it conceals beneficial ownership yet is recognised everywhere (unlike trusts, for example). But the combination of a company owned by trust is a powerful one, giving the settlor ease of control coupled with the most protean of will-substitutes.

G. Annuity Purchase

Where one person wishes to give another a right to income for life, or until a certain event (eg, remarriage), or where a person has saved a capital sum to provide an income in future (eg, on retirement), a common way to provide the income is for the donor or saver to use a capital sum to purchase an annuity, or right to a regular income payment, from an appropriate financial institution. Typically in the UK today these are insurance companies, not least because they must be solid and long-lasting institutions, and because the prices for such annuities involve actuarial calculations, which insurance companies are good at.

Such annuities often involve a form of will-substitute, in that on the death of the beneficiary there may be a second annuity (or perhaps just a lump sum) payable to a surviving member of the family (typically a spouse or partner of the deceased).

In modern Britain, governments encourage saving for retirement by giving tax relief on income saved for this purpose (though in recent years they have been gradually cutting down the total amount of tax relief granted over a lifetime). Until very recently, it was compulsory under tax legislation to use most of the capital so built up in the purchase of an annuity.[71] The rules are now being liberalised, and the annuity will no longer be compulsory. But in practice most persons retiring will still buy some form of annuity, to provide them with a basic income come what may.

Essentially, annuity purchase is a form of reverse life assurance, in the sense that the annuitant pays a lump sum to put the risk of *longevity* on the annuity company, and the annuity company accepts that risk. It is calculated in much the same way, by looking at life expectancy. Indeed, annuity business can hedge life business. Annuities can in principle be sold for a lump sum in just the same way as life interests under a trust, to reversionary societies and other investors in the marketplace.

[71] For details see ch 3 above, p 54 f.

From the point of view of the international investor, similar comments apply to the purchase of annuities as to the purchase of life policies.

H. Pension Nominations

A person entitled under the terms of a pension scheme may have the right to nominate someone to benefit from the scheme to a stipulated extent after his or her death. Originally this was intended to protect spouses, but nowadays it can be anyone, family member or not. This is an important right, particularly where the deceased member dies prematurely. The question is how far there can be a market in such nominations. If there could be, and were, such a market, there could be investor interest. In the UK pension world such nominations are a matter of private law, and depend on the drafting in the terms of the scheme.[72] Usually, however, they are not legally binding. Consequently no commercial investor will be very interested in paying for the nomination, and there is no market in them. In Australia, by contrast, where they are commonly binding, there could be a market, but none is publicly *known* to exist.

I. Wasting Assets

Historically it was sometimes useful, either for formalities or for tax reasons, to structure a transfer of an estate in land in two parts. First a lease would be granted and then the reversion expectant on the determination of the lease, or vice versa. In modern times something similar has been used to avoid the inheritance tax trap for those who seek to give away assets during their lifetimes but try to retain some rights so long as they live: so-called gifts with reservation of benefit.

The House of Lords held some years ago that, where a donor gave away the reversion expectant on a 20-year lease which the donor reserved for his or her own benefit,[73] this was not a gift with reservation of benefit.[74] The donor retained a wasting asset. The longer that she lived, the less her 20-year lease was worth. On the other hand, the longer she lived, the more the reversion was worth to the donees.

Assuming that the donor manages to guess correctly how long she will live after the gift, this technique provides a will-substitute that is—or at any rate was at that time—tax efficient. If such devices proved to be popular, and one of the parties fell on hard times and needed to raise money, a commercial investor might seek to

[72] See ch 3 above II.A.

[73] For technical reasons this was achieved by the donor transferring the whole estate to a trustee for the donor, who then granted the lease to the donor and thereafter transferred the reversion to other trustees for the intended beneficiaries.

[74] *Ingram v IRC* [2000] 1 AC 293.

buy either the wasting or the accumulating asset for an appropriately discounted or increased sum. But there is no trace of any such market in England. Any such transactions would be private and not known to any official register.

J. Newspaper-Franco Schemes?

I end with the uplifting story of a tax planning exercise that did not work. This was also a scheme to minimise or avoid capital transfer tax (the forerunner of inheritance tax). The UK legislation imposing capital transfer tax provided for an exemption for certain gifts (whether under *inter vivos* trusts or under wills) taking effect conditionally 'on surviving another person for a specified period'. The intention was no doubt to exempt from double taxation the estate which passed on A's death to B only if B survived A by a specified period. But the drafting of the statutory exemption was poor, and the death concerned was not required to have any connection with the person with whose death and estate on which capital transfer tax was charged was concerned.

A number of taxpayers attempted to take advantage of this loophole at the time that the Spanish dictator General Francisco Franco was dying. Gifts were made by donors by reference to a named person surviving Franco's death. It was expected that he would die within a few days and then the gift to the named person would be safe and escape tax. But the *Generalissimo* rather unobligingly hung on for several weeks and did not die. Time and tide, and tax-planning exercises, wait for no man, however. So tax advisers thinking of advising clients to enter into similar gifts started to use elaborate formulas to 'speed up' the deaths.

Eventually the formula most used was to refer to the death of the person whose obituary notice was top of the list in *The Times* newspaper on a certain day, with various subsidiary formulas to cope with the possibility that there was no obituary notice at all that day, or that *The Times* was not published on that day, and so on. These became known, rather curiously, as 'Newspaper-Franco' schemes. Not surprisingly, the revenue authorities challenged them.

The Court of Appeal held that the tax-planners had overreached themselves. They were right that the drafting of the legislation was poor, and there was no need for the person whose death the donee had to survive to be connected in any way with the donee, or indeed the first death. If they had waited for General Franco to die (as of course he eventually did), they would have succeeded. But by leaving General Franco on one side, and streamlining the process to depend instead on the publication of obituary notices, they had made the effective condition, not (as required by the legislation) surviving another person by a period, but *the publication of the newspaper*, and the scheme therefore failed.[75]

[75] *IRC v Trustees of Sir John Aird's Settlement* [1984] Ch 382.

But the point remains. This case involved the use of a will-substitute, an *inter vivos* trust, by which the enjoyment of an estate passed from one beneficiary to another. If the scheme had worked, the appointment of the assets to the new beneficiary would have been free of tax. A purchaser (investor) of the estate from the beneficiary might, for example, have bought before the result of the case was known, paying a price discounted to reflect the risk that the scheme did not work. There is no open market for such transactions. In the nature of things, each such opportunity will be bespoke, and will depend entirely on its own facts. Hence there is no way to know how often such transactions occur at present.

V. Conclusion

It may sometimes seem, especially to the civilian reader, as if the offshore world is ruled by tax considerations alone. These certainly have played their part in the past, and still do so today. But it would be wrong to ignore the very many non-tax reasons why offshore structures are used. Privacy, lower cost, speed and lack of red tape are equally good reasons for using offshore. So a person, who does not wish the contents or the beneficiaries of his estate to be publicly known on his death, or wants his beneficiaries to benefit straight away without waiting for court or government officials to sanction distributions, or desires to avoid forced heirship rules or some other burdensome regulation, will arrange during life for some or all of his estate to be held through one or more offshore will-substitutes. Trusts and private foundations are the most sophisticated of these, but others have their place.

The international investor market is just that: a market of international investors. Since will-substitutes present a number of greater or lesser risk-taking opportunities, they provide for a range of possible investment situations for investors with a greater or lesser appetite for risk. It is not therefore surprising that investors—and especially international investors—take advantage of them. Civil law commentators may criticise the wild Anglo-Saxon jungle that lies just outside the neat, civilian garden, for being such a cruel place, where every creature will eat another, given half a chance. Indeed, the film actor and director Woody Allen once described society as just one gigantic restaurant. But that is how life is, and will-substitutes play their part.

12

Will-Substitutes and Creditors: Canada and the US

LIONEL SMITH

I. Introduction

In this chapter, I aim to identify some of the ways in which commonly used will-substitutes interact with the rights of creditors in Canadian and US law. The assumption throughout is that a creditor had a claim against the deceased, and that this claim survives against the estate. However, to the extent that the deceased has used a will-substitute, the relevant assets do not form part of the estate. On the face of it the creditor may therefore be deprived of the assets in question. This chapter explores the extent of this problem. Much of the relevant law is provincial law or state law, which means there are dozens of jurisdictions involved; for this reason, my observations will tend to be general in nature.

A. Motivations for Using Will-Substitutes

The structure of the chapter is to address some of the most commonly used will-substitutes in Canada and the US, and to analyse their effects on creditors. Although these will-substitutes may have effects on creditors, this is not normally why people use them. The simplest advantage of using will-substitutes is that the assets will typically be received much more quickly than legacies.[1] In the Canadian

[1] See SE Sterk and MB Leslie, 'Accidental Inheritance: Retirement Accounts and the Hidden Law of Succession' (2014) 89 *New York University Law Review* 165, noting (168) that one reason for restrictive rules on the changing of beneficiary designations for retirement accounts is to ensure that the assets can be distributed quickly, by making it clear who is entitled to payment.

In Canadian estates practice, it is normal for executors to hold back a portion of the estate until the federal income tax authorities certify that there are no further liabilities of the estate. This delays the final distribution further, until the 'clearance certificate' is received. It also means that personal representatives would not wish *all* of the assets to be in will-substitutes, since this would make it impossible for them to retain a reserve.

context, another motivation is to reduce the taxes payable for the probate, or legal authentication, of the will, which are imposed by provincial law in some provinces.[2] Such taxes are tied directly to the value of the estate.[3] In the US, there is a federal estate tax and state estate and inheritance taxes;[4] these, however, are not usually mentioned as relevant motivations in discussions of will-substitutes.[5] Since the 1960s, the US probate system has been decried as cumbersome and expensive, but the expense in question seems primarily to be lawyers' fees.[6] The US system involves court supervision of the entire administration of the estate; in Canada, once the will is authenticated, the administration of the estate can take place privately if no dispute arises. There certainly seems to be a difference between Canada and the US in the extent to which citizens aim to avoid probate. In Canada, at least, people are often motivated by other considerations, the will-substitute effect being secondary. For example, life insurance is usually acquired in order to secure one's family, while pensions and retirement accounts are purchased to provide for retirement and to reduce current income tax liabilities.[7] It is primarily those who retain the estate planning services of a professional who would turn their minds consciously to the utilisation of will-substitutes.

B. Protection Through Non-Legal Norms

At the outset, it is worth mentioning that creditor protection may come through non-legal norms. In his 1984 study, John Langbein examined the reasons for what

[2] In common law Canada, there is no legal requirement that a will be probated, but an executor who acts as such without proving the will takes a significant risk of personal liability. Quebec law has the civilian system of the Latin notary; a will made before a notary is authentic and need not be proved in court. For some discussion of probate in Quebec law where it does apply (eg a holograph will), see M Piccini Roy, 'Probate Jurisdiction in Quebec: *Re Leclerc*' (2010) 29 *Estates, Trusts & Pensions Journal* 321.

[3] See Estate Administration Tax Act, 1998, SO 1998, c 34. In general I will take Ontario law as illustrative of Canadian common law. The same tax is payable for the grant of letters of administration, so even in an intestacy the existence of will-substitutes will reduce the tax burden on the estate. See ch 2 above.

[4] J Dukeminier and RH Sitkoff, *Wills, Trusts and Estates*, 9th edn (Frederick MD, Wolters Kluwer Law and Business, 2013) ch 15.

[5] The likely reason is that efforts have been made to subject nonprobate assets to equivalent taxation. See JH Langbein, 'The Nonprobate Revolution and the Future of the Law of Succession' (1984) 97 *Harvard Law Review* 1108, 1138 f, and the contribution of TP Gallanis in this volume, ch 1 above, p 12.

[6] Dukeminier and Sitkoff, above n 4, 466–69; Langbein, above n 5, 1116 f. Will-substitute transfers may also be attractive due to their privacy, or because they may allow freer choice of governing law: Dukeminier and Sitkoff, above n 4.

[7] The most important will-substitutes in Canada are beneficiary designations for life insurance and pension plans. The historical reason for the statutory validation of life insurance beneficiary designations was not so that people could avoid probate; it was simply that the doctrine of privity meant that the insurer would otherwise owe no legal obligation directly to the named beneficiary: *Vandepitte v Preferred Accident Insurance Corp of New York* [1933] AC 70 (PC) (although it would of course owe an obligation to the estate). The device was then adopted in relation to pension and savings plans. See ch 2 above, pp 11 f.

he called 'the nonprobate revolution'. One of them was that probate proceedings were less and less necessary for 'title-clearing'; ie, for the heirs to have a secure and alienable title to the assets they acquire from the deceased.[8] The other reason is more directly relevant here. While he did not mount a 'systematic empirical study', Langbein concluded, on the basis of enquiries in the commercial lending sector, 'that probate plays an inconsequential role in the collection of decedents' debts'.[9] What he found was that, apparently usually for moral rather than legal reasons, heirs very often pay the debts of the deceased, so that creditors do not need to claim against the estate. To the extent that this is true, in any jurisdiction, it means that creditors do not need to be as concerned about formal legal protections against the diversion of assets out of the estate via will-substitutes. This empirical question is beyond the scope of this chapter.

C. Procedural Issues

Let us assume that creditors do wish or need to claim against the estate. Of course, if there are sufficient assets in the estate to answer all claims, creditors will not be concerned about the effect of will-substitutes. In practice, then, we are concerned with insolvent estates.[10] This immediately raises some procedural issues. In Canada, there are two ways for an insolvent estate to be administered.[11] This can occur entirely within the provincial law governing the administration of estates, with the personal representative in control of the estate.[12] On the other hand, an insolvent estate can also be declared bankrupt, at the instance of a creditor or the personal representative. Bankruptcy is governed by federal law and a bankrupt estate will be administered by a trustee in bankruptcy.[13] Among many other effects, bankruptcy gives the trustee a range of statutory powers to set aside lifetime transfers that had the effect of diminishing the estate (and also allows the trustee to use any relevant powers available under provincial law). Moreover, it stops all proceedings by individual unsecured creditors, in favour of the collective bankruptcy proceeding. By contrast, in the US, an insolvent estate is administered under the state law governing the administration of estates, and not under federal

[8] Langbein, above n 5, 1117–20.

[9] ibid, 1120.

[10] The other possibility is that the estate is largely composed of exempt assets, which creditors cannot access. Exempt assets are mentioned below.

[11] AA Ilchenko, 'The Bankrupt Testamentary Estate' (2010) 29 *Estates, Trusts & Pensions Journal* 401. There is a more thorough (but less current) discussion in Ontario Law Reform Commission, *Report on Administration of Estates of Deceased Persons* (Toronto, OLRC, 1991) 161–83, where it is also mentioned that there is a third possibility, namely an administration action in which the estate is administered by the court. This is rarely used in Canada.

[12] In Ontario, under the Estates Administration Act, RSO 1990, c E.22 and the Trustee Act, RSO 1990, c T.23, ss 48–50, 57–59.

[13] Bankruptcy and Insolvency Act, RSC 1985, c B-3.

bankruptcy law. Since this text does not dwell on powers to set aside lifetime transfers, this difference is not that significant.

D. Dependants' Relief or Wills Variation Claims

In Canada, family members who are dependants (and sometimes non-dependants) may be able to secure an order for payment out of an estate which is greater than what they were left in the will.[14] In relation to these claims, the law may provide that the value of the estate is to be calculated so that it includes certain assets that were the subject of will-substitute transactions; moreover, that those assets can be made available to satisfy any order made in favour of dependants.[15] These claimants therefore have a powerful tool in relation to will-substitutes, but they are not treated as 'creditors' for my purposes.[16] US law does not allow dependants' relief claims.[17]

E. Exempt Assets

A final preliminary matter is to note that in both Canada and the US, some assets are exempt from claims by creditors, under provincial or state law. In this context, this is relevant because some exempt assets are also will-substitute assets.

[14] In Ontario, under Part V of the Succession Law Reform Act, RSO 1990, c S.26. 'Dependant' is defined (in s 57) to mean a spouse, parent, child or sibling of the deceased, to whom the deceased was providing support or was legally obliged to support at the time of death. For citations to the similar legislation in most other provinces, see AH Oosterhoff, *Oosterhoff on Wills and Successions*, 7th edn (Toronto, Carswell, 2011) 864. In British Columbia, the jurisdiction may be invoked by a spouse or child, whether or not they were dependent on the deceased: Wills, Estates and Succession Act, SBC 2009, c 13, ss 60–72. In Saskatchewan, an adult child can claim based on need: Dependants' Relief Act, 1996, SS 1996, c D-25.01, s 2(1) 'dependant'. Quebec law is conceptually different; it provides that the obligation of support, which is owed *inter vivos* to one's spouse, children and parents (art 585 Civil Code of Québec (CCQ)), survives against the estate of a deceased person who owes that obligation; a claim must be brought within six months of death (art 684 CCQ). See C Morin, 'Le testament: instrument de traduction' in A Popovici, L Smith and R Tremblay (eds), *Les intraduisibles en droit civil* (Montréal, Thémis, 2014) 103. Under this system, *inter vivos* gifts and some will-substitutes may be recovered to satisfy such a claim (arts 689–95 CCQ).

[15] See s 72(1) of the Ontario statute, above n 14. The list is widely drafted and covers gifts *mortis causa*, deposit accounts held in trust by the deceased, accounts or other property held in joint tenancy, revocable dispositions, life insurance proceeds on policies owned by the deceased or under group insurance, and amounts paid to designated beneficiaries in respect of pension or retirement savings plans. Not every statute has a provision of this kind; see AH Oosterhoff, above n 14, 902. See also ch 2 above, pp 47 f.

[16] Note also that by s 72(7) of the Ontario statute, above n 14, 'This section [that disregards will-substitute transactions] does not affect the rights of creditors of the deceased in any transaction with respect to which a creditor has rights'. By contrast, in Quebec law, above n 14, those who are owed support are creditors of the estate, although (as with any support claim) the amount of the claim needs to be set by the court.

[17] Dukeminier and Sitkoff, above n 4, 561 f. But see also ch 1 above IV.C.

For example, as will be discussed below, life insurance policies are often exempt even while the policyholder is alive. This is aimed at protecting dependants, and, perhaps, encouraging citizens to provide for their dependants. Pension assets are often exempt, which provides an incentive to save for retirement, and which can also provide benefits to dependants depending on the kind of pension. In the context of these exemptions, the beneficiary designation that may operate as a kind of will-substitute does not work any additional deprivation from creditors of the deceased.

II. Will-Substitutes

In this section, I will consider some commonly used will-substitutes, and how each of them may affect the interests of creditors.

A. Revocable Trusts

Inter vivos trusts are commonly listed as a kind of will-substitute.[18] Even a revocable trust, however, is created and takes effect during the settlor's life, so on a traditional trust analysis it is not a 'pure' will-substitute.[19] According to traditional trust law, even if a trust is revocable, the beneficiaries have an interest from the moment of the trust's creation.[20] This is not affected by the fact that the interest is contingent or defeasible, or deferred in possession until the death of another beneficiary. An example would be a settlor who creates a trust of a bank account, of which she is the trustee. The terms of the trust give the settlor the right to use the fund during her lifetime, so that the settlor/trustee is also a beneficiary; but the terms provide that on the settlor's death, the capital (if any is remaining) passes to the settlor's son. On a traditional analysis, the son has an interest from the moment the trust is created, even though that interest can be defeated either by revocation or by the consumption of the fund.[21] Pursuant to this present interest, which of

[18] eg MJ Rochwerg and LA Hemmings, 'Will Substitutes in Canada' (2008) 28 *Estates, Trusts & Pensions Journal* 50, 52–57.

[19] Langbein, above n 5, 1109 draws a distinction between 'pure' and 'imperfect' will-substitutes. As will be discussed below, US law classifies revocable trusts as pure will-substitutes.

[20] A power to revoke a trust is itself an asset of the settlor that creditors can seize: *Tasarruf Mevduati Sigorta Fonu v Merrill Lynch Bank and Trust Company (Cayman) Ltd Ltd and others (Cayman Islands)* [2011] UKPC 17, [2012] 1 WLR 1721; Dukeminier and Sitkoff, above n 4, 459; Gallanis, ch 1 above, p 21. This, however, would have to be done before the settlor's death.

[21] It is quite common that a beneficiary's present interest may be defeasible by the exercise of discretionary powers, as where trustees have a power to encroach on capital which may reduce the interest of the capital beneficiary. The bank account trust can be seen as an example of that structure: see J Penner, *The Law of Trusts*, 8th edn (Oxford, OUP, 2012) 20 f.

course is acquired *inter vivos*, the son is owed fiduciary obligations, has standing to enforce the trust and has rights to information about it. Moreover, since it is an *inter vivos* disposition, creditors can look to the ordinary law on voidable transactions, whether under state or provincial law, or (in Canada) under federal law if the estate is bankrupt.

Courts in the US used to apply this traditional analysis.[22] Now, however, revocable *inter vivos* trusts are generally considered will-substitutes.[23] This is partly because they share with wills the feature of revocability, but more importantly because US law takes the view that only the settlor has an interest during his life. These features together assimilate this kind of trust to a will.[24] On a traditional view, you can't have it both ways: if the other beneficiaries have no interest at all until the settlor's death, then the instrument is testamentary, so that testamentary formalities must be complied with.[25] Alternatively, if the settlor/trustee never intends to comply with formal terms of the trust, but rather retains full dominion over the property, there is a risk that the trust would be treated as a sham.[26] US law, however, does seem to allow the settlor to have it both ways: the other beneficiaries are understood to have no interest until death, but at the same time, the instrument is not testamentary.[27] Where the Uniform Probate Code (UPC) has been enacted, the non-applicability of testamentary formalities is provided for by legislative enactment.[28]

On this approach, a revocable *inter vivos* trust is properly considered as a will-substitute. This leads us to consider the most important statutory provision in US law for the protection of creditors in the context of will-substitutes, namely UPC § 6-102, which provides:

> (a) In this section, 'nonprobate transfer' means a valid transfer effective at death, other than a transfer of a survivorship interest in a joint tenancy of real estate, by a transferor whose last domicile was in this state to the extent that the transferor immediately before death had power, acting alone, to prevent the transfer by revocation or withdrawal and instead to use the property for the benefit of the transferor or apply it to discharge claims against the transferor's probate estate.
>
> (b) Except as otherwise provided by statute, a transferee of a nonprobate transfer is subject to liability to any probate estate of the decedent for allowed claims against

[22] Langbein, above n 5, 1126 f; Dukeminier and Sitkoff, above n 4, 440–45.

[23] Langbein, above n 5, 1109, 1113; Dukeminier and Sitkoff, above n 4, 445–49.

[24] Dukeminier and Sitkoff, above n 4, 449–51, noting that this assimilation has been aided by statutory interventions where courts continued to apply traditional trust law.

[25] *Cock v Cooke* (1866) LR 1 PD 241, 243: 'It is undoubted law that whatever may be the form of a duly executed instrument, if the person executing it intends that it shall not take effect until after his death, and it is dependent upon his death for its vigour and effect, it is testamentary'. See also *MacInnes v MacInnes* [1935] SCR 200; *Carson v Wilson* (1961) 26 DLR (2d) 307 (ONCA).

[26] As the Canadian Federal CA said in *Antle v R* 2010 FCA 280, [21], there is a sham when 'parties to a transaction present it as being different from what they know it to be'.

[27] Above, n 24.

[28] UPC (amended 2010), § 6-101. According to the website of the Uniform Law Commission, www.uniformlaws.org, the Code is in force in only 16 states. See ch 1 above, p 20.

> decedent's probate estate and statutory allowances to the decedent's spouse and children to the extent the estate is insufficient to satisfy those claims and allowances. The liability of a nonprobate transferee may not exceed the value of nonprobate transfers received or controlled by that transferee.

The effect of UPC § 6-102(a) is that the creation of an *inter vivos* trust that is revocable by the settlor is a nonprobate transfer.[29] The effect of UPC § 6-102(b) is that the other beneficiaries of the trust, who acquire assets after the death of the settlor, are liable to the settlor's creditors, up to the value of the assets they received. These provisions, where they are in force, clearly provide an important tool for creditor protection.

B. Pay-On-Death Accounts; Transfer-On-Death Deeds and Registrations

In US law, an important category of will-substitute is the pay-on-death account. These accounts have a named beneficiary who receives the balance, by contractual promise, on the death of the account holder. In general, validating legislation is required to avoid the applicability of testamentary formalities;[30] there is no such legislation in Canada. The result is that such an arrangement would fail, for two separate reasons. First, in line with the discussion above, the designation of the beneficiary would probably be seen as testamentary so that the relevant formalities would be needed.[31] Second, according to traditional common law principles of privity of contract, the beneficiary would not have any direct right against the financial institution where the account is held; the financial institution would owe the balance to the estate.[32]

Again by statutory intervention, US law has gone further, validating transfer-on-death arrangements for investment securities, deeds for estates in land, and even

[29] The definition of nonprobate transfer requires that the settlor had the power 'acting alone' to prevent the transfer. It has been suggested that this could allow settlors to avoid the operation of these rules relatively easily: EH Gagliardi, 'Remembering the Creditor at Death: Aligning Probate and Nonprobate Transfers' (2007) 41 *Real Property, Probate and Trust Journal* 819, 855–57. Gagliardi suggests that there is some inconsistency between the provisions of the UPC and the more general provisions in the Uniform Trust Code (UTC) on creditor access to assets in revocable trusts (UTC (amended 2010), §§ 103(14), 505), which are drafted to catch any trust 'revocable by the settlor without the consent of the trustee or a person holding an adverse interest'.

[30] Gallanis, ch 1 above, pp 15 f.

[31] See above, n 25 and text.

[32] As we will see below, in the context of other will-substitutes in Canada, there are statutory provisions obliging the debtor to pay the named beneficiary. The Supreme Court of Canada recognised a 'principled exception' to privity in 1999 (*Fraser River Pile & Dredge Ltd v Can-Dive Services Ltd* [1999] 3 SCR 108), but the scope of this remains unclear; and it is generally understood to allow third parties to take advantage of exemption clauses, but not to give them direct claims (J Neyers, 'Explaining the Principled Exception to Privity of Contract' (2007) 52 *McGill Law Journal* 757). Privity does not apply in Quebec civil law, and has been abolished by legislation in New Brunswick (Law Reform Act, RSNB 2011, c 184, s 4). US common law long ago abandoned the doctrine of privity: AL Corbin, 'Contracts for the Benefit of Third Parties' (1930) 46 *Law Quarterly Review* 12.

vehicle registrations in some states.[33] Since a bank account is a debt governed by a contract, a pay-on-death direction for a bank account can operate as a contractual promise (subject to the issues mentioned in the previous paragraph). These other structures, however, are not merely contractual promises to pay a third party, but rather bring about a transfer of rights formerly held by the deceased.

If we ask why all these structures have been implemented in US law but not in Canadian law, the answer seems to be that in Canada, there has been no comparable demand for legal structures to avoid the probate process.[34]

In the US, UPC § 6-102(b), where it is in force, will operate to make the beneficiary of any such transfer potentially liable to the settlor's creditors, up to the value of the assets received.[35]

C. Joint Tenancy

Joint tenancy is usually considered an important will-substitute in common law jurisdictions.[36] It is not a 'pure' will-substitute, inasmuch as the creation of a joint tenancy gives each joint tenant a present interest; it is not revocable.[37] This way of holding property has the characteristic that when one joint tenant dies, her interest disappears and does not pass to her estate. If there is only one other joint tenant, the result is that the surviving tenant becomes the sole owner; but her rights do not derive from the estate of the deceased joint tenant.[38]

If a joint tenant dies, the effect on his creditors is that it becomes impossible for them to attach the asset, since their debtor no longer has any rights in it.[39] One

[33] Gallanis, ch 1 above, p 16.

[34] See section I.A. The same seems to be true of England and Wales as well as Scotland. See chs 3 and 4 above, pp 76 f and p 104.

[35] Gagliardi, above n 29, 861.

[36] Joint tenancy is unknown in Quebec civil law; in that jurisdiction, undivided co-ownership operates similarly to tenancy in common in the common law.

[37] Langbein, above n 5, 1109 and 1114, draws a distinction between 'pure' and 'imperfect' will-substitutes and classifies joint tenancies as imperfect.

[38] One of the most important contexts in will-substitutes is where bank accounts or investment accounts are held jointly. These are creatures of contract, and the rights held may be purely personal; in this sense it is not clear that this is a joint tenancy in the sense understood by property law. However, the effective outcome is the creation, by contractual agreement, of the same outcome. See DWM Waters, M Gillen and L Smith, *Waters' Law of Trusts in Canada*, 4th edn (Toronto, Thomson/Carswell, 2012) 435–46. Langbein, above n 5, 1112 f treats joint accounts as 'pure' will-substitutes because one party can retain total control over the account and have the power to unilaterally end the arrangement by emptying the account.

[39] Conversely, if the creditor begins an execution process while the debtor is still alive, it may access the jointly held property. The traditional language of the common law is to ask at what point the writ of execution 'binds' the goods in question. In civilian terms, at this point the execution creditor obtains a kind of real right in the asset, which will survive the death of the debtor. Execution in relation to debts (such as bank accounts) does not always follow the same pattern; see Waters, Gillen and Smith, above n 38, 436, fn 216.

nuance to this is that where the creation of a joint tenancy is a donative transfer, it may give rise to the presumption of resulting trust in common law Canada, just as in other common law jurisdictions in the Commonwealth. For example, if A, being the sole holder of a freehold estate in land, conveys it into a joint tenancy of A and B, then depending on the relationship between A and B, it is possible that there will be a presumption that B holds his interest on trust for A. If so, then if A predeceases B, B will hold the freehold in trust for the estate of A, and this equitable interest will be available to A's creditors. In common law Canada, the traditional law regarding the presumption of resulting trust has been restated, so that the presumption of resulting trust now arises in a transfer from a parent to an adult child.[40] Conversely, in the US, it seems that it is the presumption of resulting trust that has fallen by the wayside in the context of gratuitous transfers.[41] The result is that a gratuitous transfer, even to a stranger, is taken to be a gift unless an intention to create a trust is proved by evidence.

In both Canada and the US, a joint tenancy can deprive creditors of access to an asset to which they might have had recourse, had they intervened during the life of their debtor. By UPC § 6-102(a), the survivorship interest in a joint tenancy of real estate is not a 'nonprobate transfer', which means that UPC § 6-102(b) does not apply to protect creditors. The notes to the annotated UPC explain that this is to preserve stability of title and ease of title examination, and to allow spouses to protect interests in land from creditors.[42] However, the protective provisions of UPC § 6-102(b) will apply to joint bank accounts, joint investment accounts and any other jointly held personal property. This allows creditors of the deceased to access these assets in the hands of the surviving joint tenant.

[40] *Pecore v Pecore* 2007 SCC 17, [2007] 1 SCR 795. For discussion, see Waters, Gillen and Smith, above n 38, 418–20. The traditional doctrine of equity was that the presumption of resulting trust did not arise in a gratuitous transfer from a parent to his or her child, whatever the age of the child; the transfer was taken to be a gift unless an intention to create a trust was proved by evidence. In common law Canada, this is now only true in transfers to minor children. Quebec civil law does not have any presumption of resulting trust.

[41] See AW Scott, WF Fratcher and ML Ascher, *Scott and Ascher on Trusts*, vol 6, 4th edn (Frederick, MD, Aspen Publishers, 2009) § 40.2. US law still has a presumption of resulting trust where one person pays the purchase price of an asset and directs the vendor to transfer the asset to a third party; the third party will be presumed to hold it in trust for the one who paid the price, unless an intention to make a gift is proved (ibid, § 40.1.1). Thus if A pays for an estate and directs the vendor to convey it jointly to A and B, and A dies, B would presumptively hold the estate on trust for the estate of A, making its value available to A's creditors.

[42] Note 5 to UPC § 6-102. The note also indicates that the law is different in some states: 'The exclusion of "a survivorship interest in a joint tenancy of real estate" from the definition of "nonprobate transfer" in subsection (a) is contrary to the law of some states (eg, South Dakota) that allow an insolvent decedent's creditors to reach the share the decedent could have received prior to death by unilateral severance of the joint tenancy. The law in most other states is to the contrary'.

D. Life Insurance

Life insurance can serve as a will-substitute inasmuch as the proceeds can be made payable directly to a named beneficiary, bypassing the estate. When this is done, the designation of the named beneficiary can be revocable or irrevocable; in the latter case, it can be revoked only with the consent of the named beneficiary. In Canada, the designation of a beneficiary is regulated by particular statutes;[43] because these rules appear in special statutes, they are understood to override the formal requirements of the wills legislation.[44] John Langbein suggested that the US courts reached the same result by resort to legal fictions.[45]

Typically, insurance proceeds received by a designated beneficiary pass outside the estate, and are specifically excepted from the claims of the creditors of the deceased.[46] In the US, this means that UPC § 6-102(b) will be disapplied by its opening words, '[e]xcept as otherwise provided by statute'.[47] In Canada, even during the life of the insured, the insured's rights in the policy will be protected against his or her creditors if there is a beneficiary designation in favour of a spouse, child, grandchild or parent of the insured.[48]

[43] Insurance Act, RSO 1990, c I.8, ss 190–96; relevant definitions are in s 171(1). An important part of this legislative system is s 195 which gives the beneficiary the right to sue; traditional common law principles of privity of contract would otherwise have denied such a right, above n 7, although the law has evolved, above n 32. Privity is not part of the civil law of Quebec, where the designation of insurance beneficiaries is covered by the Civil Code (arts 2445–60).

[44] See above, n 25 and text. The statutes, however, make it *permissible* to make a designation in a will, but in this case it cannot be irrevocable.

[45] Langbein, above n 5, 1128 f. Less clear is Langbein's puzzlement (1129 f) as to why courts took the view that wills legislation might apply at all. He questions 'the assumption that will-like results may be achieved only by instruments that are wills' and observes that '[t]he typical Wills Act is silent on the question of what transactions it covers—that is, what transfers must take place by will'. As noted, above n 25 and text, the Commonwealth view is that any legal act that purports to make a transfer that will only take effect upon death is a will. That is the traditional meaning of the word in the common law. It is not an *assumption* that will-like effects may be achieved only by wills; it is what 'will' means. Typically, Wills Acts impose requirements of form on some (but not all) wills, but they do not create or delimit testamentary capacity.

[46] Insurance Act, above n 43, s 196(1): 'Where a beneficiary is designated, the insurance money, from the time of the happening of the event upon which the insurance money becomes payable, is not part of the estate of the insured and is not subject to the claims of the creditors of the insured'; AH Oosterhoff, above n 14, 120 f. In Quebec, art 2455 of the Civil Code provides that the payment is not part of the estate of the insured; protection from the creditors of the deceased follows from the general principle that only the estate is liable for its debts (see *Laforest v Boudreault* 2015 QCCA 162, [22]–[23]). For US law, see Gagliardi, above n 29, 864.

[47] Gagliardi, above n 29, 863. If there were an irrevocable beneficiary designation, the resulting transfer would in any event fall outside the definition of 'nonprobate transfer' in UPC § 6-102(a).

[48] Insurance Act, above n 43, s 196(2). For discussion of some difficulties in the interpretation of this provision, see R Goodman, 'Insurance Trusts and Creditor Protection: Having Your Cake and Eating It Too?' (2010) 30 *Estates, Trusts & Pensions Journal* 89. Quebec law has wider exemptions: the policy is exempt if the beneficiary is the spouse or any ascendant or descendant of the policyholder (art 2457 CCQ); it is also exempt if the beneficiary designation is irrevocable, regardless of who is the named beneficiary, and even if it is the estate of the policyholder (art 2458 CCQ; *Perron-Malenfant v Malenfant (Trustee of)* [1999] 3 SCR 375, [38], [54], interpreting the corresponding provision in the previous Civil Code of Lower Canada; *Bank of Nova Scotia v Thibault* [2004] 1 SCR 758, 2004 SCC 29, [11]). Some provincial exemptions do not operate where the creditor is a former spouse.

E. Non-Insurance Beneficiary Designations

Beneficiary designations can be made in relation to other financial instruments. The most important ones are different kinds of pension. These may be group or individual plans, in relation to employers in the public or the private sector. There can be death benefits payable to a designated beneficiary in both defined benefit and defined contribution plans. However, since a defined contribution plan is in the nature of an individual investment account, there is the potential for a much larger payment to the beneficiary. In both Canada and the US, there are tax-sheltered retirement savings vehicles that can be created in addition to or instead of employment pensions. In Canada, these individual plans are called Registered Retirement Savings Plans (RRSPs).[49] When the holder reaches a certain age, RRSPs must be converted to Registered Retirement Income Funds (RRIFs).[50] In the US, the generic term is Individual Retirement Account or IRA.[51]

So long as applicable taxation norms are followed, contributions to all of these retirement savings vehicles, and investment growth within them, are not subject to income tax. The funds that are in the plan are only subject to income tax liability when they are taken out of it. In the case of individual pension plans (defined contribution employer plans, or RRSPs or IRAs), there may be funds remaining in the plan when the holder dies. In Canada, the estate (and not any named beneficiary) is subject to income tax on those funds.[52] In the US, the tax-sheltered status of the funds can to some extent be preserved in the hands of the beneficiary.[53]

The naming of a beneficiary allows the benefit in question to pass directly to that beneficiary, outside the estate. In the case of a death benefit payable under a defined benefit employee pension, this is analogous to what happens with life insurance benefits. The result is somewhat more striking, however, in the case of individual pension plans, whether defined contribution employer plans or RRSPs or IRAs. This is because in this case, the 'death benefit' is not in the nature of insurance, but is rather money that belonged to the deceased during his or her life (subject to the fact that income tax had not yet been paid on it).[54] In the US, where UPC § 6-102(b) is in force, it will be necessary to find a legislative exemption in order to disapply § 6-102(b) from such situations, although it appears that

[49] Rochwerg and Hemmings, above n 18, 64. See also ch 2 above I.E.i.

[50] The principal difference is that when a RRIF is created, some of the funds in the plan start to be paid out to the holder, attracting income tax liability. For the similar rule in the US, see Dukeminier and Sitkoff, above n 4, 478.

[51] Dukeminier and Sitkoff, above n 4, 479. See also Sterk and Leslie, above n 1, 169 on the popularity of these vehicles in the US. See further ch 1 above II.C.

[52] Rochwerg and Hemmings, above n 18, 64; *Laforest v Boudreault*, above n 46.

[53] Dukeminier and Sitkoff, above n 4, 478 and, for more detail, Sterk and Leslie, above n 1, 218 f.

[54] This distinction was noted by Huband JA speaking for the Manitoba CA in *Clark Estate v Clark* (1997) 15 ETR (2d) 113 (Man CA) 119. The result with this type of pension is thus comparable to the US pay-on-death account (on which see section II.B.).

these are common.[55] In Canada, the direct payment to the designated beneficiary is generally specifically provided for by provincial legislation.[56] It has been held to follow that the funds received by the designated beneficiary are immune from claims that creditors had against the deceased.[57] As with life insurance, the effect on creditors may be less dramatic than one might think, inasmuch as the plan assets may be exempt from creditors of the plan holder even while he or she is alive.[58]

In the US, it seems clear that a non-insurance beneficiary designation need not comply with testamentary formalities.[59] Some Canadian provinces have legislation authorising pension beneficiary designations in nontestamentary form.[60]

[55] See Gagliardi, above n 29, 864. Sterk and Leslie, above n 1, state (218) that 'the rights of creditors to retirement account assets are plagued by uncertainty and confusion'. They note that federal bankruptcy law protects IRAs during the plan holder's life, but state courts are divided as to whether this continues after the plan holder's death.

[56] It appears that among common law provinces, only New Brunswick and Nova Scotia lack legislation providing for this result: AH Oosterhoff, above n 14, 131 f. The legislation does not always specifically include RRSPs along with employee pensions in this respect. It was held to extend to them, however, in *Clark Estate v Clark*, above n 54, and in *Amherst Crane Rentals Ltd. v Perring* (2004) 241 DLR (4th) 176 (ONCA), application for leave to appeal dismissed (2005) 247 DLR (4th) vii. The Ontario statute was subsequently amended to cover RRSPs: Succession Law Reform Act, above n 14, s 54.1. Where the legislation applies, it is not necessary that the plan be held in the form of a trust for direct payment to operate (although outside Quebec, RRSPs are usually held as trusts if they are 'self-directed'; ie, if the holder chooses the investments from time to time). For Quebec civil law, see R Dikeakos, 'Les enjeux en matière de désignation de bénéficiaires et les successions' in Barreau du Québec (ed), *Service de la formation continue, Développements récents en succession et fiducies*, vol 391 (Cowansville, Éditions Yvon Blais, 2014) 159. In Canada, as with life insurance, it is possible to make irrevocable beneficiary designations for pensions.

[57] In *Clark Estate v Clark*, above n 54, Huband JA suggested (119 f) that creditors could claim against the designated beneficiary, invoking an analogy with *Re Diplock* [1948] Ch 465, [1948] 2 All ER 318 (CA). However, in *Amherst Crane*, above n 56, it was held that the beneficiary was not liable. Although *Amherst Crane* is binding only in Ontario, the refusal by the Supreme Court of Canada to grant leave to appeal gives the decision somewhat more authority, and the decision would be particularly persuasive in other provinces with similar legislation. See the discussion in the case note by B Corbin, 'Amherst Crane Rentals Ltd v Perring' (2005) 24 *Estates, Trusts & Pensions Journal* 206, 215 f.

[58] AH Oosterhoff, above n 14, 132, indicates that this is the law in Manitoba, Newfoundland and Labrador, Prince Edward Island, and Saskatchewan. Note that if the plan holder becomes bankrupt, federal bankruptcy legislation applies; it respects all provincial exemptions, but itself adds that RRSPs and RRIFs are exempt except for contributions made in the 12 months before bankruptcy: Bankruptcy and Insolvency Act (n 13) ss 67(1)(b), 67(1)(b.3). As noted, above n 13 and text, in Canada it is possible for an estate to be declared bankrupt.

[59] However, Sterk and Leslie, above n 1, argue that the US law governing beneficiary designations is in need of reform for several reasons: eg it does not match the law of wills regarding the presumed intention of the plan holder (as on the divorce of the plan holder), and attempts by plan holders to change beneficiary designations may be frustrated for unjustifiable reasons (such as a failure to use the correct form).

[60] In Ontario, the Succession Law Reform Act, above n 14, s 51 provides that a pension or RRSP beneficiary designation does not need to be in testamentary form, but that it is effective if it is in a will. Similar are the Alberta Wills and Successions Act, RSA 2000, c W-12.2 s 71(2); British Columbia Wills, Estates and Succession Act, SBC 2009, c 13, s 85; and Prince Edward Island Designation of Beneficiaries Under Benefit Plans Act, RSPEI 1988, c D-9, ss 2, 5–7. The statute in Saskatchewan has a provision for employment pensions; it requires the designation to comply with the terms of the plan, is not specifically extended to RRSPs, and does not mention a designation in a will: Pension Benefits Act 1992, SS 1992, c P-6.001, s 67.

In the absence of specific legislation, the problem is that the beneficiary of a revocable designation acquires no rights during the life of the insured; he or she has only a hope that the designation will not change. In this sense, one could see the designation of a beneficiary as a testamentary disposition; just like a legacy, it can be changed up to the moment of death, provided the insured retains legal capacity. Thus, one might think that the designation of the beneficiary would need to satisfy the formal requirements of the wills legislation.[61] On the other hand, it has been held that some designations may be in the nature of the exercise of a power of appointment.[62] The difficulties of applying the general common law principles to non-insurance beneficiary designations were discussed by Ralph Scane, who argued that apart from the various statutory provisions, whether or not a beneficiary designation was testamentary according to the common law depended upon whether the beneficiary received the 'identical beneficial interest, or the benefit of the same contractual right, as the plan holder held immediately before death'.[63] If not, the designation would not be testamentary. This analysis would make many non-insurance beneficiary designations testamentary, thus requiring compliance with testamentary formalities in the absence of a governing statutory provision. Even if testamentary formalities are not required, the interaction of the rules for making and changing beneficiary designations with the rules for wills creates a number of uncertainties.[64]

This issue arises not only in respect of the formal validity of a designation or revocation by the plan holder; it may also arise in relation to the powers of a substitute decision-maker, such as an attorney under a continuing power of attorney, or a court-appointed guardian, who can act when the principal is no longer capacitated. This is because such an attorney, no matter how wide his authority, cannot make a will on behalf of the incapacitated person.[65] If a beneficiary designation

[61] See above, n 25 and text. See also the debate in England referred to in ch 3 above III.B.

[62] *Baird v Baird* [1990] 2 AC 548 (PC).

[63] R Scane, 'Non-Insurance Beneficiary Designations' (1993) 72 *Canadian Bar Review* 179, 187. See also DD Oosterhoff, 'Alice's Wonderland: Authority of an Attorney for Property to Amend a Beneficiary Designation' (2002) 22 *Estates, Trusts & Pensions Journal* 16, 25–32. DD Oosterhoff argues (36) that according to Scane's test, a life insurance beneficiary designation would not generally be testamentary. She also suggests (31) that Scane's approach would mean that survivorship in a joint tenancy would be testamentary, but this seems incorrect, since survivorship is not conceptualised as involving any kind of transfer. The issue is also addressed in A Werker, 'Non-Insurance RRSP Designations—Testamentary Dispositions of Property that Do Not Form Part of the Estate?' (2003) 22 *Estates, Trusts & Pensions Journal* 103.

[64] B Corbin, 'Designating Beneficiaries' (1989) 9 *Estates, Trusts & Pensions Journal* 199, 349; Scane, above n 63; AH Oosterhoff, above n 14, 132 f. The same problem arises in England, see ch 3 above, p 75.

[65] In Ontario, this is provided for in legislation: Substitute Decisions Act, 1992, SO 1992, c 30, ss 7(2), 31(1). In *Easingwood v Cockroft* 2013 BCCA 182, it was held that the same rule is one of general application, since it arises from the principle that will-making power cannot be delegated. DD Oosterhoff, above n 63, 21 f also argues that the Ontario provisions codify the common law. She suggests that the statutes in British Columbia and New Brunswick may, however, allow the making or alteration of beneficiary designations (in the case of New Brunswick, with the approval of the court; in the case of British Columbia, through the execution of a 'enhanced agreement' that allows wider powers for the attorney).

is testamentary in character, it seems to follow that a guardian cannot make or change one, even if this would save probate fees without changing the destination of the property in question.[66]

III. Conclusion

The growth of will-substitutes might be thought to threaten the interests of creditors of the deceased, to the extent that it allows the diversion of estate assets in a way that insulates them from creditors' claims. In both Canada and the US, however, many will-substitute assets are independently protected by legislation from creditors' claims, for policy reasons relating to the protection of retirement savings and, in the case of life insurance, of dependants. While one might argue about the wisdom of such policy choices, it is not surprising that creditors may be disadvantaged by the operation of will-substitutes in these contexts.

Outside those situations, there are interesting differences between Canada and the US, which show a wider adoption of will-substitutes in the US, and a corresponding reaction in the UPC in the direction of creditor protection. First, US law treats revocable trusts as testamentary in the sense that they are not understood to create any present interest in the beneficiaries other than the settlor, while treating them also as nontestamentary in relation to formalities. Canadian common law would allow such a trust to take assets out of the estate, but only at the price of the normal incidents of trust law: if a trust is created *inter vivos*, then all beneficiaries must have a present interest (albeit defeasible or contingent). This will give them rights to information and to benefit from fiduciary obligations. Moreover, attacks on the trust could be made via the federal and provincial law on voidable *inter vivos* transactions.

Second, US law allows the creation of pay-on-death accounts, whether bank accounts or investment accounts, and increasingly allows interests in land and vehicles to be transferred on death outside probate. These structures are not found in Canada; unlike in the US, there has been no demand for a widening of will-substitutes.

Another difference relates to property in joint tenancy. In Canada, a gratuitous transfer of property (including the gratuitous creation of a joint tenancy) usually attracts the presumption of resulting trust, even if the transfer is between a parent and his or her adult child. If it is not rebutted, the presumption will lead to the finding that the property is held on a resulting trust for the estate of the deceased

[66] E Musyj and J McKim, 'Can an Ontario Attorney for Property Engage in Estate Planning?' (2014) 34 *Estates, Trusts & Pensions Journal* 79; DD Oosterhoff, above n 63; Alberta Law Reform Institute, *Beneficiary Designation by Substitute Decision Makers*, Final Report no 104 (Edmonton, ALRI, 2014). This uncertainty in Canadian law also applies to an attorney's ability to change insurance beneficiary designations.

joint tenant, making it available to estate creditors. This applies to both real and personal property, and can give creditors a measure of indirect protection. In the US, there is no such presumption. Where a joint tenancy is created without any trust, it can often operate to deprive creditors of the deceased joint tenant of access to the asset in question.

In most of these situations, however, in the US the UPC aims to protect creditors of the deceased via the general provision in § 6-102(b), that can make non-probate beneficiaries liable for the debts of the deceased up to the value of the assets they receive.[67] However, the provision is in force in only a small number of states.[68] It is somewhat paradoxical that US state legislatures are willing to widen the range of will-substitutes to satisfy a demand apparently caused by defects in the probate systems that are creations of the same legislatures, while at the same time being reluctant to enact a provision that aims to protect creditors against the operation of will-substitutes. Canadian law lacks any general provision of this kind, presumably because will-substitutes are less widely used, and where they are, the assets are already largely sheltered from creditors.[69]

[67] Although UPC § 6-102 does not usually operate in relation to joint tenancies of real estate: see section II.C.

[68] Gallanis, ch 1 above, p 21.

[69] As noted in section I.D, there is a similar provision in relation to dependants' relief claims in some provinces. In this sense, these creditors are especially favoured.

13

Will-Substitutes: The Perspective of Creditors in Germany, and England and Wales

REINHARD BORK

I. Introduction

Will-substitutes have the effect not only of benefiting a third party but also of reducing the deceased's asset pool. This can be harmful to creditors who have relied on the wealth of the deceased only to discover upon his death that the remaining assets are insufficient for the payment of his debts. The question of whether creditors enjoy legal protection against the use of will-substitutes is therefore of great significance. This chapter will consider the legal instruments available for the purposes of creditor protection. However, the scope of the investigation will be restricted in two ways. First, the investigation will limit itself to a discussion of English and German law, omitting discussion of other jurisdictions. Second, it will put thematic priority on the rules of insolvency law, which consist largely of the German *Insolvenzordnung* (InsO)[1] and the English Insolvency Act 1986 (IA).[2]

II. Will-Substitutes: Examples

Will-substitutes have been extensively explained and analysed in other chapters of this book. I will therefore refrain from repeating the catalogue of mechanisms through which the transfer of assets upon death, which would otherwise belong to the deceased person's estate, may be carried out. However, when it comes to the protection of creditors, some examples are necessary to illustrate the effects of the

[1] InsO, Insolvency Regulation, English translation at www.gesetze-im-internet.de/englisch_inso/index.html.

[2] IA; text at www.legislation.gov.uk/ukpga/1986/45/contents.

instruments chosen upon the creditors' interests. In this chapter, discussion shall be confined to three examples. The first example is a life insurance policy, in which a man names a third person (typically his wife or his children) as a beneficiary.[3] The man pays the premiums during his lifetime, and the beneficiary is entitled to claim the insured sum from the insurance company upon his death (either in the form of a lump sum or in the form of periodic payments, depending on the terms of the insurance contract). The second example is similar to the first: the man has participated in a pension scheme, with his wife (or children) being entitled to receive a lump sum or periodic payments (the mode of payment being dependent on the circumstances and the applicable national law)[4] if the man dies. The third example—which is, at least from the perspective of German law,[5] an example of a gift *mortis causa* (*Schenkung auf den Todesfall*)—is that of an individual entering into a contract with a banking institution to open a savings account, into which he deposits a certain amount of money. The account holder and the banking institution agree that a third party, in this case the wife of the account holder, shall have access to the savings in the event of the account holder predeceasing the wife. In all three examples it shall be supposed that not the wife but the couple's children shall be the heirs. Thus, the will-substitute in favour of a third party is detrimental to the heirs.

III. The Need for Creditor Protection

Such agreements can certainly also be detrimental to the deceased person's creditors.[6] During the debtor's lifetime, creditors are entitled to his or her assets

[3] The appointment of a beneficiary is expressly allowed in Germany by way of § 159 VVG (*Versicherungsvertragsgesetz*, ie Insurance Contract Act 2008; English translation at www.gesetze-im-internet.de/englisch_vvg/index.html). By contrast, English insurance law is suspicious of life insurance, as it is deemed to be unfair gambling. The Life Assurance Act 1774 therefore restricts life insurance to persons deemed as having a sincere interest in the life thus insured, and the extent of insurance is to be restricted to the value of that interest. This gives rise to astonishing results (eg, *Harse v Pearl Life Assurance Co Ltd* [1904] 1 KB 92: a policy was held to be void for lack of interest and thus illegal where a son took out a life insurance policy against his mother, who lived with him and did the housework, the insurance policy being expressly declared as intended to cover 'funeral expenses'). However, for the purposes of this chapter, there is no need to elaborate, as insurance on the insured's own life or on the life of a spouse or a civil partner is due to the very nature of the interest concerned automatically valid up to an unlimited amount, *Murphy v Murphy* [2003] EWCA Civ 1862 para 34; J Birds, *Modern Insurance Law*, 9th edn (London, Sweet & Maxwell, 2013) 46. Thus, it is always permissible to insure one's own life and to name one's spouse or civil partner as the beneficiary of that policy.

[4] Periodic payments are possible in Germany, but rather uncommon in England.

[5] The establishment of such pay-on-death accounts is very common in Germany and the US; *cf* for Germany ch 8 above at III.C. p 183 ff, for the US ch 12 above at II.B. p 257 ff. In England, joint accounts are preferred. More generally, the term *donatio mortis causa* is used here to embrace all kinds of gratuitous allotment made *inter vivos* but under the condition of the donor's death. The scope, the legal rules and the dogmatic construction for such benefaction, however, may be different in England and Germany.

[6] An inconvenient effect may also be that the creditor has to deal not only with the heirs but also with the beneficiaries, which makes it more cumbersome and probably costly to pursue his interests.

in order to recover the debt when it becomes due. If the debtor does not pay his debts when they are due, the creditors may bring claims against him or her and enforce any resulting judgments against his estate, including receivables exercisable against banks and insurance companies. The same applies if the debtor has passed away, but instead the creditors can enforce the judgment against the heirs or the executor (depending on the jurisdiction in question). As long as the (attachable part of the) estate is of sufficient value to meet all liabilities, there is no need to protect the creditors from the use of will-substitutes. They can simply enforce their claims against the estate without any problems.

In England, creditors are granted additional protection through the provisions of inheritance law. The personal representative of the deceased's estate has to ascertain the scope of the asset pool at hand,[7] and then identify the liabilities of the estate before he is permitted to distribute property to any beneficiaries. According to section 32(1) of the Administration of Estates Act 1925, wills are only permitted to take effect if the estate were still to be solvent after all liabilities have been cleared. Thus, creditors are at least protected against heirs squandering the asset pool. In Germany, there is no such protection, as there is no appointment of a personal representative to function as an extra layer of protection for creditors, and therefore in Germany, creditors lack this additional protection. Instead, it is the task of the heirs themselves to pay the deceased person's debts, primarily out of the estate and secondarily out of their own property. Creditors are therefore not protected through the involvement of an executor but rather through personal liability of heirs for the deceased person's debts (§ 1967 *Bürgerliches Gesetzbuch* (BGB)).[8]

However, the right of enforcement against the personal representative may be in vain if the debtor has already transferred the relevant assets to a third party through the use of a will-substitute. In this case, the relevant assets no longer belong to the estate;[9] if a significant amount of such assets are displaced in this manner, the remaining wealth could very well be insufficient to satisfy the creditors. If the remaining asset pool is insufficient to satisfy all the creditors who are seeking repayment of their debts in full, the creditors may file for insolvency of the debtor.[10] In this case, the insolvency practitioner[11] will sell the assets and apportion the proceeds among the creditors on a pro rata basis. He will also verify whether he can challenge the will-substitute made out to third parties, and whether he can thereby demand that the relevant assets be transferred back. This

[7] For the definition of the asset pool, see s 32(1) Administration of Estates Act 1925.

[8] ie the German Civil Code; English translation at www.gesetze-im-internet.de/englisch_bgb/index.html.

[9] *cf Ashby v Costin* [1888] 21 QBD 401, 404; *Bennet v Slater* [1899] 1 QB 45, 51.

[10] § 317(1) InsO (Germany); s 264(1)(a), 421(1) IA, pt II; s 1 Administration of Insolvent Estates of Deceased Persons Order 1986 (England).

[11] Following the terminology used in Art 2(5) of the new European Insolvency Regulation (EIR), insolvency practitioner is used here to refer to all office holders in insolvency proceedings which are listed in annex B of the EIR, eg, official receiver, administrator, liquidator, trustee or (in Germany) *Insolvenzverwalter*.

would enrich the estate and thus protect the creditors from their claims not being fully covered, particularly if the subject matter of the will-substitute was high in value.

One may question the need for creditor protection in these cases.[12] It could be argued that it is the creditors' job to protect themselves when granting the credit, for example, by requiring a pledge or lien regarding an item of the debtor's personal property. However, this presupposes that such assets to which a pledge or lien can be applied are known to the creditors, which is questionable as many assets can be easily withheld from the creditors' access to the collateral. Furthermore, creditors are usually not in the position to request that a security be provided, this holding especially true for holders of non-contractual claims, such as tort liabilities.

IV. Means of Protection

Given the need to protect the deceased's creditors against detrimental will-substitutes, solutions can be found in substantive law and in insolvency law (the latter understood as being procedural law).

A. Substantive Law

In some cases, the transfer of assets upon death by a will-substitute is void, as the transfer does not meet the legal requirements. However, these requirements are mostly established in order to protect the donor or his heirs, rather than the creditors. If, for example, the law were to require notarisation of a gift *mortis causa*, or another formality, as is the case in Germany,[13] this requirement is aimed at impeding avoidance of succession rules and at protecting the donor against hastiness, and third parties against insufficient evidence. But the legislature did not intend to protect creditors. Another example of where substantive law steps in to protect interests other than those of the creditors is where a will-substitute in favour of a mistress is invalidated on the basis of being *contra bonos mores*.[14] This invalidation is intended to protect the public order, and the members of the family who are statutory heirs, but not the creditors of the unfaithful spouse. As a result,

[12] One might hope that the heirs would be eager to pay off the debts of the deceased, so there would be no need for special creditor protection. However, the estate may be insufficient or the heirs less eager than expected, which gives cause for the subject of this chapter.

[13] This is the case in Germany under §§ 2301, 2276 BGB. *cf* OLG München 16 February 2011, 3 U 4316/07, (2011) *Zeitschrift für das gesamte Familienrecht* 1757.

[14] According to the Bundesgerichtshof (BGH), a benefit given to a mistress is only *contra bonos mores* and therefore void (§ 138 BGB) if it is granted as consideration for sexual intercourse; *cf* BGH 28 September 1990, V ZR 109/89, BGHZ 112, 259, 262; BGH 31 March 1970, III ZB 23/68, BGHZ 53, 369, 375.

looking to substantive law for the protection of creditors is not always a promising endeavour.

However, English inheritance law has a special device to protect creditors against gifts *mortis causa*, as a gift *mortis causa* is void if the transfer from the deceased person's estate is deficient.[15] If the asset has not yet been handed over to the donee at the time of death, and therefore the asset cannot be vested in the donee absolutely on the point of death, the property remains vested in the donor's estate. If the asset has already been transferred to the recipient prior to the operation of probate, the creditors may nonetheless bring proceedings against the donee for payment of debts out of the property, as the gift can easily be clawed back where the estate of the deceased donor is insolvent.[16] Under German inheritance law, there is no such automatic claw-back of gifts made immediately prior to death where the estate in question is insolvent. It is not deemed necessary to have any special rules concerning this scenario, as personal liability of heirs and the laws pertaining to transactions avoidance with regard to insolvencies should provide ample protection.

B. Insolvency Law

Therefore, the more effective way of protecting creditors is via insolvency law. How the use of the legal regime for insolvency law plays out is dependent upon whether or not insolvency proceedings have already been opened at the time of the debtor's death.

i. *Death After the Opening of Insolvency Proceedings*

If a debtor dies during the course of insolvency proceedings, the death has no effect on those proceedings.[17] However, it is questionable whether will-substitutes can come into effect at the time of death while the debtor is insolvent, since most jurisdictions will not give effect to incomplete transactions once insolvency proceedings have commenced.

a. Germany

The above is patently true with regard to Germany, as § 91 InsO hampers the acquisition of rights pertaining to the debtor's assets after the opening of the

[15] *Smith v Casen* [1718] 1 P Wms 406; *Ward v Turner* [1752] 28 ER 275—2 Ves Sen 431, 434; *Tate v Leithead* [1854] 69 ER 729—Kay 658, 659; *Re Korvine's Trust (Levashoff v Block)* [1921] 1 Ch 343, 348; *cf* also s 8(2) Inheritance (Provision for Family and Dependants) Act 1975. Opposing opinion by Warnock-Smith [1978] *Conveyancer & Property Lawyer* 130–36.

[16] R Kerridge in R Kerridge and AHR Brierley, *Parry and Kerridge: The Law of Succession*, 12th edn (London, Sweet & Maxwell 2009) para 21-08.

[17] See BGH 26 September 2013, IX ZR 3/13, (2014) *Zeitschrift für Wirtschaftsrecht* 137 para 12 (Germany); s 5(1) Administration of Insolvent Estates of Deceased Persons Order 1986 (England).

insolvency proceedings.[18] According to this rule, it appears to be impossible to give a beneficiary any right upon the debtor's death, if the death is subsequent to the opening of insolvency proceedings. However, the German Bundesgerichtshof (BGH) grants many exceptions,[19] especially if the beneficiary has a secured position before proceedings are opened. This secured position is obtained if the debtor is unable to prevent the covenantee from acquiring the right in question.[20] In the case of will-substitutes, the beneficiary will not usually have this secured position. If, for example, the asset concerned is a savings account, the debtor can withdraw and spend the money as he pleases before he dies. If the asset in question is the potential payout from a life insurance policy, he can terminate the insurance contract at will prior to his death or he can change the named beneficiary, the same being true of private pension schemes.

However, the BGH[21] does not apply § 91 InsO to insurance contracts, regardless of whether or not the appointment of the third party is irrevocable. The Court has argued that the claim of the third party against the insurance company has never been part of the deceased person's assets, and as a result it is not part of the insolvent estate. In fact, before the death of the insured person, no claim existed at all. The claim arises upon the death of the insured person, and has therefore always has been purely a claim exercisable by the third party. The only avenue which is therefore open to the insolvency practitioner, with regard to seeking access to an insurance payout for the purposes of maximum fulfilment of creditors' claims, is to seek revocation of the appointment of the relevant beneficiary before the bankrupt dies, and thus before the claim of that beneficiary comes to fruition.[22] If the appointment of that beneficiary were to be irrevocable, this would not be possible, and upon death of the bankrupt, the beneficiary would be entitled to receipt of the insured sum in full. Although to date there is no case law on this matter, the same should apply to pension schemes. Until the death of the employee, he is entitled to receive the pension payment(s) but this right ceases upon his death. Simultaneously, a new right (to a monthly pension payment or to a lump sum) arises in

[18] See further R Bork, *Rescuing Companies in England and Germany* (Oxford, OUP, 2012) paras 11.09, 11.46.

[19] *cf* BGH, above n 14.

[20] Examples in BGH 20 December 2014, IX ZB 69/12, (2015) *Zeitschrift für Wirtschaftsrecht* 233 para 10; BGH 25 April 2013, IX ZR 62/12, (2013) *Zeitschrift für Wirtschaftsrecht* 1082 para 27; BGH 20 September 2012, IX ZR 208/11, (2012) *Zeitschrift für Wirtschaftsrecht* 2358 para 13.

[21] Leading case is BGH 27 April 2010, IX ZR 245/09, (2010) *Zeitschrift für Wirtschaftsrecht* 1964 para 2. *cf* also BGH 9 October 2014, IX ZR 41/14, (2014) *Zeitschrift für Wirtschaftsrecht* 2251 para 27; G Kayser, *Die Lebensversicherung in der Insolvenz des Arbeitgebers* (Cologne, Heymanns, 2006) 55.

[22] The appointment can be revoked in accordance with § 159(1) VVG. Once insolvency proceedings have been opened, the insolvency practitioner can revoke the grant, terminate the life insurance contract under § 168 VVG, obtain the surrender value of the assets under § 169 VVG and distribute the proceeds among the creditors. This does not affect the assets of the beneficiary since according to § 159(2) VVG he only has an expectation rather than a claim or secured asset for as long as the insured event has not occurred. BGH 27 September 2012, IX ZR 15/12, (2012) *Zeitschrift für Wirtschaftsrecht* 2409 para 8; BGH 26 January 2012, IX ZR 99/11, (2012) *Zeitschrift für Wirtschaftsrecht* 636 para 8.

favour of the spouse. Thus, this is not a transfer of assets, but rather an instance of one right superseding another.

One might argue that savings accounts should be treated in the same way. However, the prevailing opinion in academic literature views the issue differently,[23] albeit without giving any rationale. The reasoning could be that attention should be paid primarily to the ultimate economic result, this being that the deposit was part of the insolvency estate prior to the debtor's death and that it is now a part of the third party's assets. That this result has not been generated by assignment of the claim against the bank, but rather by creating a new claim for the beneficiary which replaces the old claim of the deceased, cannot, and should not, make a difference.

In my opinion, the following view should be preferred: until his death, the account holder is—similar to other will-substitutes such as insurance contracts and pension schemes—entitled to withdraw its contents. However, this right dissolves upon his death, if he has agreed with the bank that upon his death another person shall be entitled to withdraw the money. In this case, the claim of the account holder ceases when he dies, and a new claim arises in favour of the beneficiary, rendering § 91 InsO inapplicable (unless the insolvency practitioner manages to seize the contents of the account prior to the death of the customer).[24]

b. England

English law comes to similar conclusions as German law. However, it does so via a different route.

First, the rights concerned are often held on trust, which means that they are not part of the deceased's assets and therefore not part of the insolvency estate. This is especially true regarding life insurance policies, where section 11 of the Married Women's Property Act 1882[25] applies, which expressly states that the insured person holds the contract on trust for the beneficiary, with the consequence being that the insured sum is not part of the estate of the deceased.[26] The same is true for pension schemes, where the right to the lump sum is held on trust for the

[23] *cf* P Gottwald in P Gottwald and J Adolphsen, *Insolvenzrechts-Handbuch*, 4th edn (Munich, Beck, 2010) § 40 para 43; HG Ganter in *Münchener Kommentar zur Insolvenzordnung*, 3rd edn (Munich, Beck, 2013) § 47 para 404; M Brinkmann in W Uhlenbruck (ed), *Insolvenzordnung: InsO*, 13th edn (Munich, Vahlen, 2010) § 47 para 49.

[24] Further explanation, see M Obermüller, *Insolvenzrecht in der Bankpraxis*, 8th edn (Cologne, Schmidt, 2011) para 2.167.

[25] s 11 MWPA reads as follows: 'A policy of assurance effected by any man on his own life, and expressed to be for the benefit of his wife, or of his children, or of his wife and children, or any of them, or by any woman on her own life, and expressed to be for the benefit of her husband, or of her children, or of her husband and children, or any of them, shall create a trust in favour of the objects therein named, and the moneys payable under any such policy shall not, so long as any object of the trust remains unperformed, form part of the estate of the insured, or be subject to his or her debts'.

[26] *Holt v Everall* [1876] 2 Ch D 266, 273 ff.

beneficiary by the trustees, albeit with the peculiarity that the trustees (or scheme administrators) have discretion in choosing the beneficiaries.[27]

Second, the rule comparable to § 91 InsO is less rigorous than its German counterpart. Under English insolvency law, the anti-deprivation rule stipulates that

> upon a man's becoming bankrupt, that which was his property up to the date of the bankruptcy should go over to someone else and be taken away from his creditors, is void as being a violation of the policy of the bankrupt laws.[28]

However, this rule only applies if the transfer of the debtor's assets to the beneficiary is triggered by the opening of insolvency proceedings, and therefore is a means of ensuring that these assets cannot be used to repay creditors. If the condition for the transfer is another event (be it a default that is not indicative of certain insolvency or be it the death of one of the contracting parties), the agreement does not infringe the anti-deprivation principle and is therefore still valid.[29] Thus, will-substitutes will not be rendered incapable of use by the anti-deprivation principle and so the beneficiary will obtain the insured sum or the lump sum from a pension scheme,[30] even if the death of the benefactor occurs after the opening of the insolvency proceedings.

c. Conclusion

So far, we can conclude the following: creditors are not adequately protected by those rules of insolvency law that halt unaccomplished acquisition processes upon the opening of insolvency proceedings. This holds true for both England and Germany. The primary reason for this is that the assets acquired by the beneficiary were not part of the bankrupt party's estate immediately upon his death. Even in cases where the deceased was entitled to full use of those assets during his lifetime, this entitlement ceases upon his death and is therefore not part of the

[27] See ch 3 above, p 54.

[28] *Re Harrison (ex parte Jay)* [1880] 14 Ch D 19. Extensive discussion of the anti-deprivation principle: *Belmont Park* [2011] UKSC 38; R Bork and M Voelker, '§ 91 InsO und die Anti-Deprivation Rule—ein Rechtsvergleich' (2013) *Zeitschrift für Insolvenzrecht* 235; J Davies, 'The Nature and Scope of the Anti-Deprivation Rule in the English law of Corporate Insolvency' (2011) 8 *International Corporate Rescue* 155, 231; R Goode, *Principles of Corporate Insolvency Law*, 4th edn (London, Sweet & Maxwell, 2011) paras 7-01 ff; LC Ho, 'The Resilience of the Principle Against Divestiture in Mayhew v King' (2010) *Corporate Rescue and Insolvency* 159 ff; S Worthington, 'Making Sense of Arguments about the Anti-Deprivation Rule' (2011) 8 *International Corporate Rescue* 26; and S Worthington, 'Insolvency Deprivation, Public Policy and Priority Flip Clauses' (2010) 7 *International Corporate Rescue* 28.

[29] Leading authority is *Re Garrud (ex parte Newitt)* [1881] 16 Ch D 522, which concerned a deprivation of property upon the debtor's default, which occurred after bankruptcy. There is slight doubt concerning this judgment, as the CA in *Belmont Park* [2009] EWCA Civ 1160 para 93 thought it was overruled by *British Eagle* [1975] 1 WLR 758. This is clearly incorrect because the ratio decidendi of *British Eagle* concerns the *pari passu* rule and not the anti-deprivation principle. Unfortunately, the Supreme Court did not clarify this in *Belmont Park* [2011] UKSC 38 (see para 82-3); *cf* Bork and Voelker, above n 28, 242 ff.

[30] However, the exemption for *donationes mortis causa* must be observed; *cf* above n 15.

deceased's estate.[31] Simultaneously, a new entitlement arises regarding the relevant beneficiary. Thus, we do not have a transfer of assets (which would be hindered by insolvency law) but rather a substitution of assets. Under the latter circumstances, creditors can only be protected if the insolvency practitioner can somehow cancel the relevant contract, withdraw the relevant sum and/or revoke the appointment of the relevant third party.

ii. Death Before the Opening of Insolvency Proceedings

If the death of the benefactor occurs before the opening of insolvency proceedings, the acquisition of the assets by the beneficiary is unquestionable.[32] However, under both English and German insolvency law, the insolvency practitioner has to ascertain whether he can challenge any will-substitutes used.

a. Germany

In Germany, gratuitous performances by the debtor can be challenged under § 134 InsO.[33] The rules are comparatively straightforward and the grounds for challenge are easy to identify. The insolvency practitioner must do little more than set out and, if necessary, prove that a recipient received some performance from the debtor,[34] without any, or without sufficient, compensation. It is then for the recipient to prove that the performance occurred more than four years prior to the insolvency application or that it constituted merely the giving of a common ad hoc gift of minor value. The complete absence of subjective or mental elements, and the fact that § 134 InsO does not necessitate the insolvency of the debtor at the time of performance, renders it a powerful instrument.

Regarding will-substitutes the main question is whether the transaction has been performed within the relevant time of four years prior to the insolvency application. This task is simple if the subject matter of the will-substitute is, for example, a savings account. The beneficiary is entitled to the sum contained within the account, but only upon the death of the donor. Prior to the settlor's death,

[31] *cf Re Palmer* [1994] Ch 316, 317: the estate does not include 'any interest in property which the debtor had had at the beginning of the day of his death but which had ceased at the moment of his death'.

[32] *cf Bennet v Slater*, above n 9, 52: in both jurisdictions, the law refers to the legal situation as it stood at the point in time of the debtor's death. In other words, a legal fiction is imposed, namely that insolvency proceedings had been opened immediately upon the death of the debtor. *cf* for Germany's approach to the issue R Bork, *Einführung in das Insolvenzrecht*, 7th edn (Tübingen, Mohr Siebeck, 2014) para 496; for England's approach *Re Palmer* [1994] Ch 316. However, this does not change the fact that the assets are not part of the insolvency estate.

[33] See further R Bork, 'Transactions at an Undervalue—A Comparison of English and German Law' (2014) 14 *Journal of Corporate Law Studies* 453; Bork, *Rescuing Companies in England and Germany*, above n 18, paras 11.23 ff; R Bork in B Kübler, H Prütting and R Bork, *Kommentar zur Insolvenzordnung*, 61st edn (Cologne, RWS, 2014) § 134 paras 1 ff; G Kayser in *Münchener Kommentar zur Insolvenzordnung*, 3rd edn (Munich, Beck, 2013) § 134 paras 1 ff; C Thole, *Gläubigerschutz durch Insolvenzrecht* (Tübingen, Mohr Siebeck, 2010) 439–82.

[34] Unlike its English counterpart, German insolvency law does not differentiate between companies (which become insolvent) and individuals (who are declared bankrupt).

he does not have any right whatsoever with regard to the deposit. Thus, the pertinent question of whether the transaction has been performed within the relevant time has to be answered by looking at the time of death, and not by looking at the time of appointment of the third party. If the death occurred within four years prior to the insolvency application, the transaction can be challenged and the beneficiary has to pay back any money he has already withdrawn from the account.

As for life insurance policies, it is undoubtedly so that benefiting a third party constitutes a gratuitous performance and can therefore be challenged under § 134 InsO.[35] With respect to the relevant time, according to the BGH, a distinction must be made between revocable and irrevocable appointments. If the beneficiary is appointed revocably, it follows from § 159(2) VVG that he had been given no secured position at all[36] with regard to his interest in the insured sum before the death of the insured person. He acquires the claim against the insurance company upon the death of the benefactor and this acquisition is challengeable under § 134 InsO if the death occurred within the relevant time of four years prior to the declaration of insolvency. If the appointment is irrevocable, the beneficiary has a contingent[37] claim under § 159(3) VVG and therefore a secured asset. The result of the asset being secured is that the appointment can be challenged by the insolvency practitioner only if the application for insolvency proceedings follows within four years of the appointment. Otherwise, the appointment as such is completely unchallengeable,[38] meaning that the beneficiary may keep his claim against the insurance company, as well as being entitled to the insured sum upon the death of the insured debtor. However, it must be taken into account that the value of the beneficiary's irrevocable position can be increased due to the debtor continuing to pay the insurance premiums. According to the BGH, an increase in the value of creditors' or third parties' assets can also be attacked and classified as a gratuitous performance.[39] The Court therefore allows a claim against a beneficiary who receives any enrichment that is a result of the debtor's payments.[40] This leaves the beneficiary with the obligation not to pay back the premiums, but rather to pay back the increase of the asset's value, ie, the difference between the insurance sum he eventually received, and the sum he would have got if the debtor had

[35] *cf* Bork, 'Transactions at an Undervalue', above n 33, 473 ff; R Bork, 'Der Lebensversicherungsvertrag in der Insolvenz des Versicherungsnehmers' in R Bork, T Hoeren and P Pohlmann, *FS für Helmut Kollhosser* (Karlsruher, Verlag Versicherungswirtschaft, 2004) 57, 65 ff; Kayser, *Die Lebensversicherung in der Insolvenz des Arbeitgebers*, above n 21, 67 ff.

[36] ie not even a contingent claim but only a position of hope.

[37] Condition is the death of the benefactor.

[38] BGH 23 October 2003, IX ZR 252/0, BGHZ 156, 350, 356; BGH 20 December 2012, IX ZR 21/12, (2013) *Zeitschrift für Wirtschaftsrecht* 223 para 13; BGH 27 September 2012, IX ZR 15/12, (2012) *Zeitschrift für Wirtschaftsrecht* 2409 para 8; BGH 26 January 2012, IX ZR 99/11, (2012) *Zeitschrift für Wirtschaftsrecht* 636 para 7.

[39] eg BGH 20 December 2012, IX ZR 21/12, (2013) *Zeitschrift für Wirtschaftsrecht* 223 para 19 (the challenging of the enrichment of a claim assigned as a security).

[40] BGH 20 December 2012, IX ZR 21/12, (2013) *Zeitschrift für Wirtschaftsrecht* 223 para 17; BGH 27 September 2012, IX ZR 15/12, (2012) *Zeitschrift für Wirtschaftsrecht* 2409 para 6.

stopped paying further insurance premiums under § 165 VVG at the beginning of the relevant time.[41]

The aforementioned principles have to be applied to pension schemes as well. If the beneficiary was appointed irrevocably and less than four years prior to the application for insolvency proceedings, the appointment is challengeable under § 134 InsO. If the appointment was revocable, the death of the benefiting employee is crucial.

However, this is only the case under two conditions: first, the relevant transaction can only be challenged if the pension scheme provides for payments to the estate in the event that a third party has not (or has not validly) been appointed. Pension schemes may be shaped in a way that payments are only granted to the retired employee during his lifetime or in the event of his death to a third party appointed by the employee, but not to his heirs.[42] In this case, the appointment is not challengeable as the challenge would not render any profit for the deceased person's estate. Second, the appointment cannot be challenged if the pension to be paid to the heirs is protected by the laws concerning attachment of assets. Assets that are not capable of being the subject of attachment are not part of the insolvency estate (§ 36 InsO). Thus, the will-substitute is not detrimental to the deceased person's creditors, as this would mean that they could not use the pension scheme in seeking repayment anyway: if the will-substitute is not challengeable, the creditors have no right against the beneficiary; if it is challengeable, the right falls back to the estate but is not attachable there. It is therefore not part of the insolvency estate (assets recoverable for the creditors). In these cases, the will-substitute as such is not challengeable because the prerequisite of avoiding transactions is always that the creditors be at a disadvantage due to said transaction (§ 129(1) InsO).[43] If, for example, a third party is appointed as beneficiary and the heirs are close relatives, the appointment of the third party cannot be challenged, as § 850(2), (3) *Zivilprozessordnung* (ZPO)[44] protects pension claims[45] of close relatives from

[41] BGH 20 December 2012, IX ZR 21/12, (2013) *Zeitschrift für Wirtschaftsrecht* 223 para 16.

[42] The result would be that there is no claim against the pension scheme at all if the employee dies before his retirement and he has not appointed a beneficiary.

[43] *cf* BGH 26 April 2013, IX ZR 220/11, (2013) *Zeitschrift für Wirtschaftsrecht* 1288 paras 4 ff; BGH 17 March 2011, IX ZR 166/08, (2011) *Zeitschrift für Wirtschaftsrecht* 824 paras 13 ff: disposal of assets which are protected against attachment and therefore do not belong to the insolvency estate does not disadvantage creditors.

[44] ie Code of Civil Procedure; English translation at www.gesetze-im-internet.de/englisch_zpo/index.html.

[45] A similar variety of protection is granted under § 805(3)(b) ZPO for pensions paid to former employees on the basis of insurance contracts if such insurance has been taken out in the interests of providing a pension to the insured or to his dependent next of kin. However, this rule is not applicable to non-dependent workers (BGH 5 November 2007, IX ZB 34/06, (2008) *Zeitschrift für Wirtschaftsrecht* 338 paras 12 ff). Upon the corresponding petition having been made and on the basis of § 850i(1) ZPO, the court may, for those persons and according to the court's discretionary estimations, leave funds to the debtor for a reasonable period of time in the amount that would remain if the income he was earning consisted of current wages or of service pay. No legal protection is provided against attachment regarding saving accounts.

attachment.[46] As a result, any challenge made would not serve to enrich the insolvency estate and therefore would not have as its purpose the protection of creditors, but rather its purpose would be purely to further the interests of the heirs. As it is the sole aim of claw-back provisions to protect the creditors, and thus not to protect the heirs or close relatives against the appointment of a third party, the entitlement of the third party remains unaffected. However, even in such cases, the insolvency practitioner remains entitled to challenge the contributions paid to the pension schemes and to reclaim the increase in value of the third party's assets which are generated by payments made by the debtor within the relevant time of four years.

b. England

Within English law, provisions similar to § 134 InsO can be found in section 238 IA concerning insolvent companies[47] (which we shall henceforth omit from discussion) and section 339 IA dealing with bankrupt individuals.[48] In accordance with both provisions, transactions can be challenged by the insolvency practitioner in formal proceedings (liquidation/administration/bankruptcy)[49] where the debtor received no consideration, or where the consideration given was of significantly less value than the performance rendered by the debtor (hence the interaction constitutes a 'transaction at an undervalue'). The first statutory requirement (with all requirements being objective under this particular provision) is that a transaction between the debtor and the recipient has taken place. Second, the performance of the debtor must either have been gratuitous, or it must be demonstrated that the consideration given in return, in money or in money's worth, was significantly lower in value than the performance rendered by the bankrupt. With regard to challenges undertaken in accordance with section 339 IA, the relevant time period during which the transaction must have occurred is the period of two years ending with the day of the presentation of the bankruptcy petition on which the individual is adjudged bankrupt. The eligible time period can be extended by three years, provided that the debtor was insolvent at the time of the transaction, or the

[46] The protection is limited by § 850c ZPO to a certain value, depending on the number of persons for whom the debtor has to provide maintenance.

[47] There are similar rules for particular situations, eg ss 52–56 Pensions Act 2004 (concerning insolvency of the employer); *cf Re Storm Funding Ltd* [2013] EWHC 4019 (Ch) para 27.

[48] See further J Armour in J Armour and H Bennett, *Vulnerable Transactions in Corporate Insolvency* (Oxford, Hart Publishing, 2003) paras 2.1 ff; Goode, above n 28, paras 13-12 ff; R Parry and S Shivji, 'Preferences' in R Parry, J Ayliffe and S Shivji, *Transactions Avoidance in Insolvencies*, 2nd edn (Oxford, OUP, 2011) paras 4.01 ff.

[49] This includes bankruptcy proceedings on the basis of the Administration of Insolvent Estates of Deceased Persons Order 1986, but does not include the administration of the estate by the personal representatives as the presence of formal insolvency proceedings is required; *cf Re Leng* [1895] 1 Ch 652, 655. However, in these cases s 423 IA does apply (Kerridge, above n 16, para 21-03) and *donationes mortis causa* can be challenged (above n 9).

debtor became insolvent as a result of the transaction.[50] All of these requirements are, in principle (exceptions apply in the event of connected parties),[51] for the insolvency practitioner to prove. It is quite remarkable that—as in Germany—no mental elements are included as requisites within this bankruptcy provision.[52]

In addition, transactions at an undervalue can also potentially be clawed back indefinitely under section 423 IA,[53] so long as the debtor (whether a company or an individual) entered into the transaction for the purpose of prejudicing the interests of a person who is making, or may at some point in time, make a claim against them.[54] It is inconsequential whether or not the debtor was insolvent at the time of the transaction. The burden of proof lies with the person challenging the transaction.

On applying these rules to will-substitutes, it seems to be common ground that life insurance policies are part of the assets of the named beneficiary and not of the deceased's estate. However, a challenge based on its status as a transaction at an undervalue is possible: although in the relationship between the parties to the insurance contract, mutual compensating performances are indeed delivered (payment of the premium against insurance protection, this being in the form of the proceeds of the policy), the latter can be owed to a third party as a beneficiary or assignee. In this case, part of the consideration is performed to a third party gratuitously, and this can result in a claim against that third party.[55] In cases where the policy is assigned, the insolvency practitioner of the insolvent assignor can therefore bring a claim against the assignee under sections 339, 423 IA,[56] and the same is true if the bankrupt held the policy on trust for a third party.[57] In both cases, the benefactor has transferred an asset (the insurance claim) to the third party which would otherwise be part of his estate. Where section 11 of the Married Women's Property Act 1882 applies, the creation of the trust can merely

[50] s 341(1)(a) and (2) IA: for the two years preceding the bankruptcy petition, it is irrefutably presumed by statute that the debtor had been insolvent; see A Keay and P Walton, *Insolvency Law*, 2nd edn (London, Jordans, 2008) para 38.2.

[51] According to s 341(2) IA, there is a presumption that the bankrupt was insolvent at the time of the transaction if the benefited person is an associate (as defined in s 435 IA) of the benefactor.

[52] With regard to insolvencies, challenges are excluded where the company has acted subjectively in good faith and for the purpose of carrying on its business, and where there were reasonable grounds to believe that the transaction would benefit the company, s 238(5) IA. This is because s 423 IA is primarily based on the subjective prerequisite of the debtor's 'purpose' being to defraud creditors. See Bork, 'Transactions at an Undervalue', above n 33, 466 ff.

[53] For details, see Armour, above n 48, paras 3.1 ff; Goode, above n 28, paras 13-136 ff; J Ayliffe in R Parry, J Ayliffe and S Shivji, *Transactions Avoidance in Insolvencies*, 2nd edn (Oxford, OUP, 2011) paras 10.01 ff.

[54] Thus, different from s 238 IA and from German law (§ 134 InsO), there is a mental element here.

[55] *cf* in general Parry and Shivji, above n 48, para 4.62.

[56] A McGee, *The Law and Practice of Life Assurance Contracts* (London, Sweet & Maxwell, 1995) paras 18.19 ff.

[57] P Hamilton, *Life Assurance Law and Practice* (London, FT Law & Tax, 1995) para A5.7; RJ Surridge, R Scott, B Murphy, N James and N John, *Houseman and Davies: Law of Life Assurance*, 12th edn (London, Butterworths, 2001) para 12.15.

be challenged if there was, parallel to section 423 IA, intent to defraud the creditors of the insured.[58] However, challenging a transaction for being seemingly at an undervalue seems to be an unorthodox approach in practice as there is no case law available concerning these situations. The reason for this could be that beneficiaries are regularly appointed more than two years prior to the death of the insured, and the insured was also not in a state of insolvency prior to death; furthermore, it is possible that the intent to prejudice creditors is exceptionally difficult to establish. Another source of uncertainty may be that the law leaves the consequences of a transaction at an undervalue largely up to the discretion of the court; according to section 339(2) IA, the court is only compelled to make an order as it sees fit with regard to restoring the position of the debtor to what it would have been had he not entered into that transaction. The courts have held that proper exercise of said discretion can include making no order at all.[59] However, it could theoretically also lead to a claw-back of the premiums paid during the relevant time[60] or of the insured sum. However, this would be quite a drastic request by the courts.

The same holds true for pension schemes. As regards the relationship between the deceased employee and the beneficiary, this can only be established as being a transaction at an undervalue if there had been an entitlement of the estate, were it not for the use of the will-substitute.[61] If the pension claim had ended upon the death of the employee, were it not for the nomination of a third party as recipient, this cannot be held to be a transaction at an undervalue. If the transaction does not prejudice the assets of the debtor,[62] it is not challengeable in the event of the debtor's insolvency. In such cases, the court could only compel the repayment of those contributions paid by the bankrupt within the relevant time. Furthermore, even if a transaction at an undervalue can be established, the beneficiary will normally not be appointed within two years prior to the onset of insolvency. The purpose of naming the recipient of the pension upon death is usually not done with an ascertainable purpose of prejudicing creditors, but rather with the specific intention to care for that person.

c. Conclusion

In summary, it can be said that will-substitutes examined in this chapter are more likely to be challenged under German insolvency law than under English insolvency law. The German rules regarding transactions at an undervalue allow

[58] *cf Holt v Everall*, above n 26, 274.

[59] *Re Paramount Airways Ltd* [1993] Ch 223, 239; *Singla v Brown* [2007] EWHC 405 (Ch) paras 51–60.

[60] *Holt v Everall*, above n 26, 274.

[61] This is unclear if the trustees (or scheme administrators) have discretion in designating the beneficiary. In such cases it is—strictly speaking—not possible to find 'an entitlement of the estate' unless the trustees have decided so.

[62] *cf Pozzuto v Iacovides* [2003] EWHC 431 (Ch) paras 27–46.

for the clawing back of gifts and transactions which were rendered four years prior to the insolvency application. Neither insolvency of the debtor at the time of the transaction, nor any mental elements need to be established. The interests of third parties (such as the beneficiary or the heirs) are only guarded in certain circumstances through the law of protection against attachment, which leads to the result that under certain conditions not the will-substitute as such, but rather payments to pension funds or insurance companies made within the relevant time, can be claimed from the beneficiary. By contrast, English law shows greater reluctance regarding the avoidance of transactions at an undervalue. Although there are no mental elements mentioned in section 339 IA,[63] insolvency of the debtor at the time of the transaction, or as a result thereof, has to be established if the transaction was carried out more than two years (but no more than five years) prior to the bankruptcy petition. Furthermore, the consequences of a transaction having been made at an undervalue are left to the discretion of the court. The reluctance of English insolvency practitioners in challenging will-substitutes may be a consequence not only of the very high costs but also of the relatively uncertain outcome of such proceedings, which is due to the great amount of discretion afforded to English courts.

[63] As opposed to s 423 IA; *cf* above n 52.

14

Will-Substitutes and the Claims of Family Members and Carers

JONATHAN HERRING

I. Introduction

'Who owns the tin opener?' is not a question which arises in healthy relationships. 'Who is in charge of the TV remote?' on the other hand is a perfectly proper matter for contention! For most couples and families the precise ownership of property is not a question to which they tend to give much attention, save in certain interactions with third parties, such as taking out a bank loan, or where there is a family business. Generally family members give no thought to the ownership of the tin opener because it simply does not matter. Family members will not seek to claim property rights as against each other in relation to their property, at least while the relationship is intact.

This means that the normal rules governing property tend not to work well in families. We cannot expect couples to set out precisely what their interests are during their relationship because it is not a question to which they give much thought. If they were asked about ownership they would probably reply they did not know and do not care who owned what. We cannot, therefore, expect them to spend effort, time or money on clarifying their legal position. It is precisely for that reason that some countries have a particular set of laws determining family ownership (eg, community of property regimes).

This ambiguity over the property ownership of couples in intimate relationships matters little generally because the issue of ownership *inter se* is only likely to be a major issue when the relationship comes to an end. Then in jurisdictions which do not have some kind of community of property regime, legal mechanisms are in place to allocate the appropriate ownership of property. In England the courts can make financial orders on divorce under the Matrimonial Causes Act 1973 (MCA) or following death under the Inheritance (Provision for Family and Dependants) Act 1975 (I(PFD) Act). Thereby the court can ensure that there is a degree of fairness and clarity in the allocation of the couple's property interests when it matters.

That is all well and good, save three points. First, these remedies may only be available in cases where couples have formalised their relationship through marriage. In England, for example, there are no orders redistributing the ownership of property available to unmarried cohabitants who separate.[1] There is much to discuss on that question, but it is not the primary issue for this chapter. The second question we can also put to one side is that ownership of family property may be important for third parties, such as creditors and those dealing with family businesses. The availability of the orders at the end of relationships does not deal with those cases. The third issue, and the one most relevant for this book, is that the party who owns the property might dispose of their property before the courts' jurisdiction applies. For example, a testator may seek to dispose of assets before death or divorce in order to avoid the court redistributing their property. The focus of this chapter is with such cases and specifically with those who by means of will-substitutes prevent the law allocating property following death between those in intimate relationships.

To address this issue we need to explore the policy issues concerning distribution of property on death carefully. We need to understand the strength of the arguments in favour of the court making orders that redistribute property following death, in order to assess whether there is anything particularly wrong with the use of will-substitutes designed to avoid the operation of that jurisdiction. The argument over the legitimacy of the courts' jurisdiction is typically presented as a clash between those who promote the freedom of the testator and those who promote the claims of family members. At a basic level, if you believe that the primary policy on disposition of property on death should be respect for the testator's wishes, then will-substitutes are of little concern to you. However, if you attach weight to the interests of family members and believe the court should protect them, then you will be much more concerned by will-substitutes, if they are used to defeat their claims.

This chapter will seek to unpack the claims that are made and the significance of these for debates over will-substitutes. It will be argued that the strongest cases for departing from testamentary disposition fall into three categories. The first is where it can be assumed the will no longer represents the deceased's wishes. The second is where there is a quasi-proprietary claim by a family member. The third is where the claimant has provided unpaid care for the deceased at a time of need. These will be explored in this chapter. It will be argued that will-substitutes should be set aside if necessary to protect the interests of claimants who fall within the last two of these three categories.

While the chapter will focus on the theoretical issues raised, it will use the approach taken by English law as an example of how these points will play out. This is helpful because as we shall see, the English legislation provides a broad

[1] J Herring, *Family Law*, 6th edn (Harlow, Pearson, 2015) chs 6 and 7.

discretion for the courts to interfere with the allocation of property through a will, without a clear ranking of the claims of the different parties. The judicial interpretation of the statute can be used to provide insight into the theoretical debates. We will start, therefore, with a brief overview of the Act.

II. The Inheritance (Provision for Family and Dependants) Act 1975

Under English law the starting point is that a testator is free to dispose of their property as they wish. The I(PFD) Act enables relatives or dependants who believe that they have not been left an adequate sum in the deceased's will or by virtue of the rules of intestacy, to apply to court for an order they be paid money from the estate. The applicant bears the burden of proving to the court the merits of their claim. Generally the courts are reluctant to interfere with the allocation of property in a will, without a strong case.

It is remarkably difficult to find statistics on the extent to which the I(PFD) Act is used. Even the Law Commission with all the resources at its disposal was only able to find figures for the number of applications issued at the Chancery Division. It found in 2007 there were 43 applications under the legislation.[2] It is hard to believe that this is the complete picture. Notably, the statistics do not cover applications in the Family Division or County Courts. Of course, there are no figures on the number of cases which were settled or dealt with informally.

A. Who can Claim Under the Act?

The following groups of people can apply:

1. The spouse or civil partner of the deceased.[3]
2. The former spouse or civil partner of the deceased, provided the applicant has not remarried or entered another civil partnership.[4]
3. A person who

> during the whole of the period of two years ending immediately before the date when the deceased died … was living (a) in the same household as the deceased, and (b) as the husband or wife [or civil partner] of the deceased.[5]

[2] Law Commission, *Intestacy and Family Provision Claims on Death* (Law Com CP No 191, 2013) para 1.9.

[3] Inheritance (Provision for Family and Dependants) Act 1975 (I(PFD) Act), s 1(1)(a).

[4] ibid, s 1(1)(b).

[5] ibid, s 1A.

The court would consider whether a reasonable person with normal powers of perception would say the couple was living together as husband and wife.[6] In using this test the reasonable person should be aware of the multifarious nature of marriages.[7] In *Churchill v Roach*[8] Judge Norris said that to live in the same household it was necessary to have

> elements of permanence, to involve a consideration of the frequency and intimacy of contact, to contain an element of mutual support, to require some consideration of the degree of voluntary restraint upon personal freedom which each party undertakes, and to involve an element of community of resources.

4. Any child of the deceased, including posthumous, adopted and grown-up children.[9] An adopted child cannot claim under this ground against their biological parents, but can claim against their adopted parents.[10]
5. Any person 'treated by the deceased as a child of the family in relation to' a marriage or civil partnership.[11] It most commonly applies in relation to stepchildren.[12]
6. Any other person 'who immediately before the death of the deceased was being maintained, either wholly or partly, by the deceased'.[13] The phrase 'maintained' in this definition is clarified in section 1(3):

    > a person shall be treated as being maintained by the deceased, either wholly or partly, as the case may be, if the deceased, otherwise than for full valuable consideration, was making a substantial contribution in money or money's worth towards the reasonable needs of that person.

There is much more that could be said about the list, but for now it is worth highlighting that it acknowledges the potential claims of those with a close personal relationship to the deceased, even if there is no blood tie. Indeed, it is notable that parents and siblings are not included as claimants in their own right. They can only claim if they are dependent on the deceased. This suggests it is the notion of financial dependence that is more important than a close blood tie.

B. The Meaning of the Reasonable Financial Provision

In determining what award is appropriate under the legislation, a somewhat subtle distinction is drawn between claims by spouses and others. If the claimant is the

[6] *Re Watson* [1999] 1 FLR 878.

[7] Although in *Baynes v Hedger* [2008] 3 FCR 151 a clandestine same-sex relationship did not fall within this category because it was not a publically acknowledged relationship.

[8] *Churchill v Roach* [2004] 3 FCR 744, 761.

[9] I(PFD)Act 1975, s 1(1)(c).

[10] *Re Collins* [1990] Fam 56.

[11] I(PFD)Act 1975, s 1(1)(d).

[12] *Re Leach* [1986] Ch 226.

[13] I(PFD)Act 1975, s 1(1)(e).

spouse, the question is simply whether the *provision* is 'reasonable'. For other cases, the question is whether the *maintenance* is reasonable. The emphasis on maintenance is important. A non-spouse applicant who is 'comfortably off' may have difficulty in persuading the court that they need to be maintained at a higher level than their current lifestyle.[14] The concept of maintenance will certainly not stretch to include luxuries.[15] A spouse may be well off, but still be able to claim the provision for them is unreasonable. Reasonable provision is not necessarily restricted to the minimum necessary to survive.[16] When considering the appropriate level for a spouse, the court will have regard to the age of the applicant, the duration of the marriage, the applicant's contribution to the welfare of the family of the deceased and the provision the applicant may reasonably have expected to receive if the marriage had been terminated by divorce rather than by death.[17] These factors may well lead the court to award spouses a larger sum than necessary simply to maintain them.

Under section 3, in considering a claim, the court should consider:

a. The financial resources and financial needs which the applicant has or is likely to have in the foreseeable future.
b. The financial resources and financial needs which any other applicant for an order … has or is likely to have in the foreseeable future.
c. The financial resources and financial needs which any beneficiary of the estate of the deceased has or is likely to have in the foreseeable future.
d. Any obligations and responsibilities which the deceased had towards any applicant for an order … or towards any beneficiary of the estate of the deceased.
e. The size and nature of the net estate of the deceased.
f. Any physical or mental disability of any applicant for an order … or any beneficiary of the estate of the deceased.
g. Any other matter, including the conduct of the applicant or any other person, which in the circumstances of the case the court may consider relevant.

These factors are largely self-explanatory. It should be noted that factors (b), (c), (d), (f) and (g) require the court to consider the position of all those who may be seeking money from the estate.[18] So, although a claimant may show a close relationship to the deceased and be in great need, their claim may fail if there are others interested in the estate who are of greater need.

[14] *Re Jennings (Deceased)* [1994] Ch 256.
[15] *Re Dennis* [1981] 2 All ER 140.
[16] *Re Coventry* [1990] Fam 561.
[17] I(PFD)Act 1975, s 3(2).
[18] *Cattle v Evans* [2011] EWHC 945 (Ch).

III. Theory: Freedom of Testamentary Disposition

Most legal systems give at least some respect to the theory of freedom of testamentary disposition, although the weight it is given varies across jurisdictions. The principle claims that a person should be entitled to decide who will receive their property on their death. Just as a person when alive can give their assets to whomsoever they choose, so they should be able to on death. Others may believe it foolish or even immoral that I spend so much money on purchasing erudite law books, but still I am entitled to do that if I so wish, or at least as long as I retain mental capacity. In a similar manner, on my death I should be able to dispose of my property to promote the publication of yet more erudite law books, if I so choose. So understood, the principle of testamentary freedom is no more than a continuation of the rights the deceased had when alive.

However, few jurisdictions give complete protection to testamentary disposition. France and Germany, for instance, rely on 'forced heirship' or 'compulsory shares' provisions to protect the claims of the deceased's spouse or children.[19] England's I(PFD) Act allows the court to make orders altering the disposition of property in a will, as we have seen. But none of these jurisdictions ignore freedom of testamentary disposition altogether. They are presented as restrictions on that freedom, rather than removal of it. They all allow testamentary freedom once the testator's obligations have been met.

The principle of freedom of testamentary disposition seems to carry much less weight in cases of intestacy. Where no effective will is left (or a will deals with only a portion of the deceased's estate) then most legal systems have provisions which determine how the estate should be divided. Typically this will require the estate to be distributed to the testator's spouse or close relatives. A lively debate arises over the extent to which the intestacy rules should seek to ascertain the wishes of the deceased, or should determine what objectively would be a fair and appropriate division of assets.[20] These are not as distinguishable as might at first appear. Surely it is not unreasonable to presume that a deceased would want a fair and just settlement. Whichever approach is taken, and we need not enter that dispute, it is a less ferocious debate than that over interferences in testamentary disposition. That is because as long as a reasonable approach is taken, there is always the argument that if the deceased objected to the legislated automatic division it was open to them to make a will. Further, at least under English law, the existence of claims under the I(PFD) Act means that any manifest injustice caused by the automatic intestate division can be remedied by a court order.

It is appropriate now to turn to the theoretical debate. Why should particular weight be attached to the principle of testamentary freedom? Here are some of the arguments used.

[19] See chs 7 and 8 above, p 173 and p 188 and ch 15 below p 304 f.

[20] See Herring, *Family Law*, above n 1, ch 13 for a summary.

A. An Aspect of Ownership

John Locke is sometimes identified as the philosophical grandfather of freedom of testamentary disposition.[21] He regarded testamentary disposition as a crucial aspect of protecting the individual and their rights over property. The alternative was that property on death fell under the control of the king and feudal property structures. John Stuart Mill went so far as to see a right of testamentary power as 'one of the attributes of property'.[22] Supporters of testamentary freedom will acknowledge that the freedom could be used in what many would regard as a capricious way. But that, they would say, is typical of many legal freedoms. Cockburn CJ in *Banks v Goodfellow* stated:

> Yet it is clear that, though the law leaves to the owner of property absolute freedom in this ultimate disposal of that of which he is enabled to dispose, a moral responsibility of no ordinary importance attaches to the exercise of the right thus given … The English law leaves everything to the unfettered discretion of the testator, on the assumption that, though in some instances, caprice or passion, or the power of new ties, or artful contrivance, or sinister influence, may lead to the neglect of claims that ought to be attended to, yet, the instincts, affections, and common sentiments of mankind may be safely trusted to secure, on the whole, a better disposition of the property of the dead, and one more accurately adjusted to the requirements of each particular case, than could be obtained through a distribution prescribed by the stereotyped and inflexible rules of the general law.[23]

What is important to note about this quote is that if a parent were, say, to deprive their children an inheritance through a will, this would be seen as a breach of moral duty by the testator, rather than any kind of interference with the legal interests of the claimant. The legal obligation and any moral obligation are kept quite distinct. Although a testator may have a legal obligation to provide for a child during childhood, once childhood comes to an end they have met their legal obligations, unless, at least in English law, there are special circumstances (eg, the adult child is living apart from a parent and has a disability or is receiving full-time education).[24] As it is during life, so too it should be on death.

B. Protecting the Interests of Elderly People

Testamentary freedom can be seen providing older people with a way of exercising power over their relatives. Even John Locke made reference to the fact that through 'hopes of an Estate the father secured their obedience to his will'.[25] While this may

[21] R Croucher, 'How Free is Free? Testamentary Freedom and the Battle between "Family" and "Property"' (2012) 37 *Australian Journal of Legal Philosophy* 9.

[22] JS Mill, *Principles of Political Economy* (1848) Bk II, ch 2 [4].

[23] *Banks v Goodfellow* (1870) 5 LR QB 549, 563–65.

[24] Children Act 1989, sch 1, para 2.

[25] J Locke, *Second Treatise of Civil Government*, ch VI, 'Of Paternal Power' (1690) para 72.

be seen as unpleasant, it should be remembered that old age can be a time of weakness and vulnerability. An older person may be particularly in need of support and care from relatives. They are in many ways powerless and dependent on others.[26] The ability to leave a gift in their will to a family member or to others who provide them with care may be one of the few tools of power they have left.

C. Showing Love

John Stuart Mill saw the ability of a parent to give a gift to a family member as a powerful way for parents to show their love and affection for them.[27] Making gifts to family members compulsory would deprive the testator of this ability.[28] Michael Sandel and other sociologists warned of the danger of making altruistic behaviour compulsory.[29] Doing so denies people the chance of being virtuous and can rob an act of its symbolic meaning. A gift under a will may be more significant than its financial value in so far as it symbolises a relationship of love or is a formal acknowledgement of the relationship. Especially given the emotional trauma that can follow a death, we should be slow to inhibit the emotional comfort that a gift can provide.

There is a broader point here and that is that if a testator does not have testamentary freedom then there is a fear that they will be less happy during their life. They will be concerned at the inability to express their love or ensure the future wellbeing of someone close to them.[30] This may cause worry. It may cause them to make inappropriate gifts during their lifetime. These points show the error in claiming that as the deceased is dead their views and interests can be ignored. For example, it has been asked: 'What sense does it make for society to allow the wishes of the deceased to trump the happiness of the living?'[31] But, that overlooks the impact of the testamentary disposition rules on those living, but contemplating the wellbeing of their loved ones after their death.

D. Discriminatory Provision

Systems of forced heirship, or those which seek to identify the moral obligations that a deceased owes, are in danger of imposing on a testator the norms and values

[26] J Herring, *Older People in Law and Society* (Oxford, OUP, 2009).

[27] Mill, above n 22, Bk II, ch 2 [3].

[28] ibid.

[29] M Sandel, *What Money Can't Buy* (London, Allen Lane, 2012).

[30] D Kelly, 'Restricting Testamentary Freedom: Ex Ante Versus Ex Post Justifications' (2013) *Fordham Law Review* 1125.

[31] L Tritt, 'Technical Correction or Tectonic Shift: Competing Default Rule Theories Under the New Uniform Probate Code' (2010) 61 *Alabama Law Review* 273, 288.

of the dominant culture. Daniel Monk has pointed out the benefit for lesbian and gay testators of testamentary freedom enabling them to provide for lovers, free from heterosexist assumptions about the nature of their relationships or obligations to family members.[32] Allowing the testator to balance the competing claims of those close to them may seem preferable to the state imposing the dominant culture's understandings of those obligations.[33] A good example of the dangers is a fascinating study by Malcolm Voyce of the response of the Australian courts to claims surrounding family farms, who found that the courts protected the interests of sons at the expense of widows and daughters.[34]

E. Incentives

Many writers on the nature of property have emphasised that property rules encourage people to work, save and invest, by enabling them to reap the rewards of labour.[35] This is also seen as a particularly important reason for allowing freedom of testamentary disposition. If we were to restrict what people could do with their property on death then it would mean that people would have less incentive to work or save.[36] Although, to be fair, we may need to balance the incentive against the fears that hope of an inheritance decreases the incentive on the donee to work or save. Andrew Carnegie famously suggested that 'the parent who leaves his son enormous wealth generally deadens the talents and energies of the son, and tempts him to lead a less useful and less worthy life than he otherwise would'.[37]

F. Conclusion on Testamentary Freedom

These arguments in favour of testamentary disposition appear to create at least a prima facie case for respecting testamentary disposition. In other words, that unless a claim can be made on behalf of the state the testator should be able to use wills to dispose of property. Without wills or will-substitutes a person facing death may have to spend their last few days organising their financial affairs through gifts. That is hard to justify as an appropriate policy. Allowing the use of wills and substitutes seems a far more preferable approach.

[32] D Monk, 'Sexuality and Succession Law: Beyond Formal Equality' (2011) 19 *Feminist Legal Studies* 231.
[33] JC Tate, 'Caregiving and the Case for Testamentary Freedom' (2008) 42 *University of California Davis Law Review* 129.
[34] M Voyce, 'Family Provision, the Family Farm and Rural Patriarchy: Three Actors in Search of a Play?' (2014) 19 *Deakin Law Review* 349.
[35] Kelly, above n 30.
[36] ibid.
[37] A Carnegie, *The Gospel of Wealth and Other Essays* (London, Penguin, 2012) 34.

IV. Theory: Claims of Relatives and Carers

Here I will explore five arguments that relatives or carers might rely on to make a claim against the estate. I will suggest that the first two (based on a moral claim and on need) are not strong enough to justify a departure from testamentary freedom, but the final three (based on claims the testator made a mistake, legal obligations and care) are.

A. Moral Claim

The claim that adult children or other family members have a moral claim against their parents seems increasingly outdated. John Stuart Mill claimed that children could be entitled to maintenance and education, and that leaving them with the abilities to be independent would be sufficient to meet parental obligations.[38] Adult children would have no further claim against their parents. His argument must be viewed in current economic conditions. John Langbein has spoken of the fact that children now 'get their inheritance early'—largely through an investment by parents in their education, especially given university costs.[39] Although, for middle-class parents, nowadays a degree of help in housing costs may be common too, at least early in their child's career. We might agree that the extent of financial support given or received by adult children from their parents varies hugely from case to case and we cannot assume, given the very significant financial contributions received by some children from their parents during their lifetime, that automatically all children should receive an inheritance.[40]

It certainly seems that, as far as England is concerned, moral attitudes towards family inheritances are changing. Increasingly sociologists recognise that family is constituted by 'doing rather than being'.[41] It is feelings of obligations and commitment which are shaped in part by social expectations and cultural values, and also by the particular qualities of the relationship between the individuals. For David Morgan a 'focus on doing, on activities, moves us away from ideas of the family as relatively static structures or sets of positions or statuses'.[42] A leading study in England is that of Janet Finch and Judith Mason who found support for a relational social existence.[43] They emphasised, however, that the notion of family was

[38] Mill, above n 22, Bk II, ch 2 [3].

[39] JH Langbein, 'The Twentieth-Century Revolution in Family Wealth Transmission' (1989) *University of Chicago Law Occasional Paper* no 25.

[40] D Reid, 'From the Cradle to the Grave: Politics, Families and Inheritance Law' (2008) 12 *Edinburgh Law Review* 391.

[41] G Douglas, 'Family Provision and Family Practices' (2014) 4 *Oñati Socio-legal Series* 222.

[42] D Morgan, *Rethinking Family Practices* (Basingstoke, Palgrave, 2011) 5 f.

[43] J Finch and J Mason, *Passing On: Kingship and Inheritance in England* (London, Routledge, 2000).

seen as flexible and dependent not on particular blood relationships or formal ties, but rather by the quality of the actual relationship. So, for example, a person may feel a close link to a sister they see regularly, but a weaker link to another sister they see only occasionally. That is not to say the kin link was irrelevant, but rather that it was less significant than the reality of the social relationship.[44] The only relationship where that was less strong was the one of child and parent:

> The core thread of fixity is the continuing relationship between parents and children. This remains at the core even in complex families … [T]he parent–child relationship is both predictable and privileged, as is seen very clearly in relation to inheritance.[45]

It flowed from this that most people did want to be able to leave something for their children and indeed that was seen as part of being a good parent. However, this was not seen as essentially tied to the mere fact of the relationship and depended to some extent on the quality of the relationship. So, we may gradually be moving away from a consensus that a parent is morally obliged to leave an inheritance to a child simply by virtue of the biological relationship.

Even if you disagree, and believe that parents ought to favour their children in the will, it is hard to see why this is any more than a moral obligation. Typically the law does not give effect to a moral claim. Of course, we might presume a parent would want to meet their moral obligations and, if there was no evidence as to what the testator wished, to assume they wished to meet their moral obligation, but that is the 'mistake' argument below. There is a further difficulty here, too. You may believe that a parent has a moral obligation to provide for an adult child in their will, but why should you impose your views on a testator who does not agree with that?

B. Need

Might the fact of need be sufficient to raise a claim of a relative to support? This, it is suggested, must be doubted. One person's need does not per se justify a claim by the one in need. More is needed such as evidence that the claimant suffered a loss as a result of caring for the testator or had relied on a promise of the testator. Such claims will be discussed later.

A claim based on need alone is not given much weight under the I(PFD) Act. In addition to the general factors, the court will consider 'the extent to which and the basis upon which the deceased assumed responsibility for the maintenance of the applicant, and … the length of time for which the deceased discharged that responsibility'.[46] The Court of Appeal, however, has suggested that it is willing

[44] Reid, above n 40.
[45] Finch and Mason, above n 43, 59.
[46] I(PFD)Act 1975, s 3(4).

to infer assumption of responsibility from maintenance.[47] However, the fact of previous maintenance is likely to exclude the most needy of claimants: those who have provided care for no payment. The courts are generally reluctant to allow adult children who have sufficient earning capacity to succeed in making a claim against their parents' estate.[48] The difficulty facing an employed adult child claimant is in showing that an award would be reasonable for his or her maintenance. Even in cases of need the courts have usually required that an adult child establish a 'moral obligation' or some other special circumstances if the claim is to succeed. In *Garland v Morris*[49] it was found to be reasonable for the deceased to make no provision given his daughter had not spoken to him for several years, despite her need. Examples of a moral obligation or special circumstances include a son who had worked on the family farm in the expectation that he would inherit it,[50] and an applicant whose father was left money by the applicant's mother on the understanding that he would leave the money in his will to the applicant but did not.[51] This seems the right approach; there are many people in need in the world and something more than that is required to justify an interference in testamentary freedom.

C. Correcting Mistakes

Now, I will start with the first of three arguments which I suggest do justify interference in testamentary freedom. One way of justifying some interference is that we need to correct mistakes in the will and ensure that the allocation of the estate meets the intent of the testator. So understood the claimant is arguing that the testator would never have made the will they made (or allowed the intestacy rules to operate) had they known of the circumstances at their death.[52] For example, a child in dire need claiming under the I(PFD) Act could argue the testator made their will with no provision for them on the assumption that they would be in a financially sound position. Had the testator known the truly awful financial position they were in they would have made a different will. In *Re Hancock (Deceased)*[53] an adult child succeeded in a claim when there was a dramatic increase in the value of the estate (from £100,000 to £650,000) from the time the will was made and death. The Court of Appeal accepted evidence that, had the deceased been aware that his estate would increase to this level, he would have provided for his adult child. Unforeseen events are, of course, the curse of the will maker. The jurisdiction is

47 *Jelley v Iliffe* [1981] Fam 128; *Bouette v Rose* [2000] 1 FCR 385.
48 *Ilott v Mitson* [2011] EWCA Civ 346; *Re Hancock (Deceased)* [1998] 2 FLR 346.
49 *Garland v Morris* [2007] EWHC 2 (Ch).
50 *Re Pearce (Deceased)* [1998] 2 FLR 705.
51 *Re Goodchild* [1996] 1 WLR 694.
52 According to I(PFD)A 1975, s 21, a statement of the deceased is admissible evidence.
53 *Re Hancock (Deceased)* [1998] 2 FLR 346.

an acknowledgement that wills are in their nature an advance prediction of what claims one may or may not face and thus are inherently prone to error.[54]

Of course, this justification will not apply to all interferences with testamentary freedom. The 'forced heirship' provisions apply even where it is absolutely clear a testator intended to disinherit their child. Similarly it is not necessarily fatal to an I(PFD) Act claim that the testator would have made the same will even if he had known the facts.

D. Legal Obligations

It is well established that before any gifts can be paid out of an estate the debts of the testator need to be paid first. The claim of any donee must be subservient to the claim of the debtor. It may be that some claims from family members and close members can fall into the category of a debt, or at least equivalent to a debt. It is uncontroversial and entirely compatible with the principle of testamentary disposition that the will only applies to the estate of the deceased that remains once debts and legal obligations are met.

This, however, creates a difficult position for spouses, especially in countries where there is no community of property regime. English law, for example, has no community of property law regime for married couples, yet on divorce there is at least a 'starting point' of an equal division of the assets.[55] This approach has been developed by the courts to acknowledge that in a marriage the parties have made an equal contribution, whether by family care or wealth creation. There should be no preference for the home maker over the money maker.[56] However, the claim of the family carer will only be recognised once the court makes a financial order on divorce. There is a sense, then, in which a spouse has an inchoate right floating above the matrimonial assets, which crystallises when the divorce order is made. This is not a formal ownership, as such, but is a recognised legal claim.

The way a spouse might put their claim is that it would be surprising if they were worse off because their marriage ended by death than if it ended by divorce. Indeed, this argument seems implicitly accepted by Parliament because under the I(PFD) Act section 3(2), the court is required

> to have regard to the provision which the applicant might reasonably have expected to receive if on the day on which the deceased died the marriage, instead of being terminated by the death, had been terminated by a decree of divorce.

However, death and divorce are distinguishable. On divorce, the crucial question is how to divide up the property fairly between the two parties. On death, there is no division required except between the spouse and the other relatives or legatees.

[54] Kelly, above n 30.
[55] *White v White* [2001] 1 AC 596.
[56] ibid.

It could be argued, therefore, that on death a spouse might expect a greater share than on divorce.[57] The I(PFD) Act recognises that reasonable provision for spouses may be in excess of what is necessary for their maintenance. For a surviving spouse reasonable financial provision means 'such financial provision as it would be reasonable in all the circumstances of the case for a husband or wife to receive, whether or not that provision is required for his or her maintenance'.[58] In *Fielden v Cunliffe*[59] the Court of Appeal suggested that the principle of equal sharing of family property promoting in *White v White*[60] could be used, with its yardstick of equality guideline, but only with caution.[61] As Wall LJ put it:

> A marriage dissolved by divorce involves a conscious decision by one or both of the spouses to bring the marriage to an end. That process leaves two living former spouses, each of whom has resources, needs and responsibilities ... However, where the marriage, as here, is dissolved by death, a widow is entitled to say that she entered into it on the basis that it would be of indefinite duration, and in the expectation that she would devote the remainder of the parties' joint lives to being [the deceased's] wife and caring for him.

The quasi-property claim based on a potential claim under the MCA can only be made by a spouse. However, increasingly in English law a successful claim to the family home may be made by a non-spousal family member, such as a cohabitant or carer. This might be done through the law on constructive trusts or proprietary estoppel.[62] Looking at the claim of proprietary estoppel, this has been understood as where a property owner has made an assurance or promise which has been relied upon by the claimant in circumstances in which it would be unconscionable for the owner to deny a claim. They can apply to promises by an owner that on death they will leave a property by a will. Increasingly the courts are being more flexible over the circumstances in which a claim can be made. In *Gillett v Holt*[63] where Walker LJ states: '[T]he fundamental principle that equity is concerned to prevent unconscionable conduct permeates all the elements of the doctrine. In the end the court must look at the matter in the round'.

Simon Gardner sees in such dicta a willingness in the courts to develop a more flexible claim for cohabitants based on the nature of their relationship.[64] He would seek to develop the law so that the remedies for property disputes for unmarried couples (based on a proprietary estoppel or constructive trust claim) would match those available for married couples under the MCA. We may be some way from that, but developments in the law are heading in that direction. In so far

[57] *P v G* [2006] Fam Law 179; *Iqbal v Ahmed* [2011] EWCA Civ 900.

[58] I(PFD)Act 1975, s 1(2)(a).

[59] *Fielden v Cunliffe* [2005] 3 FCR 593.

[60] *White v White*, above n 55.

[61] See also *Baker v Baker* [2008] EWHC 977 (Ch); *Lilleyman v Lilleyman* [2012] EWHC 821 (Ch).

[62] S Gardner, 'Material Relief Between Ex-cohabitants 2: Otherwise than Via Beneficial Entitlement' (2014) 78 *Conveyancer & Property Lawyer* 202.

[63] *Gillett v Holt* [2000] Ch 210.

[64] Gardner, above n 62.

as Gardner's assessment is correct, it provides a quasi-proprietary claim over the property which could justify the I(PFD) Act jurisdiction.

So we see in both the MCA and the use of proprietary estoppel and constructive trusts the law acknowledging that the care work within intimate relationships and the nature of a relational life generates a strong claim to family homes and other property. The I(PFD) Act can, therefore, be justified as an alternative way of acknowledging that a spouse or cohabitant could have made a claim under the MCA or for proprietary estoppel, and to give effect to that claim.

E. Care

I believe that the strongest claim comes from those who have provided care to the deceased, particularly care work which has gone unpaid. The carer of the deceased will have provided them with a clear benefit at a loss to the carer.[65] Where they are in need, as a result of that care, there seems a particularly strong basis for a claim against the estate.[66]

Let us imagine someone becomes frail and in need of care. A family member or friend starts to provide care and this gradually increases in burden and extent. The carer is suffering a significant loss in terms of money and cost. We might hope in such a case the value of the care will be recognised by the state and they will receive a degree of financial support. However, few countries provide adequate state support. In the absence of state support, the cost of the care lies where it falls. This is what currently happens and the economic and social costs of the care fall on carers, women in particular.[67] That is unacceptable and (in the absence of state support) we need to find a way of requiring the recipient of care to pay or compensate the carer.

One way of doing this would be to require the carer and the older person to enter a contract to set out their obligations and expectations. There may be some people for whom this is appropriate, but not many. In part this is because such a contract will be impossible to draft. Intimate life is messy and complex.[68] We cannot foresee now what care will be needed. Care, especially in later life, is not a matter of nine to five, with four weeks holiday. Its tasks are not easily defined. Caring is a matter of doing, and letting be. Of sitting still, being there. Of doing complex tasks, of holding close. It is not reducible to the black and white of print. It is unbounded, unpredictable.

There is another reason to avoid contracts. Sometimes the truth is hard to look at. Our society has so elevated independence that an acknowledgement of care can be

[65] J Herring, *Caring and the Law* (Oxford, Hart Publishing, 2013) ch 2 for a discussion of the losses caused by caring.

[66] B Sloan, *Informal Carers and Private Law* (Oxford, Hart Publishing, 2013).

[67] Herring, *Caring and the Law*, above n 65.

[68] J Herring, *Relational Autonomy and Family Law* (Amsterdam, Springer, 2014).

a sign of weakness. To our shame being a burden to others has become one of the great fears of old age. Putting this all down in writing: that one needs care, that the other will suffer loss, that something is owed is for many hard to face. Worse too is the contractarisation of care, and that care can lose its value. The care ceases to be marked by love, trust and mutuality. It becomes reduced to legal obligations and a reading of sub-clauses. Questions become asked that should not be: do they love me? Or are they doing this because they are contractually required so to do? Have I become an unconscionable bargain?

The resolving of payment for care ex post facto, post-death carries many benefits.[69] It means the parties need not try and set this out in advance. Only in retrospect can the costs be calculated and the value of care assessed. Then the compensation can be paid for the love shown, rather than the financial arrangements impacting the caring relationship itself. It ensures that widespread obligation of reciprocity is met, which as described by Janet Finch

> is the key to understanding how patterns of support build up over time. An expectation that assistance should flow in two directions, and that no one should end up in a position where they are receiving more than they are giving, is at the heart of many of the negotiations which take place about support in families.[70]

The problem with the I(PFD) Act, as already mentioned is that only if a carer is being maintained by the deceased (or a spouse or cohabitant of the diseased) will they fall within a category of claimants.[71] Yet the unpaid carer may well not be maintained and so fall outside the protection of the legislation. This, it is suggested, is odd given that the carer has a far greater claim than other claimants.

While inheritance issues are commonly viewed as matters of fairness between the testator and the different family members, it is important to appreciate the state interests here. Looking at the position of those who lack resources to care for themselves, unless the state undertakes the care for all those who cannot provide for themselves, there needs to be a way of sharing that burden by imposing obligations on others. Typically this is achieved through the family and the sharing of financial costs of raising children between parents and the state. A range of arguments might be made for why it is not unreasonable to impose such obligations on parents. In many countries there is a debate over the extent to which care of older people is seen as a matter of family obligation and if it is, how that is to be given legal effect.

The possibility of them using legislation such as the I(PFD) Act to ensure that carers are adequately provided for from the estate of the deceased ensures that the economic costs of the carer do not fall on the state and that the care of older

[69] TP Gallanis and J Gittler, 'Family Caregiving and the Law of Succession: A Proposal' (2012) 45 *University of Michigan Journal of Law Reform* 761.

[70] J Finch, *Family Obligations and Social Change* (Bristol, Polity Press, 1989) 240.

[71] *McIntosh v McIntosh* [2013] WTLR 1565.

people can be undertaken by family members with a degree of reassurance that they will receive some form of compensation on death.

V. Will-Substitutes and Anti-Avoidance

So far this chapter has been looking at the arguments over interferences with testamentary disposition. It has been argued that there are good reasons for the law to interfere with testamentary dispositions on the basis that the will fails to meet the intentions of the testator or legally protected obligations, or to ensure compensation for care. The I(PFD) Act and similar legislation enables the courts to do this. However, a testator might try and avoid the operation of the legislation by using a will-substitute or otherwise disposing of property prior to death. In so far as that defeats the justifications for the Act, such avoidance must be countered.

An application under section 1 of the I(PFD) Act only deals with property passing under a will; a *donatio mortis causa*;[72] statutory nominations[73] and jointly owned property that passes automatically on death to the joint owner.[74] However, it does not apply to other will-substitutes. For example, death benefits of pension schemes and life insurance benefits[75] cannot be challenged under section 1. However, the Act does include some anti-avoidance provisions through section 10 and these could apply to some will-substitutes.

Under section 10, the court can order a person who has received property from the deceased to make a payment to, or transfer property to, the estate in the following circumstances (section 10(2)):

> (a) that, less than six years before the date of the death of the deceased, the deceased with the intention of defeating an application for financial provision under this Act made a disposition, and
> (b) that full valuable consideration for that disposition was not given by the person to whom or for the benefit of whom the disposition was made (in this section referred to as 'the donee') or by any other person, and
> (c) that the exercise of the powers conferred by this section would facilitate the making of financial provision for the applicant under this Act.

Unsurprisingly the donee cannot be required to pay more than the value[76] of what they received from the testator, but it need not be the full amount.

[72] I(PFD)Act 1975, s 8(2).
[73] ibid, s 8(1).
[74] ibid, s 9(4), applied in *Lim (An infant) v Walia* [2014] EWCA Civ 1076.
[75] ibid, s 10(7) allows premiums to be covered. See ch 3 above p 58 and p 68 f.
[76] The value is the value at the time of the death.

In deciding whether to make an order and what amount to require repayment the court will

> have regard to the circumstances in which any disposition was made and any valuable consideration which was given therefor, the relationship, if any, of the donee to the deceased, the conduct and financial resources of the donee and all the other circumstances of the case.[77]

The provision covers any disposition 'payment of money (including the payment of a premium under a policy of assurance) and any conveyance, assurance, appointment or gift of property of any description, whether made by an instrument or otherwise'.[78] It was, therefore, applied without difficulty to a husband who shortly before his death transferred property to a child of a previous marriage by way of a gift, in order to limit the amount his wife would inherit.[79]

It is important to notice the limits of this provision. First, it must be shown that it was done with the intention of defeating a claim under the Act. That may prove hard to establish.[80] Second, it only covers dispositions for which there was not full valuable consideration. The payment out under a life insurance policy or pension scheme, for example, would probably not fall under that provision.

It is difficult to know how often these anti-avoidance measures are used or how the courts use their discretion. There is very little case law on them, which suggests they are rarely relied upon. They were referred to in *Dellal v Dellal*.[81] The testator, Jack Dellal, was an extremely wealthy man, who it was claimed had £445 million, although his estate on death was valued at £15.4 million. His wife claimed he had disposed of property to his children from previous relationships in order to defeat her application. The reported hearing was an application to strike out the claim, made on the basis that the wife's argument was speculative, as she had not identified precisely any dispositions. This failed on the basis that it had not been shown that the wife's claim was entirely a 'fishing expedition'. The most interesting comments are from Nicholas Mostyn, who contrasts the differences between section 10 of the I(PFD) Act and the similar provision under section 37 of the MCA designed to set aside transactions entered into in order to defeat financial claims on divorce. He notes:

> The effect of an order under section 37 is to annul or 'avoid' the transaction under attack. Moreover, the bad intention to defeat the principal ancillary relief claim is presumed for transactions done within the three year period before the avoidance claim. There is no time limit on attackable transactions. A transaction done 20 years earlier is, at any rate in theory, capable of being annulled. By contrast, a claim under section 10 of

[77] s 10(6).

[78] s 10(7), although donations *mortis causa* are excluded.

[79] *Dawkins v Judd* [1986] 2 FLR 360.

[80] It does not need to be shown to be the dominant motive behind the transaction: *Lazard Brothers and Co (Jersey) Ltd v Norah Holdings Ltd* [1988] 1 WLR 1307.

[81] *Dellal v Dellal* [2015] EWHC 907 (Fam).

> the 1975 Act does not affect the validity of the disposition under attack. If relief is granted then it takes the form of a money judgment against the disponee to pay a specified sum to the estate. There is no presumption as to the necessary bad intention and there is a six year time limit on attackable transactions.[82]

The fact that the time limit and the requirement of proof of 'bad intention' differ between the two pieces of legislation is hard to justify. Why should the claim of a spouse be weaker when the marriage has ended in death, rather than divorce? Indeed, as mentioned above, given there is only one spouse's needs to deal with on death, rather than the two on divorce, one might think her claim is all the stronger.

Do we need a more effective protection against the use of will-substitutes as an avoidance mechanism for legislation designed to protect the interests of carers and family members, such as the I(PFD) Act? I suggest it all depends on the strength of the reasons for the intervention in testamentary freedom. For those who support the priority of testamentary disposition over all other claims, will-substitutes appear to offer no concern. They are no more than another vehicle which a testator may use to ensure that their property reaches a desired beneficiary. Indeed, they may even be seen as a way of increasing that ability by providing an avenue less subject to public scrutiny. Similarly, if one believes the justification for using the I(PFD) Act is to ensure the will reflects the genuine intentions of the testator we can presume that the decision to use a will-substitute reflects the wishes of the testator.

However, it has been argued here that there are two cases where there is a legitimate restriction on testamentary freedom. The first is in so far as it protects quasi-proprietal claims, as it does in jurisdictions such as England where there is no community of property regime, and the expectation is that reallocation of property will take place at the end of a relationship to ensure a fair division. The second is where the claimant has undertaken unpaid care for the deceased. It has been argued that the provision of an award post death is the most appropriate way of dealing with that care, both as a matter of fairness between the parties and to peruse the state interests in ensuring care is provided for older people and that those who undertake that care, who are predominantly women, are not unduly disadvantaged in providing it. I would argue that these are important interests for which there is a strong interest in protecting. In these cases will-substitutes should not be permitted if they will impact on their award. If, as argued above, financial compensation for care is best provided after death, it is important there is a reasonably secure method for ensuring the provision cannot be bypassed by will-substitutes or other devices. There is, therefore, a strong case for extending the avoidance provisions under the I(PFD) Act.

[82] Ibid, [9].

VI. Conclusion

This chapter has explored cases where there is a claim by a family member or carer which is defeated or reduced as a result of a will-substitute. It has explored the case for testamentary freedom and accepted that it is a sound starting point, at least given the kind of property regimes most Western democracies use. The arguments used in favour of testamentary freedom would also support the use of will-substitutes. However, the chapter has explored the use of forced heirship law or legislation such as the English I(PFD) Act to amend the provision made by a will or the intestacy laws. It has been argued that the strongest justifications for such intervention in testamentary freedom occur where the claimant is arguing that they have a property claim or quasi-property claim over the estate or where they have provided unpaid (or underpaid) care for the deceased. These claims seem as effective against a will-substitute as they are against the will itself. Indeed it has been argued that the use of legislation such as the I(PFD) Act is an effective tool to encourage the care of older people and the best way of ensuring compensation for the costs of that care. It also pursues important state goods in ensuring that the care is provided and valued. In so far as will-substitutes defeat those goals they should be liable to be set aside in the same way wills can be.

15

Will-Substitutes and the Family: A Continental Perspective

ANNE RÖTHEL

I. Introduction

Will-substitutes can be seen as simply another type of gratuitous transfer, situated somewhere between lifetime gifts and wills. Just as lifetime gifts and wills, they express the freedom to transfer property as desired by the transferor. But will-substitutes can also be seen as specific devices, which are, so to speak, hidden in a blind spot and used with the intention to circumvent provisions otherwise applicable to 'proper' gifts or 'proper' wills. Hence, will-substitutes become an issue where the law attempts to make a clear distinction between transfers made during lifetime and transfers governed by succession law. This chapter deals with one of the instances in which such a 'distinctive line' is drawn: the rights of family members in continental jurisdictions. It is no surprise that continental civil law jurisdictions with their long-rooted tradition of family-based statutory rights take a formalistic approach to wills and that they define any instrument which can be used for the same purposes as a will, ie, for organising a revocable, gratuitous transfer of wealth upon death.[1]

The purpose of this chapter is to provide an assessment of how continental jurisdictions, and in particular German law, deal with will-substitutes in the context of family rights. On the one hand, this chapter analyses how will-substitutes are dealt with in the context of *compulsory* family rights. On the other hand, it

[1] It has been suggested that there is a distinction between 'pure' or 'perfect' will-substitutes, which do not have any legal effect during lifetime, and 'impure' or 'imperfect' will-substitutes such as joint tenancies, which also lead to lifetime consequences; see JH Langbein, 'The Nonprobate Revolution and the Future of the Law of Succession' (1984) 97 *Harvard Law Review* 1108, 1114 ff and ch 7 above, pp 163 ff and pp 167 ff. Esp with regard to the rights of the family 'impure' or 'imperfect' will-substitutes are of importance. From a broader perspective, any will has lifetime effects, whether or not they are of immediate legal relevance (expectations, motives etc). More importantly, however, a coherent approach to wills and alternative devices should also include alternative devices irrespective of their lifetime effects.

assesses how they are tackled in the context of *default* family rights. It will show that—in contrast to the findings John Langbein[2] and Thomas P Gallanis[3] have made for current US law—default provisions of succession law aimed at protecting the family, such as the automatic revocation of a will in the event of divorce ('divorce rule'), are not applied to will-substitutes. This is true at least for German law, where will-substitutes, though being efficiently subjected to compulsory shares (section III), are expressly exempted from the rules governing the interpretation of wills (section IV). However, these findings are not as contradictory as they might seem at first (section V).

The aims of this chapter are restricted. It cannot explore the legal status of each will-substitute, and the way it relates to each and every family right in every continental jurisdiction, nor can it cover all jurisdictions. Its purpose is to provide an impression of the common strands and the central ideas prevailing in continental jurisdictions. Compulsory shares and default interpretation rules were chosen as the most significant and relevant examples due to the fact that German courts have dealt with both of them. Although an exploration of the hotchpot rules is possible, their importance for will-substitutes seems of little practical significance.[4]

II. The Role of the Family in Continental Succession Laws

Before taking a closer look at will-substitutes, the role of the family in continental succession laws requires clarification. Continental succession laws share the deeply rooted principle that family members enjoy specific, pre-defined imperative rights to the estate. These laws rely on both testamentary freedom and the family, but in contrast to common law jurisdictions, family members generally enjoy fixed statutory rights in the form of the Romanic forced heirship (property rights to the estate)[5] or the Germanic compulsory share (financial claims).[6,7] For the purpose of this chapter, the term 'compulsory share' is used in a broad and

[2] Langbein, above n 1, 1149 ff; see also GMP McCouch, 'Will Substitutes under the Revised Uniform Probate Code' (1993) 58 *Brook Law Review* 1123, 1149 ff.

[3] See ch 1 above V.

[4] But see ch 6 above, p 135 and ch 7 above, pp 163 and 166.

[5] See Italy (Arts 536 ff C Civ), Spain (Arts 806 ff C Civ) and Switzerland (Arts 470 ff ZGB).

[6] See Austria (§§ 762 ff ABGB), the Netherlands (Arts 4:63 ff BW) and Germany (§§ 2303 ff BGB).

[7] For comparative studies see C Castelein, R Foqué and A Verbeke (eds), *Imperative Inheritance Law in a Late-Modern Society* (Antwerp, Intersentia, 2009); A Röthel (ed), *Reformfragen des Pflichtteilsrechts* (Cologne, Heymann, 2007); I Kroppenberg, 'Compulsory Portion' in J Basedow, K Hopt and R Zimmermann (eds), *The Max Planck Encyclopedia of European Private Law*, vol 1 (Oxford, OUP, 2012) 337–41; A Dutta, 'Entwicklungen des Pflichtteilsrechts in Europa' (2011) *Zeitschrift für das Gesamte Familienrecht* 1829–40.

functional sense, including any legal institution that guarantees family members formalised statutory rights to the estate of the deceased, irrespective of the legal nature of these rights. Unlike under English law, these rights have in common that they are neither discretionary nor dependent on individual needs or other specific reasons.[8]

Even though these imperative family rights to compulsory shares represent the most substantial limitation to private autonomy in succession law, and thus give rise to vivid debates, they remain essentially uncontested. The idea that family members enjoy a statutory entitlement to a minimum part of the estate meets with broad societal acceptance, and the corresponding legal rules are intended to be 'long lasting'.[9] Notwithstanding the fact that recent reforms of succession law in many continental jurisdictions[10] have adapted the statutory position of family members, the family's established position was never at any fundamental risk. Imperative family rights have undoubtedly achieved the status of an *institution* within succession law. This has historical reasons. The historical trajectory of compulsory family rights as a shared continental law tradition can be traced back to its beginnings in Roman law (*querela inofficiosi testamenti*)[11] and, in a second step, to the development of succession law from family law in the Middle Ages.[12] Ultimately, this historical foundation has entailed that the rules governing forced heirship and compulsory shares have taken the position of fundamental rights, as is for example the case in Germany.[13] Additionally, academics increasingly emphasise the symbolic and psychological importance of inheritance for the family members' identities and the course of their lives.[14] Others reveal

[8] See ch 14 above II.

[9] J Beckert, 'The *Longue Durée* of Inheritance Law' (2007) 1 *Archives Européennes de Sociologie* 79 ff; R Foqué and A Verbeke, 'Towards an Open and Flexible Imperative Inheritance Law' in C Castelein, R Foqué and A Verbeke (eds), *Imperative Inheritance Law in a Late-Modern Society* (Antwerp, Intersentia, 2009) 203 ff.

[10] Recent law reforms concerning succession law have been undertaken in many continental jurisdictions, see in particular, the Netherlands (2003), Italy (2006), France (2007), Denmark (2008), Catalonia (2008) and Germany (2010).

[11] R Zimmermann, 'Die Erbfolge gegen das Testament im Römischen Recht' in A Röthel (ed), *Reformfragen des Pflichtteilsrechts* (Cologne, Heymann, 2007) 97–115.

[12] J Beckert, *Inherited Wealth* (Princeton, Princeton University Press, 2007); K Gottschalk, 'Erbe und Recht. Die Übertragung von Eigentum in der frühen Neuzeit' in S Willer, S Weigel and B Jussen (eds), *Erbe. Übertragungskonzepte zwischen Natur und Kultur* (Berlin, Suhrkamp Verlag, 2013) 85 ff; B Willenbacher, 'Individualism and Traditionalism in Inheritance Law in Germany, France, England, and the United States' (2004) 28 *Journal of Family History* 208 ff.

[13] For Germany, see BVerfG 19 April 2005, BVerfGE 112, 332.

[14] F Lettke (ed), *Erben und Vererben. Gestaltung und Regulation von Generationenbeziehungen* (Konstanz, UVK, 2003); U Langbein, *Geerbte Dinge. Soziale Praxis und symbolische Bedeutung des Erbens* (Cologne, Böhlau, 2002).

the anthropological and socio-biological link between family and property.[15] Moreover, the rules on compulsory shares reflect the perception of a strong need within civilian jurisdictions for clearly defined rules to govern legal relations in a reliable manner. Without such objective, clear and stereotyping rules on compulsory shares, the courts would be overburdened with litigation claiming that the testator was lacking capacity, or that he or she was mistaken or had become a victim of undue influence, or that a will without inclusion of the family is to be declared void for violating the *bona mores*. Therefore, from a civil law perspective, statutory family rights correspond fully with the overall preference of general and practical rules facilitating foreseeable outcomes. Once again, 'rationality' of law prevails over individual justice. And finally but no less significant, the rules on compulsory shares reflect a strong emphasis on the idea of equality, where the position of children is concerned.[16]

III. Will-Substitutes and the Rights to Compulsory Shares

A. Continental Characteristics

Continental jurisdictions such as France, Austria, Switzerland, the Netherlands, Italy, Spain and Germany that acknowledge compulsory shares conceive these rights in many ways as the 'extension' or 'prolongation' of obligations and expectations of *solidarity* that had already arisen during lifetime. Family law imposes several limitations on private autonomy. These limitations become limitations to testamentary freedom imposed by succession law. However, given that the structure and the nature of family rights undergo fundamental changes, this turn from family law to succession law, and from private autonomy of the living to freedom of testation, is more complex than simply turning the page in a book. Rights that were previously based on specific conditions, in particular needs, and mainly fulfilled by monthly payments (maintenance), now change into claims for lump sums; matrimonial property rights that were deferred to the moment of death, or

[15] D Clark (ed), *The Sociology of Death: Theory, Culture, Practice* (Oxford, Blackwell, 1993); J Carrier, 'Gifts, Commodities, and Social Relations: A Maussian View of Exchange' (1991) 6 *Sociological Forum* 119 ff; U Schönpflug (ed), *Cultural Transmission. Psychological, Developmental, Social, and Methodological Aspects* (Cambridge, CUP, 2008); S Willer, S Weigel and B Jussen (eds), *Erbe. Übertragungskonzepte zwischen Natur und Kultur* (Berlin, Suhrkamp Verlag, 2013).

[16] P Steiner, 'L'heritage égalitaire comme dispositif social' (2005) 46 *Archives Européennes de Sociologie* 127 ff; for a different reasoning, see ch 14 above, pp 290 f: testamentary freedom as an instrument to counterbalance discriminatory provisions in intestate rules, eg in order to promote the equality of same-sex partners.

property rights that only existed as limitations to the power to dispose of one's property, eventually acquired the status of actual rights. Thus, from the family members' perspective, the death of a member of the family not only represents a dramatic emotional experience and a personal loss, but also *the* fundamental *turning point* concerning the legal nature of their rights over the deceased's estate.

i. Anti-Evasion Provisions

Continental laws governing compulsory shares—as much as they may differ in detail—all stipulate specific anti-evasion provisions. The fact that they all draw a distinctive line between the living family member's obligations and the deceased family member's obligations shows that they are aware of the necessity to prevent potential loopholes. In this respect, the drafters of the *Bürgerliches Gesetzbuch* (hereafter BGB) were under no illusion: the absence of such anti-evasion rules would mean that the rights to compulsory shares 'would hardly have any practical impact'.[17]

ii. Structure

Given the many differences in nature and structure of the continental rules on compulsory shares, their anti-evasion provisions operate with surprising similarity. First, they share the fact that they address *lifetime gifts* made by the deceased.[18]

A second characteristic is that they do not generally require a wrongful intent.[19] In contrast to English law,[20] the continental version of the anti-evasion provision is *formal* and *objective*. Any lifetime gift can be challenged without having to prove that the deceased intentionally wished to harm family members and to infringe their rights to compulsory shares. As such, the anti-evasion provisions aimed at protecting the compulsory shares are constructed in quite the same way as the provisions aimed at creditor protection.[21]

Third, the anti-evasion rules operate mainly by extending compulsory shares to lifetime gifts. Gifts falling under the scope of the anti-evasion rules are treated as if they were part of the succession, and family members entitled to a compulsory share

[17] *Motive zu dem Entwurf eines BGB*, vol 5 (Goldbach, Keip, 1888, reprint 2000) 452: 'Ohne eine solche Schranke würde das Institut des Pflichttheiles kaum eine materielle Bedeutung haben'.

[18] See § 2325(1) BGB, Art 922 French C Civ, Art 556(2) Italian C Civ, Arts 4:67 ff BW, § 785(1) AGBG, Art 475 Swiss ZGB as well as chs 6 and 7 above, pp 135 f and p 160.

[19] But see ch 9 above, p 201 regarding Swiss law (Art 527 no 3 ZGB).

[20] See s 10 Family (Provisions for Dependants) Act as well as chs 3 and 14 above III.E. and V.

[21] See ch 13 above IV. But for Italy and the protection of creditors with a view to life insurance contracts see the findings of ch 6 above, p 139.

are entitled to either complementary compulsory shares (*Pflichtteilsergänzung*)[22] or claw-back claims against the beneficiary, if the beneficiary is still enriched.[23]

However, continental anti-evasion provisions differ in one point, namely the issue of whether any lifetime gift or only recent lifetime gifts should be taken into account. Many jurisdictions have decided in favour of a limitation period. In Germany, the rights to compulsory shares are only extended to gifts made in the last 10 years prior to death (§ 2325(3) BGB). Swiss law takes account of any gift that has been made in the five years prior to death and also grants the right to challenge any 'assets alienated by the deceased with the obvious intention of circumventing the limitations on his or her testamentary freedom' as well as any 'advances … to the extent these are not subject to hotchpot'.[24] In Austria, Liechtenstein and the Netherlands, the time limit depends on the person of the beneficiary. Gifts in favour of 'third parties' are only taken into account if they have been effected in the last two years prior to the death (§ 783(3)2 *Allgemeines Bürgerliches Gesetzbuch* (ABGB)), whereas gifts to persons who belong to those entitled to a compulsory share are to be taken into account without consideration of any time limit (§ 785(2) ABGB).[25] Finally, the Romanic jurisdictions entitle the heir to challenge any 'exceeding' lifetime gift, however long ago it was made.

[22] See § 2325(1) BGB: '(1) Where the testator made a gift to a third party, a person entitled to a compulsory share may claim, as an augmentation of his compulsory share, the amount by which the compulsory share is increased if the object given is added to the estate' (this as well as all subsequent translations of German provisions are, unless indicated otherwise, taken from www.gesetze-im-internet.de/englisch_bgb/englisch_bgb.html). Further, see § 785(1)1 ABGB: 'On demand of a child entitled to a compulsory share or a spouse entitled to a compulsory share, gifts by the testator are to be taken into account in the calculation of the estate'; Art 475 ZGB: 'Inter vivos gifts are added to the estate insofar as they are subject to an action in abatement' (trans by the Swiss Federal Council, www.admin.ch/opc/en/classified-compilation/19070042/201407010000/210.pdf); or Art 922(2)1 French C Civ: 'The assets that were disposed of by inter vivos are added to this mass fictitiously, according to their state at the time of the donation and their value at the opening of the succession, after deducting from them the debts or the charges that encumber them' (trans Légifrance, www.admin.ch/opc/en/classified-compilation/19070042/201407010000/210.pdf).

[23] See for the German Law the dispositions of §§ 2328, 2329 BGB. § 2328 BGB states: 'If an heir is entitled to a compulsory share himself, he may refuse the augmentation of his compulsory share to the extent that he would retain his own compulsory share, including what would be due to him as an augmentation of his own compulsory share'. § 2329 BGB states: '(1) To the extent that an heir is not obliged to augment a compulsory share, the person entitled to a compulsory share may, in accordance with the provisions concerning the return of unjust enrichment, demand from the recipient of a gift that he return it for the purpose of making up the shortfall. If the person entitled to a compulsory share is the sole heir, he has the same right. (2) The recipient may avoid the return of the gift through the payment of the shortfall'.

[24] See Art 527 ZGB and ch 9 above, p 201.

[25] For Austria and Liechtenstein, see ch 9 above, p 203. The same is true for Dutch law, see Art 4:67 lit e BW. These seemingly 'odd' rules rely on two ideas: The first is of an 'emotional' nature and is based on the fact that gifts to family members may be perceived as being more hurtful than gifts to third parties. The second is of a 'systematic' nature and based on the idea that the anti-evasion provisions are not only meant to protect the family against gifts to third parties, but also to ensure a balanced attribution of shares among family members; see further A Röthel, 'Umgehung des Pflichtteilrechts' (2012) 212 *Archiv für die civilistische Praxis* 157, 170 ff.

The only time limits applicable are normal prescription periods of claims.[26] In the context of will-substitutes, however, these differences can be set aside. As will-substitutes come into effect upon death, they generally fall within the scope of the anti-evasion provisions.

iii. Relevance

There are very few English cases turning on the anti-evasion provision of section 10 Family (Provisions for Dependants) Act. Cases dealing with other aspects of the family provision legislation are equally scarce.[27] This situation is in stark contrast to the great practical importance of the rules on compulsory shares and anti-evasion provisions in continental jurisdictions.

Thanks to their broad scope as well as their formalistic and non-discretional nature, claims for compulsory shares, including complementary compulsory shares for lifetime gifts, have become standard in continental law and are brought to court in great quantities and with predictable outcomes. Thus, compulsory shares, and in particular anti-evasion rules, operate efficiently and form the core of succession law.

An empirical analysis of the sheer number of judgments rendered in Germany on matters of succession law in the last 25 years proves that cases involving the set of provisions governing compulsory shares (§§ 2303 ff BGB) are clearly above average in quantity, and count amongst the most litigated issues. The same is true of cases concerning the complementary compulsory share (*Pflichtteilsergänzung*) pursuant to the anti-evasion provision stipulated under § 2325 BGB.[28]

iv. Will-Substitutes: A Pseudo Problem?

This brief outline offers many reasons why will-substitutes should represent no major challenge for the continental succession laws governing the rights to compulsory shares, as they are protected by effective anti-evasion provisions. These work even more efficiently with regard to will-substitutes than with regard to 'pure' lifetime gifts. As will-substitutes take effect only upon death, they will always fall within the scope of application of the anti-evasion provisions. In theory, will-substitutes represent the least controversial issue in the context of family rights to succession.

[26] See Art 921 French C Civ and A-M Leroyer, *Droit des successions*, 3th edn (Paris, Dalloz, 2014) para 593.

[27] See ch 14 above, p 285.

[28] See the 'quantitative analysis of case law' undertaken by D Leipold in 2010, www.jura.uni-freiburg.de/institute/izpr2/downloads/dateienleipold/quantitativerechtsprechungsanalyse. The study reveals that out of the 5,628 chosen decisions on succession law of various German courts published between 1985 and 2010, nearly a quarter were decisions by the Bundesgerichtshof (BGH) (180 out of 834) and concerned the compulsory share, and that § 2325 BGB ranks among the five most important provisions of the BGB, only outnumbered by § 1922 BGB (universal succession), § 1967 BGB (transfer of debts), § 2084 BGB (interpretation in favour of validity) and § 2247 BGB (formalities on wills).

B. Remaining Uncertainties

However, this is not entirely true or at least not always that evident. Focusing in particular on German law, will-substitutes remain a challenge to compulsory shares and their respective anti-evasion provisions.

Since the inception of the BGB, there has been an awareness of the potential problem raised by will-substitutes and the need for effective anti-evasion provisions to protect the rights to compulsory shares. On these matters, German law is by no means stagnant. The German experience clearly shows that the only way to extricate will-substitutes from the regime of anti-evasion provisions is either to challenge their gratuitous nature—with the consequence that they would neither be subject to compulsory shares nor to complementary compulsory shares—or to argue that they are not at all, or not entirely, a gift made by the deceased. This is an issue which has recently been the subject of debate and court review in Germany in particular regarding transfers to charitable foundations (subsection III.B.i). Life insurance constitutes an additional challenge, which has yet to be resolved in Germany, as well as in various other continental jurisdictions. Very often, the insurance sum paid to the beneficiary is not wholly considered a gift made by the deceased, and is therefore not entirely included when calculating the complementary compulsory share (subsection III.B.ii).

i. Charitable Transfers: Merely 'Fiduciary Benefits'?

As Anatol Dutta has already pointed out, gratuitous transfers in favour of existing foundations, or for the creation of a foundation, can function as will-substitutes under German law, which thus leads to a potential problem for those entitled to a complementary compulsory share (*Pflichtteilsergänzung*, § 2325 BGB).[29] The legal nature of such transfers has been the subject of recurrent court scrutiny, first by the Reichsgericht and then by the Bundesgerichtshof. In a decision of 2003, the Bundesgerichtshof had to render a judgment on the legal nature of such transfers to charitable foundations.

a. Bundesgerichtshof 10 December 2003: Dresdner Frauenkirche

The following case was presented to the Bundesgerichtshof. A widowed father of an only daughter supported the Stiftung Dresdner Frauenkirche, a private charitable foundation with the purpose of reconstructing the Dresdner Frauenkirche, by making a lifetime transfer in the amount of 4.4 mio DM (€2.2 mio) to the foundation. He therefore received a *Stifterbrief*, a document in testimony of his generosity. As the donor had disinherited his only daughter and had additionally installed the foundation as his sole heir, the disappointed daughter sued the foundation for her compulsory share. She based her claim on the estate left via

[29] Ch 8 above, pp 187 f.

will to the foundation, and on the lifetime transfers previously made by her father. Even though the central issue of this case is actually that of lifetime transfers made some years before death and not that of transfers taking effect upon death, the Bundesgerichtshof had to arrive at a general decision concerning the legal nature of transfers to charitable foundations, which means that the judgment in this case is equally important for the assessment of will-substitutes.

The Oberlandesgericht Dresden had supported the view that these transfers were not gratuitous. Therefore, they were not gifts and consequently did not entail an entitlement to a complementary compulsory share (§ 2325 BGB). The principal argument was that transfers in favour of charitable foundations would not enrich the foundation as it was bound to invest the means according to its charitable purpose. Instead, these transfers were merely transitory items,[30] which was in keeping with the view that had been previously taken by the Reichsgericht.[31]

However, the Bundesgerichtshof took a different position, thus approximating German law with Swiss and Austrian law, where the legislature had expressly acknowledged the gratuitous nature of transfers for charitable purposes and in particular of those to charitable foundations.[32] The Bundesgerictshof deemed the transfer to the foundation 'Dresdner Frauenkirche' to be gratuitous, and thus qualified it as a gift entitling the compulsory heir to a complementary compulsory share.[33] The Court focused on a 'technical' line of reasoning and explained that ownership had been transferred to the foundation.[34] It rejected the argument of the Oberlandesgericht Dresden that the foundation had acquired the means only 'on trust' (*Treuhand*).[35] Instead, it held that the foundation had acquired definitive ownership without any remaining discretional rights of revocation. The mere fact that the foundation had an obligation to invest the means according to its purposes did not mean that it held the means 'only' on trust.[36]

Despite the fact that the judgment of the Bundesgerichtshof primarily revolved around the technical issue concerning the legal nature of such transfers, the Court

[30] OLG Dresden 2 May 2002, (2002) *Neue Juristische Wochenschrift* 3181 f.

[31] RG 6 February 1905, RGZ 62, 386, 390 f.

[32] See Art 82 Swiss ZGB: 'A foundation may be challenged by the founder's heirs or creditors in the same manner as a gift', and § 785(3) Austrian ABGB: 'Gifts which the deceased has made from his revenues without affecting the core of the assets (*Stammvermögen*) and for charitable purposes are not taken into account'; for the Law of Liechtenstein see the decision FL OGH 9 February 2006, 6 CH.2004.23, LES 2006, 468 as well as ch 9 above IV.

[33] See BGH 10 December 2003, BGHZ 157, 178, 182 ff.

[34] BGH 10 December 2003, BGHZ 157, 178, 182 f: 'Gegen eine Schenkung … spräche allerdings eine Zuwendung allein zu dem Zweck, es zugunsten anderer zu verwenden. … Die Beklagte verwandte die Mittel nach dem Willen des Geldgebers ausschließlich für sich selbst, so wie es in ihrer Satzung festgelegt ist … Es besteht kein Anhalt, dass die Geldzuwendungen des Erblassers nicht im Sinne eines endgültigen Vermögenstransfers erfolgen sollten'.

[35] OLG Dresden 2 May 2002, (2002) *Neue Juristische Wochenschrift* 3181 f.

[36] BGH 10 Dez 2003, BGHZ 157, 178, 182: 'Zwar war die Beklagte gehalten, die Gelder zu Stiftungszwecken … zu verwenden. Das verlieh dem Erblasser aber keine weitergehenden Rechte im Sinne eines Treuhandverhältnisses. Die für Treuhandverhältnisse typischen Merkmale … treffen auf Spenden der vorliegenden Art nicht zu'.

was indeed aware of the obvious political question underpinning the trial and made the following statement:

> Even if the reason to support charitable purposes might seem honourable and in the public interest, this does not alter the fact that such transfers actually affect the rights to a compulsory share. If such restrictions to the rights to compulsory shares appear politically justified, it remains the exclusive competence of the legislature to implement such restrictions.[37]

b. The Academic Aftermath

This judgment gave rise to an animated academic debate. Though the technical argument that lifetime transfers to charitable foundations are gifts, and not merely fiduciary contributions, was widely supported by legal scholars, many of them used a political line of reasoning to argue in favour of a general privilege of charitable transfers. Donations in favour of charitable foundations should be at least partially exempted from claims of those entitled to complementary compulsory shares. In particular, this was proposed for cases where claims invoking family rights degenerated into 'luxurious' claims, as was for example the case in the decision concerning the Dresdner Frauenkirche, where a 'greedy' daughter sued for the total sum of 3.1 million DM. Some authors suggested that charitable foundations should be treated as an additional 'fictive' child of the deceased so as to reduce the (complementary) compulsory shares of the 'real' family members.[38] Others referred to Austrian law, where the ABGB exempts transfers for charitable purposes from the compulsory share, provided that the transferred wealth derives exclusively from the revenues, and does not affect the core of the assets (*Vermögensstamm*), see § 785(3)1 ABGB.[39]

c. The Reform of 2010

However, the German legislature decided otherwise. In fact, the German anti-evasion provision, which entitles the compulsory heir to a complementary

[37] BGH 10 Dez 2003, BGHZ 157, 178, 187: 'Dass im Einzelfall die Motive durchaus anerkennenswert sein mögen und die als gemeinnützig gedachte Vermögensverschiebung im allgemeinen Interesse liegen kann, ist für die damit einhergehende Pflichtteilsverkürzung ohne Belang. Solche Eingriffe in das Pflichtteilsrecht, so sie denn rechtspolitisch gerechtfertigt erscheinen, sind dem Gesetzgeber vorbehalten'.

[38] R Hüttemann and P Rawert, 'Pflichtteil und Gemeinwohl—Privilegien für gute Zwecke?' in A Röthel (ed), *Reformfragen des Pflichtteilsrechts* (Cologne, Heymann, 2007) 73–91. Others have suggested that charitable transfers should be exempted from complementary compulsory shares as being merely gifts made out of decency (*Anstandsschenkungen*, § 2330 BGB), see W Matschke, 'Gemeinnützige Stiftung und Pflichtteilsergänzungsanspruch' in HP Westermann and K Mock (eds), *FS Bezzenberger* (Berlin, De Gruyter, 2000) 521–28.

[39] See § 785(3)1 ABGB: 'Gifts which the deceased has made from his revenues without affecting the core of the assets (*Stammvermögen*) and for charitable purposes are not taken into account'. See Hüttemann and Rawert, above n 38, 77 ff; A Röthel, 'Generationengerechtigkeit versus Gemeinwohl' (2006) *Zeitschrift für Erbrecht und Vermögensnachfolge* 8, 12.

compulsory share (§ 2325 BGB) was finally reformed in 2010, but not in the proposed direction of a specific exemption for charitable purposes. Instead, the legislature only changed the time limit applicable to claims. The ten-years rule, which had been consistently applied, was changed into a *pro-rata-temporis*-rule (*Abschmelzungsregel*).[40] The legislature expressly hoped that this reform would address the needs of charitable foundations insofar as it would be conducive to a reduction of subsequent claw-back claims.[41] Doubts remain as to whether this step was of any great consequence. The rule quite clearly failed to implement any changes regarding will-substitutes, which operate upon death. The state of affairs, as it had been described by the Bundesgerichtshof in 2003, remained unaltered by the reform. Therefore, 'charitable' will-substitutes still do not enjoy any exemption or alleviation.

ii. Providential Transfers via Life Insurance: Premiums, Last Redemption Value or Revenues?

The legal assessment of life insurance has given rise to a similar discussion. Life insurance contracts represent a typical and frequently used will-substitute on the continent—in Germany,[42] as well as in many other civil law jurisdictions, for example, France,[43] Switzerland,[44] Austria and Italy.[45] One might expect that the great practical impact would lead to clear, stable and similar evaluations across the different jurisdictions, yet the contrary is true. Life insurance is still the subject of many heated debates and recurring jurisprudential interpretation. This is not only true of France and Italy, as Cecile Pérès and Gregor Christandl have shown,[46] but also for Germany. German courts have had several opportunities to assess the extent to which life insurance is to be included in the calculation of complementary compulsory shares (*Pflichtteilsergänzung*, § 2325 BGB).

a. Reichsgericht 25 March 1930: Premiums

In contrast to the issue of charitable transfers (see subsection III.B.i above), there were no doubts, as far as life insurance is concerned, that the beneficiary of a life insurance contract had received a gift. In fact, the Reichsgericht stated as

[40] § 2325(3) BGB: 'The gift is fully taken into account within the first year prior to the devolution of the inheritance, and is taken into account by one-tenth less within each further year prior to the devolution of the inheritance. If ten years have passed since the gift was made, the gift is not taken into account'.

[41] BT-Drs. 16/13543, 7.

[42] Ch 8 above, p 183. The Association of German Insurers (Gesamtverband der Deutschen Versicherungswirtschaft) reported that in 2014, €2,500 mio were held in insurance funds, governed by some 92.5 mio contracts, www.gdv.de/wp-content/uploads/2015/07/GDV-Lebensversicherung-in-Zahlen-2015.pdf.

[43] Ch 7 above, pp 167 ff.

[44] Ch 9 above, pp 209 f.

[45] Ch 6 above, pp 137 f.

[46] See chs 6 and 7 above, p 139 and pp 153 ff and pp 169 ff.

early as 1930 that life insurance contracts enrich the beneficiary and are therefore gifts within the meaning of the anti-evasion provision.[47] But it is still contested whether the gift is equivalent in amount to the insurance sum that is finally paid to the beneficiary.[48] The Reichsgericht pointed out that a gift not only requires the enrichment of the beneficiary, but that the enrichment also has to originate from a designation by the donor. The Reichsgericht held that this was only the case for premiums paid by the contracting party, but not for the insurance sum, which in general is substantially higher.[49] Thus, the Reichsgericht had developed a position which is quite similar to current English law (section 10(7) Inheritance (Provision for Family and Dependants) Act 1975).[50]

b. Bundesgerichtshof 28 April 2010: The Last Redemption Value

Recently, in 2010, the Bundesgerichtshof expressly departed from this long line of case law. Interestingly, the Bundesgerichtshof developed a third evaluation method for the value of the complementary compulsory share with regard to life insurance. It found that any payment resulting from life insurance does not constitute a gift from the contracting party to the beneficiary, unless the value is equivalent to the fictional last redemption value that the contracting party would personally have been entitled to (*letzter fiktiver Rückkaufswert*).[51] This position had already been established by Swiss law, as the Swiss Civil Code states in Article 529 that:

> Where a life assurance claim maturing on the death of the deceased was established in favour of a third party by a disposition inter vivos or by a testamentary disposition or was transferred by the deceased during his or her lifetime to a third party without valuable consideration, such claim is subject to abatement at its redemption value.[52]

c. And the Remaining Revenues?

Hence, the insurance sum is not entirely subject to the complementary compulsory share (§ 2325 BGB), as the revenues (*Überschüsse*) cannot be challenged. Once more, the Bundesgerichtshof argued 'technically' and relied on the legal nature of gifts. The Court emphasised that the anti-evasion rule is exclusively applicable to assets that had once been at the disposal of the deceased. Therefore, a previously unattained right (by the deceased) can never be treated as a gift in the context of compulsory shares.[53]

[47] RG 25 March 1930, RGZ 128, 187, 188 f.

[48] But see for Austrian law, OGH 10 June 1997, (1997) *Österreichische Notariatszeitung* 394 ff; OGH 24 April 2003, (2003) *Österreichische Notariatszeitung* 340, 341. In both cases, the Austrian OGH held that the compulsory share has to be calculated on the basis of the insurance sum.

[49] RG 25 March 1930, RGZ 128, 187, 190.

[50] See chs 3 above III.E. and 14 above V.

[51] BGH 28 April 2010, BGHZ 185, 252, 254 ff.

[52] See further ch 9 above VI.B.

[53] However, the BGH decided otherwise with regard to § 134 InsO, the equivalent anti-evasion provision aiming at the protection of creditors. The BGH explains this difference with the fact that the

This time, the Bundesgerichtshof remained silent on the obvious political dimension of its decision. Whereas the Court did not move one iota to alleviate the burden of compulsory shares in favour of charitable purposes, it found room for some alleviation in favour of 'provisional' purposes. The subtle 'technical' distinction between direct and indirect gifts, between the deceased's contribution and the extent of the beneficiary's enrichment, has finally promoted a profoundly 'political' issue. The partial exemption of revenues generated by a life insurance contract from the entitlement to a complementary compulsory share (§ 2325 BGB) is in full accordance with a general and well-established position under German law that the accumulation of wealth destined to provide for others (*Versorgungsvermögen*) should enjoy statutory support.[54] Since their introduction in the late-nineteenth century, life insurance contracts have been perceived as 'special' and have contributed to multifaceted conceptual changes in both contract law and succession law.[55] Even though the Bundesgerichtshof did not expressly refer to this tradition of 'leniency' on life insurance contracts, it is suggested that these political reasons genuinely explain why the Court—contrary to its otherwise 'adamant' support of the compulsory share[56]—explored options and finally found a way for at least creating a partial privilege for life insurance contracts with regard to compulsory shares.

One might add another argument explaining why 'providential purposes' should be different from 'charitable purposes' with regard to compulsory shares: the typical beneficiary of a life insurance contract is not a third party, but someone related to the deceased. In many cases, life insurance contracts do not conflict with compulsory shares, in particular if the beneficiary is the spouse or civil partner. Conflicts often arise when the deceased names his cohabitant or another companion as the beneficiary. In such cases, the Bundesgerichtshof makes a minimal correction to the fact that cohabitants enjoy no legal succession rights under German law,[57] by granting life insurance contracts a partial exemption from compulsory

insolvency rules aim at restoring the assets in nature ('real'), whereas the rules on forced heirship only offer a monetary claim and thus aim at only fictionally restoring the *status quo ante*; see BGH 28 April 2010, BGHZ 185, 252, 264 and ch 14 above, p 299 f.

[54] G Hager, 'Neuere Tendenzen beim Vertrag zugunsten Dritter auf den Todesfall' in H Ficker (ed), *FS E von Caemmerer* (Tübingen, Mohr, 1978) 128–31; A Röthel, *Ist unser Erbrecht noch zeitgemäß?* (Munich, Beck, 2010) A 44.

[55] In fact, the early recognition of contracts in favour of third parties (§§ 328, 331 BGB) with the inception of the BGB in 1900 is partially due to the emergence of insurance and insurance contracts in the 19th century; see further R Zimmermann, *The Law of Obligations* (Oxford, OUP, 1996) 34 ff. German law not only recognised contracts in favour of third parties *upon death* (§ 331 BGB), but also later confirmed that these contracts can be transferred 'other than by succession law', BGH 19 October 1983, (1984) *Neue Juristische Wochenschrift* 480, 481 and ch 8 above III.C.

[56] See BGH 10 December 2003, BGHZ 157, 182 and BGH 23 May 2012, BGHZ 193, 260.

[57] Cohabitants enjoy neither intestate rights, nor are they entitled to compulsory shares (see §§ 1924 ff, § 2303 BGB); but see for a comparative overview KGC Reid, MJ de Waal and R Zimmermann (eds), *Comparative Succession Law, volume 2. Intestate Succession* (Oxford, OUP 2015) 442, 504 ff.

shares. Nevertheless, this exemption to legal rights to compulsory shares is yet to be operated in a coherent way. As of now, the exception applies only to contracts in favour of third parties, that is to say when a contracting party designates a third person as a beneficiary in his or her insurance contract. However, it is inapplicable to gifts, which the contracting party donates *directly* to another person with the same intent.[58]

C. Interim Findings

As the short overview clearly demonstrates, the continental imperative of family rights remains under threat of circumvention, but continental jurisdictions have established effective anti-avoidance provisions that by and large successfully reintegrate some functionally equivalent instruments into the regime of compulsory shares. In general, family rights are more or less equally protected against wills, will-substitutes and lifetime gifts.[59] Notwithstanding the brief existence of an exemption for charitable transfers, and a partial exemption for revenues when transferred via life insurance contracts, it must be remembered that continental jurisdictions enforce family rights against will-substitutes in an effective as well as a largely coherent manner. They are all equipped with well-functioning anti-evasion provisions, and respective claims are continuously and successfully brought to court. As the anti-evasion provisions mainly target lifetime gifts made before death, will-substitutes do not represent a genuine challenge to them.

However, it seems remarkable that one kind of will-substitute—the life insurance contract—challenges the otherwise precisely defined and neatly 'closed' system of family rights as provided for by succession laws of almost all continental jurisdictions. Germany, Switzerland, Austria and France offer a range of legal responses, grounded in statutory as well as case law, ranging from a large or at least 'unclear' exemption (France) up to no exemption at all (Austria). The fact that life insurance is dealt with so differently, despite the fact that the anti-evasion provisions generally follow a similar structure, once again underlines the degree of influence exercised by policy—irrespective of the fact that these political reasons are not expressly stated but concealed in dogmatic arguments, as is the case in Germany.

[58] See Röthel, *Ist unser Erbrecht noch zeitgemäß?*, above n 54, A 46; Röthel, 'Umgehung des Pflichtteilrechts', above n 25, 174 f; P Windel, *Über die Modi der Nachfolge in das Vermögen einer natürlichen Person beim Todesfall* (Heidelberg, von Decker, 1998) 171; K Muscheler, *Universalsukzession und Vonselbsterwerb* (Tübingen, Mohr Siebeck, 2002) 119 ff.

[59] Under German law, a 'regular' claim for a compulsory share is directed against the heir. Conversely, the right to the 'complementary compulsory share' (*Pflichtteilsergänzung*) can result in a claim against the beneficiary of the transfer (§ 2329(1) BGB). It can also result in the claim being reduced or turned down where the beneficiary is no longer enriched (§§ 2329(1), 818(3) BGB). However, the 'complementary' claims are more likely to fail due to practical reasons. Whereas the existence of testamentary dispositions and their beneficiaries can easily be identified, transfers via lifetime gifts or will-substitutes may often remain unknown or at least require closer scrutiny, see ch 6 above, pp 151 f.

IV. Will-Substitutes and Default Rules on Interpretation

A. Default 'Divorce Rules' for Wills

From the family's perspective, another important and crucial issue of succession law is whether wills favouring spouses or civil partners remain valid in the event of divorce or annulment of the partnership. Generally, continental jurisdictions are reluctant to allow the remaining family members, for instance the deceased's children, to challenge the will on grounds of error (*Irrtum*) or misconception of an implied condition (*Fehlvorstellung über die Geschäftsgrundlage*). In particular, this is true of Austrian and Italian law.[60] Germany provides the counter-example, expressly granting statutory protection to the interests of the family by way of a statutory default rule. § 2077 BGB states as follows:

(1) A testamentary provision in which the testator has made provisions in favour of his spouse becomes ineffective if the marriage is dissolved before the testator's death …

(2) A testamentary disposition in which the testator has made provision for the person to whom he is engaged is ineffective if the engagement was dissolved before the testator's death.

(3) The disposition is not ineffective if it is to be presumed that the testator would have made it even in such a case.[61]

By doing so, the German legislature has placed a 'special' emphasis on the position of children and of surviving parents, as they do not have to prove the relevance of the marriage or partnership for the deceased's decision-making process. Instead, they can simply rely on the statutory rule of § 2077(1) BGB, with the result that they are—unless the contrary is proven—entitled to the estate under the rules of intestacy.[62]

B. Non-Applicability to Will-Substitutes

Thomas P Gallanis has identified within US law a 'major trend' of extending default rules concerning wills to will-substitutes. In particular, he has pointed to

[60] Austrian, Italian and Swiss law know no express statutory provision, and the courts only seldomly rule in favour of the family. In Austria, this may change in the future (see the proposal for reform of § 726 AGBG). Concerning Italian law, I have to rely on the observations by G Christandl. Interestingly, the Italian C Civ acknowledges a default rule concerning children born after the will (§ 687 C Civ), but not in the event of a subsequent divorce.

[61] The same applies to registered partners, § 10(5) *Lebenspartnerschaftsgesetz* (LPartG).

[62] §§ 1924 ff BGB; see further W Schlüter and A Röthel, *Erbrecht*, 17th edn (Munich, Beck, 2015) §§ 7 ff.

the reformed Uniform Probate Code, which expressly extends the 'divorce rule' to will-substitutes.[63] This question only arises in jurisdictions with comparable default rules such as the divorce rule concerning wills under German law. However, the position of German law is quite clear on this point and takes the opposite view on the applicability of the divorce rule to will-substitutes. In their decisions, German courts were especially concerned to underline the differences between wills and will-substitutes.

i. Bundesgerichtshof 30 November 1994: The Contractual Nature of Will-Substitutes

The Bundesgerichtshof had several opportunities to rule on the applicability of regulations governing the validity of wills or will-substitutes.[64] All the cases brought to the Bundesgerichtshof concerned life insurance, and the Court consistently denied the application of the divorce rule to the designation of the life insurance's beneficiary—with sometimes 'tragic' effects, as the following case illustrates. A husband had concluded a life insurance and named his 'wife' ('*die Ehefrau*'), as the primary beneficiary. He had also written a will and named his wife, as well as any subsequently born children as his testamentary heirs. They separated only two years later. During the divorce procedure, the husband died at the age of 33 of a brain tumor and—one is tempted to add 'of course'—without having altered the designation of the beneficiary of his life insurance contract. The insurance company thus paid the insurance sum to the widow, and the deceased's father claimed the sum back, mainly relying on an analogy to the divorce rule, which is also applicable if death occurs during the divorce proceedings.[65]

Once again, and perfectly in line with its earlier judgments, the Bundesgerichtshof expressly rejected the analogy,[66] and thus upheld its general rule that the provisions on wills are not to be applied to will-substitutes, such as transfers upon death via a life insurance.[67] The Court mainly invoked the legal nature of wills as

[63] § 2-804(b)(1)(A) of the Uniform Probate Code, ch 1 above V.A.

[64] BGH 17 September 1975, (1976) *Neue Juristische Wochenschrift* 290; BGH 1 April 1987, (1987) *Neue Juristische Wochenschrift* 3131; BGH 14 February 2007, (2007) *Neue Juristische Wochenschrift–Rechtsprechungs-Report Zivilrecht* 976, 977; see also BGH 29 January 1981, (1981) *Neue Juristische Wochenschrift* 984 and BGH 30 November 1994, BGHZ 128, 125.

[65] Following § 2077(1) 2, 3 BGB: 'It is equivalent to dissolution of marriage if at the time of death of the testator the requirements for divorce were satisfied and the testator had petitioned for divorce or consented to it. The same applies if the deceased at the time of his death was entitled to petition for the annulment of the marriage and had filed the petition'.

[66] BGH 30 November 1994, BGHZ 128, 125, 132.

[67] See earlier concerning the 'divorce rule' (§ 2077 BGB) BGH 17 September 1975, (1976) *Neue Juristische Wochenschrift* 290; BGH 1 April 1987, (1987) *Neue Juristische Wochenschrift* 3131; see later BGH 14 February 2007, (2007) *Neue Juristische Wochenschrift–Rechtsprechungs-Report Zivilrecht* 976, 977 and recently OLG Düsseldorf 16 October 2014, (2015) *Zeitschrift für Erbrecht und Vermögensnachfolge* 274, 275 as well as OLG Bremen 11 November 1958, (1959) *Versicherungsrecht* 689; OLG Düsseldorf 13 May 1975, (1975) *Der Betrieb* 1503; OLG Hamm 29 January 1975, (1976) *Versicherungsrecht* 142; LG Saarbrücken 16 April 1982, (1983) *Neue Juristische Wochenschrift* 180. See as well the rules concerning the revocation in cases of misrepresentation (*Anfechtung*, §§ 2078 ff BGB) BGH 10 December 2003, BGHZ 157, 79, 85 f.

unilateral dispositions in contrast to the contractual nature of transfers via a life insurance. Rules such as the divorce rule only represented assumptions on the hypothetical will of the deceased, without taking into account how third parties would have reasonably interpreted the disposition. Therefore, the application of such a unilateral interpretation rule would run contrary to the 'legal nature of the designation of the beneficiary' since it would fail to take into account the perspective of the contractual party and his or her understanding of the declaration.[68] Eventually, the Bundesgerichtshof added a practical argument. The application of the 'divorce rule' might lead to laborious litigation and would thus impair the effective and prompt handling of the insurance case.[69] Another argument for not applying the divorce rule to designations of beneficiaries in life insurance contracts is that the fate of the marriage or the civil partnership is merely an 'external' fact, which does not belong to the sphere of the insurance company and should therefore not affect its contract with the deceased.[70]

Though German courts have consistently denied the application of the divorce rule (§ 2077 BGB) to the designation of a beneficiary in a life insurance contract, they have pointed out that intestate heirs can still prove that the divorce had affected the basis (*Geschäftsgrundlage*, § 313 BGB) of the transfer and was therefore revocable.[71] However, there remains an important difference as to the burden of proof. Concerning wills, the assumption is in favour of the intestate heirs, and it falls upon the named beneficiary to prove the contrary—whereas as far as life insurance is concerned, the assumption is in favour of the designated beneficiary, and it is upon the intestate heirs to challenge the transfer.[72]

[68] BGH 14 February 2007, (2007) *Neue Juristische Wochenschrift–Rechtsprechungs-Report Zivilrecht* 976, 977: 'Denn die für die Auslegung einer letztwilligen Verfügung gebotene Prüfung des hypothetischen Erblasserwillens nach § 2077(3) BGB widerspricht der Rechtsnatur der Bezugsrechtsbenennung als einseitiger, empfangsbedürftiger Willenserklärung ... Bei einer Erklärung im Rahmen einer vertraglichen Vereinbarung ist im Interesse des Vertragspartners, hier des Versicherers, weitgehend auf deren Wortlaut und darauf abzustellen, wie die Erklärung aus dessen Sicht zu verstehen ist'. ['This is due to the fact that the legal assessment of the testator's hypothetical will, as required for the interpretation of a testamentary disposition pursuant to § 2077(3) BGB, contradicts the legal nature of the designation as a unilateral declaration of intent requiring acknowledgment ... In the interest of the contractual partner, ie, the insurer, a declaration through a contractual agreement is to be interpreted on the basis of its exact wording and on the basis of how it is to be understood from the contractual partner's perspective'].

[69] BGH 14 February 2007, (2007) *Neue Juristische Wochenschrift–Rechtsprechungs-Report Zivilrecht* 976, 977; see also BGH 1 April 1987, (1987) *Neue Juristische Wochenschrift* 3131: 'Außerdem soll der Versicherer im Interesse einer schnellen und reibungslosen Abwicklung des Versicherungsfalls nicht—mitunter schwierige—Auslegungsfragen entscheiden müssen, die sich aus einer entsprechenden Anwendung von § 2077 BGB ergeben können'. ['Moreover, in the interest of the prompt and smooth processing of the insurance case, the insurer should not be required to decide on—sometimes difficult—interpretation issues, which may arise because of the corresponding application of § 2077 BGB'].

[70] See G Otte in *von Staudingers Kommentar zum Bürgerlichen Gesetzbuch* (Berlin, De Gruyter, 2012) § 2077 para 31.

[71] BGH 1 April 1987, (1987) *Neue Juristische Wochenschrift* 3131 f; BGH 30 November 1994, BGHZ 128, 125, 132.

[72] See Otte, above n 70, § 2077 para 31.

ii. And What About Succession Contracts?

Considering the strong emphasis that the Bundesgerichtshof placed on the contractual nature of the life insurance contract, and the non-contractual nature of wills, it might seem contradictory that the BGB expressly expanded the applicability of the divorce rule to binding dispositions (*vertragsmäßige Verfügungen*) made by way of a succession contract (*Erbvertrag*, see §§ 2274 ff BGB). § 2279(2) BGB states that '[t]he provision of section 2077 also applies to a contract of inheritance between spouses, civil partners or engaged persons … to the extent that a third party is provided for'.[73] However, the applicability of the divorce rule (§ 2077 BGB) to inheritance contracts between spouses (§ 2279(2) BGB) can be realigned with the non-applicability of § 2077 BGB to life insurance contracts: a transfer via life insurance contract and a transfer via inheritance contract differ insofar as the life insurance contract is a contract between the contracting party and a third party different from the beneficiary, whereas the inheritance contract between the contracting party and his or her spouse is not. Thus, it is not the contractual nature of the will-substitute alone that explains the non-applicability of the divorce rule to will-substitutes, such as life insurance contracts, but it is also the fact that life insurance contracts are contracts with a third party.

iii. Will-Substitutes as Functional Equivalents?

Even though there is no reasonable doubt about the *status quo* of German law concerning the non-applicability of the testamentary default rules to will-substitutes, legal scholars increasingly plead otherwise. Their main argument is that the designation of a beneficiary in a life insurance contract is the 'functional equivalent' of a testamentary disposition and should therefore be treated in the same way.[74] However, it still needs to be established to what degree wills and will-substitutes are indeed 'functional equivalents'. As far as the application of the divorce rule is concerned, it would seem that the functional similarity is mainly based on the assumption that designations in life insurance contracts in favour of a spouse or civil partner are generally motivated by the same reasons as a testamentary disposition.[75] However, legal scholars such as Dieter Leipold acknowledge that, unlike with 'pure' testamentary provisions, in the case of life insurance contracts,

[73] See further Schlüter and Röthel, above n 62, § 23 para 11.

[74] See D Leipold in *Münchener Kommentar zum Bürgerlichen Gesetzbuch*, 6th edn (Munich, Beck, 2013) § 2077 para 38: 'Funktional kommt jedoch die Benennung des Ehegatten als Bezugsberechtigten durchaus einer letztwilligen Verfügung gleich, und sie beruht im Regelfall im selben Maße auf der familienrechtlichen Bindung'. ['However, the designation of a spouse as a beneficiary is indeed functionally equivalent to a testamentary disposition and, as a rule, relies to the same extent on relations defined by family law'.] See also R Stürner in *Jauernigs Kommentar zum BGB*, 15th edn (Munich, Beck, 2014) § 2077 para 8; J Petersen, 'Die Lebensversicherung im Bürgerlichen Recht' (2004) 204 *Archiv für die civilistische Praxis* 832, 852 ff.

[75] Leipold, above n 74, § 2077 para 38.

the interests of third parties (insurance companies) should be taken into account, as well as practical issues such as the prompt and effective handling of the insurance case.

V. Conclusions: Will-Substitutes from the Perspective of the Family

If there was one single conclusion and one way to tie up the loose ends, I would feel tempted to summarise that, from the perspective of the family, and as far as continental jurisdictions are concerned, will-substitutes do not present a major 'danger'. Quite the contrary. The statutory rules on compulsory shares not only protect the family members against wills, but also quite similarly and effectively against 'pure' lifetime gifts, even if such gifts, as well as will-substitutes, have been made many years before death. And will-substitutes are treated as lifetime gifts and therefore share their fate, as they are all subject to claims for additional compulsory shares, redemption or claw-back (see section III above). This is very telling of the position of the family in continental succession laws. The high value that continental jurisdictions assign to the family within succession law is reflected in the decision to grant the family members rights against wills, but also against lifetime gifts and will-substitutes. The protection of the family appears a central idea of succession laws and is therefore extended to other, similar, transactions that affect the family rights in a comparable way. This observation underlines both the central position that the family occupies within continental succession laws, and the strong link between succession law, the law of lifetime gifts and family law. Or, vice versa, the civilian jurisdictions generally aspire to enforce family rights notwithstanding the legal nature of a gratuitous transfer and the time at which it is effected, be it via will, will-substitute or lifetime gift.

This is at least true regarding *compulsory* family rights. Compulsory family rights such as the right to compulsory shares are more or less likewise exercised on wills and on will-substitutes. Civil law jurisdictions show a strong concern for anti-evasion strategies and have developed effective anti-evasion provisions that ensure the reintegration of transferred wealth into the calculation of compulsory shares.

But the image changes if one looks at *default* rules aimed at the protection of the family. At least as far as the German divorce rule is concerned, we have seen that the general wish to exercise family rights against will-substitutes does not lead to the corresponding application of default rules to will-substitutes. This might seem contradictory, given the strong support of family interests in the context of compulsory shares. However, this is based on a coherent view of will-substitutes. In both cases, will-substitutes are viewed as lifetime gifts and not as wills. As for compulsory shares, will-substitutes are taken into account in their calculation.

With regard to default rules on the interpretation of wills, these norms are not applicable to will-substitutes. What remains to be resolved and what does not fit in this picture is the incoherent assessment of life insurance. Interestingly, the most used will-substitute in civil law jurisdictions is also the will-substitute that is most likely to benefit from exemptions. If there are policy reasons that support a privilege for providential transfers, then this privilege should be applied to any transfer aiming to provide maintenance for the beneficiary.

16

Exploring Means of Transferring Wealth on Death: A Comparative Perspective

ALEXANDRA BRAUN AND ANNE RÖTHEL*

I. A Blind Spot on the Legal Landscape

As we noted in the introduction to this volume, will-substitutes represent a complex area of the law that has hitherto been largely unexplored. In fact, aside from the US and Italy, will-substitutes have generally received little attention from succession lawyers, leaving much of this area under-theorised, and creating a gap between the practical and economic relevance of will-substitutes on the one hand, and their theoretical study on the other.[1]

For instance, we have seen that in France, legal scholarship has been 'in denial'.[2] The few works that have engaged with the topic are mostly concerned with anticipated succession, or the prohibition of succession pacts, rather than offering an in-depth analysis of will-substitutes.[3] In Germany, will-substitutes seem to have sparked academic interest in the 1950s and 1960s,[4] but in recent decades a greater focus has been placed on instances of anticipated succession.[5] By contrast, in Italy, academics have shown a continuing interest in the subject since the publication in the 1980s of Antonio Palazzo's book on 'anomalous successions'.[6] It would seem that, at that time, Italian legal scholarship in this field was primarily under the influence of German and French legal thinking; this was especially so for the

* The authors would like to thank Gregor Christandl for his comments on an earlier draft of this chapter.

[1] See, for instance, chs 3 and 4 above VI and I.

[2] Ch 7 above, p 178.

[3] See the works cited by Pérès in ch 7, above fn 20 and 21.

[4] See the authors cited by T Kipp and H Coing, *Erbrecht* (Tübingen, Mohr Siebeck, 1990) 438.

[5] For an exception, see PA Windel, *Über die Modi der Nachfolge in das Vermögen einer natürlichen Person beim Todesfall* (Heidelberg, R v Decker, 1998).

[6] A Palazzo, *Autonomia contrattuale e successioni anomale* (Naples, Jovene, 1983).

studies on anticipated succession in Germany and those focusing on the prohibition of succession pacts in France.[7] What is interesting to note, however, is that, in Italy, legal scholars have been somewhat ahead of legal practice, as most of the instruments discussed in literature over the past 30 or so years have little practical relevance.[8] While in the US, legal scholars have studied the topic for decades, this has not been the case in other common law jurisdictions. In England and Wales legal literature examining will-substitutes is rather limited,[9] but that may be partly due to the overarching issue that, for many years, legal scholars have neglected the law of succession.[10] Similarly in Canada, Australia, and New Zealand, relatively few authors have engaged with the subject.[11]

One reason for this relative lack of attention to the study of the modes of transfer of wealth on death other than wills or intestacy may lie in the fact that most of the instruments used in practice fulfil a number of different functions and are traditionally analysed in other contexts. Several will-substitutes can operate as purely *inter vivos* instruments, so that it is not always immediately evident that they also allow for a transfer of wealth on death. Therefore, they are usually placed outside the 'real' or 'proper' succession law. Indeed, although will-substitutes have always existed in some form or other,[12] it is still not easy to place them within a particular legal discipline, and hence they tend to go unnoticed. As a consequence, in many jurisdictions they belong to the most uncertain, intricate, and incoherent areas of private law.

Several contributors to this volume have noted that relatively little is known about the behavioural patterns of testators in their respective legal systems, that some of the individual instruments employed in practice are under-researched or not well understood,[13] and that their interaction with the law of succession has not yet been examined in sufficient detail. In many cases, the exact nature of certain legal devices is still debated and it is sometimes unclear precisely how they operate and what their legal consequences are.[14]

This does not mean that will-substitutes are not relevant in legal practice. Even though the will may sometimes be the only instrument expressly regulated by national succession laws, at least in some jurisdictions, the economic importance of will-substitutes would appear to have attained unprecedented importance, especially as certain forms of investment (eg, life insurance and pensions) have

[7] Ch 6 above, pp 131 f.

[8] ibid.

[9] See ch 3 above, p 51 f. The same is true of Scotland. See ch 4 above, pp 79 f.

[10] KGC Reid, MJ De Waal and R Zimmermann (eds), *Comparative Succession Law, volume 1. Testamentary Formalities* (Oxford, OUP, 2011) x.

[11] An exception for Canada is AH Oosterhoff, *Oosterhoff on Wills and Successions*, 7th edn (Toronto, Carswell, 2011) and for Australia, R Croucher and P Vines, *Succession: Families, Property and Death*, 4th edn (Australia, LexisNexis Butterworths, 2013).

[12] See introduction above III.

[13] For examples, see chs 11 and 4 above, p 230 and pp 79 f.

[14] For examples see, for instance, chs 4 and 6 above, pp 79 f and p 139.

increased in popularity over the past decades.[15] This is true of the US, and also of Australia and New Zealand, where a 'non-probate revolution' has taken place.[16]

However, despite the fact that several contributions refer to a rise in the use of will-substitutes,[17] there seems to be a general lack of available statistical data concerning the use of the different instruments discussed and their overall economic relevance, and in many jurisdictions it is not known how much wealth is passed through wills. Nevertheless, several contributors were able to document significant increases in the use of individual mechanisms.[18]

II. Understanding Will-Substitutes

Although the term 'will-substitutes' is commonly used in the US, readers will have noticed that most legal systems analysed in this volume, including common law jurisdictions, do not employ a term of art that captures the array of instruments that in the eyes of a US lawyer fall under the heading 'will-substitutes'. Indeed, outside the US, the term 'will-substitutes' is hardly ever found in legal literature.[19] Most legal systems do not have another term of art that denotes the different devices functionally equivalent to wills. The reason for this might be that, as the contributions to this volume have shown, the instruments employed in practice vary in nature, so that it is perhaps not possible or even desirable to identify a term capable of capturing all of them. After all, most are instruments that are in and of themselves autonomous, often fulfilling a number of other functions aside from passing wealth on death.

Nonetheless, in some jurisdictions attempts have been made to identify terms that denote the many different instruments used to pass wealth on death. For instance, in Italy, where unlike in other civilian jurisdictions will-substitutes have long been at the centre of a lively scholarly debate, the instruments used have been referred to as '*istituti alternativi al testamento*', and more recently as part of the '*successioni anomale per contratto*' or the '*fenomeni parasuccessori*'.[20] Although by

[15] As to the magnitude in the US, see JH Langbein, 'Major Reforms of the Property Restatement and the Uniform Probate Code: Reformation, Harmless Error, and Nonprobate Transfers' (2012) 38 *American College of Trust and Estate Counsel Law Journal* 1, 12 ff.

[16] Ch 5 above VI.

[17] Chs 6, 7, 5 and 3 above III.B, I, VI and I.

[18] Although we do not have precise numbers, Pérès mentions that 60% of the French population has a life insurance policy. See ch 7 above, p 167. See further ch 6 above fn 33 for numbers on Italian life insurance and text after fn 47, for numbers on private pension plans. For numbers about the use of trusts in New Zealand, see ch 5 above fn 47 and registered private pension plans in Canada, ch 2 above I.D.i.a. See further ch 3 above I.

[19] This is true of the UK, but also of Australia and New Zealand. See ch 3 above VI.

[20] For details, see ch 6 above I.A. Christandl notes, however, that only the so-called *negozi transmorte* function as true will-substitutes.

the 1950s in Germany, Gustav Boehmer had used the term '*Testamentsersatz*',[21] it seems to have disappeared from German legal literature, clearing the way for the now more common expression '*lebzeitige Verfügungen auf den Todesfall*'.[22]

In the absence of a suitable expression capable of encapsulating the different devices that, like wills, can pass wealth on death, some contributors to this volume have discussed the topic in the context of transfers *that take place outside succession*, usually meaning outside substantive succession law, rather than procedural law, as is the case in the US.[23] In fact, the term 'non-probate transfers' is not particularly useful in the context of legal systems that do not have a probate procedure in place. Interestingly, the German Bundesgerichtshof has spoken of contracts in favour of third parties taking effect upon death as instruments that the testator can choose 'instead of testamentary dispositions' and that operate 'outside succession law'.[24] A similar expression is also found in the European Succession Regulation (Brussels IV),[25] which states in article 1(2)(g) that among the matters excluded from the scope of the Regulation are

> property rights, interests and assets created or transferred otherwise than by succession, for instance by way of gifts, joint ownership with a right of survivorship, pension plans, insurance contracts and arrangements of a similar nature, without prejudice to point (i) of Article 23(2).

The Regulation refers to transfers that take place otherwise than by succession,[26] the assumption being that these instruments are not currently captured by the law of succession of the individual Member States. To what extent this is the case will be discussed later.[27] Thus, will-substitutes are somewhat difficult to capture.

[21] G Boehmer, *Grundlagen der Bürgerlichen Rechtsordnung*, vol 2/2 (Tübingen, Mohr, 1952) 82 ff.

[22] Wieacker spoke of the 'lebzeitigen Zuwendungen auf den Todesfall'. F Wieacker, 'Zur lebzeitigen Zuwendung auf den Todesfall' in HC Nipperdey (ed), *FS Lehmann*, vol 1 (Tübingen, De Gruyter, 1956) 271 ff. Also common is the term 'Rechtsgeschäfte unter Lebenden auf den Todesfall'.

[23] See chs 6, 7 and 9 above, II, I and I.

[24] BGH 19 October 1983, (1984) *Neue Juristische Wochenschrift* 480, 481. See reference in ch 8 above III.C. W Marotzke in *von Staudingers Kommentar zum Bürgerlichen Gesetzbuch* (Berlin, De Gruyter, 2008) § 1922 BGB para 54 speaks of 'Sukzessionen am Erbrecht vorbei'.

[25] Regulation (EU) 650/2012 of the European Parliament and of the Council of 4 July 2012 on jurisdiction, applicable law, recognition and enforcement of decisions, and acceptance and enforcement of authentic instruments in matters of succession and on the creation of a European Certificate of Succession [2012] OJ L201/107.

[26] The same expression had already been used in the 1989 Convention on the law applicable to succession to the estates of deceased persons at art 1(2)(d). For an explanation of the article, see the Explanatory Report by Donovan Waters at 33 f. For an examination of the provision in the Regulation, see R Frimston, 'Chapter I: Scope and Definitions' in U Bergquist, D Damascelli, R Frimston, P Lagarde, F Odersky and B Reinhartz, *EU Regulation on Succession and Wills* (Cologne, Dr Otto Schmidt KG, 2015) 38, 45–47 and esp JP Schmidt 'Rechtsgeschäfte unter Lebenden auf den Todesfall' in A Dutta and J Weber (eds) *Internationales Erbrecht* (Munich, CH Beck, 2016) EU-ErbVO Art 1, paras 64 ff.

[27] See below at section IV.C.ii.

III. The Reality of Will-Substitutes

A. Types of Will-Substitute

The picture that emerges from the various contributions is complex, as the contributors have evinced different understandings of what should fall within the category of mechanisms that are functionally equivalent to wills.[28] Also, the instruments resorted to in the legal systems examined in this volume vary and, although some carry the same or a similar name, they may operate differently across jurisdictions. Below we provide an overview of the principal instruments that have been discussed in this book, in an attempt to identify certain patterns.

i. Life Insurance

There is little doubt that life insurance policies are taken out in all of the analysed jurisdictions and that they represent a highly popular and economically important type of will-substitute. They are widely used on the European continent,[29] but they also play a very important role in common law jurisdictions.[30] Only in Australia do they appear to be 'relatively rare', most likely due to the fact that superannuation pension schemes are not only compulsory for employees, but also enjoy certain tax privileges.[31]

In many jurisdictions, life insurance was already being used in the nineteenth century and at the beginning of the twentieth century.[32] Their emergence marks the transition from extended families to middle-class 'nuclear families' at the turn of the last century, as well as changes in lifestyle, in the composition of wealth, and the way in which care is provided for in old age.[33]

What makes life insurance policies, and more specifically beneficiary designations within such policies, will-substitutes is the fact that they allow for a person to nominate a beneficiary who will take the insurance proceeds directly upon death of the former. Though life insurance across different jurisdictions are far from being

[28] For an examination of the term, see introduction above II.

[29] See ch 6 above III.A; ch 7 above II.B; ch 9 above III.B; and ch 15 above III.B.iii.

[30] See chs 1, 2 and 12 above II.B, I.C.i and II.D. Data concerning England and Wales reveals a decrease in number. See ch 3 above II.C. For Scotland see ch 4 above VI.

[31] Ch 5 above at III.E.

[32] For England, see ch 3 above II.C; for Scotland, see ch 4 above VI; for New Zealand, see ch 5 above II.E; for Switzerland, see ch 9 above VI.B; for France, see ch 7 above II.B and for Germany, see ch 15 above III.B.iii, as well as R Zimmermann, *The Law of Obligations* (Oxford, OUP, 1996) 34 ff.

[33] For the importance of social factors to the law of succession, see MJ De Waal, 'Comparative Succession Law' in M Reimann and R Zimmermann (eds), *The Oxford Handbook of Comparative Law* (Oxford, OUP, 2008) 1077–79.

regulated in the same way, many legal systems have created a favourable environment, by explicitly exempting life insurance from the application of certain succession law rules. For instance, beneficiaries of such policies often enjoy privileges over creditors (eg, in Italy, the US, Canada, New Zealand, and Australia),[34] or over claims of family and dependants (especially in France, but also in England and Wales, Germany, and Switzerland).[35] In addition, they frequently benefit from tax privileges (eg, in France, Canada, and England and Wales, but not in the US),[36] which makes them highly desirable.

ii. Pension Schemes and Retirement Plans

While life insurance is used almost everywhere to pass wealth on death, private pension schemes and retirement plans of various kinds feature prominently in common law jurisdictions such as England and Wales, the US, and Canada.[37] In Australia, they are compulsory for every employee and, therefore, represent the most common will-substitute.[38] However, in New Zealand, they do not count among the instruments usually used to transfer wealth on death.[39]

Although the schemes and plans vary from jurisdiction to jurisdiction in terms of their structure and the type of death benefit they pay out, in most of the schemes, it is possible for a member of a pension scheme or plan to designate a beneficiary who will receive a death benefit payment, normally in the form of a pension or a lump-sum payment. The exception to this is England and Wales, and to some extent Australia, where such nominations are not generally binding on the scheme administrators, while remaining revocable until death.[40] Thus, pension nominations tend to operate like a will, though in the case of pensions, the choice of potential beneficiaries is often restricted by the respective schemes, in some cases to spouses or dependants.[41]

One of the reasons why investments in private pension schemes are popular in common law jurisdictions may be that they tend to enjoy considerable tax privileges,[42] and that the death benefits are passed outside probate, so that they do not in principle enter the estate. As a consequence, they are not generally available

[34] Ch 6 above III.A; ch 12 above II.D; ch 1 above IV.B; ch 2 above I.C; ch 5 above III.E.

[35] Ch 7 above II.B; ch 3 above II.C; ch 14 above V; ch 15 above III.D.iii; ch 9 above VI.B.

[36] Ch 7 above II.B; ch 2 above I.C.i; ch 3 above II.C; ch 1 above IV.A.

[37] See ch 3 above II.A, ch 1 above II.C and ch 12 above II.E, as well as ch 2 above I.D and E.

[38] Ch 5 above I.

[39] ibid.

[40] A Braun, 'Pension Death Benefits: Opportunities and Pitfalls' in B Häcker and C Mitchell (eds), *Current Issues in Succession Law* (Oxford, Hart Publishing, 2016) ch 10.

[41] This is true for Australia. See ch 5 above III.D. In England and Wales, it depends on each scheme. See ch 3 above II.A.i and iii.

[42] This is true of England and Wales, Canada and Australia. Although Australia has no estate tax, pensions enjoy a favourable tax regime in that benefits paid from superannuation funds are taxed less than other funds. For details, see ch 5 above III.D.

to the creditors of the deceased,[43] and are frequently, though not always, outside the scope of the power of courts under the family provision legislation.[44] Thus, similar to life insurance, they usually benefit from a favourable environment, partly because they offer a way to provide for the spouse or civil partner and other dependants.

Conversely, in civilian jurisdictions, private pension plans have only recently started to function as a means through which a plan member can pass wealth on death, as in the past they did not always offer the possibility of choosing the beneficiary of their death benefits.[45] In other words on death of the member, payments would sometimes be made directly and automatically to the spouse or to dependants, or be simply absorbed by the fund, without the member having any choice. For instance, in Italy, pension death benefits of private pension schemes would automatically pass to the surviving spouse, the children and the parents, so long as they were maintained by the plan holder, and, in their absence, the money would be kept in the fund.[46] However, since 1999, it is possible for a member of an Italian private pension scheme to nominate beneficiaries.[47] In Germany, the recently introduced 'Riester-Rente' theoretically allows the contracting party to nominate a beneficiary, but where the nominee is someone outside the circle of close family members, public subsidies and tax advantages are lost.[48]

iii. Bank and Other Savings Accounts

Certain types of bank account operate not just as a savings device, but can also represent a vehicle for passing wealth on death without the need for a will. For instance, in the US, the 'pay-on-death' bank accounts (PODs) are a popular type of account, alongside joint accounts, as well as trust and agency accounts. As the name suggests, PODs are bank accounts that are created in the name of the depositor and payable on his death to another person. They are, therefore, a type of asset-specific will, with transfer taking place outside probate.[49] In other common law jurisdictions, this type of account is not or, at least, not yet available. However, money can and is often held in a joint bank account,[50] with survivorship operating on death of one of the tenants, without the need for a will.

[43] See chs 1 and 12 above IV.B and II.E. In Scotland, the protection of creditors seems to be uncertain: ch 4 above VII.B.ii.

[44] This is the case in England and Wales. See ch 3 above III.E. For Australia, see ch 5 above III.G.

[45] In France, there have been several attempts to introduce private pension plans, which so far have failed for ideological and political reasons. See ch 7 above, p 167.

[46] Ch 6 above III.B.

[47] Under the Swiss social security system, a person can only nominate the beneficiary for certain types of insurance, part of the so-called third pillar. See ch 9 above VI.A, as well as R Aebi-Müller, 'Die drei Säulen der Vorsorge und ihr Verhältnis zum Güter- und Erbrecht des ZGB' (2009) *successio* 7 ff.

[48] §§ 10a, 82 and 92 ff Einkommensteuergesetz.

[49] See ch 1 above II.D.

[50] See chs 2, 3 and 5 above I.B.i.a, II.D.iii and II.B and III.B.

One problem that has emerged regarding jointly held bank accounts is that, unlike the case with POD accounts, where the form discloses the depositor's intention to transfer title to the account only at the depositor's death, with joint accounts the intention of the transferor is not always evident. Where it is not expressed clearly, the surviving joint tenant may not obtain the benefit of the account, but may hold it on trust for the estate of the deceased.[51] In this respect, the US POD accounts appear to be a more secure estate planning instrument.[52]

An aspect to note is that bank accounts, whether POD accounts or joint accounts, do not necessarily enjoy the favourable treatment that other will-substitutes, such as life insurance and pension plans, benefit from. For instance, in England and Wales, joint bank accounts fall within the scope of the court's jurisdiction under the family provision legislation. In Australia, their use is constrained by notional estate provisions that protect family members from loss of support following the death of their spouse, partner or parent.[53] In New Zealand too they are vulnerable to claims under the Property (Relationships) Act 1976.[54] In some legal systems creditors may also be able to obtain the wealth held in a bank account.[55] For instance, in the US states where the Uniform Probate Code (UPC) § 6-102(b) is in force, it will operate to make the beneficiary of any such transfer potentially liable to the settlor's creditors, up to the value of the assets received.[56] Thus, transfers on death through bank accounts do not always operate entirely beyond the remit of succession laws.

Interestingly, Swiss legal practice offers a person the option of establishing a joint account (*compte joint*) containing a clause capable of excluding the heirs of the deceased from becoming a party to the contract with the bank (*Erbenausschlussklausel*). However, it appears that the validity of such clauses is quite controversial, and that in certain circumstances the transaction can be qualified as a gift *mortis causa*, so that inheritance rules would ultimately apply.[57]

Other civil law jurisdictions discussed in this volume do not recognise bank accounts with survivorship operating upon death. In Germany, bank accounts can be transferred via a gift that takes effect on death, but from a legal point of view, the transfer is regarded as a testamentary disposition, unless the donor has lost substantial control over the bank account during his or her lifetime. It is, however, possible for a person to enter into a contract with the bank in favour of third parties which takes effect on death. Such contracts are not usually treated

[51] In common law jurisdictions this is often the effect of the operation of a presumption, which operates however differently across legal systems. See ch 1 above II.D; ch 2 above I.B.i.a; ch 3 above II.D.iii; ch 5 above II.B and III.B; and ch 12 above II.C. The operation of the presumption is important for creditors, as the wealth will be available to estate creditors. See ch 12 above III.

[52] See chs 1, 3 and 12 above II.D, V.A and II.B.

[53] See ch 5 above I.

[54] ibid.

[55] For England and Wales, see ch 3 above II.D.iii and, for the US, see ch 12 above II.B and C.

[56] Ch 12 above II.B.

[57] Ch 9 above II.

as testamentary for the purpose of applying conventional succession laws, and are therefore a way of preventing the application of succession laws, though they cannot avoid the forced heirship regime.[58] Although in Italy it is theoretically possible to enter into similar third-party contracts with a bank, to date it is unclear whether these contracts will be regarded as void due to a potential conflict with the prohibition of succession pacts.[59] For this reason, unlike in Germany, in Italy, such third-party contracts are not a reliable will-substitute, except in the context of life insurance, where they are specifically regulated.[60]

iv. Modes of Passing Real Property on Death

Just as it is possible to hold a bank account jointly, real property too can be held in joint names, and in common law jurisdictions it is a common way of holding real property,[61] especially for couples. As mentioned in relation to joint bank accounts, one consequence of holding property as joint tenants rather than as tenants in common, is that on death of one of the tenants, the other acquires absolute title to the property directly and automatically by way of survivorship (*ius accrescendi*). However, as we have noted before in relation to joint bank accounts, although the interest passes automatically, assets are not entirely outside the reach of creditors or dependants.[62]

Somewhat similar is the operation of the French 'clause tontine', often stipulated for cohabitants or for spouses with a separate property regime.[63] This is a clause whereby two people who acquire property together stipulate that on the death of either, the property is deemed the sole property of the survivor with retroactive effect. Therefore, unlike in the case of joint ownership, where both are entitled to the entirety together right from the start, in the case of the *tontine* there was only ever one owner. Another difference is that severance is not possible so that the survivorship cannot be avoided. For this reason it is questionable whether the *clause tontine* is actually similar to a disposition in a will, which is why Pérès defines them as 'impure' will-substitutes.[64] Although they would appear to be quite uncommon in France, as they go against the desire to keep property in the family, according to Matthews they are not infrequently used by British buyers of French houses as a means of replicating the most important feature of English joint tenancy, to which they are of course accustomed, ie, *survivorship*.[65] Austrian law too has a similar mechanism called 'Wohnungseigentum der Partner im Todesfall', which is

[58] See ch 8 above III.C.
[59] Ch 6 above III.B.iv.
[60] Arts 1920 ff of the Italian C Civ.
[61] Chs 1, 2, 3 and 5 above II.F, I.B, II.D and II.B and III.B.
[62] See above at III.A.iii.
[63] Ch 7 above II.A.iv.
[64] ibid at II.A.iv.
[65] Ch 11 above IV.D.

a popular form of joint ownership of residential apartments whereby on death of one of the owners, the share accrues to the surviving partner.[66]

In Scottish law, joint tenancy of real property would appear to be available only to trustees and members of an unincorporated association. Nonetheless, similar results may be achieved through a 'special destination', which is very common for spouses and represents one of the main types of will-substitute in Scottish law.[67] As with joint tenancy, upon death of one of the co-owners, the interest of one person is carried by operation of law to the survivor. Unlike in the case of joint ownership, however, such a destination must be inserted into the conveyance by the transferor at the request of those who are seeking the creation of the special destination in their favour.

Also within the category of will-substitutes capable of passing an interest in land outside the conventional succession laws, and without the need for a will, fall Transfer-On-Death Deeds of Land (TODs), which are a fairly recent legal creature and unique to the US market. TODs provide that an individual owning an interest in land may designate one or more beneficiaries who will receive the interest on the owner's death outside probate, without the need to comply with formality requirements for wills.[68] While the owner is alive, the beneficiaries have no interest in the land, which distinguishes it from joint tenancies, the French *tontine*, the Austrian 'Wohnungseigentum der Partner im Todesfall', and the Scottish special destinations.

Finally, also within this category might fall the property entitlement claims of spouses, civil union partners and cohabitants in New Zealand, which operate as a means of transferring property to the surviving partner outside the will.[69] Although the transfer arises from an application for division made by the surviving spouse, and not from an act of *disposition* of the deceased, Peart qualifies these transfers as will-substitutes. This is because they offer a way to obtain and pass property outside succession laws, without the need for a will or the application of intestacy rules.[70]

v. Trusts

One of the oldest mechanisms for the transfer of wealth on death, especially in common law jurisdictions, are trusts, which can take various forms. Those that

[66] Regulated in § 14 *Wohnungseigentumsgesetz* of 2002. For a commentary of the provision, see C Prader, *Manz Wohnrecht, WEG 2002*, 4th edn (Vienna, Manz, 2015) and H Würth, M Zingher, P Kovanyi and I Etzersdorfer, *Miet-und Wohnrecht*, vol 2, 23rd edn (Vienna, Manz, 2015) § 14 *Wohnungseigentumsgesetz*.

[67] Ch 4 above V.

[68] Ch 1 above II.E.

[69] See ch 5 above II.A.

[70] Interesting to note in this context are also marital agreements that establish a continued community of property that seems to be common in rural areas of Bavaria, and that avoid claw-back claims of compulsory heirs. See ch 8 above VI.B.

come perhaps closest to wills are revocable trusts, as they share most of the characteristics of the will, in that: they are not asset specific; they leave the settlor with considerable freedom to enjoy and dispose of the trust fund during his or her lifetime; and they remain revocable until the moment of the settlor's death. The advantage of a revocable trust over a will is that the settlor can determine the distribution of wealth on death, often for more than one generation, whilst at the same time also avoiding probate.

Although revocable trusts are very popular in the US, as well as in offshore jurisdictions,[71] this is, perhaps surprisingly, not true of other common law jurisdictions, such as Australia, Canada,[72] and England and Wales,[73] nor do they seem to be common in Scotland.[74] This might be explained partly because of tax reasons, but also because there is a risk that due to the reservation of powers, the trust will be considered a sham and thus be void, or that assets will be held not to have been effectively segregated from the settlor's creditors.[75] In other words, it is often unclear how far the settlor can reserve certain rights.[76]

That said, even when they are not revocable, *inter vivos* trusts remain an interesting estate planning device.[77] For instance, in New Zealand, certain types of discretionary trust function as will-substitutes where the settlor is the trustee (or retains powers to remove trustees) as well as the primary beneficiary, and can nominate new beneficiaries at any time.[78] Matthews notes that will-substitute effects are typical also of so called 'thin' trusts, popular in offshore jurisdictions, whereby property is held by a trustee for a beneficiary (often the settlor) for life, with the power for the beneficiary to appoint capital to himself, and subject thereto on trust for such person or persons as the beneficiary may appoint.[79]

As Christandl and Jakob have pointed out, both Italy and Switzerland have ratified the Hague Trusts Convention,[80] and trusts can potentially be used as will-substitutes, given that the Convention does not exclude the possibility of recognising trusts in which the settlor reserves certain powers.[81] However, for that to happen the choice of the law governing the trust would need to admit revocable

[71] Ch 1 above II.A and ch 11 above IV.A.

[72] Chs 2 and 12 above, p 32 and II.A. The only exceptions are *alter ego* and joint partner trusts. See MJ Rochwerg and LA Hemmings, 'Will Substitutes in Canada' (2008) 28 *Estates, Trusts & Pensions Journal* 50, 52–54.

[73] See ch 3 above, p 53.

[74] Ch 4 above, p 80.

[75] *Tasarruf Mevduati Sigorta Fonu v Merrill Lynch Bank and Trust Company (Cayman) Ltd and others (Cayman Islands)* [2011] UKPC 17.

[76] Ch 3 above, p 53, ch 5 above, p 120, ch 12 above, pp 255 f.

[77] See ch 11 above IV.A.

[78] Unlike in England and Wales, in New Zealand, they seem to be fiscally neutral. Ch 5 above II.C.

[79] Ch 11 above IV.A.

[80] Ch 6 above, p 148 and ch 9 above, p 205.

[81] Art 2 of the Hague Convention on the Law Applicable to Trusts and on their Recognition of 1 July 1985.

trusts and there is a risk that the trust will be considered a sham in the legal system in which recognition is sought. For this reason, they do not seem to be common in Italy.[82]

vi. Foundations

Like trusts, foundations, and especially private purpose foundations, can represent an interesting vehicle for the transfer of wealth on death of a person. Although in principle they are lifetime instruments that take immediate effect, they can be structured in a way that allows the founder to pass wealth to chosen beneficiaries, which in practice are often members of the founder's family.

Private purpose foundations are quite common in civil law jurisdictions, and increasingly also in offshore ones.[83] Although in Germany the admissibility of private and family foundations was debated for a long time, today they are widely accepted by legislatures and courts,[84] even though legal scholars have raised the concern that their use may lead to the creation of a private 'parallel world' of succession law.[85] Austria has permitted private purpose foundations since 1993,[86] whereas Switzerland has recognised them since the coming into force of the Swiss Civil Code in 1911, and Liechtenstein since 1937. By contrast, in Italy and France, private purpose foundations are not recognised and therefore cannot be used as a will-substitute.

Private foundations operate as will-substitutes where they allow the founder to be a beneficiary, or even the sole beneficiary, and to reserve extensive rights to himself or herself, such as a right to change the purpose of the foundation, or to revoke it. In such cases, a foundation may achieve more or less what certain trusts can achieve and can therefore function as a useful estate planning tool. However, according to Matthews, it is rare to find a system that allows the transfer to third parties of the founder's reserved rights (where such rights are lawful in the first place) or of the rights conferred upon beneficiaries.[87] Thus, at least from the perspective of international investors, the usefulness of foundations as will-substitutes is limited.

The contributions in this volume show that such private purpose foundations can differ in nature and that, while in some legal systems they can function as reliable will-substitutes, capable of pursuing a variety of different purposes, in others their use may be restricted. For instance, Swiss private purpose foundations can function as will-substitutes, but they entail certain risks, and the use of the

[82] See ch 6 above IV.A.

[83] P Panico, *Private Foundations: Law and Practice* (Oxford, OUP, 2014).

[84] Ch 8 above V.B.

[85] A Dutta, *Warum Erbrecht—Das Vermögensrecht des Generationenwechsels in funktionaler Betrachtung* (Tübingen, Mohr Siebeck, 2014).

[86] For an overview, see S Kalss, 'Privatstiftung' in S Kalss, C Nowotny and M Schauer, *Österreichisches Gesellschaftsrecht* (Vienna, Manz Kampfl, 2008) 1295 ff.

[87] Ch 11 above IV.C.

family foundation is restricted. They are also not immune from forced heirship claims.[88] By contrast, the Liechtenstein mixed family foundations would appear to be a much more attractive and flexible device.[89]

vii. Gifts Mortis Causa

Gifts *mortis causa* represent one of the oldest will-substitutes, dating back to Roman times and possibly predating the will.[90] Though known to most common law jurisdictions, at least in the US, as well as in Australia and in New Zealand, they are not often used.[91] The same is true of Scotland.[92] Although it is difficult to judge whether they are still relevant in practice, in England and Wales recent case law indicates that they have not fallen entirely into disuse.[93]

The English *donatio mortis causa* consists of a revocable gift made during a person's lifetime, in contemplation of the donor's impending death, but which takes effect only on his death. It is a useful device insofar as it does not require any formalities, though it requires delivery of the asset to the donee during the lifetime of the donor, and can only operate when there is an impending death. In other words, in order for the donation to be valid, the donor must be considering the probability of death in the near future, and not just sometime in the future, and for a specific reason. Upon his death, the donee is automatically entitled to the property which is usually already in his possession. Thus, the *donatio mortis causa* can only be employed in certain specific circumstances. In addition, it may not represent the most reliable will-substitute.[94] In fact, one difficulty with this instrument is that due to its informal nature, it is uncertain whether there is sufficient evidence to prove that such a donation was made.

Although in the course of the codification movements the *donatio mortis causa* was abolished in some civil law jurisdictions, such as in France and Italy,[95] it still exists in some civil law jurisdictions, though perhaps in a different form. For instance, the German BGB recognises the *Schenkungsversprechen von Todes wegen* (§ 2301 BGB), which has different requirements from the English *donatio mortis causa*.[96] Indeed, unless there is a lifetime loss of ownership of the gifted asset, the

[88] See ch 9 above III.D.

[89] ibid.

[90] H Lange and K Kuchinke, *Erbrecht*, 5th edn (Munich, CH Beck, 2001) 740.

[91] Ch 1 above II.H and ch 5 above, pp 108 f.

[92] Ch 4 above, p 80.

[93] Ch 3 above II.E.

[94] Even though in common law jurisdictions the *donatio mortis causa* seems to feature similar characteristics, there are also some differences, as only England and Wales allow for real property to be the subject matter of such a gift. See ch 5 above, p 108.

[95] In Italy, there was a proposal to introduce the *donatio mortis causa*. See bill no 1043 of 27 September 2006 discussed in A Braun, 'Testamentary Freedom and its Restrictions in French and Italian law: Trends and Shifts' in R Zimmermann (ed), *Testierfreiheit/Freedom of Testation* (Tübingen, Mohr Siebeck, 2012) 58, 77.

[96] See the discussion in ch 8 above III.B.

gift is clearly subject to succession law, thus requiring compliance with formality requirements.[97]

viii. Clauses in Partnership Agreements

Clauses in partnership agreements also show features of will-substitutes but only insofar as they affect the transfer of wealth upon death. Unlike a will they are not *dispositions* made by the testator himself, but are the result of an agreement between the partners. Hence, they cannot be unilaterally revoked. Nevertheless, they are a means of passing wealth on death insofar as, in principle, partnership shares cannot be freely disposed of through the use of a will. In other words, the testator cannot nominate his or her successor to the partnership by means of a will, so that clauses in partnership agreements are not technically a *substitute*, but rather do something that a will cannot. Partnership clauses are *necessary* in order to nominate a beneficiary of one's share upon death. Under German law,[98] and contrary to Italian law,[99] the nomination of the beneficiary does not of itself transfer the share into the hands of the nominated beneficiary, unless the beneficiary is also the sole testamentary or intestate heir.

Among the jurisdictions examined in this volume, such clauses seem to be especially popular in Germany, Switzerland and Italy.[100] Notwithstanding the fact that they differ in content and form, their specific importance probably relates to the high number of family-run small and middle-sized businesses, which traditionally favour the 'personalised' partnership to 'anonymised' corporations.

Besides the various different denominations, these clauses provide first for the continuation of a partnership upon the death of a partner, by preventing its termination ('continuation clauses'), and, secondly, for the nomination of a beneficiary of the deceased's share either by way of an accrual clause ('consolidation clause'), or by rendering the partnership share heritable ('succession clause' or 'successor clause').[101] The reasons why such clauses are used are to protect the interests of the surviving partners, as well as to secure the 'personal' nature of the partnership.[102]

As partnerships are strongly linked to family-run businesses, which generally enjoy societal support, legislatures as well as courts have often been willing to exempt the succession to partnership shares from rules of succession law, which would otherwise apply. However, partnership shares are not granted the same privileges as, for instance, life insurance.[103] Indeed, in Italy, recent tax law reforms

[97] § 2301 BGB.

[98] Ch 8 above VII.B. The same is true for Austria, see S Kalss and G Probst, *Familienunternehmen* (Vienna, Manz, 2013) paras 20/30 and 20/32.

[99] Ch 6 above III.C.

[100] See chs 6, 8 and 9 above III.C, VII.B and II. For Austria, where they seem to be common too, see Kalss and Probst, above n 98, paras 20/27 ff.

[101] For an overview, see ch 10 above V.A.

[102] Ch 6 above III.C, and ch 8 above VII.A and B.

[103] See above at III.A.i.

have put an end to former tax privileges and partnership shares are now included in the taxable estate.[104] German courts consider partnership shares in every respect as part of the estate, especially as far as compulsory shares are concerned.[105] Jakob reminds us that in certain circumstances a Swiss court may qualify succession clauses as testamentary dispositions, thereby rendering them subject to the rules of succession law.[106]

ix. *Powers of Attorney and Mandates*

Certain types of powers of attorney or mandates can also function as will-substitutes where they can last beyond the death of the attorney or mandator, though usually in an indirect way. Such instruments are common in Australia and take the form of irrevocable powers of attorney.[107] German law recognises both *trans-mortem* mandates, which do not expire upon death of the mandator, and *post-mortem* mandates, which only come into force upon death.[108] Certain types of mandates or powers of attorney would also seem to be recognised in Italy and Switzerland.[109]

Such powers of attorneys and mandates are increasingly recognised, partly due to the rise of 'enduring' or 'lasting' powers of attorney that help manage property and financial affairs in case of mental incapacity.[110] What the various powers of attorney and mandates have in common is that they do not technically *substitute* wills, insofar as they do not in and of themselves *transfer* or *dispose* of wealth upon death to a specific beneficiary. That said, they enable the attorney or mandatary to make dispositions for the grantee or mandator, after the latter's death and out of the estate. Indeed, for the property to be transferred, the attorney or mandatary still has to make a gift.

Hence, for a *post-mortem* mandate to serve as a will-substitute, it must enable the attorney to make dispositions. This is not, for instance, the case with the French *mandat à effet posthume*, as it does not allow for dispositions, at least not against the wishes of the heirs,[111] and, consequently, is not a typical will-substitute.[112] Conversely, in Germany, practitioners regularly recommend testators

[104] Ch 6 above III.C, fn 66.

[105] Ch 8 above VII.B, fn 43; for further law reforms see A Röthel, *Ist unser Erbrecht noch zeitgemäß?* (Munich, Beck, 2010) A 40 ff.

[106] Ch 9 above II, text after fn 17.

[107] Ch 5 above III.H.

[108] Mentioned in ch 8 above IV.B.

[109] Ch 6 above III.D.v, and ch 9 above II.

[110] See the country report by A Röthel, 'Private Vorsorge im internationalen Rechtsverkehr' in V Lipp (ed), *Handbuch der Vorsorgeverfügungen* (Munich, F Vahlen, 2009) §§ 22–31.

[111] See Cass Civ 1ère, 12 May 2010 no 09-10.556. A Leroyer, *Droit des Successions* 3th edn (Paris, Dalloz, 2014) para 438; P Malaurie and C Brenner, *Malaurie/Aynes: Les successions, les libéralités*, 6th edn (Paris, Dalloz, 2014) para 169; for a different assessment, see M Grimaldi, *Le mandat à éffet posthume* (Issy les Moulineaux, Défrenois, 2007) 3.

[112] Ch 7 above I.

to complement wills with such *post-mortem* mandates.[113] The reason for this is that the mandatary can be given the power to act on behalf of the estate from the moment of death. In Australia, enduring powers of attorney can be used to alter the effect of a will.[114] In Italy, *post-mortem* mandates can be employed to function as a supplementary contract, for instance to savings accounts, which can therefore work more effectively.[115]

As mandates *post-mortem* or powers of attorney do not in and of themselves transfer wealth upon death, they would appear to create less tension with the otherwise applicable rules of succession law. Nonetheless, some frictions can arise. For instance, in Italy, courts are unsure about a possible clash with the prohibition of succession contracts.[116] While the Australian legislature is concerned that the interests of the beneficiary of the last will might be harmed,[117] German courts do not generally interfere, so long as the mandate remains revocable by the heirs.[118] Thus, mandates or powers of attorney do not necessarily fall outside the reach of succession law rules and in some ways are not entirely reliable.[119]

B. Trends and Common Fundamental Features

It is clear from the examination of the different modes of transfer listed above, that the mechanisms employed in practice vary greatly.[120] It would seem that US legal practice offers the greatest variety of instruments, several of which are not usually available elsewhere (eg, POD and TODs).[121] And, while Italian legal scholars have devised a number of different instruments, many are not actually used in practice.[122]

What is interesting to note is that, unlike what one might expect, there are no clear and uniform patterns within common and civil law jurisdictions. For instance, the picture emerging from the French contribution differs considerably from the

[113] See K-H Schramm in F Säcker, R Rixecker, H Oetker and B Limperg (eds), *Münchener Kommentar zum Bürgerlichen Gesetzbuch*, 6th edn (Munich, Beck, 2012) § 168 para 30 and in the context of family businesses, R Krause 'Family Business Succession Planning in Germany—Strategies for Intergenerational Transfer in a Globalized World' in I Stamm, P Breitschmid and M Kohli (eds), *Doing Succession in Europe* (Zurich, Schulthess, 2011) 299, 302.

[114] Ch 5 above III.H.

[115] Ch 6 above III.D.v.

[116] ibid.

[117] Ch 5 above III.H.

[118] Ch 8 above IV.B.

[119] See ch 6 above III.D.v and ch 9 above II.

[120] There are also other devices discussed by some of the authors, which are not included in the list above. See the many instruments discussed in Italian legal literature and examined by Christandl in ch 6 above III. See also contracts to make a will referred to in ch 4 above VIII and ch 5 above III.F, as well as instruments employed to transfer property of indigenous populations. See ch 2 and ch 5 above II.A and III.I.

[121] Ch 1 above II.D, E and G.

[122] Ch 6 above VII.

Italian study, and there are also interesting dissimilarities between Switzerland, Liechtenstein, and Germany. The same is true of common law jurisdictions. For instance, in Australia, the legal landscape is very different from the one we find in New Zealand, and even between the US and England and Wales, there are significant divergences in the type of instruments used.

That said, some instruments tend to be more characteristic of either the common law or the civil law jurisdictions. For instance, while trusts feature prominently in common law jurisdictions, foundations and contracts in favour of third parties with effect on death are more popular in civil law jurisdictions.[123] By contrast, other instruments are peculiar to particular legal systems, such as the New Zealand relationship property entitlement claims,[124] or the Scottish special destinations.[125] On the other hand, there are also some instruments that are employed almost everywhere, such as life insurance, which have become increasingly popular and often constitute the 'emblematic' will-substitute, especially in civil law jurisdictions.[126] Another trend seems to be the emergence of private pension schemes as will-substitutes, both in common and some civil law jurisdictions.

If one were to try to group these instruments together, one could say that some mechanisms represent financial instruments that provide a person primarily with an investment opportunity. For instance, life insurance, retirement and pension plans, and, to some extent, bank accounts, represent saving mechanisms, which provide for future events such as retirement, old age and illness, while also offering the option of passing a benefit on death of the person making the investment, often for the maintenance of dependants. Other mechanisms explored in this volume, though also representing investment opportunities, are primarily modes of holding, managing, and preserving property rights, such as joint tenancies, trusts, and foundations,[127] the latter two also representing instruments for the segregation of assets. Among those instruments aimed at preserving wealth, also count various clauses in partnership agreements and companies. Conversely, the *donatio mortis causa* does not have ancillary purposes, other than to benefit the donee on death of the donor. Finally, one could also distinguish between those instruments through which the person can *dispose* of wealth on death, and those that in and of themselves are not capable of effecting a *transfer* of wealth, but that allow for the succession process to be structured in a certain way. These include powers of attorney or clauses in partnership agreements.

[123] Chs 6 and 8 above II.B and III and III.C and V.B.

[124] See ch 5 above II.A.

[125] Ch 4 above V.

[126] See ch 6 above III.A; ch 7 above II.B; and ch 9 above VI.B.

[127] Among these is also the Italian *patto di famiglia*. For an analysis of the *patto di famiglia*, see ch 6 above V.

It follows from the above analysis that, in many ways, most of the instruments examined in this volume perform more functions than a will. In other words, their main purpose may not necessarily be that of determining the distribution of wealth on the death of a person. Nevertheless, they can also be used to pass wealth or, as we noted, to structure the distribution and transfer of wealth on death, which is the function they share with the will. In doing so, they do not establish an heir or legatee, but simply identify a beneficiary, usually of a particular set of assets, rather than the entire estate. Hence, the beneficiary does not succeed to an inheritance or a legacy, though functionally the benefit often looks just like a legacy under a will. Indeed, most modes of transfer examined in this book are *asset-specific*. As a consequence, for instance, beneficiary designations in a life insurance, or nominations in retirement schemes, cannot be used to transfer assets other than those invested in the life insurance policy or the pension plan. The same applies to contracts entered into, for instance, with a bank in favour of third parties that take effect on death.[128]

Another interesting aspect to note is that some of the instruments explored in the volume are contractual in nature. This is, for example, true for powers of attorney and clauses in partnerships. Moreover, in Italy as well as in Germany, contracts in favour of third parties with effect on death represent a very common will-substitute that can be employed in order to transfer different types of wealth: wealth invested in a bank account, a life insurance, or in a pension plan etc. In that sense they can serve a similar function to that served by beneficiary designations in the US or Canada, which are employed in different contexts, from insurance, to banking and pensions.

Finally, it has also emerged that some of the instruments have changed over time. For instance, pensions have shifted from being an instrument primarily designed to provide for retirement in old age or ill health, to being an instrument that is capable of passing a considerable amount of wealth to chosen beneficiaries (under favourable conditions).[129] Conversely, life insurance has almost developed in the opposite direction. Originally, they were conceived of primarily as a device operating on death of the contracting party, and were therefore regarded as pure 'risk' or 'gambling' contracts.[130] However, as several contributors have highlighted, modern day insurance policies also serve lifetime purposes and often operate primarily as 'saving devices'.[131] As a consequence, the transfer of wealth upon death represents one, but not necessarily the only, important feature of life insurance policies.

[128] Ch 8 above III.C.

[129] This is, for instance, also true of complementary private pension plans in Italy. See ch 6 above III.B.

[130] For France, see ch 7 above II.B, text at fn 54.

[131] See below at IV.B.i.

IV. Rationale Behind the Use of Will-Substitutes

A. Introduction

In most parts of the Western world, the 'paradigm' instrument for the transfer of wealth on death foreseen by the legislature is the will. The law of wills therefore represents the 'gold standard' or the 'benchmark',[132] against which will-substitutes tend to be compared. Hence, the legal discourse is likely to be centred on what will-substitutes can or cannot do and, in particular, on which rules applicable to wills they *avoid*.[133]

One of the most interesting questions in this context is in fact why people might pass wealth on death through means other than wills. As has already emerged above, many of the instruments analysed fulfil more than one function with the possibility of passing benefits on death often being a secondary purpose. Hence, it is difficult to determine which of these functions is the key factor driving testators to choose one instrument over another. The examination of the rationale behind will-substitutes is not an easy task and it is one that leads into uncertain territories, especially given the lack of empirical data or of sociological studies carried out in this field. Little is known about the subjective motives of those who use these instruments, and much is therefore speculative. Moreover, explicit or apparent reasons may hide less apparent or implicit ones. While one instrument may be used for a particular purpose in one legal system, in another that same instrument may be employed for very different purposes. Even within the same legal system, the use of individual devices may be motivated by very different reasons, such that it is often difficult to generalise. Also, in the majority of the cases, motives are more likely 'many and varied'.[134]

Nevertheless, it is certainly possible to identify features which from the perspective of a testator may render individual mechanisms particularly advantageous. Generally speaking, these can be classified into two broad categories: financial advantages and non-financial ones. As to the former, some will-substitutes may be attractive from an economic perspective due to the tax advantages they offer,[135] or because they reduce procedural costs (eg, the cost of probate or the cost of preparing a will).[136] They may also be popular because they simplify the transfer of wealth (by making it more direct,[137] less formal[138] and less time-consuming),[139]

[132] Ch 7 above III.B.

[133] See below at V.A.

[134] Ch 5 above IV; see also ch 1 above I; ch 3 above IV.

[135] Ch 2 above II.A; ch 3 above IV.C; ch 5 above IV; ch 9 above I; ch12 above I.A. But see ch 6 above VII.

[136] Ch 1 above I; ch 12 above I.A; but see ch 3 above IV.B for England and Wales.

[137] Ch 3 above IV.B for England and Wales, and ch 4 above II.C for Scotland.

[138] Ch 1 above I; ch 2 above II.A, and ch 4 above II.D.

[139] For the US and Canada, see ch 12 above I.A.

provide greater flexibility, or greater predictability,[140] especially where they can shield the beneficiaries from claims of creditors,[141] as well as family members and dependants.[142]

However, there are also non-financial factors that may encourage a person to choose one instrument over another, and these can be just as important. Will-substitutes may, for instance, be used in order to obtain and provide family members and dependants with higher yields,[143] to exercise control over future generations,[144] to preserve wealth within the family,[145] and to avoid the dissipation of assets[146] as well as the potential fragmentation of businesses.[147] They might also be used to guarantee confidentiality and privacy,[148] to allow a freer choice of governing laws,[149] or to promote family values and dynastic identity.[150] Hence, will-substitutes may serve a range of financial, as well as non-financial goals.

One might feel tempted to express a value judgement over the potential reasons or explanations just listed, and to categorise the reasons into 'good' and 'bad', or into 'welcomed' and 'unwelcomed', or even 'dubious' explanations. Sometimes it may not be easy or possible to refrain from such evaluations.[151] Depending on whether one takes the perspective of a testator, beneficiary, heir, dependant, creditor, investor, a financial adviser, or financial provider, will-substitutes may look just like another way of 'investing and passing wealth' on death,[152] or a means of avoiding rules that would otherwise be applicable.[153]

[140] Jakob in ch 9 above, p 196, states that 'the wealth distribution becomes more predictable and controllable, as a monitored step-by-step transfer of the assets is possible'.

[141] For Canada, see ch 2 above II.2.

[142] Ch 12 above I.D for Canada and the US. For the US, see also ch 1 above IV.C; ch 9 above I, and III.D for Switzerland, and ch 3 above III.E and IV.D for England and Wales.

[143] Ch 5 above IV and ch 3 above IV.A.

[144] Ch 5 above IV for New Zealand and ch 4 above II.B for Scotland.

[145] Here see ch 8 above V.B on perpetual dispositions through the use of foundations. By contrast, Jakob reports that in Switzerland, the trend of foundations goes not towards perpetuation but rather towards the distribution of all foundation assets to the beneficiaries. See ch 9 above III.A, text before fn 21.

[146] See ch 9 above I. On fragmentation of assets, see also Christandl in ch 6 above V, who points however at the fact that the will-substitutes available in Italy cannot really avoid fragmentation, not even the *patto di famiglia*.

[147] Ch 10 above III and ch 6 above V.

[148] Ch 1 above I; ch 2 above II.A; ch 3 above IV.B; ch 4 above II.B; and ch 12 above, fn 6.

[149] Ch 12 above, fn 6 for the US. See also ch 4 above, text at fn 17.

[150] Ch 9 above VII with regard to foundations; see also ch 6 above III.C with regard to family businesses.

[151] For instance, while Dutta in ch 8 above VIII thinks that will-substitutes should be regarded with suspicion, Jakob in ch 9 above VII advocates switching from a 'negative' avoidance-based approach to a 'constructive' one.

[152] This is more likely to be the common law perspective: see ch 3 above IV; ch 11 above V; and ch 14 above III.

[153] See, esp the analysis from the German and French perspective described in chs 8 above V and 7 above I. In contrast, see ch 9 above VII and ch 11 above V.

However, value judgements are frequently based on the assumption that all choices are conscious and rational, which may not always be the case. In fact, one aspect that has emerged from the contributions is that there is not always a clear estate planning strategy behind the use of particular instruments. The idea that people are perfectly aware of the (at least perceived) limitations of the will and the law applicable to wills, or the procedural aspects of the transfer on death, as well as of the various benefits of other available instruments, may actually be misleading. This is partly due to the fact that with some of these instruments, the estate planning features are not at the forefront of the person's mind. While someone writing a will usually intends to distribute assets on death and to benefit another person, pension schemes are often entered into when a person is first employed, and the idea of succession is remote.[154] Where, as in Australia, pension schemes are compulsory, an employee has no choice about whether or not to join the scheme. The circumstances for a person who sets up a trust or a foundation are likely to be different, as they would normally employ the services of a financial or legal adviser, who may alert the client to the need to also plan his or her succession.

We have further learned that there may be instances in which a will cannot be used, even if the deceased would have wanted to. For instance, in Germany and Italy, it is not possible to dispose of shares in partnerships through a will.[155] The same is true of death benefits of English private pension schemes, which require the scheme member to complete a nomination form as provided by the respective scheme.[156] We should also not forget that sometimes it is the government, the legislature, or the courts themselves that create a favourable environment in order to encourage citizens to use a certain device, for instance, through tax incentives or more favourable formality requirements,[157] or by exempting beneficiaries from claims made by creditors, family members, or dependants. It is, therefore, difficult to provide a definitive assessment of the true motivations behind the use and proliferation of will-substitutes. In fact, one could read the use of a particular instrument both as an attempt to avoid certain rules and, at the same time, as an expression of different needs, and yet equally legitimate. Even in the US, it would seem that the rise of will-substitutes is not just to be explained as a result of simple dissatisfaction with the efficiency of the probate procedures.[158]

In order to fully capture the phenomenon of will-substitutes, and the breath of different characteristics they feature, it is perhaps more useful to distinguish between motives that are essentially related to the specific traits of some of the instruments examined (below at IV.B), and motives that are related to the nature and effect of the current law of wills and succession more generally (below at IV.C).

[154] See ch 3 above IV and ch 12 above I.A.

[155] Ch 8 above VII.B.

[156] Ch 3 above II.A.iii.

[157] See ch 3 above IV.

[158] Ch 4 above, text after fn 7.

The latter include the procedural aspects of the transfer of wealth, which might be perceived as limiting or outdated, and which some testators or estate planners may want to avoid. Of course, one difficulty with this is that one sought after characteristic of a will-substitute may at the same time also represent a perceived disadvantage of the will and its related rules, so that it is not always possible to draw a clear distinction. Nevertheless, it is important not to view will-substitutes merely as mechanisms of avoidance,[159] especially since people may be wrong about the consequences, and assume that they can escape certain rules, when in reality they cannot.[160]

B. Motives Related to the Specific Nature and Characteristics of Certain Will-Substitutes

One of the reasons why people use certain will-substitutes is that usually they can offer something that wills cannot, and are at times also more 'sophisticated'.[161] In a way, the 'more' they offer lies in the fact that they are different from wills. After all, if they were too similar, what would be the point of using them?[162]

Generally speaking, most will-substitutes are less 'death-related' and, therefore, perhaps less emotive than wills. As Thomas Atkinson put it some years ago, '[a] superstitious prejudice against wills is found in many persons past middle age. Apparently they think that testamentary preparation for disposition of their property at their death will somehow hasten their demise'.[163] Will-substitutes do not usually force people to go through the tragic rituals of will-making, so that they can evade the sense of definite end that accompanies a will.[164] As noted earlier, they are often entered into at an early stage of a person's life, when they first start a job or have a family, and they are not yet in the mindset of planning their succession. One could, for instance, argue that for some people, the decision to use a life insurance has more to do with the lifetime aspects of the life insurance, and that the effects that take place upon death are a mere 'add on'. A similar argument could be made about joint bank accounts. Several contributions have shown that it is common for couples to hold bank accounts jointly, and the reason for that may be in the first instance administrative convenience,[165] rather than a conscious

[159] See ch 3 above IV; ch 4 above II; ch 9 above VII; and ch 12 above I.A.

[160] See, for instance, the part concerning claims of family members and dependants, below at IV.C.ii.b.

[161] See ch 11 above IV.

[162] See Christandl in ch 6 above, p 132: '[T]hey [will-substitutes] would not present sufficient advantages that would set them apart from wills'.

[163] TE Atkinson, *Handbook of the Laws of Wills* (St Paul MN, West Publishing Co, 1937) 122.

[164] A Zoppini, 'Contributo allo studio delle disposizioni testamentarie "in forma indiretta"' (1998) 52 *Rivista Trimestrale di Diritto e Procedura Civile* 1077, 1080, fn 6; D Clark (ed), *The Sociology of Death: Theory, Culture, Practice* (Oxford, Blackwell, 1993).

[165] Ch 2 above I.B.i.a and ch 3 above II.D.iii.

choice to benefit the surviving partner on their death. The same does not, however, apply to American PODs, which are bank accounts set up with the sole purpose of benefiting someone exclusively with effect from death of the account holder.

Aside from the mere 'symbolic' or 'emotional' attractiveness of will-substitutes, most of them involve specific lifetime effects that distinguish them from wills and that explain their attractiveness, some of which we will examine below.

i. Will-Substitutes as Saving and Investment Devices

As we noted earlier, some of the instruments analysed, such as life insurance and pension plans, are investment products and function as saving mechanisms, the primary purpose of which is to provide for future uncertain events. Their usefulness as a savings device lies not merely in the yields they generate, but also in the fact that money so invested cannot be easily taken out. The possibility of designating a beneficiary to receive the proceeds or death benefits often appears to be a welcomed side effect or advantage. This is even more so the case with pension schemes whose raison d'être is primarily to provide for retirement.[166] In a sense, the underlying motive of the scheme member in joining a pension scheme or plan is even less 'altruistic', than is the case with life insurance, as the person entering the plan is primarily providing for him or herself.[167] This is especially true where the scheme is compulsory.[168]

The fact that wealth is passed on through life insurance and pension schemes is thus also a consequence of the fact that nowadays families tend to invest their wealth differently, and no longer just in real estate.[169] Since much of the wealth is invested in financial assets, it is therefore only natural that when disposing of wealth held in such instruments, the person uses the mechanism that the financial providers offer, ie, a beneficiary designation or nomination form.[170] As Gallanis put it, 'completing these forms is faster and easier than writing a will and is essentially costless'.[171] In other words, the decision not to dispose of these assets through a will may have nothing to do with the characteristics of the will itself, or the law applicable to it.

One reason why wealth is increasingly invested in certain financial products may be that we live longer and we need more than just wealth to provide for our retirement; we also need private modes of providing for old age and care. In fact, at least in Europe, provision for old age and care has become increasingly *privatised*.

[166] For Canada, see ch 2 above I.D and ch 12 above I.A. See also ch 3 above IV for England and Wales.

[167] DB Bernheim, 'How Strong are Bequest Motives? Evidence Based on Estimates of the Demand for Life Insurance and Annuities' (1991) 99 *Journal of Political Economy* 899.

[168] Ch 5 above II.D.

[169] JH Langbein, 'The Twentieth-Century Revolution in Family Wealth Transmission' (1988) 86 *Michigan Law Review* 722, 728.

[170] Ch 3 above II.A and B and ch 4 above II.E.

[171] Ch 1 above, p 11.

It follows that the success of will-substitutes is also a by-product of an ageing society in which people are likely to need more means for their retirement, and for a longer period of time, but are also required to organise their own welfare and to accumulate assets for that purpose.[172] In addition, these instruments can offer a way to provide dependants with increased revenue, and in the case of pensions the scheme members can sometimes even determine whether the beneficiary gets a lump-sum payment or a pension. This is a choice the will does not offer.

ii. Will-Substitutes as a Way of Holding, Managing and Preserving Property

Other will-substitutes, such as trusts, foundations and joint tenancies represent ways of holding and, in some cases, also of managing and preserving property. Although these instruments can operate as will-substitutes, this is not their sole or primary purpose. They each produce specific and significant lifetime effects.

A will does not impact on the way in which the testator holds his or her property during lifetime; it only declares what shall happen upon death to the property that is left. By contrast, during a person's lifetime, wealth held jointly,[173] held on trust,[174] transferred to a family foundation,[175] or held in a partnership[176] is already governed by the rules on joint ownership, by the trust deed, foundation or partnership rules. The wealth is dedicated to a specific purpose, even though the transfer is revocable.[177] Those who acquire or transfer property in joint names, settle wealth on trust, establish a foundation, or invest in a partnership, become a joint tenant, settlor, a founder, and partner already during lifetime, and this inevitably affects how a person can dispose of their wealth.

In the case of trusts, foundations and partnerships, a 'structure' is established that can provide 'continuity and stability'.[178] In some cases, the whole purpose behind it is to shield assets from creditors and family members and dependants, and to pursue a variety of additional purposes. Among these also count the possibility for the founder or settlor to constitute a 'privately created succession regime',[179] and to potentially *control* the distribution and management over

[172] See J Finch and J Mason, *Passing on. Kinship and Inheritance in England* (London, Routledge, 2000) 136. Conversely in the US, it would seem that 'planning for old age is private no more': MA Case, 'When Someday is Today: Carrying Forward the history of Old Age and Inheritance into the Age of Medicaid' (2015) 40 *Law & Social Inquiry* 499, 501.

[173] For Canada, see ch 2 above I.B; for the US, ch 1 above II.F; for Australia and New Zealand ch 5 above II.B and III.B; for England and Wales, see ch 3 above II.D, as well as ch 11 above IV.E; and for Scotland, see ch 4 above III and IV.

[174] See, esp ch 1 above II.A; ch 5 above II.C; and from the perspective of investors, see ch 11 above IV.A.

[175] See, esp ch 9 above III and IV. See further ch 11 above IV.C.

[176] See ch 6 above III.C.

[177] See the introduction, above at II.

[178] Ch 5 above III.C.

[179] Ch 8 above V.B.

generations. The settlors or founders are also often keen to avoid fragmentation and dissipation of assets.[180]

As noted earlier, trusts and private purpose foundations function as true will-substitutes only where they leave space for active interference of the settlor or founder, so as to allow him or her to determine beneficiaries on his or her death. The reservation of powers is not only a way of financially controlling the trust and foundation, but can also entail a symbolic effect. Jakob reminds us that family foundations 'have the potential to transport more than just property'.[181] Kalss points in the same direction by highlighting that corporate property is 'special property'.[182]

However, even though trusts and foundations can operate as will-substitutes, the prospect that they allow for a 'private succession law', in the sense that the succession is organised and designed also for future generations,[183] appears to be only one of their many possible advantages. Of course, much is speculative, but given their substantial and symbolic lifetime effects, one should not overestimate the weight given to possible effects these instruments can have on death.

C. Motives Linked to the Functioning of Succession Law

Despite the fact that the transfer of wealth may not always be at the forefront of the mind of those resorting to a will-substitute, many contributions have left no doubt that will-substitutes can be used to avoid the consequences that ensue from transferring wealth by means of a will. Sometimes a person may intend to completely avoid succession law rules from applying (without wanting to resort to an instrument that would involve losing immediate control over the assets), and at other times people may try to avoid just one of the consequences of the application of succession rules. For instance, in Germany, foundations allow a founder to deviate from the succession law rules against perpetuities, but not other provisions.[184] Finally, in some instances, the intention may be to 'modify' or perhaps 'temper' the effect of certain rules, rather than to 'avoid' them entirely.[185]

Any discussion on avoidance strategies presupposes that will-substitutes are not subjected to 'ordinary' succession law, which—as the contributions to this book have shown—is not always true. For instance, provisions such as those in place to protect family members and dependants have been extended so as to capture certain will-substitutes.[186] As far as creditor rights are concerned, some instruments

[180] Ch 5 above IV. This is a concern business owners often have. For ways of tackling the risk of fragmentation and termination of a partnership or corporation see ch 10 above V.
[181] Ch 9 above VII.
[182] Ch 10 above I.
[183] Ch 8 above V.B. See also ch 4 above I, text before fn 7.
[184] Ch 8 above V.B.
[185] Ch 8 above VI.
[186] See below at IV.C.ii.b. See also ch 15 above III.

are treated more favourably than others.[187] Thus, the picture is far from uniform. However, it is certainly true that conventional succession law rules are not automatically and necessarily extended to will-substitutes. Depending on the respective legal environment and the type of instrument employed, will-substitutes can therefore deviate from wills in several respects including, but not limited to, the following: the way the estate is administrated and transferred upon death;[188] the required formalities;[189] the applicability of default rules such as those on the revocation and construction of wills;[190] hotchpot rules;[191] rules on unworthiness and forfeiture;[192] admission of binding effects;[193] liability to creditors;[194] duties towards family members and dependants;[195] and, last but not least, different tax implications.[196]

Although each and every one of these differences may theoretically constitute a reason why an individual chooses to use a particular will-substitute, some aspects are more important than others. In fact, looking at the various contributions collected in this volume, it would seem that, by and large, testators or estate planners are unconcerned with rules on unworthiness or forfeiture, or those on the construction and rectification of wills. These are aspects that at least most testators will be unaware of, or care very little about. Also, and this is perhaps more unexpected, the various contributions reveal that the avoidance of formalities prescribed for wills does not really play an important role in the decision-making process,[197] nor does it seem to be a concern to most authors.[198] In some legal systems the formalities required for will-substitutes are even stricter or more demanding than those foreseen for wills, at least in jurisdictions where oral or holograph wills are admitted.[199] Even in jurisdictions where holograph wills are not recognised, courts may have discretionary powers which allow them to admit documents to probate that do not satisfy the formal requirements for execution of a will, for example, in Australia and New Zealand.[200] In any event, most will-substitutes require at least some

[187] See above at III.A. See also chs 12 and 13 above II and IV.

[188] Ch 1 above II.

[189] Though the requirements are not as different, and formality is therefore not as big a factor as expected. See below at n 197.

[190] Ch 4 above VIII.D; ch 6 above VI.D; ch 5 above IV and but see ch 1 above V.

[191] See ch 3 above III.E and ch 6 above II.B.

[192] Ch 6 above VI.C; but see ch 5 above V for Australia.

[193] Ch 6 above I.B.

[194] Ch 6 above IV.B; ch 12 above I.E.

[195] Chs 14 and 15 above V and III. For New Zealand, see ch 5 above V.

[196] Ch 2 above II.A; ch 3 above IV.C; ch 5 above IV; from the perspective of international investors, see ch 11 above III; but see also ch 1 above IV.A.

[197] Ch 8 above III. See further ch 2 above II for Canada and ch 4 above II.D for Scotland, as well as ch 6 above VI.B for Italy.

[198] Ch 2 above II.B. See further ch 6 above VI.B.

[199] See KGC Reid, MJ De Waal and R Zimmermann, 'Testamentary Formalities in Historical and Comparative Perspective' in KGC Reid, MJ De Waal and R Zimmermann (eds), *Comparative Succession Law, volume 1. Testamentary Formalities* (Oxford, OUP, 2011) 437 ff.

[200] See N Peart, 'Testamentary Formalities in Australia and New Zealand' in Reid, De Waal and Zimmerman, ibid, 329, 349.

formalities and these do not usually differ that significantly from those required for wills.

Much more prominent would appear to be other considerations such as: (i) changing the way in which the transfer of wealth takes place, that is to say the procedural implications of the administration and transfer of the estate; and (ii) sheltering assets from claims of third parties, including creditors, family members and dependants, as well as tax authorities. Both of these considerations will be discussed below.

i. *Will-Substitutes as a Means of Changing the Way in which Property is Transferred*

We have learned that, in the US, will-substitutes have primarily developed as a probate avoidance instrument, due to the fact that the probate procedure is costly, time-consuming and overall cumbersome.[201] The mere fact that will-substitutes are explicitly defined as arrangements under which rights shift 'outside probate' or are named 'nonprobate transfers' or 'nonprobate wills' demonstrates the strong link between the emergence of will-substitutes and probate procedures. Even though Gallanis has pointed out that other considerations too may play an important role,[202] much of the attractiveness of will-substitutes stems from the—at least perceived—disadvantages of the probate process.

Interestingly, this is not true of all jurisdictions that have probate procedures in place. Neither in England and Wales, nor in Australia or New Zealand, does probate avoidance feature so prominently among the reasons for choosing a will-substitute.[203] The same applies to Canada, where probate appears to be a 'relatively rapid and straightforward affair'.[204] That said, there are some aspects of the probate process that a testator may want to avoid, even in a legal system where overall the procedure is not as cumbersome, expensive, or lengthy as in the US. For instance, by avoiding probate one can achieve a direct transfer of the wealth to the beneficiary, without it passing through the hands of a personal representative, and the transfer can thus be kept confidential, which, for a variety of reasons, may be an attractive prospect.[205] Given that it is direct, sometimes, it may also be quicker.

Civil law jurisdictions do not usually have a probate procedure but even in Germany we are told that, upon closer inspection, the transfer of an estate may give rise to difficulties a testator may wish to avoid. For instance, where a will

[201] See ch 1 above I.

[202] Notably the fact that will-substitutes are cheaper, quicker and easier to create than wills and the fact that they can often override the rights of creditors and dependants. See ch 1 above I. See further ch 4 above II.

[203] Ch 3 above IV and ch 5 above IV.

[204] For Canada, see ch 2 above II.A. In Scotland, too it does not seem to represent a problem. See ch 4 above II.

[205] Ch 3 above IV.B, but also ch 4 above II.F. See further ch 2 above II.A.

is contested, court proceedings may be necessary, which may induce some people to grant a *post-mortem* or *trans-mortem* mandate, to enable a mandatary to distribute the assets after the death of the mandator, thereby reducing the risk of a will contest.[206]

Thus, to conclude, one rationale behind the use of at least certain will-substitutes may be a desire to avoid the involvement of a personal representative (which is the case in common law jurisdictions) and/or court proceedings, and thus any form of state control or intervention.[207] At least with certain devices, we have seen that there is an underlying desire to *privatise* the succession process,[208] in order to obtain greater control over how wealth is passed and thus over the timing of the distribution.

ii. *Will-Substitutes as a Means of Sheltering Assets from Claims of Third Parties*

Besides wanting to obtain greater control over how and when the transfer takes place, testators may also desire greater control over who gets the property and how much. This can be achieved with greater certainty, where it is possible to isolate the assets from claims of creditors or family members and dependants.

a. Rights of Creditors

One of the functions of succession law is to protect creditors and to ensure that the deceased's debts are paid. Due to the fact that some of the instruments analysed allow for a transfer outside the traditional structures of succession laws, creditors may not have access to the wealth which is transferred and may be left empty-handed. However, the extent to which the desire to shelter assets from creditor claims plays a primary role is often unclear.[209] In some cases it may well represent the primary motive for investing or holding wealth in a particular way, but in others it may simply be a welcome secondary consequence.

Gallanis has shown that, in the US, where there is a trend towards harmonising the law of wills and will-substitutes, the approach taken to creditor rights in the context of will-substitutes is not yet uniform and their interests remain inadequately protected. Aside from revocable trusts, in most US states, creditors of the deceased person are denied access to wealth transferred through will-substitutes. Although the UPC aims to protect creditors of the deceased via the general provision in § 6-102(b), which can make non-probate beneficiaries liable for the debts of the deceased up to the value of the assets they receive, the provision is in force in only a small number of states. Conversely, Canadian law lacks any general

[206] Ch 8 above IV.A and B.

[207] Ch 5 above IV.

[208] See above at IV.B.ii and Dutta, *Warum Erbrecht*, above n 85. See further DJ Feder and RH Sitkoff, 'Revocable Trusts and Incapacity Planning: More than Just a Will Substitute' (2016) 24 *Elder Law Journal* (forthcoming) II.A.

[209] Ch 3 above IV.D. According to L Smith in ch 12 above I.A, avoidance of creditors' rights is not normally why people use will-substitutes in Canada and the US.

provision of the kind contained in the UPC. That said, both in the US and Canada, in many cases will-substitute assets are independently protected by legislation from creditors' claims, for policy reasons relating to the protection of retirement savings and, in the case of life insurance, of dependants.[210] In this sense, will-substitutes do not necessarily represent a threat to creditors in and of themselves.

By contrast, it would seem that in Scotland, there is more potential for will-substitutes to prejudice the rights of creditors.[211] In England and Wales, creditors can get hold of some assets, but not of others and the reasons for that are not always clear.[212] It would also seem that will-substitutes are more likely to be challenged under German than under English insolvency law, partly due to the high cost of English court proceedings as well as the uncertain outcome.[213]

In France, Pérès mentions that creditor rights are set aside both in the case of the *tontine* and of life insurance, which represents the most important will-substitute in France. In Italy too, benefits transferred by a life insurance contract enjoy the special privilege of being protected against the claims of both the insured's and the beneficiary's creditors.[214] As a consequence, where the estate is insolvent, the beneficiary of a life insurance, who is also the heir of the deceased, may disclaim the inheritance, without losing the benefits under the insurance contract.[215] Whether the same applies to death benefits paid under Italian private pension schemes is still unclear.

Thus, overall, the protection of the interests of creditors is not always guaranteed, and some of the most common will-substitutes are exempted from creditor claims, leaving the estate without sufficient assets to answer all claims. However, the question of creditor protection is not just relevant for cases where the estate is insolvent. A general problem for all creditors is that they have to find out about the existence of other instruments, besides the will, and have to identify the various beneficiaries against whom to bring a claim,[216] which makes the whole process much more cumbersome and costly for creditors.

b. Rights of Family Members and Dependants

Common law, as well as civil law, jurisdictions know of specific rights in the estate granted to family members and dependants, either in the form of discretionary 'family provisions claims', or in the form of statutory fixed rights, such as the US 'elective share',[217] the German 'compulsory share' or the Romanic 'forced heirship'.[218]

[210] Ch 12 above III.
[211] Ch 4 above II.F.
[212] Ch 3 above III.D.
[213] Ch 13 above IV.B.ii.c.
[214] Ch 6 above III.A.
[215] Ch 6 above III fn 37.
[216] See ch 3 above III.D and ch 6 above IV.C.
[217] See ch 1 above VI.A, text after fn 114.
[218] See ch 14 above III and ch 15 above III.

Despite technical differences and divergences in how testamentary freedom is considered, the way in which jurisdictions approach will-substitutes and the rights of family members and dependants, is not as different as one might expect. The analysed jurisdictions are similar, insofar as they refrain from establishing a general provision or rule that covers all types of will-substitute. Notwithstanding differences in the entitlements of family members, the jurisdictions analysed in this volume generally approach will-substitutes as specific ways of transferring wealth. They either extend the provisions protecting the rights of family members only to some types of will-substitute (eg, in England and Wales, the US, and Canada),[219] or establish that only exceptional types of will-substitute are entirely or partly sheltered from claims of family members (eg, in Germany, France, Italy, and Switzerland concerning life insurance).[220] Even though this fragmented approach reflects the asset-specific nature of most will-substitutes, many contributors in this volume have described the state of the law as 'incoherent', 'problematic', or 'unsystematic',[221] and have called for a 'reintegration' of will-substitutes into succession law.[222] This is in line with a growing trend towards expanding rather than reducing the 'strength' of rights of family members and dependants in relation to will-substitutes.[223]

Yet, another striking similarity between the jurisdictions is the focus on the intention of the deceased when deciding whether or not to treat will-substitutes as part of the law of succession. Whereas civilian jurisdictions mainly rely on the *time* at which the benefit was passed, without looking at the intention,[224] common law jurisdictions generally require there to be clear proof of the deceased's *intention* to defeat the claims of the dependants.[225] Only where that is the case, will they be able to get hold of the assets. This appears to be one of the reasons why on the European continent, claw-back claims concerning will-substitutes are 'standard procedures', whereas there does not seem to be much litigation on this under the English family provision legislation.[226] However, even where claw-back claims are common, will-substitutes still have an indirect effect on the rights of family members and dependants because it is more difficult to trace where the assets have ended up.[227] Thus, as is the case with creditors, the fragmented transfer of wealth has an effect also on family members and dependants.

In the context of the rights of family members and dependants, several contributors considered will-substitutes as a means of 'avoiding', 'evading', or

[219] Ch 3 above III.E; ch 14 above II.A; ch 1 above IV.C; ch 2 above II.B.

[220] See ch 8 above VI; ch 7 above III.A; ch 6 above VI.A; ch 9 above III; and ch 15 above V.

[221] See ch 1 above VII; ch 3 above III; ch 4 above IX; ch 5 above V; ch 7 above III; ch 12 above III; ch 15 above V.

[222] Ch 7 above III; ch 8 above VII; ch 14 above V.

[223] Ch 1 above IV.C; ch 2 above II.B; ch 5 above III.G; ch 12 above I.D, as well as ch 15 above III.B.

[224] See ch 15 above III.A.ii.

[225] See ch 3 above III; ch 5 above III.G; ch 14 above V.

[226] See ch 14 above V and ch 15 above III.A.iii.

[227] Ch 6 above VI.A, text after fn 114.

'bypassing' those rights.[228] That said, much like the case with the avoidance of creditor rights, whether the deceased actually uses a will-substitute in order to infringe the claims of family members or dependants is not always clear. After all, many of them benefit family members anyway, though often in a manner different from that established by conventional succession laws. Also, it would seem that, at least in European continental legal systems, will-substitutes do not present a major danger to the rights of family members, due to the anti-evasion rules that are in place.[229] In that sense they are often better off than creditors. As for common law jurisdictions, the avoidance of dependants' claims seems to be a concern in England and Wales,[230] and New Zealand,[231] but less so in Australia[232] and Canada.[233]

c. Tax Liabilities

One final point to mention, as a possible rationale behind the use of will-substitutes, is the desire to avoid or reduce payment of taxes.[234] Several contributions to this volume leave no doubt that tax considerations play an important role in explaining certain developments, as they can work both as an incentive and a disincentive. For instance, while in New Zealand the fiscal environment has rendered trusts a particularly attractive device,[235] in Australia, stamp duty and capital gains tax have operated as a significant disincentive for settling property on trust.

Tax incentives certainly play a role in England and Wales and explain, for instance, the significant investments in private pension schemes, as well as the lack of popularity of revocable trusts.[236] In Canada too, tax considerations seem to inform choices to join certain retirement schemes[237] and this is true even though no Canadian jurisdiction currently levies an inheritance tax on estates, but rather imposes probate fees that are tied to the value of the estate. Although Australia and New Zealand do not levy estate tax, testators may still want to avoid capital gains or income tax. By contrast, in the US, will-substitutes are subject to transfer

[228] See ch 3 above IV.D; ch 4 above IX; ch 5 above I and V; ch 8 above VI; ch 9 above VII, as well as ch 14 above V.

[229] Ch 15 above III.C.

[230] Ch 3 above IV.D and ch 14 above V.

[231] Ch 5 above V.

[232] Ch 5 above IV. The notional estate provisions prevent will-substitutes from defeating meritorious family provision claims.

[233] Ch 2 above II.B.

[234] For a general discussion, in particular from an investor's perspective, see ch 11 above III.

[235] Ch 5 above II.C.

[236] Ch 3 above IV.C. See also J Finch, L Hayes, J Masson, J Mason and L Wallis, *Wills, Inheritance, and Families* (Oxford, Clarendon Press, 1996) 35, who mention that tax explains the reduction in the number of discretionary trusts. In this sense, see also ch 11 above IV.A. In Scotland '[t]he use of will-substitutes to evade taxation is likely to be a prime objective, though the extent to which this is realistic is questionable'. See ch 4 above II.F, at fn 37.

[237] Ch 2 above I.D.

taxation, so that tax avoidance does not play the same role.[238] That said, the federal tax exemption in the US is relatively high.[239]

However as Matthews states, 'even in the civil law world the imposition of tax—or the availability of reliefs—in specified situations is a well-known instrument of policy, and decisions taken there can be as much tax driven as in the common law countries'.[240] Perhaps unsurprisingly, in Liechtenstein and Switzerland, tax planning is a significant driver behind the use of certain will-substitutes, especially for those who view them as a form of investment.[241] Tax plays a role in other jurisdictions, too. This is, for instance, shown by the contribution by Pérès. Nevertheless, she also reports that some of the devices remain in use even though, in recent times, certain tax advantages that were granted in the past were eliminated. For instance, in the past, marital property arrangements were tax efficient and clearly used for that reason, but even though since 2007 this has changed,[242] they continue to be quite popular. Similarly tax considerations used to play a considerable role in the context of life insurance, but this is also no longer true. Despite this, they represent the most common will-substitute in France. In Italy, consolidation clauses in partnerships (*clausole di consolidazione*) have enjoyed widespread use as a means of avoiding inheritance tax, but they remain popular even after a tax reform has changed the tax treatment. Conversely, private pension schemes continue to have important tax implications in Italy. Thus, although tax considerations can play an important role, it does not follow that where tax privileges are removed, people automatically stop using them. This would support the argument that tax considerations represent one among many possible reasons for choosing one mechanism over another.

V. Consequences and Potential Tensions

Two aspects that we have not yet addressed are the potential pitfalls for the person who has chosen to use a will-substitute, and the challenges these mechanisms present for legal systems as a whole, and, in particular, for the operation and functioning of their succession law.

[238] Ch 1 above I and IV.

[239] In 2015, the US federal estate tax exemption amount is $5.43 million. By comparison, in England, the current tax threshold is £325,000. See ch 3 above IV.C, at fn 135.

[240] Ch 11 above, p 234.

[241] Ch 9 above I.

[242] See ch 7 above II.A.iii.

A. Consequences for the Testator

Having addressed the advantages that the various instruments explored in this volume offer to the person who intends to pass wealth on death, it is time to examine whether will-substitutes are necessarily a 'blessing'.[243]

On the one hand, one could see it as a welcome expression of the private autonomy of a person that he or she can chose to pass wealth on death through a variety of different means and not just through the use of a will. On the other hand, this reasoning only holds true, so long as the mechanisms that are available are reliable and operate in ways that actually allow the person to fulfil his or her wishes, as well as guaranteeing that those wishes actually reflect his or her intentions. As is well known, wills are regulated by a number of intent-effecting rules that are aimed at protecting testators and ensuring that their wishes are realised. Among these count, for instance, the rules on capacity and those on formalities, as well as provisions on lapse, automatic revocation, unworthiness, and rectification and construction of wills, which are often founded on the presumed intention of the testator. In addition, some legal systems also have a probate procedure in place, one of the functions of which is to ascertain the validity of the will. However, there is no such procedure for will-substitutes and this may expose the person using them to certain risks, especially where the formalities for will-substitutes are lower.[244] In the US, for instance, this has been described as problematic, with the most recent scholarship urging improvements to beneficiary-designation forms in order to better effect the donor's wishes.[245]

There may also be other pitfalls in place due to the fact that many will-substitutes have developed in legal practice and are often not specifically regulated, so that it is not necessarily clear whether they are actually recognised as being valid.[246] For instance, Christandl notes that, in Italy, will-substitutes are constantly exposed to the danger of being caught by the trap of the prohibition of succession pacts, which makes many of them unreliable estate planning devices.[247] Similarly, in

[243] Ch 3 above V.

[244] ML Leslie, 'Frustration of Intent in the Wealth Transmission Process' (2014) *Onati Socio-legal Series* 4(2) 283, 302. The authors concludes that, '[b]ecause financial institutions have a vested interest in laws that emphasize efficiency and dispatch over the effectuation of intent, and because estate planning lawyers have only limited abilities to minimize these problems, the problem of intent-frustration is unlikely to be resolved any time soon' (303).

[245] ibid. See, esp MB Leslie and SE Sterk, 'Revisiting the Revolution: Reintegrating the Wealth Transmission System' (2015) 56 *Boston College Law Review* 61. See further SE Sterk and MB Leslie, 'Accidental Inheritance: Retirement Accounts and the Hidden Law of Succession' (2014) 89 *New York University Law Review* 165. For a discussion of possible perils, see also ch 3 above V.

[246] Writing in the 1930s, Thomas Atkinson stated that at that point in time, certain schemes used in the US were without sound theoretical basis and frequently failed in practice: Atkinson, above n 163, 123. Since then, things have changed considerably. See ch 1 above II.

[247] Ch 6 above VII.

Switzerland, certain private purpose foundations bear the risk that they might be considered illicit, and the validity of joint bank accounts with a clause excluding the heirs of the deceased from becoming party to the contact with the bank (*Erbenausschlussklausel*) is also quite controversial.[248] Hence, where the state of the law is ambiguous, will-substitutes can be unreliable.[249]

Moreover, will-substitutes may not quite achieve what was intended. We mentioned earlier that, where the intention of a person setting up a joint bank account is not clearly expressed, the surviving tenant may well end up holding the surplus on trust for the estate, rather than taking beneficially,[250] and the intention to benefit the transferee may be frustrated. It may also be the case that the person using the instrument believes that the instrument carries certain advantages (eg, that it shields the assets from potential claims of creditors or family members and dependants) when in fact that is not the case. For instance, in New Zealand, the insured's intention can be defeated if the surviving spouse or partner elects to apply for a division of relationship property under the Property (Relationships) Act 1976.[251] Similarly, in certain circumstances, French law treats the *tontine* and life insurance as gifts and subjects them to conventional succession rules.[252]

One final aspect to consider is that the use of different devices to dispose of one's wealth can actually render estate planning more complex, thus necessitating the involvement of a legal or financial adviser, which can result in higher costs.[253] In fact, although some will-substitutes can lead to a transfer that in some cases is simpler and quicker, and therefore possibly less expensive, the higher the number of instruments used, the more difficult it may get. It may happen that the person forgets whether they have designated a beneficiary in the life insurance or pension scheme, and who the beneficiary may be, especially since those schemes are sometimes joined early in the life of a person. In other words, cases of accidental succession may occur,[254] and funds may remain unclaimed. But complexity may not be the only problem. It has recently been suggested that a further issue is that estate planning is increasingly being carried out by those who 'do not have the expertise or the incentive to properly advise the client',[255] such as employees of a bank or insurance company. Thus, the increased choice of instruments comes at a cost.[256]

[248] Ch 9 above II.
[249] See also ch 2 above I.E, text before fn 79.
[250] See above at III.A.iii.
[251] Ch 5 above II.E.
[252] Ch 7 above III.A.ii.
[253] Ch 4 above II.
[254] Sterk and Leslie, 'Accidental Inheritance', above n 245.
[255] KD Schenkel, 'Testamentary Fragmentation and the Diminishing Role of the Will: An Argument for Revival' (2008) 41 *Creighton Law Review* 155, 162.
[256] ibid.

B. Impact of the Use of Will-Substitutes on the Operation of Succession Laws

Succession law, whether procedural or substantive in nature, is designed to fulfil a number of different functions. The fact that the mechanisms discussed in this volume may, to a greater or lesser extent, allow for a transfer outside the realm of conventional succession structures and provisions inevitably bears consequences for the operation of such rules. This can create tensions with policy considerations underlying current laws governing succession.

One potential effect of the transfer of wealth on death by means other than wills is that the scope of the application of current succession laws becomes more narrow, unless their reach is extended so as to capture the instruments discussed above. In addition, there are also a number of other direct and indirect effects that stem from the fact that rules of probate, as well as substantive provisions, can be bypassed.

Among the direct effects of the use of will-substitutes is the fact that the transfer, though in some cases becoming simpler and more direct (eg, in that no personal representative is involved and that they are often less formal), is in other respects rendered more opaque.[257] This is primarily a consequence of the fact that the transfer becomes increasingly fragmented, which can be problematic, as we said above, for third parties, such as creditors or family members and dependants.[258] Not only might they need to ascertain whether the deceased has made a will, but also which other instruments he or she may have used to pass wealth on death, and whom the beneficiaries of those transfers are. For instance, forced heirs might run into difficulties when determining the exact basis on which their share has to be determined.[259] Also, it may be more difficult for them to contest the validity of a will-substitute[260] and to enforce their rights through litigation, especially as financial institutions pay or transfer the assets without providing notice to the heirs or dependants.[261]

The use of will-substitutes might also complicate matters for personal representatives and heirs who are required to pay the debts of the deceased. Not only is wealth passed on in certain ways that are unavailable for the payment of the debts of the deceased, they may still count as part of the taxable estate, and therefore may need to be factored in.[262] It is also unclear who is responsible for coordinating assets to make sure that liability for taxes and debts is allocated properly.[263]

[257] Ch 6 above VI.A.

[258] Schenkel, above n 255.

[259] Ch 6 above VI.A.

[260] See ch 3 above III.C.

[261] According to Leslie and Sterk, this increases the likelihood that a 'wrongdoer' will dissipate the decedent's assets before the beneficiary realises that he or she has a valid claim. Leslie and Sterk, 'Revisiting the Revolution', above n 245, 113.

[262] Ch 3 above IV.C.

[263] Leslie and Sterk, 'Revisiting the Revolution', above n 245, 95 speak of problems with asset coordination both during lifetime and on death.

The development of will-substitutes also creates potential tensions as far as the coordination of will-substitutes with the rules of wills is concerned.[264] For instance, in England and Wales, it is unclear whether, and to what extent, a will has an effect on the distribution of pension death benefits.[265] But frictions may also arise with core principles and doctrines of the law of wills. For instance, Christandl mentions the tensions that the use of will-substitutes gives rise to with regard to the rules on unworthiness to inherit and those regulating the revocation of wills.[266] There is also an underlying conflict with the principle of universal succession due to the fact that the transfer is increasingly fragmented.[267]

Finally, the use of will-substitutes may also have an indirect impact. For instance, in some jurisdictions the use of will-substitutes seems to have influenced developments in the law of wills. For instance, according to Lawrence Friedman:

> The rise of will substitutes has, in turn, affected the law of wills itself. This is probably a key reason why the law of wills has become less formal and formalistic. After all, now one can draw up a document that looks like a will, sounds like a will, and acts like a will, but isn't a will.[268]

VI. The Perception and Treatment of Will-Substitutes

A. Will-Substitutes in Legal Scholarship

We noted earlier that the proliferation of will-substitutes has largely occurred in a discrete manner, and that in most jurisdictions succession lawyers have paid relatively little attention to them.[269] However, where they have been discussed, what was the focus of the legal discourse and what was the narrative? In other words, how have legal scholars examined the use of will-substitutes and the rationale behind it?

It is interesting to note that the legal discourse involving will-substitutes has developed differently in the various jurisdictions, which is particularly apparent in civil law jurisdictions, despite the fact that the legal practice of will-substitutes does not necessarily differ that much. For instance, in Italy, the theoretical discussion seems to have primarily focused around the prohibition of succession pacts,[270]

264 Ch 3 above III and ch 12 above I.C. See also ch 6 above VII.

265 Ch 3 above III.E.

266 Ch 6 above VI.C and D

267 Kipp and Coing, above n 4, 445. See ch 7 above, p 160.

268 LM Friedman, *Dead Hands: A Social History of Wills, Trusts, and Inheritance Law* (Stanford CA, Stanford University Press, 2009) 100 f.

269 Above at I.

270 Ch 6 above VII.

with legal scholars discussing the various instruments as potential ways to circumvent it. Although the prohibition also features in the French Civil Code, and the literature exploring its scope is rich, there is relatively little discussion about will-substitutes as such. In Germany, where succession pacts are generally permitted, much of the academic debate involving will-substitutes seems to have centred around § 2301 BGB, and the question of how to draw a clear distinction between lifetime and testamentary dispositions. Even though the provision is widely studied in scholarly literature and is under continuous scrutiny,[271] it would seem to represent one of the most 'obscure' parts of German succession law.[272] That said, in Germany, the debate has also focused on the principle of universal succession and the protection of interests of family members and dependants. By contrast, in the US, the story of will-substitutes is primarily narrated as a story about the limits of the probate system and of attempts to get round it. Much less focus is placed on other motives that may drive testators towards the use of will-substitutes, such as the avoidance of rights of creditors or dependants, which do play a role.[273]

As to the way in which will-substitutes are perceived, it is interesting to note that will-substitutes are frequently studied as avoidance mechanisms. Indeed, several contributions in this volume have described or approached will-substitutes as instruments aimed at avoiding the operation of certain succession law rules.[274] This seems to be especially true of authors reporting on developments in civil law jurisdictions. In the US too, will-substitutes are mostly discussed as probate avoidance instruments. Conversely, in other common law jurisdictions this approach would seem to be less prominent, and there is less talk of *suspicion* or *hostility* towards their propagation or use.[275] The same applies in Scotland.[276] In other words, in these jurisdictions, will-substitutes are more directly discussed as expressions of the private autonomy of a person. This difference in approach might be partly due to the fact that, at least in principle, testamentary freedom is generally more restricted in civil law jurisdictions.

B. The State of the Art of the Law

Will-substitutes have also received little attention from legislatures and the courts have been faced with the difficult task of having to tackle some of the consequences of the use of will-substitutes without much guidance. Several of the instruments discussed in this volume are products developed in legal practice or by financial providers, who regulate their use unless and until the legislature

[271] See ch 8 above III.B and C.
[272] For an interesting discussion, see Windel, above n 5.
[273] Ch 1 above, p 5.
[274] See ch 8 above III–VI; ch 9 above VII. As well as ch 7 above I, text after fn 21.
[275] Ch 14 above, pp 284 and 291, but see also chs 2, 3, 5, 11 and 12.
[276] Ch 4 above II.E.

intervenes.[277] In some cases academics and courts have provided the legal framework for instruments that have emerged in such a way. For example, Dutta has shown that the German Bundesgerichtshof has developed the rules allowing succession clauses in partnership agreements, which were later recognised by the legislature.[278] Other instruments have emerged in legal practice, such as types of *post-mortem* mandates or powers of attorney, even though legal scholars were, and sometimes still are, unsure about their validity.[279]

Overall, the attitude among the various legal systems towards will-substitutes has been quite positive. Several have encouraged their use, or at least the use of certain instruments, by granting, for instance, tax and formal privileges, or by exempting them from claims of creditors or family members and dependants.[280] This is certainly the case in the US, where the state has been 'playing an important hand in encouraging the growth of the nonprobate system',[281] and has been willing to widen the range of will-substitutes.[282] If we look at the privileges granted to certain pension plans, something similar could be said of England and Wales.[283] Pérès confirms that, in France, will-substitutes have been 'allowed to thrive',[284] which is particularly apparent if one considers the position taken in relation to life insurance.[285] Similarly, in Canada, registered plans are incentivised by tax advantages.[286]

At times, legal systems have also tried to mitigate their use, for instance, by levying tax,[287] or by extending the reach of provisions pertaining to succession law, and applicable to wills, to will-substitutes.[288] For instance, in Canada, some provinces have established statutory regimes that allow courts to retrieve the value of dispositions made by will-substitutes, in the context of dependants' relief or will variation claims.[289] In France, 'barriers' have been imposed on will-substitutes,

[277] Leslie and Sterk, 'Revisiting the Revolution', above n 245, 61 write that although Langbein had predicted that financial intermediaries would develop forms designed to ascertain and implement the intention of deceased persons and that legal doctrine would adapt the gap-filling rules developed in wills law for use with nonprobate transfers, this seems not to have happened in all instances.

[278] Ch 8 above, pp 191 f.

[279] Ch 6 above III.D.v and ch 9 above, p 197.

[280] See above at III.A.i–ii, about the favourable climate towards life insurance and private pension schemes. For instance, in Italy, pension schemes were protected from claims of creditors. For details, see G Christandl, 'Vertragliche Sondererbfolge. Der Pensionsfonds im italienischen Recht' in FA Schurr and M Umlauft (eds), *FS Eccher* (2016, forthcoming). English and Scottish statutory nominations are an example of where the legislature has encouraged the use of instruments less formal than the will. See ch 3 above II.B and ch 4 above VII.A.

[281] Langbein, 'Major Reforms of the Property Restatement and the Uniform Probate Code', above n 15, 15. See also ch 12 above, p 252.

[282] Ch 2 above III and ch 12 above II.

[283] See the discussion above, p 328. See also ch 3 above II.A.ii.

[284] Ch 7 above I, text after fn 21.

[285] Ch 7 above II.B.

[286] Ch 2 above I.D.

[287] See ch 5 above V.

[288] See above V.B.

[289] Ch 2 above II.B.

for instance, by allowing the claw-back of certain property into the estate of the deceased.[290] Other legal systems have general anti-evasion rules built into their succession law, such as Germany.[291]

The reason, why legal systems may have tolerated or even encouraged the use of certain will-substitutes, may be explained on the basis of policy or economic reasons.[292] Among these might be the need to encourage people to provide for their retirement and/or their dependants. This explains, for example, why life insurance and pension plans do not only often enjoy tax privileges, but are also generally exempted from claims of creditors of the deceased.[293] That said, Christandl has noted that, in Italy, one reason for treating life insurance differently has also been to protect the insurance companies themselves from such claims.[294] In other words, financial providers have an interest in being able to make pay-outs quickly and without incurring any liability. By paying directly the person nominated in the insurance contract, they can avoid the hassle of having to determine the heir. The importance of the economic arguments have also been highlighted by Pérès in relation to life insurance and the decision of the French courts to treat modern life insurance contracts as chance-event contracts.[295] Finally, the fact that several will-substitutes involve the presence of a third party (ie, a financial provider or a trustee) and require at least some formalities, may also be a reason why legal systems have tolerated lower formality standards for some will-substitutes.

However, it is important to note that the approach taken by individual legal systems has not necessarily been coherent. Not surprisingly, therefore, several authors in this volume are of the view that the current state of the law is unsatisfactory.[296] Although legislatures may have intervened in relation to some instruments and in certain respects, they may not have done so in others. For instance, Pérès reports that in France, the assimilation of the rules applicable to life insurance to the conventional rules of succession law is 'far from perfect'.[297] A similar fragmented picture emerged from our examination of the rights of creditors[298] and that of family members and dependants.[299] Thus, will-substitutes are in some regards treated as wills and submitted to the same provisions and requirements, and in others, they follow different rules. Moreover, in several jurisdictions the reasons

[290] Ch 7 above III.

[291] Ch 8 above III.B.

[292] Ch 6 above, pp 155 f; ch 7 above, p 171; and ch 12 above, p 264.

[293] Ch 12 above, p 264.

[294] Ch 6 above, p 139.

[295] See ch 7 above, pp 170 f. But see also the argument of the English Law Commission which preferred to extend the reach of family provision legislation to pension death benefits because that would mean interfering with the discretion of trustees. See ch 3 above, p 68.

[296] See Braun in ch 3 above VI, and Pérès in ch 7 above IV. See Carr in relation to nominations in ch 4 above VII.B.i.

[297] Ch 7 above III.B.

[298] Above at IV.C.ii.a.

[299] This is certainly true of civil law jurisdictions: see above at III.C.ii.b, as well as ch 15 above III.A.ii. However, see also ch 3 above III.E.

for treating some instruments differently from others are not clear.[300] The lack of a systematic approach may, however, be due to the fact that the instruments used vary in nature and involve very different issues. Hence, a uniform answer may not only be unfeasible, but perhaps also undesirable.

Conversely, in the US, in the beginning courts tended to treat will-substitutes as lifetime instruments, but this was strongly criticised by John Langbein who highlighted the legal fiction this involved and the distortions of legal doctrines it provoked,[301] advocating instead a uniform law of succession. As far as formalities are concerned, in the US, two systems have developed, one for probate and one for non-probate transfer, while other default rules have been harmonised, at least to a large extent. That said, as Gallanis pointed out in his contribution,[302] a counter-trend against harmonisation has taken place at the federal level, and it is unclear what the future holds. Be that as it may, the developments in the US appear to be the exception rather than the rule. No other jurisdiction examined in this volume has made an attempt to harmonise the law of wills and will-substitutes.

What other options do legal systems have? If will-substitutes are perceived as avoidance instruments, one possibility to temper their use could be to reform existing succession laws by 'improving' or changing procedural or substantive provisions that some people may try to avoid.[303] However, as noted above,[304] will-substitutes are not just the result of a desire to avoid succession laws. Therefore reform of existing laws alone may not 'solve' the issues that currently arise.

It would further be possible to create a special set of rules for will-substitutes, inspired by the rules applicable to wills, and to apply them to instruments that pass wealth with effect on death.[305] In other words, will-substitutes could be treated as a separate and special group. The problem with this is that will-substitutes vary in nature and the fact that they pass wealth on death is just one of the many features most of them have.

The better option would seem to be to simply apply the rules applicable to wills by analogy to will-substitutes which, as we saw, is partly what some jurisdictions have been doing, though not always in a systematic manner.[306] This approach

[300] See ch 3 above III and ch 4 above IX. See further ch 15 above, p 322 where Röthel argues that '[i]f there are policy reasons that support a privilege for providential transfers, then this privilege should be applied to any transfer aiming to provide maintenance for the beneficiary'.

[301] JH Langbein, 'The Nonprobate Revolution and the Future of the Law of Succession' (1984) 97 *Harvard Law Review* 1108, 1109.

[302] Ch 1 above VI.

[303] In the US, one response to the nonprobate revolution has been to reform probate. GMP McCouch, 'Probate Law Reform and Nonprobate Transfers' (2008) 62 *University of Miami Law Review* 757. According to Schenkel, the response should rather be to exempt wills from probate: Schenkel, above n 255, 156.

[304] See above at IV.

[305] To some extent this is done in France where specific forfeiture rules where developed that apply to life insurance and that mimic the laws on intestacy. See ch 7 above III.B.

[306] See ch 3 above III.

seems to be favoured by several authors in this volume.[307] One argument in favour of this option is that by treating functionally similar devices alike, greater coherence or consistency could be achieved, and therefore greater fairness obtained for creditors and family members and dependants. Moreover, as Langbein argued a few years ago: 'The subsidiary rules are the product of centuries of legal experience in attempting to discern transferors' wishes and suppress litigation. These rules should be treated as presumptively correct for will-substitutes as well as for wills'.[308] This is indeed the direction law reformers have taken in the US (even though there is a counter-trend taking place). However, unless all will-substitutes were to be automatically subject to succession law, this approach would require clear criteria in order to decide which rules to extend and to which instruments.

VII. Conclusions

A. What Will-Substitutes Teach Us

Will-substitutes tell us something about how testators think and feel about estate planning, their desires and fears and also about what they perceive to be the shortcomings of current succession rules. For instance, the developments show that testators may want to combine lifetime effects with the transfer of benefits on death, and to provide for family members and dependants in ways different from a disposition in a will. This is, for instance, possible through life insurance and pension schemes. The use of will-substitutes would also suggest that people tend to shy away from anything that is too 'death-related'.[309]

The success of certain mechanisms further indicates that some testators may want to be able to bind themselves.[310] On the other hand, others may want to increase their control over the distribution and destination of their wealth, for instance, through the use of foundations and trusts, but also obtain greater certainty as to who gets the property and how it is passed to future generations.

The response to will-substitutes also reveals that legal systems are sometimes prepared to tolerate circumventions of succession rules if it is in the interest of society or of financial providers.[311] As we have seen, they may indeed offer incentives where there are policy and economic reasons at play.[312]

307 Ch 3 above VI; ch 6 above, text after fn 118; ch 7 above III; ch 8 above VII, as well as ch 15 above V. See further Röthel, *Ist unser Erbrecht noch zeitgemäß?*, above n 105.

308 Langbein, 'The Nonprobate Revolution', above n 301, 1136 f.

309 See Atkinson, above n 163.

310 See ch 6 above III.C.

311 See above n 294.

312 Ch 7 above, pp 170 f.

Will-substitutes further reveal what the transfer of wealth looks like in practice. They teach us, for instance, that through the increase in use of will-substitutes, the transfer upon death has become fragmented and has therefore inevitably been rendered more complex, even in legal systems that enshrine the principle of universal succession.[313] The phenomenon further shows that conventional succession rules have certain limitations[314] that could be reformed and that the current laws fail to meet certain perfectly legitimate needs of testators.[315]

Will-substitutes also highlight that it is difficult to draw a clear line between *mortis causa* and *inter vivos* dispositions and that some instruments do not fit neatly into one category or another. As Ashbel Gulliver and Catherine Tilson pointed out many years ago, '[s]uch problems arise most frequently as a result of a person's use of the form of an inter vivos transaction with the objective of producing some of the major consequences normally following the execution of a will'.[316] In fact, some will-substitutes are in a 'no-man's land', as they straddle the boundary between lifetime and *mortis causa* dispositions. Particularly problematic in this sense are, for instance, joint tenancies, revocable trusts, but also the gift *mortis causa*, as well as foundations, as they produce both lifetime and *mortis causa* effects. This explains why some authors in this volume have resorted to a terminology first used by Langbein, who distinguishes between 'pure' and 'impure' will-substitutes.[317]

B. Will-Complements Rather than Will-Substitutes

One aspect that has emerged from the contributions in this volume is that the instruments that are used to pass wealth on death often can or do obtain outcomes that wills cannot usually achieve.[318] For example, will-substitutes allow for certain lifetime effects, provide for the maintenance of dependants, facilitate asset segregation, increase the control over the future disposition and management of wealth, and facilitate the preservation of assets, including businesses. Some will-substitutes also render the transfer more direct, confidential, speedy, and at times, less expensive.

However, the analysis has also shown that the will too can do things that most will-substitutes cannot. For instance, the will allows for the transfer of all of one's

[313] Ch 7 above I.

[314] For instance, in New Zealand the courts take a liberal approach to family protection claims and awards are unpredictable, so that testators may want to choose a device that gives them greater control. Ch 5 above II.C.

[315] eg the use of clauses in partnership agreements seems to respond to a perfectly legitimate need to preserve a business, which is often in the interests of the entire family.

[316] AG Gulliver and CJ Tilson, 'Classification of Gratuitous Transfers' (1941) 51 *Yale Law Journal* 1.

[317] Ch 1 above, p 3 and ch 7 above II.A and B.

[318] See above, p 340.

present and future assets, while most of the mechanisms discussed in this volume are asset-specific and can only be employed to transfer wealth that is held in a particular way or that is invested in a particular form. The only other instrument that comes close to fulfilling a similar function is the trust, but even then a 'pour-over' will is usually necessary because the trust requires segregation of assets. Moreover, in the case of a will, the owner can normally secure secrecy of his intentions during lifetime, and remains free to enjoy and dispose of his wealth in any way he or she sees fit. This, as we have seen, is not possible with most of the instruments we have analysed in this volume. Only certain trusts allow the settlor to maintain a similar freedom and control. Many of the other mechanisms require surrender of some of the control during lifetime. Thus, in order to gain control over the future destinations of assets, it is sometimes necessary to give up a certain amount of control during lifetime. Furthermore, in most legal systems the will is generally simple to make, relatively cheap, and has the advantage of being regulated by a clear set of default rules, which provide the testator with legal certainty.[319] By contrast, some of the mechanisms discussed in this volume are not regulated in a systematic manner and in many jurisdictions it is still unclear whether, and to what extent, they are to be treated as lifetime or testamentary dispositions. This may indeed depend on the specific terms of the agreement entered into with the bank, pension scheme, life insurance etc. To some extent, will-substitutes can, therefore, be unreliable.[320]

Hence, it is perhaps not surprising that in a number of legal systems explored in this volume, wills remain a popular device.[321] For instance, in England and Wales, the official rate of testation seems to be around 41 per cent, and is about the same in the US, where approximately 60 per cent die intestate. The numbers of those leaving a will are lower in France (10 per cent) and in Italy (15 per cent), as well as in Germany (25–35 per cent) but higher in Spain (50 per cent), in Australia and New Zealand (50 per cent) and in Canada (50 per cent).[322] Exactly how much wealth is transferred by will is, however, unclear as we lack data for most legal systems.

In any event, a high or low level of testation is not necessarily an indicator of whether will-substitutes are successfully employed. In fact, even in the US, will-substitutes have not completely displaced wills or probate administration, and it has been argued that they should not be viewed as irreconcilable opposites 'but rather as complementary components of an increasingly varied and complex

[319] Schenkel, above n 255, 182: 'Although post-death administration is undeniably simplified, the pre-death process of estate planning now requires more documentation, techniques, and tasks than ever before. Ironically, the will, the instrument whose undesirable post-death characteristics spawned the turn towards alternative techniques, offers the simplest and most efficient mechanism for channeling a person's testamentary desires'.

[320] See above at III.A.i–vi and viii–ix.

[321] Clear exceptions are France and Italy. For numbers on different jurisdictions see KGC Reid, MJ De Waal and R Zimmermann, 'Intestate Succession in Historical and Comparative Perspective' in KGC Reid, MJ De Waal and R Zimmermann (eds), *Comparative Succession Law, volume 2. Intestate Succession* (Oxford, OUP, 2015) 442, 444.

[322] For Canada, see ch 2 above fn 110.

system of death-time transfers'.[323] Thus, the will may in many cases just be one among a larger pool of instruments to which a person can resort to pass benefits on death.

This means that, to some extent, the expression 'will-substitutes' is a misnomer.[324] The term tells us what these instruments may do, but not what they are and how they operate, ie, their legal nature. Further, it may give the impression that they necessarily 'substitute' or replace the will, when in reality they often *complement* the will, operate where a will could not be used,[325] or work with the will to pursue a common objective.[326] Even where they are used as a substitute to dispose of certain assets, they can never be a substitute for disposing of the whole estate.

C. Denying or Facing Reality?

What has emerged from our analysis is that there may be a variety of different reasons why someone uses a certain will-substitute. Sometimes the choice is guided by specific characteristics of a will-substitute rather than by a desire to avoid any particular rule of succession law, and sometimes they go hand-in-hand. Where avoidance is the driving factor, the most common concerns seem to be escaping the complexity and costs related to the transfer of wealth by will, or shielding the transfer from third-party claims.

What is interesting to note, however, is that will-substitutes are a phenomenon common to all jurisdictions, irrespective of whether or not: (i) estate tax is payable or of the particular tax regime applying in a legal system; (ii) there is a system of probate in place; (iii) the legal system has opted for forced heirship provisions or a system of family provision claims; (iv) the legal system prohibits succession pacts or inheritance contracts; or (v) there are stringent formality requirements for wills.

This suggests that there are needs that extend beyond the specific advantages of each individual will-substitute or the shortcomings of the will and related procedural and substantive norms. These may be a more general result of the fact that we live longer, invest differently, plan differently, have more complex family structures, and that, at least in Europe,[327] care and provision for retirement is increasingly privatised. Indeed, the success of some will-substitutes seems to depend on a number of factors, including the following: the investment and

[323] McCouch, above n 303, 760.

[324] Another author, who has looked at will-substitutes from the perspective of private international law, has introduced the term 'succession substitutes', which he defines as being wider than 'will-substitutes'. J Talpis, 'Succession Substitutes' (2011) 356 *Recueil des cours de l'Académie de droit international de La Haye* 9, 24 ff, 43 f. However, this term does not seem to be particularly accurate either.

[325] Ch 1 above, p 5; ch 3 above I; and ch 9 above VII.

[326] See what Dutta says about succession clauses in partnerships in ch 8 above VII.

[327] For the US, see Case, above n 172.

saving patterns of a particular population; the nature and role of social security and retirement systems of the individual jurisdictions; the type of business structures; and the importance of private ownership in land (family homes). In other words, at least in this field of succession law, the cultural, social and economic background plays an important role, even though there are clear common trends among the jurisdictions studied.[328] Thus, there may be need for more flexibility and consequently more than one instrument to pass wealth on death.

Clearly, will-substitutes are not just a temporary phenomenon, and it is time that the issues that their use inevitably raises are addressed in a proactive manner. Whether the time is ripe for legislative reform is not clear. However, there is no doubt that this area requires a more in-depth discussion and further studies,[329] including empirical and sociological investigations. Will-substitutes represent a chance to rethink some of the existing principles and doctrines, and to investigate whether current succession rules are still at pace with our time. At the same time, they also offer an opportunity to remind us of what is unique to wills, what drives succession law, and what legal systems consider to be inherent and special to it.

[328] See what we said about life insurance, above at section III.A.i.

[329] According to Christandl, in Italy, the discussion needs a fresh start and should focus on what actually happens in practice. See ch 6 above VII. Campbell too believes that further research is worthwhile: ch 2 above III. See further Braun in ch 3 above VI; Carr in ch 4 above IX; and Pérès in ch 7 above IV.

INDEX